THE LIVES AND LEGENDS

OF BUFFALO BILL

William F. Cody

THE LIVES AND LEGENDS OF
BUFFALO BILL

BY DON RUSSELL

NORMAN AND LONDON
UNIVERSITY OF OKLAHOMA PRESS

By Don Russell

One Hundred and Three Fights and Scrimmages: The Story of General Reuben F. Bernard (Washington, D.C., 1936)

The Lives and Legends of Buffalo Bill (Norman, 1960)

(editor) *Campaigning with Crook,* by Captain Charles King (Norman, 1964)

(editor) *Five Years a Dragoon,* by Percival G. Lowe (Norman, 1965)

Custer's Last (Fort Worth, 1968)

(compiler) *Custer's List* (Fort Worth, 1969)

The Wild West, or A History of the Wild West Shows (Fort Worth, 1970)

(co-editor, with Nancy Alpert Mower) *The Plains,* by François des Montaignes (Norman, 1972)

LIBRARY OF CONGRESS CATALOG CARD NUMBER: 60–13470
ISBN: 0–8061–1537–8

8   9   10   11   12   13   14   15   16   17   18   19   20

ACKNOWLEDGMENTS

I should name at least 150 persons who have been generous with information for this book, and some of them have been mentioned for specific help in footnotes. Among those whose aid has been of broad scope, first should be the late General Charles King, who wrote and told me of Hat Creek and of much more. Chris Madsen was a stimulating correspondent. Agnes Wright Spring, state historian of Colorado, far exceeded the duties of that generous profession in giving me a packing box full of notes and material she had assembled on the show. Maurice Frink, executive director of the Colorado State Historical Society, and Nyle H. Miller, secretary of the Kansas State Historical Society, have been continuously on the lookout for material. J. Edward Leithead, Albert Johannsen, and Colonel C. D. Randolph taught me all I know about dime novels. Of the Cody family, Hiram S. Cody, Mary Jester Allen, and Lydia S. Cody were of great help.

A few among many others include: William D. Aeschbacher, Nebraska State Historical Society; Lola M. Homsher, Wyoming state historian; Victor Gondos, Jr., and Elbert L. Huber, National Archives; Stanley Pargellis, Newberry Library; Warder H. Cadbury, Adirondack Museum; Alys Freeze, Denver Public Library; Herbert Kahler, David L. Hieb, and Major Edward S. Luce, National Parks Service; Walter C. Scholl, circus collector; Fred B.

Hackett, Charles Wayland Towne, William McDonald, J. C. Dykes, Annie Fern Swartwout, the late Elmo Scott Watson, and the late Stanley Vestal.

DON RUSSELL

Elmhurst, Illinois

CONTENTS

vii

ILLUSTRATIONS

MAPS

THE LIVES AND LEGENDS

OF BUFFALO BILL

1

THE CODYS WERE NOT GOOD AT SPELLING

BUFFALO BILL WAS DESCENDED neither from Irish kings, as his younger sister supposed when she wrote a biography of him, nor from Italian *condottieri*, as Mussolini's propaganda agency claimed at a time when Fascism was as prolific in discoveries and inventions as was Russian Communism in subsequent years. Buffalo Bill's most remote definitely known ancestor was one Philip, whose surname appears in various surviving records as Legody, Lagody, McCody, Mocody, Micody (and from an easy misreading of some of these, Moody), as well as Codie, Gody, Coady, and Cody. Public and church officials were ingenious in their phonetic spellings of names. In 1698, Philip purchased a house at Beverly, Massachusetts, and occupied it for twenty-five years, farming an adjacent six acres. He and his wife, Martha, were members of the First Church of Beverly, and five of their six children were baptized there. Investigation tends to identify Philip and Martha with a Philippe Le Caude of Jersey and a Marthe Le Brocq of Guernsey, who were married in the parish of St. Brelades, Island of Jersey, on September 15, 1692. With further variant spellings, including Lecaudey, Lescaudey, and Lescaude, this family can be traced back to 1566 on Jersey. Although the names are French, the Channel Islands, of course, have been English since the Middle Ages.[1]

[1] Helen Cody Wetmore, *Last of the Great Scouts*, xi–xii; editorial, "Bologna

At all events, in 1720, Philip, by this time calling himself Cody, acquired land at Hopkinton, Massachusetts, moved there within two or three years, and stayed until his death. A will probated in 1743 (in which the name is spelled Coady) indicates that he died that year.

Ancestral carelessness in the spelling of the family name may not have been passed on to Buffalo Bill, but he had a fine disregard for the orthography of proper names in his autobiographical writings. Bill was sixth in descent from Philip, those intervening being Joseph, 1700–56, whose wife was Mary Martin; Philip, 1729–1808, whose wife was Abigail Emerson; Philip, 1770–1850, whose wife was Lydia Martin; and Isaac, who deserves more attention than he has received in biographies of his illustrious son. Grandma Lydia Martin may be responsible for the family legend of the Irish kings, for she boasted that her ancestors were of Irish nobility. However, genealogists tracing another Cody family, mostly settled in the South and apparently not related to Buffalo Bill, derived the name from the Irish Odo, which became MacOdo, then Codo, and finally developed into Cody.

Isaac, the son of Philip and Lydia Martin Cody, was born in Toronto Township, Peel County, Upper Canada, on September 15, 1811, the sixth of a family of four sons and five daughters. When Isaac was seventeen years old, the family came to Ohio and occupied a farm near Cleveland, in the vicinity of subsequent Euclid Avenue and Eighty-third Street. Six years later Isaac was married to Martha Miranda O'Connor, who died shortly after the birth of a daughter, Martha, in 1835. Isaac was married again, to Rebecca Sumner of Medina County, Ohio, but she also died within a short time, leaving no children. In 1839, Isaac started a series of wanderings, accompanying his elder brother, Elijah, and family to Missouri. Traveling by boat down the Ohio River, they stopped at Cincinnati, and there Isaac met Mary Ann Bonsell Laycock. Their romance developed rapidly, for although Isaac continued his journey, he did not stay long in Missouri. He returned to Cleveland

on Buffalo Bill," *Chicago Daily News*, March 11, 1937; "Ancestors of 'Buffalo Bill' Had Place in Essex County," *Salem*, Mass., *News*, undated clipping; Ernest William Cody, "The Piercing of the Veil," Cody Family Association.

for his daughter, Martha, then retraced his route to Cincinnati, where in 1840 Isaac and Mary were married.[2]

The mother of Buffalo Bill was descended from Josiah Bunting, who is said to be the person holding the parchment in the paintings showing William Penn signing his treaty with the Indians. The Buntings came from Derbyshire, England, in 1690 and settled in Derby, Pennsylvania. Mary's mother, Hannah Taylor Laycock, died in 1830; Mary's father, Samuel, married again and shortly afterward was drowned at sea. When her stepmother remarried, Mary went to live with her brother William in Cincinnati, and had been there for three years when she met Isaac Cody. She is said to have been a school teacher.[3]

Isaac Cody was one of those pioneers who were always looking for something bigger and better around the next bend of the river. He may have taken a look at the new Territory of Iowa the previous year; at all events he took his new wife and his daughter down the Ohio and up the Mississippi to Davenport. There he prospered as an Indian trader and within a year bought a house in LeClaire (named for Antoine LeClaire, interpreter credited with translating the story of Black Hawk into a synthetic autobiography). At the same time Isaac Cody filed a claim on a tract about two miles west of LeClaire. He kept the house during most of the fourteen years he spent in Scott County, using it as headquarters for various ventures. This first time he stayed long enough for his eldest son, Samuel, to be born there on February 22, 1841. Meanwhile Isaac built a four-room log house on his claim and was living there when his and Mary's oldest daughter, Julia Melvina, was born on March 28, 1843. Happily, the Codys were still living in the log cabin when William Frederick was born on February 26, 1846.[4]

The first of multitudinous arguments about Buffalo Bill concerns

[2] *The Cody Family Handbook-Directory*, 4–27; Lydia S. Cody, *The Cody Family in America*, 1–6.

[3] Julia Cody Goodman, "Memoirs of Buffalo Bill" (hereinafter cited as Mrs. Goodman MS).

[4] F. M. Fryxell, "The Codys in LeClair," *Annals of Iowa* (July, 1929); James Colby, "Buffalo Bill's Old Boyhood Home Is Still Standing in Scott Co.," Davenport, Iowa, *Democrat and Leader*, March 14, 1948; *History of Scott County, Iowa*, 1097; *Atlas of Scott County, Iowa* (Davenport, 1905), 152; Harry E. Downer, *History of Davenport, and Scott County, Iowa*, I, 362, 764.

the year of his birth, for in the earliest of his autobiographies he said he was born in 1845. It has been suggested that this was done to add a year to his age, thereby making some boyhood adventures more believable, but he nullified this advantage in the same book by getting himself to Kansas, where his adventures began, two years too early. He was careless with dates, but corrected the year of his birth in later autobiographies to 1846, verified by the family Bible and the United States Census.[5]

In 1847, Isaac contracted to clear a six-hundred-acre farm on the Wapsipinicon River for William F. Brackenridge, who was recalled by members of the Cody family as "Colonel" and "Senator." Coincidence suggests that our hero might have been named for William F. Brackenridge, who visited Iowa only once but gave Isaac Cody full authority to employ some twenty-five men with plows and ox-teams that spring to open up the land, while other men were hired to cut stone in a quarry on the tract, and to build a house of eight to ten rooms. In this stone house, still standing with additions, Isaac Cody lived as farm manager, surely one of the leading citizens of the community. While the stone house was being built, the family occupied a log cabin near the river.[6]

Born to adventure, Will, as he was called by the family, was only one year old when he had his first narrow escape from death. Mrs. Cody was entertaining visitors from LeClaire, ladies in white dresses, Julia tells us, which indicates that frontier conditions were not entirely on a calico basis, even though deer were commonly seen leaping over the newly built rail fences that surrounded the farm. A boat ride on the river was suggested, and one of the hired men was called upon to row the skiff. It hit a rock and overturned, spilling out the ladies, the white dresses, our infant hero, and his four-year-old sister. The rower waded out with a child under each arm. This first adventure seems to lack something, and undoubtedly

[5] *Census Returns, 1850*, Vol. 33, p. 733, town of LeClaire, copy from C. E. Kopf, Iowa State Department of History and Archives; W. F. Cody, *The Life of Hon. William F. Cody, Known as Buffalo Bill* (hereafter cited as Cody, *Life*, 17; *An Autobiography of Buffalo Bill* (hereafter cited as Cody, *Autobiography*, 3.

[6] Elmer Jens, clerk of the District Court, Scott County, and his assistant, Minnie Dilly, identified the tract owner as William F. Brackenridge; Colby locates the old stone house as on the McCausland farm, two miles south of McCausland and west of Butler No. 5 School ("Buffalo Bill's Old Boyhood Home," Davenport *Democrat and Leader*, March 14, 1948).

Buffalo Bill press agents could have made more out of it, but they seem to have missed this boat.

A second hitherto unrecorded adventure does not offer much more, except to illustrate the future great horseman's fearlessness at an early age. He toddled toward the doctor's horse, tied near the stone house, and just escaped a vicious kick as his sister pulled him away.[7]

It has become a legend, not only fostered by motion pictures, but also apparently by Buffalo Bill himself, that he never went to school a day in his life. On the contrary, however, he was exposed to schooling at an earlier age than is generally possible. In the fall of 1847, Isaac Cody hired Miss Helen Goodrige to teach a school of twelve to fifteen pupils in a log building with board benches. Martha, Samuel, and Julia went to school, and as Mrs. Cody was cooking for the crew of men hired for the farm, and as the teacher could not object since Mr. Cody paid most of her salary, little Willie, less than two years old, was sent along in charge of his sisters. It is not recorded that he made any notable educational progress.[8]

Isaac Cody, living in the big stone house, bossing a big gang of workmen, and setting up the community school, must have appeared the successful citizen; but, typical of his pioneer generation, he ever looked for brighter prospects beyond the horizon. This time it was news of gold in California, and Isaac Cody resigned as manager of the Brackenridge farm and moved his family to the house in LeClaire, getting ready for a covered-wagon trip across the plains. Julia recalled that her father became ill and that the party of twenty went on without him. Dennis Barnes said that the LeClaire contingent, consisting of himself, Isaac Cody, and George Long, planned to join a party captained by George Dodge of Port Byron, Illinois, at Leavenworth, but that Long was frightened by tales of Indian atrocities and the fate of the Donner party, and without him, Barnes and Cody were unable to finance the trip.[9]

Isaac Cody drove his covered wagon to Davenport, where he exchanged it for an ambulance—a vehicle that has perhaps best

[7] Mrs. Goodman MS.

[8] Twentieth Century–Fox, *Buffalo Bill* (1944); Dan Muller, *My Life with Buffalo Bill*, 61; Dan Muller to Don Russell, July 25, 1949; Mrs. Goodman MS.

[9] Fryxell, "The Codys in LeClair," *Annals of Iowa*, July, 1929; Mrs. Goodman MS; her date, 1848, is more logical.

been described as a primitive ancestor of the station wagon. With it he took a contract to carry mail and passengers between Davenport and Chicago, making one trip a week. He crossed the Mississippi to Rock Island, then took a road along the river where the children from the Iowa side could watch him pass. Will tells of being taught his A, B, Cs' at the LeClaire school, but implies that he spent most of his time setting figure-four traps to catch quail, stealing apples, and getting into other mischief. He tells of stealing a boat with two other boys, losing their oars in the middle of the Mississippi, and being rescued by a man in a canoe.

In 1852, Isaac Cody sold out his stage business and also his LeClaire property and again contracted with Brackenridge to manage a large farm, this time at Walnut Grove, near Long Grove, on the Dubuque road. Here he employed fifteen to twenty German immigrants, who built small log houses with grass roofs, forming what was called the German village. Cody was not long satisfied.[10]

An event that profoundly affected the entire family was the death in the fall of 1853 of Samuel, the oldest boy, then twelve. Sam had the chore of bringing the cows from a pasture two or three miles away, and to do this, he rode a high-spirited mare. One evening he got to the main road just as school was letting out and probably wanted to show off his horsemanship. The mare, Bettie, reared and threw herself over on him. He was carried by the teacher and pupils to a near-by house, and his parents were summoned. Will, then seven, says in his first autobiography that he was riding with Sam and dashed off to call their father, who was at a political meeting at Sherman's tavern, a mile away. Julia, then ten, does not mention this, but says she was left alone that night to see to putting Willie, Eliza, and Nellie to bed. Sam was carried home next day to die.

The family agrees that Sam's death stimulated the removal from Iowa, but it took less than that to set Isaac Cody's feet to itching for travel. He had begun to hear about Kansas, and wrote to his brother Elijah, then living in Weston, Missouri, across the river from Leavenworth, for information. Elijah urged Isaac to come on. Isaac also wrote to members of Congress, who assured him that an

<hr/>

[10] Elizabeth Jane Leonard and Julia Cody Goodman, *Buffalo Bill: King of the Old West*, 290.

act opening Kansas and Nebraska to settlement would probably be passed at the winter session.

About the first of April, 1854, Isaac left Walnut Grove and came back to LeClaire, but as he had already sold all his property there, the family stayed for a few days with Isaac's companion of the California project, Dennis Barnes.[11]

[11] Colby, "Buffalo Bill's Old Boyhood Home," Davenport *Democrat and Leader,* March 14, 1948; Fryxell, "The Codys in LeClaire," *Annals of Iowa,* July, 1929; Cody, *Life,* 21; Mrs. Goodman MS—her dates check.

THE CODYS IN BLEEDING KANSAS

IT IS A POPULAR IMPRESSION that covered-wagon pioneers were poverty-stricken failures impelled by the hope of finding a more independent life by squatting on free land. Overlooked is the cost of the covered wagon itself, of the livestock to move it, and of provisions for the long journey. Pioneering was done by those willing to risk what they had to get more.

With attention focused on the long journeys over the Oregon Trail by its many diaries and journals—for strangely enough many pioneers recognized the historic importance of their adventure by keeping a record of it—we think of the Westward Movement as ever rolling steadily westward. Actually there were many backtrackings and crosscurrents.

Isaac Cody was no exceptional pioneer when he moved southward, from Iowa to Kansas, nor when he equipped himself with what his daughter declares was as nice an outfit as ever came to the new territory. There was a big, four-horse wagon loaded mostly with clothing, driven by a young man, George Yancey, hired for the purpose. There was a big family carriage, drawn by two horses and having three seats—not too much room for a family that now included, besides the parents, Martha, Julia, William, Eliza Alice, born in 1848, Laura Ella (also called Nellie and Helen), born in 1850, and Mary Hannah, six months old.

As they were traveling in a settled region, they did not camp out. Instead they traveled from county seat to county seat; sometimes finding a hotel of sorts; sometimes arranging to spend the night in a private house. In Missouri the children had their first experiences with Negroes and slavery. It is a curious commentary on the isolation of that period that Willie, born in a log cabin and brought up under what we consider pioneer conditions in Iowa, did not know the difference between Negroes and Indians.[1]

It was a leisurely journey of about a month; William even tells of a stop along the way to enter one of their animals in a horse race. At Weston they were welcomed by Elijah Cody, who made available to them temporarily a house on his farm about two miles from town. Within a few days Elijah proposed that as he had business at the Potawatomi Indian Reservation, eighty miles westward, he and Isaac should take their wives and look over prospects in Kansas Territory. Willie was allowed to go along.[2]

They ferried across the Missouri River and went through the Fort Leavenworth reservation. Willie was impressed by a full-dress parade of dragoons—the Wild West show idea perhaps began to germinate during these early days. From the top of Government Hill[3] they looked down upon the beauties of Salt Creek Valley, and that spot Isaac and Mary Cody immediately picked for their future home, a determination that was not shaken by subsequent exploration. But Willie was more impressed by the hundreds of white-covered freighters' wagons, waiting to start their trips westward on government contracts to supply army posts on the farther frontier. At the agency he saw his first Indians and rode Indian ponies.

Isaac let no grass grow under his feet. On his return he went with Elijah to the fort, met the quartermaster, and obtained permission to graze his horses in Salt Creek Valley. As a result he got a government contract to put up hay for use at the fort, and eventually permission to erect a cabin for his temporary use. Meanwhile

[1] Mrs. Goodman MS; Wetmore, *Last of the Great Scouts*, 4–9 (Grosset & Dunlap edition [hereafter G&D], 4–10); Cody, *Life*, 21–25.

[2] Mrs. Goodman locates it at Marysville, probably St. Marys.

[3] Government Hill is marked by co-ordinates 347:749 on *Typographical Map, Fort Leavenworth and Vicinity*, General Service Schools, Fort Leavenworth, 1924; and on U. S. Geological Survey, *Kansas-Missouri, Leavenworth and Vicinity*, 1911, reprinted 1922.

he and Willie camped out in the valley. They traded for Indian ponies, one a gentle bay mare they named Dolly; the other an unbroken sorrel stallion that Willie named Prince. One evening they met a young man camped near by with a party of Californians bringing back a herd of mustangs for market. He proved to be Horace Billings, a nephew of Isaac and Elijah Cody, the son of their sister Sophia. Horace's whereabouts had been unknown to his family for several years, during which time he had been in Hawaii as well as in California and had been a horse rider with a circus. Horace undertook to break Willie's Prince and taught that plains-bred animal to kneel and do other tricks. Horace demonstrated his own skill by riding standing on one of the better-trained Cody horses. His visit was brief, as he soon returned to mustanging, but here was another contribution to the future Buffalo Bill's Wild West.

Meanwhile the act to organize the Territory of Kansas was passed by both houses of Congress and approved by President Pierce on May 30, 1854. Isaac Cody heard of it on June 10, and on that day took his family and possessions across the Rialto Ferry and headed for the cabin he had built in Salt Creek Valley, thus claiming to be the first legal settler to enter Kansas. He surveyed the quarter-section lines of his claim, filed his claim at Fort Leavenworth, and hired men to help him erect a seven-room log house.

Perhaps after all it was Isaac Cody who was responsible for Buffalo Bill's Wild West. A Fourth of July celebration seemed essential in those days, but neighbors were few except for Kickapoos, Delawares, and Cherokees, for whom M. Pierce Rively had operated a trading post since 1852. The Reverend Joel Grover was missionary. Cody, Rively, and Grover planned a barbecue and picnic, purchasing a wagonload of supplies, as well as two beeves— one for the whites, who roasted their animal in a pit and served it on a long table made of boards and sawhorses; the other for the Indians, who butchered it after the manner of hunting a buffalo and ate it the same way, inside and out, to hide and bones. The Indians gave war dances, played games, and took part in horse races; the whites had patriotic speeches. Such a barbecue was a standard frontier event, but seldom were Indians invited.

Other events at Rively's store were less peaceful. Isaac Cody may have been the first legal settler, but others had preceded him, and on the day Cody moved his family to Kansas after receiving word of the act of Congress, a group of squatters met at Rively's store to organize for the mutual protection of their rights to claims they had entered without authority—a common practice in the westward movement, and usually successful. The Salt Creek Valley Resolutions of June 10, 1854, however, attracted attention in the press because of two added provisions: "That we recognize the institution of slavery as always existing in this Territory and recommend that slaveholders introduce their property as soon as possible," and "That we afford protection to no Abolitionists as settlers of Kansas Territory."[4] That Rively himself was a prime mover in this organization is suggested by the fact that he later was a member of the convention that drafted the proslavery Lecompton constitution.

Isaac Cody was not particularly disturbed by the Salt Valley Resolutions since he did not consider himself an abolitionist. There is no indication that he came to Kansas as a Free Soil crusader and every indication that his main idea was to attain material success in the new territory. He had dabbled in politics; two daughters and a son say he had been elected to the Iowa legislature, although there is no record that he ever served. It seems doubtful that he considered any political activity in Kansas until he was pushed into it. He ran surveys for some of his neighbors among the Missouri squatters, and was not reticent in giving them his opinion that slavery would not flourish in Kansas.[5]

On September 18, 1854, as he was passing Rively's store on horseback, he was hailed and asked to address a settlers' meeting. He tried to beg off, but some of the settlers took him to a large dry-goods box as platform and demanded a speech. As reported by his son "as nearly as I can recollect," Isaac Cody explained that he had

[4] Jesse A. Hall and LeRoy T. Hand, *History of Leavenworth County, Kansas;* A. T. Andreas, *History of Kansas* (Chicago, 1883), 83; Samuel A. Johnson, *The Battle Cry of Freedom* (Lawrence, Kan., 1954), 73; for Rively, see Robert W. Johannsen, "The Lecompton Constitutional Convention," *The Kansas Historical Quarterly,* Vol. XXXIII, No. 3 (Autumn, 1957), 241.

[5] Mrs. Goodman MS; Wetmore, *Last of the Great Scouts,* 16 (G&D, 17); Cody, *Life,* 16. William J. Peterson, superintendent of the State Historical Society of Iowa reported on January 18, 1951, that a researcher had "consulted a half dozen different sources, none of which revealed that Isaac Cody ever served in the General Assembly of the State of Iowa."

voted to make Iowa a *white* state—"that negroes, whether free or slave, should never be allowed to locate within its limits; and, gentlemen, I say to you now, and I say it boldly, that I propose to exert all my power in making Kansas the same kind of a state as Iowa. I believe in letting slavery remain as it now exists, and I shall always oppose its further extension."

He was shouted down as an abolitionist; one or two spectators tried to drag him from the platform, and when he attempted to continue, he was stabbed with a bowie knife by Charles Dunn, an employe of Elijah Cody. This was going too far for the temper of the time, and there was no interference when Dr. Hathaway, a neighbor who also had Free Soil sentiments, took Isaac into Rively's store, attended to his wound, and then suggested that he be taken to Elijah's home in Weston, where he could receive better attention. Mrs. Cody was sent for; she brought a wagon and a driver. Isaac was taken to his brother's home, where he stayed in bed three weeks. His lung had been hit. He recovered and resumed his normal pursuits, although his death three years later was attributed to this injury, at least as a contributing factor.

This is the story as told by Buffalo Bill in his 1879 autobiography and as told by his sister Julia. He makes no heroic claim further than to say that his father "shed the first blood in the cause of freedom in Kansas." That claim may be valid, but as the cause of freedom in Kansas had not yet become a major issue, the event, which was an altercation rather than a riot, attracted little notice. Because of exaggerations giving Willie a heroic role, doubt has been expressed whether Isaac Cody ever was stabbed.

That he was, much as his son tells it, is confirmed by a contemporary newspaper account—no friendly one, but rather showing a ferocity of feeling that is surprising at this early stage of Kansas settlement. The *Democratic Platform* of Liberty, Missouri, reported on September 28: "A Mr. Cody, a noisy abolitionist, living near Salt Creek, in Kansas Territory, was severely stabbed, while in a dispute about a claim with Mr. Dunn, on Monday week last. Cody is severely hurt, but not enough it is feared to cause his death. The settlers on Salt Creek regret that his wound is not more dangerous, and all sustain Mr. Dunn in the course he took."[6] This is the only

[6] In the Kansas State Historical Society (hereafter referred to as KSHS) Library.

mention of a land dispute, a not uncommon accompaniment of arguments over the slavery issue in Kansas.

By a somewhat devious path, a Buffalo Bill legend was built upon this episode. According to his sister Julia, Willie was at home when the assault was reported, and said he wanted to kill the bad man when he got big. It was his sister Helen who brought Will to the scene: "As father fell, Will sprang to him, and turning to the murderous assailant, cried out in boyhood's fury: 'You have killed my father! When I'm a man I'll kill you!' . . . Mr. Hathaway and Will then carried father to a hiding place in the long grass by the wayside. The crowd dispersed so slowly that dusk came before the coast was clear. At length, supported by Will, father dragged his way homeward, marking his tortured progress with a trail of blood. The path was afterward referred to in the early history of Kansas as 'The Cody Bloody Trail.'"[7]

Just how the hiding was accomplished in the midst of a crowd dispersing so slowly or how much support was given his father by eight-year-old Will is not made clear. In Cody's last autobiography, whose editors seem sometimes to have elaborated Helen's stories, Will is made to say, "Somehow I got off my pony and ran to his assistance, catching him as he fell. His weight overbore me but I eased him to the ground. . . . With the help of a friend I got father into a wagon when the crowd had gone. I held his head in my lap during the ride home."[8] The wagon is back and "The Cody Bloody Trail" is gone, but it is still melodramatic. Apparently a family legend grew from a small boy's wanting to kill the bad man to a rescue of the father and face-to-face defiance of the bad man. Dan Winget, claiming to have been Will's boyhood companion, goes further and says Will in later years tracked down and killed the assailant. Actually all that seems to have happened to Dunn is that he lost a job working for Elijah Cody.[9]

Trouble was growing, and Isaac Cody's neighbors manifested their disapproval of his sentiments by driving off his horses. He also attributed to them the mysterious burning of three thousand tons of hay he had put up on the contract with the Fort Leaven-

[7] Wetmore, *Last of the Great Scouts*, 18 (G&D, 19).
[8] Cody, *Autobiography*, 12.
[9] Dan Winget, *Pipe Dreams, Smoker* (August, 1924), 10; *Pipe Dreams—Third Smoke* (October, 1925), 31.

worth quartermaster. However, he was not frightened off, but filed a pre-emption on his claim in Kickapoo Township in the fall of 1854, paying $1.25 an acre for it.[10]

He had considered joining in the development of the townsite of Leavenworth until he was sought out by A. J. Whitney, James Frazier, H. B. Jolley, and Robert Riddle, who persuaded him to join them in locating a new townsite. So great was his reputation as locator and surveyor that they agreed to help him complete his house so that he would be free to go. The result of their exploration was the founding of Grasshopper Falls, which became Valley Falls. They organized a company to put up a sawmill and a gristmill. By spring six or eight families were settled there.[11]

With his house in Salt Creek Valley completed, Isaac Cody established a school in the cabin the family had vacated and hired Miss Jennie Lyons to teach it. A dozen children were rounded up, including two Kickapoo boys from the reservation six miles away. The young Indians became Will's particular friends. The school lasted three months. It ended when a delegation from the Salt Creek Valley Squatters Association told Miss Lyons that they did not intend to allow any damned abolitionist to have a school and that if they came again, they would burn the schoolhouse and all in it, as most of the pupils were Cody's brats anyhow. The frightened teacher handed her resignation to Mrs. Cody, as Isaac was at Grasshopper Falls.[12]

Isaac, however, was not frightened off; he continued improving his Salt Creek Valley home. He started a well in the fall. In the spring he got down sixty feet without striking water and quit. He had left a pick at the bottom and proposed to lower Willie down after it. That was one adventure our hero ducked. Julia volunteered, much to the consternation of her mother, who found out about it just as Julia was crawling out the top, pick in hand.

The well failure made necessary a long haul from a spring that gave occasion for an unsuccessful encounter of the future Buffalo

[10] Mrs. Goodman MS; Hall and Hand, *History of Leavenworth County*, 410: "Cody's farm was on the south side of the Fort Riley Road and old Oregon Trail, now [1921] part of Weisinger and Seymour farm, north of the Hurd farm."
[11] Mrs. Goodman MS, A. T. Andreas, *History of Kansas*, (Chicago, 1883) Vol. I, 205 (sketch of Isaac Cody, p. 508); they staked their claims December 25, 1854.
[12] Mrs. Goodman MS; Edwin L. Sabin, *Buffalo Bill and the Overland Trail*, 14.

Bill with the wildlife of the plains. One night Will and his father started for the spring after dark. They found the spring in possession of a horde of wild beasts, but were able to ward off attacks with swinging pails and retreat to the house. Armed with guns and a lantern, they returned. They fired again and again at shining eyes reflected in the lantern's light with terrible effect, but with even more terrible effect on the surrounding atmosphere. Victorious, they filled their pails and returned, but the water was unusable, and their clothing had to be buried. The next morning they also buried the bodies of a dozen skunks near the spring.[13]

Besides fighting skunks and going to school, nine-year-old Will with the aid of twelve-year-old Julia and their ponies plowed ten acres and planted it in corn—one of the few times in his life he worked as a farmer.

On May 10, 1855, the last of the Cody children was born. He was named Charles Whitney, the Whitney for his father's partner in the Grasshopper Falls enterprise. Charles died at the age of nine, on October 10, 1864.

Isaac Cody was busy that spring of 1855 guiding emigrants to Grasshopper Falls and surveying and locating claims for them. There is no indication that he was active in the cause for which he had suffered. The November election of a delegate to Congress, who would serve only until March 4, had aroused little interest, even though it had been carried by bands of ballot-box stuffers from Missouri.

When votes of Missouri visitors carried an election of a territorial legislature on March 30, 1855, the Free State forces were aroused. The "Bogus Legislature," as it was called by Free State men, rode the victory with a high hand. Governor Andrew H. Reeder called new elections in seven districts where fraud seemed provable. The legislature declined to accept the credentials of any Free State men and adjourned to Shawnee, convenient to the Missouri border. The Governor declared the removal illegal. At this point a scandal over land speculation forced the removal of Governor Reeder by President Pierce.

Ominous of the future was the arrival at Osawatomie on April 20 of John Brown, a fanatical abolitionist beyond doubt. Much less

[13] Mrs. Goodman MS.

17

fanatical were the settlers whose way had been paid by the New England Emigrant Aid Society, for many of them had come along for the free ride. Other Free Staters were not abolitionists at all. Their ranks included Whigs, Free Soilers, Know-Nothings, Democrats, Hards and Softs, and Hunkers, and other varieties of the confused political parties of the period. They spent the summer holding conventions in an attempt to find points of agreement—no less than six were held at Lawrence from June through August, followed by another at Big Springs in September and a constitutional convention at Topeka in October. Its chairman was James H. Lane, former Democratic lieutenant governor of Indiana, opportunist, anti-abolitionist who insisted on a referendum, which carried, barring free Negroes from Kansas, subsequently major general of the militia of this pseudo-government, and leader of the Free Soil fight.

The Topeka constitution was adopted on December 15. An election was called for January 15, 1856, in which Charles Robinson of the New England Emigrant Aid Company was elected governor, Mark William Delahay to Congress, and Isaac Cody to the legislature as representative from the Twelfth District.

Mark William Delahay is a baffling character to Lincoln biographers. Carl Sandburg refers to him as "the only man of whom it was known that Lincoln promised him money for personal political promotion" and as "a shady Kansas politician." Delahay was born in Maryland in 1819. His wife was said to have been a Hanks, of the family of Lincoln's mother. He practiced law in Springfield, Illinois, and came to Leavenworth, Kansas, in the fall of 1854, possibly as an observer for Lincoln—at all events he acted in that capacity.

Lincoln promised him money for coming from Kansas to Chicago for the Republican convention that nominated Lincoln in 1860. In 1861 the two associates in the Topeka movement, Lane as captain and Delahay as first lieutenant, took a Frontier Guard of White House Defenders to Washington to protect Lincoln during the inaugural. Lincoln appointed Delahay surveyor-general for Kansas and Nebraska, and subsequently United States Circuit Court judge for Kansas, from which position Delahay resigned when threatened with impeachment for incompetency, corruption, and drunkenness on and off the bench.[14]

Delahay, possessed of these many capacities, appeared on July 4, 1855, editing the first issue of *The Kansas Territorial Register* at Leavenworth. A contemporary diarist said it "is a Democratic Union, non-committal sort of a Free State paper and is ably edited. . . . If he comes out Free State, in the river he goes—this National Democrat dodge won't work in Kansas."[15] This proved an accurate forecast, for on December 22 of that same year presses and type were thrown into the Missouri River by the Kickapoo Rangers, who were none other than Isaac Cody's Kickapoo Township neighbors, formerly the Salt Creek Valley Squatters Association. Delahay was away at the time, at a state convention of the Topeka Movement, but even though he met with no physical violence, his career as journalist was ended, permanently.[16]

Isaac Cody met Delahay during the summer of 1855, and it was Delahay who interested Cody in the Topeka Movement. It is probable that Cody's first service was as elections officer and returns judge for the vote on ratifying the constitution of December 15.[17] A month later he was elected to the legislature. The Free State party made no attempt to open polls in proslavery strongholds for this election. However, at Easton, near Leavenworth, Border Ruffians threatened to stop the voting and a Free State militia company, captained by Reese P. Brown who was also a candidate for the legislature, was called out to guard the polls. The following day Kickapoo Rangers, Cody's unpleasant neighbors, caught Captain

[14] Carl Sandburg, *Abraham Lincoln: The War Years* (4 vols., New York, 1939), III, 451; see also I, 236, 371, and *Abraham Lincoln: The Prairie Years* (2 vols., New York, 1926), II, 327-30, 340, 385-86; Carl Sandburg, *Lincoln Collector: The Story of Oliver R. Barrett's Great Private Collection* (New York, 1950), 64, 154-56; H. Miles Moore, *Early History of Leavenworth City and County* (Leavenworth, 1906), sketch of Delahay, p. 265; Henry Clay Whitney, *Life on the Circuit with Lincoln*, ed. by Paul M. Angle (Caldwell, Idaho, 1940), 333; Don C. Seitz, *Lincoln the Politician* (New York, 1931), 145; *Transactions of the KSHS*, VI, 287, 295, 361, 415; John G. Clark, "Mark W. Delahay: Peripatetic Politician," *The Kansas Historical Quarterly*, Vol. XXV, No. 3 (Auumn, 1959), 301-12.

[15] Moore, *Early History of Leavenworth City and County*, 120.

[16] Hall and Hand, *History of Leavenworth County*, 218, 262; Johnson, *Battle Cry of Freedom*, 144-45.

[17] William E. Connelley (ed.), "The Topeka Movement," records of the Free State Provisional Government, *Collections of the KSHS*, XIII, 125-249. "B. G. Cody" was paid $24.16 for services as election officer and returns judge (p. 161); "Isaac," carelessly scribbled, might be read "B. G."

Brown alone and hacked him to death with hatchets, one of the most atrocious murders of the border war.[18]

Isaac Cody was one of the most active members of the Topeka legislature. He was one of thirty-three, out of a membership of sixty, who answered roll call to establish a quorum when it convened on March 4, 1856. Sessions continued through March 15, and apparently Cody was present at every meeting, sometimes three a day, morning, afternoon and evening. Of some fifty roll calls, his vote is recorded on all except three. He served on the Ways and Means Committee and the Accounts Committee. He received one vote through two ballots in an election for members of a committee to select a capital. After its adjournment on March 15 the House of Representatives attempted to meet again on July 4, 1856, but was dispersed by Colonel E. V. Sumner of the United States Army. When a session called for January 6, 1857, lacked a quorum because many members were under arrest, a recess was taken until June. As no roll calls were taken for the July and January sessions, it is not known whether Isaac Cody attempted to attend them.[19]

As it has been said by a historian of some standing that Isaac Cody "had no influence on the free state cause, took no part in it, was not stabbed as has been stated, and was never mistreated in any way by border ruffians,"[20] the proved facts may be emphasized: that he was stabbed in an argument over slavery is confirmed by a contemporary newspaper; that he was elected a member of the Topeka legislature and faithfully attended its regular sessions; that he lived in Kickapoo Township where flourished the Kickapoo Rangers who threw into the river the press of his close associate Delahay and murdered a fellow member of the legislature. With this much verified, certain further adventures recorded by members of his family seem not unreasonable.

One night Isaac Cody came home ill and went to bed in an

[18] Oswald Garrison Villard, *John Brown* (Garden City, N. Y., 1939), 129; Hall and Hand, *History of Leavenworth County*, 218; Johnson, *Battle Cry of Freedom*, 145.

[19] Journal of the House, *Collections of the KSHS*, XIII, 166–235.

[20] Richard J. Walsh, *The Making of Buffalo Bill*, 38, quoting William E. Connelley. J. C. Dykes has supplied penciled notes that Connelley made on a copy of Walsh's book; on p. 38 he wrote "True," and on p. 35, regarding the stabbing, "Never happened" and "Nothing to it." Yet Connelley edited the legislative journal in which Isaac Cody's name appeared forty or fifty times.

upstairs room. Next morning, a man whom Will and Helen identify as a justice of the peace named Sharpe rode up and demanded a meal. As Martha began preparing food, he asked Mrs. Cody where her damned abolitionist husband was. She replied that when she had last heard from him, he was at Grasshopper Falls but was expecting to go to Topeka. Sharpe sat on a chair, sharpening a long knife on a whetstone, and declared he was going to take Isaac Cody's lifeblood with it when he caught him. Mrs. Cody then told Julia and Willie to take the three younger children upstairs. There Isaac Cody told Willie to get his gun and Julia to get an ax, ordering Willie to stand ready to shoot if Sharpe started up the stairs, Julia to attack with the ax if Willie missed. Of course, this is Julia's story; no one else would concede that the future Buffalo Bill could miss a shot, even at nine or ten years of age. Mrs. Cody, who seems to have had her share of the family courage, kept on talking to the unwelcome visitor, and apparently her calmness was convincing, for he ate his dinner and went on his way, doing no other damage than stealing Mr. Cody's saddlebags.[21]

Between alarms, farm life went on in normal ways. Julia spent the winter in Leavenworth, going to school with Mollie Delahay and doing some work in exchange for her board. This family friendship continued for several years; Julia tells of meeting Abraham Lincoln when he visited the Delahay home during his Kansas tour in 1859. Isaac Cody spent most of his time at Grasshopper Falls, where he had taken all the cows except two. Willie had the usual farm boy's chore of driving the remaining two cows to pasture. His sister says he usually took a gun along to practice firing at a mark, the two Kickapoo boys who had attended school with him often being his companions.

Mr. Cody returned home in the spring of 1856, accompanied by a number of armed men—possibly on his way to the session of the Topeka legislature. He noticed that the pasturage was good and suggested that Willie and Julia drive back the cows from Grasshopper Falls. They made the long ride on their Indian ponies in one day and spent the night at the home of Dr. Lorenzo Northrup—his family had spent the winter of 1854–55 in the Cody home while

[21] Mrs. Goodman MS; Cody, *Life*, 51–52; Cody, *Autobiography*, 14–15; Wetmore, *Last of the Great Scouts*, 23–24; there are some discrepancies.

waiting to move to the falls. Willie and Julia started home the next day, but the seven cows slowed them down so that they were only halfway home by dark. They stopped at the house of Mr. Lellie, where they were made welcome, although a wedding was about to take place and approximately fifty homesteaders were on hand to see Daisy in her lawn dress printed with large flowers and to dance most of the night to the music of two fiddlers. Willie and Julia slept in the barn with other guests—girls at one end of the loft, boys at the other—and next morning they got their breakfast, paid for their entertainment (no record of how much), and took the cattle on home. This is the sort of episode that makes the Buffalo Bill legend seem so impossible a century later, not because anything happened, but because nothing did. Mr. Cody, riding with an armed party in fear of murderous Border Ruffians, thought nothing of sending his thirteen-year-old daughter and ten-year-old son on a three-day trip through a sparsely settled and lawless frontier country to get a few cows. It was another age; in all the charges of atrocities by both sides in the border war, no crimes against women or children were recorded.

As the summer wore on, the children picked strawberries, raspberries, wild plums, crabapples, and grapes. The corn grew tall. Willie and Julia rode their ponies to Leavenworth for mail and to shop. A neighbor named Harney, who had a contract from the Fort Leavenworth quartermaster for hay, brought twenty-five workers to a camp near the Cody farm. When some of them came to buy milk, Mrs. Cody talked with them about her troubles with the Border Ruffians, and they offered to help her. One night a wagon was heard approaching, its drunken crew shouting at the tops of their voices what they intended to do to the "damned old abolitionist." The children were sent to ask help from the hay camp. When the wagon stopped in front of the house, Mrs. Cody told the Border Ruffians that her husband was not at home, but that he would arrive soon with Jim Lane's band. About that time the haymakers let out a shout and fired off a few guns. The Border Ruffians whipped up their horses and got out, not stopping to pick up a keg of powder that rolled off their wagon. They had planned to blow up the Cody house, or so they had boasted at the store where they had bought the powder.[22]

Pro-Slavery men established a guard at a distance from the house, planning to intercept Isaac Cody when he returned home from Grasshopper Falls. Dr. Hathaway came to warn the family and urge them to get word to Mr. Cody. Willie was in bed with the ague and had just had a chill, but he got up and insisted on taking the message. Julia saddled his pony, Prince, while Mrs. Cody wrote a letter which Willie hid inside his stocking. He started slowly, as he was wobbly from being sick. At Stranger Creek, eight miles out, he saw a camp; one of the men there, catching sight of him said, "That is the damned abolitionist boy; let's go for him." They had to catch their horses and saddle them, thus giving Willie time to get to the top of the hill sloping away from the creek and to the prairie. By that time several men were galloping after him. He pushed his pony to the limit, but kept only a few hundred yards ahead. He recalled that the farm of a friend, Mr. Hewette, was about nine miles from the creek. As Hewette employed several men, Willie would be safe there. The boy lost his hat; he got sicker and sicker, but reached the Hewette gate a little ahead of his pursuers. The farmer and his hands were just coming out from dinner, and their appearance was enough to frighten off the Border Ruffians. Hewette inquired what the trouble was, and well he might. Willie had puked all over his pony, which was also white with foam, yet the boy insisted on going on to warn his father. Hewette told him that he had talked with his father that morning and that he had no intention of going home until the last of the week, so there was no hurry. Hewette also warned Willie that if he did not rest his pony he would kill it. They dragged the boy off his pony and put a man to walking it while Mrs. Hewett took charge of Willie, bathed him, and put him to bed. Exhausted, he slept all night, awoke apparently cured of the ague, found Prince to be all right, and rode the remaining five miles to meet his father at Grasshopper Falls.[23]

Isaac Cody read the letter and decided that instead of going

---

[22] Mrs. Goodman MS, Cody, *Life*, 50–51; Wetmore, *Last of the Great Scouts*, 25–26; there are more discrepancies.

[23] Mrs. Goodman, needless to say, is the only narrator who tells of our hero's puking all over his horse; she says she got these details from Mr. and Mrs. Hewette in 1876. This seems to clinch the story of Willie's rising from a sick bed. Cody, *Life*, 45–46; Cody, *Autobiography*, 13–14; Wetmore, *Last of the Great Scouts*, 27–29.

home he would join General Lane, who had marched his "Army of the North" to Lawrence. Willie went along, and it was ten days before the family knew what had become of them. Then two men rode up and asked to spend the night, saying they had come from Jim Lane's camp. When questioned, they identified Little Billie as a boy who had made quite a reputation by defeating men of the camp at rifle shooting, and Isaac Cody as among the important men there, always making speeches. This was a period when Lane's army had a number of skirmishes with Border Ruffians with several killings on both sides, but it is unlikely that Isaac Cody had any part in them, as he and Willie arrived home a few nights later.[24]

The father was ill from exposure, yet it was unsafe for him to stay in the house, as watchers could still be seen on a distant height. A bed was made for him in a cornfield. In daytime he wore a skirt and cape and a pasteboard sunbonnet, so that he would look like a woman from the distant hill. Dr. Hathaway attended him for two weeks, at the end of which time he felt sufficiently recovered to attempt to go to Fort Leavenworth for refuge. He was barely able to walk, and it took him three days to make four miles, keeping to the cornfields, and away from roads. Willie and Julia accompanied him by the main road, carrying food, water, quilts, and blankets from one stopping place to the next. After sleeping out two nights, he reached the home of a Mr. Lawrence, who took him to the fort.

The army at that time was declining to protect Free State refugees; therefore, Mr. Cody consulted Delahay, who suggested that he go East and assist in recruiting immigrants for Kansas. Delahay gave Cody letters of introduction to a number of persons who might be of help, among them Abraham Lincoln. Isaac Cody took steamboat and train to Cleveland, where he visited his brother Joseph and to some degree recovered his health, enough that the two brothers went to Chicago to attend a Republican meeting, and there Isaac Cody presented his letter from Delahay to Lincoln. Mr. Cody stayed away about two months; by the time he returned, Kansas had quieted, and there is no record of his being further disturbed. The tide of emigration had turned against the proslavery

[24] Lane was in and about Lawrence from August 1 to September 14, 1856. The fight at Hickory Point took place on September 14. Mrs. Goodman's dating indicates August for the visit of the Codys.

forces, and they now had little hope of success. To this end Isaac Cody contributed in some degree, for that fall and the following spring he was busy locating families at Grasshopper Falls.

Prince, first of Will's famous steeds, was stolen by Border Ruffians and recovered in several surprising ways in Buffalo Bill books. Julia's story lacks sensationalism. She says Prince was stolen toward the end of the border troubles. Shortly afterward the Kickapoo Rangers decided to disband for the winter of 1856. They posted notices on trees and fences that anyone who thought his horses were in their camp should claim them on a certain day. Willie read the notice and went to the camp to look for Prince. He found one stall closed and locked; when he whistled, a horse answered. Willie then went to the captain and said he had come to claim his pony. The captain asked him to prove he had an animal in the camp. Willie told him to have stall ten unlocked and the animal in it untied. When Willie whistled, Prince nickered once, then ran out of the stall and up to Willie, nosing him affectionately. "Take him home," said the captain. Julia says Will met this captain again years later and they became good friends.[25]

During his eastern tour Isaac Cody had invited emigrants he recruited to make his home their headquarters. By March the house was full and tents were set up in the yard. Scarlet fever and measles broke out, causing four deaths. Isaac Cody, busy trying to help, suffered a chill while working in the rain. Dr. Hathaway was called and reported the condition serious. Elijah was notified, and brought another doctor from Weston, but Isaac grew worse, and on March 10, 1857, he died. He was buried in Pilot Knob Cemetery, Leavenworth.[26]

Isaac Cody's family attributed his death to the stab wound of three years before. More directly it might be said that he gave his life in aiding the emigrants who saved the Free State cause in Kansas. A harsher judgment might point to a mixture of patriotism and profit, and note that his devotion to the cause of freedom was closely allied to his speculative interest in Grasshopper Falls. In this he

[25] Although Mrs. Goodman does not name him, he was probably John W. Martin, captain of the Kickapoo Rangers and member of the proslavery Lecompton constitutional convention.

[26] Lydia S. Cody, *The Cody Family*, 35; Ernest William Cody, secretary, Cody Family Association, confirms March 10 as date of Isaac's death.

was no different from most of the heroes of "Bleeding Kansas." He was no fanatic like John Brown, no crusader for a cause, but typical of the average Kansas settler unexpectedly pitched into a major political battle and forced to take sides.

Moreover, Isaac Cody was typical of the frontier generally—restless, never satisfied with what he had, always sure that the promised land was just beyond the next horizon. The principal legacy he left his son was this restless pioneering urge toward the pot of gold at the end of the rainbow. Will followed a rainbow trail all his life, but never quite caught up with the pot of gold, although many a time it vanished when almost within his grasp.

William F. Cody at four years of age.

Buffalo Bill's statue at Cody, Wyoming

Courtesy Northern Pacific Railway

3

BOY ON THE PLAINS

GRANTED MORE TIME, Isaac Cody might have left his family prosperous. His death in the midst of ever expanding projects left them land poor. Joseph Cody, Isaac's brother, came from Cleveland to manage the Grasshopper Falls property. He established the first newspaper in Jefferson County, but abandoned it after four months, and apparently he was similarly unsuccessful in bringing any immediate prosperity to the Cody family. In addition, according to Helen, the Isaac Cody family was threatened with a suit for one thousand dollars for a debt that had already been paid. This was settled in their favor late in the summer, but meanwhile Mrs. Cody had sold a team of horses, discharged the hired help, and rented the farm. The renters took care of a long-neglected job of fencing, but that had the effect of cutting off the house from the Military Road, eliminating much of the hotel business the family had done with traders and other travelers.

Willie went to work for a neighbor, driving an ox-team to Leavenworth for fifty cents a day. When the hauling job was completed, he told his mother he would like to work for Majors and Russell, so she took him along the next time she went to Leavenworth to trade at the company store. Alexander Majors, while waiting on her, noticed Willie tugging at his mother and asked what the boy wanted. She said he wanted a job. Majors asked if Willie could ride. Willie replied that he had often run races in Salt Creek Valley with William H. Russell, the other partner in the firm. They consulted Russell, who offered Willie a job as express boy, carrying messages between the firm's office and the telegrapher at Fort Leavenworth, a distance of three miles. Willie jumped at the offer, and was given a place to sleep, assigned a mule to ride, and told to report at eight o'clock the next morning. He was there bright and early and was given messages to be taken to the fort. When Willie entered the office a short time later, Russell supposed he had not yet gone and scolded him, but when Willie delivered the answers from the fort, he was commended for his promptness, although cautioned that the messages were not so important that he should ride the mule to death.

The firm of Majors and Russell eventually grew into an intricate organization of interlocking partnerships, involving also William B. Waddell and John S. Jones, that is almost as tangled as some holding-company complications of the twentieth century. The most famous of these partnerships was Russell, Majors and Waddell, which operated the Pony Express in 1860. When Willie first became its messenger boy, the firm of Majors and Russell was on the verge of its first big expansion. In 1855 it had obtained a two-year contract from the government giving the firm a monopoly on transporting military supplies west of the Missouri River. That contract was renewed for one year on February 25, 1857, and during April and May the trains of huge freight wagons drawn by oxen left with the annual supplies for frontier forts. Normally this would have completed the government business for the year, and Majors and Russell would have turned to private hauling to keep their wagons rolling; but in June, 1857, the quartermaster at Fort Leavenworth called upon the partners to transport three million pounds of additional supplies for the somewhat grandiloquently styled Army of Utah—it consisted of parts of two regiments of infantry, a regiment of dragoons, and a battery of artillery—which was being mobilized for the equally grandiloquently styled Mormon War—a war without casualties.

Trouble with the Mormons was nothing new in that period. Driven out of Missouri, then out of Illinois after their leader Joseph Smith was killed by a mob, they had traveled across the plains to the unwanted deserts of Utah. There Brigham Young set up a patriarchal government, but accepted the appointment of terri- torial officials from Washington. Some of them had little sympathy with the religion of the Church of Jesus Christ of Latter-day Saints or with Mormon ways of life, and clashes were inevitable. Brigham Young was reported to be fomenting rebellion. The army got under way in late July, and Majors and Russell strained their resources getting together the fifty-nine wagon trains they sent out that sea- son. While they were scraping the bottom of the barrel of their equipment and manpower, it is reasonable to suppose that they made such use as they could of their young employee Willie Cody.

Cody tells of three trips across the plains in this period, but his chronology of them is hopelessly confused. The sequence of events following is a reasonable interpretation after fitting certain epi- sodes that are corroborated to others that may be assumed to have occurred approximately as told by Cody or his sisters.

Willie carried messages between the freighting company office and the fort telegrapher for some two months, but there was too much sitting around offices and too little riding to suit a country boy. John Willis, a friendly wagon train boss, suggested that Willie ask for a transfer to help him herd his oxen while they were re- cuperating between trips. To this Majors and Russell consented. As the oxen were grazed about eight miles from the Cody home, the boy was able to make frequent visits to his family, and Julia tells how he strutted when he rode in, wearing strapped around him a revolver John Willis had given him. When this job ended, Willie returned home.

There had been no school since Miss Lyons had been frightened off by the Border Ruffians, but when a young man boarding at the Cody home until he could locate a claim said he had been a teacher in Illinois, Mrs. Cody proposed to organize a school. Willie and Julia scouted the neighborhood and turned up fifteen to eighteen pupils for him at two dollars a month each, including Willie, Eliza, and Helen—Julia was too busy with housework to go. Classes opened in midsummer in a cabin on an abandoned claim.

At this point our story first acquires a heroine, Mary Hyatt by name, with whom Willie admits he was "dead in love—in a juve- nile way." The boys built playhouses or arbors for their sweethearts, and Willie built such an affair for Mary, only to have it torn down by his rival, Stephen Gobel, about three years his senior. They tangled, and Willie got a licking. The teacher heard about it, and whipped both of them. The former cowboy carried a bowie knife in his bootleg, and when Steve continued his teasing and started to kick down the rebuilt playhouse, Willie slashed him in the thigh. Steve bled a little and shouted that he was killed, thus bringing the teacher and other pupils on the run. Willie ran too, but in the direction where he knew John Willis was camped with a wagon train. Late in the afternoon, Steve, his father, elder brother, and the constable were seen approaching, and Willie hid in one of the wagons. As Willie had last been seen heading in that direction, they proposed to make a search, but Willis, who was something of a plains lawyer, asked to see their warrant, and when the constable admitted he did not have one, suggested that they should have one before trying to arrest a boy for what amounted to little more than play. Willis offered so much argument they gave up. Late in the evening Willis brought Willie home and proposed that Mrs. Cody allow the boy to go along with the train to Fort Kearny, a journey of forty days, by which time the excitement would have died down and probably trouble would be avoided. She consented. Of this first trip across the plains Bill says, "The trip proved a most enjoyable one for me, although no incidents worthy of note occurred on the way."[1]

John R. Willis disagreed with Bill about the lack of incident. Forty years later Buffalo Bill's Wild West played Memphis, on October 4, 1897, and the wagon-master and prairie lawyer, now a judge at Harrisburg, Arkansas, wanted to see it. Because he missed it, we have this letter: "Dear old Friend it has bin a long time scince I have herd from you. Seeing in the Dailys that you would be in Memphis today I thought I would like to hear from you personly and I would have come over but it seems that I am out of luck at this time. I am county judge of Poinsett County, Arkansas, only three hours from Memphis and I have to hold court today and I see that you will be in Memphis only one day. I would like very much to shake your hand, Billy, and talk over the old grand hours

[1] Cody, *Life*, 53–57; Mrs. Goodman MS; Wetmore, *Last of the Great Scouts*, 56–61.

30

you rode at my heels on the little gray mule while I was killing Buffalo. oh them were happy days. of course you recolect the time the Buffalo run through the train and stampeded the teams and you stoped the stampede. Well write as soon as you get this or send answer by Telegraph to Harrisburg, Ark., as I will be holding court there all day. Your Freind and old Wagon Master, John R. Willis."[2]

Undoubtedly this incident is the one in which Cody describes the train as strung out to a considerable length between the foot of the sand hills and the river, some two miles away. A large herd of buffalo was grazing between the road and the river. A party of returning Californians dashed into the herd and stampeded it toward the hills, and "about five hundred of them rushed through our train pell-mell, frightening both men and oxen. Some of the wagons were turned clear around, and many of the terrified oxen attempted to run to the hills, with the heavy wagons attached to them. Others turned around so short that they broke the wagons' tongues off. Nearly all the teams got entangled in their gearing, and became wild and unruly, so that the perplexed drivers were unable to manage them. The buffaloes, the cattle, and the drivers were soon running in every direction, and the excitement upset nearly everybody and everything. Many of the cattle broke their yokes and stampeded. One big buffalo bull became entangled in one of the heavy wagon-chains, and it is a fact that in his desperate efforts to free himself, he not only actually snapped the strong chain in two, but broke the ox-yoke to which it was attached, and the last seem of him he was running towards the hills with it hanging from his horns. A dozen other equally remarkable incidents happened during the short time that the frantic buffaloes were playing havoc with our train."[3]

That is all he says of it, with not a word about his stopping the stampede, which would imply remarkable horsemanship for a boy eleven or twelve years old. It helps to explain why almost every army officer with whom Buffalo Bill served as scout referred to him as a modest man—an incomprehensible adjective to those who

[2] *Letters from Buffalo Bill* (ed. by Stella Adelyne Foote), 46 (facsimile), reprinted by permission.
[3] Cody, *Life*, 73–74; Cody, *Autobiography*, 21–22.

look upon him as a braggart. It also explains why he sometimes exasperated those who sought to publicize him. Prentiss Ingraham did his best on the opening provided by Cody's "A dozen other equally remarkable incidents happened." With this slight invitation Colonel Ingraham concocted one of the tallest tales of the Buffalo Bill saga. Thousands of stampeding buffalo were racing directly toward the young hero, according to Ingraham. To escape, Billy leaped to the branches of a cottonwood tree, but from that vantage point he was able to see the cause of the stampede—a band of Indians. The Indians, of course, were heading directly toward the tree. His only escape was to leap to the back of a huge buffalo bull and ride him out. It made a spirited picture for the cover of the first issue of Beadle's Boy's Library. How did Billy get off, you may well wonder. Wild Bill, the only man on the plains capable of such accuracy, raised his rifle and dropped the buffalo. "From that day the boy was known as Buffalo Billy," says Colonel Ingraham, accounting for everything.[4]

Willis would have given a good account of Billy's value, particularly in the stampede, and Lewis Simpson next asked for him as an "extra hand." Mrs. Cody raised objection as she had heard that Simpson "was a desperate character, and that on nearly every trip he had made across the plains he had killed some one." Mr. Russell assured her that this account was exaggerated and that Simpson was regarded as one of the most reliable wagon-masters on the plains. After she had talked with Simpson, she gave her consent. Cody describes the organization of this train:

"The wagons were known as the 'J. Murphy wagons,' made at St. Louis especially for the plains business. They were very large and were strongly built, being capable of carrying seven thousand pounds of freight each. The wagon-boxes were very commodious —being as large as the rooms of an ordinary house—and were covered with two heavy canvas sheets to protect the merchandise from the rain. These wagons were generally sent out from Leavenworth each loaded with six thousand pounds of freight, and each drawn by several yokes of oxen in charge of one driver. A train consisted of twenty-five wagons, all in charge of one man, who was

[4] Col. Prentiss Ingraham, *Adventures of Buffalo Bill from Boyhood to Manhood*, 1, 5–6.

known as the wagon-master. The second man in command was the assistant wagon-master; then came the 'extra hand,' next the night herder; and lastly, the cavallard driver, whose duty it was to drive the lame and loose cattle. There were thirty-one men all told in a train. The men did their own cooking, being divided into messes of seven. One man cooked, another brought wood and water, another stood guard, and so on, each having some duty to perform while getting meals. All were heavily armed with Colt's pistols and Mississippi yagers." He explains that in the language of the plains, the wagon-master was called the "bull-wagon boss," the teamsters, "bull-whackers," and the whole train a "bull outfit."[5]

It was on this trip, says Cody, that he first became acquainted with James B. Hickok, later famous as "Wild Bill." Hickok, ten years older than Cody, was "a tall, handsome, magnificently built and powerful young fellow, who could out-run, out-jump and out-fight any man in the train. He was generally admitted to be the best man physically in the employ" of Majors and Russell. In telling of the beginning of their friendship, Cody says, "One of the teamsters in Lew. Simpson's train was a surly, overbearing fellow, and took particular delight in bullying and tyrannizing over me and one day while we were at dinner he asked me to do something for him. I did not start at once and he gave me a slap in the face with the back of his hand—knocking me off an ox-yoke on which I was sitting, and sending me sprawling to the ground. Jumping to my feet I picked up a camp kettle full of boiling coffee which was setting on the fire, and threw it at him. I hit him in the face, and the hot coffee gave him a severe scalding. He sprang for me with the ferocity of a tiger and would undoubtedly have torn me to pieces, had it not been for the timely interference of my new-found friend, Wild Bill, who knocked the man down. As soon as he recovered himself, he demanded of Wild Bill what business it was of his that he should 'put in his oar.' 'It's my business to protect that boy, or anybody else, from being unmercifully abused, kicked and cuffed, and I'll whip any man who tries it on,' said Wild Bill; 'and if you ever again lay a hand on that boy—little Billy there—I'll give you such a pounding that you won't get over it for a month of Sun-

---

[5] Cody, *Life*, 64–66; Raymond W. and Mary L. Settle, *Empire on Wheels*, 27–32.

days.' From that time forward Wild Bill was my protector and friend, and the friendship thus begun continued until his death."[6]

Wild Bill is not among those mentioned in the story of the capture of the wagon train by Lot Smith's Mormon militia a few days later. According to Cody this took place during a noon halt, when Simpson, his assistant George Woods, and Billy were driving the cattle a mile and a half to water and thus were separated from the main camp. As the story continues, Cody's autobiography lapses into language reminiscent of melodrama, perhaps in fact lifted bodily from *May Cody; or, Lost and Won*, a play about the Mormon War in which Cody had appeared the year before his autobiography was published.

While on their way back to camp a party of twenty men intercepted them. "The next moment three guns were leveled at Simpson. 'If you make a move you're a dead man,' said the leader.

"Simpson saw that he was taken at a great disadvantage, and thinking it advisable not to risk the lives of the party by any rash act on his part, he said: 'I see now that you have the best of me, but who are you, anyhow?'

" 'I am Joe Smith,' was the reply.

" 'What! the leader of the Danites?' asked Simpson.

" 'You are correct,' said Smith, for he it was.

" 'Yes,' said Simpson, 'I know you now; you are a spying scoundrel.'

"Simpson had good reason for calling him this and applying to him a much more approbrious [*sic*] epithet, for only a short time before this Joe Smith had visited our train in the disguise of a teamster, and had remained with us for two days."[7]

This language of the melodrama and the dime novel might cause some to put this down as an instance where Cody confused what had happened with the parts he had played or the adventures written about him. There is another explanation. Cody found what he once called "pen trails," tough ones to follow, and if the trail had been blazed by some predecessor, he was apt to take advantage of it. Of course, he knew no such words were spoken on that occasion, but he also indicates quite clearly that he knew the "appro-

[6] Cody, *Life*, 60–72.
[7] *Ibid.*, 75.

brious" words that were actually used were not printable—certainly not in 1879.

Here are the facts: On the night of October 4, 1857, Major Lot Smith's Mormon party captured and burned Majors and Russell's Trains 21 and 25 in charge of Wagon-masters John M. Dawson and R. W. Barrett at Simpson's Hollow on Green River. The bullwhackers of these trains were set afoot and had to walk twenty miles to Camp Winfield. On the following day Smith's party captured Train 26 in charge of Wagon-master Lewis Simpson some fifteen miles to the rear on Big Sandy Creek. Simpson succeeded in talking Smith out of one wagon, oxen to draw it, clothing, provisions, and even their arms. Lot Smith left his own account of the capture, in which he said, "Captain Simpson was the bravest man I met during the campaign." In all his melodramatic dialog, Cody does no violence to any known fact. His characteristic blunder in referring to Lot Smith as "Joe" is indication that his story is told from memory.[8]

Simpson's crew in their single wagon went on to Fort Bridger and spent the winter there with the troops of the Army of Utah and remnants of wagon-trains personnel. Bill Cody's presence there is confirmed by Trooper Robert Morris Peck of the First U. S. Cavalry, who wrote his reminiscences for the *National Tribune* in 1901. Trooper Peck says Cody "was then a boy of 11 or 12 years old, employed by Lou Simpson, a bull-train wagon boss, as an extra hand or 'cavvyyard' driver, or something of that kind.

"He gave no visible signs then of future fame, and only impressed me as a rather fresh, 'smart-ellick' sort of a kid. The bull-whackers had made quite a pet of him and one of them informed me that Billy was already developing wonderful skill at riding wild horses or mules, shooting and throwing a rope, etc. I had almost forgotten that I had ever seen the little dirty-faced bull-whacker when, just after the war, I heard the name of 'Buffalo Bill' mentioned frequently in connection with frontier affairs. I thought at first it was another nick-name that had been conferred on 'Wild Bill,' whom I had known on the plains by several sobriquets, as 'Injun Bill' and 'Buckskin Bill,' but on asking an old comrade who

[8] Leroy R. and Ann W. Hafen (eds.), *The Utah Expedition* (Glendale, 1958), 220–46; J. Cecil Alter, *James Bridger* (Columbus, 1950), 291–94; Settle, *Empire on Wheels*, 19–20.

had been with me in Utah, 'Who is this Buffalo Bill I hear so much about?' he answered 'Why don't you remember Bill Cody, that smart little fellow that was with Lou Simpson's bull-train as an extra hand?' my recollection of him was revived."[9]

Peck was not libeling Bill in calling him "dirty-faced." Sister Julia gives some details not usually included in adventure stories. One morning Will's whistle was heard from the top of a hill near the farm, and the dog Turk rushed out to greet the returning hero. The three sisters and the mother followed, but their enthusiasm suffered a sharp restraint. He was not fit to go into the house. They cut off his long hair, which was matted and covered with bugs. They took his filthy clothes away from him and burned them. After he had had a bath and had put on clean clothes, they let him in the house. The next thing he wanted to do was eat, for he had been living for weeks on bacon, hardtack, and black coffee.

To this period belongs the much-debated story in the Buffalo Bill legend of his killing his first Indian at the age of eleven—or was it twelve? It was on a cattle drive, another angle of the supply services of Majors and Russell, the beef herd being in charge of Frank and Bill McCarthy. At Plum Creek on the South Platte, thirty-five miles from old Fort Kearny, Indians stampeded the herd during a noon rest, killing three herders. The McCarthy brothers rallied the rest of the men, armed with Mississippi yagers (carrying a bullet and two buckshot) and Colt's revolvers, and a volley checked the Indians, although one herder was shot in the leg. Frank McCarthy ordered a dash for a slough, the bank of which would give some protection. The little party worked its way down the slough toward its junction with the South Platte, then down the river toward Fort Kearny. A raft of poles was made for the wounded man. Night found them still following the river bank—but here is the story as Cody told it in 1879:

"I being the youngest and smallest of the party, became somewhat tired, and without noticing it I had fallen behind the others for some little distance. It was about ten o'clock and we were keeping very quiet and' hugging close to the bank, when I happened to look up to the moon-lit sky and saw the plumed head of an

[9] *National Tribune*, May 9, 1901, transcript from Mrs. Raymond H. Milbrook, Detroit.

Indian peeping over the bank. Instead of hurrying ahead and alarming the men in a quiet way, I instantly aimed my gun at the head and fired. The report rang out sharp and loud on the night air, and was immediately followed by an Indian whoop, and the next moment about six feet of dead Indian came tumbling into the river. I was not only overcome with astonishment, but was badly scared, as I could hardly realize what I had done. I expected to see the whole force of Indians come down upon us. While I was standing thus bewildered, the men, who had heard the shot and the war-whoop and had seen the Indian take a tumble, came rushing back.

" 'Who fired that shot?' cried Frank McCarthy.

" 'I did,' replied I rather proudly, as my confidence returned and I saw the men coming up.

" 'Yes, and little Billy has killed an Indian stone-dead—too dead to skin,' said one of the men, who had approached nearer than the rest, and had almost stumbled upon the corpse. From that time forward I became a hero and an Indian killer. This was, of course, the first Indian I had ever shot, and as I was not more than eleven years of age, my exploit created quite a sensation."

The party continued down the river, reaching Fort Kearny shortly after reveille. A company of cavalry and one of infantry followed the trail of the Indians to the head of Plum Creek, then gave up the chase. As only a few cattle were recovered, the company agent at the fort sent the party back to Leavenworth. "On the day that I got into Leavenworth, sometime in July," says Cody, "I was interviewed for the first time in my life by a newspaper reporter, and the next morning I found my name in print as 'the youngest Indian slayer on the plains.' I am candid enough to admit that I felt very much elated over the notoriety." He names the reporter as John Hutchinson, who "now lives in Wichita, Kansas." In a later account he names the newspaper as the *Leavenworth Times,* published by D. R. Anthony.[10]

That newspaper account has not been found, possibly because the episode cannot be dated accurately. The confusion involves the

[10] Cody, *Life,* 61–62; Cody, *Autobiography,* 20. Miss Helen M. McFarland, librarian, KSHS, checked files of the *Leavenworth Times* for July, 1858, and July, 1859, without finding the item, so Cody probably is mistaken about the name of the newspaper.

three expeditions. None of them was made before the death of
Bill's father in March, 1857. It is improbable that he could have
made more than two in one year, and Cody himself says he only
made two trips in any one year. Both Bill and his sister Julia agree
that the trip with the McCarthys, in which the first Indian was
killed, followed the two others. However, he says it took place between May and July, 1857, and she dates it 1859. Splitting the difference and making it 1858 is confirmed by a further circumstance.
Bill says he returned home in July to learn of the marriage of his
half-sister, Martha, to John Crane or Craine. The marriage took
place on February 7, 1858. Crane was revealed to be a bigamist,
and Martha died—of grief, the family believed—that November.
Julia says Bill did not learn of Martha's death until he returned
from another expedition, which all seem to agree followed the one
with the McCarthys.

With the date thus established, the remaining question is: Did
the incident happen at all? The story grew in the telling; few episodes in Buffalo Bill's career were subject of more exaggeration.
A favorite addition is that the Indian had an arrow, or gun, or
rifle aimed at one of Bill's comrades and that Bill's shot saved a life.
Bill's comrades, it may be recalled, were some distance ahead, and
it was night. Indian attempts to stampede and steal stock were not
uncommon on the plains at this period, and while it was less usual
to get a chance at a shot at one of the Indians, Bill's story is not so
remarkable as to seem an invention. That the newspaper account
of it has not been found proves little, for more frontier newspapers
than Indians became casualties in early Kansas. Whether Bill killed
an Indian at eleven, or twelve, or thirteen years of age is of scant
importance, but as he seldom told any tale without some basis of
fact, it seems probable that he did.

Cody's story continues that shortly after his return from this
expedition in July, he went out with another wagon train, with
Buck Bomer in charge, taking supplies to Fort Laramie. From
there, Cody says, they were ordered to take supplies to a new post
being established at Cheyenne Pass, which appears in his book as
Fort Wallach. Obviously this is Camp Walbach, named for Brevet
Brigadier General John DeBarth Walbach, veteran of the War of
1812. It was established at Cheyenne Pass, about eighty miles from

Fort Laramie and twenty-five miles northwest of present Cheyenne, in September, 1858, and was abandoned in April, 1859.[11]

The wagon train returned to Fort Laramie about November 1,
and Bill says he "joined a party of trappers who were sent out by
the post trader, Mr. Ward, to trap the streams of the Chugwater
and Laramie for beaver, otter, and other fur animals, and also to
poison wolves for their pelts." Seth Edward Ward was post trader
and sutler at Fort Laramie from 1857 to 1871. This trapping venture lasted less than two months, did not prove very profitable, and,
says Cody, "was rather dangerous on account of the Indians." They
returned to the fort in December.[12]

Bill, still a boy, it should be remembered, found some time to
play with Indian boys his age at Fort Laramie, to learn something
of sign language and other Indian ways, and to make some friends.
However, when he learned in January, 1859, that Lew Simpson
was ordered back to Leavenworth as brigade trainmaster of three
wagon trains traveling a day apart, Bill was eager to accompany
him, and go home.

After passing Ash Hollow, the trains followed the North Platte,
seeking better dried grass than would be available along the well-
traveled South Platte route.

One morning Simpson took George Woods, his assistant wagon-master, and Billy to ride with him from the rear train to the one
ahead. They had gone about seven miles on their mules, and were
on a big plateau back of Cedar Bluffs when they discovered a band
of Indians coming out of a ravine half a mile distant.

"I thought that our end had come this time, sure," says Cody.
"Simpson, however, took in the situation in a moment, and knowing that it would be impossible to escape by running our played-
out mules . . . jumped from his own mule and told us to dismount
also. He then shot the three animals, and as they fell to the ground
he cut their throats to stop their kicking. He then jerked them
into the shape of a triangle and ordered us inside the barricade."
The Indians, some forty in number, charged. The three fired their

[11] Cody, *Life*, 85; Cody, *Autobiography*, 28 ("Walback"); Francis B. Heitman, *Historical Register and Dictionary of the United States Army*, II, 554; information from Fort Laramie records by David L. Hieb, National Park Service.

[12] Cody, *Life*, 85; Merrill J. Mattes, "The Sutler's Store at Fort Laramie," in
Annals of Wyoming, Vol. XVIII, No. 2 (July, 1946), 102–13.

Mississippi yager rifles—a single-shot weapon carrying a conical or Minié ball and so named because it was made famous by the Mississippi volunteer regiment commanded by Colonel Jefferson Davis in the Mexican War. Their Colt's revolvers, also cap and ball, were used next, and these may have been a surprise to the Indians, as repeating arms were still uncommon on the plains. Billy remarks that only two or three of the Indians had firearms. The Indians balked their charge, as they usually did when meeting resistance, and started circling while shooting arrows, one of which struck Wood in the shoulder, but without putting him out of action for long. After all this shooting, a survey showed three Indians and one horse dead—a modest claim compared with those usually made for Indian fights. The Indians charged again, and again stopped short of the barricade. No further casualties are reported. The foe then drew back some distance, surrounding the three, and tried to burn them out, but the late winter grass was too short. Night came on. The besieged trio dug in with their knives to strengthen their fortification. At dawn the Indians tried another charge, but gave up when they saw that the three were alert and not out of ammunition. At ten o'clock the loud and sharp reports of big bull-whips were heard. As the first wagon of the rear train came into view, the Indians made a half-hearted charge, fired a last volley of arrows, and rode away.[13]

After some buffalo hunting along the Platte near Plum Creek, adding to the experience that later made Billy a skilled hunter, Simpson sent Billy with two men identified as Scott and Charley to take the train-book record ahead, so that the teamsters' money would be ready when the trains reached Leavenworth. After Indians on the other side of the Little Blue had chased them futilely for two hours, Billy, Scott, and Charley hid in a deep ravine. Billy found a hole in the bank into which they crawled, but when Charley struck a match to light his pipe, they saw they were surrounded by skeletons. Bones of massacre victims in a cave sounds like something out of one of Colonel Ingraham's dime novels, but likely they had stumbled into an Indian burying ground. They did not tarry to investigate, but got going. Next night they reached Oak Grove Ranch, where Scott and Charley went on a three-day spree. As

[13] Cody, *Life*, 79–84; *Autobiography*, 30.

Billy was only thirteen and says he got home with money in his pockets, he probably did not join them. He reached home in February, 1859.

Most unbelievable in these adventures is Billy's age—and once again we find him where he belongs at that age, in school. Mr. Valentin Divinny was the teacher, and Cody says, "My mother wished me to attend it, and I did so for two months and a half—the longest period of schooling that I ever received at any one time in my life." This is the fifth school he is recorded as attending. His formal education ended in the late spring of 1859 when he was struck by the "Pike's Peak or Bust" gold rush excitement. Billy was one of those who busted. Green Russell, one of the Georgians who had found gold on Cherry Creek, passed through Leavenworth on his way home to recruit a party for further prospecting. His reports were not optimistic, but he was assumed to be trying to cover up. Billy joined a party headed for Auraria, the future Denver.

"We pushed on to the gold streams in the mountains," says Cody, "passing up through Golden Gate, and over Guy Hill, and thence on to Black Hawk [the January discovery of John H. Gregory]. We prospected for two months, but as none of us knew anything about mining, we met with very poor success, and . . . turned our faces eastward." They built a raft and attempted to navigate it down the Platte, but were wrecked at Julesburg, losing baggage and provisions. A bull train came by, and as Billy knew the wagonmaster, he hired to go back to Auraria with it and then return home to Leavenworth.

That fall the Cody family moved into what they called the Big House, which they planned to run as a hotel. Billy contributed by inviting some of his friends to board there during the winter. Julia names them as James B. Hickok (not yet Wild Bill), Lew Simpson, John Willis, and George Ross.

In November, Billy started on a trapping expedition with Dave Harrington. The story he tells sounds like something concocted for Beadle's Dime Library, but its essentials are confirmed by his unimaginative sister Julia, who had a personal interest in that she carried on a flirtation with Dave Harrington. He being twenty-three and she sixteen, it came to nothing, says she. The partners bought a wagon, a yoke of oxen, provisions, and traps, and set out for the Republican River. From Junction City they worked north to the mouth of Prairie Dog Creek. There one of the oxen slipped on ice, dislocating its hip, and had to be shot. This stopped them, and they camped to trap beaver. They built a dugout in the side of a hill, covered it with grass, brush, and dirt, put up a fireplace, and got in some wood. One night a bear attacked the surviving ox. Dave wounded the bear, which charged him. Billy, with a lucky shot in the dark, killed the bear. A few mornings later, while stalking a herd of elk, Billy slipped on the ice and dislodged a large stone, which fell on his leg and broke it. Dave set and bound the broken bone and carried Billy to the dugout.

As Billy would be laid up most of the winter, it seemed obvious that Dave should start at once for the nearest settlement, borrow a yoke of oxen, and come back for the wagon, Billy, and their pelts and gear. This would take twenty days, they estimated. Dave chopped wood to last that time, put the provisions within Billy's reach, and rigged a can on a string and stick so that Billy could pull it through a window to get snow for water. For the first eleven days after Dave left, Billy had little to do but lie still. He read the Bible through and a few other books—one of the rare times he mentions reading anything. Like Robinson Crusoe (which may have been one of the books) he cut a notch in a stick each day to keep track of time.

On the twelfth day he was awakened by a touch on his shoulder, and looked up to see an Indian's face, daubed with war paint. The dugout was soon full of Indians, with more peeping in the door. An elderly Indian pushed through; Billy recognized old Rain-in-the-Face, whom he had often visited at Fort Laramie. Cody says he was taught the Siouan language by the sons of this chief, including "the son who succeeded to the name of Rain-in-the-Face, and who years later, it is asserted, killed General George A. Custer." Recent students discredit stories that Rain-in-the-Face killed either General Custer or his brother, Captain Tom Custer.

The elder Rain-in-the-Face recognized Billy and persuaded his young men to spare the boy, although they took his rifle and pistol, cooking utensils, sugar, coffee, and matches. They cooked a lot of his provisions, but "were polite enough to give me some of the food after they had cooked it," Cody recorded in their favor. They left him part of a deer, flour, salt, and baking powder.

The second day after they left it began to snow. Snow continued for three days until the doorway was blocked and the dugout covered to a depth of several feet. The snow delayed Dave, and it was not the twentieth, but the twenty-ninth day, when his voice was heard shouting to his oxen and calling to Billy.

Dave gathered their traps, loaded their furs, which the marauding Indians had missed, and arranged a bed in the wagon for Billy. They had three hundred beaver skins and one hundred otter skins. After eight days of toiling through snow, they came to a ranch house, where they rested two days, then went on to the farm where Dave had borrowed the team. For its use they paid twenty-five beaver skins, valued at sixty dollars. At Junction City they sold furs and wagon, and joined a government mule train, arriving home in March, 1860.[14]

[14] Cody, *Life*, 85–101; Mrs. Goodman MS.

4

BOY OF THE PONY EXPRESS

WHILE BILLY CODY AND HIS COMPANIONS were demonstrating that it was necessary to know something about mining to extract gold from the Pikes Peak region, his recent employer, Russell, was succumbing to an attack of gold fever. Russell, older and more experienced than Billy, knew it was easier to take gold out of the miners than out of the mines. The obvious way would have been through the freighting business he knew so well. Instead, he also tried something he knew nothing about. It took him longer to learn his lesson, but the result was the same.

Russell's first reaction to the gold fever was to invest in the Denver City Town Company, organized by his friend General William Larimer of Leavenworth. That gave Russell about thirty acres in the middle of the future capital of Colorado. Second guessing a hundred years later could not have done better than that. Then, with John S. Jones, always ready to form a partnership with any of the famous three, Russell organized the Leavenworth and Pike's Peak Express Company. He neglected to consult Majors or Waddell about this venture, in which they were soon to become heavily involved, whether they liked it or not. A minor setback came when Auraria instead of Denver got the post office. Russell overcame that obstacle because there was no way of sending mail except by the Leavenworth and Pike's Peak Express Company.

However, he had no contract to carry mail, and to get one, he bought J. M. Hockaday and Company, which had a mail contract between the Missouri River and Denver. This involved extending his route. His main line followed the Oregon Trail, while coaches for Denver forked off at a crossing that soon became known as Julesburg. The overextended company was bankrupt by October 28, 1859, and the firm of Russell, Majors and Waddell took it over to save its partner. With losses from the Mormon War unsettled, affairs of Russell, Majors and Waddell were precarious.

The principal asset of Russell's venture was the Hockaday mail contract, worth $130,000 a year. The mail contract to California, worth $600,000 a year, was held by John Butterfield's Overland Mail Company, controlled by Wells Fargo, Adams, American, and National express companies. Butterfield's "ox-bow" route dipped from Little Rock to Preston, Texas, almost touched the Mexican border at Fort Fillmore, then went by way of Fort Yuma to San Diego, turning northward to San Francisco. It was 2,800 miles long, and it took twenty-five days to get mail from the Missouri River to San Francisco. It was obvious to anyone who looked at a map that the central route was shorter. Russell, Majors and Waddell put on a huge advertising campaign to prove that the central route was the most practical. That campaign was the Pony Express.[1]

Whether Russell or someone else conceived the idea of the Pony Express has been disputed, but the idea was neither particularly new nor original. Marco Polo found messages speeded by using relays of riders on horseback in Kublai Khan's domain long before America was discovered. George Wilkins Kendall, pioneer war correspondent, established a pony express to send his Mexican War dispatches to the *New Orleans Picayune*. To establish a regular service of this character, however, required a high degree of organization.

Russell, Majors and Waddell had a start on that organization in their mail line to Salt Lake City, but stage stations were too far apart. At first, Pony Express stations were set up at intervals of twenty-five miles, but even this proved too far for horses to travel at top speed, and the distance was cut in half. Beyond Salt Lake

[1] Mannel Hahn, "The Pony Express," *The Westerners Brand Book* (Chicago), Vol. III, Nos. 1, 2, 3 (March, April, May, 1946).

City an entirely new line of stations was laid out. Required in all were 190 stations, 500 horses, and 80 riders—and an investment of $100,000.

Special saddles were designed to cut down weight. They were made to take a *mochila*, a leather sheet that fitted over the saddletree. It had a hole to put over the horn and a slit to pass over the cantle. In the corners were four leather pouches called *cantinas*, each with a brass padlock. Keys for three cantinas were held only at the principal stations: Fort Kearny, Fort Bridger, Fort Laramie, Salt Lake City, and Carson City. The fourth was for way letters and the time card, signed at every station. The *mochila* could be changed in a very brief time—the record was said to be eleven seconds. Opening the pouch, signing the card, and relocking took longer. The rider stood in his stirrups as he neared the station, pulled the *mochila* out from under him, dismounted, threw the *mochila* over the saddle of the waiting horse, mounted, and was ready to go as soon as the station agent had scribbled the data on the time card. A rider made seven to twelve such changes in his day's ride of seventy-five to one hundred miles. After he met his relay, he rested a day or two, then rode back to his home station over the same route.[2]

As the Pony Express was primarily an advertising venture, its inauguration on April 3, 1860, was accompanied by all the glamour and fanfare that could be devised. There is still some argument over who rode the first relay out of St. Joseph, Missouri—it was not Buffalo Bill—but most riders of the first run, both ways, are known. One was Pony Bob Haslam, long associated with Buffalo Bill's Wild West in later years. The time of the first trip from San Francisco to St. Joseph was ten days. It took four more days to get the mail to New York by railroad. Important messages could be telegraphed from St. Joseph. The story of the Pony Express is also that of a race with a telegraph line, moving both westward and eastward toward a junction. The lines were joined on October 24, 1861, providing through service from New York to San Francisco. The last run of the Pony Express was on November 18. Russell, Majors and Waddell failed to get the mail contract they sought for their Central Overland, California and Pike's Peak Express Company, last of

[2] Arthur Chapman, *The Pony Express*, 83–90.

their numerous business organizations. The Pony Express was run at a loss—that was expected. But the failure to get the mail contract, added to their other troubles, caused the downfall of the partnership in all its ramifications. The triumph for which they are remembered bankrupted them.[3]

Why is it remembered? It was spectacular and it had much contemporary publicity, yet a recent historian notes that almost nothing was written about it for half a century after its brief existence. Undoubtedly the Pony Express owes much of its continuing glamour to one of its riders, William F. Cody. For three decades a representation of the Pony Express was a spectacle at every performance of Buffalo Bill's Wild West. No other act was more consistently on its program. It was easy to stage, and it had the interest of a race, as well as re-creating a romantic episode. It is highly unlikely that the Pony Express would be so well remembered had not Buffalo Bill so glamorized it; in common opinion Buffalo Bill and Pony Express are indissolubly linked.

Actually Bill Cody's riding was far from being of outstanding importance to the operation of the Pony Express, however much he contributed to its bright and shining tradition. Some skeptics have vociferously denied that he ever rode Pony Express at all, but they offer no argument against it except his age. Billy was fourteen when the Pony Express started and not quite sixteen when it ended. It is commonly stated that Russell, Majors and Waddell required riders to be at least twenty. They did not. The average age of some forty Pony Express riders about whom biographical details are available was under nineteen.[4]

Alexander Majors wrote, "Among the most noted and daring riders of the Pony Express was Hon. William F. Cody, better known as Buffalo Bill." This would be conclusive on Cody's services except for its appearing in a book closely connected with publicity for Buffalo Bill's Wild West. The book was dedicated to Cody, had a preface signed by him, and he guaranteed the $750 cost of printing it. Its title page names Prentiss Ingraham as editor, but it is far too dull a book to have been ghost-written by the author

[3] Olaf T. Hagen, "The Pony Express Starts from St. Joseph," *Missouri Historical Review*, Vol. XLIII, No. 1 (October, 1948).

[4] Raymond W. and Mary Settle, *Saddles and Spurs*, 111; Gene Morgan, "*Westward the Course of Empire . . .*" (Chicago, 1945), 3.

of Buffalo Bill dime novels. It seems unlikely that the partner responsible for the pledge required of all employees to refrain from profanity, drinking, or dishonesty would have endorsed a complete falsehood. It is of record that Majors protested some exaggeration edited into it.

A disinterested witness to Cody's Pony Express riding was Edward E. Ayer, the wealthy contractor who founded the American Indian collection in the Newberry Library, Chicago. In a private journal Ayer wrote: "About six or seven years ago I attended a reception and dinner given by all the diplomats of Paris to Buffalo Bill. I said it wasn't necessary to introduce me to Bill Cody; that I had crossed the plains in 1860, and that he was riding by our train about a month, and would give us news in a loud voice as he rushed by, so that we all became much attached to him. At the reception Bill wouldn't let me get out of his sight, and insisted that I should sit at his side, thereby disarranging the seating plan at the banquet."[5]

Cody makes a poor witness for himself by getting his dates tangled. He says he arrived at Julesburg as the Pony Express started, but gives the date as 1859. George Chrisman, a former wagon-master was station agent—on that Cody is correct. Chrisman bought the ranch from René Jules, or Jules Reni, for whom the station was named. Chrisman "hired me at once as a pony express rider," says Cody, "but as I was so young he thought I would not be able to stand the fierce riding which was required of the messengers. . . . He gave me a short route of forty-five miles, with the stations fifteen miles apart, and three changes of horses. I was required to make fifteen miles an hour, including the changes of horses. . . . I stuck to it for two months, and then upon receiving a letter informing me that my mother was very sick, I gave it up and went back to the old home."

In the summer of 1860, he says, he met Lew Simpson in Leavenworth, and was invited to go with a wagon train from Atchison to Fort Laramie. He went home to tell his family of his plans, then joined Simpson in Atchison. There Billy met Russell, who gave him a letter to Joseph A. Slade, in charge of the division from Julesburg

[5] Frank C. Lockwood, *The Life of Edward E. Ayer* (Chicago, 1929), 28; original journal located by Stanley Pargellis, librarian, Newberry Library.

to Rocky Ridge, with headquarters at Horseshoe Station. When the wagon train arrived there, Slade employed Billy as Pony Express rider.[6]

Joseph Alfred Slade was born in Carlyle, Illinois, about 1824, and served in the Fifth Illinois Volunteers in the Mexican War. He stayed in the West and was reputed to have killed twenty-six men, although the name and address of only one is known. Benjamin F. Ficklin, route superintendent, sent Slade to Julesburg to get rid of Jules, believed to be sheltering a gang of thugs preying on the company. Slade ousted Jules; then Jules dry-gulched Slade with a double-barreled shotgun. Ficklin caught Jules and hanged him, but his outlaw companions cut him down and revived him. When Slade recovered, he raided the outlaw hideout near Rocky Ridge and captured Jules. Slade tied Jules to a corral post, filled him full of bullets, and cut off his ears, nailing one to the post and drying the other for a watch fob.[7]

Slade was a rough character. He was dismissed as agent for the Overland after he shot up the post canteen at Fort Halleck. He was hanged by Vigilantes at Virginia City, Montana, on March 10, 1864, after shooting up that town while drunk once too often and defying the miners' court. Yet Mark Twain found Slade "so friendly and so gentle spoken that I warmed to him in spite of his awful history." Billy Cody had a similar impression: "Slade, although rough at times and always a dangerous character—having killed many a man—was always kind to me. During the two years I worked for him as pony-express-rider and stage-driver, he never spoke an angry word to me."[8] It was on Slade's division that Billy made his most notable Pony Express ride.

Alexander Majors told the story thus: "His route lay between Red Buttes and Three Crossings, a distance of 116 miles. It was a most dangerous, long and lonely trail, including the perilous crossing of the North Platte River, one-half mile wide, and though generally shallow, in some places twelve feet deep, often much swollen and turbulent. An average of fifteen miles an hour had to be made,

---

[6] Cody, *Life*, 91; Settle, *Empire on Wheels*, 113.

[7] Isaac H. Elliott, *Record of the Services of Illinois Soldiers* (Springfield, 1882), 209; Hoffman Birney, *Vigilantes* (Philadelphia, 1929), 309–37; Thomas J. Dimsdale, *The Vigilantes of Montana* (Norman, 1953), 194–205.

[8] Mark Twain, *Roughing It* (Hartford, 1884), 79–96; Cody, *Life*, 105.

including change of horses, detours for safety, and time for meals. Once, upon reaching Three Crossings, he found that the rider on the next division, who had a route of seventy-six miles, had been killed during the night before, so he was called upon to make the extra trip until another rider could be employed. This was a request the compliance with which would involve the most taxing labors and an endurance few persons are capable of; nevertheless young Cody was promptly on hand for the additional journey, and reached Rocky Ridge, the limit of the second route, on time. This round trip of 384 miles was made without a stop, except for meals and to change horses, and every station on the route was entered on time. This is one of the longest and best ridden pony express journeys ever made."

Comparing this with Cody's account reveals several discrepancies. Cody gives his original route, Red Buttes to Three Crossings as 76 miles, not 116, and the added route to Rocky Ridge as 85 miles, not 76, making the total ride 322 miles instead of 384. The longest Pony Express ride is credited to Pony Bob Haslam during the Paiute War in Nevada and was 380 miles; second was Howard R. Egan with a run of 330 miles. Cody's third longest was not occasioned by Indian troubles; Miller, the man he replaced, had been killed in a drunken brawl. Majors protested exaggeration in the editing of his book, and undoubtedly he complained of these juggled figures that made it appear that Cody had made the longest ride. There is circumstantial evidence that is conclusive. Cody's subsequent *True Tales of the Plains* pretends to quote from Majors' book, but the mileage is given as 321, not 384. The quotation with corrected figures also appears in Frank C. Cooper's press-agent book, *Stirring Lives of Buffalo Bill and Pawnee Bill*. Cody himself never claimed to have made the longest Pony Express ride, and the mileages he gives check on the map. He says he made the 322 miles in twenty-one hours and forty minutes, using twenty-one horses.[9]

In his original autobiography Cody related only one other Pony Express adventure: "As I was leaving Horse Creek one day a party of Indians 'jumped me' in a sand ravine about a mile west of the

---

[9] Alexander Majors, *Seventy Years on the Frontier*, 176–77; Cody, *Life*, 104–105; Settle, *Empire on Wheels*, 119; W. F. Cody, *True Tales of the Plains*, 30; F. C. Cooper, *Buffalo Bill and Pawnee Bill*, 34.

station. They fired at me repeatedly, but missed their mark. I was mounted on a roan California horse—the fleetest steed I had, and lying flat on his back, I kept straight on for Sweetwater Bridge— eleven miles distant—instead of trying to turn back to Horse Creek. The Indians came on in hot pursuit, but my horse soon got away from them, and ran into the station two miles ahead of them. The stocktender had been killed there that morning, and all the stock had been driven off by the Indians, and as I was therefore unable to change horses, I continued on to Ploutz's Station—twelve miles further—thus making twenty-four miles straight run with one horse."

Whatever else may be said about this episode, it was obviously written down by Cody himself, for the station was Plant's and the only way so simple a name could come out as "Ploutz's" was for the printer to so decipher Cody's handwriting. Another case of the same sort of error comes up in this same period. Cody records that in September Indians robbed a stage between Split Rock and Three Crossings, "killed the driver and two passengers, and badly wounded Lieut. Flowers, the assistant division agent." The assist- ant division agent so wounded was Lem Flowers, and again Cody's handwriting was misread. This affair became badly entangled in the Buffalo Bill legend by being post-dated six years to his stage- driving days—with Bill as the hero of the occasion.[10]

The Indians drove off most of the horses, causing a suspension of service. Some forty riders, stock tenders, and stage drivers left idle organized a company to seek the stolen animals. James B. Hickok was elected captain. The company followed the Indian trail to Powder River, Crazy Woman's Fork, and Clear Creek, where a large Indian village was discovered. Hickok suggested that they wait until near dark, then creep close to the village, and at a signal dash through it, opening a general fire on the Indians, and attempt to stampede the stock. The plan worked; the Indians were taken by surprise, and before they could rally, the horse herd was on its way. All Pony Express horses were recovered, and a hundred Indian ponies were brought along. A grand spree at Sweetwater Bridge Station celebrated the victory. Slade came to take a hand, got into a quarrel with a stage driver, and shot and killed him.

[10] Cody, *Life*, 105–106; J. V. Frederick, *Ben Holladay*, 70.

Billy became "a sort of supernumerary rider" at Horseshoe Station, and describes his duties during the winter of 1860 and spring of 1861 as taking care of stock and occasionally riding a Pony Express run. He had time for hunting. One day when he had shot only a couple of sage hens, he happened upon what he took for a trappers' dugout. He knocked, and when the door opened, he saw eight men, two of whom he recognized as teamsters discharged by Simpson on suspicion that they had robbed and murdered a rancher. They did not appear to recognize Billy, so he put on a bold front and proposed to get his horse and spend the night. Hoping to allay suspicion, he suggested leaving his rifle, but this did not work; two of them accompanied him. After getting his horse, he purposely dropped one of the sage hens and asked one of the men to pick it up. While the bandit was stooping to do so, Billy struck him on the back of the head with a revolver, then quickly turned and shot and killed the other man, leaped to his horse, and spurred away. Closely pursued, he turned his horse loose and scrambled up a mountainside. The bandits kept on after the galloping horse. Billy got back to the station just before daylight. Slade organized a party of twenty to hunt the horse thieves, but found the dugout abandoned and a trail leading toward Denver. A new-made grave confirmed Billy's having killed one of them.[11]

The significant point of this story is that it is the only one, of anything signed by Cody, in which he tells of killing a white man. This episode and the raid on the Indian village are among the few incidents in Cody's original autobiography for which there is no corroboration. However, they are so inconclusive and unimportant that there seems no reason to doubt them. Some other Pony Express exploits are almost certainly apochryphal. One of them in *True Tales of the Plains* goes thus:

"As I was galloping around a curve on a hillside trail one day, I rode flush up to a leveled pistol. The man behind it told me to throw up my hands. I obeyed. There is no use arguing with a leveled pistol. Frontiersmen in those days shot to kill. The road agent dismounted and walked up to me to take my saddle-bags. I tried to look scared and harmless. He lowered his revolver as he reached for the bags. Just then I whirled my pony around. The little horse's

[11] Cody, *Life*, 107–18.

plunge knocked the man off his feet, and a stray kick from one of
the iron-shod hoofs grazed the fellow's head, knocking him sense-
less. Having no further interest in him I was glad enough to make
my escape, and rode in safety in time to the next station." In another version, Billy tied up the bandit and took him along, and in
still another all this took place during his famous long ride. What
makes it unreasonable is the fact that there was nothing in Pony
Express saddlebags to interest a bandit. No gold was carried at
five dollars a half-ounce.[12]

In another yarn Billy tells of arriving at a stage station that
was being stampeded by a buffalo bull. He shot the buffalo when it
was only fifteen yards from a three-year-old girl playing with a
wooden doll. A variant version names the girl as Mamie Perkins,
with an emigrant party and on her way to a river for a bucket of
water when the buffalo charged. Billy, in a passing government
wagon train, snatched up his rifle and killed the buffalo when it
was within a dozen feet of the terrified child. Perhaps something
of the kind happened at one time or another, but the stories are
badly garbled.[13]

In the closing Pony Express days Hickok had his encounter
with "the McCanles gang" that gave him his name of "Wild Bill."
Exaggerated stories of this affair added greatly to the reputation
of Wild Bill and also became badly entangled in the Buffalo Bill
legend. Wild Bill did not kill ten men with gun and knife. A record
of the court of Justice of the Peace T. M. Coulter shows that on
July 12, 1861, David C. McCanles, his nephew James Woods, and
James Gordon, a rancher, were killed at Rock Creek Station. Arrested on charges of murdering them were Hickok and J. W. Brink,
known as "Doc," stock tenders, and Horace Wellman, station agent.
After a hearing, the defendants' pleas of self-defense were sustained and they were discharged. There is no report of testimony,
but it is conceded that Hickok shot all three, killing McCanles and
wounding the others. His co-defendants were charged with killing
the wounded men.

Sixty-six years after the fight, Monroe McCanles, who had wit-

[12] Cody, *True Tales of the Plains*, 23–24; W. F. Cody, *Adventures of Buffalo
Bill* (hereafter cited as Cody, *Adventures*), 141–46; Frank Winch, *Thrilling Lives
of Buffalo Bill and Pawnee Bill*, 36.

[13] Cody, *True Tales of the Plains*, 24–26; Wetmore, *Last of the Great Scouts*, 36.

nessed it as a boy of twelve, said his father and the two other victims were unarmed. This seems careless of them, as Monroe quotes his father as threatening Wellman with the words, "Send him out or I'll come in and drag him out." McCanles went in and was shot by Hickok, who then wounded Woods and Gordon as they came running up. McCanles had sold the Rock Creek property to the Overland for a Pony Express station, and threatened to take his property back by force when he was not paid. Wellman resisted, although he had gone to the division office in Brownsville in an attempt to get the payment due. Further investigation indicated that McCanles, as sheriff of Watauga County, North Carolina, had absconded with trust funds in 1859, and had brought with him to Nebraska one Sarah Shull, also known as Kate Shell. After he homesteaded, he sent for his wife and family. It is said that Sarah (or Kate) then took up with Hickok. McCanles is also said to have bullied Hickok, which, as it proved, was unsafe. Motives seem sufficient, but the Civil War has also been dragged in.[14]

Despite contrary opinions recorded by Ned Buntline and Nebraska Ned, Buffalo Bill had nothing to do with it.[15]

[14] Connelley (ed.), *Collections of the KSHS*, XVII, 19–27; George W. Hanson, "True Story of Wild Bill–McCanles Affray," *Nebraska History*, Vol. X (April–June, 1927); Frank J. Wilstach, *Wild Bill Hickok*, 40–77; Richard O'Connor, *Wild Bill Hickok*, 17–31.

[15] Nebraska Ned, *Buffalo Bill*, 111–14.

In Ned Buntline's Drama, *Scouts of the Prairie*, in 1873

Left to right: Ned Buntline, William F. Cody, and Jack Omohundro ("Texas Jack").

Buffalo Bill's stage troupe, 1876–77

5

PRIVATE CODY IN THE CIVIL WAR

FROM THE VIEWPOINT of a century later the boyhood adventures of Billy Cody seem unbelievably fantastic. The twentieth-century boy is surrounded by a degree of family protection that would have been inconceivable to Tom Sawyer. While Billy Cody was bull-whacking across the plains, Horatio Alger, Jr., was finding home-less boys in New York living in packing boxes and supporting themselves as bootblacks and newsboys—and those who missed be-coming Alger heroes became juvenile delinquents. Had the Cody family remained in Cleveland, Ohio, Billy might have worked in a livery stable or have driven a grocer's delivery wagon. Because he was near Leavenworth, Kansas, he was found at the corral of Rus-sell, Majors and Waddell, driving their ox-teams or riding Pony Express. This seems romantic because Buffalo Bill, his press agents, and dime novelists made it so. After a closer look at what Billy said about himself, the conclusion might be drawn that he was a juve-nile delinquent of the plains. His first activity in the Civil War was as a horse thief.

Billy Cody for once was out of step with his epoch. In World War II and the Korean War there was much agitation against sending boys to battlefronts at the age of eighteen. About one-fourth of Civil War volunteers were under eighteen; drummers and fifers could be legally enlisted at sixteen. Billy Cody was fifteen in

1861, but he did not regularly enlist until he was eighteen. In later years he explained that he had promised his mother not to enlist while she lived. She died just before his eighteenth birthday. Apparently she had less objection to his joining the militia. During most of the war he was employed in some semi-military capacity.

The volunteer system resulted in great irregularities in organizations, some of which verged upon being private armies. Major General David Hunter, reporting on Kansas when the war was nearly one year old, said, "The State had recently twelve regiments nominally, ten quasi regimental organizations, and attempts were in progress to raise two more Kansas regiments for service in New Mexico." This seemed a huge army, but out of all of it he could round up only 1,600 soldiers on duty.[1] There were home guards for local defense against guerrillas led by Colonel William C. Quantrill and other successors of the Border Ruffians of an earlier day. Independent companies were raised by local leaders, who shopped around before joining a regiment. The first organization Billy Cody joined was one of these private armies carrying on its own private war. It was such a discreditable episode in his life that we can be sure he told the truth about it.

Billy says he quit the Pony Express at Horseshoe Station and arrived in Leavenworth about June 1, 1861. There, he says, "I met several of the old, as well as the young men, who had been members of the Free State party all through the Kansas troubles, and who had, like our family, lost everything at the hands of the Missourians. They now thought a good opportunity offered to retaliate and get even with their persecutors, as they were all considered to be secessionists. That they were all secessionists, however, was not true, as all of them did not sympathize with the South. But the Free State men, myself among them, took it for granted that as Missouri was a slave state the inhabitants must all be secessionists, and therefore our enemies.

"A man by the name of Chandler proposed that we organize an independent company for the purpose of invading Missouri and making war on its people on our own responsibility. He at once

[1] *The War of the Rebellion: A Compilation of the Official Records of the Union and Confederate Armies,* Serial Vol. 8, Series I, Vol. VIII (hereafter written as *O.R.* (8) I, VIII), 616.

went about it in a very quiet way, and succeeded in inducing twenty-five men to join him in the hazardous enterprise. Having a longing and revengeful desire to retaliate upon the Missourians for the brutal manner in which they had treated and robbed my family, I became a member of Chandler's company. His plan was that we should leave our homes in parties of not more than two or three together, and meet at a certain point near Westport, Missouri, on a fixed day. His instructions were carried out to the letter and we met at the rendezvous at the appointed time. Chandler had been there some days before us, and, thoroughly disguised, had been looking about the country for the whereabouts of all the best horses. He directed us to secretly visit certain farms and collect all the horses possible, and bring them together the next night. This we did, and upon reassembling it was found that nearly every man had two horses. We immediately struck out for the Kansas line, which we crossed at an Indian ferry on the Kansas river, above Wyandotte, and as soon as we had set foot upon Kansas soil we separated with the understanding that we were to meet one week from that day at Leavenworth.

"Some of the parties boldly took their confiscated horses into Leavenworth, while others rode them to their homes. This action may look to the reader like horse-stealing, and some people might not hesitate to call it by that name; but Chandler plausibly maintained that we were only getting back our own, or the equivalent, from the Missourians, and as the government was waging war against the South, it was perfectly square and honest, and we had a good right to do it. So we didn't let our consciences trouble us very much. We continued to make similar raids on the Missourians off and on during the summer, and occasionally we had running fights with them; none of the skirmishes, however, amounting to much.

"The government officials hearing of our operations, put detectives upon our track, and several of the party were arrested. My mother, upon learning that I was engaged in this business, told me it was neither honorable nor right, and she would not for a moment countenance any such proceedings. Consequently I abandoned the jay-hawking enterprise, for such it really was."[2]

[2] Cody, *Life,* 125–27.

The ultimate fate of Chandler and his company appears in official records. Captain Irving W. Fuller, First Missouri Cavalry (Federal) reports that on January 24, 1862, "I was notified by Mr. Irving, of Missouri, at 3 o'clock A.M. that 15 jayhawkers had robbed his farm in Missouri and taken therefrom 40 horses and mules and 6 negroes; that they dragged his family, among whom there are several females, out of bed, insulting them in the most revolting manner, robbed them of their jewelry, and finally left and proceeded in the direction of Elwood. I immediately concluded to go in search of this party, and Mr. Irving offering himself and a few neighbors as guides, I consented thereto, but dispatched him in advance. I overtook him at Geary City, where I found that his party had caught 2 and killed the captain (by name Chandler) of jayhawkers, and wounded another."[3]

Billy, loafing about Leavenworth, ran into Wild Bill Hickok, who was in charge of some ox-trains purchased by the government from Jones and Cartwright—the same Jones who was mixed up in the affairs of Russell, Majors and Waddell—and was loading supplies for the Federal post at Rolla, Missouri. Hickok persuaded Billy to come along "as a sort of assistant under him," and from Rolla they took a freight shipment to Springfield, Missouri, then returned to Rolla. Since Wild Bill had a fast running horse he wanted to enter in the fall races at St. Louis, they went there, betting everything they had, including the horse, on the race. Billy rode as jockey, but they were badly beaten, and, says Cody ruefully, "We were 'busted' in the largest city we had ever been in." Wild Bill went to army headquarters next morning and got a job as scout, and Billy records, "I being so young failed in obtaining similar employment." Hickok borrowed money and bought a steamboat ticket to send Billy back to Leavenworth. Hickok went to Springfield.[4]

Still in the fall of 1861, Billy says, he made a trip to Fort Larned, carrying military dispatches, and that winter he assisted George Long in buying horses for the government.

In the spring of 1862, he was guide and scout for the Ninth Kansas Volunteers under Colonel Clark in an expedition "to the

[3] O.R. (8) I, VIII, 54–56.
[4] Cody, Life, 127, 131–32.

Kiowa and Comanche country, on the Arkansas river, along which stream we scouted all summer between Fort Lyon and Fort Larned, on the old Santa Fe trail. We had several engagements with the Indians, but they were of no great importance." Official records show that Lieutenant Colonel Charles S. Clark with seven companies of the Ninth Kansas Cavalry was stationed at Ohio City, Kansas, on May 10, and some time between then and August 7 marched to Fort Lyon and Fort Larned, Colonel Clark being in command of Fort Larned in November. One engagement is recorded, at Locust Grove, Indian Territory, on July 3, one enlisted man of the regiment being killed.[5] Julia says that in Santa Fe, Will met Kit Carson, then colonel of the First New Mexico Volunteer Infantry.

Billy came home in the fall, and that winter joined the Red Legged Scouts, so called because they wore red leggings made from the red sheepskin used by shoemakers in those days. This was a quite informal militia or home guard organization, and Julia says Billy went to school during part of the winter, riding with the Red Legs when called out. Early in the war this organization of scouts was the idea of Brigadier Generals Thomas Ewing and James G. Blunt. Originally it had included a number of "Jennison's Jayhawkers," but most of them had joined Colonel Charles R. Jennison in forming the Seventh Kansas Cavalry in October, 1861. Even then some unkind observer had defined a Red Leg as "more purely an indiscriminate thief and murderer than a Jayhawker." That reputation was not improved by Billy's commander, Captain William S. Tough, also spelled "Tuff" and "Tuft," and, on the authority of Quantrill of the guerrillas, "Tufft." Tough was born in Savannah, Georgia, and had lived in Baltimore, Maryland, before coming to St. Joseph, Missouri, in 1860; thus all his antecedents were Southern. He was inclined to the Southern side after a band of Jayhawkers stole his mules, but received a greater injury from the other side—a band of bushwhackers shot him. Without authority from either side, Tough raised a company of seventy-five men at Leavenworth, took after the bushwhackers, and hanged five of them. From then on Tough and his company were counted on the Union

[5] *O.R.* (19) I, XIII, 377, 637, 808–11; *Official Army Register of the Volunteer Force*, Part VII (Washington, 1867), 353–54; Cody, *Life*, 134.

side, and despite other revengeful killings, had considerable official standing at the time Billy joined.

Cody mentions as members "Red Clark, the St. Clair brothers, Jack Harvey, an old pony express rider named Johnny Fry," but does not name Hickok, who is reported to have been a Red Leg at an earlier period. Cody describes their work as "many a lively skirmish with the Younger brothers, and when we were not hunting them, we were generally employed in carrying dispatches between Forts Dodge, Gibson, Leavenworth, and other posts."[6]

Official records contain little mention of the Younger brothers, the later associates of Frank and Jesse James in banditry, but do have some further information on Captain Tough. General Blunt appointed Tough his chief of scouts with pay of $250 a month. They were traveling with a wagon train accompanied by a small escort, including an army band, on October 7, 1863, when Quantrill's cavalry in blue uniforms appeared between them and the post at Baxter Springs. Tough recognized them as enemies, and he and the General opened fire. Quantrill pulled out after killing the escort and bandsmen and burning the wagon train. Among the dead was Johnny Fry, the Pony Express rider mentioned by Cody. General Blunt, accompanied by Tough and six or eight men, followed Quantrill's retreat, until he crossed the Neosho going south.[7]

Cody says that during the summer he "engaged to conduct a small train to Denver for some merchants," arriving there in September, 1863. In Denver he received a letter from Julia telling him that his mother was dangerously ill, so he hurried home. She died on November 22, 1863.[8]

Previously Julia was married to James Alvin Goodman. Her story puts Billy in the unusual role of matchmaker. She says that in the fall of 1862 she remarked to Willie that she knew he would not stay home, and as it was apparent that their mother would not live long, she was concerned about living in the Big House with the three young girls and no man to protect them. Willie suggested

---

[6] Cody, *Life*, 134–35; William E. Connelley, *Quantrill and the Border Wars* (Cedar Rapids, 1910), 411; Frank W. Blackmar, *Kansas: A Cyclopedia of State History* (2 vols., Chicago, 1912), II, 553–54.

[7] *O.R.* (32) I, XXII, 694, 698, 701.

[8] Cody, *Life*, 135; Mrs. Goodman MS; she says she sent the letter by a member of his company, meaning Red Legged Scouts.

that she get married, but he found objections to several eligible young men she mentioned. However, to Al Goodman, then living across the road on a rented farm, he could take no exception; Al was a steady, industrious young man who did not drink or use tobacco. Willie declared him to be just the one. Julia agreed, and put the question to Al on the purely business relationship of his agreeing to care for the younger members of the family. Al accepted the conditions, and they were married on December 22, 1862.

Billy was in no great rush to serve his country after his mother's death. In his own words, he went to Leavenworth and "entered upon a dissolute and reckless life—to my shame be it said—and associated with gamblers, drunkards, and bad characters generally. I continued my dissipation about two months and was becoming a very 'hard case'." On February 4, 1864, the Seventh Kansas Volunteer Cavalry, known as Jennison's Jayhawkers and including many men who had been in the Red Legged Scouts, arrived in Leavenworth for thirty days' veteran furlough. Volunteer regiments in the Civil War usually enlisted for "three years or the war," and at the end of three years a considerable effort was made to persuade members of the regiment to re-enlist in a body. Those who did so were sent home on veteran furlough—a chance for the boys to parade their uniforms before the home folks and to seek recruits from among the home town boys to fill vacancies. The regimental history says that the Seventh was the only Kansas regiment to re-enlist with a full organization.

Bill Cody is quite frank in telling how he came to be recruited. "Among them [the veterans] I met quite a number of my old comrades and neighbors, who tried to induce me to enlist and go south with them. I had no idea of doing anything of the kind; but one day, after having been under the influence of bad whisky, I awoke to find myself a soldier in the Seventh Kansas. I did not remember how or when I had enlisted, but I saw I was in for it, and that it would not do for me to endeavor to back out." He enlisted on February 19, 1864, giving his home as Leavenworth; he was mustered in on February 24 and was assigned as a recruit to Company H, commanded, through most of his service, by Captain Charles L. Wall. The official record shows William F. Cody as "age, 18; born

61

in Scott County, Iowa; occupation, teamster; eyes and hair, brown; complexion, fair; height 5′ 10″."[9]

The regiment reassembled under command of Colonel Thomas P. Herrick on March 12, 1864, and moved by way of St. Louis to Memphis, where it arrived on June 6 and was assigned to escort working parties along the Memphis and Charleston Railroad. During this spring, Grant was hurling the Army of the Potomac against Lee's Confederates in the battles of the Wilderness in Virginia, and Sherman was beginning his advance from Chattanooga toward Atlanta. Behind Sherman, to the Ohio River on the north and across the Mississippi to the west, there were no Confederate forces of size, but there was one of consequence. The great cavalry leader Nathan Bedford Forrest had a small command, but he usually got there first with the most, to the great discomfiture of the Union forces and with peril to Sherman's communications. In February, about the time Cody was enlisting, Forrest had defeated the cavalry column of Brigadier General William Sooy Smith at Okolona, Mississippi, and had driven it back on Memphis. In March, while the Seventh Kansas was moving toward the front, Forrest took Fort Pillow, killing most of its garrison of Negro troops. An advance detachment of the Seventh Kansas arrived at Colliersville on the Memphis and Charleston Railroad in June just in time to reinforce the retreating command of Brigadier General Samuel D. Sturgis, which had been roundly defeated by Forrest at Brice's Cross Roads.[10]

To oppose Forrest, the Union forces were reorganized under Major General Andrew J. Smith. His infantry consisted of two brigades of the Sixteenth Corps under Brigadier General J. A. Mower, an able strategist. On June 18, Major General Cadwallader C. Washburn, commanding the District of West Tennessee, ordered all the cavalry along the railroad to concentrate at La-Grange, Tennessee, where it formed a cavalry corps under Brigadier General Benjamin H. Grierson. As the cavalry corps moved from LaGrange to Ripley on July 5, the Seventh Kansas was the

[9] Cody, *Life*, 135; *Report of the Adjutant General of the State of Kansas*, I, 625; *Official Military History of Kansas Regiments* (Leavenworth, 1870); S. M. Fox, *The Seventh Kansas Cavalry; Official Army Register of the Volunteer Force*, Part VII, 351–53.
[10] *O.R.* (77) I, XXXIX, Part I, 202; (78) Part II, 126.

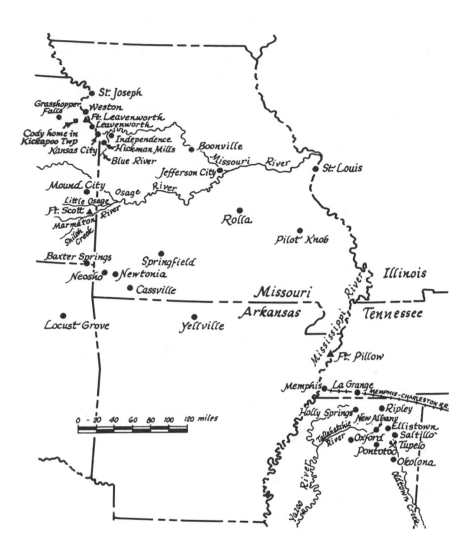

CIVIL WAR CAMPAIGNS OF PRIVATE W. F. CODY,
7TH KANSAS CAVALRY, 1864–65

advance guard and skirmished with an enemy brigade for about an hour. Smith's entire command was at Ripley on July 8 and moved out toward New Albany and Pontotoc, with the Seventh Kansas as advance guard for the entire movement, and the rest of the cavalry covering the left flank by parallel roads. At Pontotoc the Seventh Kansas struck Colonel Robert (Black Bob) McCulloch's Confederate brigade and held it in front while Grierson moved the rest of the cavalry to the east of the town, forcing the enemy out of it. As the march was continued toward Tupelo on July 13, the Seventh Kansas became the rear guard, since it was left facing the enemy while the rest of the army moved around it. During that day the Seventh Kansas was constantly engaged, several times setting ambushes for superior forces. Its support, the 1st Brigade, United States Colored Troops got into some of the fights.

Smith's command met Forrest's main body on July 14 in the Battle of Tupelo, sometimes called the Battle of Harrisburg, of which one of Forrest's biographers says, "There is no doubt that it was a defeat for the Confederates which, with more dash and boldness on the part of A. J. Smith might have been turned into a disaster." The Seventh Kansas Cavalry on that day was on the extreme right of the line and was engaged only with the enemy's pickets. A detachment of the Kansans under Major F. M. Malone moved north along the Mobile and Ohio Railroad toward Saltillo, destroying bridges and water tanks. On July 15 the Seventh Kansas was again in advance, skirmishing with the enemy and capturing a few prisoners while moving toward Old Town Creek. As rear guard the following day, the Seventh tangled again with McCulloch, fighting a brisk action at Ellistown with the Confederate Second Missouri Regiment. On July 17 the Seventh had a quieter day on the left flank, and was detailed to escort the wounded from Salem to LaGrange, where the regiment arrived on July 19, closing this phase of the campaign. "On several occasions," Colonel Herrick reported, "my regiment was engaged with the enemy and severely punished him, without corresponding loss to ourselves. In the whole of my experience I have never known the enemy's firing to be so much at random and so far above range, as in the several engagements during the late expedition." The Seventh lost two men killed, two wounded, and six horses shot.[11]

This was the most important campaign of Bill Cody's Civil War career. It was worth boasting of being in a fight in which Forrest was defeated—that did not happen often. In his autobiography Cody gives it two sentences: "General A. J. Smith re-organized the army to operate against Forrest, and after marching to Tupalo [*sic*], Mississippi, we had an engagement with him and defeated him. This kind of fighting was all new to me, being entirely different from any in which I had ever before engaged." Many years later—in 1911—Buffalo Bill's show played Tupelo, and Cody wrote to Julia, "Busy day here. The people found out I had been in the Battle of Tupelo—And a committee of leading citizens took me out to the battlefield to explain to them the positions of both armies as I am the first Northern Soldier to do it who was in the battle."[12]

That is all he says about it, and his biographers, instead of hunting out a few details, get involved in a dime-novel type of spy story. Sister Helen, who gets events of the period considerably tangled, tells how Bill captured an old acquaintance named Nat Golden, who was serving as a Confederate spy. Taking the papers that all captured spies always have conveniently on their persons, Bill Cody boldly entered the tent of General Forrest himself and volunteered to serve the Confederate commander as scout. However, Golden inopportunely escaped, and as he appeared in the Confederate camp, Bill jumped on a horse, eluded pursuers, and delivered another bundle of precious spy papers to General Smith. Frank Cooper has the same Nat Golden captured, but it is to General Braxton Bragg that Bill takes the spy papers.[13] It seems more probable that Private Cody spent most of his time in the ranks of Company H.

On August 1, 1864, the cavalry moved out again toward Holly Springs, Mississippi, and, joined by two of Mower's brigades of infantry, forced a crossing of the Tallahatchie River, pursuing the enemy to Hurricane Creek, where there was a sharp fight. On August 13 the Seventh Kansas took part in an assault on Oxford. In this campaign First Sergeant Alonzo Dickson of Cody's com-

[11] Robert Selph Henry, *"First With the Most" Forrest* (Indianapolis and New York, 1944), 324; O.R. (77) I, XXXIX, Part I, 247–51.

[12] Cody, *Life*, 136; *Letters from Buffalo Bill*, 73.

[13] Wetmore, *Last of the Great Scouts*, 115–23; Winch, *Thrilling Lives of Buffalo Bill and Pawnee Bill*, 39–49; F. C. Cooper, *Buffalo Bill and Pawnee Bill*, 37–51.

pany, H, was killed. Instead of continuing the drive against Forrest, Smith, for want of supplies, fell back, and Forrest raided into Memphis itself, capturing, among other things, General Washburn's dress uniform, which Forrest politely returned under a flag of truce. Washburn, not to be outdone in the amenities of war, had Forrest's Memphis tailor make up a Confederate uniform and sent it to the rebel leader.

This was of little concern to Bill Cody or the Seventh Kansas Cavalry; their interest in General Forrest was over for the war. On September 6 the Seventh Regiment was ordered to Memphis with all baggage in readiness to go to Missouri, threatened with invasion by Major General Sterling Price, with such able subordinates as Joseph O. Shelby and John S. Marmaduke. While the Seventh was moving northward to defend St. Louis, Price crossed the Missouri line on September 19, and eight days later was held up at Pilot Knob, eighty-six miles from St. Louis, by a makeshift force assembled by Brigadier General Thomas Ewing.

The Seventh Kansas was not in this fight, although Cody says, "The command of which my regiment was a part hurried to the front to intercept Price, and our first fight with him occurred at Pilot Knob. From that time for nearly six weeks we fought or skirmished every day." That is all he says of the entire campaign. However, the part taken by the Seventh Kansas was quite important, as is shown in the report of Major General William S. Rosecrans, just transferred to command the Department of Missouri after his defeat at Chickamauga, who said that at this time General Smith's 4,500 infantry, the Seventh Kansas, just in from Memphis, a part of the Thirteenth Missouri, and recruits for Merrill's Horse, a total of 1,500 cavalry, were all that stood between Price's men and the capture of St. Louis. Price reported that he had 8,000 armed men and 4,000 unarmed men; hence the possibility of capturing St. Louis did not look quite so attractive from his point of view—with more federal troops arriving every day to oppose him.[14]

The Seventh Kansas moved out under command of Brigadier General John B. Sanborn. A detachment of the Thirteenth Missouri under Captain James M. Turley made a reconnaissance that developed the enemy left at Boonville and then followed the enemy

[14] O.R. (77) I, XXXIX, Part I, 319; Fox, *Seventh Kansas Cavalry*.

trail, while Sanborn led his force, including the Seventh Kansas toward a junction with the main body. On October 20 they became part of a cavalry division, commanded by Major General Alfred Pleasanton, who formerly had commanded the cavalry of the Army of the Potomac in Virginia. The Seventh Kansas was assigned to the division's Second Brigade, under Brigadier General John Mc-Neil, for whom Cody says he did some scouting.[15]

On October 22, 1864, McNeil's brigade crossed the Little Blue and attacked two brigades of Price's army, driving them back to the edge of Independence, Missouri. A charge with the saber through Independence was led by the Thirteenth Missouri, brilliantly supported, says General McNeil, by the Seventh Kansas and the Seventeenth Illinois. In the charge two guns were captured and heavy casualties were inflicted on the Confederates. The pursuit was pushed to Hickman's Mills, where McNeil's brigade found itself in contact with Price's entire force. The Seventh Kansas and Merrill's Horse were out in front as a skirmish line, and, according to McNeil's report, most gallantly pressed up to the center of the main line until the skirmish line was recalled. McNeil hung on, hoping for reinforcements, but during the night the Confederates withdrew.

Nearly half a century later Cody was visiting a business partner, Colonel D. B. Dyer, at his country home near Kansas City when Cody recognized that he was on the battlefield of the Little Blue and pointed out that Price's forces were "right on the edge of this bluff." He also recalled the capture of Major General John Sappington Marmaduke, commander of Price's cavalry. Marmaduke had two horses shot under him at Little Blue, and was captured shortly afterward while fighting a rear-guard action at the Marais des Cygnes River. In his last autobiography Cody says he was with the scouting party that captured the General near Mound City, that he shared his lunch and a bottle of whiskey with the General, and later was assigned as guard to conduct the prisoner to Fort Leavenworth. Marmaduke spent the rest of the war at Fort Warren, Massachusetts. In later years he was elected governor of Missouri.

[15] *O.R.* (79) I, XXXIX, Part IV, 126; (83) I, XLI, Part I, 308; (85) I, XLI, Part III, 408; Cody, *Life,* 136.

By the time Cody returned to his command, Price was in full retreat. On October 25, McNeil's brigade, after a ten-mile gallop, charged across the Marmaton River and routed the enemy, pursuing to Shiloh Creek. There McNeil's brigade was joined by the cavalry division's Fourth Brigade, commanded by Lieutenant Colonel Frederick W. Benteen, in later years one of the controversial figures of Custer's last fight.[16]

In summarizing a campaign hastily, it is easy to forget that all these movements from one point to another on a map were actually made by men who were doing a lot of hard riding and fighting, getting little sleep, and galloping far ahead of supply wagons. General McNeil's report brings this side of the picture to life at Shiloh Creek. There Price's entire army was drawn up in a line four men deep—perhaps the unarmed men Price mentions were in the fourth line. But even at four deep, the Confederate line stretched out on both sids of the two small Federal cavalry brigades. To avoid being enveloped, McNeil ordered a charge in the hope of breaking the enemy center, but the horses could not be made to trot or gallop. They just walked. As the Federal cavalry walked, the equally tired Confederates walked away, and finally moved off in a confused mass. The cavalry was too tired to follow; they bivouacked right there. Next morning the cavalry found a cornfield, fed their horses, and were then able to take up the pursuit. They picked up Price's abandoned wagons, with much ammunition and equipment, and continued the chase through Shanghai to Newtonia, which they reached on October 28. At that point McNeil's brigade was ordered back to Rolla. That was the end of the Price campaign, as far as the Seventh Kansas Cavalry was concerned, and the raid was, in fact, over. Early in November, Cody's regiment was ordered to St. Louis.[17]

Cody says that he became a noncommissioned officer and was put on detached service as a scout during the Price campaign. The records show he was discharged from the army as a private, but he may have attained sergeant's stripes temporarily. As for scouting, the only story he tells is reasonable enough. He was riding

<hr>

[16] O.R. (83) I, XLI, Part I, 310, 371, 388, 628; *Kansas City Star*, September 30, 1911; Cody, *Autobiography*, 77–79.
[17] O.R. (83) I, XLI, Part I, 371.

ahead of the command, he says, dressed in gray clothes, or Missouri jeans, and stopped at a farmhouse where he saw a man, also dressed in gray costume, sitting at a table eating bread and milk.

"You little rascal, what are you doing in those 'secesh' clothes?" was the greeting, and Cody recognized Wild Bill Hickok disguised as a Confederate officer. While they had bread and milk together, Hickok reported that he had been spying in Marmaduke's division, and thought it would be useful to stay on for a while. He gave Cody some papers to take to General McNeil. That's the story. Although the spy papers and the disguise are melodramatic fare, such things actually went on during the Civil War. The most fantastic part of the story is Wild Bill and Cody sitting down together with bowls of bread and milk.[18]

Another of Cody's adventures has nothing to do with spying. A day or two later, says he, he was riding with the advance guard when he stopped at a farmhouse for a drink of water. He found a woman with her two daughters much frightened at the prospect of having a Yankee army march past. As they gave him something to eat and were friendly, he posted himself as a sentinel in front of the house and turned away stragglers until after the army had passed. The grateful housewife invited him to stay for dinner. While he was eating, three men burst into the room and pointed shotguns at his head. However, they proved to be the husband and two sons of the hostess, and when the situation was explained, they thanked Bill for his help but advised him to move on before less appreciative bushwhackers happened along.

The third story does not concern Cody at all, but concludes the adventure of Wild Bill Hickok. It is placed as not far from Fort Scott, Kansas. The two armies were facing each other, says Cody, when two horsemen were seen, apparently trying to ride from the Confederate to the Union lines. One was shot and killed; the other, who proved to be Wild Bill, was rescued by seven companies of the Seventh Kansas. As a result of his report to Generals Pleasanton and McNeil a charge was ordered, and the Confederates were driven back. There is no corroboration for this story, but it can be proved that Wild Bill was a scout or spy at this period. The following exchange of letters is of official record:

[18] Cody, *Life,* 136–37; Cody misspells the General's name—"McNiel."

Cassville, Mo., February 10, 1865

Brigadier General Sanborn:

I have been at Camp Walker and Spavinaw. There are not more than ten or twelve rebels in any squad in the southwest that I can hear of. If you want me to go to Neosho and west of there, notify me here. It was cold; I returned back.

J. B. Hickok

And the reply:

Headquarters, District of Southwest Missouri
Springfield, Mo., February 11, 1865

J. B. Hickok,
Cassville, Mo.

You may go to Yellville or the White River in the vicinity of Yellville and learn what Dobbin intends to do with his command now on Crowley's Ridge, and from there come on to this place.

JOHN B. SANBORN,
Brigadier General, commanding.[19]

The "Dobbin" mentioned presumably was Colonel Archibald S. Dobbin, who commanded a brigade of Fagan's division of the Confederate Army of Missouri. This letter proves Cody correct in saying that Wild Bill was a scout making his headquarters in Springfield, Missouri. Cody says that at the end of the Price campaign, he "returned to Springfield, Missouri, for a rest and for supplies, and Wild Bill and myself spent two weeks there in 'having a jolly good time,' as some people would express it." He makes no mention of their having bread and milk on this occasion.

Following Price's retreat across the Arkansas River, Bill Cody may well have done some scouting; in fact, the entire regiment, after returning to St. Louis, was scattered in detachments of a company or two at various posts to guard against guerrillas, and was largely engaged in scouting activities. One company was sent to guard bridges along the Iron Mountain Railroad between De-Soto and Mineral Point. Lieutenant T. W. Phillips with a consolidated detachment of the Seventh Kansas was ordered to pursue twenty to twenty-five guerrillas toward Marshall and to burn the

[19] *O.R.* (101) I, XLVIII, Part I, 810, 819.

houses of any citizens harboring those guerrillas. Lieutenant William W. Crane with twenty men of the regiment surprised a band of guerrillas at McKenzie's Creek, killing four men and capturing six horses. Lieutenant J. H. Wildey reported that he had killed one-third of the guerrilla Jeff's command: "Number killed, 1; number of command, 3; aggregate, 3. This is all the rebel force there was." Reports of warfare of this character run on well after the surrender of General Lee in Virginia on April 9, 1865.[20]

Bill Cody's company, H, was ordered from St. Louis to DeSoto on December 11, 1864, when six companies of the regiment were rounded up from scattered posts in the Pilot Knob area. At the end of 1864 three companies were at Pilot Knob, three were at Patterson, and the remaining four were at St. Louis. Private Cody is recorded as detached for duty in a hospital at Pilot Knob on January 23, 1865, and was detailed for special duty as orderly at Headquarters, District of St. Louis, on February 19, an assignment connected with the activities of the Freedman's Relief Society. Except for a furlough to Weston, Missouri, beginning April 5, he remained on this duty until September 13, when he was ordered to rejoin his regiment.[21]

Meanwhile his company was at Fredericktown at the end of February and back at Pilot Knob on April 30. The Seventh Kansas was reassembled on July 21 for a western expedition. From Omaha it marched to Fort Kearny and Camp Rankin, which it garrisoned in August.

Trouble with the Indians had continued throughout the war, and Brigadier General Patrick Connor hoped to end it by a large expedition in three columns against the Sioux in the Powder River country, while volunteer troops were still available. He was not successful, but the Seventh Kansas was among troops called in to replace organizations assigned to the expedition.

On August 25, 1865, the Seventh Kansas was ordered to return from Fort Kearny to Fort Leavenworth, arriving there on Septem-

---

[20] *O.R.* (86) I, XLI, Part IV, 368, 459, 510, 830, 831, 866, 979; (101) I, XLVIII, Part I, 346, 535-36, 1033-34; (102) I, XLVIII, Part II, 142, 226, 268-69, 496, 510, 808, 937, 1112-13, 1175.
[21] C. H. Bridges, the adjutant general, to Addison E. Sheldon, Nebraska State Historical Society, May 8, 1929, states that Cody was not with the regiment on its move west in July, 1865.

ber 14, one day after Cody was ordered to rejoin his company. He was mustered out as a private with the regiment on September 29. The regimental history says of him: "One of the members of Company H has since become famous—W. F. Cody, 'Buffalo Bill.' He entered as a veteran recruit and was mustered out with the regiment."[22]

Cody served one year, seven months, and ten days with the Seventh Kansas Cavalry. During his year of active service with his company, the regiment did considerable fighting and campaigning. It was mustered out with a strength of 501, a sizable regiment for the end of the Civil War, in contrast to several Kansas regiments that were consolidated with others because of diminishing strength. Cody missed no battle, campaign, or skirmish credited to the regiment during his seven months of detached service, his company being in garrison during that entire period. During his service as headquarters orderly he probably carried dispatches over the district, giving substance to the story that he served as scout, for that was part of a scout's duty.

[22] Fox, *Seventh Kansas Cavalry,* 20; *Report of the Adjutant General of the State of Kansas,* I, 625.

"Buffalo Bill–Yellow Hand Duel," July 17, 1876

From a painting by Robert Lindneux, in Buffalo Bill Museum, Cody, Wyoming.

Wild Bill Hickok

Engraving from Webb's *Buffalo-Land* (1872).

MR. CODY ATTEMPTS DOMESTICITY

DURING THE TIME he was on special duty as orderly in St. Louis, Will Cody met Louisa Frederici—she says on May 1, 1865. In his story for publication, and in hers, this meeting appears quite romantic, but when he was seeking a divorce in 1905, he charged he was tricked into marriage. In his autobiography he says that when he was discharged from the army, "after a brief visit at Leavenworth I returned to St. Louis, having made up my mind to capture the heart of Miss Frederici, whom I adored above any young lady I had ever seen." In her story of their first meeting, Will was brought to her house by her cousin William McDonald. Finding her dozing over *The Family Fireside,* they jerked the chair from under her, provoking her to slap Cody under the impression that she was assailing her cousin. This practical joke was so successful that they concocted another. She and Cody were to pretend that they were engaged, for the benefit of an admirer with whom she had a date that night. This scheme also worked well, and Will became a regular visitor.[1]

A quarter of a century later, testifying in his unsuccessful divorce suit, Cody said, "Boylike, I thought it very smart to be engaged. I asked her to marry me, or asked her if she would marry

[1] Cody, *Life,* 141; Louisa F. Cody and Courtney Ryley Cooper, *Memories of Buffalo Bill,* 1–13, 27–36 (hereafter cited as Mrs. Cody, *Memories).*

me if I would come back after the war was over. And jokingly she said 'yes.' Shortly after that I was ordered away from St. Louis and I accompanied the army as the troops or command that I was with was ordered away from St. Louis and I had nearly forgotten all about this little engagement when the war was over and I was discharged from the army. I returned to Leavenworth, Kansas, which she knew was my home, and I received several letters from her, asking me to keep my word and I desiring to keep my word if I had asked her to marry me after the war, I concluded to do it. I went to St. Louis and arrived there, I think, two days before we were married, which ceremony was performed by a justice of the peace at her father's house at about 11 o'clock in the morning." They were married on March 6, 1866.[2]

If he visited her immediately after his discharge, as both say, it was for a brief time. He says he drove a string of horses from Leavenworth to Fort Kearny that fall. His first postwar scouting job fits in here.

During the triumphant engagement in London of Buffalo Bill's Wild West, General William Tecumseh Sherman wrote, "All I aim to accomplish on this sheet of paper is to assure you that I fully recognize your work, and that the presence of the Queen, the beautiful Princess of Wales, the Prince, and the British public,. are marks of favor which reflect back on America sparks of light which illuminate many a house and cabin in the land where once you guided me honestly and faithfully in 1865–6 from Fort Riley to Kearney in Kansas and Nebraska."[3]

General Sherman was vague about the year, but shortly after his assignment as commanding general of the Military Division of the Mississippi, he made an inspection tour of his new command. He left St. Louis at the end of September—about the time of Cody's discharge from the Seventh Kansas—and in the course of this tour went from Fort Riley to Fort Kearny. Cody failed to mention his service to Sherman in his 1879 autobiography, but in *True Tales of the Plains* and in subsequent books explained that he was employed as scout and dispatch bearer in the fall of 1865 for General

[2] *The Westerners Brand Book* (Chicago), Vol. II (1945–46), 29.
[3] W. F. Cody, *Story of the Wild West*, 766; Cody, *True Tales of the Plains*, 62–63.

Sherman and peace commissioners from Fort Zarah to Council Springs, where they met Kiowas and Comanches. Fort Zarah, commonly misspelled by Cody and everyone else, was named for Major Henry Zarah Curtis, killed in the fight at Baxter Springs on October 5, 1863. Council Springs, on the Arkansas River at the mouth of the Little Arkansas, is now Wichita.

During this journey Cody told a lieutenant that Dick Curtis, the chief scout, was leading the party too far west. The lieutenant took Cody to Sherman, and when Curtis admitted he was unsure of the route, Cody was told to lead the party, riding with the General for twelve miles until the Indian camp at Council Springs came into view. Cody had been there before with Charley Rath, Indian trader. At Council Springs, Colonel Jesse Leavenworth, Indian agent at Fort Leavenworth (named for his father), made treaties on October 18, 1865, with Kiowas and Comanches. After the council, Cody says, he guided Sherman to Fort Kearny and to Leavenworth.[4]

Then, or about this time, Bill drove a string of horses from Leavenworth to Fort Kearny. There he was employed by Bill Trotter, division agent of the Overland Stage Line, to drive the stage between Fort Kearny and Plum Creek. Cody continued in this occupation until February, 1866. At this time the Overland was owned by Ben Holladay, who contributed toward glamorizing stagecoach drivers by dressing them in broad-brimmed sombreros, corduroys trimmed with velvet, and high-heeled boots. A nine-foot rawhide whip, its handle usually decorated in silver, was the insigne of office. The trotting teams often made eight miles an hour, and occasionally ten or twelve. Fastest was a six-horse, snow-white team on the Georgetown division in Colorado Territory, but Cody's four-horse team of grays was rated among the fast groups.[5]

In his autobiographies Cody tells of no adventures as stagecoach driver, but an apochryphal story, often repeated, is told in

[4] Robert G. Athearn, *Willliam Tecumseh Sherman and the Settlement of the West* (Norman, 1956), 18–25; Athearn to Don Russell, August 7, 1957: "The only trip Sherman made between Ft. Riley and Ft. Kearney was in the fall of "65"; Cody, *Autobiography*, 81–90; Cody, *True Tales of the Plains*, 56–58; Ernest Wallace and E. Adamson Hoebel, *The Comanches* (Norman, 1952), 306–309; Clarence Wharton, *Satanta* (Dallas, 1935), 76.

[5] Frederick, *Ben Holladay*, 72, 75–76, 87; Cody, *Life*, 105, 141–42.

The Great Salt Lake Trail, of which he is listed as co-author, although his share of the book consisted only of the inclusion of chapters from his autobiography. The story is told in the third person:

"While driving stage between Split Rock and Three Crossings, he [meaning Cody] was set upon by a band of several hundred Sioux. Lieutenant Flowers, assistant division agent, sat on the box beside Cody, and there were half a dozen passengers well armed inside. Cody gave the reins to Flowers, applied the whip, and the passengers defended the stage in a running fight. Arrows fell around and struck the stage like hail, wounding the horses and dealing destruction generally, for two of the passengers were killed and Flowers badly wounded. Cody seized the whip from the wounded officer, applied it savagely, shouting defiance, and drove on to Three Crossings, thus saving the stage."[6]

This is a typical Buffalo Bill adventure, but it did not happen. For that, the authority is Buffalo Bill himself. In telling of Indian depredations in 1860, he describes this scene, including the wounding of "Lieut. Flowers," actually Lem Flowers. It is clear that he does not intend to imply that he was there.[7]

Instead of fighting Indians, Cody went to St. Louis to be married.

Louisa Frederici would probably have had a much happier life had she married Louis Reiber, the suitor scared off by the practical joke she and Will Cody perpetrated. To have settled down as housewife in the Old French town section of St. Louis would have suited her temperament. If she was swept away by the romantic idea of marrying a hero of Indian fights and plains adventure, as her book written by Courtney Ryley Cooper implies, it was the only time glamour touched her. Of the stuff that made pioneers she had none. For the West she had no sympathy, no understanding. Very likely she was deathly afraid of it. Show business she detested. As a result, their separations were long and frequent. It is doubtful that Will in his entire married life stayed home for longer than six consecutive months.

---

[6] Col. Henry Inman and Col. William F. Cody, *The Great Salt Lake Trail,* 220.
[7] Cody, *Life,* 106; Westmore, *Last of the Great Scouts,* 136–39; Frederick, *Ben Holladay,* 75–76, 170.

Of her background she tells little; her father, John Frederici, was an immigrant from Alsace-Lorraine; her mother was named Smith and was American-born. Louisa was educated in a convent; for how long is not stated. During her long residence in North Platte she was not neighborly. In the divorce suit Cody charged she embarrassed him by wearing a dirty wrapper while receiving guests. If she received any of Will's guests, it probably was unintentional. Dan Muller, who was brought up by the Codys, tells of her eating with him in the kitchen while Will entertained in the dining room. Cooper once wrote, "The poor old woman hardly knew the parade had gone by—Buffalo Bill's life was largely a haze to her."[8]

An hour after they were married they were on their way to Leavenworth by river steamboat. Bill says some Missourians aboard shunned him as a "Kansas jay-hawker and one of Jennison's house burners," an accusation not far from the truth. At one landing horsemen galloped up, threatening to shoot "the black abolition jay-hawker." Mrs. Cody fainted as deck hands pulled in the gangplank and the captain got the boat under way. Will telegraphed friends in Leavenworth, hoping for a reception that would indicate that he was not regarded as a bandit in his home country. Some sixty of his friends gathered with a brass band at the boat landing, a form of charivari not uncommon in those days. A formal reception was held at the home of his sister Eliza, who had recently been married to George Myers.

For a while Bill tried to settle down to normal pursuits. From Dr. Joel J. Crook, who had been assistant surgeon in his regiment, Bill rented the house in Salt Creek Valley that had belonged to his mother, and attempted to run it again as a hotel. Says his sister Helen, "Will radiated hospitality, and his reputation as a lover of his fellowman got so widely abroad that travelers without money and without price would go miles out of their way to put up at his tavern. Socially he was an irreproachable landlord; financially his shortcomings were deplorable." After six months he gave up and sold out the Golden Rule House, deciding, as he put it, that he could make more money out West on the frontier than he could

---

[8] Dan Muller, *My Life with Buffalo Bill*, 52; Courtney Ryley Cooper to Don Russell, April 13, 1929.

at Salt Creek Valley. This resulted in his first separation from Louisa, who stayed for a while with Helen in Leavenworth, later returning to St. Louis.[9]

It was a turning point in his life; had his inclinations been more domestic, there would have been no Buffalo Bill. He says he "started alone for Saline [now Salina], Kansas, which was then the end of track of the Kansas Pacific Railway." At Junction City he met Wild Bill Hickok, who was employed as scout at Fort Ellsworth. Cody went there with Hickok and was hired in the same capacity. "During the winter of 1866–67," he says, "I scouted between Fort Ellsworth and Fort Fletcher." As there was little demand for scouts in winter, it is probable his employment was irregular. Henry A. Northrop testified that he spent that winter with Cody in a dugout, remains of which are still visible on Mulberry Creek in Saline County. Early in 1867, Cody helped haul goods for a store established in Ellsworth by Arthur Larkin, a former neighbor in Leavenworth.[10]

Fort Ellsworth, which gave its name to the city of Ellsworth, was established in 1864 by the Seventh Iowa Volunteer Cavalry and named for its second lieutenant Allen Ellsworth. In 1866 the garrison was moved to a new site near present Kanopolis. The new post was named Fort Harker for Brigadier General Charles Harker. Fort Fletcher was established in 1865 on Big Creek, about fifteen miles southeast of the present Hays. Cody says he was at Fort Fletcher when Brevet Major General George A. Custer, just appointed lieutenant colonel of the new Seventh United States Cavalry, came through there on his way to join the expedition led by Major General Winfield Scott Hancock in the spring of 1867. Cody was still at Fort Fletcher later in the spring when heavy floods on Big Creek drowned out the fort and it was abandoned. The garrison was moved to a new post named Fort Hays, about a mile south of present Hays, Kansas.

[9] Wetmore, *Last of the Great Scouts,* 147–49.

[10] Cody, *Life,* 145; Henry A. Northrop, affidavit, Saline County Historical Society, 1925; locates the dugout as "on the south side of Mulberry Creek on the North East Quarter (N.E.¼) of the South West Quarter (S.W.¼) of Section Nine (9) Township Fourteen (14) Range Three (R. 3) west of the Sixth P.M., Saline County, Kansas"; George Jelinek, *Ellsworth, Kansas, 1867–1947* and *Ninety Years of Ellsworth.*

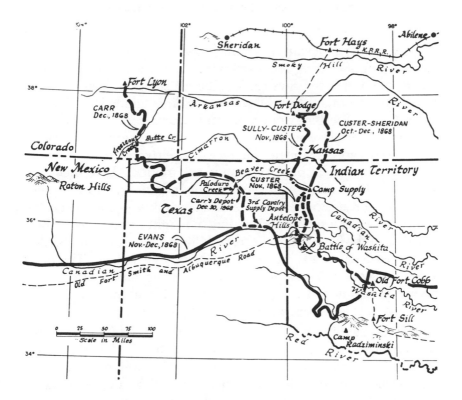

INDIAN CAMPAIGN, 1868

As this is the beginning of Cody's employment as scout, it might be well to explain something about the job he did so much to glamorize. Scouting is a part of an army's looking where it is going, which in later days came to be called reconnaissance, and usually is performed by well-trained soldiers, guided by detailed maps. On the Western frontier the only maps were those made by military exploring expeditions, and the unmapped gaps on routes were often wide. Trappers, hunters, trail drivers, or anyone else familiar with the country were sought as guides. Many such men were well acquainted with the ways of Indians and were experienced in fighting them. While such knowledge was an asset, the primary duty of a scout was scouting, not fighting Indians, as Buffalo Bill might have you believe, or killing Indians (or not killing them), as some of his critics might have you believe. The main value of a scout was his familiarity with a particular area that could be put to use in following a trail, in guiding a command, or in carrying messages from one command to another.

Scouts, guides, and several other kinds of civilian employees such as teamsters and packers were hired by the Quartermaster Department of the army, usually through a post or regimental quartermaster. Scouts were hired by the month and were under no obligation to stay beyond that period, nor were they guaranteed continuous employment. Their pay ranged from $60 a month to $150, or even more for especially hazardous missions. A regiment or an expedition might be authorized to employ a number of scouts, in which case one of the most reliable of them was designated chief of scouts and was paid accordingly. In large organizations an officer was also designated chief of scouts; equivalent to the reconnaissance officer or G-2, intelligence officer of the present day.

While scouts were not hired primarily for fighting, they usually did fight, for Indian warfare resembled twentieth-century warfare in that there were no neutrals and no noncombatants. Occasionally, possibly by stretching regulations, scouts were hired specifically for fighting, as in the case of the company of fifty serving under Brevet Colonel George A. Forsyth who fought the battle of Beecher's Island. Indians were hired both for scouting and fighting, and at one period one troop of each cavalry regiment was made up of

Indian scouts. As a scout Cody had his share of fighting, but in 1866 and 1867 he was employed for the most part as guide and dispatch bearer.

In this connection Cody records his first ride with General Custer, who had come to Fort Hays "from Fort Ellsworth with an escort of only ten men. He wanted a guide to pilot him to Fort Larned, a distance of sixty-five miles across the country." Custer arrived at Fort Hays on April 19, 1867, after an Indian chase from Fort Larned, and stayed until June 1. He was back in July on an unauthorized trip to Fort Harker, and on to Fort Riley to see his wife, for which journey he was tried by court martial. Probably Cody guided Custer in June on the trip of which he makes something of a tall tale. Bill was riding a mule, and the General expressed doubt whether the animal could keep up—Custer always prided himself on his horses. For the first fifteen miles as against Custer's thoroughbred and other officers' horses, Cody's mouse-colored mule had trouble, but after they hit the sand hills across the Smoky Hill River, the mule proved to have more endurance and led the rest of the way, about half the party trailing far behind. Custer was impressed with Cody's ability in leading the escort across country where there was no trail, and offered to employ him as scout any time he was free from his employment at Fort Hays. However, this was Cody's only active service with George Armstrong Custer.[11]

"A few days after my return to Fort Hays," says Cody, "the Indians made a raid on the Kansas Pacific Railroad, killing five or six men and running off about one hundred horses and mules." He says he was sent as scout and guide for the expedition, which was commanded by Brevet Major George Augustus Armes, captain of Company F, Tenth United States Cavalry, with his troop and a mountain howitzer. To continue Cody's account: "On the second day out we suddenly discovered on the opposite side of the Saline River, about a mile distant, a large body of Indians, who were charging down upon us. Major Armes, placing the cannon on a little knoll, limbered it up and left twenty men to guard it; and

[11] Cody, *Life,* 145–47; Elizabeth B. Custer, *Tenting on the Plains,* 349–402; George A. Custer, *My Life on the Plains,* 22–98; plea before a court-martial, Custer Battlefield Museum, copy from Maj. E. S. Luce.

then, with the rest of the command, he crossed the river to meet the Indians. Just as he had got the men over the stream, we heard a terrific yelling and shouting in our rear, and looking back to the knoll where the cannon had been stationed, we saw the negroes, who had been left there to guard the gun, flying towards us, being pursued by about one hundred Indians; while another large party of the latter were dancing around the captured cannon, as if they had got hold of an elephant and did not know what to do with it. Major Armes turned his command back and drove the Indians from the gun. The troops then dismounted and took position there. Quite a severe fight ensued, lasting about two hours. Five or six of the soldiers, as well as Major Armes, were wounded, and several of the horses were shot. . . .

"Major Armes, who was wounded and lying under the cannon —which, by the way, had become useless—called me up and asked if I thought there was any show of getting back to the fort. I replied that there was. Orders were accordingly given by Major Armes for a retreat, the cannon being left behind. During the movement several of our men were killed, but as night came on and dense darkness prevailed, we succeeded in making good headway, and got into Fort Hays just at daylight next morning, in a very played-out condition."[12]

According to Major Armes's report there were thirty-four troopers against three hundred Indians in this fight of August 2, 1867, on Saline River, Kansas. It was the first fight of the Tenth United States Cavalry, a new regiment made up largely of veterans of the United States Colored Volunteers and other organizations of Negroes raised during the Civil War. Company F had been organized only since June 21. Armes reported a scout present, but did not name him. Cody's account is in accord with the official report except in a few details. Sergeant William Christy was the only soldier killed, not "several"; Major Armes was the only one wounded, not "five or six." Cody consistently misspelled the major's name as "Arms."[13]

It was a period in which the government devoted much effort

[12] Cody, Life, 147–48.
[13] George A. Armes, Ups and Downs of an Army Officer, 247; Annual Report of the Secretary of War, 1867.

to negotiations in a hope for permanent peace with the Indians. The object of General Hancock's expedition, of which Custer's Seventh Cavalry was a part, was to overawe the Indians with a display of force. It succeeded in persuading a tribe or two to profess peaceful intentions. There had been no fighting when Custer swung out in a thousand-mile scout, winding up in need of supplies and further orders about halfway between Fort Wallace and Fort Harker. He sent his empty wagon train to Fort Wallace for supplies and Major Joel H. Elliott with an escort of ten men to Fort Harker for orders before he learned that, while carrying orders to him, Lieutenant Lyman Kidder, with ten enlisted men and an Indian guide, had been waylaid and the party slaughtered to the last man. Custer rode for his wagon train, arriving just in time to drive off attacking Indians. Major Elliott got through safely. It was then that Custer made his journey to Fort Riley. Found guilty of unauthorized absence from his command, Custer was suspended for a year, ending his campaigning for the season.

Major Armes was not seriously wounded in the fight of August 2, and was sufficiently recovered to lead Company F to a more satisfactory encounter with Indians on Prairie Dog Creek on August 21 and 22. Allison J. Pliley guided Armes on this expedition.

The Indians continued raids and murders of settlers until October when the Medicine Lodge Treaty insured perpetual peace as long as the weather was cold enough to keep them in their lodges. Far to the north, General Sherman was present at the negotiation of another peace treaty at Fort Laramie. Red Cloud refused to sign, besieged Fort Phil Kearny, and slaughtered Colonel William J. Fetterman's command in December. Yet in the fall of 1867 prospects for peace still seemed favorable south of the Platte.

7

WILLIAM F. CODY BECOMES BUFFALO BILL

CODY NEVER QUITE ATTAINED domesticity—but he tried. The inducement this time was his daughter, Arta, born on December 16, 1866. Mrs. Cody says he came home in time to be consulted about the baby's name, another indication that his employment as scout through the winter was not continuous. It was shortly after the Saline River fight, in August, 1867, that Cody quit scouting again. He had been sent with dispatches from Fort Hays to Fort Harker, and while visiting in Ellsworth, he met William Rose, who had a grading contract for the Kansas Pacific near Fort Hays. Rose proposed that he and Cody form a partnership to establish a town on the west bank of Big Creek where the railroad was scheduled to cross, about a mile from the fort, and that they open a store and saloon there. Cody accepted, and they hired a railway surveyor to lay out a town, to which they gave the name of Rome. They bought supplies and started a store; Cody quit his job as scout and brought his wife and daughter to Rome. They lived in the rear of the store. Rose and Cody donated lots to anyone who would build on them, reserving corner lots for future profit. Within a month, says Cody, they had a town of two hundred frame and log houses, three or four stores, several saloons, and a hotel.

Then one day there appeared one Dr. William E. Webb, agent or prospector for the railroad, who proposed that he be admitted to partnership in the flourishing town. Rose and Cody rejected the idea, as they supposed they had the best site in the area. Dr. Webb moved on only a mile or so and laid out Hays City, letting it be known that the railroad would establish a roundhouse and machine shops there. Within three days, says Cody, Rome was deserted, its populace having moved, houses and all, to the new site. Again Cody is telling a tall tale satirizing himself; Kansas historians say Rome lasted a year or two, surviving a cholera epidemic in 1868, and died when the railroad raised its approaches to Big Creek bridge, leaving Rome behind a high embankment.[1]

Rose still had a contract with the Shoemaker and Miller Company for five miles of grading, and the partners went to work on that. Mrs. Cody retreated to St. Louis. As time passed, Cody became better acquainted with Webb; they went buffalo hunting together, and Cody found Webb after all not such a villain as he had supposed.

Cody's mentions of buffalo hunting are infrequent up to this time, but he already had his "celebrated horse Brigham, the fleetest steed I ever owned," so named because he had been bought from a Ute Indian from Utah, then dominated by Brigham Young. On one occasion Cody, mounted on Brigham, and Webb, riding a Thoroughbred bay, outran a band of thirteen Indians, after bantering them by waving their hats and firing a few shots. On reaching Hays, Webb wanted to organize a party to pursue the Indians, but Bill talked him out of that idea. Bill had enjoyed the race, perhaps, but he did not hunt Indians for sport. This completes Cody's story of his relations with Dr. Webb, who in 1872 was to give Buffalo Bill his first book publicity in *Buffalo Land*. Oddly enough, *Buffalo Land* mentions none of the episodes described by Cody.[2]

Cody and Rose, with their visions of wealth dissipated—even though Dr. Webb kindly gave each of them a lot in Hays—were now hard put to it to meet the grading contract. Brigham was reduced to the lowly status of work-horse on a scraper. However, Bill was not so impressed with responsibility that he would decline to res-

[1] Mrs. Cody, *Memories,* 51–54; Cody, *Life,* 149–52; *Collections of the KSHS,* XII, 440; *ibid.,* X, 279.

[2] Cody, *Life,* 152–53; W. E. Webb, *Buffalo Land,* 145–50, 194, 196, 212, 234, 268, 422–23.

cue Brigham from this duty when occasion offered. One day a small herd of buffalo appeared. The scraper was abandoned, the harness thrown off, and Bill sallied forth bareback, having no time for saddling up. He was armed with what he called a needle gun, a common name in those days for the .50-caliber Springfield rifle converted to breechloading. The needle gun, a recent popular invention, had a needle-like firing pin that went through the powder to strike a primer at the front end of the cartridge. However, anything new that had a firing pin, particularly the new Army breechloader, was a needle gun to most frontiersmen. Because of its deadliness, he had dubbed this firearm Lucretia Borgia, probably getting the idea from Victor Hugo's "emotional drama" *Lucretia Borgia; or, The Poisoner*, which Mrs. Julia Dean Hayne was playing in those days. He may have seen it in St. Louis.

Thus equipped, Bill had not gone far when he met five officers from Fort Hays who looked upon his apparent work-horse in some amusement. They assured the rider they would give him the meat after killing the buffalo, as "it required a fast horse to overtake the animals on these prairies." Bill pretended ignorance and trailed along. His description of what followed revealed something of his buffalo-hunting methods: "There were eleven buffaloes in the herd and they were not more than a mile from us. The officers dashed ahead as if they had a sure thing on killing them all before I could come up with them; but I had noticed that the herd was making toward the creek for water, and as I knew buffalo nature, I was perfectly aware that it would be difficult to turn them from their direct course. Thereupon, I started towards the creek to head them off, while the officers came up in rear and gave chase. The buffaloes came rushing past me not a hundred yards distant, with the officers about three hundred yards in the rear. . . . I pulled the blind-bridle from my horse, who knew as well as I did that we were out for buffaloes—as he was a trained hunter. The moment the bridle was off, he started at the top of his speed, running in ahead of the officers, and within a few jumps he brought me alongside the rear buffalo. Raising 'Lucretia Borgia' to my shoulder I fired, and killed the animal at the first shot. My horse then carried me alongside the next one, not ten feet away, and I dropped him at the next fire. As soon as one buffalo would fall, Brigham would take me so close to the next, that I could almost touch it with my gun. In this manner I killed eleven buffaloes with twelve shots."

Two things are to be noted about this method: that the buffalo were killed from the rear forward so as not to stampede or scatter the herd; and, second, that the shooting was done at very close range. As Cody explained to the officers, his running buffalo without saddle or bridle was not particularly notable with a horse trained to bring his rider alongside the animal—a type of training similar to that employed by cowboys for horses used in cutting out steers from a herd.

Another tall story? It seems unlikely, as Cody names the officers as Captain Graham and Lieutenants Ezekial, Thompson, Reed, and Emmick. Captain George Wallace Graham commanded Company I of the Tenth Cavalry at Fort Hays at that time. First Lieutenant Israel Ezekial and Second Lieutenant John Milton Thompson were both officers of the Thirty-eighth Infantry, companies of which were stationed there. "Emmick" is undoubtedly First Lieutenant Myron J. Amick of the Tenth Cavalry. First Lieutenant William I. Reed, Fifth Infantry, was also stationed at Fort Hays at that period, as is shown in a special order of September 3, 1867, appointing him to the post council of administration. As usual, Cody's story checks with names and circumstances. Cody presented the officers with the tongues and tenderloins of the buffalo and loaded a wagon with hindquarters as food for the workmen.[3]

Cody once told R. Farrington Elwell, the artist who served his apprenticeship doing Wild West posters, that "Buffalo Bill" was first applied to him by Captain Graham's party. There seems some confirmation for this in a mention in the Leavenworth *Daily Conservative* of November 26, 1867, of "Captain Graham . . . Buffalo Bill and other scouts," which might imply that Cody was known as "Buffalo Bill" to Graham. Meanwhile, Cody had begun his buffalo hunting for the Kansas Pacific, which gave his nickname wide circulation.

Captain Graham solicited Cody's services as scout in case of an expedition, but Bill doubted that he could get away from his

[3] Cody, *Life*, 155–56; *Official Army Register for 1868;* Fort Hays, Kansas Special Orders Book, 1866–68; S.O. 88, Sept. 3, 1867, and S.O. 94, Sept. 12, 1867. mention Amick and Reed, KSHS; I am obliged to Nyle H. Miller and Joe Snell for these citations.

grading contract. As it happened, says Cody, that night Indians raided the work camp and ran off five or six teams of horses. Bill applied to the fort for help, and Captain Graham's troop was assigned to pursue the thieves. Cody went along as a civilian seeking to recover property, not as employed scout. He located an Indian camp along the Solomon River, but a trooper's premature shot alarmed the raiders and they fled.

Cody soon had opportunity to employ his buffalo-hunting skill professionally. With grading contracts such as Cody's completed, the main body of track layers, twelve hundred strong, reached the heart of the buffalo country. Accordingly, Goddard Brothers, who had a contract for boarding the workers, employed Cody to kill twelve buffalo a day, for which he was to be paid five hundred dollars a month. That was large pay for those days, but was offered because there was danger from Indians and because the services of a hunter of considerable skill were required. Looked at from the employers' angle, it was a bargain, for the meat would cost somewhere around one cent a pound, depending on how much of the animal was used—Cody says only the hump and hindquarters.

It is curious that no critical eye has applied elementary mathematics to this contract. In Cody's original autobiography he says, "During my engagement as hunter for the company—a period of less than eighteen months—I killed 4,280 buffaloes." These figures appear in nearly every book and in almost every biographical article about Cody, including many brief notices in books of reference.[4] There are two things wrong with the statement. A moment's calculation will show that at twelve buffalo a day, in a year and a half he should have delivered 6,570 buffalo to Goddard Brothers—and surely he was not boasting of failure to fulfill his contract by more than one-third of the animals called for. The second thing wrong is that he could not possibly have worked for the contractors for as long as eighteen months or anywhere near that length of time.

Cody says he ended this work in May, 1868, when end-of-track reached Sheridan. That statement is correct, as the contracts of

[4] Cody, *Life*, 161–62; Cody, *Autobiography*, 118; Wetmore, *Last of the Great Scouts*, Mrs. Cody, *Memories*, 147; but twelve months in Cody, *True Tales of the Plains*, 68.

both Shoemaker and Miller and Goddard Brothers expired at Sheridan in May. Dating back eighteen months from May, 1868, wipes out everything Cody says happened to him in 1867. That, of course, was not his intention, and the obvious answer is a typographical error. Read "eight" for "eighteen," and he would have started his buffalo contract in October, 1867, a time which is in agreement with his account of his activities that year. In eight months he should have delivered 2,928 buffalo; the figure 4,280 exceeds his contract by 1,352, or some five or six a day.

A contemporary newspaper account of one hunt indicates his growing reputation and that of his horse Brigham. The Leavenworth *Daily Conservative* of January 11, 1868, quotes the Hays City *Advance*: "Bill Cody and 'Brigham' started on a hunt Saturday afternoon, and came in Tuesday. The result was nineteen buffalo. Bill brought in over four thousand pounds of meat, which he sold for seven cents per pound, making about $100 per day for his time out." Another article shows that he had time for other pursuits. Said the *Conservative* on March 5, 1868, again quoting the *Advance*: "Bill Cody has made a match to run the Brigham pony ninety miles in twelve hours. Brigham is to 'tote' 175 pounds, and the race is to come off next month."[5]

Some of Cody's publicity says that he did his buffalo killing for the Union Pacific Railroad, and this has been cited as an attempt to connect him with the completion of the first transcontinental railroad. The actual name of the railroad for which Cody did his buffalo hunting was Union Pacific, Eastern Division, a name adopted by its promoters in the hope that if they were first to make junction with the Central Pacific, they might be declared the main line. The name caused endless confusion and was changed in 1868 to Kansas Pacific. Under either name it had no corporate connection with the Union Pacific, but in 1880 it was absorbed by the Union Pacific, thus adding to the confusion.[6]

There seems no doubt that it was his buffalo killing during the construction of this railroad that made Cody widely known as Buffalo Bill. As he tells it: "It was at this time that the very appropriate

---

[5] From the files of the KSHS.

[6] Cody, *True Tales of the Plains,* refers to "the Kansas Pacific Railroad (now the Union Pacific)"; see also p. 66.

name of 'Buffalo Bill' was conferred upon me by the road-hands. It has stuck to me ever since and I have never been ashamed of it." In *True Tales of the Plains,* he implied that the application of the nickname was not entirely complimentary. The workers grew tired of a steady diet of the same meat, and would say, "Here comes this old Bill with more buffalo!" Finally, says Cody, "they connected the name buffalo and Bill together and that is where the foundation was laid to the name of 'Buffalo Bill.'" A jingle said to have originated at the time added to the legend:

> *Buffalo Bill, Buffalo Bill,*
> *Never missed and never will;*
> *Always aims and shoots to kill*
> *And the company pays his buffalo bill.*[7]

The idea that no Western character was authentic unless he had been patented with a geographical or descriptive title seems to have taken root in the Civil War period, coming to full flower in the heraldry of the dime novels. At first these nicknames were not necessarily exclusive property. The "California Joe" of Berdan's Sharpshooters in the Civil War was Truman Head. The "California Joe" about whom Custer wrote without knowing his name was Moses E. Milner. The "Texas Jack" who was scout in the Civil War and the Indian wars was not the "Texas Jack" who was hanged in Indian Territory, nor was he the "Texas Jack" who had a Wild West show that toured the country.

There were other Buffalo Bills. Some of them gained contemporary fame. On December 10, 1862, from Fort Benton on the Missouri River in Montana Territory, Edward Shelley, an English traveler, wrote in his diary: "Buffalo Bill, a personage whom I have hitherto regarded as a myth, came in this morning from the other side of the mountains and brought a few papers of rather later date than anything I have seen since I left Laramie." This probably was Buffalo Bill Cramer, who is on record as having bought a herd of mixed cattle from the American Fur Company at Fort Benton in

[7] Cody, *Life,* 162; Cody, *True Tales of the Plains,* 67; Mrs. Cody, *Memories,* 113; D. Harper Simms, "How Buffalo Bill Got His Name," in *Corral Dust* (Potomac Corral of Westerners), Vol. IV, No. 1 (March, 1959), 6; Leavenworth *Daily Conservative,* November 26, 1867.

1864. "Buffalo Bill" (William J.) Wilson was hanged at Lincoln, New Mexico, on December 10, 1875, for the murder of Bob Casey, so he probably was not the "Buffalo Bill" reported on March 30, 1876, to have killed "a few weeks ago" the sheriff of Young County, Texas. "Buffalo Billy" Brooks, buffalo hunter, peace officer at Newton and Dodge City, Kansas, in the 1870's, could possibly have been the "Buffalo Bill," professional buffalo hunter, who scouted for June Peak's Texas Rangers on the trail of Sam Bass. W. C. Tomlins, known as the "Buffalo Bill of the Black Hills," was a meat hunter before he took up ranching on the Belle Fourche.[8]

A vociferous claimant to the title of the "original Buffalo Bill" was William Mathewson. His story pops up in several versions, but the most definite is that of Frank Winch, press agent for the Buffalo Bill show. In 1911, according to Winch, Cody received the following letter from Mathewson: "You have no right to call yourself 'Buffalo Bill' and you know you haven't. You claim to have won that title from Comstock. You know I am the original Buffalo Bill and was known by that name ten years before you ever worked for the Kansas Railroad. When I was post trader I was called Buffalo Bill because I killed buffaloes to supply meat for them that didn't have any meat or couldn't get it and I never charged them a cent for it. When you and your show come to Topeka I aim to tell you to your face that you are using a title that doesn't belong to you."

In all probability this is correct, and Winch says Cody accepted it. The nickname was scarcely exclusive, but by this time Cody had a considerable property interest in it. He had recently won an injunction in a suit against an imposter attempting to use the name for a show. Since it was desirable to avoid unfavorable publicity, Winch was sent to Topeka, he says (he may be mixed up as Mathewson lived in Wichita), to see what could be done.

He found that Mathewson was hard up, and had recently sold a cherished rifle, which Winch recovered and presented to "the

[8] Herbert O. Brayer, "The Western Journal of Edward Shelley," *The Westerners Brand Book* (Chicago), Vol. XIII, No. 11 (January, 1957), 88; Larry Gill, "From Butcher Boy to Beef King," *Montana*, Vol. VIII, No. 2 (Spring, 1958), 51; Ed Bartholomew, *Biographical Album of Western Gunfighters* (Houston, 1958); Wilmington *Delaware Gazette*, March 30, 1876, identifies the killer as W. F. Cody, but Cody was on the stage at the time; Charles L. Martin, *A Sketch of Sam Bass, the Bandit* (Norman, 1956), 120; Richard B. Hughes, *Pioneer Years in the Black Hills*, ed. by Agnes Wright Spring (Glendale, 1957), 36.

original Buffalo Bill" in Cody's name. That broke the ice, and when the show arrived, Winch brought Cody and Mathewson together. The quarrel evaporated, and Mathewson was an honored guest at the afternoon performance. Characteristically, Cody arranged to take care of Mathewson's needs unknown to the recipient. Winch arranged with a newspaperman to "buy" (with Cody's money) weekly installments of Mathewson's life story. It might have been worth publishing.[9]

The title of Buffalo Bill is said to have been at issue in the buffalo-shooting contest between Cody and Billy Comstock, but Cody's original autobiography does not mention it. Cody is called "Buffalo Bill" in an advertisement for the event reproduced by Courtney Ryley Cooper. It reads: "Grand Excursion to Fort Sheridan, Kansas Pacific Railroad. Buffalo shooting match for $500 a side and the championship of the world between Billy Comstock (the famous scout) and W. F. Cody (Buffalo Bill), famous buffalo killer for the Kansas Pacific Railroad."[10]

William Comstock was not customarily called "Buffalo Bill." Said to have been part Cheyenne Indian, he was post guide and interpreter at Fort Wallace in 1866. Throughout the 1867 campaign he accompanied Custer as chief scout, then returned to Fort Wallace. Late that year or in January, 1868, he killed a contractor named Wyatt at the sutler's store in an argument over a debt. Comstock was brought to trial and pleaded guilty before M. S. Joyce, colorful justice of the peace at Hays. The judge's ruling is reported as, "Ye are a damned fool for tellin' it. I discharge ye for want of evidence." Comstock was said to be hiding out at his Rose Creek ranch near by when General Sheridan sought him out shortly after assuming command of the department on March 2, 1868. Sheridan named Comstock, Abner Sharp Grover, and Richard Parr as mediators, scouts, and guides, being persuaded that their influence among the Indians might go far toward preserving the peace. Lieutenant Fred H. Beecher was in charge of their activities.

[9] Frank Winch, "Buffalo Bill—Frontiersman," *Ace-High*, Vol. XLVII, No. 3 (First April Number, 1929), 395–402.

[10] Mrs. Cody, *Memories*, 122; Courtney Ryley Cooper, "The Life and Times of Buffalo Bill," *Kansas City Star*, May 9, 1926; that the contest was for the title "Buffalo Bill" is stated in Wetmore, *Last of the Great Scouts*, 164; Cody, *Autobiography*, 123.

Beecher sent Comstock and Grover to the Cheyenne village of Chief Turkey Leg, with whom they had a long friendship, but while they were there, a runner came in with news that four Indians had been killed and ten wounded in a fight with troops on the Saline. Comstock and Grover were told to leave the camp, yet they were unsuspicious when joined about two miles away by seven young Cheyennes who professed to be friendly. While they were all riding along together, the Indians suddenly opened fire, killing Comstock instantly and severely wounding Grover. Grover played dead, hiding in the grass the night of August 16 and all the next day, then dragged himself to the railroad, where he was picked up by a passing train and was taken to Fort Wallace.[11]

The contest between Comstock and Cody is one of the most enduring in the Buffalo Bill legend, and almost anyone in Kansas can point out exactly where it occurred, but no one seems to know exactly when. The place, according to George Allaman, a scout and meat hunter, and Pete Ziegler, an early-day rancher, was two and one-half miles west of Monument, Kansas, in a draw leading northwest from the railroad tracks—Cody said twenty miles east of Sheridan. Archaeological evidence supports this location; Charles Tauscher, Union Pacific section boss found several hand-blown beer and champagne bottles at this site, undoubted evidence that Buffalo Bill slept here. As the event was arranged by officers at Fort Hays and Fort Wallace, backing their respective scouts with a bet of five hundred dollars a side, it probably took place after Cody had quit meat hunting and returned to scouting.

The advertising brought about one hundred spectators on a special excursion train from St. Louis. Among them were Mrs. Cody and Arta, who came to take up residence at Hays. According to Cody, the hunt was to last from eight o'clock in the morning until four in the afternoon. The hunters were to go into the same herd at the same time, each "making a run," killing as many buffalo as

[11] Report of Bvt. Col. H. C. Bankhead, captain 5th Infantry, commanding, Fort Wallace, Aug. 19, 1868, to Hq., District of the Upper Arkansas; Mrs. Frank C. Montgomery, "Fort Wallace and Its Relation to the Frontier," *Collections of the KSHS*, XVII, 225–26; P. H. Sheridan, *Personal Memoirs*, II, 286–87, 292–93; Homer W. Wheeler, *Buffalo Days*, 244–49; "Father He Gets Scairt at Turkey Leg's Village," as told to E. S. Sutton by Frank Yellow Bull (MS from Edward M. Beougher); *Lawrence Weekly Tribune*, August 27, 1868; W. J. Carney, "Billy Comstock, Government Scout," *Collier's*, Vol. XXVI, No. 5 (November 3, 1900).

possible. A referee was to follow each as official scorekeeper. Comstock was armed with a Henry repeating rifle, which fired faster but was of lighter caliber than Cody's "Lucretia Borgia." Cody, of course, was mounted on Brigham. But let Cody tell the story:

"Comstock and I dashed into the herd, followed by the referees. The buffaloes separated; Comstock took the left bunch and I the right. My great forte in killing buffaloes from horseback was to get them circling by riding my horse at the head of the herd, shooting the leaders, thus crowding their followers to the left, till they would finally circle round and round. On this morning the buffaloes were very accommodating, and I soon had them running in a beautiful circle, when I dropped them thick and fast, until I had killed thirty-eight; which finished my run. Comstock began shooting at the rear of the herd, which he was chasing, and they kept straight on. He succeeded, however, in killing twenty-three, but they were scattered over a distance of three miles, while mine lay close together. I had 'nursed' my buffaloes, as a billiard player does the balls when he makes a big run."

The St. Louis excursion party now set out a lot of champagne—the archaeological evidence—"which proved a good drink on a Kansas prairie, and a buffalo hunter was a good man to get away with it," says Cody. While this was going on, another herd was sighted, and the contestants charged into it, Cody killing eighteen and Comstock fourteen; score: Cody, fifty-six; Comstock, thirty-seven. The champagne was brought out again, this time with lunch, and under these benign influences Cody decided to show what he could do without saddle or bridle on the next run. They had to move about three miles to find another small herd, of which Cody killed thirteen, "the last one of which I had driven down close to the wagons, where the ladies were," and killed within fifty yards of one of the wagons. Again Buffalo Bill was showing signs of becoming a showman. This brought the score to Cody, sixty-nine; Comstock, forty-six. The match was then declared over, and Cody was proclaimed champion buffalo hunter of the plains.[12]

Cody recounts two Indian adventures of his meat-hunting period. For one of them there is a version taken down by a newspaper reporter on December 12, 1872, seven years before his autobi-

[12] Cody, *Life*, 171–75.

ography was published. When questioned at an Omaha banquet, Cody said: "That was the time of the railroad construction, and the Indian war was going on. One day I had rode twenty-one miles from the line of the road, and was alone. Just as I came out on a little rise of ground I saw a lot of Kiowa Indians. They discovered me at the same time, and eighteen or twenty jumped up to go for me. They were at breakfast and their horses were right by their sides. When they are on the war path they are always armed, so that each only had to put a bit of rope into his horse's mouth and he was ready. I saw at a glance what they were doing and I wanted to be home. You may bet I would like to be out of that, and I got out as fast as I could. I looked over my shoulders and saw them just a whooping and howling after me. I didn't like that country— not a bit. It was almost entirely level, and they were at times during the first three miles within 200 yards of me. Once when I came to a little hog wallow in the prairie I turned long enough to fire at the fellow that was ahead and I must have hit him, for he stoped, [*sic*] but I never could find him afterwards. I had every confidence in my horse and I noticed that the Indians soon began to string out. If I had been out with a poor one I would have lost all hold [hope?]. I know he was good bottom, though the Indians had a great advantage because their horses were fresh and mine had gone twenty miles before they saw me. It was a long run and a wild one. They fired several shots but they did not happen to hit me at all. One advantage I had was that they carried long muzzle loading guns, and could not load again when they had once fired. I could see how they came on and changed places just as the horses gave out. Mine kept ahead. Finally the guard at the camp saw us. At that time there were only six Indians following me. All the rest had played out. Soldiers came out to meet me and we easily killed those six."[13]

This story has every indication of being Cody's own, unretouched, and we may concede that the reporter must have taken it down just about as he told it. In the autobiography a few details are added: that the chase began at the Smoky Hill River, that the horse was Brigham, and that the rescue party was headed by Cap-

[13] Unidentified newspaper clipping dated December 12, 1872, quoting *Omaha Herald* (from Everett Graff); Cody, *Life*, 162–67.

tain Nolan of the Tenth Cavalry. This would be Captain Nicholas Nolan, who commanded Company A at this time.

On the other occasion Cody was accompanied by a butcher known as "Scotty," who was driving a two-mule wagon loaded with the meat of fifteen buffalo Cody had killed. When they saw about thirty Indians riding out of a ravine, they unhitched the mules and tied them to the wagon, along with Bill's horse, not Brigham this time. Buffalo hams were thrown to the ground around the wagon to form a breastwork, and the two, armed with three or four extra revolvers and a box of ammunition, were ready to stand siege. The Indians charged, but were stopped by the fire of rifles and pistols at a distance of about one hundred yards. The Indians charged back and forth several times, says Cody, and three of them who got within fifty yards were shot down. Meanwhile Cody had set a grass fire to windward, as a signal to the troops along the railroad, eight miles away. The Indians dismounted and continued firing from a bank or knoll until they saw the cavalry approaching, then mounted and rode off. Cody gives the total casualties as five Indians killed. The meat, with a few arrows sticking in it, was put back on the wagon and taken to camp.[14]

There were also contemporary newspaper stories, copied from newspaper to newspaper across Kansas and even as far as St. Louis, that indicate a growing Cody legend. By February 14, 1868, he was called "Cody, the noted guide and hunter" in the Lawrence *Kansas Weekly Tribune*, which said: "At Hays City considerable anxiety exists in regard to the safety of a party of citizens who were out buffalo hunting. There were ten in all in the company, among whom were George and Henry Field, brothers of Mr. Samuel Field of this city, and Mr. Parks, the traveling correspondent of the *Journal*, all under the direction of Cody, the noted guide and hunter. They left Hays ten days since, and were to return on Friday last, but have not been heard of since. Fears are expressed that they have been captured or killed by the Indians, who have shown decided symptoms of hostility of late. Some efforts are being made toward organizing a party to go in search of them." "Friday last" was February 7, so they were a week overdue. Apparently Cody

14 Cody, *Life*, 167–69.

96

the noted guide and hunter brought the party back safely, as no further account has been found.

An item in the *Topeka Leader* of March 28, 1868, stated: "W. F. Cody, government detective, and Wm. Haycock, Deputy U. S. Marshal, brought eleven prisoners and lodged them in our calaboose on Monday last—a band of robbers having their headquarters on the Solomon, charged with stealing government property and desertion."[15]

Army quartermasters hired "detectives"—so designated on pay rolls—as well as scouts during this period, and W. F. Cody may well have been hired in that capacity to lend a hand to his friend Wild Bill Hickok, for there is no doubt that the "Wm. Haycock" mentioned was Wild Bill. Uncertainty is dispelled by Theodore R. Davis, correspondent for *Harper's Weekly*, who commented on the indefiniteness of Wild Bill's legal name, which was "printed as Wm Hitchcock—Wm Hancock and Wm Hickok, also Wm Haycock, and you were told that 'Jim' Hickock was correct."

Davis told of an expedition to hunt deserters from General Hancock's 1867 expedition. The deserter hunt was instigated by Henry M. Stanley, correspondent for the *Weekly Missouri Democrat* and the *New York Tribune,* later famous for finding Livingstone in Africa. Stanley's horse equipment had been stolen. Davis says Stanley was seeking the Leatherstocking element on the Kansas frontier, "of which, as he said, not a shadow materialized—both garments and character of honest old Natty Bumpo seemed a shocking misfit for the self-named Wild Bills and Texas Jacks." This discovery seems shocking a century later when Wild Bill's fame has far wider impact that that of James Fenimore Cooper's fictional hero.

Wild Bill failed to impress Davis, who reports: "The man was by nature a dandy. . . . In his usual array Wild Bill could have gained unquestioned admittance to the floor of most fancy dress balls of metropolitan cities. When we ordinary mortals were hustling for a clean pair of socks, as prospective limit of change in wearing apparel, I have seen Wild Bill appear in an immaculate boiled shirt, with collar and cuffs to match—a sleeveless Zouave

[15] Newspapers in the files of KSHS.

jacket of startling scarlet, slashed with black velvet—the entire garment being ornamented with buttons which, if not silver, seemed to be. The trousers might be either black velvet or buckskin, and like his jacket, fitted with buttons quite beyond useful requirement. The french calfskin boots . . . fitted admirably, and were polished as if the individual wearing them had recently vacated an Italian's armchair throne on a side street near Broadway. The long wavey hair that fell in masses from a conventional sombrero, was glossy from a recent anointment of some heavily perfumed mixture. As far as dress went only, Wild Bill was to border plainsmen what 'Beau' Neil was to the Army of the Potomac— faultlessly clad under surprising circumstances. In fact I don't believe that it would have occasioned comment had the scout produced and deliberately fitted on kid gloves matching perfectly his expensive necktie."

Stanley suggested "that deserters had a cash value, attractive to members of the scout contingent, who beside were very desirous of seeing themselves flatteringly mentioned in print," so he and Davis enlisted a few, picking Wild Bill "as the most available individual for chief operator, although our confidence in the critter was slim." Their confidence, however, was not misplaced. "It was Wild Bill who piloted the party to its quarry, and when the ranch was surrounded, Wild Bill, upon his own suggestion, stole noiselessly and alone to the door, gaining admittance after a short parley," which resulted in the surrender of the deserters.[16]

In that same year a correspondent of *Harper's Monthly* gave the first big boost to the Wild Bill legend.[17] The fame of Buffalo Bill grew more slowly, yet he had dramatized himself as buffalo hunter for the Kansas Pacific, and publicity-minded officials had buffalo heads mounted and displayed at stations, where soon they were pointed out as having been shot by Buffalo Bill.

When end-of-track reached Sheridan in May, Goddard Brothers no longer required Cody's services. As Cody no longer required Brigham, he raffled off his poky-looking horse by selling ten chances at thirty dollars each. Ike Bonham of Wyandotte, Kansas,

---

[16] *The Westerners Brand Book* (Chicago), Vol. II (1946), 97–106.
[17] George Ward Nichols, "Wild Bill," *Harper's Monthly*, Vol. XXXIV, No. 201 (February, 1867).

had the lucky number. After winning races against five Thorough-breds with Brigham, he sold him to Superintendent of Construction Wilcox of the Kansas Pacific. While Cody was in Memphis in 1876 on a theatrical tour, he was invited by Wilcox to visit Brigham. Said Cody, "It seemed as if he almost remembered me." Buffalo Bill's sentimental attachment for horses has sometimes been exaggerated.

Lulu and Arta retired to Leavenworth, and Cody was hired by the quartermaster at Fort Larned, then commanded by Captain Daingerfield Parker of the Third Infantry.[18]

[18] Cody, *Life*, 175–77; he leaves the first "i" out of Daingerfield.

SHERIDAN FINDS CODY'S SERVICES

"EXTREMELY VALUABLE"

THE PERIOD FROM MAY TO AUGUST, 1868, was the last in which the movements and actions of Cody are relatively obscure. It is possible that he was not regularly employed, as army authority did not encourage the employment of scouts except during active campaigning, and this was a time of uneasy peace on the plains under the Medicine Lodge Treaty. The Indians had promised to go to specified reservations, but made no move toward them. There was delay in ratifying the treaty, hence in paying annuities in the form of goods promised by the government. Sheridan did all he could to meet the treaty obligations. "An abundant supply of rations is usually effective to keep matters quiet in such cases, so I fed them pretty freely," he said.[1] The Indians were not particularly hungry. The 4,280 buffalo killed by Cody, in whatever time, had not materially reduced the huge herds roaming the Kansas plains in 1868.

Cody served as guide and courier for Brevet Major General William B. Hazen, superintendent of Indian affairs for the Southern Plains, who was at Fort Larned charged with carrying out the treaty provisions. The first sign of trouble came in July when the Cheyennes raided the Kaws and robbed the houses of several white settlers near Council Grove. Because of this raid, the post commander at Fort Larned hesitated to issue arms and ammunition to

[1] Sheridan, *Personal Memoirs*, II, 286.

the Comanches and Kiowas who demanded them as promised in the treaty. They scorned food and other supplies offered. When Brevet Brigadier General Alfred Sully came from Fort Dodge to investigate, Satanta of the Kiowas and other chiefs persuaded him that only a few bad young men of one tribe had misbehaved, and pleaded that the peaceful Indians needed guns to hunt buffalo. Sully accepted this explanation and issued the arms. While Comanches and Kiowas were still encamped near Fort Larned, two hundred Cheyennes, four Arapahoes, and twenty visiting Sioux began on August 10 a series of rapes and murders of settlers along the Saline and Solomon rivers. Thirteen men and two women were killed before troops arrived—Captain Benteen with a detachment of the Seventh Cavalry dashing to the rescue of settlers fortified in the cabin of a Mr. Schermerhorn. During this same month Billy Comstock was killed by Cheyennes who coveted his pearl-handled Colt's revolver.

Cody went to Fort Hays, probably carrying dispatches, and was taken on as scout again by Major Armes of the Tenth Cavalry. The expedition failed to find hostile Indians, but we get a glimpse of Cody in Major Armes' diary entry of August 24: "We marched out at sunrise, met Colonel Benteen, Seventh Cavalry, en route to Harker. He was relieved in the field by Colonel Carpenter, who marched twenty-five or thirty miles and has discovered quite a number of Indian signs. Bill Cody (Buffalo Bill), one of our scouts and one of the best shots on the plains, keeps us well supplied with plenty of buffalo and deer. He gets $60 per month and a splendid mule to ride, and is one of the most contented and happy men I ever met."[2]

On the day Major Armes recorded his appreciation of Buffalo Bill, General Sheridan augmented his forces by directing his assistant inspector-general, Brevet Colonel George A. Forsyth, to enroll "fifty first-class hardy frontiersmen to be used as scouts against the hostile Indians," with Lieutenant Beecher as second in command. Within five days this company was organized at Fort Hays and Fort Harker—an indication that a considerable number of hardy frontiersmen were competing with Buffalo Bill for scouts' jobs—and took the field, scouting across the headwaters of the Solomon River

[2] Armes, *Ups and Downs of an Army Officer*, 272.

and along Beaver Creek. At Fort Wallace, Forsyth learned of an attack on a wagon train by a small band of Indians. While following this trail, his company bumped into Roman Nose with 970 warriors. In the fight at Beecher's Island—so named for the lieutenant who was among the slain—on the Arickaree Fork of the Republican River, the mounted Indians charged the little force and were not turned away until the scouts had poured into them seven volleys from their Spencer repeating carbines, then fired revolvers into the faces of the Cheyennes. The Indians rallied and charged again, and again failed. Roman Nose was killed. The scouts were held under siege from September 17 to 25, when they were rescued by a detachment of the Tenth Cavalry commanded by Colonel L. H. Carpenter, mentioned in Armes' diary. Cody never claimed to have been in the Beecher's Island fight, although he was described as being there in irresponsible books.

Major Armes left Fort Hays on September 2 on an expedition to Walnut Creek, this time with Wild Bill Hickok as scout. Cody had returned to Fort Larned. The earliest official record that has been found relating to Cody's army employment shows that from September 9 to 14, 1868, he was hired as a laborer resacking forage at thirty dollars a month, paid by Second Lieutenant L. W. Cooke, acting assistant quartermaster at Fort Larned.[3] It is possible that the quartermaster employed him at any job authorized in order to keep him available in case his services as scout were needed. In fact, they were.

Cody tells of guiding General Hazen with a small escort from Fort Larned to Fort Zarah. General Hazen continued on to Fort Harker, but Cody was sent back alone to Fort Larned. He was captured by Indians, he says, but managed to persuade Chief Satanta that he had been sent for cattle to be issued to the Kiowas. This ruse gave him temporary respite, but the Kiowas failed to see any cattle, and they did see Cody high-tailing it for Fort Larned. They pursued him to the vicinity of the fort, where he met a small party of soldiers and a scout named Denver Jim, sent out to recover the bodies of seven or eight woodchoppers and herders killed that

---

[3] Report of persons hired by 2nd Lt. L. W. Cooke, acting assistant quartermaster, Ft. Larned, Kan., records of the Office of the Quartermaster General, National Archives, called to my attention by Elbert L. Huber.

morning by Satanta's warriors. A trap was set for Cody's pursuers and two of the Indians were killed.[4]

What is definitely known is that Cody was sent from Fort Larned to Fort Hays, sixty-five miles away, to inform General Sheridan that the Kiowas and Comanches were on the warpath. Sheridan himself tells the rest of the story: "This intelligence required that certain orders should be carried to Fort Dodge, ninety-five miles south of Hays. This too being a particularly dangerous route—several couriers having been killed on it—it was impossible to get one of the various 'Petes,' 'Jacks,' or 'Jims,' hanging around Hays City to take my communication. Cody learning of the strait I was in, manfully came to the rescue, and proposed to make the trip to Dodge, though he had just finished his long and perilous ride from Larned. I gratefully accepted his offer, and after four or five hours' rest he mounted a fresh horse and hastened on his journey, halting but once to rest on the way, and then only for an hour, the stop being made at Coon Creek, where he got another mount from a troop of cavalry. At Dodge he took six hours' sleep, and then continued on to his own post—Fort Larned—with more despatches. After resting twelve hours at Larned, he was again in the saddle with tidings for me at Fort Hays, General Hazen sending him, this time, with word that the villages had fled to the south of the Arkansas. Thus, in all, Cody rode about 350 miles in less than sixty hours, and such an exhibition of endurance and courage was more than enough to convince me that his services would be extremely valuable in the campaign, so I retained him at Fort Hays till the battalion of the Fifth Cavalry arrived, and then made him chief of scouts for that regiment."[5]

Sheridan seems to have calculated the distance 50 to 60 miles too long. Fort Larned to Fort Hays, 65 miles, was made twice; Fort Hays to Fort Dodge is 95 miles; Cody gives the distance from Fort Dodge to Fort Larned as 65 miles, which is too low. This totals 290 miles, not 350. Cody makes the riding time fifty-eight hours. Figuring at the minimum, this makes an average of 116 miles of riding a day, a feat that can be little appreciated in these days when few know much of horseback travel. For a part of the journey he

[4] Cody, *Life,* 178–87.
[5] Sheridan, *Personal Memoirs,* II, 300–301.

was riding parallel with the Indians he was carrying information about. Cody tells of stumbling into a hostile camp the first night and narrowly escaping, something which could well have happened. Few will doubt one further point he adds—that he filled a canteen with brandy before he started.

This may account for his final absurdity—that he was thrown by his mule, which then kept just beyond his reach while he walked thirty-five miles, until he became so exasperated that he shot it within sight of his destination. This story is typical of the tall tales Cody included for humorous effect—not always successfully.

Cody's story might seem to be an exaggeration of Sheridan's, except for the fact that Sheridan's book was published nine years after Cody's. It is one of the few cases in Cody's first autobiography in which he seems to exaggerate. Another interpretation might be that he attached little importance to it, and added other events of about the same time to it—for nowhere was he very accurate in keeping the order of events straight.

However, his press agents never dreamed up a more dramatic story than is provided in a simple statement in official records. There it appears that on September 14, 1868, Second Lieutenant L. W. Cooke, Third U. S. Infantry, acting assistant quartermaster at Fort Larned, Kansas, discharged W. F. Cody as a laborer sacking forage at $30 a month, and that on September 15, Lieutenant Cooke put W. F. Cody on the pay roll as a scout at $75 a month—the top pay authorized for a scout at that time. Never again would Buffalo Bill be so little known as his employment on September 14 indicates.[6]

Buffalo Bill had not long to wait for the arrival of the Fifth Cavalry, the regiment with which he was to win his greatest fame as scout. When Sheridan moved his headquarters to Fort Hays, a few days before Cody brought him the information on which he says his plans for his winter campaign were based,[7] there were available for that campaign only 2,600 men—the Seventh and Tenth regiments of cavalry, the Third and Fifth regiments of in-

[6] War Department, Office of the Quartermaster General, QM 201 AP-C-(A & C Div.) Cody, William F., May 19, 1939, transcript of Cody's record prepared at the request of Rep. Thomas F. Ford (hereafter OQM 1939). A similar transcript compiled at the National Archives adds a few details.

[7] Sheridan, *Personal Memoirs*, II, 301.

fantry, and four companies of the Thirty-eighth Regiment of infantry. He called for a regiment of Kansas volunteers—it was raised as the Nineteenth Infantry by Governor Samuel J. Crawford, who took the field as its colonel—and asked that all available cavalry be sent to Kansas.

Seven companies of the Fifth Cavalry were assembled in a remarkably short time for that period. Companies H and L left Aiken, South Carolina, on September 12 by railway to Columbus, Kentucky, took a riverboat for St. Louis, and train again to Fort Harker, where they arrived on September 23. Two days later, F from Richmond, Virginia, M from Gallatin, Tennessee, and B from Nashville arrived. On September 27, A and I from Raleigh, North Carolina, completed the battalion that Major William B. Royall marched against the Indians on October 1.[8]

The Fifth Cavalry, organized in 1855 as the Second Cavalry— horse regiments previously in the army were known as dragoons and mounted riflemen—had served against Indians in the Southwest until 1861. Then it acquired its higher number and lost to the Confederacy such distinguished officers as Robert E. Lee, Albert Sidney Johnston, William J. Hardee, Earl Van Dorn, Edmund Kirby Smith, and John B. Hood. Union generals from the Fifth included George H. Thomas and George Stoneman, Jr. Many famed officers served subsequently in the Fifth Cavalry, in the Civil War and in the Indian wars, yet in its long fighting record as part of the First Cavalry Division in World War II and in Korea, the Fifth Cavalry was usually identified as the regiment for which Buffalo Bill had been chief of scouts.

The Fifth halted at Fort Hays long enough to receive Sheridan's orders and to pick up its scout, then continued its reconnaissance along the Kansas Pacific Railway toward Prairie Dog Creek, where Forsyth had seen signs of an Indian camp during his expedition.

After marching a couple of days, Major Royall suggested that Cody go out and kill some buffalo to feed the command.

"All right, Colonel, send along a wagon or two to bring in the meat," Cody said.

[8] Capt. George F. Price (compiler), *Across the Continent with the Fifth Cavalry* (a regimental history compiled by its adjutant from official records), 131–32.

"I am not in the habit of sending out my wagons until I know that there is something to be hauled in," Royall replied. "Kill your buffaloes first, and then I'll send out the wagons."

Cody killed half a dozen buffalo, then reported back for the wagons.

The next afternoon he was sent out again. This time he did not ask for wagons, but "coming up with a small herd, I managed to get seven of them headed straight for the encampment, and instead of shooting them just then, I ran them at full speed right into the camp, and then killed them all, one after the other in rapid succession." Royall demanded an explanation.

"I didn't care about asking for any wagons this time, Colonel; so I thought I would make the buffaloes furnish their own transportation," said Cody.[9]

While this has some earmarks of being another tall tale, the action was not beyond his abilities and perhaps not beyond his effrontery. Major Royall, whom Cody properly addressed in the brevet rank of colonel which he had held since the Civil War, had entered the army with Missouri volunteers during the Mexican War, remaining in service with the First Dragoons until transferred to the cavalry. He was senior first lieutenant when the regiment was organized and had been with it ever since, becoming major in 1863.

Arriving at Prairie Dog Creek, Royall established a camp with Company L as guard, and sent out the rest of the battalion in two detachments under Captains William H. Brown and Gustavus Urban to scout toward Beaver Creek and the Republican River. The detachments found no Indians, but while they were away, Tall Bull and his band of Cheyennes attacked the camp and its guard, killed one trooper, wounded another, and drove off twenty-six horses. Buffalo Bill was not in this fight, since he was with one of the detachments. As soon as they returned, the pursuit was taken up, without result, to Buffalo Tank on the railroad, where the battalion arrived on October 22.[10]

There Brevet Major General Eugene A. Carr, senior major of

[9] Cody, *Life*, 207–209; he misspells it "Royal."
[10] Price, *With the Fifth Cavalry*, 132, 672; for Royall, pp. 292–98; Cody, *Life*, 209.

the Fifth Cavalry, arrived to take command. As he was in command during most of Buffalo Bill's service with the regiment, it is well to take a close look at this bearded Cossack, of whom it has been said that he would rather be colonel of a cavalry regiment than President of the United States. Few officers of his time had more experience in Indian warfare. From the time of his graduation from West Point in 1850 to the Civil War, he made almost annual expeditions against the Indians. A native of Erie County, New York, assigned to the Regiment of Mounted Riflemen as a second lieutenant, he accompanied expeditions to the Rocky Mountains in 1852 and 1853. He was severely wounded in a fight with Mescalero Apaches near Mount Diavolo, Texas, on October 10, 1854. For gallantry in this affair he was promoted to first lieutenant in a new regiment that became the Fourth Cavalry. He took part in the Sioux expedition of 1855, was on field service in Kansas in 1856, was employed in the Kansas border troubles in 1857, as captain led a company in the Mormon War of 1858, served with the expedition to the Antelope Hills in 1859, and fought Kiowas and Comanches in 1860.

At the outbreak of the Civil War he escaped from the Confederate forces taking over western posts and marched his company from Fort Washita to Fort Leavenworth, arriving in time to take part in the Missouri campaign of 1861. In that graveyard of many Civil War reputations he was one of the few who gained credit. At Wilson's Creek, Carr, still captain of a company of the Fourth Cavalry, led off the field the only organized remnant of Franz Sigel's shattered brigade. Carr was brevetted lieutenant colonel for gallant and meritorious service in this battle and was offered the colonelcy of the Third Illinois Volunteer Cavalry, which he accepted. He commanded a division at the battle of Pea Ridge and was awarded the Congressional Medal of Honor for "directing the deployment of his command and holding his ground under a brisk fire of shot and shell in which he was several times wounded." He was promoted to brigadier general of volunteers and at almost the same time to major of the Fifth Cavalry in permanent rank— during the Civil War officers held several kinds of commissions simultaneously. In the campaign against Vicksburg, Carr commanded the Fourteenth Division of the Thirteenth Army Corps, which fought at Magnolia Church, Port Gibson, Jackson, Edward's Station, and Champion's Hill. Carr's division began and ended the engagement at Big Black River Bridge for which he was brevetted colonel. His division made the first lodgment in the enemy's works at Vicksburg on May 22, 1863, and he was reported conspicuous for coolness under fire and for holding his command so steady that not a regiment faltered. He was awarded three more brevet commissions, as brigadier general of volunteers for the capture of Little Rock, as major general of volunteers for the campaign against Mobile, and as major general "for gallant and meritorious services in the field during the War of the Rebellion."

When General Carr assumed command of the battalion of the Fifth Cavalry at Buffalo Tank, he was joined by Forsyth's scouts, now commanded by Lieutenant Silas Pepoon of the Tenth Cavalry. Carr moved out with the entire force on the following day toward the Republican River. On October 25 the advance guard, Company M under Lieutenant Jules C. A. Schenofsky, and Pepoon's scouts struck a party of Sioux and Cheyennes estimated at four or five hundred. The Indians were driven across the south fork of the Beaver and Shuter Creek. A running fight continued until dark. That night the Indians fired on the camp from a bluff, and Cody says that while he was eating supper with three officers, a bullet broke the plate of Lieutenant Alfred B. Bache. One cavalryman was wounded and thirty Indians were reported killed in the day's fighting. The next morning the pursuit was continued toward Prairie Dog Creek, with skirmishing all day, but that night the Indians got off to a better start and were seen only occasionally on October 27. Scattering trails were followed until the end of the month.[11]

One of these marches was toward the headwaters of the Beaver, and General Carr asked Buffalo Bill the distance. Cody gave it as twenty-five miles, a one-day march. After they had gone some distance, the General rode out to Cody and told him that Pepoon's scouts believed he was heading wrong and that he would find no water in the direction he was leading the troops. Cody was sure he would find water, held back by beaver dams, within eight miles.

[11] Price, *With the Fifth Cavalry*, 132–33; Cody, *Life*, 210–14; he spells the lieutenant's name "Schinosky."

When he was proved to be right by finding an ideal campsite along a branch of the Beaver that lacked a name, General Carr ordered that it should be known as Cody's Creek.

In telling of a skirmish the following morning, Bill admits he missed his shot! As he tells it: "We pulled out early next morning for the Beaver, and when we were approaching the stream, I rode on ahead of the advance guard, in order to find a crossing. Just as I turned a bend of the creek, 'bang!' went a shot, and down went my horse—myself with him. I disentangled myself, and jumped behind the dead body. Looking in the direction whence the shot had come, I saw two Indians, and at once turned my gun loose on them, but in the excitement of the moment I missed my aim." He saw a few lodges moving away, as mounted warriors kept shooting at him. "I sent a few shots after them to accelerate their speed, and also fired at the one on the other side of the stream," but still he does not say that he hit anyone.

"When General Carr came up, he ordered Company I to go in pursuit of the band. I accompanied Lieutenant Brady [Second Lieutenant Charles B. Brady], who commanded, and we had a running fight with the Indians, lasting several hours. We captured several head of their horses and most of their lodges."

At the end of October the battalion came in to Fort Wallace for three weeks. Cody hunted as usual, and records, "One day while I was out with a small party, we were 'jumped' by about fifty Indians. We had a severe fight of at least an hour, when we succeeded in driving the enemy. They lost four of their warriors."[12]

Another expedition had gone out from Fort Dodge under General Sully, including a battalion of the Third Infantry, of which he was lieutenant colonel, and the Seventh Cavalry under Major Elliott. It moved slowly and cautiously and found no Indians. Sheridan was so dissatisfied with Elliott's leadership that he petitioned the Secretary of War to remit Custer's suspension, which still had several months to run, and return him to duty.

Carr's battalion marched to Fort Lyon, Colorado Territory, arriving November 20, where it was ordered to prepare for a winter campaign. Sheridan's plan was his customary strategy of converging columns to keep the Indians from breaking out of their normal

[12] Cody, *Life*, 214–17.

range. His main column, as he explained it, "was to push down into the western part of the Indian Territory [Oklahoma], having for its initial objective the villages which, at the beginning of hostilities, had fled toward the head-waters of the Red River, and those that had gone to the same remote region after decamping from the neighborhood of Larned at the time General Hazen sent Buffalo Bill to me with the news." This column, which Sheridan accompanied, included Custer's Seventh Cavalry, Crawford's Nineteenth Kansas, and five companies of infantry under Brevet Major John H. Page. Before the Kansas cavalry reached Camp Supply, the assembly point, the trail of a returning war party was seen, and Custer's Seventh was ordered to follow it. The result was the Battle of the Washita, the only considerable fight of the campaign. Elliott, smarting under Sheridan's distrust, charged into a group of Indians, saying, "Here goes for a brevet or a coffin," and was killed with nineteen who followed him. Custer destroyed Black Kettle's village of Cheyennes and withdrew after finding that he had stirred up several other villages in the immediate vicinity. Buffalo Bill, needless to say, was not in this fight, although one biographer has him "with a revolver in either hand" carving his way "through the surging mass of redskins."[13]

The other columns found more hardships than fighting. Colonel A. W. Evans led six troops of the Third Cavalry and two companies of infantry from New Mexico by way of Fort Bascom toward western Indian Territory. Carr's seven troops of the Fifth Cavalry, with Cody as chief of scouts, was to march southeast from Fort Lyon toward the North Canadian and there join five troops of cavalry already in the field under Brevet Brigadier General William H. Penrose, captain, Third Infantry, then move toward the Antelope Hills and the headwaters of Red River.

Carr left Fort Lyon on December 2, with Penrose three weeks ahead of him. Penrose had only a small pack train and was expected to be short of supplies. The Fifth Cavalry customarily traveled with full wagon train, despite which it made some amazing marches in pursuit of Indians. There were seventy-five six-mule wagons, says Cody, in addition to ambulances and pack mules. The

[13] Sheridan, *Personal Memoirs*, II, 307–308; Carl Coke Rister, *Border Command*, 94–99; J. W. Buel, *Heroes of the Plains*, 321–22.

trail was followed for three days, but a heavy snowstorm then halted Carr's command at Freeze-out Canyon. As snow had obliterated the trail, Cody with four scouts was sent to see if he could find Penrose. Scouts with the regiment included Tom Renahan, Hank Fields, and a character called "Nosey."

After riding twenty-four miles through the snowstorm, the scouts found one of Penrose's old camps along a tributary of the Cimarron. Cody rode back alone to bring up the troops. At eleven o'clock that night he reached Carr's camp. As the battalion got under way early next morning the snow was so heavy that a way had to be shoveled through drifts for the wagons. Penrose's trail was traced on the west side of the Cimarron, but as that route appeared too rough for wagons, Carr followed along the opposite bank for a day's march, which ended on a high tableland in the Raton foothills (Cody spells it Rattoon), overlooking a creek valley. The bluff was not too steep for mounted men, but Carr thought the wagons could not make it. Buffalo Bill assured the General the wagons would get there. When the train came up, Cody was brusque in ordering one of the drivers to "run down, slide down or fall down—any way to get down." The driver feared the wagons would overrun the mules, but Cody had had long experience with wagons under the best teachers on the plains—the drivers of Russell, Majors and Waddell. Here is how he describes it:

"Telling Wilson, the chief wagon-master, to bring on his mess-wagon, which was at the head of the train, I said I would try the experiment at least. Wilson drove his team and wagon to the brink of the hill, and following my directions, he brought out some extra chains with which we locked both wheels on each side, and then rough-locked them. We then started the wagon down the hill. The wheel-horses—or rather the wheel-mules—were good on the hold-back, and we got along finely until we nearly reached the bottom, when the wagon crowded the mules so hard that they started on a run and galloped down into the valley and to the place where General Carr had located his camp. Three other wagons immediately followed in the same way, and in half an hour every wagon was in camp, without the least accident having occurred."[14]

It was afterward learned that the wagon train's daring descent

[14] Cody, *Life*, 206, 218–23.

of the hill had gained seven days on Penrose, for on the other side of the Cimarron he had been halted by a cliff that even pack mules could not descend and had turned back, losing three days' time each way. Along San Francisco Creek, Cody ran into two soldiers of the Tenth Cavalry, who hailed him as their old scout Buffalo Bill. They reported Penrose's command in a starving condition. Carr ordered Major Brown with two troops and fifty pack mules loaded with provisions to push ahead, with Cody as guide. Three days later Penrose's command was found on Paloduro Creek— Cody makes it "Polladora," which is close enough. Penrose's men had been on one-quarter rations for two weeks, and two hundred horses and mules had died of fatigue and starvation.

Carr unloaded his wagons and established a supply camp on December 30 at this point, now the southeast corner of Texas County, in the Oklahoma Panhandle. The wagons were sent back for more supplies. Meanwhile, Carr picked five hundred of the best men and horses to be sent with the pack train on a forty-mile march due south into the Texas Panhandle toward the Canadian River. Cody went with this expedition, as did Wild Bill Hickok, who had been scout for the Penrose expedition. They struck the South Fork of the Canadian, or Río Colorado, a few miles above Adobe Walls, scene of the later fight between buffalo hunters and Comanche Indians.

Here scouts arrived from a supply camp for the Evans expedition, only twelve miles away. These scouts also reported that the Evans camp was expecting a bull train with a large amount of beer. Cody and Hickok decided to hijack the beer. The Mexicans who had brought it from Fort Union had no objection to selling it twelve miles short of their destination. Says Cody, "It was sold to our boys in pint cups, and as the weather was very cold we warmed the beer by putting the ends of our picket-pins heated red-hot into the cups. The result was one of the biggest beer jollifications I ever had the misfortune to attend."

General Carr records that "during the winter of 1868, we encountered hardships and exposure in terrific snow storms, sleet, etc., etc. On one occasion that winter, Mr. Cody showed his quality by quietly offering to go with some dispatches to General Sheridan, across a dangerous region, where another principal scout was reluctant to risk himself." Cody tells of Hickok's carrying dispatches under similar circumstances, but does not mention his own trip—another exasperating instance of his failing to take credit where he has supporting evidence.[15]

After scouting along the Canadian without results, Carr returned to his supply camp. There occurred a ruckus so little to the credit of either Cody or Hickok that Bill's version may be accepted as authentic:

"Among the scouts of Penrose's command were fifteen Mexicans, and between them and the American scouts there had existed a feud; when General Carr took command of the expedition—uniting it with his own—and I was made chief of all the scouts, this feud grew more intense, and the Mexicans often threatened to clean us out; but they postponed the undertaking from time to time, until one day, while we were all at the sutler's store, the long-expected fight took place, and resulted in the Mexicans getting severely beaten.

"General Carr, upon hearing of the row, sent for Wild Bill and myself, he having concluded, from the various statements which had been made to him, that we were the instigators of the affair. But after listening to what we had to say, he thought that the Mexicans were as much to blame as we were.

"It is not to be denied that Wild Bill and myself had been partaking too freely of 'tanglefoot' that evening; and General Carr said to me: 'Cody, there are plenty of antelopes in the country, and you can do some hunting for the camp while we stay here.'"

Cody's account again underplays the situation. According to Sergeant Luke Cahill, who commanded the hunting party, scurvy had broken out, many men were sick, and fresh meat was a necessity. Twenty wagons with drivers, a wagon-master, and twenty infantrymen were assigned to accompany Cody. After a four days' march, a buffalo herd was sighted. Cody stampeded the herd into a deep arroyo full of snow, and fifty-five were killed. Some wagons were loaded and sent back. The next day Cody killed forty-one buffalo, exhausting two buffalo horses. The recoil of his Springfield rifle left his right shoulder and breast so much swollen that he

[15] *Ibid.*, vi–viii, "Introductory" letter from Carr dated July 3, 1878; Col. Homer W. Wheeler, *Buffalo Days*, 264–65.

113

could not put on his coat without help. It took two days to gather up the scattered carcasses, and by that time Cody was ready to go again.[16]

The Fifth Cavalry returned to Fort Lyon on February 19, 1869, "without having encountered hostile Indians or accomplished any material results, although the companies were conspicuous for their energy, untiring pursuit, and rapid movements. Company L made one march of seventy-five miles in twenty-six hours during a blinding snow storm." Thus the regimental history sums it up, and it might have added that Carr's column accomplished just what Sheridan expected it to do in blocking the Indians from drifting off westward, enabling the two other columns to accomplish the campaign objective. Evans captured a village of Nakoni Comanches on the North Fork of Red River on Christmas Day and drove off this band. When Sheridan moved out again after Custer's fight on the Washita, he found the Kiowas and Comanches ready to negotiate. Custer then moved against the Cheyennes. He refrained from attacking because two women prisoners were in their camp. The women were surrendered, and a peace was concluded on March 15, 1869.[17]

Carr's speedy relief of Penrose's command, along with the subsequent campaign in snow, with temperatures twenty-eight to thirty degrees below zero, was no small accomplishment, and Cody's trailing, his handling of the wagon train, and his hunting were important factors. For his work he gained recognition where it most counts—on the pay roll.

The red tape—actual red tape about a quarter-inch wide that I found still around these records in the National Archives—unties somewhat as follows. When General Sheridan retained Bill as scout after the famous ride, Cody was put on the pay roll of Lieutenant Cooke, quartermaster at Fort Larned, at $75 a month. At the end of September, 1868, he was transferred to the pay roll of Captain A. J. Kimball, assistant quartermaster at Fort Hays. He remained

[16] Cody, *Life*, 227–28; Luke Cahill, "An Indian Campaign and Buffalo Hunting with 'Buffalo Bill,'" *Colorado Magazine*, Vol. IV, No. 4 (August, 1927), 125–35; Cahill MS in library, State Historical Society of Colorado (hereafter SHSC); Cody to Cahill, March 8, 1913.

[17] Price, *With the Fifth Cavalry*, 133; Rister, *Border Command*, 94, 131–34, map, p. 68.

on that pay roll through November 30, at $75 a month, with the notation that he was "on the plains" under the direction of the major general commanding, meaning Sheridan. On February 1, 1869, Cody was transferred to Captain E. B. Kirk, assistant quartermaster at Fort Lyon, and paid off. On February 26, General Carr, by Special Order No. 46, Headquarters, Expedition from Fort Lyon, Colorado Territory, commanded Lieutenant Hayes, quartermaster of the Fifth Cavalry, to employ William Cody as scout at $125 a month to date from October 5, 1868. The effect of this order was to give Bill back pay at the rate of an additional $50 a month for all the time he had been with the Fifth Cavalry. This explains his saying that General Carr "at my request kindly granted me one month's leave of absence to visit my family in St. Louis," for ordinarily scouts were not retained by the army beyond the end of a campaign.[18]

So, with money in his pocket, Bill started off to see Lulu and Arta—and proceeded to get himself into another unnecessary jam. Quartermaster Hayes, with Carr's approval, allowed Cody to take a horse to ride and a mule on which to pack his belongings to end-of-track at Sheridan, and told him to leave the animals at the quartermaster's corral at Fort Wallace. Instead of doing as he was told, Cody left them with Perry, a hotelkeeper at Sheridan. While Bill was in St. Louis, a quartermaster's agent reported to Brevet Brigadier General Henry C. Bankhead, captain Fifth Infantry who commanded Fort Wallace, and Captain Samuel B. Lauffer, quartermaster there, that Cody had left the country and had sold a government horse and mule to the hotel owner. The animals were seized and taken to Fort Wallace.

When Cody returned to Sheridan, Perry told him what had happened, and Bill's first act was to give the quartermaster's agent "just such a thrashing as his contemptible lie deserved." Bill then went to the fort and demanded the horse and mule, for which, of course, he was responsible to Lieutenant Hayes. Both General Bankhead and Captain Lauffer ordered the scout off the reserva-

---

[18] S.O. 46, Hq., Expedition from Ft. Lyon, C. T., Feb. 26, 1868, attached to Report of Persons Hired by Lt. Hayes, Ft. Wallace, Kas., or in the Field for November, 1868, on which is a notation that Cody was employed as per order of Maj. Gen. P. H. Sheridan. Records of the Office of the Quartermaster General, National Archives.

tion. Bill went back to town and beat up the quartermaster's agent again. That night Bill was arrested by soldiers from the Thirty-eighth Infantry, under Captain Ezekial, an old friend. Bill protested that the Captain could have made the arrest without bringing the Negro regiment with him, but quotes the officer as saying, "I know that, Bill, but as you've not been in very good humor for the last day or two, I didn't know how you would act." Bill was taken to the guardhouse, but since Captain Graham's company, with which Bill had scouted, was on guard, he was not locked in a cell but was allowed to sleep in a sergeant's bunk.

Bill addressed a telegram to General Sheridan, but the operator took it to Bankhead, who tore it up. Hearing of this, Bill demanded to be taken to the telegraph office under guard to send the telegram. Bankhead then gave up, allowed Bill to take the horse and mule on Bill's promise to let the quartermaster's agent alone, and sent the scout on his way to Fort Lyon. That is Bill's story, which leaves Bankhead's willingness to compromise unexplained, although it might be pointed out that Bankhead had overstepped his authority in arresting a civilian off the reservation and holding him in a guardhouse. Oddly enough, in later years General Bankhead was among those who endorsed Buffalo Bill in glowing terms for Wild West show publicity.[19]

Bill's heedlessness of army procedures is characteristic. His occasional formidable outbursts of temper such as caused his beating up of the quartermaster's agent were less so, for this is one of few cases recorded where he resorted to violence—and to his credit be it noted that there was no gunplay. That the charge of horse stealing should be credited so near his usual haunts indicates that even yet his reputation had not traveled far.

Shortly after his return to Fort Lyon, Bill found himself on the other side of a case of horse stealing. Some horses and mules, including a horse belonging to General Carr and a mule owned by Lieutenant W. C. Forbush, were stolen from the post. Cody says he was commissioned a "United States detective" to recover them. The thieves had been traced to the vicinity of old Fort Lyon, purchased from the fur trader William Bent and abandoned for a new location when floods threatened to undermine it. There Bill Green,

19 Cody, *Life*, 229–33.

a scout, had lost the trail in tall grass, but had marked the spot. Cody followed the trail a bit farther, into a grove where a number of animals had been tied and taken out separately to confuse the trail. With Green, Jack Farley, and another scout, Cody made a five-mile circuit around this point and picked up the trail of four mules and eight horses. Such trailing is described in many a western novel, but Cody did it where other scouts had failed. After this new trail was followed down the Arkansas and up Sand Creek, it became confused again, but Cody was then convinced that he would find the animals at the Saturday auction in Denver.

Going there, he rented a room overlooking the Elephant Corral from Ed Chase. When from this vantage point he saw Lieutenant Forbush's mule put up at auction, Cody went down and arrested a thief named Williams. "He recognized me and endeavored to escape, but I seized him by the shoulder," says Cody. "He was armed with a pair of pistols, which I took away from him." Farley and Green took the prisoner out of town and threatened to hang him, under which threat Williams was quick to betray his partner. At an unoccupied house three miles further down the Platte River, Bill Bevins was covered with Cody's rifle before he could draw his revolver. The stolen animals were rounded up, and the party returned to Denver, where the two horse thieves were jailed overnight "in charge of my friend, Sheriff Edward Cook." Cody probably means Dave Cook, city marshal, who had just been nominated for the office of sheriff.

The next day the two prisoners were tied to mules, and the party started for Fort Lyon. The first night, while Farley was on guard, he was kicked into the fire by Williams. Bevins jumped over the fire carrying his shoes in his hands. Cody knocked Williams down with a revolver, but Bevins got away, dropping one of his shoes. He was followed for eighteen miles through snow and prickly pear by Cody and Green and finally was run down on the banks of the Platte. Cody expressed his admiration for "the most remarkable feat of the kind ever known either of a white man, or an Indian. A man who could run bare-footed in the snow eighteen miles through a prickly pear patch, was certainly a 'tough one' and that's the kind of a person Bill Bevins was." After Bevins had cut the thorns out of his foot with Cody's knife, he was allowed to ride

117

Cody's horse back to camp. Bevins caused no further trouble, for his foot was swollen to enormous size. However, on a subsequent dark and stormy night, Williams got away. Bevins was turned over to civil authorities at Boggs' ranch on Picket Wire Creek (the Purgatoire). As soon as he recovered the use of his foot, he escaped from a log jail where he was awaiting trial.

Bevins, also known as Bevans and Blivins—in this case Cody's spelling is possibly as good as any other—was afterward notorious for a series of stagecoach holdups along the Black Hills Trail in 1876. Calamity Jane claimed to have ridden with him, but Calamity Jane was apt to boast acquaintance with anyone in the public eye. Bevins was arrested at Lander and sentenced to ten years in prison. He escaped from jail at Laramie and resumed stage robbing, but was caught again. He failed in another jailbreak in 1877 at Cheyenne. Cody, writing in 1879, said Bevins was confined in the Nebraska state prison, to which he had been transferred after the penitentiary burned in Laramie. Bevins was released in 1886 and died shortly afterward.[20]

[20] Cody, *Life,* 233–34; Melvin Schoberlin, *From Candles to Footlights* (Denver, 1941), 41, 119, 195; William Ross Collier and Edwin Victor Westrate, *Dave Cook of the Rockies* (New York, 1936); Agnes Wright Spring, *Cheyenne and Black Hills Stage and Express Routes,* 211–12, 215; also information from Mrs. Spring regarding Chase, Bevins, and the Elephant Corral.

Buffalo Bill and Sitting Bull

Courtesy Denver Public Library Western Collection
Photograph by W. Notman, Montreal

Red Cloud, Buffalo Bill, and American Horse

9

THE SECRETARY OF WAR HEARS OF CODY

IT WAS A SOMEWHAT DEMORALIZED ARMY that took the field against the Indians in the spring of 1869. Congress by an act of March 3 cut the army from 54,641 to 37,313, reducing the number of infantry regiments from forty-five to twenty-five, although retaining the five regiments of artillery and ten of cavalry. This meant a significant reduction in the number of officers, and a Benzine Board—the reference is to a dry-cleaning fluid—was soon getting rid of the less desirable ones.

A regiment of cavalry consisted of a headquarters and band and twelve companies, often called troops, although that designation did not become official until 1883. Field officers included a colonel, a lieutenant colonel, and three majors. Headquarters included an adjutant, a quartermaster, and, until 1870, a commissary, detailed from first lieutenants, three additional officers being allowed for the purpose. The noncommissioned staff included a sergeant-major, a quartermaster sergeant, a commissary sergeant, a saddler sergeant, and an attached veterinary surgeon who ranked as a sergeant-major. Available for the band were the chief musician, chief trumpeter, and twenty-four trumpeters assigned two to each company.

There were three officers in each company: a captain, a first lieutenant, and a second lieutenant. The noncommissioned officers were a first sergeant, a company quartermaster sergeant, five sergeants, and eight corporals. There were also a farrier, a blacksmith, a saddler, and a wagoner. The minimum number of privates was sixty; the maximum, seventy-eight. Thus a cavalry regiment would aggregate between 1,024 and 1,240 men.

Two companies serving together formed a squadron, commanded by the senior captain. Any larger number of companies less than the full regiment was called a battalion.

This was the cavalry regiment on paper. The actual regiment was much smaller. In the spring of 1869 the colonel of the Fifth Cavalry was W. H. Emory, on duty in his brevet rank of major general in command of the unreconstructed state of Louisiana at New Orleans. The lieutenant colonel, Thomas Duncan, was on duty as brevet brigadier general, at Nashville, Tennessee. The senior major, Carr, also a brevet major general, was commanding the regiment, and Major Royall was on field duty. The junior major, Eugene W. Crittenden, joined the regiment at Fort Lyon in November, 1868. Through the companies many officers were absent on special duty, for tables of organization provided no officers for many necessary staff positions. Rarely did a company boast two of its three officers; often only one was on company duty. Despite this shortage, there were few vacancies; not enough to take care of the small annual graduation class from West Point. Surplus graduates were commissioned brevet second lieutenants. Happily these officers were paid in their brevet rank, so no West Pointers starved to death on the plains. However, the courtesy title that accompanied brevet rank was sadly deficient. All second lieutenants, whether of brevet or full rank, were just "Mr." in the regiment. Seldom were they allowed to exercise authority. In the absence of other officers, the senior sergeant took charge—always showing the utmost of deference and respect toward the second lieutenant. Such was the lowly condition of the "shavetail," so named because recruit mules, not yet broken to saddle, pack, or harness, had their tails shaved to indicate that they were not ready for serious work.

The enlisted men included a few veterans of the Civil War, many immigrant foreigners who found the army a refuge when no other jobs were open, a few adventurous youngsters, and a certain number who joined the army to get transportation to the Far West for various reasons, most of them bad. Desertion was high, re-enlistments low, with the result that there was a large proportion of untrained recruits in every summer's campaign.

Army economy demands got down to William F. Cody, who was cut back to $75 a month as the spring campaign opened.[1] The seven companies of the Fifth Cavalry marched from Fort Lyon on May 1, by way of Cheyenne Wells. At Fort Wallace, Cody made his peace with General Bankhead. Bill tells a standard army tall tale on himself and Brevet Major William H. Brown, captain of Company F, who seems close akin in spirit with Cody's humor. Cody says he and Major Brown went to Sheridan to purchase provisions for their mess, "but unfortunately we were in too jolly a mood to fool away money on 'grub.' We bought several articles, however, and put them into the ambulance, and sent them back to the camp with our cook." A day's march later, the cook asked where the provisions were. Major Brown insisted that the provisions had been brought by the cook, who reported that he had found only "a five-gallon demijohn of whiskey, a five-gallon demijohn of brandy, and two cases of Old Tom-Cat gin." Another mess, supplied with another kind of provisions, proved willing to make an exchange; they got more provisions for their liquor, says Bill, than the amount of money paid for it would have bought.[2]

As the battalion went into camp on Beaver Creek on May 13, Cody discovered a large Indian trail. General Carr sent Lieutenant Edward W. Ward and twelve troopers with Cody to investigate. Some five miles downstream the lieutenant and Cody crawled to the top of a knoll, from which they saw an Indian village three miles away. Ward wrote a report and handed it to a trooper, telling him to take it to General Carr with all speed. As the detachment cautiously retreated, two or three shots were heard, and the messenger was seen galloping back, pursued by four or five Indians. Ward and his men charged, driving off the Indians. Cody then volunteered to carry the message.

When Cody reached camp, General Carr mounted five com-

[1] Cody was hired as scout at $75 a month on May 10, 1869, by Lt. W. C. Forbush, in camp near Fort McPherson, O.Q.M. 1939. Cody had been continuously employed, however, as Carr reported on May 22 (see note 5 below).

[2] Randolph B. Marcy, *Border Reminiscences* (New York, 1872), 20–21, preceded Cody with another version of this tall story.

panies, leaving two to guard the wagon train, and moved toward the village, picking up Ward's detachment on the way. As the battalion attacked an estimated five hundred Indians at Elephant Rock at three o'clock, Company B, commanded by Lieutenant C. A. Schenofsky, was cut off and had to be rescued. This company lost three of four men killed; three men were wounded. Thirty Indians were reported killed or wounded. After dark the Indians retreated toward the Republican River.[3]

Their trail was followed for three days. At noon on May 16 the advance guard of forty men under Lieutenants John B. Babcock and William J. Volkmar of Company M with Cody as guide were surrounded at Spring Creek by two hundred Indians. The troopers dismounted and formed a circle, holding their horses while firing and falling back to the main body, three miles away. Said General Carr in 1878, "They all, to this day, speak of Cody's coolness and bravery. . . . Reaching the scene we could see the Indians in retreat. A figure with apparently a red cap rose slowly up the hill. For an instant it puzzled us, as it wore the buckskin and had long hair, but on seeing the horse, I recognized it as Cody's 'Powder Face' and saw that it was Buffalo Bill without his broad-brimmed sombrero. On closer inspection I saw his head was swathed in a bloody handkerchief, which served not only as a temporary bandage, but as a chapeau—his hat having been shot off, the bullet plowing his scalp badly for about five inches. It had ridged along the bone and he was bleeding profusely—a very 'close call,' but a lucky one."[4]

The Cheyennes were fighting to cover the retreat of their women and children, and abandoned ponies, lodges, and belongings as they fled across the Republican River. Toward evening the troops gave up the chase. Supplies were exhausted; Fort Kearny was the nearest depot. General Carr says Cody "decided it would

[3] Price, *With the Fifth Cavalry*, 134-35, 459, 518, 524; Cody, *Life*, 245-48.

[4] Price, *With the Fifth Cavalry*, 135, 457, 460, 484; Cody, *Life*, vii, 248-49; Carr's letters of December 29, 1906, in *The Rough Rider*, Vol. IV (1907), 7, and in Buffalo Bill's Wild West Official Program, 1907. Cody does not mention being wounded, but tells of being wounded in this manner at South Fork of Loup River, Nebraska, April 26, 1872. It seems unlikely Carr could be mistaken in reporting so vivid a recollection; Cody's memory confused the two fights.

be best to undertake the job himself—a point characteristic of him as he never shirked duty or faltered in emergencies. . . . Cody made a ride of fifty miles during the night, arriving at Fort Kearny at daylight. He had chased and fought Indians all day, been wounded, and when, through his rare frontier instinct, he reached us he had been almost constantly in the saddle and without sleep for forty hours." The troops resumed their march up Spring Creek and across the divide to the Platte River, arriving at Fort McPherson on May 20.

No scout ever received a greater tribute in an official report than General Carr gave Buffalo Bill at the conclusion of this campaign. He said, "Our Scout William Cody, who has been with the Detachment since last September, displayed great skill in following it [the trail] and also deserves great credit for his fighting in both engagements, his marksmanship being very conspicuous. He deserves honorable mention for this and other services and I hope to be able to retain him as long as I am engaged in this duty."

Carr's official report was accompanied by a separate letter in which he said, "I have the honor respectfully to request that authority be given to pay my scout William Cody, one hundred dollars extra for extraordinarily good services as trailer and fighter in my late pursuit of hostile Indians; see my report of this date, page 6. I was only authorized by the Commanding General, Department of the Missouri, to employ two men as scouts and guides, of which he is one."[5]

That letter went through military channels to the War Department in Washington and resulted in an order signed by E. D. Townsend, the adjutant general of the army, dated June 1, and addressed to Brevet Major General C. C. Augur, commanding Department of the Platte. It read: "Referring to your endorsement of the 27th ultimo, forwarding copy of Report of Brevet Major General E. A. Carr, Major 5th Cavalry, of his request that authority be given to pay his scout William Cody $100 extra for extraordinarily good services as a trailer and fighter in the pursuit of hostile In-

[5] Carr's report, Hq. Det. 5th Cav., camp at Ft. McPherson, Neb., May 22, 1869, to Bvt. Brig. Gen. Geo. D. Ruggles, Asst. Adj. Gen., Hq. Dept. of the Platte, Omaha; and accompanying letter, Carr to Ruggles, same date. Records of the Adjutant General, National Archives.

dians, I have the honor to inform you the Secretary of War authorized the $100 to be given Mr. Cody."[6]

This citation in a War Department order was unique in a day when there were no medals, decorations, or campaign ribbons save the Congressional Medal of Honor, which was awarded Cody on another occasion. That the army's entire chain of command up to the Secretary of War should have acted favorably to grant Cody $100 was recognition no other scout could boast. Yet Cody never boasted of it. There is no mention of it in all the voluminous Buffalo Bill literature.

In his autobiography Cody does note that General Carr recommended to General Augur that "I be made chief of scouts of the Department of the Platte, and informed me that in this position I would receive higher wages than I had been getting in the Department of the Missouri. This appointment I had not asked for." This transfer of a scout from one department to another was also an unusual tribute to Cody's abilities. Colonel Wheeler notes, "When the Fifth Cavalry was relieved from the Department of the Missouri, all the scouts were discharged with the exception of Cody, who went to old Fort McPherson, Nebraska, with the regiment." This was effected by transferring Cody on June 1 to the payroll of Lieutenant F. C. Grugan, regimental quartermaster of the Second Cavalry and acting assistant quartermaster at Fort McPherson. On the following day, June 2, Cody was transferred back to Lieutenant Hayes of the Fifth Cavalry in a routine document that classified Mr. Cody with pack mules and other property; it ordered "transfer to the Quartermaster of the expedition for the Republican under General Carr thirty (30) pack mules equipped, five (5) packers mounted, material for hopples and forage sacks, with two civilian scouts, William Cody and — Garry." Lieutenant Hayes took up Cody on the payroll on June 9, the day the expedition started, still at only $75 a month. The regimental history makes it formal that "Cody was appointed chief scout and guide for the Republican River expedition of 1869."[7]

[6] Headquarters, Department of the Platte, Letters Received, 1867–69, National Archives and Records Service, Record Group 98 (hereafter Dept. of the Platte, Letters), microfilm in Nebraska State Historical Society (hereafter NSHS).

[7] Wheeler, *Buffalo Days*, 257; OQM 1939; Walsh, *The Making of Buffalo Bill*,

By this time all of the Fifth Cavalry except Company K had arrived in the West, but three companies were assigned to garrison and other duties, so that General Carr had actually only one more troop available than in the previous campaign. According to the regimental history, the expedition consisted of "four squadrons of the regiment (A, B, C, D, E, G, H, and M), with Major Frank North's Pawnee scouts and the celebrated guide, William F. Cody."[8]

In 1864, Frank North was a clerk at the Pawnee Agency trader's store near Genoa, Nebraska, when Major General Samuel R. Curtis came that way on a campaign against the Sioux and Cheyennes and asked for a company of Pawnee scouts. It was raised with Joseph McPhadden, another clerk at the store, as captain, and North as lieutenant. General Curtis became so impressed with North's ability that he asked North to raise a second company of scouts in 1865.

Frank North was commissioned captain by the governor of Nebraska Territory, and his company as part of the Civil War Volunteer forces was not mustered out until June, 1866. An act of Congress of July 28, 1866, authorized the enlistment of Indian scouts "who shall receive the pay and allowances of cavalry soldiers, and be discharged whenever the necessity for their further employment is abated, or at the discretion of the department commander." There was no provision for officers, so North and his subordinates were enrolled as civilian employes of the Quartermaster's Department, just as Cody was, with the difference that they were hired as major, captains, and lieutenants. North as captain received one horse, one ration per day, camp equipage, and $150 a month. His first and second lieutenants received the same allowances and $130 a month each.

A battalion of four companies of Pawnee Scouts under Frank North as major was raised in the winter of 1866–67 to guard construction of the Union Pacific Railroad. This time Major North was joined by his brother, Luther H. North, who became captain of Company A. Luther had served an enlistment in the Second Ne-

text and facsimile, Bvt. Brig. Gen. Wm. Myers, Chief Quartermaster, Hq., Dept. of the Platte, to Lt. Grugan; Price, *With the Fifth Cavalry,* 584.

[8] Price, *With the Fifth Cavalry,* 135.

braska Cavalry during the Civil War and had accompanied his brother as a volunteer in the spring expedition of 1866. The battalion remained in service until January, 1868. In May of that year, two companies were called out, remaining in service until the end of the year.[9]

Company A of the Pawnee Scouts under Captain Luther North arrived at Fort McPherson on February 12, 1869. It consisted of one captain, one first lieutenant, two sergeants, and forty-eight Pawnees. Company B under Captain James Murie was mustered on April 24 at Fort Kearny. On June 8, the day the expedition was to start, Major North was asked to raise a third company. He acted quickly, for he mustered it two days later, and joined General Carr in the field with Company C on June 17.[10]

The expedition again was directed against Tall Bull's Dog Soldiers, a term that has been somewhat confusing. The Hotamitaneo or Dog Men Society was a warrior group that set itself up as a separate band—or else all members of one band joined this society —and this band became known as the Dog Soldiers. Tall Bull's Dog Soldiers have been called an outlaw group, as the main body of Cheyennes had made peace with Custer. However, Indian tribal action was not considered binding on anyone not taking part in it, and it is doubtful that Tall Bull's band lost any credit with the rest of the Cheyennes because of its continued raiding and fighting. Tall Bull had been joined by a band of Arapahoes, traditional allies of the Cheyennes, and a band of Sioux.

On May 30, while the Fifth Cavalry was reorganizing at Fort McPherson, Tall Bull's band attacked settlers along the Solomon River, carrying off Mrs. Thomas Alderdice and Mrs. G. Weichel after strangling Mrs. Alderdice's baby and killing Mrs. Weichel's husband. Susanna Zigler Daily Alderdice was the wife of Thomas Alderdice, one of Forsyth's scouts in the fight at Beecher's Island. Maria Weichel, from Luneberg, Hanover, Germany, had been in

[9] *The Journal of an Indian Fighter: The 1869 Diary of Major Frank North* (ed. by Donald F. Danker), reprinted from *Nebraska History*, Vol. XXXIX, No. 2 (June, 1958); George Bird Grinnell, *Two Great Scouts and Their Pawnee Battalion;* Robert Bruce, *The Fighting Norths and Pawnee Scouts;* George E. Hyde, *Pawnee Indians,* 205–206, 219, 223, 238, 240.

[10] Post Returns, Fort McPherson, N. T., February, April, 1869, National Archives.

the United States only two months.[11] Rescue of these two women was a primary objective of Carr's expedition.

The first encounter came at 5:00 P.M. on June 15 when the Indians attempted to stampede the mules while they were being watered. According to Cody, "One of the herders came dashing into camp with an arrow sticking into him. My horse was close at hand and mounting him bare-back, I at once dashed off after the mule herd, which had been stampeded. I supposed certainly that I would be the first man on the ground. I was mistaken, however, for the Pawnee Indians, unlike regular soldiers, had not waited to receive orders from their officers, but had jumped on their ponies without bridles or saddles, and placing ropes in their mouths, had dashed off in the direction whence the shots had come, and had got there ahead of me."

Colonel Royall, with Companies A, B, and M, took up the pursuit, which was continued for fifteen miles until darkness. In this raid Privates E. C. Bean of Company H and C. E. Elwood of Company M were wounded.[12]

It will be noted that Cody was riding a horse, not a mule. On May 30, General Carr had requested two good horses for the guides and scouts, pointing out that the risks they took were much greater because of mounting them on mules.[13] Cody was not yet satisfied, for, during the chase, he admired a horse ridden by one of the Pawnees and later arranged a trade. This horse Cody made famous as "Buckskin Joe," continuing to ride him until the end of his scouting service in 1872. Since Buckskin Joe was a government-issue horse, Cody did not own the animal.

A few days after the mule raid, the Pawnees hunted buffalo, and by surrounding a small herd, killed thirty-two. Cody then asked Major North to hold the Pawnees back to give Buckskin Joe a chance to see what he could do. Buffalo Bill, following his usual method, killed thirty-six in a half-mile run. From then on, says he, he was a big chief among the Pawnees.[14]

Colonel Royall, with Companies A, E, and M and a company

[11] Robert Lynam (ed.), *The Beecher Island Annual* (Wray, Colo., 1930), 105; Carr to Ruggles, May 22, 1869, Dept. of the Platte, Letters.
[12] Cody, *Life*, 251–53; Price, *With the Fifth Cavalry*, 136, 658, 672.
[13] Carr to Ruggles, May 30, 1869, *Dept. of the Platte*, Letters.
[14] Cody, *Life*, pp. 252–253; *1869 Diary of Major Frank North*, 133.

of fifty Pawnee Scouts under Lieutenant Gustavus W. Becher, made a scout to the right of the column, and on July 5 surprised and defeated a party of Cheyennes in sand hills near Frenchman's Fork. According to Cody, who states definitely that he was not in the action, the trail then found was the one the expedition followed. Neither had Cody anything to do with a fight on July 8 at Dog Creek, when Corporal John Kyle and three men of Company M killed three of thirteen Indians who surrounded them and drove off the rest. Cody must have been present when the camp of the main body on Rock Creek was raided at midnight of the same day in an unsuccessful attempt to stampede the horses and mules. One Pawnee scout was wounded in this fight.[15]

[15] Cody, *Life,* 254–55; Price, *With the Fifth Cavalry,* 136, 658, 672.

The Triumph of the West

Cartoon from *Life* (December 15, 1887).

Iron Tail

of the buffalo nickel and Buffalo Bill's Wild West.

Courtesy Fred B. Hackett

THE BATTLE OF SUMMIT SPRINGS

MOST OF THE OFFICERS AND ENLISTED MEN of the Fifth Cavalry who rode with Cody that summer gave him top rating as scout on the basis of his accomplishment in the campaign and battle of Summit Springs. The fight was the last in that section of the plains, freeing Kansas and some surrounding country of serious Indian troubles. Eight companies were in action, which makes it a major battle by Indian wars' standards. Fiction and motion pictures of masses of cavalry dashing to the rescue have given the impression that such encounters were common. Actually, most of the 968 actions fought by the Regular Army against Indians between 1865 and 1898 were small affairs involving no more troops than an under-strength company or two, and many were fought by even smaller detachments. The slaughter observed in Hollywood depictions of these events is not at all borne out by facts. Total casualties were 1,944, which means that it took two fights to get one soldier killed and three wounded. Many authorities believe the Indians did not suffer as heavy losses.[1]

Summit Springs, however, was one of a very few of these fights that would satisfy Hollywood and the writers of Westerns. The

[1] Heitman, *Historical Register and Dictionary of the United States Army*, II, 295; Stanley Vestal, *New Sources of Indian History*, 132-41; "How Good Were the Indians as Shooters?" *Guns* (December, 1956), 20-23, 74-75.

cavalry charged with bugle blowing, a woman was rescued (and later married a soldier), the slaughter of Indians was large—as attested by a board of officers who counted the bodies—and the troops suffered no losses. It is not surprising that it became a subject for spectacle in Buffalo Bill's Wild West, with dramatic exaggerations that provoked some skepticism regarding Cody's part in the battle.

Cody has been denied his due, however, for a more serious reason. Several popularly read books on the Indian wars base their descriptions of Summit Springs on the reminiscences of Luther North.[2] That is not surprising, for Luther made his reminiscences available in at least nine printed versions. That no two of them agree with each other, and that none of them agree with accounts of the fight from army records, was not noticed. Luther told his tale too often. Whether he was able to persuade himself that he was telling what he had actually seen is beyond guessing, but some of it is not so. That he was moved by great prejudices, he makes evident. One is his prejudice against General Carr. Frank North discharged his brother Luther on August 7, less than a month after the fight, and Luther explains, "I had a few words with General Carr and when we got to the Fort I resigned and came home."[3] His prejudice against Carr extends to other officers and to the regiment. Consistently he disparages the cavalry and attempts to give the Pawnee Scouts principal credit for the victory.

Luther's jealousy for the reputation of his brother Frank has more subtle implications. In telling his stories, Luther was always humbly modest (except when recounting his own exploits) and always insistent on the greatness of Frank. Titles that resulted included *Two Great Scouts and Their Pawnee Battalion* and *The Fighting Norths and Pawnee Scouts*. Thus the younger brother who quit in the middle of one campaign and missed a couple more becomes the co-equal of the elder brother who was the responsible organizer and leader. If Luther was jealous of (instead of *for*) his elder brother, which is psychologically probable, he put it over.

[2] George Bird Grinnell, *The Fighting Cheyennes*, 310–18; Paul I. Wellman, *Death on the Prairie* (New York, 1934), 90–91; Wellman, *The Indian Wars of the West* (Garden City, N. Y., 1956), 95–96; Stanley Vestal, *Warpath and Council Fire*, 164–74.

[3] *1869 Diary of Major Frank North*, 146.

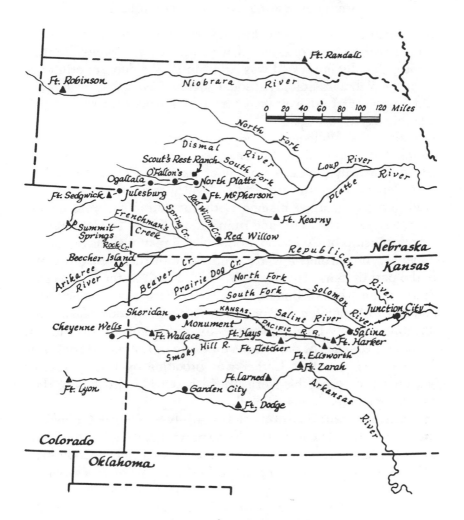

SCENES OF CODY'S SCOUTING, 1867–72

George Bird Grinnell, who knew Luther well for many years, seems never to have questioned his statements, however contradictory. Equally impressed was Addison E. Sheldon, superintendent of the Nebraska State Historical Society,[4] as was many another who sought out Luther in his later years for eyewitness accounts of heroic days.

Jealousy of William F. Cody, common among scouts of the period, was amplified in Luther's case until it became a positive hatred. Primarily it was a corollary of his other violent prejudices. That General Carr and the Fifth Cavalry favored Cody had no small part in it. Luther blamed Cody for detracting from honors due the Pawnees as scouts and from Frank's fame. The later ranching partnership of Cody and Frank North may well have had an influence, for partnerships are productive of disputes, especially on the part of heirs. The death of Frank North as the result of an injury in the arena of Buffalo Bill's Wild West may reasonably be assumed to be another factor. There is no indication of any disagreement at any time between Cody and Frank North. But the increasing violence of the attacks on Cody in Luther's stories over the years suggests that Luther was brooding over some real or fancied injury. Since his stories have had wide circulation, they must be examined in some detail.

It was about the time of the fights of July 8, 1869, that it became known definitely to General Carr's command that Tall Bull's Cheyennes held captive Mrs. Alderdice and Mrs. Weichel. Cody says, "Wherever they had encamped we found the print of a woman's shoe." The trail pointed northward, indicating that the Indians were heading toward the Powder River country by way of the Laramie Plains and Wyoming's Black Hills. Carr hoped to intercept the hostiles and rescue the women before they crossed the South Platte, so pushed his command to the limit, making 150 miles in four days.

On July 10 he passed two of Tall Bull's camps along Frenchman's Fork, and encamped on a third, which apparently the Indians had left that morning. With this gain of three days on the leisurely-moving Cheyennes, Carr pushed forward even more rapidly. That night he left his wagon train to follow along, with

[4] Bruce, *The Fighting Norths*, 66–67.

Company M as escort, and took with him "all available men; that is all whose horses were fit for service, and they amounted to two hundred and forty-four (244) officers and soldiers and fifty (50) Pawnee Scouts, out of seven companies of the 5th Cavalry and one hundred and fifty (150) Pawnees."[5] The final dash began at 2:00 A.M. on July 11, which was to prove the day of battle. When the command reached the breaks of the Platte Bluffs, the Pawnees reported seeing two horsemen, and the entire command was taken into a ravine.

All accounts derived from Luther North say that at this point the trail split into three forks, and to quote one of them, "General Carr with part of his men and about a half dozen Pawnees took the left hand trail to the northwest. Major Royall with all the rest of the white soldiers, except those who were coming along in the rear with the wagon train, William F. Cody, and a number of the Pawnees, took the right hand trail to the northeast. The North brothers, Captain Cushing and about forty Pawnees took the middle trail straight north." This set the stage for Luther's claim that Cody missed the fight entirely. It has led to such interpretations as that Carr wanted to follow the broadest trail, but was dissuaded by the Norths, and that Carr also missed the fight.[6]

General Carr in his report made a few days after the fight did not see it that way. He said: "The trail appeared to divide here, a small portion going to the right, but the main part keeping to the left on the table land. Taking for granted, however, that it must go to the Platte for water, of which also we were in much need, I moved directly towards that stream." Captain Price, the regimental historian who commanded Company A in the fight, says that Carr, "having ascertained the general direction in which the Indians were retreating, moved his command by rapid marches beyond their right flank, and gained a position in their front from which he was enabled to strike a blow that almost annihilated

[5] Bvt. Maj. Gen. E. A. Carr, Hq., Republican River Expedition, Fort Sedgwick, C. T., July 20, 1869, to Bvt. Brig. Gen. George D. Ruggles, a.a.g., Hq. Department of the Platte; Journal of the March of the Republican River Expedition, both in Letters Received, 1867–69, Department of the Platte, National Archives.

[6] Clarence, Reckmeyer, "The Battle of Summit Springs," *The Colorado Magazine*, Vol. VI, No. 6 (November, 1929), 212. See also Grinnell, *Fighting Cheyennes*, 311–12; Grinnell, *Two Great Scouts*, 195; Vestal, *Warpath and Council Fire*, 170.

them." And Cody says, "Acting on my suggestion, the General made a circuit to the north, believing that if the Indians had their scouts out, they would naturally be watching in the direction whence they had come." Is this an exaggeration of Cody's contribution? Carr himself endorsed it at a later date, saying, "Cody's idea was to get around, beyond, and between them and the river."[7]

But what of Luther North's frequently told story that Cody missed the fight entirely because he accompanied Major Royall at this time? All that is wrong with it is that Cody was not with Royall, and that Royall's squadron did not miss the fight. Reverting to Carr's report, he tells of moving through bad sand for several miles, "when a report was brought in of a herd of animals in the valley near the stream to the right while at the same time came a report from the left of mounted Indians seen. I determined to detach Colonel Royall with three companies to move direct for the animals and with the rest move towards where the Indians were reported as that was the direction of the main trail. I sent the pack mules back to the train, which was in sight, and both parties struck out on a gallop. In a few minutes I received information that Tepees had been seen in the direction I was pursuing; I sent to Colonel Royall to send me a company as soon as he could spare one, and he promptly sent me his strongest company."

That this information was brought by Cody is added by Price, who records "the arrival of the guide, William F. Cody, who reported large herds of ponies about six miles distant in a southwesterly direction, which was indubitable evidence that Tall Bull and his warriors were encamped and unconscious of approaching peril, as the pickets, who were watching their rear, had made no danger signals." Price further credits Cody with having "guided the Fifth Cavalry to a position whence the regiment was enabled to charge the enemy and win a brilliant victory." The regimental quartermaster, Lieutenant Edward M. Hayes, who was in the charge, also credited the surprise in broad daylight as "due in great measure to the daring and guidance" of Cody, who "discovered the village and led the troops to the position they were to occupy in the attack without the knowledge of the Indians. This was considered

[7] Price, *With the Fifth Cavalry*, 137; Cody, *Life*, p. 235; *The Rough Rider*, Vol. IV (1907), 7.

the greatest of the many great achievements of this wonderful scout."[8]

Luther North says, "It was six of our Pawnee Scouts with General Carr that discovered the Camp of Tall Bull." Cody clarifies this point, saying, "I was ordered to pick out five or six of the best Pawnees, and go in advance of the command. . . . We discovered the village. . . . Here I left the Pawnee scouts to keep watch, while I went back and informed General Carr that the Indians were in sight."[9]

Price locates the village as "southwesterly," and Carr's report says "the attack was made from the northwest." This demolishes Luther North's story of following three trails, for if the troops had been following the Indians' trail, the attack would have come from the southeast. Even Grinnell, who accepted Luther's story of the three trails, quotes Cheyenne informants as saying they were surprised by an attack from the north.[10] It will be recalled that Luther says Cody was not in the fight because he was with Royall following one of these trails, but Carr says he detached Royall to investigate a report of a herd of animals. Carr further states that just before the attack, "Colonel Royall rejoined with his command, having found that the animals reported were bushes." The official journal of the expedition also says that when the village was located, "the column took the gallop and maintained it until 1:30 when Col. Royall rejoined; the supposed herd having proved to be only bushes." Price records, "Major Royall and his command joined just as the village was captured and participated in the subsequent operations."

Actually, as the blow fell, Carr's forces, which had been somewhat scattered, were well concentrated. The three companies he had retained were in the lead, joined by the company first sent back by Royall. Royall's remaining two companies, still in the rear, formed a reserve. The Pawnee Scouts, who had been reconnoitering the river bank to see if the Indians had crossed, arrived on the

---

[8] Carr to Ruggles; Price, *With the Fifth Cavalry*, 137, 448, 584; *The Rough Rider*, Vol. IV, p. 9.

[9] L. H. North, "Pioneering with Capt. Luther H. North," *Winners of the West*, Vol. XI, No. 10 (September 30, 1934), 3; Cody, *Life*, 255.

[10] *The Fighting Cheyennes*, 311–12.

left at the last moment. And Carr records that the wagon train, guided by Company M, was in sight.

Lieutenant Price's Company A was on the right, and as it had the farthest to go, the charge guided on it. Captain Leicester Walker commanded Company H on the left. These two troops were to turn the enemy's flanks, dash to the rear, and capture the herds that could be seen on the hills some two miles away. Company C under Captain Thomas E. Maley and Company D under Captain Samuel S. Sumner formed a center squadron that was to drive straight for the middle of the village. Major Eugene W. Crittenden, in immediate command of the battle line, rode with this squadron, and, according to Price, the Pawnee Scouts went in with the center squadron, although they were "free lances, riding everywhere."

As Lieutenant Price signalled he was ready, the line moved forward at a slow trot, the undisturbed village lying before it about twelve hundred yards away. It was about two o'clock in the afternoon—a little after, according to Carr's report—and thus in broad daylight this large body of horsemen moved undiscovered across an open plain toward the Indian village. A heavy gale blowing from the west prevented the noise of hoofbeats from disturbing the Indians. However, a fifteen-year-old boy guarding the herd in the hills beyond the village, discovered the charging troops and began a wild dash on a white pony to give the alarm. His shouts could not be heard because of the gale, but if he could arrive first by a minute or two, the advantage of surprise would be lost. To spur the troopers on, Carr ordered the charge sounded.

The differences that occur in eyewitness accounts, particularly after a lapse of time, are well illustrated in variant stories of this unimportant episode. In his report, General Carr merely said "sounded the charge." In 1907 he recalled the story thus: "When we all got started, I told the bugler behind me to sound 'the charge,' and he said, 'I—I disremember it, sir'; but it came to him directly, and he sounded it while all were going at full speed."

Price wrote in 1883: "The chief trumpeter was ordered to sound the charge. Only those who were near him could hear the short sharp notes, but every man saw him going through the motions. That was enough. All knew that there was only one call to sound then; and away dashed the gallant troopers in one of the most superb charges ever made by the Fifth Cavalry."

Cody's version was written in 1879: "As we halted on top of the hill overlooking the camp of the unsuspecting Indians, General Carr called out to his bugler: 'Sound the charge!' The bugler for a moment became intensely excited, and actually forgot the notes. The General again sang out: 'Sound the charge!' and yet the bugler was unable to obey the command. Quartermaster Hayes—who had obtained permission to accompany the expedition—was riding near to him, jerked the bugle from his hands and sounded the charge himself in clear, distinct notes. As the troops rushed forward, he threw the bugle away, then drawing his pistols, was among the first men that entered the village."[11]

Cody's story indicates that he was with the headquarters group, where he belonged. Even on a technicality, he happens to be correct. Many an old-timer will recall that cavalry had trumpeters, whereas buglers sounded calls for the infantry. That was not true in 1869. Cavalry regiments had a "chief bugler" until the army appropriations act of 1872 changed the title to "chief trumpeter" —as Price records on page 593 of his regimental history despite his anachronism on page 138.

As the Indian herder, dashing to give the alarm, reached the south side of the ravine (lying east and west) in which the village was situated, the troops were at the north edge, with only fifty yards to go. With a shout, the cavalrymen struck. The Cheyennes had no time to seize their weapons or get their horses, and fled in panic in all directions. The herder who might have warned them was killed fighting in the middle of the village. Price turned the left flank, killed seven warriors, and captured three hundred animals. Walker, on the right, was delayed by a sharp drop in the ravine, and a few Indians escaped there while he was fighting through it. Major Crittenden's two center troops and Major Frank North's Pawnee Scouts charged through the village, driving all before them. It was a short, sharp fight that completely broke the power of the Dog Soldiers.

General Carr appointed a board, consisting of Majors Royall

[11] Carr to Ruggles; Cody, *True Tales of the Plains*, 154, quoting Carr; Price, *With the Fifth Cavalry*, 138–39; Cody, *Life*, 256. Cody misspells Hayes as "Hays."

and Crittenden and Second Lieutenant Robert A. Edwards, recorder, to determine the casualties and account for the captured property. They reported fifty-two killed on the field, and seventeen women and children captured. In Carr's forces, one man was slightly scratched by an arrow. Property taken included 85 lodges, 274 horses, and 144 mules. Tall Bull's band had been successful raiders. The report shows 56 rifles, 22 revolvers, 40 sets of bows and arrows, and 50 pounds of powder.[12]

Who rescued the surviving woman captive is more a mystery than who blew the bugle. Luther North said that when he with his brother Frank, Captain Cushing, and Sergeant Sam Wallace stopped near a lodge, Mrs. Weichel came out of it screaming, caught Cushing around the legs, and would not let go until Frank North was able to persuade her that she was safe. Another story is that she came running out from among the tipis as the troops charged, that the troopers shouted for her to lie down, and the charging line leaped over her. Cody says she was rescued by the company ordered to seize the village. In the Wild West show spectacle he was represented as having a large part in the rescue, but he never personally made the claim. She was wounded—the details are vague—and recovered at Fort Sedgwick, where she married the hospital steward who took care of her there. Of $1,300 found in the village, loot of the Saline River raids, $900 was given to her.

Mrs. Alderdice, the other captive, was killed by an Indian woman, says Price, and Cody says the woman was Tall Bull's wife. It is agreed that she was brained with a tomahawk. She was buried on the field.

Tall Bull, or Tatonka Haska, was killed in the fight. As he was the reputed leader in many raids on the frontier, the fact that he was killed was important. Who killed him was not, and was not mentioned in any contemporary report. In the Fifth Cavalry it was generally understood that Cody fired the fatal shot. Only one person denied it, and that was Luther H. North, whose story grew in the telling.

Luther North's earliest published story crediting his brother

[12] Report of Special Board, attached, Carr to Ruggles; see also General Orders No. 48, Department of the Platte, Aug. 3, 1869; and Record for the Month of July, 1869, Medical History of Post, Fort McPherson, National Archives.

Frank with the killing of Tall Bull was told to George Bird Grinnell for *Pawnee Hero Stories and Folk Tales* in 1889. That was twenty years after the fight and three years after Frank's death. Cody was not mentioned. In 1915, Grinnell drew on Luther again for *The Fighting Cheyennes*. Here seems to be the first appearance of the story that Cody rode off with Major Royall, but Grinnell does not say they missed the fight—there is just no further mention of them. Luther told his story to Grinnell again in 1928 for *Two Great Scouts and Their Pawnee Battalion*. This time Luther says that the troops returned from the pursuit about six o'clock, and, "Just as they reached the village a terrific storm of rain and hail came up and while all hands were trying to get under shelter in the lodges, Cody rode into camp. He had been with Colonel Royall and had missed the fight. Later by Ned Buntline (E. C. Judson) he was given the credit for having killed Tall Bull, but he was not in the fight at all." In the same year, 1928, Luther wrote a letter to Richard J. Walsh, quoted in *The Making of Buffalo Bill*, telling much the same story, with such minor discrepancies as making it five-thirty instead of six o'clock, but insisting that Cody was not in the fight—pointing out, however, that this was no fault of Bill's as he was ordered elsewhere.[13]

Luther spoke less kindly of Bill a year later in a pamphlet, *Blake's Western Stories*, in which Herbert Cody Blake quotes Luther as saying, "Well, Cody was on the expedition, attached to the Cavalry. He had a pair of 'I. C.' (inspected and condemned) Government plugs hooked up to a wagon loaded with stuff such as soldiers would buy—tobacco, groceries, 'Air-tights' [canned goods] and 'fluids'—a sort of mobile canteen, a moving grocery." Thus in a year's time Luther had demoted Cody from scout to camp follower. Also in 1929, Luther toured the battle site with Clarence Reckmeyer, who wrote an article for *The Colorado Magazine* in which Luther again tells of Cody's being with Royall, but ups his return another hour: "It must have been seven o'clock and the storm was about over when Buffalo Bill rode into the village and got off his horse at our lodge." Luther, it has been noted, had other prejudices besides that against Cody. One of them seems to be expressed in this article's gratuitous statement, "I don't know where

[13] Grinnell, *Two Great Scouts*, 201; Walsh, *The Making of Buffalo Bill*, 150–51.

Crittenden was, but probably he was with the wagon train." In an article signed by Luther North in this same magazine in 1934, he says, "My recollection is that there was not more than four officers of the Fifth Cavalry, besides General Carr, in the fight."[14]

Actually, twenty or more officers of the Fifth Cavalry were in the fight, and Major Crittenden led the central squadron in the charge. Brevets were recommended for Lieutenant Volkmer, whose company, M, was with the wagon train, and for the four troop commanders in the charge, Lieutenant Price and Captains Maley, Sumner, and Walker. Their officers were First Lieutenants George F. Mason, Edward P. Doherty, Calbraith P. Rodgers, and Peter V. Haskin, and Second Lieutenants Frank C. Morehead and Robert A. Edwards. With General Carr were First Lieutenants Hayes, quartermaster, and Jacob Almy, adjutant. Major Royall's officers were Captains Philip Dwyer and John H. Kane, First Lieutenant Robert P. Wilson, and Second Lieutenant J. Edward Leas. How did Luther miss seeing all these officers? He gave himself away when he told Reckmeyer, "Frank, Captain Cushing and myself, with about twenty-five of our men, followed a band of perhaps a hundred and fifty men, women and children, for ten miles or more, but we only killed two of them. . . . It was about six o'clock, I suppose, when we got back to the village." If he rode twenty miles between two o'clock, when the fight began, and six, there must have been a lot of the fight he did not see.[15]

There are many discrepancies in Luther's several stories, but let us now consider the killing of Tall Bull. General Carr in his official report stated: "Tall Bull" the chief, finding how matters were going, determined to die. He had a little daughter on his horse and one of his wives on another. He gave the daughter to his wife and told her to escape and take the white woman who was prisoner, and she might use her to make terms for herself when peace was made. The wife begged him to escape with her, but he shut his

[14] *Blake's Western Stories*, 18–19; Reckmeyer, "The Battle of Summit Springs," *The Colorado Magazine*, Vol. VI, No. 6 (November, 1929), 216; Capt. L. H. North, "My Military Experiences in Colorado," *The Colorado Magazine*, Vol. XI, No. 2 (March, 1934), 69.

[15] Price, *With the Fifth Cavalry*, 179–585 (Military Records of Officers); Reckmeyer, "The Battle of Summit Springs," *The Colorado Magazine*, Vol. VI, No. 6 (November, 1929), 216.

ears, killed his horse, and she saw him killed fighting. She then surrendered and was saved with her daughter of eight and brother of twelve years."

Luther's stories generally agree that as he and Frank were passing the bank of a canyon, the chief raised his head, fired a shot at Frank, and then dropped out of sight. Frank tumbled from his horse so quickly that Luther supposed his brother had been hit, but Frank got up, handed his bridle rein to Luther, and told Luther to ride on toward the Pawnees, who were farther up the hill; or, as one of his recorders puts it, Luther was "acting as a lure to bring Tall Bull out of the ravine where he was hidden." When the Indian heard the horses leaving, he raised his head from his hiding point. Frank shot the Indian through the head.

As Luther told the story first, to Grinnell in 1889, "A hundred yards up the ravine was found his war pony, stabbed to the heart, and by it sat his squaw, awaiting with Indian patience whatever fate might come to her." As Grinnell retold Luther's story in 1915, "he found a place for the wife and child where they would not be exposed to fire, and returning to the mouth of the ravine, stabbed the horse behind the foreleg . . . climbed the bank nearest to the soldiers. . . . Major North pulled the trigger, and the Indian fell back without discharging his gun. . . . Later in the day the dead chief Tall Bull was found in the ravine directly under this spot. Shortly after this another head appeared at the same spot—the head of a woman. She reached the top of the bank, pulled her little six-year-old girl after her, and making signs that she wished to talk, walked to Major North, and passed her hands over him, asking for pity. Major North sent her to the rear, where she would be safe. She proved to be the wife of Tall Bull." Grinnell's 1928 story adds the details that the stabbed horse was orange colored, and says that Frank learned that the woman was Tall Bull's wife from an interpreter three days later.[16]

Luther told his story thus to Reckmeyer in 1929: "Tall Bull took his beautiful cream-colored horse into the canyon with him, and, perceiving that it might be captured by the enemy, he held his gun close to its breast and fired. It ran out of the mouth of the

[16] George Bird Grinnell, *Pawnee Hero Stories and Folk Tales*, 329–30; Grinnell, *The Fighting Cheyennes*, 316–17; Grinnell, *Two Great Scouts*, 198.

canyon and dropped dead. Luther noticed the smoke from the gunpowder issuing from the wound as the horse lay dying. . . . Tall Bull's wife, with her six-year-old daughter, then motioned to Frank from the canyon where Tall Bull fell, that she desired to surrender. Unlike long-haired heroes who have often delighted in killing women and children, Frank sent her to Tall Bull's lodge across the creek with other prisoners."[17]

As Luther told his story to Mr. Blake, Tall Bull was riding a magnificent yellow or cream-colored horse with a white mane and tail, which he killed, whether by shooting or stabbing is not specified. After the Indian fell, "a squaw and a girl about 12 years old climbed out of the canyon and came up to us. The woman put her hands up in front of her face and bent her head down; this meant, 'have pity, mercy, on me.' "[18]

At this stage the Indian killed by Frank North cannot be positively identified as Tall Bull by his orange or yellow or cream-colored horse that was stabbed behind the foreleg at the mouth of the canyon, stabbed to the heart one hundred yards up the ravine, shot in the breast so that it ran out of the canyon with gunsmoke issuing from the wound, after being ridden to one or more of these places either by the chief or by his wife and daughter, who was either six or twelve years old. However, the woman who waited stoically beside the horse and was there captured, or motioned from the top of the canyon that she desired to surrender, or came to Frank North and made signs that she desired to surrender, was identified three days later, says Luther North, as the wife of Tall Bull by Leon Pallady, interpreter at Fort Sedgwick, and she, says Luther North, pointed to Frank North as the one who had killed Tall Bull.

In a court of law the discrepancies in Luther North's stories would be sufficient to discredit him as a witness. Certainly they show that he was no reliable authority on either the Battle of Summit Springs or the death of Tall Bull.

Cody's testimony is much less dramatic. As he first told the story, he was much more interested in Tall Bull's horse than he was

[17] Reckmeyer, "The Battle of Summit Springs," *The Colorado Magazine*, Vol. VI, No. 6 (November, 1929), 214–15.
[18] *Blake's Western Stories*, 22.

in the chief. He says that while the loot of the camp was being burned, some Indians returned, and a fight went on all around the camp. "I was in the skirmish line, and I noticed an Indian, who was riding a large bay horse, and giving orders to his men in his own language—which I could occasionally understand—telling them that they had lost everything, that they were ruined, and he entreated them to follow him, and fight until they died. His horse was an extraordinary one, fleet as the wind, dashing here and there, and I determined to capture him if possible, but I was afraid to fire at the Indian for fear of killing his horse.

"I noticed that the Indian, as he rode around the skirmish line, passed the head of a ravine not far distant, and it occurred to me that if I could dismount and creep into the ravine I could, as he passed there, easily drop him from his saddle without danger of hitting his horse. Accordingly I crept into and secreted myself in the ravine, reaching the place unseen by the Indians, and I waited there until Mr. Chief came riding by.

"When he was not more than thirty yards distant I fired, and the next moment he tumbled from his saddle, and the horse kept on without his rider. Instead of running toward the Indians, however, he galloped toward our men, by one of whom he was caught. Lieutenant Mason, who had been very conspicuous in the fight and who had killed two or three Indians himself, single-handed, came galloping up to the ravine and jumping from his horse, secured the fancy war bonnet from the head of the dead chief, together with all his other accoutrements. We both then rejoined the soldiers and I at once went in search of the horse; I found him in the possession of Sergeant McGrath, who had caught him. The Sergeant knew that I had been trying to get the animal and having seen me kill his rider, he handed him over to me at once.

"Little did I think at that time that I had captured a horse which, four years afterwards, was the fastest runner in the state of Nebraska, but such proved to be the fact. I jumped on his back and rode him down to the spot where the prisoners were corralled. One of the squaws among the prisoners suddenly began crying in a pitiful and hysterical manner at the sight of this horse, and upon inquiry I found that she was Tall Bull's wife, the same squaw that had killed one of the white women and wounded the other. She

143

stated that this was her husband's favorite war-horse, and that only a short time ago she had seen Tall Bull riding him. I gave her to understand that her liege lord had passed in his mortal chips and that it would be sometime before he would ride his favorite horse again, and I informed her that henceforth I should call the gallant steed 'Tall Bull' in honor of her husband."[19]

It has been pointed out that there are glaring discrepancies between this story and that told of the killing of Tall Bull in subsequent autobiographies of Buffalo Bill. This offers an interesting example of Cody's indifference to what was printed about him, even under his own name and of an almost inconceivable recklessness with facts on the part of his Wild West publicity department. There are actually only two principal stories. It will be noted that Cody has said that he fired the shot when Tall Bull was "not more than thirty yards distant." In the other, Cody as author is made responsible for saying that he killed Tall Bull "at a range of fully four hundred yards."

The "four hundred yards" story appeared first in *Story of the Wild West*, published in 1888. This book contains biographies of Daniel Boone, Davy Crockett, and Kit Carson, and the autobiography of Buffalo Bill. Whether Cody wrote the biographies is not of concern here, but it is obvious that he spent little time on his autobiography, except possibly on an added chapter bringing it up to date, for it appears to be a reprinting of the 1879 book with most of the original illustrations. Actually it is some seventy-three pages shorter, but most of the cutting was done on large chunks of extraneous matter—a long story of Forsyth's fight, for example—and occasional condensation.

Except for these omissions and minor condensations, the wording of the two autobiographies is the same—until page 583 is reached in *Story of the Wild West*. That page contains every word that is on page 256 of the 1879 autobiography, except the last two lines. In both books you may read of the surprise maneuver at Summit Springs, the charge on Tall Bull's camp, the incident of the bugler's forgetting the call, and the entry into the village.

The last two lines of the original autobiography's page 256 read: "General Carr had instructed the command that when they

[19] Cody, *Life*, 260–61.

entered the village, they must keep a sharp look out for"—and that is the bottom of the page. You will not find what they were to look for on the next page of *Story of the Wild West*. What the command was to look out for was the women prisoners, but poor Mrs. Weichel, who left a footprint on page 582 of *Story of the Wild West,* is never heard of again in that book, never gets wounded, never gets rescued, never marries the hospital steward. You never learn whether Mrs. Alderdice lived or died. Instead you read in this 1888 book: "The pursuit continued until darkness made it impossible to longer follow the Indians, who had scattered and were heading off in every direction like a brood of young quails." Not only have the women prisoners vanished; so also has the Battle of Summit Springs in that one sentence.

For three pages you read a jumble of words about Indian fighting that at no point bears any relation to what is said in the original autobiography, or to anything said anywhere else about the campaign and battle of Summit Springs. But when you get to the second paragraph of page 588, Cody's narrative starts again, word for word and paragraph for paragraph as it appears beginning at the top of page 263 in the 1879 Cody autobiography.

Now it takes no great literary detective to deduce that something happened to pages 257 through 262 of the original autobiography, and the obvious solution is that those pages were torn out of the copy from which the printer was setting the type for the book published in 1888. The printer had on his hands the cut of an illustration originally captioned "The Killing of Tall Bull," and nothing to tell what it was about. With Cody not available, perhaps before he had returned from the 1887 tour of Great Britain or while the show was on the road in 1888, whoever was in charge of editing *Story of the Wild West* rose to the emergency. He faked three pages bearing no resemblance at all to Cody's original story, but magnificent. The Battle of Summit Springs became three fights, providing no less than one Indian battle a page, all drawn out of thin air and imagination. It went something like this:

Three days after the charge halted so abruptly (on page 583), a band of six hundred Indians was encountered. The Indians attacked, compelling the troops to retire to a ravine (the picture shows Cody in a ravine). The Indians made two desperate charges, but were driven back with heavy loss. An especially well-mounted Indian was seen several times riding in a circle around the besieged troops. Cody crawled up the ravine and shot the Indian—at a range of four hundred yards. Some days later in Fight No. 3, three hundred warriors were killed and Tall Bull's widow was captured. She made the statement that Tall Bull had been killed by "the Prairie Chief," meaning Cody.

Crude as this story was, its inventor not only got away with his improvisation for the immediate emergency, but also succeeded in having it spread about much more widely than the original. Cody apparently never caught up with the faked yarn until he came to write the series of articles for *Hearst's* magazine in 1916, which became his posthumous autobiography. Then he went back to his original story. Meanwhile, *Story of the Wild West* ran through numerous editions under the imprints of half a dozen publishers— it was listed in a catalog of Sears, Roebuck and Company as late as 1902. That was not all. The improvised story was copied in several other autobiographical works signed by Buffalo Bill.

The name of William F. Cody appeared on the title page of *The Great Salt Lake Trail* in 1898 as co-author, apparently because he allowed Colonel Henry Inman to quote liberally from the autobiography in *Story of the Wild West*. Inman, an old army man, should have known something was wrong. It is evident that he read it, for he left out one sentence and made a couple of minor changes, but he swallowed the synthetic triple battle hook, line, and sinker: he even made the jumble more unintelligible because of the missing sentence.[20]

In 1904 came a new book, *The Adventures of Buffalo Bill*, signed by Col. William F. Cody as author. In this book the faked yarn of the killing of Tall Bull is restored to its full glory as developed that day when the pages turned up missing, eliminating Inman's apochryphal meddling. This book also went through several editions and was reissued in 1944 as a paperback to advertise a motion picture.[21] That was not yet all.

After Cody's death in 1917 a new title appeared, *Buffalo Bill's Own Story of His Life and Deeds . . . Brought Up to Date Including*

[20] Inman and Cody, *The Great Salt Lake Trail*, 414–17.
[21] Cody, *Adventures*, 71, 75 (Boblin edition, 58–61).

a Full Account of His Death and Funeral ..., by William Lightfoot Visscher. Only the title and Colonel Visscher's added chapters were new; Cody's "own story" was lifted bodily from *Story of the Wild West*, including—you have already guessed—that false yarn that strung out Tall Bull's demise through two subsequent fictitious battles. This book was put out by three or four publishers with variant titles—as late as 1939, Mrs. Johnny Baker published an edition as *Life and Adventures of Buffalo Bill* for sale near Cody's grave on Lookout Mountain.

All of this proves that error can give truth a long run for more money, and that William F. Cody should have read the fine print before signing his name to so many books.

Luther North's variant stories cannot be so logically accounted for. If he has been correctly quoted by his several Boswells, much of what he said was demonstrably false. It is to be remembered, however, that six of his nine and more stories were told after he was eighty-three years of age, and more than sixty years after the fight. In that time memories grow dim, assumption may seem to become observed occurrence, and prejudice may warp judgment. Yet there may be some residual fact in his stories. Frank North may have killed a chief in one of the manners Luther describes. The identification depended on Mrs. Tall Bull, and to her one white man may have looked very much like another.

Cody's story, as he told it before his press agents so valiantly helped him out, has factual corroboration. In later years General Carr wrote, "Buffalo Bill had got pretty well around the village when he went in on Captain Price's right." Lieutenant Mason, who, Cody says, got the war bonnet, was in Price's company and was cited as distinguished for gallantry in the fight. Carr continues, "As he [Cody] advanced he saw a chief on a horse charging about, and haranguing his men. He and his party laid for him and, as he came near, Buffalo Bill shot him off his horse and got the horse.... When he came into camp 'Mrs. Tall Bull' said that was her husband's horse. So that left no doubt that Buffalo Bill killed the chief."[22]

Brigadier General William P. Hall, who joined the Fifth Cavalry as second lieutenant immediately after the fight, wrote Cody

[22] *The Rough Rider*, Vol. IV (1907), 7; Cody, *True Tales of the Plains*, 155-56.

in 1907: "I recall that you shot Tall Bull, and captured his celebrated gray race horse which you named Tall Bull and with which you captured the stakes in a great many horse races afterward." Brigadier General Charles King, who joined the Fifth Cavalry as first lieutenant within two years of the fight, wrote in 1929, "Never before this year did I hear of it being doubted or questioned that Cody killed Tall Bull." William H. McDonald, of North Platte, who as a boy lived near the fort, and first knew Cody when he returned from this expedition, told me in 1955, and he has put it in writing, "I know it was generally understood at Fort McPherson, where the 5th Cavalry came immediately after the Battle of Summit Springs in July, 1869, that Cody killed Tall Bull."[23]

It is unfortunate that a dispute so inconsequential should have obscured the fact that Buffalo Bill is credited with guiding the Fifth Cavalry to a position whence it was enabled to win a brilliant victory. It was scouting and guiding that he was hired to do.

[23] *The Rough Rider*, Vol. IV (1907), 9; Charles King, in *New York World*, March 31, 1929; interview with W. H. McDonald, September 6, 1955; W. H. McDonald to Miss Margaret McCann, April 6, 1929, manuscripts file, NSHS.

Vincent Orapeza, famous roper

Courtesy Franklin J. Meine

Antonio Esquivel, champion vaquero rider

Courtesy Denver Public Library Western Collection

Johnny Baker, the "Cowboy Kid"

BUFFALO BILL GAINS NATIONAL FAME

THE VICTORY AT SUMMIT SPRINGS was hailed as freeing Kansas, and Nebraska south of the Niobrara, from the horrors of Indian warfare—although Indians continued to steal horses, and soldiers to pursue them. General Carr's expedition, having accomplished its objective, marched to Fort Sedgwick, near Julesburg, Colorado, to rest and refit. Rotation, an army policy popularized in the Korean War, was not unknown in that earlier series of "police actions," the Indian wars. The battalion of the Fifth Cavalry was reorganized at Fort Sedgwick by exchanging Companies A, E, and M, which had taken part in the campaign, for Companies F, I, and L, which had been in garrison at Fort McPherson. The three companies from Fort Sedgwick arrived at Fort McPherson on July 23. The replacement troops moved out the next day under command of the senior captain, Brevet Major William H. Brown of Company F, with orders to pursue the Indians who had raided O'Fallon's Station on the Union Pacific Railroad. Cody had been ordered to go by railroad to accompany the expedition as scout.[1] The expedition was not important except to Cody, who on this occasion first met Edward Zane Carroll Judson, sometimes known as Ned Buntline, author and dime novelist.

Judson served as a private in Company K, First New York

[1] Price, *With the Fifth Cavalry*, 141, 404, 633, 642, 646; Cody, *Life*, 263.

Mounted Rifles, for two and one-half years of the Civil War, during which he fought in no battles but did spend some time behind bars for desertion. He claimed to have been "chief of scouts with the rank of colonel," a dime-novel formula that Cody's press agents were to make familiar. He had acquired the name of Ned Buntline more legitimately by signing it to an enormous amount of printed matter and by editing *Ned Buntline's Own* magazine, which was sunk and refloated on his precarious financial seas a number of times. He was not the originator of the dime novel, but he took advantage of the successful innovation of Beadle and Adams as an able and prolific storyteller and boasted that he wrote as many as six novels a week. He was reputed to have made as much as $20,000 a year, and he supported half a dozen wives, several of them simultaneously.

He had other claims to distinction. He had once been hanged. The lynching did not take because the rope broke, or was cut. The rope was applied after he had shot in a duel a Nashville man who accused him of intentions somewhat less than the honorable to be expected of a dime-novel hero. After that Ned concentrated on his own wives and tried to let other men's wives alone. In New York, Judson *alias* Buntline had been jailed for instigating a riot against William Charles Macready, an English actor, by partisans of Edwin Forrest. Sticks and stones backed the rioters' critical judgment that the American was the greatest Shakespearean. The militia was called out in this dramatic dispute, and several rioters, as well as more or less innocent bystanders, were shot. Ned Buntline was arrested and spent a year in jail, but was welcomed as a hero when he was released. In St. Louis, Ned staged another riot. As organizer for the American, or "Know-Nothing," party, he stirred up a mob against the German element in that city, then fled the state after being indicted by a grand jury.[2]

Quite a myth has grown up about the meeting of Buffalo Bill with Ned Buntline. This is not surprising, as nothing in the Buffalo Bill legend has been more exaggerated than Ned Buntline's part in it. Writing people, like those of other professions, delight in making a hero of one of their own kind. Their story goes that Ned

[2] Jay Monaghan, *The Great Rascal;* Richard Moody, *The Astor Place Riot* (Bloomington, 1958); Harold K. Hochschild, *Township 34,* 114–47.

Buntline was under contract to write a series of stories, and went West seeking a hero of the new postwar frontier, a frontier that had receded greatly since the days of Natty Bumpo and Seth Jones. Ned read newspaper accounts of the Battle of Summit Springs and sought the hero of that conflict, Major Frank North, at Fort McPherson. Frank North, the myth continues, was averse to the kind of publicity projected, but directed the dime-novel writer to Bill Cody, lying asleep under a wagon. Ned Buntline dragged Cody out from under the wagon, dubbed him "Buffalo Bill," and then and there invented the entire Buffalo Bill legend.[3]

The genesis of this myth lies with Luther North, whose unreliability can rarely be questioned, and who never shared his brother's alleged aversion to publicity. The wagon is the grocery wagon Luther invented for Cody to take on the Summit Springs expedition. In this case not only Luther's story but also every assumption built upon it proves erroneous.

Ned Buntline did not come West seeking a hero; instead, he was returning from California after an unsuccessful tour as a temperance lecturer. The Trans-Mississippi West was already a familiar subject to dime-novel readers, and Buntline, for all his prolificacy, made no large contribution to the Western type. He did not write a series of stories about Buffalo Bill; he wrote one story only, then dropped the subject for some three years. His total output of Buffalo Bill dime novels was four. The story he wrote in 1869 was not about the postwar frontier, but about border fighting in the Civil War. His discovery of a Western hero was, then, quite coincidental.

The theory that Ned Buntline invented the nickname "Buffalo Bill" does not hold up; there is nothing in the novel he wrote suggesting the need for such an invention, and even less demonstrating the creative imagination to have had so happy an inspiration. Moreover, there is evidence that Cody was known as Buffalo Bill some two years before the publication of Ned Buntline's novel. On November 26, 1867, the Leavenworth *Daily Conservative* recorded that "Buffalo Bill, with fifteen or twenty citizens volun-

---

[3] *Blake's Western Stories*, 5; see also Walsh, *The Making of Buffalo Bill*, 155; Stuart H. Holbrook, *Little Annie Oakley and Other Rugged People*, 78, 86–92; Monaghan, *The Great Rascal*, 3–8; Glenn Shirley, *Pawnee Bill*, 15, 47.

teered to go out and look for" Judge Corwin, who had strayed from a hunting party of Ohio and eastern Kansas gentlemen who had left Fort Hays on November 22. After a long ride, the lost man was found about five miles from the fort, nearly starved and almost exhausted. Since the same newspaper on January 11, 1868, refers to "Bill Cody and 'Brigham'" hunting buffalo from Fort Hays and we know about his scouting under Major Armes from Fort Hays the previous August, there seems no doubt that the "Buffalo Bill" of the dispatch was Cody. This was the period of his buffalo hunting contract, during which, according to his own story, he acquired the nickname. The published diary entry of Major Armes for August 24, 1868, refers to "Bill Cody (Buffalo Bill), one of our scouts," but his book was not published until 1900.

Similarly, W. E. Webb in *Buffalo Land* speaks of "making the acquaintance of those two celebrated characters Wild Bill and Buffalo Bill, or, more correctly William Hickok [so he has it] and William Cody," and notes that "Buffalo Bill has since figured in one of Buntline's Indian romances." Webb certainly gives the impression that he knew Cody as Buffalo Bill before he appeared in the Buntline romance.[4]

There seems no valid reason to doubt that Cody had been "Buffalo Bill" since his buffalo-hunting days for the railroad contractors. Hunting buffalo to feed the troops was one of the duties of a scout, and Luke Cahill's story of the hunt, in which he says Cody "never shot an animal but once and not one of the buffalo escaped,"[5] is sufficient to show that he still deserved to be called "Buffalo Bill."

The theory that Ned Buntline invented not only the name "Buffalo Bill" but also the entire Buffalo Bill legend could be formulated only by those who had neither read Ned Buntline's work nor investigated Cody's pre-Buntline career. The theory is based on the myth that Cody was "just another scout" who would never have been heard of had not Ned Buntline written novels about him, and who, in the words of a recent writer, "ever after lived in a

[4] Nyle H. Miller and Joseph W. Snell, "Some Notes on Kansas Cowtown Police Officers and Gun Fighters," *Kansas Historical Quarterly*, Vol. XXVI, No. 2 (Summer, 1960), 198; Armes, *Ups and Downs of an Army Officer*, 272; Webb, *Buffalo Land*, 145, 149.

[5] "An Indian Campaign," *Colorado Magazine*, Vol. IV, No. 4 (August, 1927), 132.

thick fog of wonder, honestly incapable of discriminating between what had happened in his life and what Buntline swore had happened." Another writer had it that "When the scouting ended in October, Cody found himself stranded at Fort McPherson with no occupation and no income," and, "He was out of a job and his wife expected a baby." The fact is that Cody was never off army payrolls from the time he made his famous ride for General Sheridan in September, 1868, until he resigned to go on the stage in December, 1872. As for the baby, since he was a civilian employe living on the post, his wife was entitled to the services of the post surgeon, and it is recorded in the medical history of Fort McPherson that she got such services. As for that thick fog of wonder, it must have been thick indeed if Cody honestly believed that he had twin sisters named Lillie and Lottie, whose mission in life was to be kidnaped singly, alternately, or as a pair by Dave Tutt, Jake M'Kandless, Indians, Border Ruffians, and other misspelled villains of the Wild Bill legend, which is what Ned Buntline swore had happened.

Luther North set the momentous meeting at Fort Sedgwick, but those who have copied him make it Fort McPherson, which is more logical. If Ned Buntline went to Fort Sedgwick after reading newspaper accounts of Summit Springs, he moved fast if he met Frank North there. A preliminary account of the fight was released in St. Louis on July 14. Frank arrived at the fort on July 15 and took a train for home, Columbus, Nebraska, at 2:00 P.M. on July 17. A detailed account of the fight was released on July 19, and Cody arrived at Fort McPherson from Fort Sedgwick on July 23. Incidentally, neither newspaper dispatch mentioned either Frank North or Cody.[6]

Ned Buntline did in fact stop at Fort Sedgwick on his way east, then went on to Fort McPherson. He might have been looking for Cody, who was there. He would not have been looking for North, who had gone home. The legend assumes that Buffalo Bill was unknown, but if Ned had talked with officers and enlisted men of the Fifth Cavalry at Fort Sedgwick, he would have heard favorable accounts of Cody. A good reporter might have turned up an order from the Secretary of War commending William Cody for

[6] *New York Herald*, July 14, 17, 1869; *1869 Diary of Frank North*, 141.

"extraordinarily good services as a trailer and fighter in the pursuit of Indians." A dime-novel writer in search of a frontier hero would have looked no farther.

There is only one flaw in this deduction. In the story Ned Buntline wrote, there is no mention of Cody's scouting on the plains or of the battle of Summit Springs. Luther North and those who have written after him have said that Ned Buntline wrote of the killing of Tall Bull by Buffalo Bill.[7] There is no citation to page or publication. There is no mention of an Indian named Tall Bull in any of the four Buffalo Bill dime novels written by Ned Buntline.

Anyone who reads this masterpiece—and obviously those who have written so glibly about it have not—might formulate another theory. So far as it is based on anything that happened, and not much of it is, it expands on exploits of Wild Bill Hickok. It could be that Wild Bill was the hero Ned sought, and it could be that he ran down Cody to get his reminiscences of Wild Bill. A further deduction is that he was struck with the alliterative value of the name "Buffalo Bill" and so used it in his title. The name was about all he got from Cody, for the story is largely about Wild Bill, and it has only vague suggestions of Cody's Civil War experiences.

Cody himself did not theorize. He stated flatly that Ned Buntline's object in coming to Cottonwood Springs and Fort McPherson was to deliver a temperance lecture. Cody's story of their meeting lacks the glamour that has been built up around it, but is in reasonable agreement with known facts. Cody reports that they were introduced just as the expedition was ready to start. Obviously the dime novelist had arranged to go before Cody arrived at the fort the previous night. Cody quotes Ned as saying, "No lectures for me when there is a prospect of a fight." Could it be that this was his only motive, that he was not looking for Buffalo Bill or Wild Bill, or even Major North?

Cody describes Ned as "a gentleman who was rather stoutly built and who wore a blue military coat, on the left breast of which were pinned about twenty gold medals and badges of secret societies. He walked a little lame as he approached us. . . . As

[7] Grinnell, *Two Great Scouts*, 201; Monaghan, *The Great Rascal*, 672; Shirley, *Pawnee Bill*, 15, 47.

he came up, Major Brown said: 'Cody, allow me to introduce you to Colonel E. B. C. Judson, otherwise known as Ned Buntline.' "[8]

Right there a single capital letter explodes a popular theory that Ned Buntline wrote Buffalo Bill's autobiography. Judson's initials were E. Z. C. Ned would not have had his own name wrong. Cody consistently got all names wrong.

Since Major Brown became a character in the resulting dime novel, there is no doubt about its being this expedition that Ned accompanied. That pin-points the meeting of Ned Buntline and Buffalo Bill as on July 24, 1869, the day Major Brown led forth his scouting party. If it continues to interest anyone, Major Frank North on that day was in Omaha as interpreter at a murder trial of some Pawnee Indians.

Cody was much impressed when Ned, who was diffident about his ability as a horseman, was first to swim his mount across the South Platte, wide and high because of recent rains. Cody has little more to say about Ned than that "he asked me a great many questions." Cody lent his horse Powder Face to Ned, and thereby that animal gained dime-novel notoriety. At O'Fallon's Station, Cody found the trail of the Indians the expedition was seeking. The trail was followed to the North Platte, but the Indians were then two days ahead, and the chase was given up, the expedition going on to Fort Sedgwick.[9] No more is said of Ned Buntline, who presumably resumed his trip eastward.

During this interval, pay call was heard at Fort Sedgwick, and in those days that meant galloping horses instead of galloping dominoes. Cody matched Tall Bull with a horse ridden by Lieutenant Mason and won a hundred-dollar race and two hundred dollars in side bets with Reuben Wood, the post trader. Bill put it all on Tall Bull in a race against the pick of the Pawnee Scouts' horses. Tall Bull won again, and Cody was up to seven hundred dollars. As he could get no more bets on Tall Bull, he arranged a four-hundred-yard race for Powder Face against one of Luther North's horses. Powder Face won, but Cody got few bets. Based on these incidents is a story that Cody made his living racing horses.

[8] Cody, *Life*, 263–64.
[9] Price, *With the Fifth Cavalry*, 141, 633, 642, 646.

He did all right, but he was also on the quartermaster's pay roll as scout.

As General Carr had gone on emergency leave after the Summit Springs fight, Major Royall on August 2 marched out the re-organized battalion of seven companies of the Fifth Cavalry, the Pawnee Scouts, "and the guide, William F. Cody," on a scout toward Frenchman's Fork of the Republican River. Pawnee Killer's band of Sioux was discovered within ten miles of the fort; there was a running fight, and the Sioux were pursued across Frenchman's Fork and northward across the South Platte. Major North rejoined the regiment from his home on August 6, and it was on the next day that he paid off his brother Luther and sent him home. The pursuit continued across the North Platte and eight miles beyond the Niobrara. Forty-two Indian ponies were found abandoned, but the expedition also had its troubles in the sand hills. "I have lost 17 animals and am leading many barely able to walk," Royall reported. Since rations also were exhausted, the pursuit was abandoned on August 11. The troops went to Fort McPherson, arriving there on August 22.[10]

Regimental headquarters of the Fifth Cavalry was established at Fort McPherson with the arrival of its colonel, Brevet Major General William H. Emory, on July 10. The lieutenant colonel, Brevet Brigadier General Thomas Duncan, was also present, an unusual assembly of brass for a regiment in Indian-fighting days. Cody was assured of regular employment, and sent for Lulu and Arta. General Emory had promised to have a log house built, but the family arrived, in late August, before it was ready. After a few days with William Reed of the trading post, they were able to move in. Mrs. Cody says the walls were lined with condemned tents after the logs had been chinked with mud, and Bill tried to hang wall paper he had brought from Cheyenne, but made a mess of it. An old army stove served for cooking and heating. Mrs. Cody also records that it was at this time that she first saw Bill in the vogue then in favor for scouts of the plains: "Where his close-cropped hair had been were long, flowing curls now. A mustache weaved its way outward from his upper lip, while a small goatee showed black and spot-like on his chin."[11]

[10] Ibid.; 1869 Diary of Frank North, 146–47.

He also found time for horse racing. Lieutenant Edward P. Doherty won twenty dollars, but when Major North tried his luck, he records ruefully on September 9, "I made a horse race with Cody and got beat."

On September 15, however, another expedition set forth, this time with General Duncan in command. According to the regimental history it consisted of Companies B, E, F, and M of the Fifth Cavalry, Companies D, C, and M of the Second Cavalry, Major North's Pawnee Scouts, "the guide, William F. Cody," and another scout, John Y. Nelson, whom Cody called "a good fellow though as a liar he has few equals and no superior." In later years Nelson, whose Indian name was Cha-sha-cha-Opoyco, meaning "Red-Willow-Fill-the-Pipe," traveled with Buffalo Bill's stage shows as interpreter and was a fixture in Buffalo Bill's Wild West— full-bearded John Nelson, his Sioux wife, and their children are prominent in many pictures of that aggregation.[12]

No officer who ever had Cody in his command is on record as having complained about the scout's being drunk while on duty, but Bill himself never hesitated to tell of his drinking. On the morning after the first day's march from the fort, General Duncan, whom Cody calls "a jolly, blustering old fellow," proposed a shooting match. Says Cody, "I can assure the reader that I did not feel like shooting anything except myself, for on the night before I had returned to Fort McPherson and spent several hours in interviewing the sutler's store, in company with Major Brown. I looked around for my gun, and found that I had left it behind. The last I could remember about it was that I had it at the sutler's store." Cody appealed to Major Brown, who sent back for Bill's rifle. Meanwhile Bill borrowed a gun from Nelson to fire the match with the General, "which resulted in his favor." Undoubtedly this was one time Buffalo Bill was happy over being outshot.

This expedition was a pursuit of the remnant of the Cheyennes and Sioux under Pawnee Killer, Whistler, and Little Bull. There was much buffalo hunting, probably to stretch out the rations. On September 23, Major Frank North recorded, "The Gen.

[11] Mrs. Cody, *Memories*, 153, 161.

[12] Post Returns, Ft. McPherson, September, October, 1869; Price, *With the Fifth Cavalry*, 141; *1869 Diary of Frank North*, 155–61; Cody, *Life*, 271–75.

Cody and I killed 13 Buffalo our men killed lots." On September 26, at Prairie Dog Creek, which Cody says was not far from the place where he had been laid up with a broken leg while trapping with Dave Harrington, Buffalo Bill and Major North went hunting in advance of the command and killed a few buffalo while looking for a campsite. Frank dismounted to rest, while Bill rode back over the next hill to look for the advance guard. As soon as he spotted it, he also dismounted and lay down to rest.

"Suddenly I heard three or four shots," says Cody, "and in a few moments Major North came dashing up towards me, pursued by eight or ten Indians. I instantly sprang to my saddle, and fired a few shots at the Indians, who by this time had all come in sight, to the number of fifty. We turned our horses and ran, the bullets flying after us thick and fast—my whip being shot from my hand and daylight being put through the crown of my hat."

Major North in his diary told the story in much the same way: "Today we marched 24 miles and I and Cody came ahead to the Creek and 6 Indians got after us and gave us a lively chase you bet. I got my men out and they killed one Indian and got two ponies a mule and lots of trash."

Lieutenant Price, acting adjutant of the expedition, and Lieutenant Volkmar, acting engineer and signal officer in charge of the pioneer detachment, were in the advance with a few Pawnee Scouts. As soon as the pursuing Indians saw troops coming, they retreated. North rode his horse in a circle, a traditional plains signal for "enemy in sight." His Pawnee Scouts "broke ranks pell-mell and, with Major North at their head, started for the flying warriors." They were pursued so closely that they abandoned their village, which was destroyed next morning. "It was afterward learned," says Price, "that the band traveled ninety miles without halting, and thereafter marched as rapidly as possible until they arrived at Standing Rock Agency."[13]

Lieutenants Price and Volkmar were mentioned in the official report of this action "as meriting the highest praise for dash and gallantry" and for having "undoubtedly saved the lives of Major Frank North (commanding the Pawnee Scouts) and the guide,

[13] Cody, *Life*, 274; *1869 Diary of Frank North*, 158; Price, *With the Fifth Cavalry*, 141–42, 444, 461; Grinnell, *Two Great Scouts*, 210.

William Cody." Cody in his account gives credit only to Volkmar (misspelling it "Valkmar"). There are those who view with suspicion anyone who praises Buffalo Bill, so it may be well to mention that the name of Price does not appear anywhere in Cody's autobiography. As Cody's book was published before Price compiled his regimental history, the officer might well have resented the slight and minimized mention of Cody.

As the pursuit continued, an old woman was picked up whom Nelson recognized as a relative of his wife and the mother of Pawnee Killer, who with Whistler had led the Sioux band that was with Tall Bull's Cheyennes at Summit Springs. But by October 23 there seemed little hope of overtaking this hostile band. Rations were running low and snow impeded travel; therefore, the expedition turned back to Fort McPherson, where it arrived on October 28, and was disbanded. Headquarters of the Fifth Cavalry and Companies F, H, I, L, and M were assigned as garrison. Companies A, B, C, D, E, and G were ordered to take station at Fort D. A. Russell, Wyoming. Major North and his Pawnee Scouts were discharged on October 28.

William F. Cody was discharged as scout on October 31. However, he was not out of a job. The records show that he was hired as chief herder the following day, November 1, at the same salary. All that this means is that Lieutenant Hayes did not want to be called upon by some inspector general to explain what need he had for a scout while the regiment was in garrison. Cody remained on the pay roll as chief herder at seventy-five dollars a month until July 1, 1870, when he again became a scout, this time at one hundred dollars a month.[14]

That winter he received his first wide acclaim. On December 23, 1869, there appeared in the *New York Weekly* the first installment of Ned Buntline's serial story, *Buffalo Bill, the King of Border Men*. It was advertised as "the wildest and truest story he ever wrote." Full acceptance of that claim would not require that it contain any large amount of truth. It did not. Just what Ned got out of his western trip aside from the names of Major Brown and Buffalo Bill would mystify any reader. Perhaps his only real

[14] Post Records, Fort McPherson; O.Q.M. 1939; Price, *With the Fifth Cavalry*, 142.

discovery was the alliterative magic of the name Buffalo Bill, for the name had far more impact than the story.

Cody was flattered and appreciative. When his eldest son was born on November 26, 1870, Bill naïvely proposed to name the baby "Elmo Judson, in honor of Ned Buntline; but this the officers and scouts objected to. Major Brown proposed that we should call him Kit Carson, and it was finally settled that this should be his name."[15]

Major Brown must have read Ned Buntline's story. He is the only person, contemporary or recent, who offers this much evidence of having done so. In all probability it was much more widely advertised than it was sold. It was published at the time only as a serial in a "story paper" and was not reprinted complete until 1881. Ned was not encouraged to write a sequel, and dropped the subject until Buffalo Bill gained wider acclaim some three years later.

It is not surprising that so many commentators have assumed that Ned Buntline wrote of Summit Springs and Tall Bull, for it is hard to believe that an experienced writer would so ineptly saddle the wrong horse as Ned did with his phony yarn of Civil War border fighting, at a time when Cody himself was contributing largely to the Buffalo Bill legend.

No scout in the army had built up as extensive a record as had Cody during the year in which he met Ned Buntline. From the time Cody joined the Fifth Cavalry as chief of scouts on October 5, 1868, until he returned to winter quarters at Fort McPherson on October 28, 1869, one year and twenty-three days later, he took part in seven expeditions against Indians and in nine Indian fights. Few if any men in the regiment he served saw this much action. Not one of the eleven companies of the Fifth Cavalry in the West during that time was in all these fights and expeditions. Detachments of the regiments are credited with only four small fights at which Cody was not present.

[15] Cody, *Life*, 275. Walsh, *The Making of Buffalo Bill*, 162, cited by Monaghan, *The Great Rascal*, 9, who says Major Frank North suggested "Kit Carson." The Norths can't allow Cody to name his own infant!" Major North probably was not at Fort McPherson in November, 1870, as the Pawnee Scouts were not called out until December. Ned Buntline's story was advertised in *Harper's Weekly*, December 11, 1869.

He had been acclaimed for several remarkable scouting achievements, by General Carr, by General Sheridan, and even by order of the Secretary of War. Red tape had been knotted through loopholes to keep Cody on the pay roll, and it was through this action that a scout, instead of being a casual employee hired by the job, became an institution in the Indian-fighting army. Generals Carr, Emory, Augur, and Sheridan made no small contribution to the Buffalo Bill legend—perhaps as great as that of Ned Buntline.

HUNTING PARTIES OF THE PLAINS

THE FIFTH CAVALRY had only one Indian fight in 1870—and Buffalo Bill had a large part in that one. Early on the morning of June 7, marauding Indians got twenty-one horses belonging to John Burke, government contractor, and Ben Gallagher and Jack Waite, ranchers along the North Platte, near Frémont Creek, as well as some from the Fort McPherson herd, including Cody's Powder Face. As "Boots and Saddles" sounded, Cody, on Buckskin Joe, galloped for the herd, arriving in time to see the Indians disappearing over a range of hills. He reported to General Emory that he could pick up the trail.

The first troop ready for action was Company I, commanded by Second Lieutenant Earl D. Thomas. He had reported to the regiment from West Point on September 30, 1869, and thus had missed that year's campaigns. Inexperienced in Indian warfare, he was no untried shavetail, however, for he had been private, corporal, and sergeant-major of the Eighth Illinois Cavalry in the Army of the Potomac through three years of the Civil War. As he was ready first, General Emory started his troop with the order, "Follow Cody and be off quick." He was told that reinforcements would follow.

Starting at eight o'clock in the morning without rations, the troop pushed ahead at a gallop wherever possible, delayed only by examining side trails and by rain that threatened to wash out the tracks. By dark, sixty miles had been covered. The lieutenant then halted his men and had them stand to horse until daylight. Cody was confident the Sioux would camp at Red Willow Creek, four miles away. He scouted in that direction and discovered horses feeding across the creek. He led the troop into hiding along the creek bottom. At five in the morning the Indian camp was visible only one hundred yards away. Says the commendatory order of the district commander, General Carr: "The whole Command rushed across the stream which owing to the miry swamps on each side was a difficult and hazardous undertaking worthy of the highest commendation." The Indians fired a few shots, then fled, abandoning everything except the horses they rode. Cody tells of firing a shot at a range of thirty feet that went through the backs of two Indians mounted on the same pony. He took their war bonnets, later presenting them to the daughters of General Augur. But the Sioux mounted on Powder Face got away. The troops rounded up thirty-three horses and mules, more than had been stolen.

Cody then urged Thomas to get out away from that place, and when the lieutenant suggested waiting for the reinforcements, reminded him that his order was to "follow Cody." Bill explains, "I didn't take the trail we had followed in. I knew a shorter route, and besides, I didn't want to meet the support that was coming. I knew the officer in command, and was sure that if he came up he would take all the glory of the capture away from Lieutenant Thomas. Naturally I wanted all the credit for Thomas and myself as we were entitled to."

When the support arrived, its scout, Texas Jack Omohundro, reported the trail of Company I as headed back for the fort. "The major was hotter than a wounded coyote," says Cody. "He told the general that it was all my fault, and that he did not propose to be treated in any such manner by any scout, even if it were General Sheridan's pet, Buffalo Bill. He was told by the general that the less he said about the matter the better it would be for him."

Cody has been accused of glory-grabbing in this instance, but by army custom, if the parties had joined, the senior officer would have taken command, and without stretching a point very far, could report the fight as by a part of his force. Since Cody rarely expresses adverse opinions of anyone, there may be a reason when he does. The reinforcement was Company M. The officer, then, is probably its captain, Edward H. Lieb, brevetted major and lieutenant colonel for Civil War action, who "ceased to be an officer of the army" in 1877, as the regimental historian delicately puts it. Elsewhere the harsher term "dismissed" is used.

Official reports show that Company I returned to the post on the day of the fight, July 8, arriving at 7:00 P.M. after a march of 120 miles in two days. Says Cody, "This being the first fight Lieutenant Thomas had ever commanded in, he felt highly elated over his success, and hoped that his name would be mentioned in the special orders for gallantry; sure enough when we returned both he, myself, and the whole command received a complimentary mention in a special order." This refers to General Order No. 7, District of the Republican, General Carr commanding, dated June 22, in which this sentence is included: "Lieutenant Thomas especially commends scout Cody for the manner in which he followed the trail, particularly at night, during a storm of rain, and for gallant conduct in the fight."[1]

Although this was Cody's only Indian fight in 1870, he was not idle during the rest of the year. Hunting buffalo and other game as an addition to the staple rations supplied by the Subsistence Department was a normal part of a scout's duties. Guiding important persons who came to Fort McPherson to hunt game contributed to the same end and justified providing them with escorts at government expense. No doubt Cody enhanced his income by guiding hunting parties. They contributed materially to his rapidly growing legend.

The romantic aspects of the Wild West, soon to be exploited by Buffalo Bill, were appreciated in Europe earlier than they were in America. Bill as a boy in Leavenworth had marveled at the equipage of Sir St. George Gore, whose slaughter of 2,500 buffalo during one hunting trip disgusted Jim Bridger and caused the

[1] Record of Events, June, 1870, Post Returns, Fort McPherson, Nebr.; General Orders No. 7, Headquarters District of the Republican, June 22, 1870; General Orders No. 27, Headquarters Department of the Platte, July 1, 1870, Records of the War Department, National Archives; Price, *With the Fifth Cavalry*, 142–43, 374–77, 526, 584, 673; Cody, *Life*, 269–71; Cody, *Autobiography*, 203–205.

government to take notice. Completion of the transcontinental railroad in 1869 stimulated visits of sportsmen. One of the most systematic was Sir John Watts Garland, who in 1869 established permanent camps, where he left horses and dogs with caretakers. Thereafter he came from England for hunts at about two-year intervals. He would pay as much as one thousand dollars for a trained buffalo horse. He adopted the California saddle and the American habit of drinking a cocktail before breakfast, says Cody, who guided Sir John in the winter of 1870–71.[2]

Outstanding among British sportsmen was the Earl of Dunraven, who was Lord Adair when Cody first guided him, in 1871, and who later became Windham Thomas Wyndham-Quin, fourth earl of Dunraven and Mount-Earl, to give him his full name and titles. He wrote several books, was correspondent for the *Daily Telegraph* during the Abyssinian War of 1867 and the Franco-Prussian War of 1870–71, and in 1872 and 1874 bought 60,000 acres in Estes Park, Colorado Territory, for a game preserve. In 1893 and 1895 he tried vainly to win the America's Cup with his yachts *Valkyrie II* and *Valkyrie III*. He was also at one time under-secretary for the colonies in the British cabinet.

Dunraven's first trip was arranged at General Sheridan's headquarters in Chicago. There he saw the head of an elk, or wapiti, a present to the General from Fort McPherson. Dunraven had never sighted an elk, and he immediately determined to have as fine a specimen. General Sheridan obliged by writing to the fort's commander, "requesting him to give me any assistance in his power, and if possible to let me have the valuable services of Mr. William Cody, otherwise Buffalo Bill, the government scout at the fort," the Earl recorded.[3]

Dunraven was met at the station by Buffalo Bill and Texas Jack. His descriptions of them before they became showmen indicate what the scout of the plains considered proper attire. "Bill was dressed in a pair of corduroys tucked into high boots, and a blue flannel shirt. He wore a broad-brimmed felt hat, or sombrero,

2 W. F. Cody, "Famous Hunting Parties of the Plains," *Cosmopolitan*, Vol. XVII, No. 2 (June, 1894), 131–43 (hereafter cited as Cody, "Hunting Parties"); Clark C. Spence, "A Celtic Nimrod in the Old West," *Montana*, Vol. IX, No. 2 (April, 1959), 56–66.

3 The Earl of Dunraven, *Canadian Nights*, 51–55; *Past Times and Pastimes*, Vol. I, 72–139.

and had a white handkerchief folded like a little shawl loosely fastened round his neck, to keep off the fierce rays of the afternoon sun. Jack's costume was similar, with the exception that he wore moccasins, and had his lower limbs encased in a pair of comfortably greasy deer-skin trousers, ornamented with a fringe along the seam. Round his waist was a belt supporting a revolver, two butcher knives, and in his hand he carried his trusty rifle, the 'Widow.'

"Jack, tall and lithe, with light brown close-cropped hair, clear laughing honest blue eyes, and a soft and winning smile, might have sat as a model for a typical modern Anglo-Saxon—if ethnologists will excuse the term. Bill was dark, with quick searching eyes, aquiline nose, and delicately cut features, and he wore his hair falling in long ringlets over his shoulders, in true Western style."[4]

Dunraven accompanied a scouting party along the Platte to Little Sandy Creek. On the second day he got his first elk. Within a few days he recorded a scene of slaughter such as he had never viewed before. It took two days to cut up the elk for meat with axes. Not an ounce was wasted, he records. Cody explains, "The elk hunt of those days was managed in about this way: six or seven of us would start at sunrise on our prairie horses and get as close as possible to the elk, which would be feeding in the open, two or three hundred, perhaps, in a bunch. These long-legged beasts were swifter than the buffalo, and they would let us get within a half mile of them before they would give a mighty snort and dash away after their leader. Then came the test of speed and endurance. They led the horses a wild race, and it put our chargers to their mettle to overtake the game. Right in among them we would spur, and, dropping the reins, use the repeating rifle with both hands. The breech-loading Springfield piece of fifty-calibre, the same as used in the regular army, was our favorite rifle at that time."[5]

A hunter of quite different character who came to Fort McPherson in 1870 was Othniel Charles Marsh, of Yale College, the first professor of paleontology in the United States. His expedition of students sought the remains of animals of the Miocene

[4] *Ibid.*, 55–56.
[5] Cody, "Hunting Parties," 136.

and Pliocene periods. Cody was scheduled to accompany the party, but explains, "The day before the Professor arrived at the fort I had been out hunting on the north side of the Platte River, near Pawnee Springs, with several companions, when we were suddenly attacked by Indians, who wounded one of our number, John Weister. We stood the Indians off for a little while, and Weister got even with them by killing one of their party. The Indians, however, outnumbered us and at last we were forced to make a run for our lives. . . . The General wanted to have the Indians pursued, and said that he could not spare me to accompany Professor Marsh."

However, Cody rode out with him several miles "as he was starting his bone-hunting expedition. . . . He gave me a geological history of the country; told me in what section fossils were to be found; and otherwise entertained me with several scientific yarns, some of which seemed too complicated and too mysterious to be believed by an ordinary man like myself; but it was all clear to him."[6]

Annals of the expedition tell how Professor Marsh, "all aglow with the achievements his imagination pictured as in store for him, related to the open-mouthed company as they rode along that the Rocky Mountains were once the bottom of a shallow sea, that the region in front of them was once covered by a fresh-water lake, and that the fossils he hoped to find had been buried on its bottom or along its shores.

"In the evening Buffalo Bill remarked, 'The Professor told the boys some pretty tall yarns today, but he tipped me a wink as much as to say, "You know how it is yourself, Bill." ' "[7]

This is a typical example of Cody's tall-tale humor. Of course he was mystified, but he played innocent on his own ignorance, and the boys voted it the choicest yarn brought back. Professor Marsh was amused at being accepted as a teller of tall tales, and he never forgot Bill. Years later, in writing of a buffalo hunt, he spoke of "coming alongside, ready to shoot, in the exact manner my first guide Buffalo Bill had taught me long before." Marsh continued scientific expeditions to the West for many years. In

[6] Cody, *Life*, 279–80; Webb's *Buffalo Land* is probably based in part on this expedition. The day was July 14, 1870; Record of Events, Fort McPherson.

[7] Charles Schuchert and Clara Mae LeVene, *O. C. Marsh, Pioneer in Paleontology*, 103, 129.

1874 he narrowly escaped massacre by the Sioux, but made a friend of Red Cloud, took the story of that chief's wrongs back to Washington, and provoked a scandal in the Department of the Interior. Bill says it was Marsh who first drew his attention to the possibilities of the Cody, Wyoming, region. And whenever Buffalo Bill's Wild West played New Haven, Cody, in all his regalia, called at the home of Yale College's eminent scientist.

This is the sort of thing that provoked Luther North's jealousy. Major Frank North and two Pawnees guided Marsh's 1870 expedition. The expedition members found Major North "quite modest and retiring—a good shot and, contrary to the idea that eastern people hold of the western frontiersman, drinks no liquor."[8] Yet the professor and the boys forgot about Major North, who guided them ably, but remembered the yarn-spinning of Buffalo Bill, who was with them only one day.

These visits by hunters, curiosity seekers, and eminent persons added rapidly to the growing reputation of Buffalo Bill, who was never lacking in natural showmanship. He tells of arranging horse races for the amusement of a party including George Boyd Houghton, London caricaturist. Cody's horse Tall Bull by this time had so considerable a reputation that it was difficult to get a race for him. One was arranged with a horse from Captain Edward J. Spaulding's company of the Second Cavalry under peculiar conditions. Says Cody, "I had made a bet that Tall Bull would beat the Second Cavalry horse around a one mile track, and, during the time that he was running, I would jump off and on the horse eight times. I rode the horse bareback; seized his mane with my left hand, rested my right on his withers, and while he was going at full speed, I jumped to the ground, and sprang back upon his back, eight times in succession. Such feats I had seen performed in the circus and I had practiced considerably at it with Tall Bull so that I was certain of winning the race in the manner agreed upon."

Where and when did Bill see a circus? It is one of the peculiarities of the Westward Movement that show business followed the flag much closer than did the Constitution. Dan Castello's Great Show, Circus, Menagerie, and Abyssinian Caravan made a coast-

8 *Ibid.*, 103.

to-coast tour in 1869. When it played Savannah, Georgia, in February, there was no transcontinental railroad. Just sixteen days after the Golden Spike was driven at Promontory Point, Frank North saw the show in Omaha on May 26. It reached San Francisco on July 26, playing both coasts within six months.

Its date in three-year-old North Platte was May 29. The battalion of the Fifth Cavalry arrived at near-by Fort McPherson on May 20 from Fort Lyon, after skirmishing with Tall Bull's band on the way. It did not resume its chase of Tall Bull until June 9. You can be sure that everyone who could get away that Saturday, including Buffalo Bill, rode over to see the circus.[9]

Tall Bull passes from the scene in the fall of 1870. Says Cody, "While I was a witness in a court martial at Fort D. A. Russell I woke up one morning and found that I was dead broke. . . . To raise necessary funds I sold my race horse Tall Bull to Lieutenant Mason, who had long wanted him." He probably means Captain Julius W. Mason, as Lieutenant George F. Mason, who assisted in the original capture of the horse, was shot and killed March 1, 1870, by a quartermaster's clerk after an altercation. Cody had promised Lulu to buy furniture, but lost the money at roulette.[10]

The only Indian fight of the Fifth Cavalry in 1871 was a Birdwood Creek, Nebraska, on May 24. Lieutenant Hayes, regimental quartermaster, led thirty men from Companies G, I, H, and L in the surprise and capture of six Sioux with sixty horses and mules. Cody was scout and was mentioned for "conspicuous and gallant conduct" in the fight, but nothing about it appears in any of his writings. It was his last fight of official record with the Fifth Cavalry for five years.[11]

Lieutenant Charles King recorded as his notable memory of a brief assignment at Fort McPherson in late 1871, "a glorious hunt or two with Buffalo Bill, our chief scout." He probably refers to an expedition Cody describes as a "twenty days' scout, not so much for the purpose of finding Indians, but more for the object of taking some friends on a hunt," a Mr. McCarthy of Syracuse,

[9] Cody, *Life*, 268–69; George L. Chindahl, *A History of the Circus in America* (Caldwell,, 1959), 89–93; *1869 Diary of Frank North*, 126.

[10] Cody, *Life*, 275; *Autobiography*, 212.

[11] Price, *With the Fifth Cavalry*, 149, 448, 584, 638; Record of Events, May, 1871, Post Returns, Fort McPherson.

New York, a relative of General Emory, and a couple of Englishmen. Cody led McCarthy into an ambush faked by Captain Luther North's company of Pawnees. The visitor was so frightened that he dropped his hat and gun and could not be stopped until he had galloped his horse into the main camp. Cody sometimes laid on his practical jokes with a heavy hand. Only a few days later Cody guided two troops with "Mr. Royal Buck whose father had been killed with his entire party by Pawnee Killer's band of Indians on Beaver Creek. . . . We found . . . an old letter or two which Mr. Buck recognized as his father's handwriting. We then discovered some of the remains, which we buried."[12]

The expedition of 1871 that contributed most largely to the Buffalo Bill legend was that referred to in the press as General Sheridan's party of buffalo hunters, or facetiously, as "New Yorkers on the warpath." The party included James Gordon Bennett, editor of the *New York Herald*; Charles L. Wilson, editor of the *Chicago Evening Journal*; and Henry Eugene Davies, a major general of volunteers in the Civil War, who wrote a pamphlet, *Ten Days on the Plains*, describing the hunt. Others were Lawrence R. Jerome, Leonard W. Jerome, and Carroll Livingston of New York; Major General John Charles Hecksher, Colonel John Schuyler Crosby, and Captain M. Edward Rogers of Philadelphia; General Anson Stager of the Western Union Telegraph Company; General Charles Fitzhugh of Pittsburgh; Samuel Johnson of Chicago; Colonel Daniel Henry Rucker, the acting quartermaster general; Brevet Major Morris Joseph Asch, assistant surgeon of General Sheridan's staff; and Colonel M. C. Sheridan, the General's brother.

Cody's rapidly growing reputation is indicated in the first dispatch sent to the *New York Herald* immediately after the arrival of the party at Fort McPherson on September 22, 1871: "General Sheridan and party arrived at the North Platte River this morning, and were conducted to Fort McPherson by General Emery [*sic*], commanding. General Sheridan reviewed the troops, consisting of four companies of the Fifth Cavalry. The party start across the country tomorrow, guided by the renowned Buffalo Bill and under the escort of Major Brown, Company F, Fifth Cavalry. The party expect to reach Fort Hays in ten days."[13]

[12] Charles King, *Memories of a Busy Life*, 23; Cody, *Life*, 290–92.

General Davies recorded in his pamphlet: "At the camp we were introduced to the far-famed Buffalo Bill, whose name has lately been used to 'point a moral and adorn a tale,' in the *New York Ledger,* and whose life and adventures have furnished the material for the brilliant drama that under his name has drawn crowded and delighted audiences at one of our metropolitan theatres. We had all heard of him as destined to be our guide. . . . William Cody, Esquire, which title he holds of right, being in the county in which his home is a justice of the peace, was a mild agreeable, well-mannered man, quiet and retiring in disposition though well informed and always ready to talk well and earnestly on any subject of interest. . . .

"Tall and somewhat slight in figure, though possessed of great strength and iron endurance; straight and erect as an arrow, and with strikingly handsome features, he at once attracted to him all with whom he became acquainted and the better knowledge gained of him during the days he spent with our party increased the good impression he made upon his introduction."[14]

"I rose fresh and eager for the trip," says Cody, "and as it was a nobby and high-toned outfit which I was to accompany, I determined to put on a little style myself." The impression he made is thus described by General Davies: "The most striking feature of the whole was the figure of our friend Buffalo Bill riding down from the Fort to our camp, mounted upon a snowy white horse. Dressed in a suit of light buckskin, trimmed along the seams with fringes of the same leather, his costume lighted by the crimson shirt worn under his open coat, a broad sombrero on his head, and carrying his rifle lightly in his hand as his horse came toward us on an easy gallop, he realized to perfection the bold hunter and gallant sportsman of the plains."[15]

The showman in Cody was developing rapidly. He is credited with originating in his Wild West show days the style of ten-gallon Stetson hats for cowboys, and this broad sombrero was also noticed by the Earl of Dunraven. The elaborate costume is evi-

[13] *New York Herald,* September 23, 28, 1871; Record of Events, September, 1871, Post Returns, Fort McPherson; Price, *With the Fifth Cavalry,* 619–49; Cody, *Life,* 382.
[14] H. E. Davies, *Ten Days on the Plains,* 25–26.
[15] Cody, *Life,* 282–90; Davies, *Ten Days on the Plains,* 29.

dence that Buffalo Bill was prosperous—he even adds the detail
that the crimson shirt was handsomely ornamented on the bosom.
He fitted well the elaborateness of this expedition, which had a
train of sixteen wagons for baggage, supplies, and forage, including
one wagon for ice; three four-horse ambulances in which members of the party who became weary might ride and rest; a light
wagon drawn by a pair of Indian ponies belonging to Lieutenant
Hayes, quartermaster of the expedition; five greyhounds brought
along to course antelopes and rabbits; and linen, china, and glass-
ware for the multi-course dinners prepared by French chefs and
served every evening by waiters in evening dress. It is recorded
that "for years afterward travellers and settlers recognized the
sites upon which these camps had been constructed by the quan-
tities of empty bottles which remained behind to mark them."[16]

Yet it was not all champagne and skittles, and of course Cody
was not hired as an entertainer. General Davies records that "a
good deal of time and some trouble were required to pass our
teams over to the south of the stream on which our camp for the
night was to be established, as a bridge had to be built for the
wagons to cross on, and it was necessary to double all the teams
to pull up the steep hill that formed the northern bank. At this
work our friend Buffalo Bill proved as skillful as he was in killing
buffalo, and by his science in bridge building and success as
teamster, acquired new titles to our confidence and respect."

Somehow or other the members of the party also found time
to do some hunting. General Fitzhugh was awarded a silver drinking set as a trophy for downing the first buffalo. Lawrence Jerome,
"by the exercise of his unrivaled powers of persuasion, succeeded
in obtaining from Buffalo Bill the best hunting horse in the whole
party—a dismal-looking, dun-colored brute rejoicing in the name
of Buckskin Joe, but like a singed cat, much better than he looked.
He was a wonderful beast for hunting, as his subsequent conduct
proved, and on his back Jerome did wonders for one brief day
among the buffalo." On the following day, however, Jerome dismounted to make a steady and careful shot, and thoughtlessly let
go of the bridle. He missed his shot, the buffalo started to run, and
Buckskin Joe took off after him, as he had been trained to do,

[16] Cody, "Hunting Parties," 137–40; Cody, *Life*, 289–90.

leaving Jerome afoot. Buckskin Joe turned up at Fort McPherson three days later. Jerome got another horse "warranted not to run under any provocation."[17]

That night at Camp Cody, named, says General Davies, "after our guide, philosopher, and friend," Lawrence Jerome was tried by kangaroo court "for aiding and abetting in the loss of a government horse." Although Jerome contended that the horse had lost him, Chief Justice Cody delivered the opinion of the court-martial, which was a suspended judgment.

The party hunted for 194 miles along the ranges bordering Medicine Creek, across the Republican River and its branches, and then along Beaver Creek and the Solomon and Saline rivers. More than six hundred buffalo and two hundred elk were killed.

Cody says of *Ten Days on the Plains*, "I have taken the liberty in this chapter to condense from the little volume, and in some places I have used the identical language of General Davies without quoting the same; in fact, to do the General justice, I ought to close this chapter with several lines of quotation marks to be pretty generally distributed by the reader throughout my account of our ten days' hunt. . . . I would have inserted the volume bodily in this book, were it not for the fact that the General has spoken in a rather too complimentary manner of me."[18] Cody has often been represented as a boaster, but not one of the complimentary remarks made by General Davies was quoted by Cody.

There was a forecast of new acclaim for Buffalo Bill in one of the last dispatches recording the progress of the buffalo hunters. Said the *Salt Lake Tribune* as the party arrived at Fort Hays on October 2, "Enough game will be left, we hope, for the Grand Duke Alexis when he takes a scurry over the hunting grounds."

[17] Davies, *Ten Days on the Plains*, 42, 47; Cody, *Life*, 289–90.
[18] Cody, *Life*, 289–90.

THE HUNT OF THE GRAND DUKE ALEXIS

Newspapers that recorded in scattered paragraphs the adventures of the New York buffalo hunters devoted columns to the movements of the Grand Duke Alexis, third son of Alexander II, czar of all the Russias. From some twenty-five reigning royal families in Europe there came in the entire nineteenth century fewer royal visitors to the United States than have been seen in a single year from the few remaining royal families after the world wars of the twentieth century. It is difficult now to recapture the interest Americans then had in a somewhat secondary prince. It is comparable with the interest in the 1959 visit of Nikita Khrushchev, but with a difference. Russia was then regarded as a friendly power that had acted to curb British and French sympathy for the South in the Civil War and more recently had ceded the territory of Alaska to the United States.

Alexis was headline news in eight-page newspapers that had little room for headlines. On September 26, 1871, it was recorded that the Grand Duke had sailed from Falmouth, England, escorted by a Russian battle fleet. In the same issue J. W. McKinley, merchant tailor of Broadway, advertised "Grand Duke Alexis walking and overcoats, just out and ready made." A month later, with all ready for the royal reception in Washington, the Grand Duke and the Russian fleet were still unreported. The unaccountable delay failed to diminish the flattering attention given him when he finally arrived in New York and then Washington.

Alexis had expressed a desire to see the prairies, about which he had heard much, but seemed in no hurry about it, for in his slow progress westward it was the end of the year when he reached Detroit.[1] This gave General Sheridan adequate time to prepare for the royal buffalo hunt, for he started his mobilization on November 1. One of his first steps was to assure the services of the country's most famous hunting guide, Buffalo Bill. Action was necessary, for the Fifth Cavalry, for which Cody had been chief of scouts for three years, had been ordered to Arizona Territory—its companies at Fort McPherson left for Fort McDowell on November 27. It had been planned to retain Cody, despite his lack of knowledge of the terrain or Apache ways of warfare, until a letter was received from General Sheridan instructing the commanding officer "not to take Cody."

Early in January, General George Forsyth and Dr. Asch of Sheridan's staff arrived at Fort McPherson to plan for the hunt. Cody suggested Red Willow Creek, forty miles south of the fort, and guided the staff officers and Lieutenant Hayes, Fifth Cavalry quartermaster who also had been retained, to the area. "Camp Alexis" soon was established not far from the present site of Hayes Center.[2] The staff officers asked Cody to find the Sioux chief Spotted Tail and persuade him to bring one hundred Indians to camp near by for the entertainment of the royal visitor. Cody knew that Spotted Tail's band, which had permission to hunt buffalo in the Republican River region, was on Frenchman's Fork, 150 miles from Fort McPherson. The trip was not without danger, for however friendly Spotted Tail might be at any particular time, some of his young men might be capable of killing a lone white man for his gun and horse if given the opportunity. However, Cody reached the village safely, and when Todd Randall, agent and interpreter, explained the request, Spotted Tail readily agreed to join the show and put on a buffalo hunt and war dance. On his

[1] *New York Herald*, September 30, October 3, 6, November 8, December 21, 29, 1871.

[2] Willis T. Lee and others, *Guidebook of the Western United States, Part B*, U. S. Geological Survey *Bulletin 612* (Washington, 1915); Price, *With the Fifth Cavalry*, 448–49; Cody, *Life*, 295–97; information from Dr. Lawrence Frost.

way back Cody found Captain James Egan with a company of the Second Cavalry and a wagon train at Camp Alexis, leveling off the ground and setting up wall tents, which were floored and carpeted, heated with stoves, and equipped with furniture.

The Grand Duke arrived at North Platte on January 13, 1872, in a special train in charge of Frank Thompson of the Union Pacific. There are several versions of Buffalo Bill's presentation, but this one appeared in a newspaper dispatch from North Platte:

"Your Highness," said the General, "this is Mr. Cody, otherwise and universally known as Buffalo Bill. Bill, this is the Grand Duke."

"I am glad to know you," said the hero of the Plains.[3]

Cody described Alexis as "a large, fine-looking young man," and newspaper reporters present found the prince "a fine democratic fellow," "a live one," and "a jovial lively body." A Cincinnati reporter throws some light on the extent of Cody's reputation in saying, "Buffalo Bill is a famous Western scout, employed by Sheridan for Indian service, and one who is efficient and reliable. Bill is about 30 years of age [he was twenty-five], is over six feet in height, and with other proportions. . . . Bill was dressed in a buckskin coat, trimmed with fur, and wore a black slouch hat, his long hair hanging in ringlets over his shoulders."[4]

At few times could the United States Army have produced a greater array of brass and gold braid to greet a distinguished visitor. The Civil War produced as many generals as World War II, with a smaller population and a much smaller army, while brevet ranks permitted them uniforms far beyond their actual assignments. Of greatest interest was Brevet Major General George A. Custer, only four years from his doom on the Little Big Horn. The one with the highest actual rank except Sheridan, the only lieutenant general in the army, was the department commander, Brigadier General E. O. C. Ord, of course also a brevet major general. There were three brevet brigadier generals, Innis N. Palmer, in actual rank colonel of the Second Cavalry; George A. Forsyth, known as

[3] Unidentified clipping dated North Platte, January 13, in a collection kept by Mrs. George A. Custer, with notes by her, Custer Battlefield Museum (hereafter cited as Mrs. Custer, clippings).

[4] Mrs. Custer, clippings, from *Cincinnati Daily*—(rest of name cut off), Camp Alexis, January 14.

"Sandy," the hero of Beecher's Island; and James William Forsyth, known as "Tony." Both Forsyths were lieutenant colonels on Sheridan's staff.

These generals had quite an army to command, for that period. The escort included two companies of infantry, two companies of cavalry, and the regimental band of the Second Cavalry. Cody conservatively estimated the entire hunting party at five hundred persons.[5]

The party moved immediately to the camp at Red Willow. That night the Indians put on the war dance Bill had arranged for, to the great admiration of the visitors. Cody says Alexis paid much attention to a handsome redskin maiden and that General Custer carried on a mild flirtation with one of Spotted Tail's daughters—Custer in his own writings is so open in describing his interest in Indian girls that the "mild" may be accepted as literal. Mention is also made of Cody's prowess as a yarn spinner. A *New York Herald* headline referred to "Buffalo Bill as Guide, Tutor, and Entertaining Agent."[6]

In his role as tutor Bill was questioned closely by the Grand Duke about buffalo-hunting methods, whether gun or pistol was used, and whether a trained horse was needed. He was assured that he would have Cody's celebrated buffalo horse, Buckskin Joe, and was told that he could use either weapon. In gun lore a curious legend had gained currency to the effect that Alexis so admired a Smith and Wesson .44-caliber revolver that Buffalo Bill carried that he persuaded the Russian Army to adopt it. Actually Alexis while in the East had visited the Smith and Wesson factory, which was already making its Russian model, and was presented with one of the revolvers, inlaid with gold and pearl with the arms of Russia and the United States engraved on it.[7]

The first hunt started at nine o'clock next morning, and after a herd was sighted, every effort was made to give the royal visitor the first shot. He needed several. He had decided on a revolver,

[5] Cody, "Hunting Parties"; "H. V. B.," "Corks Popped and Buffalo Fell When the West Feted Royal Guest," in *Kansas City Star*, June 8, 1939.

[6] *New York Herald*, January 16, 1872; notes by Mrs. Custer also mention Cody's prowess as storyteller.

[7] Herschel C. Logan, "Royal Buffalo Hunt," *The American Rifleman*, Vol. C, No. 10 (October, 1952), 37–42.

and, says Bill: "He fired six shots from this weapon at buffaloes only twenty feet away from him, but as he shot wildly, not one of his shots took effect. Riding up to his side and seeing that his weapon was empty, I exchanged pistols with him. He again fired six shots without dropping a buffalo. Seeing that the animals were bound to make their escape without his killing one of them, unless he had a better weapon, I rode up to him, gave him my old reliable 'Lucretia' and told him to urge his horse close to the buffaloes, and I would give him the word when to shoot. At the same time I gave old Buckskin Joe a blow with my whip, and with a few jumps the horse carried the Grand Duke to within about ten feet of a big buffalo bull.

" 'Now is your time,' said I. He fired and down went the buffalo. The Grand Duke stopped his horse, dropped his gun on the ground, and commenced waving his hat." Another member of the party adds that he "cut off the tail as a souvenir, and then, sitting down on the carcass, waved the dripping trophy and let go a series of howls and gurgles like the death song of all the foghorns and calliopes ever born." "Very soon the corks began to fly from the champagne bottles," Bill reports, "in honor of the Grand Duke Alexis, who had killed the first buffalo."[8]

Some newspapermen reported that Cody actually killed the buffalo for Alexis, Bill informs us, and the slander has been repeated since. The Grand Duke was mounted on Bill's Buckskin Joe, one of the best-trained buffalo horses on the plains; the Grand Duke was using Bill's rifle, and his hand was virtually held by Buffalo Bill while he shot, but there seems little reason to doubt that Alexis pulled the trigger. Cody assures us that "the way I have related the affair is the correct version." He also says that the Grand Duke killed eight buffalo during the five-day hunt. He got the second the same day when a small band rushed past at a distance of thirty yards. Alexis raised his pistol and fired, killing a buffalo cow. Thirty yards is still a good revolver range and Bill comments that it surprised the Grand Duke as well as everybody else. Another celebration was in order, and Bill observes, "I was in hopes that he would kill five or six more buffaloes before we

[8] Cody, *Life*, 301–305; James Albert Hadley, "A Royal Buffalo Hunt," *Transactions of the KSHS*, X (1907–1908), 578.

reached camp, especially if a basket of champagne was to be opened every time he dropped one."

The last day of this Wild West exhibition was given over to the Indians, Spotted Tail's Sioux demonstrating their methods of hunting buffalo. They surrounded a herd, and Alexis saw Two Lance, celebrated for this exploit, shoot an arrow entirely through a buffalo. Another Indian, with a lance ten feet long, its steel head a foot long, and the shaft possibly three inches in diameter, was seen "singling out a gigantic bison and thrusting his spearhead, while both raced at full speed, straight into the creature's heart. . . . Considerable skill was necessary to apply the momentum of the horse in just the right way to send the stroke home, it being necessary for the hunter instantly to let go the lance or be pulled from his steed."[9]

Buffalo Bill was showman to the end of the Grand Duke's visit. As the party was returning to the railroad, Alexis and General Sheridan rode in what Cody describes as "a heavy double-seated open carriage, or rather an Irish dogcart, and it was drawn by four spirited cavalry horses" not too much used to harness. The Grand Duke expressed admiration for the driving of Bill Reed, an Overland stagecoach driver who had brought the party to camp. When the General remarked that Cody was also a stagecoach driver, Alexis wanted a demonstration, and Bill took the reins. With Sheridan egging him on, Buffalo Bill let out the horses more than he had intended. There were no brakes on the carriage, and when they began descending a hill, he could not hold the horses in, so there was nothing to do but let them go. "Every once in awhile the hind wheels would strike a rut and take a bound, and not touch the ground again for fifteen or twenty feet," says Bill, who believed he made six miles in about three minutes.

When they parted Alexis gave Cody valuable presents—a purse of gold and a diamond stickpin, says one account; a Russian fur coat and jeweled cuff links and studs, says another. The family still has the cuff links. The presents were the least valuable return Buffalo Bill received for this famous exhibition. He had put on his first Wild West show, and he had made newspaper headlines. The account of the first day's hunt in the *Kansas City Times* read:

[9] Cody, "Hunting Parties," 141; Cody, *Life,* 304–305.

AT IT
Alexis on the Untamed Bison's
Native Heath
He Is Introduced to Buffalo Bill and
Follows His Lead

Another said, "General Sheridan and 'Buffalo Bill' Lead the Way."[10]

The Grand Duke went on to Denver, then returned with General Custer by way of Louisville to New Orleans, where he was met by a Russian warship. Cody's part in the royal entertainment was completed at North Platte, so much to Sheridan's satisfaction that both he and Ord urged Cody to apply for a commission. Bill perhaps recognized his educational deficiencies; besides, as scout at one hundred dollars a month, he was close to a lieutenant's pay.

Bennett and the other buffalo hunters had invited Cody to visit New York, and Sheridan told him he would never have a better opportunity. With only two companies at Fort McPherson, it was unlikely there would be an Indian expedition until the arrival of the Third Cavalry, which was exchanging stations with the Fifth. Cody was given a leave of absence with pay, for he remained on the pay roll of Lieutenant Hayes until March 31, 1872, when he was transferred to that of Lieutenant J. C. Thompson of the Third Cavalry.[11]

General Stager sent Cody railroad passes—in those days only unimportant people paid railroad fare—and Bennett sent five hundred dollars for expenses. Bill arrived in Chicago in February, and his buffalo-hunting friends took him to a ball in Riverside, where he found it more difficult "to face the throng of beautiful ladies than it would have been to confront a hundred hostile Indians. This was my first trip East, and I had not yet become accustomed to being stared at." Buffalo Bill in a dress suit was something to stare at. On the train to New York, he met Professor Henry A. Ward of Rochester, for whom he had collected animal specimens. Professor Ward took Bill to Niagara Falls and then to Rochester— Bill's first view of a city he was to make his home for a time.

---

[10] *Kansas City Times,* January 14, 1872; Mrs. Custer, clippings, unidentified article.

[11] Post Records, Fort McPherson, O.Q.M. 1939; Cody, *Life,* 306.

It was Bill who needed a scout and guide in New York City, for there he got off the trail. He was met at the station by J. G. Hecksher and guided to the Union Club, where Bennett, Leonard Jerome, and other buffalo hunters had arranged a dinner and informal reception. After dinner Cody persuaded Hecksher to put him on the trail of Ned Buntline, whom they found at the Brevoort Place Hotel. Both Ned and the hotel proprietors, Overton and Blair, insisted on Cody's becoming their guest, and he agreed to divide his time between them and his friends at the Union Club. This plan did not please Bennett, especially when Bill became so confused by many invitations that he forgot to attend a dinner given in his honor by Bennett. He was forgiven, however, and managed not to forget a dinner given by August Belmont. He also attended the Liederkranz masked ball, where in buckskin garb he "took part in the dancing, and exhibited some of my backwoods steps, which, although not as graceful as some, were a great deal more emphatic."[12]

It has been intimated that Ned Buntline had something to do with inviting Cody to New York, on the assumption that the dramatization of *Buffalo Bill: The King of Border Men* was about to have its *première*. Of course this is incorrect, for General Davies had seen the play before the 1871 buffalo hunt. Obviously Ned Buntline had been in and out of too many riots and jails to have been an intimate of any of Bill's hosts. Moreover, Ned was living at the Brevoort with his fourth wife, Anna, whom he had married the previous October 3, much distressing his third wife, Kate, who did not get around to divorcing him until the following November 27. His second wife, Lovanche, was less troublesome and agreed to forget the whole thing for a cash settlement. But in New York's better social circles in those days, three wives were regarded as excessive.[13]

External evidence suggests that Ned Buntline had exhausted his interest in Buffalo Bill until Cody blunderingly sought him out. But Ned was an opportunist and was quick to take advantage of his former hero's acclaim and popularity. The melodrama Fred G. Maeder had written from Ned's story was revived at the Bowery

---

[12] Cody, *Life,* 305–306.
[13] Monaghan, *The Great Rascal,* 8–13, 77, 231.

Theater, and on the opening night Bill from a box saw himself depicted by J. B. Studley with Mrs. W. G. Jones as leading lady. When the audience, learning that the real Buffalo Bill was present, demanded his appearance, the manager, Freleigh, persuaded Cody to face the footlights. Bill had a bad attack of stage fright.

"I made a desperate effort, and a few words escaped me, but what they were I could not for the life of me tell," says Cody. "My utterances were inaudible even to the leader of the orchestra, Mr. Dean, who was sitting only a few feet in front of me. Bowing to the audience, I beat a hasty retreat. . . . That evening Mr. Freleigh offered to give me five hundred dollars a week to play the part of 'Buffalo Bill' myself. . . . I told him it would be useless for me to attempt anything of the kind, for I never could talk to a crowd of people like that, even if it was to save my neck, and that he might as well try to make an actor out of a government mule." This story gets pretty tall, in view of the fact that he changed his mind completely within a few months.[14]

When General Sheridan came by, Bill told him, "I had struck the best camp I had ever seen," and asked for ten more days to enjoy it. Sheridan granted the request, but urged Cody then to hurry back to Fort McPherson, as the Third Cavalry would be needing him. Cody took advantage of the extension to visit relatives in West Chester, Pennsylvania, near Philadelphia. Oddly enough, Ned Buntline accompanied him on this domestic expedition. Bill met his uncle, Brevet Brigadier General Henry R. Guss; a cousin, Lizzie Guss; and "an elderly lady who was my grandmother, as he informed me." She was not; she was his mother's stepmother. There was a complicated double relationship. Bill's mother, Mary Laycock, was the daughter of Hannah Taylor, who died in 1830, and Samuel Laycock, who died at sea after marrying a second time. The stepmother, whom Bill met, had married the father of General Guss. General Guss had married his stepmother's stepdaughter, who was Eliza Laycock, sister of Bill's mother, and consequently his aunt. She had died before Bill visited West Chester and the General had married again.

Ned Buntline took Bill to the Chestnut Street Theatre to see the play *Peril; or, On the Beach at Long Branch* at the invitation

[14] Cody, *Life*, 310–11.

of its author, B. T. Campbell. The next night the pair visited the Commandery Degree of the Patriotic Order of Sons of America, which probably was the main objective of Ned's trip, as he was professional organizer of that fraternal order. He had other angles, too. For once he actually appears as Buffalo Bill's press agent, for the *Philadelphia Public Record* of February 16 contained an interview with Cody on the Grand Duke Alexis' hunt and recorded the visit of "a young man who has obtained considerable celebrity as a daring hunter and an Indian fighter on the plains."

Said the reporter: "From the wild cognomen, 'Buffalo Bill,' it has been the impression of many persons that he was a sort of semi-barbarian, or a regular border ruffian. On the contrary Mr. Cody is a fine specimen of a well-bred, bright-minded western pioneer. In fine, one of a class of men to whom the country owes much in its occidental developments. He is thirty years old [it was his twenty-sixth birthday], rather slim and wiry, and over six feet high. He wears a mustache and goatee, and allows the hair of his head to hang in ringlets over his shoulders."

Cody's eastern sojourn was near its end, and Ned Buntline scarcely waited until he was out of town before setting pen to paper to produce his second Buffalo Bill dime novel, taking advantage of the widespread publicity given Cody in connection with the Grand Duke's hunt and Cody's subsequent trip east. *Buffalo Bill's Best Shot; or, The Heart of Spotted Tail* started serially in the *New York Weekly* on March 25, 1872. The timely subject may have been sparked by the *Public Record* interview, for the reporter made much of the fact that Spotted Tail and his Indians could not believe that the Grand Duke was the son of another "great father" living across the waters. Ned followed this account almost immediately with another, *Buffalo Bill's Last Victory; or, Dove Eye, the Lodge Queen*, which ran from July 8 to October 14.

The name of Buffalo Bill also appeared for the first time in a bound book this year, for W. E. Webb's *Buffalo Land* was published in 1872. It was a tome of 503 pages, with many illustrations, including portraits of Buffalo Bill and Wild Bill. While its title page calls it "an authentic narrative of the adventures and misadventures of a late scientific and sporting party" and its "Professor Paleozoic" suggests O. M. Marsh, events of 1868 and 1869 are mixed in with those of 1870, perhaps to be purposely confusing. However, Webb pays high tribute to Buffalo Bill: "Cody is spare and wiry in figure, admirably versed in plain lore, and altogether the best guide I ever saw. The mysterious plain is a book that he knows by heart. He crossed it twice as a teamster, while a mere boy, and has spent the greater part of his life on it since. He led us over its surface on starless nights, when the shadow of the blackness above hid our horses and the earth, and though many a time with no trail to follow and on the very mid-ocean of the expanse, he never made a failure." And, of course, Webb did not miss the fact that "Cody had all the frontiersman's fondness for practical jokes."[15]

None of this added fame for Cody was lost on Ned Buntline, who was inspired by his own dime novel, *Buffalo Bill's Last Victory*, to hatch a new idea that any press agent would term colossal. Meanwhile Buffalo Bill returned to the plains for another "last victory."

[15] Pages 149, 161, 194–95.

The Grand Duke Alexis

Buffalo Bill on the show lot

THE MEDAL OF HONOR

IN HIS LAST AUTOBIOGRAPHY Buffalo Bill tells a tall tale of a dash across the country to join an Indian expedition. Telegraphic orders from Sheridan arrived while he was at one of Bennett's dinners. Cody left next morning—but then delayed his dash twenty-four hours longer to go fox hunting with his West Chester relatives and to make his tall tale a little taller. "I was familiar neither with the horse, the saddle, the hounds, nor fox-hunting, and was extremely nervous," says Bill. He rode sedately with his uncle until they came to a tavern. "I went in and nerved myself with a stiff drink, also I had a bottle filled with liquid courage, which I took along with me," Bill explains. "Just by way of making a second fiasco impossible, I took three more drinks while I was at the bar, then I galloped away and soon overtook the hunters." Taking stone walls and hedges with the master of the hounds, he was in at the death.

Frank Thompson of the Pennsylvania Railroad lent Cody a private car to speed him to Chicago. There further orders were to proceed immediately to Fort McPherson, as the expedition .ras waiting for him. At Omaha he had only time to be entertained between trains by friends who insisted on seeing Buffalo Bill in a dress suit. He was still wearing it when they put him aboard a train, filling his stateroom with champagne but forgetting his trunk, left behind at the Hotel Paxton. When he arrived at Fort

McPherson, the expedition had moved out, leaving Buffalo Chips White behind to guide Cody. There was nothing for Cody to do but to mount Buckskin Joe in evening dress, with his long hair tucked up in his stovepipe hat, and in this attire he reported in the field to his new commanding officer, Brevet Major General J. J. Reynolds, colonel of the Third Cavalry.[1]

At this time there was no such expedition requiring his services, and the entire story of his leisurely dash across country is probably a build-up for his appearance at Fort McPherson in full dress because he had forgotten his trunk at a drinking party. He was fully capable of that, as well as of telling the tallest of tall tales on himself.

In his first autobiography, Cody told a sober story of his first Indian expedition of 1872, giving himself much less credit than was expressed by his commanding officer. "Shortly after my return," he says, "a small party of Indians made a raid on McPherson Station, about five miles from the fort, killing two or three men and running off quite a large number of horses." Company B, Third Cavalry, under Captain Charles Meinhold and First Lieutenant Joseph Lawson, was sent in pursuit.

Meinhold, a German immigrant, had joined the organization as private in 1851 when it was the Regiment of Mounted Riflemen, guarding western trails. Ten years later he was sergeant-major, and at the outbreak of the Civil War he was commissioned first lieutenant in Kit Carson's New Mexico Volunteers. He gave that commission up to take a second lieutenancy in his old regiment, renamed the Third Cavalry, got two brevets in the Vicksburg campaign, and at the end of the war held the permanent rank of captain. Lawson was a Civil War veteran of the Eleventh Kentucky Cavalry. Texas Jack Omohundro was also a scout on this expedition.

After two days on the trail, Company B reached the South Fork of the Loup River, Nebraska, on April 26, 1872. There the Indians had scattered. The troop encamped while Cody with a detachment of six men commanded by Sergeant Foley scouted the area. Cody discovered an Indian camp and horses grazing not

[1] Cody, *Autobiography*, 245–49.

186

more than a mile away. Says Captain Meinhold's official report: "Mr. Cody had guided Sergeant Foley's party with such skill that he approached the Indian camp within fifty yards before he was noticed. The Indians fired immediately upon Mr. Cody and Sergeant Foley. Mr. Cody killed one Indian; two others ran toward the main command and were killed."

Cody says that the Indians went for their horses across a creek, and that he, on Buckskin Joe, followed, but the cavalry horses refused to jump. The troopers dismounted and crossed to Bill's aid. Two mounted warriors fired at him. He returned the fire and saw one Indian tumble from his horse. Cody pursued the other, rode alongside, and shot him through the head. As the troop arrived, the Indians fled.

"While this was going on," says the official report, "Mr. Cody discovered a party of six mounted Indians and two led horses running at full speed at a distance of about two miles down the river. I at once sent Lieutenant Lawson with Mr. Cody and fifteen men in pursuit. He, in the beginning of the chase, gained a little upon them, so that they were compelled to abandon the two led horses, which were captured, but after running more than twelve miles at full speed, our jaded horses gave out and the Indians made good their escape."

Captain Meinhold concludes, "Mr. William Cody's reputation for bravery and skill as a guide is so well established that I need not say anything else but that he acted in his usual manner."[2] On the basis of this report, "Mr. Cody" was awarded the Medal of Honor on May 22, 1872; and because he was "Mr. Cody" and for no other reason, his name was stricken from the rolls under an act of Congress of June 16, 1916, "on the ground that at the time of the act of gallantry he was neither an officer nor an enlisted man, being at that time a civilian." The Medal of Honor was the only medal awarded at this period, but Cody seemed to consider this fight as of no great consequence. His account slips in saying six Indians were killed instead of the three of the official report, but,

[2] Post Records, Ft. McPherson, Meinhold's report, April 27, 1872; The Adjutant General's Office to Rep. Thomas F. Ford, May 16, 1939 (A.G. 201 Cody, William F. [5–11–39] ORD); Cody, *Life*, 313–15.

most surprisingly, he speaks of receiving a scalp wound, apparently confusing this fight with the one in 1869 in which General Carr vividly recalled Bill's scalp wound.

Cody disposed of the rest of the year's scouting in a paragraph: "I made several other scouts during the summer with different officers of the Third Cavalry, one being with Major Alick Moore, a good officer, with whom I was out for thirty days. Another long one was with Major Curtis, with whom I followed some Indians from the South Platte river to Fort Randall on the Missouri river in Dakota, on which trip the command ran out of rations and for fifteen days subsisted entirely on the game we killed."

Alick Moore is Alexander Moore, captain in the Third Cavalry since December 15, 1870, who won his brevet as major at Gettysburg. Curtis got his brevet as major for Shiloh and Atlanta. An official report gives some detail on his expedition:

"Agreeably to Special Orders No. 90, Headquarters, Fort McPherson, Neb., Captain James Curtis, Second Lieutenant Edgar L. Steven and 50 enlisted men of Company 'I' 3rd Cavalry left post June 5, 1872, to resume the pursuit of a party of Indians who had stolen horses from the vicinity of McPherson Station in April last. Acting Assistant Surgeon A. L. Flint, Scout William F. Cody, and Guide Clifford accompanied the expedition." A further record shows that Company I returned July 21 after a march of 496 miles.[3]

A record in the medical history of the post was of more personal interest to Cody. The post surgeon on August 15, 1872, noted: "3 P.M. Mrs. Cody, wife of Mr. William Cody, Post guide and interpreter, delivered of a daughter." This was Orra Maude, their third child.

That fall the Earl of Dunraven returned for a six weeks' hunting trip with three friends. They were escorted by a detachment under Brevet Lieutenant Colonel Anson Mills, captain, Third Cavalry, with Cody as guide. Before they were ready to return, a party of General Sheridan's friends arrived, and, of course, they had to have Buffalo Bill as guide. Cody turned over his duties with the Earl's party to Texas Jack, remarking, "The Earl seemed to be somewhat offended at this and I don't think he has ever forgiven

[3] Post Records, Ft. McPherson, Record of Events, June, July, 1872; Cody, *Life*, 315.

me for 'going back on him.' "[4] However, Texas Jack made good
and was employed by the Earl again in 1874.

Texas Jack was John Burwell Omohundro, Jr., born near Pal-
myra, Virginia, on July 26, 1846, just five months younger than
Cody. His first Civil War service was as civilian mounted orderly
for Major General John Buchanan Floyd. Jack enlisted as private
in Company G, Fifth Virginia Cavalry, on February 15, 1864, four
days before Cody joined the Seventh Kansas. Jack's regiment was
in Brigadier General Lunsford L. Lomax's brigade in Major General Fitzhugh Lee's division of Lieutenant General J. E. B. Stuart's
Cavalry Corps. Jack was courier and scout during the Shenandoah
Valley campaigns. Joel Chandler Harris, of "Uncle Remus" fame,
made Texas Jack a master spy in a series of stories called *On the
Wing of Occasions*. After the war Jack started for Texas, but a
leaky ship grounded him in Florida, where he taught school. His
link with Texas is vague, but he was in at least one expedition
against Indians there, for he rescued a boy whose parents had
been killed. Not knowing his own name, the boy took that of Texas
Jack, Jr., and made it famous in a Wild West show that once
employed Will Rogers. Omohundro came north on a trail drive,
may have been at the signing of the Medicine Lodge treaty, knew
California Joe and Wild Bill at Fort Hays, and was employed as
scout at Fort McPherson and also by the Indian Service in 1872
to accompany the Pawnees on a buffalo hunt.[5]

While Texas Jack was guiding the Earl, Buffalo Bill returned
to the Chicago party, one of whom, Milligan of the firm of Heath
and Milligan, proved a lifesaver for actor Cody a few months later.
Milligan is described as "a regular velocipede," which meant the
life of the party. He was eager for an Indian fight until Cody
spotted a band of about thirty Indians. Then Milligan decided it
was not one of his fighting days and that he had urgent business
in camp. This was not one of Bill's jokes on a tenderfoot, however,
as Captain Gerald Russell, commander of the escort, ordered a
pursuit, which proved fruitless. Also on this hunt were E. P. Green,

[4] Anson Mills, *My Story*, 153; the Earl of Dunraven, *The Great Divide;* Cody, *Life*, 316.

[5] Logan, *Buckskin and Satin;* Albert Johannsen, *The House of Beadle and Adams*, II, 217; Buel, *Heroes of the Plains*, 543.

son-in-law of Philo Remington, the rifle manufacturer, and Alexander Semple.

On another hunt with United States District Attorney Neville, in stovepipe hat and swallow-tail coat, Judge Dundy, and Colonel Watson B. Smith, Cody records, "I lariated, or roped, a big buffalo bull and tied him to a tree—a feat which I had often performed, and which the gentlemen requested me to do on this occasion for their benefit."

It is frequently mentioned that Cody was also a justice of the peace during this period, but a couple of tall stories constitute all that has been told of his activities. One concerns a writ of replevin for a missing horse. Cody did not understand the legal term, but found his rifle, Lucretia Borgia, an acceptable substitute. More famous is a tale of his being called upon to perform a marriage ceremony. He could not find the words of the ceremony, so recited what he could remember, winding up with "whomsoever God and Buffalo Bill have joined together, let no man put asunder." These yarns were cover-up for a more serious side of the office. Cody was recommended for it by General Emory. In those days the army had little weight beyond the limits of a military reservation, and usually just beyond those limits there grew up a community of sharpers devoted to separating the soldier from his pay and not averse to dealing in stolen government property. Since local authorities often were sympathetic to fellow citizens who stole from the government, there was advantage to the army in having a justice of the peace who was army connected and at the same time had civilian status making him eligible for the position.[6]

Apparently Cody was a successful public official, for some of his friends at a convention in Grand Island secured his nomination as Democratic candidate to represent the Twenty-sixth District in the legislature of Nebraska. As the district was predominantly Republican, Cody had no hope of being elected and made no campaign. But the name of Buffalo Bill was potent, and the returns showed his election by forty-four votes. Cody was proud of this victory. "That is the way in which I acquired my title of Honorable," he said in his first autobiography, and he frequently used that title until it was superseded by an honorary title of

[6] Cody, *Life*, 276–78, 316–18.

colonel. However, in 1872 the Honorable William F. Cody had important business elsewhere and failed to show up at the capitol to claim his seat.

Meanwhile a contest had been filed on behalf of his opponent, charging that the returns, as filed, were incomplete. The Twenty-sixth District consisted of seven counties and an unorganized territory attached to Harlan County, with the board of canvassers sitting in Lincoln County. Six counties reported properly returns showing that Cody had carried four counties by a vote of 407 to 363. The county clerk of Harlan County, to which the unorganized territory was attached, had blundered. Instead of sending his returns to the board in Lincoln County, he had sent them to the city of Lincoln, the state capital. This vote was 169 to 83 against Cody. The House Committee on Privileges and Elections on January 14, 1873, declared that there was no contest before the committee in view of the fact that nothing had been heard from Cody, and that despite the fact that the votes had been improperly returned, they should be counted, thus giving D. P. Ashburn Cody's seat by a majority of 42.

H. C. Green, who had filed the contest, said that he had served written notice on Cody stating his grounds. Cody probably accepted Green's figures as correct and went on about his business.[7]

[7] House Journal of the General Assembly of the State of Nebraska, Ninth Regular Session, 1873, pp. 74–75; *Omaha Daily Bee*, January 16, 1873; *Beatrice* (Neb.) *Express*, October 31, 1872; Louis A. Holmes, "William F. Cody and the Nebraska Legislature," in *The Westerners Brand Book* (Chicago), Vol. XIV, No. 12 (February, 1958), 90–91; Cody, *Life*, 319.

"THE SCOUTS OF THE PRAIRIE"

DURING THE SUMMER AND FALL of 1872, says Cody, he received a
number of letters from Ned Buntline urging him to go on the stage
to represent himself. When Bill recalled his stage fright at the
Bowery Theatre, Ned assured him that he could overcome his shy-
ness. Ned was right. Officers of the post, including General Reynolds, distrusted the dime novelist, and urged Cody to stay where
he was well off. But Ned's magic words, "There's money in it,"
persuaded Bill to give it a try, for he had much of the speculative
nature of his father, always ready to pioneer in new fields.[1]

Lulu was ready for a trip home to St. Louis, and Bill admits
that was a factor in getting him started. At Omaha, however, where
he was entertained as a newly elected legislator, it was said that
he was on his way to Washington and would be back for the opening of the session. This report may have stemmed from General
Sheridan's offer of a horse-buying assignment if Bill got stranded.
Ned Buntline also hedged by coming to Chicago prepared to become a fire-insurance agent. Texas Jack was eager to try the stage,
and helped to persuade Bill. Cody was paid off as scout on November 30, and arrived in Chicago on December 12. Ned was cha-
grined that Bill and Jack had not brought along the Indians advertised in that day's *Chicago Evening Journal*. The advertisement

[1] Cody, *Life*, 320–21.

announced the appearance at Nixon's Amphitheatre on Monday, December 18, of "The real Buffalo Bill, Texas Jack and ten Sioux and Pawnee chiefs in Ned Buntline's great drama *Buffalo Bill.*" The hiring of ten Sioux and Pawnees was not practicable even had the scouts stood ready to feed and transport them.[2]

Ned's advertising the play as *Buffalo Bill* lends some credence to Cody's story that Ned had not yet written the play, and when Nixon canceled his contract, Ned went to a hotel, employed all its clerks as copyists, and produced the play in four hours. The clew to this tall tale, which everyone wants to believe, is the name of the drama's heroine, "Dove Eye." Available were the installments of *Buffalo Bill's Last Victory; or, Dove Eye, the Lodge Queen,* and it may not have taken more than four hours to turn Ned's *New York Weekly* serial into a melodrama. Its new title was announced in the *Chicago Evening Journal* on December 17. Headed in boldface, "Ned Buntline—Col. E. Z. C. Judson," its more modest type announced, "The real heroes of the Plains, Buffalo Bill and Texas Jack in a great sensation drama entitled, *The Scouts of the Prairie,* written expressly for them by Ned Buntline. Morlacchi as Dove Eye. Matinees Wednesday and Saturday—Every lady visiting the matinees will be presented with portraits of the boys."

Cody's propensity to poke fun at himself somewhat obscures what happened on the opening night. His tall tale has generally been repeated without question. He says:

> Buntline, who was taking the part of "Cale Durg" appeared, and gave me the "cue" to speak "my little piece," but for the life of me I could not remember a single word. Buntline saw I was "stuck," and a happy thought occurred to him. He said—as if it were in the play:
> "Where have you been, Bill? What has kept you so long?"
> Just then my eye happened to fall on Mr. Milligan, who was surrounded by his friends, the newspaper reporters, and several

[2] *Omaha Herald,* quoted in unidentified newspaper dated December 12, 1872; Monaghan, *The Great Rascal,* 19–20; Monaghan, "The Stage Career of Buffalo Bill," *Journal of the Illinois State Historical Society,* Vol. XXXI, No. 4 (December, 1938), 411–14; Lloyd Lewis, "An Idol Is Born," *Chicago Daily News,* December 9, 1935; *Chicago Evening Journal,* December 12, 1872 (Monday was December 16, not 18).

military officers, all of whom had heard of his hunt and "Indian
fight"—he being a very popular man, and widely known in Chicago. So I said:

"I have been out on a hunt with Milligan."

This proved to be a big hit. The audience cheered and ap-
plauded; which gave me greater confidence in my ability to get
through the performance all right. Buntline, who is a very versatile man, saw that it would be a good plan to follow this up,
and he said:

"Well, Bill, tell us about the hunt."

I thereupon proceeded to relate in detail the particulars of the
affair. I succeeded in making it rather funny, and I was frequently
interrupted with rounds of applause. Whenever I began to "weak-
en," Buntline would give me a fresh start by asking some question. In this way I took up fifteen minutes, without once speaking
a word of my part; nor did I speak a word of it during the whole
evening. The prompter, who was standing between the wings,
attempted to prompt me, but it did no good; for while I was on
the stage I "chipped in" anything I thought of.[3]

Having implied that there was no play, Cody proceeds to describe it. The parts of the ten Sioux and Pawnee chiefs were taken
by actors found walking the streets of the Blue Island Avenue
neighborhood in Chicago. They were costumed in tan-colored
frocks and cambric pantalets. "We would kill them all off in one
act," says Bill, "But they would come up again ready for business
in the next. Finally the curtain dropped; the play was ended; and
I congratulated Jack and myself on having made such a brilliant
and successful debut. There was no backing out after that."

What the play was supposed to be like may be reconstructed
from a synopsis appearing in a New York program later in the
season:

Act I. On the Plains—Trapper and the Scouts. The Renegade's
Camp—Peril of Hazel Eye. Ned Buntline's Temperance Lecture.
Cale Durg at the Torture Post, The Indian Dance—The Rescue.

Act II. Texas Jack and his Lasso. The Loves of Buffalo Bill.
The Death of Cale Durg. The Trapper's last Shot.

Act III. The Scout's Oath of Vengeance. The Scalp Dance—

[3] Cody, Life, 326–27.

The Knife Fight. The Triumph of the Scouts. The Prairie on Fire.[4]

"The papers gave us a better send-off than I expected," says Cody, "for they did not criticize us as actors."

Such was the case in the *Evening Journal,* which said: "Nixon's Amphitheatre was last night the scene of a most extraordinary character and one in which the audience bore quite as prominent a feature as did the occupants of the stage. The occasion was the first appearance of Ned Buntline's play with the blood-curdling and hair-raising title of *The Scouts of the Prairie; or Red Deviltry As It Is,* being a descriptive affair of life on the plains and in the mountains of the West, and in which the noted characters 'Buffalo Bill' and 'Texas Jack' in their own original selves were presented, as well as 'Ned Buntline' the author of the play. Last night not less than 2,500 boys and young men crowded the amphitheatre to catch a glimpse of their heroes. Mlle. Morlacchi, the Italian danseuse, essayed the part of the Indian maiden Dove Eye with great success, . . . largely sustained the dramatic interest from first to last and was an interesting connecting link in the chain of events."

The *Journal* critic did his best for the one professional in the cast, Mlle Morlacchi, whose part was summed up by the *Tribune* critic as that of "a beautiful Indian maiden with an Italian accent and a weakness for scouts." He was more accurate than he knew, for within a few months she became the wife of Texas Jack. Giuseppina Morlacchi, born in Milan in 1846, studied dance at La Scala, and made her debut at the Carlo Felice Theatre in Genoa in 1856. She appeared in Naples, Florence, Turin, London, and Lisbon before coming to America in 1867 under the management of John DePol. DePol invented a press-agentry device in insuring her legs for $100,000 before her appearance in *The Devil's Auction* at Banvard's Museum in New York. In Boston in the same play on December 23, 1867, she introduced the cancan to America. The

[4] A. Johannsen, *The House of Beadle and Adams,* II, 173; W. F. Cody, "The Great West That Was," *Hearst's International* (May, 1917), 377; Logan, *Buckskin and Satin,* 71–73; program in Buffalo Bill Memorial Museum, Lookout Mountain, Colorado.

cancan was thereafter her trademark as she appeared in *Lurline, Seven Dwarfs, The French Spy,* and *The Wizard Skiff.*[5]

Cale Durg was an alias that Judson, *alias* Ned Buntline, had invented the previous month for a recital at Stamford, New York, his occasional home. This feature was summed up by the *Tribune*: "Buntline delivered some opinions on the use of liquor which he said was injurious and had done a great deal of harm." Cody quotes the *Inter-Ocean* as regretting that Cale Durg had not been killed in the first act—before the temperance speech—instead of in the second, and the *Times* as saying that if Ned Buntline had actually spent four hours in writing that play, it was difficult to see what he had been doing all that time. No one has been able to find that statement in the *Times*. The *Times* did say this: "On the whole it is not probable that Chicago will ever look upon the like again. Such a combination of incongruous drama, execrable acting, renowned performers, mixed audience, intolerable stench, scalping, blood and thunder, is not likely to be vouchsafed to a city for a second time—even Chicago."[6]

No critic was ever more wrong than that. With a reported $2,800 in the till for the first night, Buffalo Bill himself was to bring something almost as bad to Chicago every year for a decade, and from that day to this something very like *The Scouts of the Prairie* was to meet similar condemnation from successive generations of Chicago stage, motion picture, radio, and television critics. The *Times* reporter had witnessed the birth of the Western. It is not surprising that he did not recognize it, for neither did its creator, Ned Buntline. Buffalo Bill, knowing less about the stage, just possibly did.

Ned Buntline brought no novelty to the stage in the atrociousness of his play or the lack of talent of its actors. Within a week or two the *Times* critic could see Charlotte Cushman in *Macbeth, Henry VIII,* and *Meg Merrilies,* but drama of that caliber was as much the exception in the theater then as it is on television near

[5] *Chicago Evening Journal,* December 17, 1872; Monaghan, *The Great Rascal,* 20–22, and "The Stage Career of Buffalo Bill," *Journal of the Illinois State Historical Society,* Vol. XXXI, No. 4 (December, 1938), 416; Logan, *Buckskin and Satin,* 101–18.

[6] Cody, *Life,* 327–28; A. Johannsen, *The House of Beadle and Adams,* II, 57, 173.

nine decades later. In presenting a mass-entertainment play dealing with the contemporary West, Ned Buntline followed the lead of Civil War dramatists who brought out *New Orleans; or, The Crescent City Is Ours, The Battle of Manassas, McCulloch's Raid,* and *The Fall of Atlanta* within a few days of the events they celebrated. It seems doubtful that these were less execrable than *The Scouts of the Prairies.* The appearance of contemporary heroes Buffalo Bill and Texas Jack followed such precedents as the casting of William Tillman, who escaped from a Confederate privateer, and Miss Major Pauline Cushman, Union spy and scout.[7]

Buffalo Bill won no laurels as actor, but from the first night he proved his showmanship, and his development into one of the world's greatest showmen divorced Ned Buntline's Western from the topical, the contemporary, and eventually from the historical, into a peculiar category of its own beyond space and time. That is Cody's contribution to American legend and tradition.

After a benefit for Buffalo Bill and Texas Jack on Friday night and a benefit for Ned Buntline on Saturday night, marked by the first appearance of Señorita Eloe Carfano as "Hazel Eye"—not to be confused with "Dove Eye," played by Morlacchi—the troupe moved to St. Louis. Mrs. Cody attended the opening at DeBar's Opera House on December 23; and Bill, spotting her in the third row, leaned over the footlights to yell, "Oh, Mamma, I'm a bad actor," to the delight of the audience. Bill was quick to take advantage of this break, and went on, "Honest, Mamma, does this look as awful out there as it feels up here?" The crowd was with him and shouted for Louisa to get on the stage, and he urged her on: "You can't be any worse scared than I am. Come on up." When her stage fright was only too apparent, he went on, "Now you can understand how hard your poor old husband [he was twenty-six!] has to work to make a living."[8]

The Chicago *Evening Journal* of December 27, 1872, recorded: "Ned Buntline of the Buffalo Bill troupe was arrested at St. Louis yesterday for having participated in a riot there twenty years ago." This is the complete article, buried in a column headed "News

[7] O. G. and Lenyth Brockett, "Civil War Theater: Contemporary Treatments," *Civil War History,* Vol. I, No. 3 (September, 1955).
[8] *Chicago Evening Journal,* December 21, 1872; Mrs. Cody, *Memories,* 249–50.

Items." Publicity came hard in those days, but note it is "the Buffalo Bill troupe." That would not have pleased Ned Buntline. He had jumped bail after the anti-German riot he had instigated as organizer of the American, or "Know-Nothing," party. Again he was able to arrange bail, and the show went on. Presumably he jumped bail again.

When *The Scouts of the Prairie* opened in Pike's Opera House, Cincinnati, on December 30, the *Daily Gazette* critic caught the idea that Ned Buntline's Western was something new, saying, "The play is beyond all precedent in the annals of stage lore. . . . It has in it all the thrilling romance, treachery, love, revenge, and hate of a dozen of the richest dime novels ever written. . . . The play bids fair to have a most wonderful run, for its novelty is so striking, and its subject is such a popular one with so many readers of thrilling border tales, that the temptation to see the real actors in those tragedies can not be resisted."

This tie-up between dime novel and stage, a large element in the success of Buffalo Bill, is an idea for which Ned Buntline deserves full credit. That year he wrote, or instigated, *Texas Jack; or, Buffalo Bill's Brother* for *DeWitt's Ten Cent Romances,* and kept his troupe before the public in a *New York Weekly* serial, *Texas Jack, the White King of the Pawnees,* beginning on March 24, 1873.

The troupe moved eastward, through Rochester and Buffalo. A week in Boston, opening March 3, 1873, grossed $16,200. An idea looking toward the Wild West show might be gleaned from the endorsement of the *Boston Traveler:* "The Indian mode of warfare, their hideous dances, the method they adopt to 'raise the hair' of their antagonists, following the trail, etc., or in the way their enemies deal with them, manner of throwing the lasso, &c., are forcibly exhibited, and this portion of the entertainment alone is worth the price of admission." The *Boston Transcript* agreed that "Those who delight in sensations of the most exciting order will not fail to see the distinguished visitors from the western plains before they leave"; and the Boston *Journal* opined, "The play of itself is an extraordinary production with more wild Indians, scalping knives and gun powder to the square inch than any drama ever before heard of."

Somewhere along the line the ten Blue Island Indians of the Chicago opening had been replaced by twenty—one playbill makes it twenty-five—presumably real Indians. Authenticity seemed assured by the parts of the Pawnee chiefs: Ar-fi-a-ka, played by Grassy Chief; As-ge-tes, by Prairie Dog; As-sin-an-wa, by Water Chief; Te-co-tig-pown, by Big Elk; Kit-kot-tons, by Great River; and Chuk-kak, by Seven Stars, although other Indian parts were played by Joseph J. Winter and George B. Beach.

As was then the custom, the drama was preceded by a farce or skit. Boston saw "a Beautiful Terpsichorean Comedietta, written by Colonel Judson, to introduce the Graceful MORLACCHI in Four Exquisite Dances, entitled *Love's Battle! Or, Fairy Transformations.*" A New York performance commenced with the roaring farce, *A Kiss in the Dark,* and another with "an entirely new farce, written expressly for this occasion by Ned Buntline, entitled, *The Broken Bank; or, A Rough Corner in New York.* As Cody had remarked, Ned Buntline was a very versatile man.

New York's leadership as a dramatic center was not as exclusive in 1873 as it became since, but success there was important. Competing with *The Scouts of the Prairie* were Joseph Jefferson in *Rip Van Winkle;* Lawrence Barrett, a friend of General Custer, in *Julius Caesar,* and E. A. Sothern in *Lord Dundreary*, a play in which his famous son, E. H. Sothern, later starred. New York critics who attended the opening in Niblo's Garden were possibly a shade less kind than those in Chicago. Bennett's *Herald* might be expected to favor Cody, but Bennett had a long-standing feud with Ned Buntline, whose part was described as being represented "as badly as is possible for any human being to represent it. . . . Ned Buntline is simply maundering imbecility. Ludicrous beyond the power of description is Ned Buntline's temperance address in the forest." As for Buffalo Bill, he "is a good-looking fellow, tall and straight as an arrow, but ridiculous as an actor. Texas Jack is not quite so good-looking, not so tall, not so straight, and not so ridiculous." The *Herald* critic summed it up: "Everything is so wonderfully bad it is almost good," and he may have had something there!

The *World* critic had another idea: "As an exhibition of three remarkable men it is not without interest. The Hon. W. F. Cody enters into the spectacle with a curious grace and a certain characteristic charm that pleases the beholders. He is a remarkably handsome fellow on the stage, and the lithe, springy step, the round uncultured voice, and the utter absence of anything like stage art, won for him the good-will of an audience which was disposed to laugh at all that was intended to be pathetic and serious." The *Times* came closest in explaining Buffalo Bill's success in his exhibiting "a surprising degree of aplomb, notable ease of gestures and delivery, and vocal power quite sufficient readily to fill a large theatre. . . . His use of the revolver and rifle indicate extensive practice, and were vastly relished by the audience. . . . It is only just to say that the representation was attended by torrents of what seemed thoroughly spontaneous applause; and that whatever faults close criticism may detect, there is a certain flavor of realism and of nationality about the play well calculated to gratify a general audience."

The New York Times critic's "flavor of realism and nationality" came closest to the idea Buffalo Bill would capitalize on. In 1873 such words as regionalism, folklore, and legend, were almost unknown as applied to the United States; yet newspapermen groped toward something beyond the tawdry melodrama's unmitigated bloodshed. After two weeks in New York, March 31 to April 13, the troupe moved on to the Arch Street Theatre in Philadelphia. On April 21, the critic of *The Age* noted that Buffalo Bill "looks able and willing to do many of the deeds in earnest which are represented on the stage." The *Richmond Whig*, on May 12, hailed "the best thing in the sensational way that has ever visited us. . . . all who miss seeing and hearing this company will have to regret having missed one of the most striking and stirring dramas of the age, performed by men who have gone through in stern reality what they simulate on the stage." The *Richmond Enquirer* agreed, but less enthusiastically: "Were it not . . . that they represent in a measure real scenes of which they have been the actual heroes, and having bonafide Indians on the stage, the performance would be tame and unprofitable indeed."[9]

The season closed at Port Jervis, New York, on June 16, 1873.

[9] Logan, *Buckskin and Satin*, 79–85; Monaghan, *The Great Rascal*, 26–29; Walsh, *The Making of Buffalo Bill*, 181–82.

Cody was disappointed that he had cleared only $6,000 instead of the fortune he had expected, but there is no hint that he ever contemplated abandoning this new way of life he had adopted, he says, so reluctantly. He had learned much. In his Milligan story on his first night, in his asides to Lulu at St. Louis, he discovered a rare faculty of projecting his personality to his audience. Never again would he fear the crowd. If he could not be actor, he could be showman. He was more successful than the play he was in.

Both he and Texas Jack had gained confidence in themselves, and they decided to dispense with Ned Buntline. No one knows why. Ned was full of great plans; to play *The Scouts on the Prairie* on horseback under canvas, which might have led a little sooner to Buffalo Bill's Wild West; to take the show to London; to open early in August for a long season. Perhaps much of this was talk, and the scouts had been exposed to a lot of it. Ned Buntline must have been difficult to live with, although a view of upstate New York neighbors is expressed as, "For all Ned's derelictions, he seems to have been a person one couldn't hate; he was utterly irresponsible but not mean or vicious." If the break was violent, "calling each other names not fit to print," as has been stated, neither Cody nor Buntline ever gave a hint of it.[10]

Ned wrote a new play, based on another 1872 dime novel, *Dashing Charlie, the Texas Whirlwind,* and produced it with Dashing Charlie in person and Arizona Frank as the heroes, backed by a troupe of Comanches or Modocs. The formula, without Buffalo Bill, failed to work, and Ned retired from drama permanently. Says his biographer, "The Buffalo Bill incident never loomed as large in his life as the subsequent fame of Cody made it appear." Little in the Buffalo Bill legend has been more exaggerated. Their brief association was over in June, 1873, except for Ned Buntline's fourth, and last, Buffalo Bill dime novel in 1885, *Buffalo Bill's First Trail; or, Will Cody, the Pony Express Rider.* The contribution of these to Cody's fame may be gauged by the fact that Ned wrote half as many about the long-forgotten Texas Jack—Ned's second on that hero, *Texas Jack's Chums; or, The Whirlwind of the West,* was published in 1883.

[10] Hochschild, *Township 34,* 145; Leon Mead, "Ned Buntline," *Dime Novel Round-Up,* Vol. IX, No. 101 (January, 1941).

Ned Buntline capitalized on Buffalo Bill's reputation much more than he contributed to it. He wrote the first Buffalo Bill dime novel, but failed to make it either contemporary or western. He brought Buffalo Bill to the stage, but failed to understand the value of Cody's showmanship. Ned's translation of dime novel to melodrama suggested a publicity device that served Cody well, but Ned failed to see its possibilities. His greatest failure, however, was in not discovering the Western; after pointing the way, he turned his back on it. Because of his notoriety he came to typify the dime-novel writer in his own day and since. It is commonly assumed that he wrote hundreds about the West. Bibliographers have listed not more than twenty-five or thirty western titles.[11]

Ned's departure left the company's publicity in the capable hands of Major John M. Burke, whose contribution to the Buffalo Bill legend also has been greatly exaggerated. Burke, born in Washington, D. C., had been a stock company actor, manager of a tent-show dramatic troupe, and newspaper editor. He came to *The Scouts of the Prairie* as manager of Mlle Morlacchi. His hand may be seen in favorable notice for the dancer in reviews of the first season. Whether he bestirred himself as actively at this time for Buffalo Bill is doubtful. He served as advertising manager and was promoted to general manager of the new combination.

Burke devoted thirty-four years of his life to the exploitation of Cody, from the beginning to the end of Buffalo Bill's Wild West, and the Major liked to project that loyalty backward to the beginning of Buffalo Bill's stage career. He was there, but his first loyalty then was to Morlacchi. When Buffalo Bill and Texas Jack came to a parting of the ways, Burke went with Jack—and Jack's wife, Morlacchi.

"Press agent," "publicity director," and "public relations" were terms as yet unheard, and Major Burke always held some other position, although these departments were under his direction. In addition to managerial, advertising, and publicity chores, he often was an actor. In associating with the scouts, he wore his hair long and became "Arizona John," although it is doubtful that he had ever been west of the Missouri before he met Bill and Jack in Chicago. In his writing he was a master of the adjective to the exclu-

[11] Monaghan, *The Great Rascal*, 29, 256, 321–33

sion of other parts of speech, and he seldom constructed an intelligible sentence, although he so entangled flowers and figures of speech that the lack of a mere verb was unnoticeable. However, he was at his best in getting someone else to do the writing—and make it favorable to Buffalo Bill. A good storyteller, jovial and friendly, he was welcome in every newspaper office, and almost without seeming to, he always got what he was after. He was one of the founders of the art of press-agentry, and to him goes much of the credit for making the name of Buffalo Bill a household word. It is also possible that the subsequent deterioration in the reputation of Buffalo Bill is due to Burke's exaggerations, his inconsistencies, his flagrant misquotations, and his lazy carelessness.

"THE SCOUTS OF THE PLAINS"

A NEW MODE OF LIFE now began for Cody. From fall to spring each year he toured theaters, usually with a new melodrama each season that was much the same as the one he had played the preceding season. During most of his decade on the stage, his productions were advertised as the "Buffalo Bill Combination." A combination was a traveling theatrical troupe organized primarily to present one play, although at least one other play was usually held in reserve for emergencies. Thus a combination was distinguished from a stock company, which offered a repertory of frequently changing plays and might remain indefinitely at the same theater. The Buffalo Bill Combination usually disbanded in late May or June, and often was an entirely new organization the next fall. Cody spent most of his summers guiding hunting parties or returning to his old occupation as scout. This kept alive the tradition that he was still the plainsman he depicted—and he was. On several occasions his summer experiences gave him material for a new play.

In the summer of 1873, Texas Jack and Buffalo Bill took a New York party to Fort McPherson for a hunt in western Nebraska. The hunters were Elisha P. Green, who had been on the hunting party with Milligan that served Cody so well in his stage debut, Eugene Overton, and a Mr. Scott, hatter of Chicago. However, the scouts spent little time on the plains. Their season closed late, and preparing for a new one without Ned Buntline's aid was a serious undertaking.

Cody had moved his family to Rochester—another indication that he had accepted his inevitable role as showman. Texas Jack was also attracted to Rochester—there on August 31, 1873, he and Giuseppina Morlacchi were married in St. Mary's Roman Catholic Church. She had been in a dancing troupe during the summer, and immediately after the ceremony they left for Buffalo, where the concluding performance of her season was scheduled.

The play selected for the new Grand Company or Combination was called *The Scouts of the Plains,* to the endless confusion of almost everyone who has ever written about it, including Cody. Newspaper billings, reviews, and contemporary programs make it clear that the first season's play by Ned Buntline was *The Scouts of the Prairie* from the beginning of the tour to its end, and that the second season's play was just as invariably *The Scouts of the Plains.* The casts of characters were quite different, except for Buffalo Bill and Texas Jack, who appeared in both as themselves. Mlle Morlacchi in *The Scouts of the Plains* played Pale Dove instead of Dove Eye, no great change to be sure, but other parts included Jim Daws, played by the "popular actor" Frank Mordaunt; and Uncle Henry Carter, a friend of the scouts, by J. V. Arlington, long associated with Buffalo Bill Combinations. Advertising guaranteed "living horses," but said nothing about "genuine Indians"; the Indians were W. A. Reid, B. Meredith, H. Mainhall, and J. W. Buck. A Comediette featuring three dances by Morlacchi and her singing of "Cavatina" from the opera *Ernani* immediately preceded the "sensational drama presented by the entire combination."[1]

The Scouts of the Plains was written by Fred G. Maeder, author of the original *Buffalo Bill, the King of Border Men,* which became an alternate play during the season of 1873–74. Maeder came from a famous theatrical family. His mother was Clara Fisher, who had been a sensation in England as a child prodigy playing

---

[1] Logan, *Buckskin and Satin,* 68–95, 111–16; Cody, *Life,* 324, 328–29. Both Mrs. Wetmore, *Last of the Great Scouts,* 205, and Cody, *Autobiography,* 257, incorrectly put Hickok in the first year's drama.

adult roles. Her arrival in the United States started a "Clara Fisher craze" that swept America and jammed box offices. She was married in 1834 to James Gaspard Maeder, an Irish composer. Their sons were Frank, who became a theatrical agent and manager, and Frederick, who was an actor and playwright.

As co-star to replace Ned Buntline, the two scouts and their manager, Hiram Robbins, invited Wild Bill Hickok to join them. Hickok had gained fame since his scouting days with Cody in 1869. That year, while carrying dispatches alone, he was jumped by Indians at Sand Creek, Colorado Territory, and was severely wounded by a lance before he escaped. He was released as scout at Fort Wallace and returned to his home in Troy Grove, Illinois, to recuperate. There he was employed by Henry Wilson, afterwards vice president of the United States, for what seems to have been the first family tour of the West with sight-seeing as its sole objective. The party returned to Hays City, Kansas, shortly after Sheriff Thomas Ganlon was killed. Wild Bill was persuaded to accept appointment as acting sheriff on August 23, 1869, and was also named city marshal. He served until January 3, 1870. There, and at Abilene, Kansas, where he was city marshal from April 15 to December 13, 1871, he made his reputation as frontier peace officer.

Descriptions by Buffalo Bill and others of Wild Bill as stage-shy and hating the theater are somewhat at variance with other facts in Hickok's career. Before and after his appearance in *The Scouts of the Plains,* Wild Bill experimented with various types of show business. After he left Hays City, he went north along the Republican River to Beaver Creek, where he captured six buffalo. He had conceived an idea that was close to Buffalo Bill's Wild West before Cody ever thought of it. Wild Bill hired a number of Comanche Indians and took his outfit to Niagara Falls, where he advertised a buffalo chase for July 20. He had a crowd estimated at five thousand, but had neglected to build a fence around his show and had to pass the hat. He did not get enough to pay expenses. To add to these troubles, a spectator turned loose a trained cinnamon bear belonging to one of the Indians, and the bear took after a vendor of baked sausages. The bear disposed of the predecessors of the hot dog, and the costs thereof disposed of the predecessors of the Wild West show.

The Scouts of the Plains opened at Williamsport, Pennsylvania, September 8. At Titusville, Pennsylvania, on November 6, a hotel owner asked the actors to stay out of the billiard room, where a crowd of drunks had boasted that they would clean out the Buffalo Bill Combination. Cody as usual was willing to avoid trouble, but Wild Bill slipped into the billiard room, laid out four or five of the drunks with a chair, and drove the rest from the hotel.

Hiram Robbins says Hickok was given a secondary part because he "had a voice like a girl." At Philadelphia a calcium light was used, and Hickok very much admired its effects on Buffalo Bill and Texas Jack. He demanded that the light be thrown on him, also, threatening to shoot the manipulator if it were not. When it was turned on him full center, Wild Bill "with his weak eyes blinded by the intense light" shouted, "Turn the blamed thing off," and spoiled the scene. This is one of several references to Hickok's having trouble with his eyes in his last years.[2]

Cody's principal complaint was that Wild Bill amused himself by shooting too close to the legs of the "supers" who played the parts of Indians, causing powder burns that interfered with their dying on the stage. This matter came to a crisis at Rochester on March 10, after Cody had asked Wild Bill especially to be on his good behavior. Hickok again powder-burned a "super." Cody told him to stop it or leave the troupe, and he walked out. Later in the evening the two men met at a hotel and settled accounts amicably. Hickok was paid off, and Buffalo Bill and Texas Jack gave him one thousand dollars as a bonus.

A reporter for the *Rochester Democrat and Chronicle* spotted Wild Bill on the street after the combination had left and stopped him for an interview. Hickok intimated that General Sheridan had recalled him for service as a scout. "He will first proceed to New York where he has some business to transact, remain there a few days and then go direct to the frontier," the interviewer reported. "He had nothing but kind words to speak of the boys, as he familiarly termed the other scouts." His business in New York probably was to sign up with another theatrical troupe, since that is what he did. The new combination was the Stevens Daniel Boone

---

[2] Hiram Robbins, interviewed in "Wild Bill's Humors," *Arkansas Traveler,* undated extract; *Titusville Morning Herald,* November 4, 1873.

Company, and when it failed to make as much money as Hickok thought it should, he quit. Its manager, who had invested in posters advertising Wild Bill, engaged an actor to play the part. Hickok demanded that this impersonation be stopped, and when his demand was ignored, went up on the stage at Binghampton and threw the bogus Wild Bill through a set of scenery and the manager over the footlights. He then stood off a riot squad of policemen, but surrendered to the smallest officer when the little man crawled through a window and told him politely that he was under arrest. Hickok was fined three dollars.[3]

Although this was Wild Bill's last appearance on any stage, he was not through with show business. He went to Cheyenne, where he spent most of his time gambling until he met a widow, Mrs. Agnes Thatcher Lake, whom he had befriended when her circus showed in Abilene. They were married in Cheyenne on March 5, 1876, and he toured with the circus as far as Cincinnati. He was lured to Deadwood by the Black Hills gold strike, and there he was shot in the back by Jack McCall and died on August 2, 1876.

Buffalo Bill and Texas Jack continued their tour, which included Lockport, Buffalo, and Erie, after the defection of Hickok at Rochester. They closed the season at Boston on May 13, 1874, and Jack left immediately for Denver to guide the Earl of Dunraven on a hunting trip. From the Earl's description—he thought at first he was seeing a comet, but on coming nearer, found it was "the diamond shirt-studs and breast-pin shining in the snowy bosom of my friend Texas Jack"—it may be deduced that the tour of *The Scouts of the Plains* was a success financially. Buffalo Bill went to New York, where Thomas P. Medley, of London, England, offered him $1,000 a month as a guide on a hunting expedition. Dr. W. F. Carver, "who then resided at North Platte, and who has recently acquired considerable notoriety as a rifle-shot, hunted with us for a few days," Cody recorded.[4]

The hunting party returned to North Platte, and Cody went

[3] Logan, *Buckskin and Satin,* 94–95; Howard C. Hosmer, "How Wild Bill Quit the Stage," in unnamed newspaper, 1958, quoting John Fennyvessy, *The First 90 Years of the Rochester Opera House,* and Amy H. Croughton's reminiscences of William Thompson.

[4] Logan, *Buckskin and Satin,* 89–95; Earl of Dunraven, *The Great Divide,* 33; Cody, *Life,* 336–37.

to Fort McPherson, where he was hired by Lieutenant P. H. Breslin of the Fourth Infantry, acting assistant quartermaster, as guide at $150 a month for the Big Horn Expedition commanded by Brevet Lieutenant Colonel Anson Mills. Buffalo Bill served in this capacity from August 7 to October 2, 1874.[5]

Colonel Mills became notable two years later for his part in the battles of the Rosebud and Slim Buttes, but is more widely remembered as the originator of the Mills web-belt equipment, still the model for army cartridge belts and pack equipment. The Big Horn expedition did not result in any fights with Indians, and thus received little attention. However, it accomplished its objective, to which end the work of Buffalo Bill was not unimportant.

Indians, presumed to be from villages on the North Fork of the Powder River, had committed murders and robberies at Fort Steele, Rawlins, and Seminole, in southern Wyoming Territory. While it was not to be expected that they would await the assembling of an expedition to pursue and punish them, it was at least hoped that the presence of troops in their area would discourage further raids. The expedition included Companies F, H, and M of the Third Cavalry, B and D of the Second Cavalry, H of the Fourth Infantry, and D of the Thirteenth Infantry; four Pawnee Indian Scouts; and "citizens: Two guides (Mr. Cody or "Buffalo Bill" and Tom Sun), six scouts, twenty packers, and thirty teamsters; one ambulance, 28 wagons, and 70 pack mules."[6]

Mills mentions White as one of the scouts, undoubtedly Buffalo Chips White, whose first name is the subject of confusion among historians. Captain Charles King calls him "James"; the Chicago newspaper correspondent, John F. Finerty, makes it "Charley, alias Frank," but the marker where he was killed at Slim Buttes reads "Jonathan White," which presumably is how he signed the pay roll. White had come to Fort McPherson to be treated at the hospital for an injured leg, but was turned down until Bill intervened and offered to pay the bill. White, who had served under General J. E. B. Stuart, proved to be a good rifle shot and an excellent horseman, and after his recovery attached himself to Cody.

Says Captain King: "For years he had been Cody's faithful

[5] O.Q.M. 1939; Cody, *Life*, 337–39.
[6] Anson Mills, *Big Horn Expedition*.

follower—half servant, half 'pardner.' He was Bill's 'Fidus Achates'; Bill was his adoration. . . . He copied Bill's dress, his gait, his carriage, his speech—everything he could copy; he let his long yellow hair fall low upon his shoulders in wistful admiration of Bill's glossy brown curls. He took more care of Bill's guns and horses than he did of his own; and so, when he finally claimed, one night at Laramie, the right to be known by some other title than simple Jim White—something descriptive, as it were, of his attachment for Cody and life-long devotion to his idol 'Buffalo Bill,' a grim quartermaster (Morton, of the Ninth Infantry) dubbed him 'Buffalo Chips,' and the name was a fixture."[7] Buffalo chips were the dried dung that was the universal fuel on the treeless plains, but was so useful and so often a lifesaver that the nickname may not have been intended to be quite as uncomplimentary as it sounds. White met his death while trying to stalk Indians entrenched in a ravine at Slim Buttes in 1876.

Cody tells that one morning near the head of Powder River, where the expedition hoped to find the hostile Indians, a solitary horseman was seen approaching. He proved to be California Joe Milner, armed with an old Sharps rifle, a revolver, and a knife. He said he was out for a morning ride; Joe had been prospecting, and was saying nothing. After he had trailed along with the expedition for two or three days, Colonel Mills suggested that he be hired as a scout. Cody says, "It was worth the money to have him along for company's sake, for he was a droll character in his way, and afforded us considerable amusement"—General Custer's opinion also. Oddly enough, California Joe also was killed in 1876; he was murdered in the Black Hills.

Colonel Mills knew that the Indians had had every opportunity to learn of his expedition by the time it was ready to move from Rawlins, but hoped they would expect him by the usual trail, by way of Fort Reno. Instead, he ascended the Big Horn Mountains, keeping within their cover until north of the supposed location of the Indian villages, so that he would be able to strike them from the rear. Little was known about the country of the Big Horns, by Cody or by anyone else, for sensible travelers had been accustomed to take an easier route. The expedition had bad

[7] *Campaigning with Crook*, 113–14.

Buffalo Bill and General Miles

viewing the hostile Indian camp near Pine Ridge Agency, S.D., January 16, 1891. At the right are Captain Frank D. Baldwin and Captain Marion P. Maus.

Courtesy National Archives

Indian war correspondents, 1890

At center rear are (l. to r.) Frank Grouard, Buffalo Bill, and (at r.) Lieut.
Charles Taylor, Ninth Cavalry. Front row (l. to r.) are unidentified man,
E. A. O'Brien, Associated Press; Edward B. Clark, *Chicago Tribune*;
Edgar F. Medary, *New York Herald*; Charles G. Seymour, *Chicago
Herald*; K. V. Zilliacus, of Helsingfors, Finland, European correspondent;
Dent H. Roberts, *St. Louis Post-Dispatch*; Alfred I. Burkholder, *New
York Herald*; John B. McDonough, *New York World*; Gilbert E. Bailey,
Chicago Inter-Ocean; Major John M. Burke, manager, Buffalo Bill's Wild
West; Charles II. Coppenharve, *Omaha Bee*.

Photograph by J. C. H. Grabill, Deadwood

luck at the start; on the first day of September a severe snow-storm started. It lasted for thirty-six hours and brought snow two feet deep. One horse died as he stood that night, and Colonel Mills attributed the loss of twenty-three horses to this one storm.

After the snow stopped falling, says Colonel Mills, "the mountains looked quite formidable to our front, so I sent, early, Cody to the southwest, who soon returned and reported a pass to a stream of water seven miles distant." Cody here was depending entirely on his sense of terrain. The expedition marched through this pass on September 5, and on the following day crossed the highest peaks on the range. On the other side was found a stream tributary to No Water Creek or No Wood Creek—whichever it was did not sound promising, and "Cody who had followed it down some seven miles, reported its direction as too much to the west of us, so we turned about, due east." After crossing several streams, "Cody and I while riding in advance with the Indians [the Pawnee Scouts] came abruptly upon a she-bear and two cubs, all of which we dispatched in less than two minutes." They then found themselves descending into a canyon which the scouts reported impassable. Tom Sun was sent to find a way out. He discovered a pass, but it led into a truly remarkable blockade—a spot that seems to be directly out of a Buffalo Bill dime novel. Going in advance with Cody, Colonel Mills used his binoculars to scan a valley into which large and well-beaten trails of animals led, ordinarily evidence of a passable route, but in this case even the animals had been fooled; there was no practicable outlet. Lieutenant Frederick Schwatka of the Third Cavalry, later famed as an Arctic explorer, this time found the way out by a steep climb.

After another day's march, the guides and scouts were sent to Pumpkin Buttes, the presumed position of the Indian villages, but all were found abandoned. Apparently the offending Indians had been gone for about six weeks. The expedition returned by way of Salt River and the lower bridge of the North Platte to Red Buttes and Horse Creek, and then back to Rawlins Station. Colonel Mills planned further scouting toward the Tongue River, but on September 25, General E. O. C. Ord, the department commander, ordered the expedition dissolved, its object having been accomplished—to be sure that the Indians had left the area.

An encounter with a bear accounts for the expedition's only casualty. On September 28, Colonel Mills records: "Marched at 10 A.M. and camped at 3 P.M. on Little Creek, distance 12 miles. During the day's march the men of Major Moore's Company encountered a bear on the muddy Creek, wounded and chased him into a clump of Willows on the creek when Private Miller dismounted and entered the willows against the remonstrance of California Joe, a scout so much spoken of by General Custer, when he was seized by the bear and horribly mangled and would have been killed had not some of the men rode in and dispatched the bear, not without firing three shots at him, however, while the bear and Miller were down struggling together. Miller died of these wounds soon after reaching his post—Fort McPherson, Nebraska. One man riding too close had several pounds torn from his horse by a stroke of the bear's paw."

In concluding his report, Colonel Mills mentioned only three of his civilian employes: "Mr. Cody (Buffalo Bill) sustained his old reputation as an excellent and invaluable guide, Mr. Sun also is a good guide, and I will recommend him for future employment should occasion require it. Mr. Parker acquitted himself well with the pack train."[8]

Cody was not discharged as guide until October 2. His acceptance of employment on an expedition leaving so late in the year indicates that he was in no hurry to organize another theatrical tour. Because Texas Jack was still hunting with the Earl of Dunraven, Buffalo Bill went it alone, again in *The Scouts of the Plains*. "Scouts" being in the plural, a substitute for Texas Jack was needed. The new scout was advertised as Kit Carson, Jr. Since no member of the immediate family of the great Kit Carson was ever in show business, this was probably the stage name of an actor hired for the occasion.[9] After completing his shortened tour, Buffalo Bill spent the summer of 1875 in his new home at Rochester, possibly the only summer of his life in which he remained quietly at home.

Texas Jack was back that fall, and the old combination was reorganized for their last season together. Morlacchi again played Pale Dove, and Major Burke was back as manager. As *The Scouts*

---

[8] Mills, *Big Horn Expedition;* Mills, *My Story,* 155.
[9] Kit Carson III to Don Russell, June 25, 1953.

of the Plains opened a two-day engagement at Springfield, Massachusetts, on April 20, 1876, Cody was handed a telegram from Colonel G. W. Torrence, of Rochester, informing him of the serious illness of the Codys' only son, five-year-old Kit Carson, or "Kitty," with scarlet fever. Bill played the first act, after which Major Burke substituted so that Bill could take a nine o'clock train. He was met at the station by Moses Kerngood, who drove Bill home. Kit died that night.[10]

[10] Cody, *Life,* 339; *Letters from Buffalo Bill,* 13.

17

THE DEATH OF YELLOW HAND

OFFICIAL RECORDS SHOW that William F. Cody took part in fourteen fights against Indians after he became chief scout of the Fifth Cavalry in 1868. Unhappily a mildly exaggerated story of the last of them appeared in his first autobiography, perhaps written to bring it into harmony with the re-enactment he presented in the following season's melodrama. Subsequently the story grew and grew until some versions of it were past belief. The resulting controversy centered so largely on this one episode that Cody's entire reputation as a scout seemed to depend on whether he did, or did not, kill Yellow Hand.

The fact is, he did. What actually happened can be reconstructed in detail, and beyond reasonable doubt, from contemporary evidence. It is notable that contemporary evidence has received little attention in most of what has been written about Buffalo Bill.

Many persons who know nothing else whatever about Buffalo Bill recognize the exploit variously termed "The Duel on the War Bonnet," "The Death of Yellow Hand," and "The First Scalp for Custer." It was not a duel. It was not on the War Bonnet. The victim's name was not Yellow Hand. Much argument has been wasted in attempts to prove that Yellow Hand, by whatever name known, did not ride between the opposing lines of troopers and Indians to challenge Buffalo Bill to single combat. He did not.

The place where he died is located on Hat Creek near present Montrose, Nebraska—Indian Creek, it was called in regimental returns, and War Bonnet Creek in some later official records. On modern maps all three names appear for separate creeks. "Hat" and "War Bonnet" are translations of the same Indian name for a creek tributary to the Cheyenne River, or Mini Pusa, but the creek now called War Bonnet is thirty to forty miles south of Hat Creek.[1]

As for the name, *Hay-o-wei* was translated "Yellow Hand" at the time by Baptiste Garnier, known as Little Bat, a Fifth Cavalry scout. The correct translation is "Yellow Hair," referring to the scalp of a white woman taken by *Hay-o-wei*, who was the son of Cut Nose, a Cheyenne chief, although the mistranslation indicates Yellow Hand's obscurity until he provided "the first scalp for Custer." A photograph and a painting of him have been produced, but it is unlikely he ever sat for either.[2]

Yellow Hand came to his death in a fight of some importance in the Sioux war of 1876, interest in which has centered almost exclusively in Custer's last fight. Custer's 1874 expedition, which discovered gold in the Black Hills, put him dramatically on the spot for his last stand on the Little Big Horn two years later. He had invaded the sacred ground of the Sioux—sacred to them only since they had chased the Kiowas out of the Black Hills a decade or two earlier. Sitting Bull and Crazy Horse, against whom the 1876 campaign was waged, had led their bands far beyond white influence and a long way from the Black Hills.

The Commissioner of Indian Affairs in his annual report for 1875 stated: "It is not probable that as many as 500 Indian warriors will ever again be mustered at one point for a fight; and with the conflicting interests of the different tribes, and the occupation of the intervening country by advancing settlements, such

[1] Charles King, "Long-distance Riding," *Cosmopolitan*, Vol. XVI, No. 1 (January, 1894), 296; Chris Madsen, "Chris Madsen Finds the Spot," *Winners of the West*, Vol. XI, No. 12 (November, 1934).

[2] *News from Home* (Home Fleet of Insurance Companies), Vol. V, No. 3; *The T. B. Walker Collection of Indian Portraits: 125 Reproductions of Paintings by Henry H. Cross* (Madison, Historical Society of Wisconsin, 1948), 137.

an event as a general Indian war can never occur in the United States." On November 9, 1875, Indian Inspector E. C. Watkins complained of the attitude of certain wild and hostile Indians, "composed of a small band of 30 or 40 lodges under Sitting Bull, who has been an out-and-out anti-agency Indian, and the bands of other chiefs and headmen under Crazy Horse, an Ogallalla Sioux, belonging formerly to the Red Cloud agency, numbering about one hundred and twenty lodges." On his recommendation, approved by the Indian Commissioner and the Secretary of the Interior, it was ordered "that these Indians be informed that they must remove to a reservation before the 31st of January, 1876, and that in the event of their refusal to come in by the time specified, they would be turned over to the War Department for punishment."

By the time this order got out to the Indian country it seemed to mean something else, for many other bands of Sioux were off reservations; it was not practicable for them to pick up and move in midwinter; but apparently they thought the order applied to them, whereupon their trend was toward Sitting Bull, not toward the reservations. The result was the Indian war that the commissioner was so sure would never occur, and his estimate of the number who could be mustered at one point for a fight was exceeded some 1,000 per cent. Yet "up to this moment," said the General of the Army, Sherman, meaning the moment of Custer's last stand, "there was nothing official or private to justify an officer to expect that any detachment could encounter more than 500, or at the maximum, 800, hostile warriors."[3]

Shortly after the expiration of the time limit, the division commander, Sheridan, issued orders for action. When Brevet Major General Alfred H. Terry, brigadier general commanding the Department of Dakota, received them on February 10, the Seventh Cavalry was scattered at several posts. Heavy snow and severe cold delayed its assembly. General Custer, scheduled to command the column in his brevet rank as major general, was summoned to Washington to testify in a Congressional investigation of the War Department. Custer's willingness to talk displeased Presi-

[3] *Annual Report of the Commissioner of Indian Affairs*, 1874, p. 4–5; *ibid.*, 1875, p. 4; *Annual Report of the Secretary of War*, 1876, p. 30.

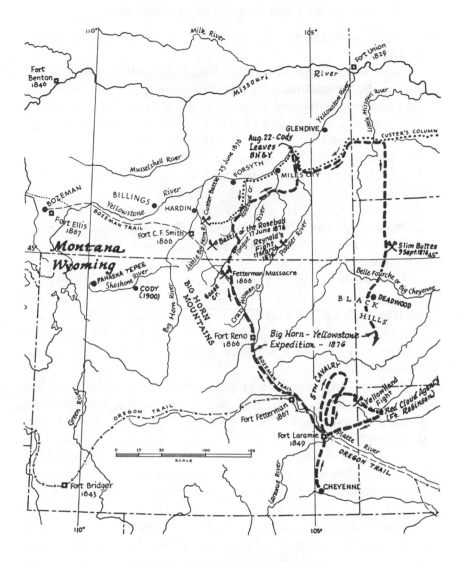

ROUTES OF FIFTH CAVALRY AND
BIG HORN AND YELLOWSTONE EXPEDITION
IN THE SIOUX WAR OF 1876

dent Grant, with the result that Custer nearly missed the year's campaign.

Brevet Major General George Crook, brigadier general commanding the Department of the Platte, acted more promptly. Cody's former commander, General Reynolds, with five companies of the Second Cavalry, five of the Third, two of the Fourth Infantry, and a pack train left Fort Fetterman on March 1. On March 17 the cavalry struck a camp on Powder River assumed to be that of Crazy Horse but possibly that of Two Moon's Cheyennes. The camp was captured and burned, but Reynolds, under fire from Indians in the hills, "left so precipitously," in the words of General Crook, "that our wounded men were left to fall into the hands of the Indians." Reynolds was tried by court-martial and suspended from command for a year.

At the western end of Terry's department, Brevet Major General John Gibbon, colonel of the Seventh Infantry, assembled the "Montana Column" at Fort Ellis and was on his way by April 1. When he reached the mouth of the Big Horn, he was halted with the news that Crook's column had withdrawn and Terry's had never started.

Action on larger scale was planned for summer. Custer got free of his Washington entanglements only on condition that his command be confined to that of his actual rank of lieutenant colonel. General Terry took charge in person, leaving Fort Abraham Lincoln, near Bismarck, on May 17 with twelve companies of the Seventh Cavalry, three of infantry, and a platoon of Gatling guns. General Crook set forth on May 29 with fifteen companies of cavalry and five of infantry.

In the same month, eight companies of the Fifth Cavalry, which had returned from Arizona Territory and the Apache wars, were ordered to Cheyenne and Fort Laramie to scout between the columns of Crook and Terry. Early in June its battalion was assembled—Headquarters and Companies A, B, D, and K from Fort Hays; C and G from Camp Supply and I from Fort Gibson, Indian Territory; and M from Fort Lyon, Colorado.

Thus four commands were in the field in a typical Sheridan containing movement, designed to keep the Indians south of the Missouri River, north of the Niobrara, and away from frontier settlements. As no one had any idea that all the Indians would be found at one spot, on the Little Big Horn, no converging movement of the columns was planned. Sheridan's report on the campaign makes that quite clear in saying, "General Terry further was informed that the operations of himself and General Crook would be made without concert, as the Indian villages are movable and no objective point could be fixed upon, but that, if they should come to any understanding about concerted movements, there would be no objection at division headquarters." Actually the Indians were not assembled at any such objective point when this order was issued. Indians depended on day-to-day hunting for food, and a gathering of thousands would exhaust the game of any region in a few days. The assembly of the Sioux and their allies lasted just long enough to annihilate Custer.

Crook struck the fringes of the gathering concentration one week before Custer did. His battle of the Rosebud on June 17 beat off the Indian attack, driving the Sioux northward as contemplated in Sheridan's plan. From that point of view it was regarded as a victory. Crook had seriously wounded men to care for; his supplies of food and, more important, ammunition were used up; therefore, he fell back to Goose Creek to reorganize.

Colonel Anson Mills, who had reported Cody an "excellent and invaluable guide," wrote several letters during the spring of 1876 urging Cody to join Crook's command. That there were several letters indicates that Buffalo Bill could not drop everything when duty called him to the plains. He had obligations to his theatrical combination. Even the death of his son Kit did not immediately affect his decision, for the show went on for six weeks after that. However, he closed his season unusually early, and seven days after his benefit performance in Wilmington, Delaware, he was again on a quartermaster's pay roll as scout on June 10, 1876, in Cheyenne.[4]

When Cody told his audience that he was through with play-acting and was off to the Indian wars, presumably it was in response to the letters of Colonel Mills. However, when Cody reached Chicago, he learned that the Fifth Cavalry was in the field and

[4] O.Q.M. 1939; Cody, *Life*, 340; King, *Campaigning with Crook*, 112; Wilmington *Every Evening*, May 27, 1876; Wilmington *Morning Herald*, June 3, 1876; *Delaware Gazette*, June 8, 1876.

that General Carr had written to Sheridan's headquarters to learn of Cody's whereabouts. It was no doubt pointed out to Cody that he could not immediately join Crook's column, then on its march to the Rosebud, but that he could find his old regiment by taking a train for Cheyenne.

He was met at the station by Lieutenant Charles King, with whom he went to the near-by camp, where he was welcomed with cheers. Brown, an enlisted man, wrote, "At noon on the 9th W. F. Cody (Buffalo Bill) joined the command as scout and guide. There is very little change in his appearance since I saw him last in '69, except that he looks a little worn, probably caused by his vocation in the East not agreeing with him. All the old boys in the regiment upon seeing General Carr and Cody together, exchanged confidences, and expressed themselves to the effect that with such a leader and scout they could get away with all the Sitting Bulls and Crazy Horses, in the Sioux tribe."[5]

On June 11, the day after Cody signed the pay roll, the battalion left for Fort Laramie. General Sheridan arrived there on June 14 with Brevet Major General James Barnett Fry, colonel and assistant adjutant general, and General Forsyth, and Cody accompanied them to Red Cloud Agency.[6] Thus he missed the Fifth's first move in the campaign, as it went northward on June 22 to seek the trail used by Indians leaving Red Cloud and Spotted Tail agencies to join the hostiles. The trail was found crossing the valley of the South Cheyenne, or Mini Pusa, and the Fifth stayed there to watch it. Meanwhile, Crook fought his Rosebud battle on June 17, Terry and Gibbon joined forces on June 21, and on June 25 came Custer's disaster—all unknown along the Mini Pusa.

On July 1, Brevet Major General Wesley Merritt succeeded General Emory as colonel of the Fifth Cavalry, taking command the same day. This was possible because Merritt was already in the field as inspecting quartermaster of the department. His advancement in the army had paralleled that of Custer. Both became brigadier generals of volunteers at the same time, just before Gettysburg; both had commanded cavalry divisions in the Civil War under Sheridan.

[5] *Ellis County Star*, Hays City, Kansas, June 29, 1876, p. 4.
[6] Cody, *Life*, 341; he spells it "Frye."

Cody accompanied the new colonel to his command. Merritt wasted no time. At dawn next day he marched the battalion closer to the trail, sending two companies to scout the surrounding country. On July 3, Company K was called from breakfast to head off Indians coming up the valley. As its captain, Julius W. Mason, and Lieutenant King led the troop through timber and out upon the sandy surface of a dry stream bed, the first man they saw was Buffalo Bill, waving his hat and pointing the way. As they galloped up the stream bed and on to grassy slopes, two or three scouts on a ridge ahead, signaled them to swing left. Company I was close behind and to the left. "As we near the ridge and prepare to deploy, excitement is subdued," King records, "Buffalo Bill plunging along beside us on a strawberry roan, sixteen hands high, gets a trifle of a lead, but we are tearing up the crest in a compact body, reach it, rein up, amazed and disgusted—not an Indian to be seen for two miles across the intervening swale." But scouts beckon again, and the troops turn toward the Cheyenne. After a thirty-mile chase the Indians are sighted from a high ridge, miles ahead and streaking it for the Powder River country. A few shots had been exchanged, so the unsuccessful chase goes in the battle record of the Fifth Cavalry as the fight "near the south branch of the Cheyenne River, Wyo." It also is credited with compelling the Cheyennes to abandon supplies they were taking to the enemy.

Such as it was, Cody had a prominent part in it, but more important, it led directly to his most publicized exploit. As it had given away the presence of the troops to the Indians, Colonel Merritt felt that further patrol of the Mini Pusa crossing was useless. The following morning he sent Major John J. Upham with three companies northwestward up the Mini Pusa, with orders to make a wide swing southward and rejoin the command at the head of Sage Creek. General Carr with three companies went eastward toward the Black Hills with similar orders. The two companies that had worn out their horses in the chase were sent southward along the valley of Old Woman's Fork directly to the rendezvous. None of the detachments found any Indians. They reassembled at Sage Creek while a courier was sent to Fort Laramie.

King tells of the news brought back on July 7: "A party of junior officers were returning from a refreshing bath in a deep pool in the stream, when Buffalo Bill came hurriedly towards them from the general's tent. His handsome face wore a look of deep trouble, and he brought us to a halt in stunned, awe-stricken silence with the announcement, 'Custer and five companies of the Seventh wiped out of existence. It's no rumor—General Merritt's got the official dispatch.'" It had taken twelve days for the news to reach this column engaged in the same campaign.

On July 11 the Fifth Cavalry was ordered to join Crook's command. For two days it marched toward Fort Laramie. At reveille on July 14 came a report from the commander at Camp Robinson that one thousand Cheyennes were planning to bolt from near-by Red Cloud Agency. The objective of all movements of the Fifth Cavalry had been to prevent such an occurrence. Within one day of Fort Laramie, Merritt turned back eastward to the Rawhide Creek crossing of the trail between Fort Laramie and Camp Robinson. From there Company C was sent to the agency, and with it rode Major Thaddeus Harlan Stanton of the Pay Department.

Major Stanton, later paymaster general of the army, was Sheridan's personal representative in the field and his substitute for an intelligence department. Stanton had been with Reynolds in March and had advised the early moves of the Fifth Cavalry. At noon Saturday Stanton reported, endorsing the Camp Robinson commander's estimate of the situation. Within an hour seven companies of the Fifth Cavalry started the first of several "lightning marches" with which Merritt added to the regiment's fame. For acting to stop the Cheyennes, he was commended by General Sheridan; for delaying the march of the Big Horn and Yellowstone Expedition for a week, he was blamed by General Crook.

The objective was to get ahead of the Cheyennes and capture or drive them back. As King explained it, he must "march over three sides of a square while they were traversing the fourth, and must do it undiscovered." The first move was to backtrack the trail by which they had just come, so that any Indians watching them would assume they were headed westward. At Rawhide Creek, fourteen miles, the horses were watered, then a turn was made to the northwest. At sunset they reached the Niobrara. At 10:00 P.M. they unsaddled at the Running Water near the Cardinal's Chair, thirty-five miles. At midnight Captain W. P. Hall arrived with the wagon train. At 3:00 A.M. the troopers were turned out for bacon and coffee, then started a fifty-mile Sunday march. At 10:15 A.M. they halted for lunch at the head of Sage Creek, where infantry was on guard. Here Captain Hall left his heavy supply wagons, taking only the company wagons with three days' rations. Two companies of infantry were picked up at Sage Creek, and rode in the wagons to guard them. The wagons camped that night at Beaver Dam. After a halt at noon the cavalry slowed to four and one-half miles an hour, to avoid raising dust that might be seen by the Indians. Halts were few and brief. At sunset scouts reported the trail in view, with no Indians in sight. By 9:00 P.M. the troopers were unsaddled along Hat Creek, not at all concerned whether that was its proper name, for they had marched eighty-five miles in thirty-one hours to attain this objective.[7]

All were soon asleep except Captain Mason's Company K, detailed for guard and picket. Its Lieutenant King commanded an outpost toward the southeast, from which direction the Cheyennes were expected. On a butte not far from King's position was a trooper of Company A, Chris Madsen, ready to send messages with signal torch or flag to Merritt's headquarters. Madsen, a recent Danish immigrant, was a veteran of the Danish-Prussian and Franco-Prussian wars and had served with the French Foreign Legion in Algeria. In later years he was one of the "Three Guardsmen" of peace officers in Oklahoma Territory, the others being Bill Tilghman and Heck Thomas, concerned with the Daltons, Bill Doolin, Al Jennings, and other desperadoes.[8]

At first light on the morning of July 17, Cody, who had been reconnoitering, came to Madsen's post and told the signalman to notify the command that the Cheyennes, camped not far away after a leisurely twenty-eight-mile march from Red Cloud Agency, were preparing to move. However, Cody did not wait, but rode on to the camp and delivered his message to Merritt personally

---

[7] Gen. Charles King and Brig. Gen. W. C. Brown, *Map, Big Horn and Yellowstone Expedition of 1876; King, Campaigning with Crook*, 9–24; Price, *With the Fifth Cavalry*, 158–95.

[8] Harold L. Mueller and Chris Madsen "Four Score Years a Fighter," *The Farmer Stockman*, Vol. LIV, Nos. 9–24, Vol. LV, Nos. 1–4 (May 1, 1941, to February 15, 1942); Homer Croy, *Trigger Marshal: The Story of Chris Madsen; Daily Oklahoman*, November 4, 1934; *Guthrie Daily Leader*, January 10, 14, 1944.

before the signalman at that end had completed receiving the message. At the same time King sent word that Indians were coming over a ridge to the southeast. He and Corporal Wilkinson were observing from a conical hilltop, while four men of the outpost held the horses in a ravine to the rear. Merritt, Carr, and two or three staff officers joined King at the lookout station. By 5:00 A.M. Indians were in view across a front of three miles, moving slowly and making no effort to conceal themselves from the direction in which the troops were located, but peering over ridges toward the west and dodging behind slopes that hid them from that direction. This puzzling behavior was understood at 5:30 when the white tops of Hall's wagons came into view. As infantry was hidden in the wagons, no fear was felt for the safety of the train.

"Have the men had coffee?" asked General Merritt.[9] "Yes, sir," reported the adjutant, Lieutenant William C. Forbush. "Then let them saddle up and close in mass under the bluffs," was Merritt's order. Carr left to oversee its execution.

Cody, with Scouts Tait and Buffalo Chips White, had come to the hilltop, from which Cody noticed thirty or forty Indians scurrying about excitedly. The observers soon saw why. Two horsemen were riding ahead of the wagon train. They were Troopers Harry Anderson and Gordon W. Keith of Company C. Their company, detached on July 14 to patrol the crossing of the Fort Laramie and Red Cloud trails on Running Water, had started two days later to follow the battalion. It was to report this movement to Merritt that Anderson and Keith were sent ahead of the command. A small group of Cheyennes started for these couriers.[10]

"By Jove! General," said Cody, sliding down the hill toward his horse, "now's our chance. Let our party mount here out of sight, and we'll cut those fellows off."[11]

"All of you keep out of sight," Merritt ordered. "Mount now,

---

[9] "His exact words"—note by King on MS of "My Friend, Buffalo Bill" (as told to Don Russell), *The Cavalry Journal*, Vol. XLI, No. 173 (September–October, 1932); King, *Campaigning with Crook*, 29.

[10] Frederick Post, sergeant, Co. C, in 1876, in a letter to Charles King, May 2, 1929, identified Keith and Anderson; names verified on Muster Roll, Co. C, 5th Cav., June 30–Aug. 31, 1876, Old Army Branch, National Archives, by Victor Gondos, Jr.

[11] King, *Campaigning with Crook*, 34–35; *New York Herald*, July 23, 1876.

and when the word is given, off with you. Watch them, King. Give the word when you are ready."

Cody, first to see the opportunity and to suggest the action, was given the honor of leading the party, which included Scouts Tait and White, and five or six troopers of Company K.[12] King, alone on the hill, watched the approach of seven Indians through binoculars. Out of sight behind the slope crouched Merritt, Forbush, and Second Lieutenant J. Hayden Pardee of the Twenty-third Infantry, acting aide-de-camp. Near by were Sergeant Schreiber and Corporal Wilkinson of the outpost.

King, in later years a novelist, appreciated the drama of the scene: "Savage warfare was never more beautiful than in you. On you come, your swift, agile ponies springing down the winding ravine, the rising sun gleaming on your trailing war bonnets, on silver armlets, necklace, gorget; on brilliant painted shield and beaded legging; on naked body and fearless face, stained most vivid vermilion. On you come, lance and rifle, pennon and feather glistening in the rare morning light, swaying in the wild grace of your peerless horsemanship; nearer, till I mark the very ornament on your leader's shield. And on, too, all unsuspecting, come your helpless prey. I hold vengeance in my hand, but not yet to let it go. Five seconds too soon, and you can wheel about and escape us; one second too late, and my blue-coated couriers are dead men."[13]

The less poetic Madsen saw "just a plain Indian riding a calico or paint pony." Yet when King described the scene to me half a century later, the color and drama were still there.

As the Indians dashed by the front of the hill, King shouted: "Now, lads, in with you."[14]

Merritt and the rest sprang to the hilltop to see the action, but both parties were already out of sight in broken country. A shot was heard, then another. While all looked toward the sound, Corporal Wilkinson glanced to the front to see a mounted Indian stop, also curious. Asking permission of Merritt, Wilkinson fired. The Indian dropped behind his pony, and almost immediately a shot whistled by the General's ear. King was sure the Indian fired from

---

[12] King, *Campaigning with Crook*, makes it five; *New York Herald*, six.
[13] King, *Campaigning with Crook*, 36.
[14] *Ibid.*, 37; *New York Herald*, July 23, 1876; the words are the same.

under the horse's neck, but Wilkinson thought he killed the Indian, and at one time claimed that this Indian was Yellow Hand, though not too seriously.[15]

As these shots were fired, Cheyennes were seen all along the ridge, and King shouted, "Here they come by the dozens." Merritt ordered, "Send up the first company," and the watchers on the hilltop rushed for their horses.

Madsen, however, was still on signal duty. Here is what he saw: "Cody was riding a little in advance of his party and one of the Indians was preceding his group. I was standing on the butte where I had been stationed. It was some little distance from the place where they met but I had an unobstructed view of all that happened. Through the powerful telescope furnished by the Signal Department the men did not appear to be more than 50 feet from me. From the manner in which both parties acted it was certain that both were surprised. Cody and the leading Indian appeared to be the only ones who did not become excited. The instant they were face to face their guns fired. It seemed almost like one shot. There was no conversation, no preliminary agreement, as has been stated erroneously in some novels written by romantic scribes.

"They met by accident and fired the moment they faced each other. Cody's bullet went through the Indian's leg and killed his pinto pony. The Indian's bullet went wild. Cody's horse stepped into a prairie dog hole and stumbled but was up in a moment. Cody jumped clear of his mount. Kneeling, he took deliberate aim and fired the second shot. An instant before Cody fired the second shot, the Indian fired at him but missed. Cody's bullet went through the Indian's head and ended the battle. Cody went over to the fallen Indian and neatly removed his scalp while the other soldiers gave chase to the Indian's companions. There is no doubt about it, Buffalo Bill scalped this Indian, who, it turned out, was a Cheyenne sub-chief called Yellow Hair."[16]

Madsen's blow-by-blow story of the fight as he saw it is in almost

[15] *New York Herald, ibid.*, King, "My Friend, Buffalo Bill," *The Cavalry Journal*, Vol. XLI, No. 173 (September–October, 1932), 19.

[16] Chris Madsen, "Comments on King's *Campaigning with Crook*," MS, 1937; Madsen to Don Russell, correspondence including 5-p. MS account of fight, 1938; Mueller and Madsen, "Four Score Years a Fighter," *The Farmer-Stockman*, Vol. LIV, No. 14 (July 15, 1941).

complete harmony with testimony of other witnesses. However, he sharply disagreed with much that is in King's account and once prepared a commentary listing twenty-eight points on which he believed King to be in error. He may have been right about some of them having to do with directions and distances; King himself in mapping the route marked a section "approximate." But Madsen was definitely wrong on two important points. In connection with the first, perhaps he was only vaguely aware of some wheeled vehicle in the background, but it became fixed in his mind that it was the Black Hills stage, not the wagon train. And he ridiculed King's mention of infantry guarding the wagons. General Merritt's report proves King right on both counts, but it is even more convincing to have a witness who clarifies discrepancies by reporting the killing of Yellow Hand as he saw it from the wagon train.

We have that story, thanks to the enterprise of the editor of a Kansas weekly newspaper. It is not surprising that these dispatches have been neglected by historians since 1876, for who would guess that the *Ellis County Star* had more war correspondents in the field than the *New York Herald,* the *Chicago Times,* or the *San Francisco Call?* There were few Thursdays that summer when the *Ellis County Star* did not print a long, newsy, and informative letter from "Powers," "Brown," or "Mac." The weekly had an interest in the Indian war that will be understood by newspapermen —a local angle. The families at Fort Hays and the friends in Hays City of the men of Companies A, B, D, and K were readers of the *Star,* and its editor employed Powers and Brown to write the news for the folks at home, probably paying them in part at least with subscriptions to the newspaper, directions for forwarding which were included in some letters. When Company E left for the front at a later date, "Mac" was similarly employed.

Sergeant John Powers of Company A was in charge of the signal department of the command, and it probably was in connection with this duty that he rode with the wagon train. What he saw from the other side of the hill after Cody crossed the ridge that hid his movements from the watchers on the hilltop is recorded in a dispatch from Fort Laramie dated July 22, 1876, which was printed in the *Star* on August 3.

Powers says: "On the morning of the 17th two men of 'C' company overtook us, bearing dispatches to Col. Merritt, who was down the creek about five miles. They pushed on, but had not gone more than a mile when we saw a large body of mounted men on a ridge east of us. At first we took them to be a portion of our command, but soon discovered that they were Indians. The two companies of Infantry that were with us tumbled out of the wagons remarkably lively and took their places beside them.

"Three or four Indians started out on a run to cut off the dispatch bearers. They had not seen the command, and were not aware that we were in the vicinity; but Bill Cody and his scouts were watching them, and when he saw what they [were] up to, he thought that several more might play at the same game. He then got around the Indians and when they felt sure of the couriers, Cody raised up from behind a little hill and shot the pony of one of the redskins. Then starting after his victim he soon had him killed and his scalp off. As soon as he fired the command charged . . . and [ran] them right into Red Cloud Agency. . . .

"The Indian killed by Buffalo Bill proved to be Yellow Hand, a sub-war chief of the Southern Cheyennes. . . ."[17]

This article, written at the time for home folks, confirms King's statement regarding the presence of the wagon train, its guard of two companies of infantry, Cody's leading the party, his firing the first shot killing Yellow Hand's pony, his killing that Indian, and the charge of the cavalry after his shots were fired.

Official reports do not name Cody, but the details of the fight conform with those of the article. General Merritt, in a telegraphic report to General Sheridan, filed July 18 at Camp Robinson, said: "At daylight yesterday morning I saddled up to move on the trail towards the agency. At the same time a party of seven, 7, Indians were discovered near the command, moving with the intention of cutting off two couriers who were approaching from Sage Creek. A party was sent out to cut these off, killing one of them. The command then moved out at once after other Indians seen in this direction and pursued them, but they escaped, leaving four, 4, lodges and several hundred pounds of provisions behind."[18]

[17] *Ellis County Star*, August 3, 1876, p. 4; I am indebted to Mrs. Minnie D. Millbrook, Detroit, for uncovering this series of seven articles, to Nyle H. Miller and staff of the Kansas State Historical Society for providing transcripts, and to Mr. Gondos for checking the identity of Powers on the Muster Roll of Company A.

Muster rolls, compiled every two months, contained a section headed "The Record of Events." That of the Field, Staff and Band, Fifth Cavalry, June 30 to August 31, 1876, says: "Early on the morning of July 17th, a party of seven Indians was discovered trying to cut off two couriers, who were on the way to this command with dispatches. A party was at once detached in pursuit, killing one Indian." The Regimental Return and the returns of Companies A, B, and D tell the story in similar language, agreeing that one Indian was killed. Company I has "two or three of them being killed." Returns of Companies G, K, and M give no details.[19] King's contemporary diary lists two killed. Powers recorded three more killed and five wounded. He was the only person to report a casualty among the troops: "Private Seffers of 'D' company was hurt by the falling of his horse down an embankment." Private James B. Frew of Company D recorded in his diary: "Two couriers arriving from agency being in danger Cody fired on them, killing the chief, Yellow Hand. The rest tried to rescue him but we charged, killing six."[20]

A dispatch to the *New York Herald* was filed from Fort Laramie on the same day as that to the *Ellis County Star*, but the *Herald* got it in type the next day, Sunday, July 23, only six days after the fight. King said he wrote a brief account for the *Herald* at the request of Cody, who had received a telegram asking for it. They went to the telegraph office with two civilians unknown to King. When King first saw the article in type more than half a century later, he disclaimed any part of it. However, as some of its phrasing is identical with what he wrote in 1880 in *Campaigning with Crook*, it seems probable that one of the civilians was a *Herald* correspondent who incorporated King's account with other material he had gathered.

Here is this version of the killing of Yellow Hand: "Company K was instantly ordered to the front. But before it appeared from behind the bluff, the Indians, emboldened by the rush of their

[18] Merritt to Sheridan, Red Cloud Agency, July 18, 1876, Letters Received, Miscellaneous Branch, No. 52–1–6858, Adjutant General's Office papers, National Archives.

[19] Record of Events, Muster Rolls, Fifth Cavalry, June 30–August 31, 1876.

[20] *Winners of the West*, Vol. XIII, No. 5 (April 30, 1936); *Chicago Tribune*, May 28, 1936; A. E. Long, "Cody–Yellow Hand Duel Is Bunk," MS, KSHS.

friends to the rescue, turned savagely on Buffalo Bill and the little party at the outpost. The latter sprang from their horses and met the daring charge with a volley. Yellow Hand, a young Cheyenne brave, came foremost, singling Bill as a foeman worthy of his steel. Cody coolly knelt, and, taking deliberate aim, sent his bullet through the chief's leg and into his horse's head. Down went the two, and, before his friends could reach him, a second shot from Bill's rifle laid the redskin low."[21]

In the phrase, "singling Bill as a foeman worthy of his steel," may be seen the germ of the later elaborated legend of a duel between the lines. But Cody did not exaggerate in writing to Lulu from Red Cloud Agency on the day after the fight. He then said: "We have had a fight. I killed Yellow Hand a Cheyenne Chief in a single-handed fight. You will no doubt hear of it through the papers. I am going as soon as I reach Fort Laramie the place we are heading for now send the war bonnet, shield, bridal, whip, arms and his scalp to Kerngood [who had a clothing store in Rochester] to put up in his window. I will write Kerngood to bring it up to the house so you can show it to the neighbors. . . . I have only one scalp I can call my own that fellow I fought single handed in sight of our command and the cheers that went up when he fell was deafening."[22]

Before Cody wrote his autobiography in 1879, the *New York Weekly* had published *The Crimson Trail; or, Custer's Last Warpath, A Romance Founded upon the Present Border Warfare, as witnessed by Hon. W. F. Cody*, and the same Hon. W. F. Cody had appeared on the stage in *The Red Right Hand; or, Buffalo Bill's First Scalp for Custer*. Perhaps it was the easiest way out to take his story from these sources. Be that as it may, he starts with a running fight that lasted several minutes, with three Indians killed as they retreated toward their main body. Then "one of the Indians, who was handsomely decorated with all the oranments usually worn by a war chief when engaged in a fight, sang out to me in his own tongue: 'I know you, Pa-he-haska; if you want to fight, come ahead and fight me.' The chief was riding his horse

[21] *New York Herald*, July 23, 1876; King, "My Friend, Buffalo Bill," *The Cavalry Journal*, Vol. XLI, No. 173 (September–October, 1932).

[22] *Baltimore Sun*, December 21, 1936; the letter was then in the possession of Mrs. Harry G. Schloss, daughter of Moses Kerngood.

back and forth in front of his men, as if to banter me, and I concluded to accept the challenge. I galloped towards him for fifty yards and he advanced towards me about the same distance, both of us riding at full speed, and then, when we were only about thirty yards apart, I raised my rifle and fired; his horse fell to the ground, having been killed by my bullet.

"Almost at the same instant my own horse went down, he having stepped into a hole. The fall did not hurt me much, and I instantly sprang to my feet. The Indian had also recovered himself, and we were now both on foot, and not more than twenty paces apart. We fired at each other simultaneously. My usual luck did not desert me on this occasion, for his bullet missed me, while mine struck him in the breast. He reeled and fell, but before he had fairly touched the ground I was upon him, knife in hand, and had driven the keen-edged weapon to its hilt in his heart. Jerking his war bonnet off, I scientifically scalped him in about five seconds. . . .

"As the soldiers came up I swung the Indian chieftain's topknot and bonnet in the air and shouted: 'The first scalp for Custer.' "[23]

It is too bad that Prentiss Ingraham and J. V. Arlington could not let a good story alone. The entire matter of the spoken challenge was, as General King bluntly put it, "bosh,"[24] and the more dramatic event, the rescue, had to be left out to account for it. The knifing episode suggests that the demand for hand-to-hand fighting did not originate with the movies, but Cody insisted that the incident was true in a private conversation with King at Pine Ridge Agency many years later. "We still have the knife on the mantelpiece at home," he said. King also wanted to doubt the scalping, but the evidence is strong for it.

That morning Cody wore one of his stage costumes, a brilliant Mexican *vaquero* outfit of black velvet slashed with scarlet and trimmed with silver buttons and lace. Of course he knew that in all likelihood there would be a fight, and undoubtedly he donned the costume so that he could tell audiences the following winter

[23] Cody, *Life*, 343–44.
[24] King's written comment on original draft of MS of "My Friend, Buffalo Bill" for Russell.

that he was wearing the authentic attire of a scout of the plains—a part of his always evident showmanship.

His first story was exaggerated only in mild degree, far from the legend that grew out of it. The word "duel" seems first to have appeared in the book by Bill's sister, Helen Cody Wetmore. His reputation suffered greatly from her adulation. Her story, unlike Bill's, has almost no resemblance to the fight as described by those who took part in it. Frank Winch, writing a show-publicity biography in 1911, drew on Mrs. Wetmore's story and added details of his own: "The chief drew his men to line and rode back and forth in front, bantering Buffalo Bill with challenges for a duel."[25] The idea that emerges of a medieval tourney between opposing lines in battle is utterly foreign to Indian warfare, yet oddly enough many of those most assiduous in "proving" that Buffalo Bill did not kill Yellow Hand have swallowed this part of the legend whole.

All of the stories denying that Buffalo Bill killed Yellow Hand are equally impossible, and most of them come from persons who were nowhere near the place. One who was, however, is Little Bat, or Baptiste Garnier, scout with the Fifth Cavalry during the campaign, although nothing of record places him in the fight of July 17. As King frequently mentions him favorably, it seems unlikely he would have overlooked naming Little Bat had he been with Cody's scouts in the encounter. Little Bat has never been directly quoted as claiming that he killed Yellow Hand. His son, John Garnier, known as Johnny Bat, is quoted as saying, "When Yellow Hand challenged some one to come out and meet him with knives Bill rode out to meet him despite Dad and the rest telling Bill the Indian would cut him to pieces." Then to save Bill's life, "my Dad just pulled up on his rifle and took a single shot at Yellow Hand and he rolled off his horse."[26]

A more commonly cited story of Little Bat's shot comes by the more devious route of a letter written on March 10, 1927, by Norman M. Kelley, reporting a story he had heard fifteen years before in his pool hall at Scenic, South Dakota, about an event which

[25] Wetmore, *Last of the Great Scouts*, 217 (G&D, 233–34).
[26] Lewis A. Lincoln to Don Russell, February 3, 1959; he says he had the story from Johnny Bat in 1919; A. E. Long, "Cody–Yellow Hand Duel Is Bunk," MS, KSHS.

took place thirty-six years before that, as told by two men who were not there at the time. The two were Baptiste Pourier, or Big Bat, a scout with the Crook column, and John W. Russell, or Buckskin Jack. Big Bat's story was that Little Bat and a man named Tate, when jumped by a few Cheyennes while hunting, took refuge in a buffalo wallow, from which they killed two Indians, one of them being Yellow Hand. Big Bat is quoted: "Later we learned that Cody was with the 5th Cavalry and he had said for so long that he wished to scalp an Indian. We went to the rear of the troops the following day, found Bill, and told him we had killed an Indian in full war dress and then Cody went to the body and came back wearing the war bonnet and other war dress." The publisher of this far-fetched yarn produced another letter, from Charles J. Miller, of El Paso, dated September 11, 1925, in which Miller says he was "with the outfit," whatever that means, gets the date wrong, and says Cody scalped a chief "and he was good and dead, being out in the sun a couple of days."[27]

Sergeant Jacob Blaut, Company I, Fifth Cavalry, is cited as having thought that he himself might have killed Yellow Hand: "Bill and I fired at the same time, and I think my bullet killed him." Blaut was another who told his tale too often. In an earlier story he had left out most of Cody and all of the doubt. Then he said that Merritt "ordered me with Buffalo Bill, Green, two orderlies, and my three men to charge the Indians, which we did, shouting and shooting. When Chief Yellow Hand's horse dropped he was taking refuge behind a knoll, aiming his revolver at me. I shot and stripped Yellow Hand. We killed 11 Indians besides Yellow Hand, captured 12 horses and one mule." Twelve dead Indians make this by far the biggest story, which is perhaps enough to say of it. King, who commanded the outpost Blaut was talking about, had never heard of Blaut.[28]

Blaut's mention of Green was probably a nod to Jules Green, whose posthumous story also appeared in the veterans' paper, *Winners of the West*. The only point of agreement in the two stories

[27] *Blake's Western Stories*, 27–28.
[28] Associated Press dispatch, Newark, N. J., July 25, 1927; Jacob Blaut, "Who Killed Yellow Hand?," *Winners of the West*, Vol. II, No. 9 (August, 1925), 7; see also *ibid.*, Vol. III, No. 6 (March, 1926), for Blaut's equally fantastic story of his part in the Ute campaign; Walsh, *The Making of Buffalo Bill*, 192.

is that Yellow Hand was killed. Surprisingly, Green gave the credit to Cody. "I was close enough to have killed him with my pistol," said the modest Green, who instead obligingly ran the Indian out of a canyon so that Buffalo Bill could fire the fatal shot. The incident is said to have occurred while Green and Cody were riding alone on a scout in advance of the regiment. This impossible yarn did not come directly from Green, but was told in a letter by a friend who said he had heard Green tell it at some time or other.[29]

Billy Garnett, sometimes called Billy Hunter, is also reputed to have said that he killed Yellow Hand. If so, he told variant yarns, for in another story he gives Cody full credit for killing Yellow Hand—in a duel with knives that lasted for more than an hour within sight of the garrison of Camp Robinson—thirty-five miles from the spot where *Hay-o-wei* died.[30]

An obituary of Colonel Frank H. Mayer, who died at the age of 102 in Fairplay, Colorado, on February 12, 1954, says that he "scoffed at William F. (Buffalo Bill) Cody's story of shooting Chief Yellow Hand. Colonel Mayer said it was a friend of his, Alex Vimy, who killed the chief." Mayer's name is not on lists of Regular Army officers and Vimy's identity is a mystery.[31]

It is surprising how many of these claimants immediately recognized their victim as Yellow Hand when that was not his name. So obscure was he that we have only one glimpse of him in his previous life, and that in a narrative by his sister, Josie Tangleyellow Hair. Said she, "I remember that Yellow Hair, my brother, and Buffalo Roads, my uncle, were appointed to go out scouting for soldiers, . . . saddled their horses and left from our tent, and I did not see them leave camp. . . . According to the general opinion and talk of the Indians, Yellow Hair was killed by one of the bullets fired by the soldiers, and was not killed in single combat by Buffalo Bill." Her story was accompanied by a story told by Beaver Heart, a member of the Rough Face Band, ostracized because of the theft of a horn from the sacred buffalo hat of the

[29] "Death of Yellow Hand, Cheyenne Chief," *Winners of the West*, Vol. VI, No. 10 (September, 1929), "as told by Jules Green, late scout 5th Cavalry, to the late Ellis T. Pierce, Hot Springs, S. D."; letter from Pierce now in possession of R. S. Ellison, Casper, Wyo.

[30] *Denver Post*, February 23, 1923.

[31] *New York Times*, February 12, 1954.

Cheyennes. According to Beaver Heart, Yellow Hair "rode down the line of soldiers away from me. The soldiers were firing at him all the time, but he reached the end of the line of soldiers before his horse was killed. . . . He then started to walk off. The soldiers were firing at him and he didn't go far before he fell dead."[32] It is clear that both deponents had been briefed on one of the more extravagant versions of the duel between the lines.

According to a popular saying commonly attributed, probably erroneously, to Sheridan, that "the only good Indian is a dead Indian," Yellow Hand was the best Indian who ever lived, for no other of his race ever died so often, in so many different places, by so many different hands. Returning from gossip, rumors, and lies circulated half a century and more after the event to the record written for the officers and enlisted men of the Fifth Cavalry who were there at the time and knew what happened, perhaps it is best summed up in the words of the regimental history: "William F. Cody, the favorite scout of the regiment, was conspicuous in the affair of the morning, having killed in hand-to-hand conflict, Yellow Hand, a prominent Cheyenne chief."[33]

[32] E. A. Brininstool, "Who Killed Yellow Hand," October Life—Outdoor Recreation, Vol. LXV, No. 2 (February, 1930), containing the stories of Beaver Heart and Josie Tangleyellowhair, as taken down February 13 and May 27, 1929, by C. B. Lohmiller, superintendent of the Lame Deer Agency, Willis Rowland, interpreter; the Nebraska State Historical Society has a file of possibly two hundred letters and clippings relating to the Yellow Hand controversy that seem to add little more to the stories here outlined.
[33] Price, *With the Fifth Cavalry,* 158.

18

CHIEF OF SCOUTS, B. H. & Y.

THE SEVEN TROOPS of the Fifth Cavalry pursued the defeated Cheyennes into Red Cloud Agency, a march of thirty miles or more that took most of the day. There the hostile eight hundred, washed of war paint and by no means imposing, were indistinguishable from other blanket Indians of the reservation, except that, as Lieutenant King tells us, "one and all they wanted to see Buffalo Bill, and wherever he moved they followed him with awestruck eyes." The fact that Bill was still wearing the black velvet costume slashed with scarlet undoubtedly added to their awe. The tired troopers were hoping for a day of rest after their long marches, but by noon next day Lieutenant Hall arrived with the wagon train—his lightning marches with the supplies continued to be the wonder of the campaign—and by two-thirty o'clock that afternoon, July 18, Merritt's command was on its way to Fort Laramie.[1]

An entire regiment was seldom assembled in the Indian wars as was the Seventh Cavalry at the Little Big Horn, but an effort was made that summer to get all of the Fifth Cavalry to Crook's command. Company C joined at Red Cloud Agency, making eight troops in the field. The remaining four were ordered out on the day of the Hat Creek fight. Company E, commanded by Captain

[1] King, *Campaigning with Crook*, 41–52.

Price, from Fort Hays and Company F from Fort Dodge went by railroad to Cheyenne, then headed for Fort Laramie by forced marches. Company H from Fort Wallace and Company L from Fort Lyon also got as far as Cheyenne, but from there were ordered to Camp Robinson to guard the Cheyennes at Red Cloud Agency who had already delayed the regiment, to the annoyance of General Crook and the benefit of Buffalo Bill's subsequent theatrical season. These two companies missed the summer campaign but took part in Brevet Major General Ranald S. Mackenzie's winter campaign against Dull Knife's Cheyennes.

It was from Fort Laramie that the world learned of Cody's exploit in the *New York Herald* of Sunday, July 23, through a dispatch sent Saturday, possibly by R. B. Davenport, the *Herald's* correspondent with the Crook expedition—and old neighbors at Fort Hays and Hays City learned of it in Sergeant Powers' letter, sent the same day but not printed in the weekly until August 3. The Fifth Cavalry did not linger at Fort Laramie. The weary troopers had arrived at three o'clock Friday afternoon. Saturday was spent drawing supplies and loading them, shoeing horses, and making other preparations for a long campaign. At six o'clock Sunday morning, while newsboys in New York were delivering the *Herald* telling of the killing of Yellow Hand, the fighting men of that skirmish were on the march to Fort Fetterman, where they arrived on Tuesday, July 25.

There a miscellaneous assortment of strays, awaiting a chance to join Crook's column, was picked up. In those days officers on leave hastened to join their commands when they heard an expedition was afoot. In this category were two Fifth Cavalry officers, Captain Calbraith P. Rodgers and Lieutenant George O. Eaton. A cousin of Rodgers, Lieutenant William C. Hunter, on leave of absence from the navy, came along to see the excitement, as did two officers of the Fourth Infantry whose companies were not assigned to the expedition, Second Lieutenants Robert H. Young and Satterlee C. Plummer. All of these were attached to the Fifth Cavalry as volunteers—it was a day when such things were done, which may go some of the way to explain Buffalo Bill.

There was no delay at Fort Fetterman. The regiment reached there in mid-afternoon, crossed the North Platte at once, amalgamated the strays into the column, and was off at eight o'clock the next morning. On the night of July 28, in the pitchy darkness of the valley of the North Fork of the Mini Pusa, the faint tones of a cavalry trumpet sounding "Officers' Call" was heard, and General Merritt ordered his trumpeter to repeat the call. The two trumpeters continued repeating "Officers' Call" until Companies E and F were guided into camp after their long march from Cheyenne. This became a regimental tradition, and the same call was used to guide the relief expedition in 1879 after Major T. T. Thornburgh was killed in the Ute uprising.

As the march toward Crook's column continued, the only glimpse of Buffalo Bill we get is King's mention that somewhere between Crazy Woman's Fork and Clear Fork on August 1, "Several small herds of buffalo were sighted, and some few officers and men were allowed to go with Cody in chase." This was hunting for rations; there was no delay; the troops pushed on, past Lake De Smet and the sites of Fort Phil Kearny and the Fetterman fight. Late on the afternoon of August 3 the Fifth Cavalry and its strays reached the camp of General Crook on Goose Creek, about where Sheridan, Wyoming, now stands.

Crook, as King describes him, "in worn shooting jacket, slouch felt hat, and soldier's boots, with ragged beard braided and tied with tape, with twinkling eyes and half-shy embarrassed manner," did not look much the soldier, but to most of those who served with him, he was the greatest Indian fighter of them all—as well as the one who had the best understanding of Indian nature. While he spent some time in fishing and bear hunting, he also drilled his troops each day, unusual in the field in that period. He was eager for another blow, but he had correctly gauged the enemy strength, and wisely waited to bring his full available force into action.

Crook had received a considerable reinforcement before the arrival of the Fifth Cavalry, notably seven infantry companies from Fort Fetterman and 213 Shoshones under Chief Washakie—both Bourke and King refer to them as "the best light cavalry in the world," although that expression may previously have been applied to mounted Indians of the plains. When the entire command was assembled, it was organized as a task force in World

War II terms; then it similarly got a name, the Big Horn and Yellowstone Expedition, and as is an ancient army custom, it was commonly known by initials, the "B. H. & Y." General Merritt became chief of cavalry, commanding a provisional brigade, and General Carr resumed command of the Fifth Cavalry. Brevet Colonel Royall, Buffalo Bill's old friend of the Fifth Cavalry, now lieutenant colonel of the Third, commanded a provisional regiment of detachments from the Second and Third regiments of cavalry. Brevet Major General Alexander Chamber commanded the infantry, ten companies from the Fourth, Ninth, and Fourteenth regiments. Colonel T. H. Stanton commanded irregulars and citizen volunteers. Brevet Colonel George M. Randall, captain, Twenty-third Infantry, was chief of scouts and Indian allies —the equivalent of the reconnaissance officer of more recent army organization.

William F. Cody was officially designated "Chief Scout with the Big Horn and Yellowstone Expedition," in which capacity he was paid $150 a month by Lieutenant W. P. Hall, the quartermaster. Some twenty civilian scouts were employed by various units of the B. H. & Y., many of them of considerable fame in frontier annals, but regardless of high opinion of Buffalo Bill's ability, he probably got the appointment through the old army rule or seniority and experience.[2]

Outstanding was Frank Grouard, often called Crook's favorite scout, and certainly one with experience peculiarly qualifying him for his duties in war against the Sioux. Frank was born September 20, 1850, on the island of Anaa, one of the Friendly Islands. His father was Benjamin F. Grouard, a Mormon missionary from an old New Hampshire family, and his mother was Nahina, daughter of the Polynesian chief of Anaa. When he was two years old, Frank's parents brought him to California, where he went to school in San Bernardino. He was reared in the family of Addison Pratt, his father's fellow missionary, and left their home in Utah to become a teamster in Montana. He may have been captured by Indians, but he lived voluntarily among the Hunkpapa Sioux for several years, on intimate terms with Sitting Bull and Crazy Horse. Because of his Polynesian appearance, Grouard was assumed by

[2] O.Q.M. 1939.

239

THE LIVES AND LEGENDS OF BUFFALO BILL

the Indians to be one of themselves. He left the Sioux in 1875 and was employed at Red Cloud Agency. He was scout with the Reynolds expedition in March, 1876, and continued with General Crook. Many officers and scouts who knew something of his past, doubted his loyalty. The Sioux looked upon him as a renegade.[3]

Baptiste Pourriere, sometimes "Pourier" and known as Big Bat, was another veteran scout. He and Grouard accompanied Lieutenant Frederick William Sibley of the Second Cavalry on the "Sibley Scout" that was one of the heroic exploits of the 1876 campaign. Louis Richaud and Ben Arnold carried the dispatches that on July 10 brought Crook his first news of the Custer disaster. Richaud, often "Richard" and "Reshaw," and probably originally "Richeau," helped his father, John, build a famous toll bridge across the Platte at what is now Casper. Louis was one-quarter Sioux. He was interpreter on one of the trips of the Sioux chiefs to Washington. He wore mustache and goatee, perhaps in imitation of Cody. Louis's sister Josephine was the wife of Big Bat.

A courier named Graves was sent to Fort Fetterman on July 16, arriving there July 22. When he started back on August 2, he was accompanied by one who was to be long associated with Buffalo Bill—Captain Jack Crawford, the Poet Scout. He was credited with carrying dispatches on a highly perilous route of four hundred miles alone to Fort Fetterman, where he had arrived on July 29. When he reached Crook's camp on the Rosebud on August 8, Cody gave him another accolade: "Jack informed me that he had brought me a present from Colonel Jones of Cheyenne [proprietor of the Jones House.] Jack Crawford is the only man I have ever known that could have brought that bottle of whiskey through without *accident* befalling it, for he is one of the very few teetotal scouts I ever met." Cody shared his gift with General Carr and Barbour Lathrop of the *San Francisco Call*.[4]

John Wallace Crawford was born in County Donegal, Ireland, on March 4, 1847, coming to the United States as a boy. At fifteen he enlisted in the Forty-eighth Pennsylvania Volunteers, in which

[3] Dr. John S. Gray, "Frank Grouard: Kanaka Scout or Mulatto Renegade," *The Westerners Brand Book* (Chicago), Vol. XVI, No. 8 (October, 1959); Joe De-Barthe, *The Life and Adventures of Frank Grouard*.

[4] Cody, *Life*, 349–50; *John Hunton's Diary* (ed. by L. G. Flannery, II, entries for July 22, 29, August 2, 1876; Capt. Jack Crawford, *The Poet Scout*, (1879) 25–36.

his father was serving. Jack was wounded at Spotsylvania, and while in Saterlee Hospital, West Philadelphia, he was taught to read and write by a Sister of Charity. He rejoined his regiment at Petersburg and was wounded again on April 2, 1865. After both parents died, he went west. He carried mail from Sidney, Nebraska, to Red Cloud Agency in 1875. He was one of the early invaders of the Black Hills, becoming a member of the Board of Trustees of Custer City, and chief of scouts of the Black Hills Rangers, E. Wynkoop commanding. He probably became "Captain Jack" when he took command of this company. He was also a correspondent for the *Omaha Bee*.[5]

The scouts under Cody faced tough campaigning as the B. H. & Y. got under way on August 5. Crook attempted to make his force as mobile as that of the Indians. He left all tents and wagons behind, setting an example by retaining for himself only a half-shelter tent and no kitchen equipment except a tin cup. Rations for fifteen days and ammunition were carried on 299 pack mules—Crook was largely responsible for the development of pack transportation in the army. For the Indian wars it was an imposing body of troops that struck out in the valleys of Goose and Prairie Dog creeks. In the lead was a long column of infantry with half a dozen scouts on the flanks—Lieutenant King, riding with the Fifth Cavalry in rear, noted that "we miss our friends Cody and Chips, who hitherto were our scouts, and no one else's." The Crow scouts covered the exposed flank of the Fifth; the Shoshones were with the advance guard. The other cavalry column was a mile away. Crook's net was spread wide.

Tongue River was reached on the first day's march. On the day following, that river was crossed thirteen times, despite which the expedition made twenty-two miles up its narrow canyon. On August 7 the troops climbed to the summit of the divide between the Tongue and Rosebud rivers, and then down into the Rosebud valley. The site of Crook's battle of June 17 was passed, and signs were studied of the trap then set. Says Captain Bourke, "Confidence in Crook was increased tenfold by the knowledge that he

[5] Crawford, *The Poet Scout*, (1886) v–xiii; entries on Crawford in *Who's Who in America*, VI; *International Encyclopedia*, second edition; Stanley J. Kunitz and Howard Haycraft, *American Authors, 1600–1900* (New York, 1938).

had outwitted the enemy on that occasion."[6] Here was found the site of a Sioux village, abandoned for ten or twelve days, according to Grouard, and for the first time Crook's command realized the extent of the Indian concentration. The circles made by tipis stretched for ten miles along the river, and estimates of the number of Indians who had occupied them ranged from seven to ten thousand—the camp that Custer struck was estimated at five to nine thousand by those who saw its site after the battle. Bourke had noted the beauty of the battlefield during the Rosebud fight, but now all was barren, for the Indians had burned off the grass, the beginning of a tactic that was to bring the cavalry horses to starvation before the campaign was over.

The next morning, August 8, the troops started in a thick, smoky haze, which made it evident that the Indians were burning grass not far ahead, although the trail was estimated by Major Stanton on the advice of scouts to be four days old. A sharp lookout was kept for patches of grass that the Indians had missed, and a long halt was made after noon to take advantage of some of them. At 6:00 P.M. came orders to saddle up, and the march was continued until well after dark. At daybreak the column moved on in a misty drizzle that became a cold, driving rain by mid-morning. That night ice formed on shallow pools along the river. A bright sun next morning soon made it August again, the column kicking up a cloud of dust and ashes from the burned-over grass that could be seen for miles.

Buffalo Bill, riding ahead of the column, discovered a similar immense cloud of dust some ten miles away, which at first he supposed to be made by the Sioux. However, with a field glass he saw what appeared to be marching troops, and sent a scout to General Crook to report that General Terry's command was in sight. Cody feared for a moment that he might have been mistaken as he saw Indians to the front, but soon identified the Seventh Cavalry forming a line of battle. "I galloped down towards the skirmish line, waving my hat," says Cody, "and when within about one hundred yards of the troops, Colonel Weir, of the Seventh Cavalry, galloped out and met me." Lieutenant Edward S. Godfrey of the Seventh Cavalry recorded in his diary on August 10 that as the Crows re-

[6] John G. Bourke, *On the Border with Crook*, 349–50.

ported Sioux ahead and put on their war paint, "we saw persons approaching and immediately formed a skirmish line with the 2nd Cavalry deployed as skirmishers in our rear. Soon after Bill Cody, *alias* 'Buffalo Bill,' rode up to our lines from Genl Crook's command."[7]

Far in rear, Lieutenant King recorded that as the dust cloud was sighted, Crows and Shoshones threw off their blankets, while the troops massed in close column behind bluffs, ready for action. As he put it, "It may be said that we were surprised at the meeting, and it can be established that they were astonished." The mystery of what had become of the Sioux was solved by the scouts. At the point of meeting of the two columns, the Sioux trail turned from the Rosebud across the divide that separates it from the Tongue.[8]

The time had come when, in the terms of General Sheridan's orders, if Terry and Crook "should come to any understanding about concerted movements there would be no objection at division headquarters." Although it has been said that Terry did not assume command over the combined columns, and apparently he did not formally, yet technically as the senior officer he was in command from the moment the two forces joined. There is some indication that Crook chafed at this situation. In all of the acrimonious disputes about the Custer disaster, Terry has escaped with relatively little criticism, perhaps because, as Bourke says, "Terry was one of the most charming and affable of men. . . . He won his way to all hearts by unaffectedness and affability. In his manner he was the antithesis of Crook. Crook was also simple and unaffected, but he was reticent and taciturn to the extreme of sadness, brusque to the verge of severity. . . . Of the two men Terry alone had any pretensions to scholarship, and his attainments were so great that the whole army felt proud of him." Yet even the circumspect Bourke drops a hint: "In Terry's face I thought I could sometimes detect traces of indecision."[9] King noted. "He had with him a complete wagon train, tents and equipage of every description. We had a few days' bacon and hard-tack, coffee and sugar,

[7] Cody, *Life*, 350–51; *The Field Diary of Lt. Edward Settle Godfrey*, 33; Bourke, *On the Border with Crook*, 350–51.

[8] King, *Campaigning with Crook*, 76–78.

[9] Bourke, *On the Border with Crook*, 351–52.

and a whole arsenal of ammunition on our mules, but not a tent, and only one blanket apiece. He had artillery in the shape of a few light field pieces, and was making slow, cautious advances up the Rosebud at the rate of eight or ten miles a day. . . . Even the Seventh Cavalry were housed like Sybarites to our unaccustomed eyes. 'Great guns!' said our new major, almost exploding at a revelation so preposterous. 'Look at Reno's tent—he's got a Brussels carpet!' "[10]

Cody, seldom unkind, reflects a common opinion in saying, "General Terry had his wagon train with him, and everything to make life comfortable on an Indian campaign. He had large wall tents and portable beds to sleep in, and large hospital tents for dining-rooms. His camp looked very comfortable and attractive, and presented a great contrast to that of General Crook, who had for his headquarters only one small fly tent; and whose cooking utensils consisted of a quart cup—in which he made his coffee himself—and a stick, upon which he broiled his bacon. When I compared the two camps, I came to the conclusion that General Crook was an Indian fighter; for it was evident that he had learned that, to follow and fight Indians, a body of men must travel lightly and not be detained by a wagon train or heavy luggage of any kind."[11] This may help to explain why Custer was eager to cut loose from Terry, to the point of meeting disaster in his effort to follow and fight Indians, and suggests that Crook might also have had it in mind to go it alone whenever he could.

However, the delays that hampered the pursuit of the Sioux after the junction of the two expeditions were not chargeable to Terry. Crook's column, as had been planned, drew rations from Terry's wagon train on the day after the two forces met, and the combined forces moved out on the Indian trail that afternoon. The Sioux had been moving northward, parallel with Terry's march southward, but at too great a distance to be detected, and had escaped from between the two forces by turning eastward toward the Tongue valley. If the Sioux again turned northward, it was possible that they might continue on toward Canada—as Sitting Bull later did. Terry throughout the campaign had been obsessed

[10] King, Campaigning with Crook, 79, 82.
[11] Cody, Life, 351.

with stopping the Indians from crossing the Yellowstone—the objective of Gibbon's movements from the beginning of the year. On August 11, Brevet Major General Nelson A. Miles, colonel of the Fifth Infantry who had reinforced Terry with six companies of his regiment after the Custer disaster, was detached and sent northward to guard the river crossings. He took back with him to the mouth of the Rosebud the empty wagon train and also Terry's artillery that had so interested Crook's campaigners. This battery, under Lieutenant W. H. Low, consisted of one twelve-pound and two ten-pound rifled field guns; a Gatling-gun battery had been with Terry's force since he had marched out of Fort Abraham Lincoln with Custer.

The steamer *Far West* took the artillery aboard, and General Miles used that vessel to distribute his garrisons along the Yellowstone. The *Far West*, rated at 398 tons and drawing only twenty inches when unloaded, was captained by Grant Marsh. She started the campaign by taking on supplies at Fort Abraham Lincoln shortly after Custer's Seventh Cavalry left that post. The *Far West* made possible the junction of Terry's and Gibbon's forces at the mouth of the Powder. She carried supplies, established depots, and ferried troops. At the time of Custer's fight she was warped up the Big Horn to the mouth of the Little Big Horn by using her two capstans with lines attached on both banks. She had taken the wounded from that fight—and Captain Keogh's horse Comanche, the only survivor—in a record seven-hundred-mile trip in fifty-four hours. The first news of Custer's last fight was given to the world when the *Far West* arrived at Bismarck.

The combined columns of Terry and Crook found heavy going along the Sioux trail. On the first night a heavy storm struck, flooding the entire country by morning. The rains continued so heavily that no movement was attempted until after noon on August 12, and only ten or eleven miles were made that day. When the Tongue River was reached, the Indian trail split three ways. Crook's scouts reported the main trail headed for the Powder. The expedition turned eastward, across Pumpkin Creek to Mizpah Creek and down Mizpah Creek to the Powder. The rains continued, increasing in volume. Captain Bourke noted that of 116 officers on the expedition only 47 were in active service sixteen years later, and he attributed much of that loss to the hardships of the August storms.[12]

There was little hope of overtaking the Sioux. The expedition found the Indian trail again divided, and this time gave it up. Rations had been reduced to salt meat and hardtack, and there was a threat of scurvy. The combined forces bivouacked along the Yellowstone from August 17 to 24. The steamers *E. H. Durfree* and *Far West* brought supplies, and the wagon train that General Miles had left at the mouth of the Rosebud came overland.

When the *Far West* arrived, Buffalo Bill and Louis Richaud were taken aboard as scouts for General Miles. "The idea of scouting on a steamboat was indeed a novel one to me, and I anticipated a pleasant trip," said Bill, although he was somewhat surprised when they were told to bring their horses. The object was for the scouts to watch from the pilot house for any signs indicating that the Sioux might have crossed the Yellowstone. When Cody saw some objects he thought might be Indian ponies, he and Richaud were landed with their horses and two companies of infantry. The objects proved to be Indian graves.

At the mouth of Glendive Creek, Brevet Lieutenant Colonel Edmund Rice, first lieutenant, Fifth Infantry, had built a system of defenses using a trowel bayonet, one of several types of entrenching tools with which the army was experimenting. His fortifications had proved their worth in a skirmish with Indians the previous day. Miles sent Bill overland with reports to Terry; Bill says he "rode seventy-five miles that night through the bad lands of the Yellowstone, and reached General Terry's camp next morning, after having nearly broken my neck a dozen times or more." Aside from mention of Rice's fight, he fails to say the country was swarming with Indians, but Captain Marsh recalled warning, "Bill, don't try it. You'll never get through alive."[13]

On August 22, Cody was discharged as chief of scouts of the B. H. & Y. Because he thereby missed the Slim Buttes fight in

[12] John F. Finerty, *Warpath and Bivouac;* Bourke, *On the Border with Crook,* 355–60; King, *Campaigning with Crook,* 84–90; Price, *With the Fifth Cavalry,* 161.

[13] Joseph Mills Hanson, *The Conquest of the Missouri,* 335–47; Cody, *Life,* 353–55 ("Richard" for Richaud and "Mills" for Miles; correctly "Miles" in *Adventures,* 69–71, *Autobiography,* 273–80); Lewis A. Lincoln, "Down the Trail with the Pioneer Kid," *Record Stockman* (January 8, 1959), 4.

which his partner Buffalo Chips was killed, excuses have been made for his quitting at this time. Bill made none, but said bluntly, "There being but little prospect of any more fighting, I determined to go East as soon as possible to organize a new 'Dramatic Combination,' and have a new drama written for me, based upon the Sioux war. This I knew would be a paying investment, as the Sioux campaign had excited considerable interest." King generously explains that "theatrical engagements demanded his presence in the East early in the fall; and most reluctantly he, too, was compelled to ask his release." The *Chicago Times* had a report that Cody told off both Crook and Terry, charged they did not want to fight, and demanded his pay vouchers. He was capable of so doing. When interviewed in Chicago, Cody said he would ask Sheridan for permission to raise a company of one hundred frontiersmen to fight through the winter.[14]

Actually Cody had no theatrical commitments. When he left the stage in the spring, he ended his partnership with Texas Jack Omohundro, which was never again revived. Texas Jack and Mlle Morlacchi organized their own combination in the fall of 1876, taking with them Major John Burke, so that Buffalo Bill was left with no one particularly interested in his return to the stage save William F. Cody, who occasionally took personal charge of his own destiny.

Cody's opinion that the campaign was over was widely shared in the rain-soaked camp on the Yellowstone. Chief Washakie and his Shoshones went home, Bourke says because they thought Terry's improvised pack train using mules from the wagon train was too slow. King says, "Several of them urge additional reasons indicative of the fact that the ladies of the tribe are not regarded by their lords as above suspicion in times of such prolonged absence." The Ute scouts also left and the few Crows remaining were divided between the commands. The sick and the disabled were sent back. Some correspondents were persuaded that no more news would develop in the Indian country that season. Crook may have been responsible for the impression in implying that he was about ready to march his troops back to his department. What he did

---

[14] *Chicago Times*, September 15, 26, 1876; Cody, *Life*, 355–56; King, *Campaigning with Crook*, 94.

not say was that the march would be in the direction he supposed the Sioux to be, through the Bad Lands north of the Black Hills.[15]

The expedition had awaited results of Cody's scout by steamboat,[16] and on August 24 the combined columns moved up the Powder, away from the Yellowstone. On the same day Cody embarked on the steamer *Yellowstone,* headed for Fort Buford and civilization. The *Yellowstone* had gone only twenty miles downstream when it met the *Josephine* coming upstream with reinforcements for Terry under Brevet Brigadier General Joseph Nelson Garland Whistler, lieutenant colonel, Fifth Infantry. When the steamers stopped to exchange news, Cody was happy to find Texas Jack aboard, employed carrying dispatches for the *New York Herald.* When Whistler learned that Terry had left the mouth of the Powder, he asked Cody to take Sheridan's dispatches to Terry, "saying that it would only detain me a few hours longer; as an extra inducement he offered me the use of his own thorough-bred horse, which was on the boat. I finally consented to go. . . . I delivered the dispatches to General Terry that same evening."

Sheridan's dispatches informed Terry that it had been determined to hold the Yellowstone Valley during the winter; that he would have fifteen hundred men for that purpose; and that he would establish winter quarters at or near the junction of the Tongue and the Yellowstone. Terry ordered Whistler and his two companies on the *Josephine* to go to the mouth of the Tongue and commence building huts for the winter camp. Resuming Cody's story, "After I had taken a lunch, General Terry asked me if I would carry some dispatches back to General Whistler, and I replied that I would. Captain Smith, General Terry's aide-de-camp, offered me his horse for the trip, and it proved an excellent animal; for I rode him that same night forty miles over the bad lands in four hours and reached General Whistler's steamboat at one o'clock."[17]

---

[15] Bourke, *On the Border with Crook,* 355–56; King, *Campaigning with Crook,* 86.

[16] King, *Campaigning with Crook,* 93.

[17] Report of Gen. Terry, Nov. 21, 1876, in *Annual Report of the Secretary of War,* 1876; Robert G. Athearn (ed.), "A Winter Campaign Against the Sioux," *Mississippi Valley Historical Review,* Vol. XXXV, No. 2 (September, 1948); Cody, *Life,* 356.

Now comes the important message of all this riding. "During my absence," says Cody, "the Indians had made their appearance on the different hills in the vicinity, and the troops from the boat had had several skirmishes with them." He then goes on to quote Whistler as saying, "Cody, I want to send information to General Terry concerning the Indians who have been skirmishing around here all day. I have been trying all evening long to induce some one to carry my dispatches to him, but no one seems willing to undertake the trip, and I have got to fall back on you. It is asking a great deal, I know, as you have just ridden eighty miles; but it is a case of necessity, and if you'll go, Cody, I'll see that you are well paid for it."

This is the first mention of pay, and Cody says he answered, "Never mind about the pay, but get your dispatches ready, and I'll start at once." Here again, as in so many other cases, Cody was ready to go when others shunned the danger, and had no fear of eluding the Indians who had been skirmishing about all day, even though he had a tired horse—he says he rode the same one back—and he himself had been on the go with little rest or sleep. He made 120 miles within twenty-two hours. "It was two o'clock in the morning when I left the boat, and at eight o'clock I rode into General Terry's camp just as he was about to march." This was the morning of August 26, and says Cody, "General Terry, after reading the dispatches, halted his command, and then rode on and overtook General Crook, with whom he held a council; the result was that Crook's command moved on in the direction which they had been pursuing, while Terry's forces marched back to the Yellowstone and crossed the river on steamboats."[18]

With definite orders to guard the line of the Yellowstone, Terry could not ignore the Indians who had appeared on its banks; thus it was this report from Whistler, carried by Cody, that resulted in the parting of the two commands, giving Crook his chance to continue pursuit of the main body of Sioux into the Bad Lands and to strike them one more blow at Slim Buttes.

Terry's command crossed the Yellowstone on August 27 on

[18] *Field Diary of Lt. Godfrey*, August 25; Cody, *Life*, 356–57; Hanson, *Conquest of the Missouri*, 349–50; Bourke, *On the Border with Crook*, 360; King, *Campaigning with Crook*, 96.

the steamers *Carroll* and *Yellowstone*. Terry asked Cody to accompany his forces on a scout north of the river toward the Big
Dry Fork of the Missouri. After a march of three days, signs were
seen indicating that Indians had been hunting buffalo in the area.
Terry sent Cody to the stockade at Glendive with this information.
Bill started at 10:00 P.M. in a drizzling rain through a section of
country with which he was unacquainted. By daylight he had made
only thirty-five of the eighty miles. As there were wide prairies
ahead, he decided to spend the day in hiding. He rode into a ravine
and went to sleep, to be awakened by the rumble of a herd of
buffalo pursued by twenty or thirty Indians. He saddled his horse,
ready for flight, but his trail was not discovered. For two hours
he watched the Indians kill and butcher their game. They then
rode off in the direction he intended to take.

At nightfall, Cody resumed his journey, making a wide detour
to avoid the Indians, and reached the Glendive stockade at daylight. Colonel Rice and his company had been skirmishing with
Indians almost every day, and since the Colonel wanted to inform
Terry of that fact, Cody made a return trip. Lieutenant Godfrey
recorded on August 30 that "Buffalo Bill and Herndon scouts who
had been sent to Glendive on 28th, rejoined us." By "Herndon,"
Godfrey probably meant George Herendeen, scout with Reno in
the Little Big Horn fight. Cody says he overtook Terry at the head
of Deer Creek, "while on his way to Colonel Rice's camp. He was
not, however, going in the right direction." As Deer Creek is downstream from Glendive, he probably was not. Cody guided Terry's
column toward the stockade. On arriving there, Bill found the *Far
West* just leaving for Fort Buford, and went aboard for Bismarck,
from which point he went by railroad to Chicago and his home in
Rochester.[19]

Official records show that on September 6, 1876, Captain H. J.
Nowlan, 7th U. S. Cavalry, acting assistant quartermaster, paid
William F. Cody $200 for services as scout with General Terry's
Expedition operating in Montana Territory, by the job in accord-
ance with a contract of that date. The time he served is not stated,
but if he was on duty until September 6 it was two weeks. That

[19] *Field Diary of Lt. Godfrey*, 44; Cody, *Life*, 357–59; Hanson, *Conquest of
the Missouri*, 350–55.

was the highest rate of pay he ever received as scout, but at no time did he more deserve it, for he was almost constantly riding alone carrying dispatches through country overrun with hostile Indians. It was Cody's last employment as a scout.[20]

[20] O.Q.M. 1939.

THE BUFFALO BILL COMBINATION

THE AMERICAN STAGE IN 1876 was in a state of disorganization suited to the talents of a novice like Buffalo Bill. It had occurred to some in show business that there might be a place for a middle-man between the owner of a dark theater and a wandering "com-bination" of players with no place to act, but as yet the booking agent was unknown. The "advance man" did the booking, seldom more than one jump ahead, for he was also publicity agent when he was not doubling back to take a part on the stage. It was all very informal. This loose organization perhaps explains why Cody, after quitting his job as scout, was not disturbed when delays oc-casioned by "just one more ride," because other scouts would not take a chance with the Sioux, stretched out into two weeks. Even-tually he arrived at Rochester, ready to begin to plan for another season of melodrama.

The breaking off of the partnership with Texas Jack was ap-parently amicable, as indicated in their meeting on the Yellow-stone. Quite likely each thought he could do as well financially alone as in the double-starred company. In some ways the Texas Jack Combination looked the better of the two. He had, of course, his wife, "the peerless Morlacchi"; he also billed Miss Maude Os-wald; he had "the great chief and scout Donald McKay and his Warm Springs Indians," who had been notable in the Modoc War of 1873; and he had Major John M. Burke. Said the *St. Louis Globe Democrat* in reviewing *Texas Jack in the Black Hills* that winter: "Arizona John, whose other name is Burke, is a member of the Texas Jack Combination. . . . In all of Texas Jack's retinue there is no one who can annihilate whole tribes of Indians with greater facility than 'Arizona John.' Armed with a revolver filled with blank cartridges, he kills six of the 'red demons' at a single fire." In his spare time, if any, Arizona John may have practiced press-agentry, but perhaps his loss to Cody at this time was not as heavy a blow to public relations as might be supposed.

To conclude the career of Texas Jack: He was well received in New York in the old reliable *The Scouts of the Plains* in 1877–78. He appeared in Denver in 1880 in *The Trapper's Daughter,* and a few weeks later Morlacchi was billed in Leadville in *The Black Crook,* called the first musical comedy. Jack wrote frequently for *The Spirit of the Times.* He died in Leadville on June 28, 1880.[1]

Cody's idea for 1876 was timely and topical. When he arrived in Rochester in late September he sought out J. V. Arlington, who had played "Uncle Henry Carter" in *The Scouts of the Plains.* Arlington "arranged for the stage" a new drama "founded on incidents of the late Indian War," called *The Red Right Hand; or Buffalo Bill's First Scalp for Custer,* perhaps based on the dime novel published "as witnessed by Hon. W. F. Cody" and later attributed to Prentiss Ingraham. Cody describes it as "a five-act play, without head or tail, and it made no difference at which act we commenced the performance. . . . It afforded us, however, ample opportunity to give a noisy, rattling, gunpowder entertainment, and to present a succession of scenes in the late Indian war, all of which seemed to give general satisfaction." J. Clinton Hall, manager of the Rochester Opera House, where the play opened, undoubtedly gave professional advice and assistance in organizing the combination, which included Cody, proprietor, C. F. Blanchett, business manager, C. B. Waite, stage manager who doubled as actor, and A. H. Meyering, orchestra leader.[2]

---

[1] Logan, *Buckskin and Satin,* 96–100; A. Johannsen, *The House of Beadle and Adams,* II, 218.

[2] Cody, *Life,* 360; A. Johannsen, *The House of Beadle and Adams,* II, 58.

Captain Jack Crawford, who brought the news of Slim Buttes "through 300 miles of hostile country, and outstripped, by killing several horses, all other messengers" for the *New York Herald,* came to Rochester, and was added to the Buffalo Bill Combination as it went to New York City for an engagement at the Grand Opera House of Poole and Donnelley. As the tour continued on through the East and middle states, Cody advertised his play by displaying the scalp and headdress of Yellow Hand in show windows, until the clergy and press of New England denounced "the blood-stained trophies of his murderous and cowardly deeds"— perhaps the first attack on Cody in connection with the Yellow Hand affair. Under this pressure, Cody withdrew the trophies from show windows, which had unexpected results in stimulating curiosity to see them at the theater, adding to the gate receipts. The controversy also won for Cody the sympathy of his comrades in arms, who forgot any objection they may have had to his exploitation of his heroism in their resentment against partisans of the peace policy from the lands of the Pequots and Iroquois.[3]

Possibly in deference to the New England view, but more likely because of Combination custom, Cody revived his alternate play of the previous season, *Life on the Border,* described as "Depicting true Frontier life." It was of a somewhat different character from the Combination's usual thrillers, as Cody took the part of "Buffalo Bill, a Western Judge, Jury, and Executioner." The plot involved Regulators and a vigilance committee headed by Captain Huntley, played by Charles B. Waite—but let the play's hero describe him: "This Captain Huntley is known to me as the most cowardly villain in this territory, and the sooner he is swung off the better. I could surprise some folks to tell what I know. But perhaps this paper could give you some idea."

But the paper, this time, does no good. Buffalo Bill is arrested by General Clark, who does not know that the villain directs a band of counterfeiters disguising themselves as Indians to place the blame on "a noble red man of the Far West," played by Charles Younger, presumably not one of the Younger Brothers of contemporary notoriety. The arrest hampers Buffalo Bill in his search for

[3] Crawford, *The Poet Scout* (1879), v, quoting *New York Herald,* July 8, 1877; King, *Campaigning with Crook,* 42–43.

Scout Jim Reynolds, played by R. J. Evans, father of Bill's sweetheart, Emma Reynolds, played by Miss Emma Wellesley. But Bill has a trick up his sleeve as he exclaims bitterly with this tongue twister: "Because I will be dead to them that want me dead and to them who would murder me if they had a chance. Yes, murder me! I am in the way of Captain Huntley and his gang."

That villain is about to force marriage on the heroine. Her mother, Mrs. Reynolds, played by Mrs. R. C. Grierson, speaks: "Our last hope now is in Heaven. God is good and will not forsake us in the hour of need." But she had overlooked Buffalo Bill.

He enters, disguised as a Mexican, and at an appropriate point in the ceremony, rises and throws off his disguise, saying, "Yes, I can show just cause why this ceremony should not take place." He then exposes Captain Huntley, and gets away with it this time. Jim Reynolds is discovered and reunited with his wife, and the lovers live happily ever after also.[4]

There are many more characters contributing to the happy ending. J. W. Crawford plays "Capt. Jack, can trail an Indian from the Missouri to the Pacific." Arlington depicts "Old Slote, A Trapper, one of the boys, age unknown." Robert Darton has the part of "Wolfy Dick, who came West to grow up with the country, but grew too fast." Grasshopper Jim, Huntley's right bower, was acted by Harry Melmer, and Toothpick Ben, Huntley's left bower, by W. S. MacEvoy. Miss Jessie Howard, third woman in the cast, was Betty Mullaney, "a true-hearted Italian girl from Cork." These descriptions of the characters, taken from a program, suggest that these melodramas were not taken too seriously by those who produced them.

The clichés quoted are the worst to be found in these scripts from the sentimental years of melodrama, and they are not very bad. If *Life on the Border* were to replace a television Western without warning, it is doubtful that one in a million listeners would know the difference—except in missing a few slightly less antiquated clichés that haunt that medium.

In 1877, Cody announced the first of his many "farewell tours." A contemporary newspaper gave full details: "This will be the last

---

[4] Prompt books, *Life on the Border*, manuscript file, SHSC; A. Johannsen, *The House of Beadle and Adams*, II, 58–59.

season that Buffalo Bill (W. F. Cody) will travel as a theatrical star. The company he now has is engaged for fifteen months, one month of which is to be passed on vacation. The troupe, about the middle of June, will arrive in Omaha, and then they will be transported at the manager's expense to his ranch on the North Platte, where they will be at liberty to do as they please. Toward the end of June they will start for San Francisco and play there for four weeks. Thence through California, Oregon, Nevada, and Utah, back to Omaha, where they will disband, Buffalo Bill going to his ranch, to remain there the rest of his life as a cattle dealer and gentleman farmer. He now has 4,500 head of cattle, and hopes to have 10,000 by the close of next year. He will, therefore, retire from the stage with an ample competence."[5]

Except that Cody did not stay on his ranch for the rest of his life, this program was generally carried out. Cody proved an astute manager in deciding to go to the Pacific Coast, "against the advice of friends who gave it as their opinion that my style of plays would not take very well in California." Cody was first to discover what all producers of "Westerns" ever since have proved—that the wholly imaginery and fictitious West of stage, book, or screen is most popular in the real West it mistakenly represents. It is a matter of local pride. When Owen Wister's *The Virginian* was criticized for the unrealistic language of its cowboys, one old-timer remarked with candor, "Well, maybe we didn't talk that way before Mr. Wister wrote his book, but we sure all talked that way after the book was published."

Money talked the right language to Cody, for he had a $1,400 house the opening night at the Bush Street Theatre in San Francisco—big money when the scale of prices was one dollar for dress circle and parquette, fifty cents for the second tier, and twenty-five cents for the gallery. Cody had talked of four weeks, but engaged the theatre for only two. He stayed five, a long run for those days and times.

Captain Jack records that there were insufficient "supers" for the San Francisco opening, and "Bill sent me on a little scout to find some more Indians. I soon returned with half a dozen robust

---

[5] Unidentified clipping from Mrs. Agnes Wright Spring, state historian of Colorado.

Hoodlums," for whom "the pleasure of being slaughtered by B. B. had an irresistible fascination." When the engagement closed, they begged to be taken to the next stop, Sacramento. After that engagement, they disappeared. When a wardrobe trunk was opened in Virginia City, several Indian costumes were missing. Late in the day the supers showed up, carrying the stolen costumes. They had worn their regalia and war paint, knowing that Indians were allowed to ride free on trains, but a conductor heard them rehearsing Shakespeare on a back platform and kicked them off at Reno. They had walked in. Said one, "If we can't eat until after the show, we're liable to drop without bein' shot." Bill fed them and put them back to work.[6]

Cody's earnings for the 1876–77 tour were reported at $13,000. At its close he met his family in Denver, where his sisters, Nellie and May, were then residing. The Buffalo Bill Combination disbanded at Omaha, as planned. There occurred an episode that was the beginning of a long series of domestic disagreements, materially changing Bill's ways of life. How he kissed the girls goodbye in 1877 became an issue in a divorce suit Bill filed against his wife in 1905. Here is his story, as he testified in court:

"In paying off the company, I went to one of the rooms where the four ladies who were the four actresses of the company were waiting to receive their final settlement, which I paid them and got their receipts in full. The ladies were having a glass of beer in this room, and one or two of the gentlemen, members of the company, were in this room and we all had a glass of beer or two, or a drink of some kind, and we were talking of the past season, and we were a little jolly, laughing and talking. When I went to leave the party the ladies all jumped up and they said, 'Papa, we want to kiss you good bye.' They called me papa, the ladies did in the company that season. And I kissed them good bye and we were all laughing and joking."

You will have gathered that Lulu was not among those present. She was in her room down the hall, getting angrier by the minute. Bill could not understand it, then or later. As he explained:

"I do not think that most wives would have felt a little angry to know and hear her husband in an adjoining room on Sunday

[6] Crawford, *The Poet Scout,* (1879) 23–24.

morning, drinking beer and kissing the theatrical girls of his company. I think they would have been rather proud of a husband who had six or seven months work with a party of people who were in his employ, to know and feel that they were on a kindly footing with their late manager, that they were sorry they were going to be separated from a good, kind manager who had always paid their salaries himself. Not only one of them got up and kissed papa good bye, but all four of them rushed up and kissed papa, their old manager, good bye and wished him well and much happiness and success. Actresses are not a narrow-minded people. They do not go off behind the door or to some dark room if they want to kiss a man. They boldly walk up to him and with their enthusiasm, they are willing to let the world know that they like him and do not hesitate to show it in their voice and by their lips. . . . You ask how old papa was at that time? He wasn't too old to be kissed then, and that has been a good many years ago, and he is not too old now. I was just 31 then, just the right age."[7]

A common assumption is that Cody was always surrounded by astute publicity advisers. In 1905 his staff of press agents failed to stop him from making a fool of himself. Even one good lawyer might have helped.

Getting back to 1877, when he kissed the girls good-bye, he did take up ranching. The ranch, in partnership with Major Frank North, had been established on the South Fork of Dismal River, sixty-five miles north of North Platte. Cody met North at Ogallala, then end-of-trail for Texas cattle drives. There they bought and branded their first herd and drove it to their range, an undertaking that required most of the summer. No more, however, is heard of Bill's retirement to the life of a rancher.

Bill left early in the fall for Red Cloud Agency, where for the first time he engaged reservation Indians for one of his shows. "Real Indians" had been advertised previously, and perhaps some had been employed, but more frequently they had been red men of the type of Captain Jack's Hoodlums. Cody took his family and his Indians to Rochester to prepare for a new season. His daughter Arta was put in a young ladies' seminary there. Lulu and Orra traveled with Bill and the Indians.

[7] *The Westerners Brand Book* (Chicago), Vol. II (1945–46), 27–31.

Cody again had an eye for the timely. John D. Lee, after a long trial, was convicted of complicity in the Mountain Meadows massacre of 1857, and his execution by firing squad took place at the scene of the crime on March 23, 1877. Since Cody, as will be recalled, had played a minor part in the Mormon War, thus recalled to public notice, his play that fall was based on Mountain Meadows. The play was *May Cody; or, Lost and Won.* May Cody was Bill's sister, who made several appearances in dime-novel literature. The author was Major Andrew Sheridan Burt. He had enlisted as a private in the Sixth Ohio Volunteer Infantry in 1861 and within a month was commissioned first lieutenant in the Eighteenth U. S. Infantry. He was brevetted captain for gallantry at Mill Spring and major for the Atlanta campaign and Jonesboro, and was a captain in the Ninth U. S. Infantry at the time he became a dramatist. Subsequently he became brigadier general of volunteers in the Spanish-American War and attained that rank in the Regular Army in 1902.

Major Burt's drama had a New York opening, at the Bowery Theatre, on September 3, 1877. "It was the best drama I had yet produced," said Cody, "and proved a grand success both financially and artistically. The season of 1877–78 proved to be the most profitable one I had ever had." A cash book for a part of this season has been preserved, and while it is not balanced, it gives some idea of how he was doing. It opens with a $428 house at New Bedford, Massachusetts, on October 26. Expenses there were $284. The next day he took in $448 at Lynn. There was no performance scheduled on Sunday.

For the following week here is the record:

Date	Place	Receipts	Expenditures
October 29	Salem, Mass.	$ 410	$215
October 30	Glouster [*sic*]	401	142
October 31	Lawrence	340	153
November 1	Concord, N. H.	308	145
November 2 & 3	Manchester	853	264
Totals		$2,312	$919

There was a weekly pay roll of $317 as follows: Austin Bro., $100; Blanchett, $30; Charles and wife, $35; Winter, $20; Arlington, $20;

Prof. Raymond, $20; MacEvoy, $15; Melmer, $15; Harvey, $15; Foeriston, $15; Ogden, $20; Thoen, $12.

At this point the net was $1,076 for the week, but there were other expenses. There is a note on printing bills of "about $1,000," probably for lithographed posters that would last the season. There is mention of "Ogden's account," probably the advance man. Daily expenses varied considerably; a representative one is that at Rockland, Maine, on November 8, where a total of $118.22 was offset by receipts of $215.00. It breaks down thus: railroad, $21.00; billposting and boards, $9.00; extra billboard, $7.50; hall rent, $20.00; license, $5.00; *Opinion*, $2.00; *Gazette*, $2.00 (newspaper advertising); music, $7.00; supers, $2.50; hotel, $30.22; baggage, $3.00; coach, $4.25; meals, lunch, $3.00. There are occasional additional items such as scenery, $4.00; red fire, $3.60; and ushers, $2.00.

On the whole, the take was well over double the daily expenses. There were good days, such as the ones that grossed $599 at Springfield and $525 at Lowell, and average days of $370 take with average expenses of $155. There were bad days, around $200, but only one as bad as Waterville on November 12, where only $118 was taken in as against $70 expenses. On this page some hand, not Cody's, wrote: "God Dam the Town. Never to be played again. Blacked Balled." The only page in the book in Cody's hand registers bank deposits of $1,000, $400, and $600.

In two months three theaters were played for three nights each, seven for two nights each, and twenty-nine cities had one performance each.[8]

Mrs. Cody enjoyed the prosperity but not the one-night stands. We have it on Bill's authority that "in February, 1878, my wife became tired of traveling and proceeded to North Platte, Nebraska, where, on our farm adjoining the town, she personally superintended the erection of a comfortable family residence, and had it all completed when I reached there, early in May. In this house we are now living [1879] and we hope to make it our home for many years to come." She did make it her home, but Bill was not there much.

He devoted the summer of 1878 to his ranch, where he first

[8] Cash book, Buffalo Bill Combination, October 26 to December 25, 1877, manuscript file, SHSC.

took notice of that most famous of all western characters romanticized by his showmanship—the cowboy. He says a regular annual spring "round-up" had been organized by Keith and Barton, Coe and Carter, Jack Pratt, the Walker brothers, Guy and Sim Lang, and Arnold and Ritchie. Writing in 1879, Cody found it necessary to define both "round-up" and "cow-boy" and to put both terms in quotation marks. He was to make both household words.

He explains: "The word 'round-up' is derived from the fact that during the winter months the cattle become scattered over a vast track of land, and the ranchmen assemble together in the spring to sort out and each secure his own stock. They form a large circle, often of a circumference of two hundred miles, and drive the cattle towards a common centre, where, all the stock being branded, each owner can readily separate his own from the general herd, and then he drives them to his own ranch. In this cattle driving business is exhibited some most magnificent horsemanship, for the 'cow-boys,' as they are called, are invariably skillful and fearless horsemen—in fact only a most expert rider could be a cow-boy, as it requires the greatest dexterity and daring in the saddle to cut a wild steer out of the herd."

The Wild West show is simmering here, but he is not yet ready to glamorize this way of life: "As there is nothing but hard work on these round-ups, having to be in the saddle all day, and standing guard over the cattle at night, rain or shine, I could not possibly find where the fun came in, that North had promised me." But he admits, "It was an exciting life, and the days sped rapidly by; in six weeks we found ourselves at our own ranch on Dismal river, the round-up having proved a great success, as we had found all our cattle and driven them home."[9]

Later in the summer he bought a trail herd from Bill Phant at Ogallala and drove it to the ranch. He spent a few weeks with his family at North Platte, where he was visited by his sisters Helen, now Mrs. Alexander C. Jester, and May, whom he had publicized in melodrama, now Mrs. Edward Clark Bedford. He also went to Kansas to see Julia, Mrs. J. A. Goodman, and Eliza, Mrs. George Myers.

When it came time to reorganize his Dramatic Combination,

[9] Cody, *Life*, 361–63.

he went to Indian Territory and hired a band of Pawnees, with C. A. Burgess as interpreter and Ed. A. Burgess as "Boy Chief of the Pawnees." His season opened in Baltimore at the opera house managed by John T. Ford, whose theater in Washington was the scene of President Lincoln's assassination.

The capital was the next stop, and during the run there, Cody learned from newspapermen that his employment of Indians was of concern to the Indian Bureau. He went to Carl Schurz, secretary of the interior, and was told that Commissioner of Indian Affairs E. A. Hayt held that the native actors were wards of the government, absent from their reservations without leave. Cody pointed out, "I thought I was benefitting the Indians as well as the government, by taking them all over the United States, and giving them a correct idea of the customs, life, etc., of the pale faces, so that when they returned to their people they could make known all they had seen." This argument was sound, for the government from earliest times had adopted a policy of bringing delegations of Indians to Washington at public expense primarily for this very purpose. He might also have pointed out that he was giving the Indians employment, so that they were self-supporting, but such an idea would have been almost revolutionary.[10]

Cody's argument proved sufficient. Secretary Schurz and Commissioner Hayt accepted the idea that the Pawnees might benefit from a backstage view of civilization and regularized the situation by appointing Cody a special Indian agent, putting him under bond to return his actors to their reservation at the conclusion of their contract. The tour continued to Richmond and Savannah, but was halted at the Georgia port by an epidemic of yellow fever such as periodically swept the seacoast in that period. Cody jumped to Philadelphia, then headed northeast.

At this time he arranged to have "the well-known author and dramatist, Colonel Prentiss Ingraham, to write a play for me." *The Knight of the Plains; or, Buffalo Bill's Best Trail* had its *première* in New Haven, and proved a huge success, encouraging Cody to try a six weeks' tour of the Pacific Coast and Far West early in 1879. In San Francisco, Cody and Captain Jack Crawford had a violent quarrel. Captain Jack's complaint was that a benefit night

10 *Ibid.*, 364–65; Hayt appears "Haight."

for Captain Jack had not benefited Captain Jack enough. Seeking to persuade him to come back, Cody wrote, "I have just finished a big engagement at the California Theatre. My share was nearly $6,000. . . . I think you had better stayed with me when I offered you $200 a month." This is a substantial advance over any salary shown in the account book of 1877.[11]

Something more on the Wild West order, however, was demanded by the Central City *Daily Register Call* on July 31, 1879, which said: "As might have been expected, the opera house was filled to overflowing last night to see the great scout of the plains, his wild Indians, black bears, buffaloes and jack rabbits, all of which the flaming posters on the dead walls announced would be present. But the small boy and the lover of western romance were disappointed. There were no buffalo, no black bears, no wild Indians; but instead a third-rate dramatic company, playing at some sort of a sickly play without point or pith. There was not a passable artist in the crowd, and if there had been there was nothing in the play to bring him or her out. Bill himself did remarkably fine in a character he has created and which he has played thousands of times. The support was simply vile, and unworthy the Alhambra Varieties in its palmy days. But yet the house was crowded."

Little as this critic liked the play, he had praise for Cody. Cheyenne was less critical: "W. F. Cody, popularly known as Buffalo Bill, made his Cheyenne debut on August 2 and 3 in a double bill entitled *May Cody; or, Lost and Won,* and *Knights of the Plains; or, Buffalo Bill's Best Trail.* Managed by N. C. Forrester." Here the alternate play was used to insure audiences for two days' stay.

Successful or sickly, the play of Prentiss Ingraham was the first significant association of Cody with the writer who was to make Buffalo Bill known throughout the world. Prentiss was the son of the Reverend J. H. Ingraham, author of *The Prince of the House of David* and other stories his son somewhat irreverently called dime novels about the Bible. Prentiss preferred to write about pirates. He is credited with writing one thousand adventure yarns and living some of them. He fought with the Confederates at Port Hudson, with Juárez in Mexico, and in the Battle of Sadowa in

[11] Cody to Crawford, April 22, 1879, Western History Department, Denver Public Library.

Austria. A colonel of Cuban rebels, he was condemned to death by the Spanish as filibuster, but made a daring escape. By 1872 he averaged two dime novels a month. His first Buffalo Bill story was published in 1879; he was still writing Buffalo Bill stories when he died in 1904. He also wrote dime novels signed by Texas Jack and Dr. Frank Powell—and some of those signed by Buffalo Bill.[12]

[12] A. Johannsen, *The House of Beadle and Adams*, II, 151–60; Wm. R. Eyster, *A Rolling Stone: Incidents in the Career on Sea and Land as Boy and Man of Col. Prentiss Ingraham*, Beadle's Boy's Library No. 13 (March 8, 1882).

Indian prisoners from Fort Sheridan, Ill., 1891

who went to Europe with Buffalo Bill's Wild West. Back row, standing, l. to r.: Revenge, Take the Shield Away, Bring White Horse, Know His Voice, One Star, Kills Close to Lodge, Hard to Hit, One Bull or Lone Bull, Standing Bear, Scatter, Sorrel Horse, Horn Eagle, High Eagle; front row: Crow Cane or White Beaver, Medicine Horse or Plenty Wound, Call Her Name or Run By, Kicking Bear, and Short Bull.

Courtesy Fort Sheridan Tower, *Signal Corps*
Photograph by George E. Spencer, Chicago

Beadle and Adams Dime Library cover, 1890

Courtesy Colorado State Historical Society

20

BUFFALO BILL, AUTHOR

THE LEGEND IS FIRMLY ENTRENCHED that all books, dime novels, and articles signed "by Buffalo Bill" were the work of ghost writers. Any suggestion that any of them were not seems preposterous. It cannot be doubted that Cody never wrote, read, or looked at much that appeared under his name. There is indisputable evidence, however, that he did write some of it.

Commonly all of the ghost writing is ascribed to Ned Buntline, although Ned wrote not one line signed by Buffalo Bill. The evidence is incontrovertible—Ned just was not there when it was done. Ned Buntline and Buffalo Bill had come to a permanent parting of the ways two years before anything was published as by Buffalo Bill.

Major John M. Burke, a pioneer press agent and a lazy man with a pen, did some ghost writing for Buffalo Bill but not much. What little he did can be easily identified, for his florid rhetoric is unmistakable. Such internal evidence suggests that he wrote or directed the writing of *True Tales of the Plains*, certain prefaces, speeches, and obvious publicity matter.

Colonel Prentiss Ingraham, a prodigious and prolific pen-pusher, spared time from his output of one thousand or so dime novels to write a few signed by Buffalo Bill. It is doubtful that he could be persuaded to do much more.

The first literary production signed "by Buffalo Bill" was a short story, "The Haunted Valley; or, A Leaf from a Hunter's Life," in *Vickery's Fireside Visitor* for April, 1875. The first of twenty-four dime novels signed "by Buffalo Bill," *The Pearl of the Prairies; or, The Scout and the Renegade*, began in the *New York Weekly* on August 9, 1875. The *Saturday Evening Post* added Buffalo Bill to its authors when *Prairie Prince, the Boy Outlaw; or, Trailed to His Doom* appeared in its issue of October 16, 1875. Meanwhile a serial, *Deadly Eye, the Unknown Scout*, started in the *Saturday Journal* on September 11, 1875, and was concluded on October 23 as another started, *The Prairie Rover; or, The Robin Hood of the Border.*

During the theatrical season of 1874–75 which preceded this burst of literary activity, Cody was going it alone, without the services of Major Burke, who had gone off with Morlacchi and Texas Jack. Burke has never been definitely connected with dime-novel writing, but the fact that Cody was separated from all his publicists at the time he first appears as author lends weight to the theory that he might have written these productions himself. Albert Johannsen, foremost authority on dime novels, has assembled evidence to indicate that this is the case, and maintains that early productions signed Buffalo Bill are not of such literary excellence as to be beyond Cody's capacity.

Ingraham seems to eliminate himself as ghost writer of these early tales in stating that the border novel had brought Cody to the front as a writer and that Cody had dictated his first novel to a stenographer.[1] Presumably it is "The Haunted Valley" to which Helen Cody Wetmore refers when she says, "The first sketch Will wrote for publication was destitute of punctuation and short of capitals in many places," his excuse being, "Life is too short to make big letters when small ones will do; and as for punctuation, if my readers don't know enough to take their breath without those little marks, they'll have to lose it, that's all."[2]

While this statement suggests Cody's tall-tale exaggeration (one of his qualifications for authorship), it also parallels the penciled manuscript by his other sister, Julia Cody Goodman, which

[1] A. Johannsen, *The House of Beadle and Adams*, II, 59–61.
[2] Wetmore, *Last of the Great Scouts*, 239–40.

is similarly devoid of punctuation and capital letters; and as for stops to take breath, it sometimes rambles on for page after page, which, with her constant use of the connective "and," make in effect a sentence that continues indefinitely. Julia says her education almost exactly paralleled Will's; if his early manuscripts were like Julia's, they might give an editor a struggle; but if a story was there, it could be dug out.

Helen goes on to say that Will "now had leisure for study and he used it to such good advantage that he was soon able to send to the publishers a clean manuscript, grammatical, and well spelled and punctuated." This coincides with the fact that he spent the summer of 1875 at his home in Rochester, with the stories and dime novels beginning to appear in August.

R. Farrington Elwell, notable western artist who served his apprenticeship painting subjects for Buffalo Bill's Wild West lithographs, describes himself as with Cody for many years in as close a relationship as father and son. He says, "As to the Colonel's literary work, yes, he did write some of his very earlier work himself; I really should say that quite a number of novels were written entirely by him and used just as written."

When O. J. Victor retired as editor of the Beadle publications in 1897, Cody wrote a letter to be included with letters of other Beadle authors in a tribute presentation. In this letter, not intended for publication, Cody said, "In every respect your advice has been valuable over the Pen Trails I have followed in my claim to authorship, and your just criticisms and suggestions have helped me in my efforts, I am most glad to freely acknowledge."[3]

Absolute proof that Cody did write some of the material appearing under his name lies in the fact that at least one manuscript in his own handwriting has been preserved. It shows no sign of editing, and only a little of the improved spelling and punctuation his sister recorded; yet it was a clean manuscript that an editor could have used with a minimum of editing. It is headed *Grand Duke Alexis Buffalo Hunt,* and it starts thus:

"Probably if I have been asked once I have been asked twenty thousand times. What kind of a time did the Grand Duke have on the plains hunting buffalo was he a good rider. Was he a nice fel-

[3] A. Johannsen, *The House of Beadle and Adams,* II, 59–61.

low socialy. could he speak good english. how many buffalo did he kill did you have to hold the buffalo for him was he a good horse-man. could he shoot well. and thousands of other questions . . . ."[4] The quotation stops here because of a word not readily decipher-able. But what is wrong with that beginning that a few capitals and question marks will not repair? Do you want the answers to his questions? If so, he proves himself an author.

Three dime novels appeared in 1876. *Kansas King; or The Red Right Hand* was in the *Saturday Journal* from March 25 to May 27. *The Crimson Trail; or, On Custer's Last Warpath,* "as witnessed by Hon. W. F. Cody (Buffalo Bill)" seems to dodge authorship. It ran from September 23 to October 30 in the *New York Weekly* of Street and Smith. It was reprinted in the Nugget Library in 1889 as by Ingraham and in the Diamond Dick Library in 1896 as by Buffalo Bill. These were echoed in that fall's melodrama *The Red Right Hand; or, Buffalo Bill's First Scalp for Custer,* arranged for the stage by J. V. Arlington. *The Saturday Journal* ran *The Phantom Spy; or, The Pilot of the Prairie* from September 23 to November 18, starting simultaneously with the *New York Weekly's* Buffalo Bill serial.

Two years elapsed before Buffalo Bill again appeared as author. Then, from May 11 to August 3, 1878, the *Saturday Journal* ser-ialized *Lost Lulu; or, The Prairie Traveler, A Romance of Life and Love in a Frontier Fort.* Since Lulu was Bill's pet name for his wife, it may be assumed that he had something to do with this one, and it may be further assumed that Lulu was not amused, remem-bering, no doubt, his kissing the girls good-bye, for when the in-stallments were assembled as a dime novel in Beadle's Dime Li-brary No. 52 (October 9, 1878), the title was changed to *Death Trailer, the Chief of Scouts; or, Life and Love in a Frontier Fort,* leaving Lulu out of it.

It was almost a year before another novel by Buffalo Bill ap-peared serially in the *Saturday Journal.* From March 29 to May 31, 1879, *Gold Bullet Sport; or, The Knights of Chivalry* was printed. It was just about this time that Cody appeared in the opening per-formance of Ingraham's drama, *The Knight of the Plains; or, Buf-falo Bill's Best Trail.* The story became Beadle's Dime Library No.

[4] Original MS in Buffalo Bill Museum library, Cody, Wyoming.

83 on December 17, with the subtitle changed to *The Knights of the Overland*. The similarity of titles suggests that Ingraham may have novelized his play or dramatized his own dime novel. The suspicion that he was the author is strengthened by the appearance of Ingraham's first Buffalo Bill dime novel in the *Saturday Journal* that same year: *Buffalo Bill, the Buckskin King* ran from November 29, 1879, to February 14, 1880.

It is possible that at this point Ingraham took over the writing of all dime novels signed "by Buffalo Bill." It is almost certain that he wrote some of those that followed, but less probable that he did any considerable Buffalo Bill ghost writing prior to 1879.

Surely no ghost writer was needed to produce *The Phantom Spy; or, The Pilot of the Prairie*. Ingraham at his worst had better plot structure. When the Phantom Spy, with long white "vail" (there is enough misspelling to warrant attributing the authorship to Cody) floating out behind, rides her steed as white as snow around a wagon train, ruin and bloodshed at the hands of the Hermit Chief's band is sure to follow. The Prairie Pilot runs down the Phantom Spy, but since no dime-novel hero can get rough with a fair villainess, he releases her after exacting a promise that she will not bring disaster to the train he is guiding. Following her trail to the bandit cave, the Prairie Pilot is captured. With the aid of his "pard," Bravo Bob, and the Phantom Spy, the Pilot not only escapes, but also rescues another captive, Ruth Radcliffe, daughter of the colonel commanding the fort at Blue Water. The Colonel in gratitude makes the Prairie Pilot his chief of scouts, but in ingratitude orders the arrest of our hero for no other crime than falling in love with Ruth. The Prairie Pilot kills two guards ordered to make the arrest and escapes.

We learn that Colonel Radcliffe is the son of the Hermit Chief. The Phantom Spy and her brother, Captain Ralph, who has led the robbers on many a ruthless raid, suppose the Hermit Chief to be their father, but actually he is their cruel stepfather, who has murdered their mother, then lured them into a life of crime while plotting to seize a legacy that will come to them when the Phantom Spy is of age. Eventually the Prairie Pilot is revealed as the elder brother of Captain Ralph and the Phantom Spy and the avenger of their wrongs. Singlehandedly he hunts down members of the outlaw band and captures the Hermit Chief. After full disclosure of the plot, which by this time no one, including the author, can understand, the Hermit Chief conveniently dies of a wound received while trying to escape, leaving the survivors to live happily ever after.

There is not a character in the story, with the exception of the innocuous heroine, Ruth, who could not be convicted of some crime or other. Dime-novel morality took little account of such matters. It is not surprising that this form of literature was subject to widespread condemnation. It would be little tax on the writing ability of Buffalo Bill. Completely unconvincing and unreal, it is interesting and exciting only because of the continuous action.

Internal evidence suggests that *Gold Bullet Sport* was the product of Ingraham's art. It is a common assumption that anyone can guess the outcome of a dime novel after reading the first chapter. However, it would be safe to defy any reader to work out the intricacies of the plot of *Gold Bullet Sport* at any point before the dénouement. A familiar device of nineteenth-century melodrama was the double—the characters who looked alike and thereby developed all sorts of plot complications, as in *The Two Orphans, The Prisoner of Zenda, The Masquerader, The Prince and the Pauper,* and *A Tale of Two Cities,* among the many that might be named. The device enabled the stage star to show his versatility by playing two roles, a great boon to Combinations that could afford only a limited number of actors. The *Gold Bullet Sport* takes the championship in this regard, for its heroine is triplets! Moreover, no one of the three knew of the existence of any other until the deathbed confession in Chapter XXVII—but do not make the error of skipping to Chapter XXIX, which is headed "Trebly Unmasked," for that concerns another matter. If you are a shrewd dime-novel reader, you may suspect that Captain Satan, leader of the villainous Knights of the Overland, is one of two apparently respectable denizens of Central City, but it is highly unlikely you will guess that he was both of them. There were masters of disguise in those days. The Gold Bullet Sport himself was also two other persons, a minor matter in these tribulations by trios. It seems unlikely that Cody could have kept all this straight, but it is much in the Ingraham manner.

The fact that Ingraham and Cody were first associated in 1879, the date of publication of Cody's first autobiography, makes Ingraham a logical candidate for its authorship. Attributing it to Ned Buntline is without merit, for Cody and Judson had had no association for the preceding six years. A clincher is the incorrect initials for Judson on page 263. Bibliographies and bookdealers' catalogs have listed the autobiography under the name of Frank E. Bliss, presumably because it was copyrighted by him, so soon is it forgotten that only a few years ago almost all books were copyrighted by their publishers. A prospectus for the book makes this point clear, saying, "Agents wanted in every town—address Frank E. Bliss, publisher, Hartford."[5]

Francis Edgar Bliss was born September 23, 1843, the son of Elisha Bliss, Jr., and Lois A. Thayer Bliss. In 1866 he became connected with the American Publishing Company, headed by his father, and was its president from 1887 until his death on November 9, 1915. Among authors published by that house were Mark Twain, Marietta Holley, Bret Harte, and Charles Dudley Warner. Mark Twain carried on a long feud over the company's retaining copyright on his books. Frank Bliss is said to have been the first publisher to sell books by the subscription method. *The Life of Hon. William F. Cody* apparently was one of his early experiments with that method. A prospectus that has been preserved has a long list of subscribers living in Hartford. The book sold for $2.00 bound in cloth, or $2.50 in leather. With about half of that commission, a book agent could make a good living at a time when Cody could hire actors at $18.00 a week. Cody's sister Helen had the general agency for the state of Ohio.[6]

With Cody opening in Ingraham's play in New Haven in the spring of 1879 and the book published by Bliss at Hartford the same year, it is not stretching coincidence far to assume that the autobiography was launched at a meeting of these three. That theory puts Ingraham on the spot as ghost writer, to which theory there is one witness objecting—the book itself.

No self-respecting professional writer of the nineteenth cen-

[5] Prospectus, *The Life of Hon. William F. Cody*, in library, NSHS.

[6] Thompson R. Harlow, director, Connecticut Historical Society, to Don Russell, June 20, 1955; Samuel Charles Webster, *Mark Twain, Business Man* (Boston, 1946); Wetmore, *Last of the Great Scouts*, 223.

tury could have written the straightforward, unpretentious recital that was Cody's original autobiography—certainly not Ingraham, who was usually florid and always sensational. The book is not sensational. No one interested in publicizing Buffalo Bill would have missed so many of his real claims to distinction or have included so many of the less creditable episodes of his career.

Who else but Cody would have mentioned his brief and unrecorded service with the jayhawkers and horse thieves whose leader was killed by federal police action? It is impossible to imagine Ingraham or Burke or Ned Buntline putting in a manuscript intended for publication the fact that Cody volunteered for Civil War while so drunk he did not know what he was doing. Anything any of them wrote about this episode—in fact, what they did write—dripped with patriotism. Who else but Cody would have been so uninhibited in relating other drunken incidents?

In a day when the *Army Register* was standard equipment in most publishing offices, no competent ghost writer would have allowed so many names to appear misspelled. Moreover, although spelling was certainly not one of Cody's strong points, not all of the errors were his. When a simple name like Plant's Station comes up "Ploutz's," when Lem Flowers appears as "Lieut. Flowers," when J. B. Omohundro, Texas Jack, gets the initials "T. B.," and when General Mills is confused with General Miles, there can be only one explanation: the printer could not read Cody's handwriting. These errors and others like them indicate that the manuscript of the book was written in Cody's hand.

The frequent errors in dates and minor details are further evidence that Cody himself is responsible, depending entirely upon memory, which was about as accurate as other memories unchecked by notes or records. A story that is dictated fouls up background and circumstances, particularly in dealing with military matters. That is never the case here. Cody's story checks out; its errors are easily corrected.

The style of the book is consistent with Cody's surviving manuscript, with many of his personal letters, and with many published interviews in which reporters seem to have got him down much as he talked. Burke's press agent's vocabulary of lurid adjectives and his sentences that never quite track from subject to predicate would be unmistakable. Had Ingraham or Ned Buntline, or for that matter Arlington, Burt, or other writers of Buffalo Bill melodramas had a hand in it, there would be much more dime novel about it. What Ingraham would have done with the same material he did do in his *Adventures of Buffalo Bill from Boyhood to Manhood,* which appeared on December 14, 1881, as No. 1 in Beadle's Boy's Library of Sport, Story, and Adventure. This made some pretense of being a biography, and alternate chapters were cribbed from Cody's autobiography, but those in between are dime novel of purest ray serene, including a preposterous story of the boy Billy riding a buffalo in a wild herd that was the subject of the cover illustration.

There are, of course, a few florid passages in the autobiography. One is the Mormon War episode, in which the conversations are set down in traditional dime-novel language. Another is the Yellow Hand affair, with a somewhat mild version of the challenge and fight between the lines. It is easy to attribute such elaborations to an editor seeking to pep up the narrative, but it is easier to trace them to the subject matter of melodramas in which Cody had appeared on the stage. What would be more expected than for him to echo the lines he had spoken many a night in the theater? In his naïveté Bill may have thought that here, at least, he had parts of his life recorded by professional authors, and he might as well take advantage of it—as he did in lifting page after page from *Ten Days on the Plains,* by General Davies, omitting the passages in praise of the scout and guide.

Cody's attribution of traditional tall stories to his own experience is another indication that he was not too much concerned with strictly factual narrative. It probably never occurred to him that he was a historic character. Exaggerations, however, are few. Army records of 1868 to 1876 show him to have been present at all the expeditions and fights he tells about and often give him more credit for his services than he gives himself. With this much of the book proving out and much more corroborated by contemporary evidence, it may be fairly assumed that the rest is not very far from fact.

Internal evidence suggests that the editing the manuscript received was mainly concerned with getting Bill's scribbling into grammatical English, with a slight bow to the formalities expected in book-writing of the period.

Cody's autobiography might have been accepted at face value had it remained as published by Bliss. Instead, it was butchered, and then the rehash was mined for several subsequent autobiographical works, with most of which Bill obviously had little to do. The first reappearance of the autobiography was in a tome of 766 pages published in 1888: *Story of the Wild West and Camp-Fire Chats, by Buffalo Bill (Hon. W. F. Cody), A Full and Complete History of the Renowned Pioneer Quartette, Boone, Crockett, Carson and Buffalo Bill.* Did Cody write the biographies of the three pioneers? A preface, signed in facsimile, is almost convincing. He writes: "A considerable part of Carson's life was spent in the service of the Government and from departmental records I have therefore extracted much of the information given herein concerning him, and which I find frequently conflicts with the statements of those who in writing his life have made facts subservient to wild exaggerations just as many romancers have done while soberly pretending to record the incidents in my own life." This is probably the only time Cody comments in print on exaggerations in what had been written about him.

He tells of meeting neighbors and friends of Boone in Missouri from whom he got many incidents "that I have been permitted to record for what I believe is the first time." However, the biographies do not come up to the billing; for the most part they are rewriting of traditional materials.

To his own part of the book, Cody added a chapter, bringing his story down to date. It contains some of his characteristic yarns, but is patched up with quotations from newspapers and publicity material. Although the rest of the autobiography appears to be a reprint of the Bliss edition, including the original illustrations, actually many changes were made, cutting thirty-one chapters to twenty-two, and 365 pages to 292, with much rewriting. That Cody had little to do with it is proved by the missing pages in the middle of the description of the Battle of Summit Springs, for the matter written to fill the gap has no resemblance either to Cody's original account or to facts of the battle it pretends to narrate.

Story of the Wild West was one of the most successful of the books signed by Buffalo Bill. It was sold by subscription by a number of distributors; the title page provided blank space for the insertion of their names as publishers. These include Historical Publishing Company, Philadelphia; R. S. Peale and Company, Chicago; Charles C. Thompson Company, Chicago; a Richmond imprint; and an 1889 edition by Eastern Publishing Company, Boston. An edition with the variant title *The History of the Wild West* was published in Chicago in 1901.

Great chunks of Buffalo Bill's autobiography were copied into *The Old Santa Fe Trail,* by Colonel Henry Inman, published in 1897 with a three-page preface signed W. F. Cody, "Buffalo Bill," to whom the book also was dedicated. A companion volume, *The Great Salt Lake Trail,* published the following year carried the names of Colonels Inman and Cody as coauthors. Cody's contribution, some 75 pages in a 530-page book, consists of two complete chapters and a few other extracts from his autobiography, including the garbled version of the killing of Tall Bull, indicating that the extracts were lifted from the autobiography in *Story of the Wild West.*

In 1904 the autobiography was mined for another narrative called *The Adventures of Buffalo Bill,* an oddity consisting of two parts. The first part, of four chapters, was a condensation and rewriting of parts of the autobiography. The second, of six chapters, called "The Life of Buffalo Bill," is written in the third person and starts over again with the boyhood of the subject. It must have been quite confusing to juvenile readers, especially as Cody was named as author, presumably of both sections.

True Tales of the Plains followed in 1908. This book is about two-thirds autobiographical, the remaining chapters discussing Wild Bill Hickok, Fort Phil Kearny, Custer's fights on the Washita and on the Little Big Horn, and other incidents of plains warfare. Many of these stories were told in some detail in the 1879 autobiography, but were cut down or left out of *Story of the Wild West.* In *True Tales of the Plains,* they have been written anew and not particularly improved. Similarly the autobiographical sections have been reworded, with extensive use of quotations from books, articles, newspaper reports, and documents. Unhappily, the quotations are not always accurate. Chapters on Sitting Bull and the

Sioux War of 1890–91 resemble program material signed by Major Burke; his grandiloquent language is unmistakable. In all probability, *True Tales of the Plains* is mainly a compilation by various press agents.

The final autobiography was an entirely new work that appeared serially in *Hearst's International Magazine* from August, 1916, to July, 1917, under the title "The Great West That Was: 'Buffalo Bill's' Life Story." When published as a book by Cosmopolitan Book Corporation in 1920, the title page read, *An Autobiography of Buffalo Bill,* and the binder's title was *Buffalo Bill's Life Story: An Autobiography.* Of all the books signed by Cody, it would seem least likely that he should have written this one, for it contains many blunders that Bill could not have made. But he did write something that formed its basis. On October 2, 1916, while it was appearing serially in *Hearst's* magazine, Cody wrote to his sister Julia: "I hardly know what I will do this winter. Wm. Randolf Hearst wants me to write a book, on my show life includeing my tours in Europe and Royalty ive met. bringing it up to the openening of the big horn basin. And what irrigation has done for the arid West. And Keep Short Monthly Stories running in the Hearsts Magazine. Has Created Such a demand, That the Hearst publishing company Can't fill the orders. The Hearst has a circulation of Seven hundred thousand coppies monthly. if I do this writeing I may go to Mays house to do it. Last winter I wrote the story of the Great West that was at Annas. I have to be where its quiet, and where I am not annoyed when I write."[7]

What he meant was that he did not want to go to the home of Julia, to whom he was writing, because she was taking in roomers and boarders at the time. He did go to May's home in Denver that winter, but not to write more articles for Hearst. He died there in January. Anna is the wife of George Cody Goodman, Julia's son. What he wrote of "The Great West That Was" at Anna's home accounts for some corrections and additions found in this last autobiography.

It is obvious, however, that whatever he wrote was edited and rewritten before it appeared in print. The editors cribbed from Helen Cody Wetmore's *Last of the Great Scouts* in telling the story

[7] *Letters from Buffalo Bill,* 78, quoted by permission of the editor, Mrs. Foote.

of Cody's first theatrical venture, thereby putting Wild Bill Hickok on the stage in Buffalo Bill's debut in Ned Buntline's drama, as she does—although that installment in the magazine was illustrated by a reproduction of one of the first year's programs showing that Wild Bill was not in the cast.[8]

A worse foul-up occurs in the account of the Battle of Slim Buttes, where Buffalo Chips White was killed, which battle Cody failed to mention in his original autobiography. When Captain Charles King was writing the articles for the *Milwaukee Sentinel* that became *Campaigning with Crook,* Cody asked King to pay tribute to Buffalo Chips, and King did so in an added article. Cody himself got around to it in *True Tales of the Plains,* in which he added the detail that he had given Chips "my best overcoat, hat, and other togs," which caused the Indians to suppose that the scout killed was Buffalo Bill. In the *Hearst's* magazine version this became "an old red-lined coat, one which I had worn conspicuously in a number of battles, and which the Indians had marked as a special target on that account." Moreover, the rewrite men did not read their source closely, because Cody distinctly says, "I remained with General Terry's command," whereas the *Hearst's* version says, "We were making a raid on an Indian village." This is wrong on two counts: Cody was not there, and the Slim Buttes fight was not a raid on an Indian village.[9]

Then Cody is made to say, "For a long time the Indians believed that I would be a menace to them no more. But they discovered their mistake later, and I sent a good many of them to the Happy Hunting-Grounds as a sort of tribute to my friend." Actually, Cody left General Terry's employ about the time of the fight at Slim Buttes, and never again was in any Indian fight. Cody, of course, never saw these chapters in print, for they were published in the magazine months after his death.

In 1917 another autobiography appeared under the title, *Buffalo Bill's Own Story of His Life and Deeds . . . ,* "brought up to date including a full account of his death and funeral" by William Lightfoot Visscher, "Col. Cody's boyhood chum and lifelong

[8] *Hearst's International* (May, 1917), 377.
[9] King, *Campaigning with Crook,* 111–17; Cody, *True Tales of the Plains,* 223; *Hearst's International* (June, 1917), 471; Cody, *Autobiography,* 290–91.

friend." Visscher was journalist, author, poet, actor, and lecturer. He was born in Owingsville, Kentucky, on November 25, 1842, fought in the Civil War, and served his newspaper apprenticeship on the *Louisville Journal* under George D. Prentice. While Visscher was with the *Kansas City Journal of Commerce,* he first knew Will Cody, then shooting buffalo for construction workers on the Kansas Pacific. A previous contribution to Buffalo Bill literature was Visscher's *A Thrilling and Truthful History of The Pony Express* (1908). His *Poems of the South and Other Verse* includes "Buffalo Bill, A Knight of the West." A verse of it goes thus:

> *A sovereign born and citizen of this fair Western land,*
> *He rose among his fellows in the custom of command;*
> *His boyhood heard the wailing that was echo of the yell*
> *When the savage made the border seem the environs of hell;*
> *With his dying father's spirit, his hunting-knife and gun,*
> *He drove the bronze barbarians into the setting sun.*[10]

The Cody autobiography edited by Visscher is lifted bodily out of *Story of the Wild West* with all its condensations and blunders. Originally issued as a memorial volume by the John R. Stanton Company of Chicago in 1917, it was reprinted as *Life and Adventures of "Buffalo Bill"* by the Wilsey Book Company, New York, in 1927, then was published again by Mrs. Johnny Baker, Lookout Mountain, Golden, Colorado, in 1939, for sale at the museum at Cody's grave.

Some of these several autobiographical works were designed for sale at the Wild West show, an idea perhaps derived from P. T. Barnum, who also had an autobiography in numerous editions that he advertised for sale at his circus. Much other literature was offered at Buffalo Bill's Wild West, so much that one wonders if it were not as much a traveling bookstore as an entertainment, and certainly enough to uphold Major Burke's emphasis on the exhibition as educational. The most widely sold publication, of course, was the annual souvenir program, which in the 1890's ran to sixty-four double-column pages of "historical sketches" and pictures for ten cents. At London in 1887, the American Exhibition

[10] Pages ii, vi, 170–74. Published in Chicago in 1911.

offered in a pink wrapper *The Life and Adventures of Buffalo Bill; Habits and Customs of the Indians; and Cowboy Life in the Wild West* at two pence. Also available was *Buffalo Bill, His Life & Stirring Adventures in the Wild West.* In Paris in 1905, the souvenir program was a seventy-eight-page biography of Cody, *Le Dernier des Grands Éclaireurs,* by René d'Hubert, at fifty centimes. Germany went in for picture books such as *Buffalo Bill's Wilder Westen: Ein Bilderbuch zum Austellen für Kinder,* by J. F. Schriber of Stuttgart, and *Buffalo Bill's Wild West, Skizzen von Carl Henkel.*

The show hit one of its high spots at the Chicago Columbian Exposition in 1893, with accompanying publicity matter. For one book published that year Cody was more responsible than he was for some of his autobiographical works. He had found his employer of Pony Express days, Alexander Majors, living in Denver in dire poverty and trying his hand at writing. His bundle of papers was turned over to Ingraham, as editor, and *Seventy Years on the Frontier* was published in Chicago in 1893 with a preface by "General W. F. Cody," a military title he did not long use. Cody paid $750 printing costs. Major Burke's *"Buffalo Bill" from Prairie to Palace* was brought out the same year by the same Chicago publisher. Paperback editions of both were for sale at the show.[11]

These were prosperous days, and Cody set up his brother-in-law, Hugh A. Wetmore, in the newspaper business in Duluth. Wetmore had literary pretensions and produced a poem or so in praise of Buffalo Bill. Likely he gave a hand to his wife, Bill's sister Helen, whose *Last of the Great Scouts* was published by the Duluth Press Printing Company in 1899.

This book was sold with the show, as Joseph Mayer recalled: "It cost us fourteen cents a copy to print. We sold it for one dollar, with a fifty-cent show ticket thrown in, and one season Buffalo Bill and Mrs. Wetmore and I split $80,000. . . . In the morning before the parade I would take out a stock on a wagon with Sammy Lone Bear, an Arapahoe who got away from Carlisle before Glenn Warner arrived, and at every corner where there was a beer saloon

---

[11] Settle, *Empire on Wheels,* 119; W. F. Cody proposal, March 30, 1893, and contract, March 25, contract archives, Rand McNally and Company, Chicago, copy from Robert West Howard.

Sammy would put on the war dance, sun dance or mating dance of his nation, and then while he was inside drinking beer I would sell books. When the books were all gone I would put Sammy in the wagon and drive back to the lot."[12]

Mrs. Wetmore's book probably outsold all the Buffalo Bill auto-biographies combined. It ran through several editions, some illustrated by Remington, and after Cody's death it was reissued in a Grosset and Dunlap reprint with foreword and afterpiece by Zane Grey, whose name was even more potent than Sammy's dancing in adding to its circulation. It is full of extravagances, exaggerations, and misinformation, and is probably largely responsible for the skepticism with which subsequent generations have viewed the exploits of Buffalo Bill.

The combination of Buffalo Bill with Pawnee Bill challenged the press agents to join the fame of the junior partner in the show to that of the more widely publicized senior partner. Two books thus produced, both plainly marked "Price $1.00," no doubt in accordance with the practice explained by Joseph Mayer, probably were sold exclusively with the show. *Thrilling Lives of Buffalo Bill and Pawnee Bill*, by Frank Winch, was published in 1911 with alternating chapters on its two heroes. It ran through at least three editions before being replaced the following year, in almost identical format, by Frank C. Cooper's *Stirring Lives of Buffalo Bill and Pawnee Bill*, a new work divided in two parts, "History of Buffalo Bill" and "Adventures of Pawnee Bill." The fine distinction may have a point, for the "adventures" of Pawnee Bill are quite different in the two books, while the "history" was quite as historic as an indiscriminate selection from previous biographies and auto-biographies of Buffalo Bill could make it.

Besides adding to the always indefinite take of show business, books sold with the show served another purpose, that of directed publicity. John Wilstach records that Major Burke saw to it that each interviewer got a copy of the current official book. News-papermen curious about Bill's heroic deeds were referred to the printed versions.[13]

[12] A. J. Liebling, interview with Joseph Mayer in *New York World-Telegram*, November 10, 1932.
[13] "Buffalo Bill's Last Stand," *Esquire*, Vol. XXI, No. 6 (June, 1944), 46-47, 126.

While almost everything written by or about Buffalo Bill had some connection with show publicity, its relationship to a group of paperback biographies is somewhat devious. Early in the 1890's there began to appear a sequence of book-size paperbacks in dime-novel format bearing no copyright notices for reasons that appear obvious. Perhaps the earliest of these, dated by a back-cover advertisement for 1891 models of Lovell Diamond bicycles, is *Buffalo Bill, the Scout,* by Clarence E. Ray, published by the Regan Publishing Corporation, Chicago. This is No. 8 in their Wild West Series. Number 9 is *Buffalo Bill and the Heroes of the Plains.* There are twenty-three chapters in *Buffalo Bill, the Scout,* of which seventeen chapters are exactly repeated, but in different order, in *Buffalo Bill and the Heroes of the Plains.* Thus Chapter I in No. 8 of the series becomes Chapter X in No. 9, Chapter III of No. 8 becomes Chapter XIV of No. 9, and so on.

Another book, *Buffalo Bill and His Wild West Companions* (anonymous) was published bound in cloth by the Henneberry Company, Chicago, and as a paperback with slightly variant title by M. A. Donohue & Company, Chicago and New York, about 1893. This work consists of thirty chapters, which reproduce verbatim twenty-one of the twenty-three chapters of *Buffalo Bill, the Scout,* and twenty of the twenty-two chapters of *Buffalo Bill and the Heroes of the Plains*—in another variant combination.

This is not all. *Buffalo Bill, King of Scouts,* by Harry Hawkeye, copyright, 1908, by I. and M. Ottenheimer of Baltimore contains seven chapters that were in all three previous books, and one more that was in two of them. Harry Hawkeye is said to be the pseudonym for Paul Emilius Lowe, who also wrote *The Dalton Brothers* for Ottenheimer. Any resemblance between it and *The Dalton Brothers in Their Oklahoma Cave,* by Clarence E. Ray, is, no doubt, coincidental.

In 1915, I. and M. Ottenheimer published *Buffalo Bill and His Daring Adventures in the Romantic Wild West,* by Nebraska Ned, but this was an original effort, so original in fact that four chapters describing a Buffalo Bill adventure in Mexico come directly from one dime novel or another. Buffalo Bill gets credit for Wild Bill's exploits as peace officer of Hays and Abilene in several of these books. The method of production is illustrative of the curiosities of the dime-novel period.

Dime novels were closely tied to show publicity, and after *Fancy Frank of Colorado* in 1880, Cody did not appear again as author until stimulated by the founding of the Wild West in 1883. That year he did three: *Wild Bill, the Whirlwind of the West, Texas Jack, the Prairie Rattler,* and *The Pilgrim Sharp; or, The Soldier's Sweetheart.* He followed these in 1884 with a series of three having as hero his friend Dr. Frank Powell: *White Beaver, the Exile of the Platte, The Wizard Brothers; or, White Beaver's Red Trail,* and *White Beaver's One-arm Pard.* In 1885 he dropped to one, *The Dead Shot Nine; or, My Pards of the Plains.*

This burst of literary activity ended in 1886 with *Montebello, the Magnificent; or, The Gold King of Colorado,* a title that surely only Colonel Ingraham could have thought up. As a matter of fact he did, for three years later he wrote *Montebello, the Gold King; or Buffalo Bill's Best Bower.* At first glance this would seem to be one of those cases in which Ingraham's ghost writing was revealed by a reprint of the story under his name but for one important fact: it is not the same story.

Buffalo Bill, or his ghost writer, then abandoned literary pursuits for eight years. In 1894 the show played Brooklyn, and proximity to the nation's literary capital inspired Cody to his greatest year as novelist. *Wild Bill, the Dead Center Shot; or, Rio Grande Ralph, the Cowboy Chief* was advertised as written for Beadle's Dime Library by special contract with the author. It has added interest in that it is one of the very early novels featuring a cowboy, for the cowboy had not yet become the national hero. It was followed quickly by *Wild Bill, the Wild West Duellist, White Beaver's Still Hunt, Texas Jack, the Lasso King,* and *The Ranch King's Dead Shot; or Texas Jack's Proxy.*

The last dime novel by Buffalo Bill, *The Dread Shot Four; or My Pards of the Plains,* started serially in *The Banner Weekly* of April 10, 1897, and was left hanging in mid-air when Beadle abandoned that publication with the issue of May 22. The publishers hastened to publish the complete story in their Dime Library on June 16. Cody's only later attempt at fiction is a short story, "The

White Captive," which was published in the magazine *10-Story Book* in September, 1903.

Dime novels signed by Buffalo Bill number twenty-four different stories. Including serials later assembled in a single publication, there were twenty-seven reprints. In all he had made fifty-one appearances in eleven periodicals. Three short stories have been mentioned.

Magazine articles signed by Buffalo Bill were few and factual, and it seems likely that he contributed personally to them more than to other material signed by him. "Famous Hunting Parties of the Plains," in *Cosmopolitan* for June, 1894, contains much information about his hunting experiences not found in his autobiographies. Newspaper articles signed by him in most cases were publicity material prepared by press agents from the autobiographies. Signed announcements in programs he probably approved but did not write.

How much Cody actually contributed to the sizable amount of material printed under his name, of course, remains speculative, but that he actually wrote some of it is beyond doubt. We can wish that he had taken more interest in the work of his ghost writers and that they had evinced more curiosity about their subject. Apparently he told them little or nothing, another instance of that unexpected modesty in talking about himself that was so often remarked by officers under whom he served as scout and notables for whom he was a hunting guide. A corollary, perhaps, was his complete indifference to the extravagances published about him.

It seems doubtful that he ever read a Buffalo Bill dime novel, or anything else printed about himself, including books signed with his name. Evidence of his reading anything is scanty. He says he read the Bible and "a few other books" when as a boy he was marooned with a broken leg during the trapping expedition with Dave Harrington. An English reporter, visiting Cody's tent at the show in 1887, noted a library of three books—*Life of General Custer*, probably that of Frederick Whittaker; *U. S. Infantry Tactics*, presumably General Emory Upton's official manual; and a book of newspaper cuttings. Cody read little, yet he was fully aware of the historical significance of the frontier of which he had been a part—

the whole theme of his showmanship—although at the same time he had no sense of having played any important part in that history. His books were merely publicity for his showmanship.

Cody's press agents seem never to have caught his vision. They took the available material and sought to rearrange it in ways that would appear new, much as the makers of the paperback biographies rearranged the same chapters in different order to produce a new book. His press agents collected endorsements as if they were selling a patent medicine. All of their exploitation went into the making of a dime-novel hero, none into documenting his historical career that then and ever since has typified the West that he and they were interested in exploiting.

All of the writings by and about Buffalo Bill were designed to publicize the show, but the show is barely mentioned in them. This is understandable, for press agents often exploit their product by indirection. What they did not know was that the show, while transitory and ever changing, was permanently important. Cody and his press agents may have done a poor job for history, but they were tremendous in their creation of a tradition. That creation was the romance of the West—the romance of the West that ever since has continued in fiction, on the stage, in motion pictures, in radio, in television—and even in history. The credit—or the blame—for starting all this goes to Cody; to what was written by him, for him, and about him, and about Buffalo Bill's Wild West.

"Buffalo Bill's in Town!"

Courtesy Denver Public Library Western Collection

Buffalo Bill's Wild West in action

Courtesy Fred B. Hackett

21

BUFFALO BILL'S WILD WEST

IN CONCLUDING HIS 1879 AUTOBIOGRAPHY, Cody told of plans to take Prentiss Ingraham's play *The Knights of the Plains* to London for the following season—one of the early indications that he was thinking along the lines that were to bring him his Wild West show triumph there eight years later. Happily he awaited fuller development of his idea. Meanwhile, Ingraham wrote a new play for the 1879–80 season, *Buffalo Bill at Bay; or, The Pearl of the Prairies.* It was in four acts and employed sixteen characters.

Publication of the autobiography and of Prentiss Ingraham's dime novels about Buffalo Bill gave the theatrical tours a much-needed boost, but it is not to be supposed that Cody traveled in a constant fanfare of publicity. Actually his closing years on the stage were the most obscure and unadvertised in Buffalo Bill's lifetime. A newspaper item in 1880 recorded that Buffalo Bill dropped nine hundred dollars shooting dice in a saloon. That was paying a high price for a minimum amount of not-too-favorable publicity.

The arrival of the Buffalo Bill Combination in Chicago in the fall of 1881 went unnoted until a trained donkey of the troupe kicked, bit, and routed the crew of a Loop livery stable. That was good for half a column of humorous comment in the *Tribune*, including bare mention of the animal's owner and show. The opening of the "thoroughly successful drama," *The Prairie Waif*, by

John A. Stevens (author of *Unknown*) at Sprague's Olympic Theatre for one week only, commencing Monday, September 5, got
only this grudging notice: "A crowd that filled every seat, swel-
tered in the aisles, and filled the lobbies was present at the Olympic
Theatre last evening to welcome back Buffalo Bill and his Indian
warriors in their soul-stirring, blood-curdling drama of *The Prairie
Waif*. The audience appeared to thoroughly enjoy the entertainment offered for their amusement."[1]

Two points should not be overlooked: there was a standing-
room-only crowd, and "the audience appeared to thoroughly enjoy the entertainment." The troupe of twenty-four included four
Winnebago chiefs, a Pawnee chief, and an Indian maiden. In Act
IV they appeared "in their wild and weird Songs and Dances as
follows: The Scalp, Sun, Horse, Squaw, and other dances under
control of Eddie Burgess, Interpreter and Boy Chief of the Pawnees." There was the trained donkey that had disrupted the orderly business of J. H. Beardsley's livery stable on Randolph Street.
Mr. Cody gave "an exhibition of Fancy Rifle Shooting, in which he
is pre-eminent and alone. *Note*—The audience will please take particular notice of the twenty different positions that Mr. Cody holds
his rifle in making his fancy shots." On occasion there were added
shooting exhibitions by Dr. Frank Powell, known as White Beaver,
companion of Buffalo Bill in many a dime-novel adventure and
contract surgeon at Fort McPherson when Cody was there as chief
of scouts. It is of record that they were in at least one Indian fight
together—it took place in the green room of Chicago's Olympic
Theatre on Friday night of the week's engagement when the
Winnebagoes went on a firewater rampage.[2]

Another long-time associate of Cody's who shows up in *The
Prairie Waif* playing the part of Hans, the Dutchman, is Jule Keen,
for many years treasurer of Buffalo Bill's Wild West. Lew Parker
tells a story about him: "It was absolutely essential that the part
of the Waif should be played in the first act. . . . The lady who
played the part of the Waif, in Chicago, was not particularly

[1] *Chicago Tribune*, August 8, 1880; September 5, 6, 1881.
[2] Leonard and Goodman, *Buffalo Bill*, plate 27, p. 225; Mary Hardgrove, Hebbard, "Notes on Dr. David Franklin Powell, Known as 'White Beaver,'" *Wisconsin
Magazine of History*, Vol. XVI, No. 6 (Summer, 1952), 306–309; Buel, *Heroes of
the Plains*, 416.

friendly to Keen, who, at that time, was the stage manager, as well as acting the Dutch part in the piece. At a matinee one day, at the time of the raising of the curtain, the Waif had not arrived; there was no understudy for the part, but the curtain went up just the same, and the play went on; just as the curtain descended at the close of the first act, the lady entered the theatre. She came in with a sweep and a flashing eye and exclaimed: 'What is going on here? How dared you raise that curtain without my being here?' Keen turned around slowly and drawled: 'Why, weren't you here.' "[3]

Apparently Buffalo Bill melodrama was still as informal as it was lacking in dramatic talent, but it needed neither play nor acting to be profitable; it only needed to be western. Critics found merit in the Indian dances, shooting exhibitions, and pageantry, and some were disappointed in not finding more of this groping toward folklore and tradition—and toward the Wild West show.

Cody's search for a more truthful medium was not the result of any discouragement over financial returns from his theatrical ventures, however. In the season of 1880–81 he is said to have netted $48,000, and the two following seasons were equally successful. Whether it was *Vera Vance; or, Saved from the Sioux* or *From Noose to Neck,* he made money. In his final season before founding the Wild West show, that of 1882–83, when he played *Twenty Days; or, Buffalo Bill's Pledge,* Cody says, "I found myself richer by several thousand dollars than I had ever been before, having done a splendid business at every place where my performance was given that year."[4]

The Wild West show, closely associated with rodeo, was an original and distinctively American type of entertainment. It seems self-evident that it was originated by Buffalo Bill. However, almost everyone who had any connection with its beginnings has put in a claim to its invention. The general idea, of course, was not new. P. T. Barnum in 1843 bought fifteen calf buffalo that were exhibited in a tent at the Bunker Hill celebration when Daniel Webster dedicated the monument. Barnum took his $700 investment to Hoboken, where he advertised a Grand Buffalo Hunt—

---

[3] Lew Parker, *Odd People I Have Met,* 21–22.
[4] Walsh, *The Making of Buffalo Bill,* 214–15; *Letters from Buffalo Bill,* 26; Cody, *Story of the Wild West,* 693.

Free of Charge. The catch was that Barnum had bought up all the ferries for the day. The buffalo calves, however, refused to co-operate until stampeded by shouts of the audience, then crashed through a fence and fled to a swamp. C. D. French, the star per-former, lassoed one calf before the stampede, and put on a roping exhibition. Barnum had failed to solve the problem of putting on such a show and did not try it again.[5]

In 1856, Mabie Brothers Menagerie and Den Stone's Circus were combined with Tyler's Indian Exhibition, which used Indians in spectacles portraying a buffalo hunt, a corn gathering, Poca-hontas rescuing Captain John Smith, and dances. Wild Bill Hickok attempted a buffalo-hunt show at Niagara Falls in 1871, but he met the same problem Barnum faced, without a ferry business to fall back on. Ned Buntline proposed to produce *The Scouts of the Prairie* outdoors, with horses, and when Buffalo Bill and Texas Jack backed out on him, tried it unsuccessfully with Arizona Frank and Dashing Charlie.[6]

None of these schemes was as broad in scope as Buffalo Bill's Wild West proved. The idea for it was claimed by Nate Salsbury, who later became Cody's partner in the venture. Nate recalled that, on returning from a tour of Australia in 1876 with the Sals-bury Troubadours, he had debated with J. B. Gaylord, an agent of the Cooper and Bailey Circus, about the merits of Australian jockeys in comparison with American cowboys and Mexican riders. As a result, he says, "I began to construct a show in my mind that would embody the whole subject of horsemanship and before I went to sleep I had mapped out a show that would be constituted of elements that had never been employed in concerted effort in the history of the show business." In thus describing his concept, he makes it clear that what he had in mind was that part of the show that became the "Rough Riders of the World," with no hint of the pageant of the West that became the outstanding element in Buffalo Bill's Wild West. Salsbury says that some years later "I decided that such an entertainment must have a well known figure head to attract attention and thus help to quickly solve the

---

[5] P. T. Barnum, *The Life of P. T. Barnum* (London, 1855), 215–18.

[6] Elbert R. Bowen, "The Circus in Early Rural Missouri," *Missouri Historical Review*, Vol. XLVII, No. 1 (October, 1952); Monaghan, *The Great Rascal*, 29–31.

problem of advertising a new idea. After careful consideration of the plan and scope of the show I resolved to get W. F. Cody as my central figure."

The two men met in 1882 while both were playing in New York, and "As he was about at the end of his profit string on the theatrical stage I dare say he was pleased at the chance to try something else, for he grew very enthusiastic over the plan as I unfolded it to him and was sure that the thing would be a great success. It was arranged at the lunch that I would go to Europe the following summer and look the ground over with a view to taking the show to a country where all its elements would be absolutely novel. I was quite well aware that the Dime Novel had found its way to England especially and wherever the Dime Novel had gone Cody had gone along. . . . I went to Europe the following summer and looked the ground over. I came to the conclusion that it would take a lot of money to do the thing right and told Cody that we must be well provided with money when we made the plunge and that so far as I was concerned I did not feel rich enough to undertake my share of the expense and that I would have to wait another year before I could go into the scheme in proper shape. To this Cody did not demur but said that he was in about the same fix as myself. So far we had arrived at a perfect understanding that we were to share and share alike in the venture. . . . But Cody must have agreed to drop the matter for another year with a strong mental reservation for I was astonished in the Spring of 1883 to get a telegram (which I now have in my possession) asking me if I wanted to go into the show for this country if *Dr. Carver did not object*. Of course I was dumbfounded and replied that I did not want to have anything to do with Doctor Carver who was a fakir in the show business and as Cody once expressed it 'Went West on a piano stool.' Events proved that Cody did not wait for our plan to go to Europe to ripen but no sooner had my ideas than he began to negotiate with Carver who had a reputation as a marksman to go in with him and was kind enough, when they had laid all their plans, to let me in as a partner. Of course I turned them down and they went on the road and made a ghastly failure."[7]

[7] Nate Salsbury, "The Origin of the Wild West Show," *The Colorado Magazine*, Vol. XXXII, No. 3 (July, 1955), 205–208.

It is easy enough to see Cody's point of view in this negotiation. Far from being merely a figurehead in a form of entertainment devised by Salsbury, he had been moving toward the Wild West show idea for many years. He certainly had staged quite a show for the Grand Duke Alexis as well as for General Sheridan's hunting friends. His stage appearances had tended more and more toward western spectacle. When Nate Salsbury came to him with a concrete proposal, contributing to the concept with his idea of a show that would "embody the whole subject of horsemanship," Cody welcomed the suggested partnership; but when Salsbury wanted to postpone the venture, Cody might well assume that Salsbury was cooling off to the project.

Tipping the balance was Cody's success with the "Old Glory Blow Out," or Fourth of July celebration, at North Platte, which proved that the idea was as good on home grounds as it was for Europe. William McDonald, of North Platte, who was there at the time, remembers the circumstances. He says that Cody, just home from his theatrical tour, came into the store of Charles J. Foley when Charles F. Ormsby, onetime mayor, and other prominent citizens were there. Cody asked what was planned for July 4 and was told that nothing had been planned. "Cody mumbled something to the effect that he was surprised that nothing had been planned for the Fourth of July," said McDonald, "then went up the street to the saloon, but he hardly stayed long enough to get a drink. He wasn't one to take a drink just to get his mouth wet. He came back, protesting that it was not patriotic not to have a Fourth of July celebration. Ormsby and Foley said, 'O.K., Bill, you are chairman to get up a celebration.'" North Platte at that time had a race track with a fence around it, and Bill proposed to use it to give a demonstration of how he had killed buffalo, using steers and blank ammunition. It was McDonald who recalled that M. C. Keefe had a small herd of buffalo and suggested that perhaps they could be used. Cody persuaded his fellow citizens to offer prizes for shooting, riding, and bronco busting, and sent out five thousand handbills announcing the events and prizes. He estimated that he might get one hundred cowboy entrants; he actually got one thousand. Then it was that he began to see what he had on his hands. McDonald insists that Cody at this time announced his intention of organizing a wild west show, using that name for it.[8]

Louis E. Cooke summed it up in press-agentese: "The attendance was unprecedented for that section, the whole country for a radius of over one hundred and fifty miles being temporarily depopulated. Thus in a still distant and debateable region, a wilderness over which the buffalo roamed and the hostile savage prowled; under most difficult and dangerous conditions; in furtherance of a purely patriotic purpose was roughly organized an ephemeral celebration, destined through Col. Cody's efforts and masterful personality to become not only the progenitor of all the 'Frontier Day' State and Inter-State tournaments since and still given in the West, and ranking as the most popular attraction at its greatest holiday gatherings, but to serve as the basic idea for an American revelation; border warfare and illustriously illustrative educational entertainment; the only one of its kind, and which has electrified and conquered the civilized world, and all the rulers and greatest soldiers, statesmen, educators, scientists, artists, horsemen and historians thereof."[9]

This is typical of the language of the great outdoor-show era, but it scarcely exaggerates in saying that Cody's exhibition, staged under the frontier conditions he was attempting to depict, was the original, not only of the Wild West show, but of the rodeo, although that word did not gain currency until long after 1911 when Cooke wrote of it.

Rodeo undoubtedly had its origin in informal and impromptu races, contests, and show-off at open range roundups, such as the one Cody attended with Frank North. Captain Mayne Reid, author of boys' books of western adventure, wrote from Santa Fe on June 10, 1847, "This round-up is a great time for the cowhands, a Donneybrook fair it is indeed. They contest with each other for the best roping and throwing, and there are horse races and whisky and wines." At a Fourth of July celebration in 1869 at Deer Trail,

[8] Interview with William McDonald, North Platte, September 6, 1955; Unidentified clipping, "First Wild West Show 50 Years Ago; North Platte to Observe Anniversary."

[9] F. C. Cooper, *Buffalo Bill and Pawnee Bill*, 210–24; Winch, *Thrilling Lives of Buffalo Bill and Pawnee Bill*, 176–77; *The Billboard*, October 2, 1915, December 29, 1934.

Colorado, the title, "champion bronco buster of the plains," and a suit of clothes were awarded to Emilne Gardenshire of the Milliron Ranch. The riding of a wild steer was featured at a Fourth of July celebration in Cheyenne in 1872.[10]

Cody's timing was perfect in launching his Wild West in 1883. The idea was in the air. In April of that year, A. B. Grady organized a company of cowboys in Texas to give exhibitions of roping and horsemanship, putting on two shows at San Antonio in May, almost simultaneously with the opening of the Buffalo Bill show. That July 4, Pecos, Texas, staged a roundup contest with prizes.

The outdoor show was just entering its period of greatest popularity. In 1885 more than fifty circuses were on the road, the top number ever to tour the United States. The circus was derived from Europe and boasted of its foreign character, but it was peculiarly American in its spectacular bigness, combining in one aggregation the horse show, the trained-animal show, the traveling menagerie, the museum of freaks, and the hippodrome track for races. It was the period of great, free street parades, of two and three performances a day, of railroad excursions to cities where the big shows played—the period of P. T. Barnum and W. C. Coup, James A. Bailey, Adam Forepaugh, W. W. Cole, Sells Brothers, John Robinson, and Yankee Robinson, before the mergers in the closing years of the century. Ringling Brothers started their circus in 1884.

Cody apparently went to work immediately after the Old Glory Blow Out, signing up talent and seeking properties, for he was able to assemble his show early in the spring of 1883, despite continuing his theatrical season of 1882–83 as usual. While in New York on that tour, he saw Nate Salsbury and found him not ready with cash backing. Quite possibly Cody thought he was being given the runaround. On this same tour Cody met Dr. W. F. Carver in New Haven and agreed to form a partnership. As Carver once told it, Cody "came to my home in New Haven, Conn., down and out. I told him I was getting ready to bring out the Wild West Show, and he gave me his solemn promise not to drink another drop if I would take him outdoors with me, and I agreed to do so. The result was

[10] C. P. Westermeier, *Trailing the Cowboy,* 343–40; Chuck Walters, "The Legend of Rodeo," *1955 Annual Rodeo Sport News* (January, 1955), 29.

that I invested $27,000 in the enterprise and signed a note with him on the First National Bank of Omaha for $2,000, all of which I had to pay. In addition to this, he failed to live up to his promise and was dead drunk all summer. So we separated."[11]

Carver liked to boast that the Wild West was his idea, yet one of his first quarrels with Cody was over Cody's calling it that in billing he had ordered printed, Carver preferring "Golden West." According to McDonald, whose family's bank in North Platte backed Cody's show, Carver put up no money at all for the Wild West. Cody's drinking that summer unquestionably contributed to their troubles, but according to observers, Carver bent an elbow quite as often as Cody. Carver's claim to have originated the Wild West is thin on all counts. He was in Europe on an exhibition-shooting tour while Cody was staging the Old Glory Blow Out and was too busy with shooting exhibitions to take any part in organizing the show, according to his own accounts.

Carver's exhibition shooting was notable, but his self-conferred title of "world's champion marksman" was exaggerated, and he claimed feats that violated the laws of physics and ballistics. In endurance shooting he made several records. On July 13, 1878, at Brooklyn Driving Park, he broke 5,500 glass balls out of 6,211 shots fired within 500 minutes. In six days ending January 17, 1885, at Lincoln Skating Rink, New Haven, he hit 60,016 wooden blocks tossed in the air out of 64,881 shots fired, and bettered his 60,000-hit record at Minneapolis in 1888 with only 650 misses. Contrary to Carver's claims, however, his records did not stand long. Within a year B. A. Bartlett of Buffalo broke the 60,000-mark with only 280 misses, and the record was really shattered in 1907 when Adolph T. Topperwein hit 72,500 targets with only nine misses.[12]

His records can be checked, but nothing seems to be known of his life as a plainsman except what he said of himself, and it so happens that he seldom agreed even with himself. In a biographi-

[11] "The Letters of Doc Carver" (ed. by Raymond W. Thorp), *Outdoor Life—Outdoor Recreation*, Vol. LXV, No. 4 (April, 1930), 89; R. W. Thorp, *Spirit Gun of the West*, 138.

[12] E. L. Stevenson, "These Carver Yarns," *Outdoor Life—Outdoor Recreation*, Vol. LXVI, No. 2 (August, 1930), 84; H. F. Williamson, *Winchester, the Gun That Won the West* (Washington, 1952), 183–85; Charles Askins, "Ad Topperwein," *The Gun Digest*, 1956 (Chicago), 97–100.

cal sketch in a program for his Wild West combined with the circus of Adam Forepaugh, Jr., in 1888, Carver claimed an important part in the Sioux war in Minnesota in 1862, saying, "Dr. Carver's acquaintance with the country, his familiarity with the savages' methods of fighting, together with his magnetic influence over the band of scouts—of which he was the chief—united in crowning his labors with brilliant success, and the defeat, capture and subsequent hanging of 'Little Crow' was due largely to his courage, strategy, and sleepless zeal." Yet in a biography based entirely on Carver's manuscripts and notebooks it is said that Carver was hundreds of miles away at the time of the Sioux war in Minnesota and that he knew nothing of it until long after it was over.[13]

As scouts, cowboys, Mexican *vaqueros*, Indians, buffalo, elk, mountain sheep, bucking horses, stagecoach, and emigrant wagons were assembled that spring of 1883, Cody insisted on authenticity in every detail. This brought near disaster at the first rehearsal at Colville (later Columbus), Nebraska.

The stagecoach was hitched to a team of almost unbroken mules, with a veteran driver, Fred Mathews, at the reins. Mayor "Pap" Clothier and members of the town council were passengers and honored guests. Frank North headed the Pawnees who were to make the attack. When the Pawnees shrieked their war whoop and charged, firing blank cartridges, the mules bolted. The Indians took up the chase with noise and vigor. Buffalo Bill's rescuers tried to head off the stampede, but were swept along with it. Around the race track went the entire company until the mules tired and could be halted. The Mayor was restrained with difficulty from attempting to beat up Cody.

Frank North had this caustic comment: "Bill, if you want to make this damned show go, you do not need me or my Indians. You want about twenty old bucks. Fix them up with all the paint and feathers in the market. Use some old hack horses and a hack driver. To make it go you want a show of illusion, not realism."[14]

[13] *The Combined Dr. W. F. Carver Wild West and Adam Forepaugh, Jr., Exhibitions,* 1888; Thorp, *Spirit Gun,* 28–29; Charles B. Roth, "The Biggest Blow Since Galveston," *The Denver Westerners Monthly Roundup,* Vol. XII, No. 1 (January, 1956), 9.

[14] L. O. Leonard, "Buffalo Bill's First Wild West Rehearsal," *Union Pacific Magazine* (August, 1922), 26–27.

Cody never took this advice entirely, although he learned in time the value of illusion. To the end he insisted on authenticity wherever practicable. The stagecoach, always billed as the old Deadwood Stagecoach, was genuine. He had telegraphed Luke Voorhees, manager of the Cheyenne and Black Hills Stage line, for a coach. Voorhees sent him one that had originally cost $1,800. Cody had ridden in it in 1876. At one time it had been abandoned for three months after having been attacked by Indians near Indian Creek. It also had seen service in Colorado on the North Park line to Teller. It survived the sinking of the show on a Mississippi River steamboat the following year. It is reported still in existence in the museum of the United States Post Office Department in Washington.[15]

The Wild West, Hon. W. F. Cody and Dr. W. F. Carver's Rocky Mountain and Prairie Exhibition, as it was sometimes billed, opened at the Omaha Fair Grounds on May 19, 1883. Dr. Carver had an off day, perhaps because of too much celebration of the opening—a celebration that lasted five weeks according to some accounts. When the crowd yelled for Buffalo Bill, Cody tried his hand at the glass balls with a borrowed gun. It is not to be supposed that Bill had neglected the inaugural festivities, despite which he shot so well that his act became a permanent part of the show.[16]

Considering Dr. Carver's jealousy of rivals, it is surprising that top billing, next to the two proprietors, was given to Captain A. H. Bogardus, listed on the program as the Champion Pigeon Shot of America, who "will give his great exhibition using the Ligowsky clay pigeon." Bogardus was making history, for pigeon shooting then meant live passenger pigeons, lured to the marksman's trap by a "stool pigeon," a captive pigeon tied by a leg to a stool, thereby bringing a picturesque expression into the language. "Bogardus Rules" governed matches at which contestant shot at passenger pigeons released from traps, but Bogardus himself deplored this slaughter. He began the manufacture of glass balls and of spring traps, the traps triggered to throw out the balls in simulation of

[15] Spring, *Cheyenne and Black Hills Stage and Express Routes*, Appendix B; *Sheridan* (Wyo.) *Express*, December 29, 1900.

[16] Dexter Fellows and Andrew A. Freeman, *This Way to the Big Show*, 69; Shirley, *Pawnee Bill*, 98–99; Walsh, *The Making of Buffalo Bill*, 229.

bird flight. He was too late to halt the slaughter, which reached its peak between 1878 and 1882 when the heavy demand for squabs as a delicacy caused the killing of millions of passenger pigeons at their nesting grounds. The last passenger pigeon died in the Cincinnati zoo in 1914.

While Bogardus was unsuccessful in saving the passenger pigeon, his exhibitions saved the trapshooter from following the bird into extinction and established a popular sport. Adam Bogardus, born in Albany County, New York, on September 17, 1833, came to Illinois in 1856, where he became a market shooter at Elkhart, Logan County. He defeated Abe Kleinman, Illinois champion, then challenged Ira Paine, champion wingshot of America. Paine conceded the national title to Bogardus in 1871 after a series of matches. At Brighton, England, on August 6, 1878, Bogardus defeated the English champion, Aubrey Coventry, seventy-nine to seventy-eight, in a one-hundred-bird match. His four sons, Eugene, Peter, Edward, and Adam, Jr., all expert shots, appeared with Bogardus in the Wild West show.[17]

Major Frank North, of course, got top billing. Others introduced as "notables of the Far West" were Colonel Tom Wilson and George Clother. The staff was headed by John M. Burke as general manager. Thereafter the talents of that great press agent were devoted exclusively to the fortunes of Buffalo Bill. Also recruited from theatrical combinations was Jule Keen, beginning his long service as treasurer. E. W. Woolcott was business manager and F. Whitiker was superintendent.

Major North brought along as interpreter for the Pawnees twenty-three-year-old Gordon William Lillie, who had been secretary to the agent and teacher in the industrial school at the Pawnee agency, Indian Territory. Lillie later became well known as "Pawnee Bill" and as "the White Chief of the Pawnees." He was born in Bloomington, Illinois, on February 14, 1860, the son of Newton W. and Susan Ann Lillie. He received a high school education and afterward worked for about six months as bookkeeper in his father's flour mill. The family then moved to Wellington, Kansas,

[17] William Bushell, *The Life of Captain Adam Bogardus*; Eugene T. Peterson, "Passenger Pigeons and Stool Pigeons," *Michigan Alumnus Quarterly Review*, Vol. LXII, No. 18 (May 26, 1956), 262–66.

to establish a mill, but Gordon decided to strike out for himself at the age of sixteen. He spent one season trapping with Tom Evans and sold the catch in St. Joseph, Missouri. In August, 1882, he went on a roundup for the Zimmerman ranch on Skeleton River before accepting appointment at the Indian agency. Gordon Lillie's seven years on the frontier made him something more than a tenderfoot when he joined the Wild West at its second stand, Council Bluffs.[18]

Besides Major Burke, there was one other member of the original company destined to remain with Buffalo Bill as long as he was in show business. This was Johnny Baker, soon to be known as "The Cowboy Kid." Johnny was authentically western. His father, Lew, and his mother settled at O'Fallon's Bluffs in 1862. When the Pony Express and stage station became a ghost town, they moved to North Platte. There nine-year-old Johnny tagged Buffalo Bill around town to hold the Scout's horse. Cody was always kind to children, and soon made the boy a companion, virtually adopting him. As the Wild West was projected, Johnny begged to go along.

After Omaha and Council Bluffs the exhibition went to Springfield and then eastward, reaching Boston's Beacon Park on July 2. The show had no tentage and no lighting, so was confined to afternoon engagements in borrowed fair grounds or other large enclosures. At Aquidnuck Fair Grounds, Newport, Lord Mandeville became the first of many English notables to ride in the Deadwood coach. The *Hartford Courant* called it the "best open-air show ever seen. . . . The real sight of the whole thing is, after all, Buffalo Bill. . . . Cody was an extraordinary figure, and sits on a horse as if he were born in the saddle. His feats of shooting are perfectly wonderful. . . . He has, in this exhibition, out-Barnumed Barnum."

This sort of praise did not sit well with the "world's champion marksman" who was co-star of the show. Dr. Carver did not have the personality nor the background to put himself over. In addition, the "Evil Spirit of the Plains" had an evil temper, and when he missed his shot one day at Coney Island, he smashed his rifle over his horse's ears and punched his helper. Nate Salsbury saw the show in New York and found little merit in it, but that was because "they had not developed my ideas in putting it together

[18] J. H. DeWolff, *Pawnee Bill;* Souvenir, Pawnee Bill's Historic Wild West (1893); Souvenir of Buffalo Ranch and Its Owners (1911).

at all." He declared the season "a ghastly failure," which was an exaggeration.[19]

The show lacked adequate management and needed discipline, to which neither Cody nor Carver contributed much. Its general idea, however, was sound, and its program contained many of the features that were to make Buffalo Bill's Wild West a continuing success. The Pony Express and "The Startling and Soul-Stirring Attack Upon the Deadwood Mail Coach" were permanent fixtures, as was "Cow-Boys' Fun!" introducing bucking and kicking ponies. Roping, tying, and riding wild Texas steers was another event that would continue into rodeo. There was a variety of races: a bareback pony race of Indians, a one-hundred yard race between an Indian on foot and a mounted Indian, turning a stake at fifty yards; and a dash of mounted cowboys. The closing spectacle was "A Grand Hunt on the Plains," deriving from the Old Glory Blow Out. It introduced buffalo, elk, deer, wild horses, and cattle.[20]

One outstanding event, however, was seen only that first season. This was billed as "Lassoing and Riding the Wild Bison of the Plains." According to Pawnee Bill, the top riders of the show had succeeded in riding all the buffalo with the show except one big bull called Monarch. All were afraid of him, and they purposely missed roping him. At Indianapolis, Cody insisted that Monarch be ridden. Buck Taylor and Jim Lawson threw him, but Jim Bullock, top steer rider, refused to attempt the ride. Cody himself then got aboard. Monarch ran a short distance, then bucked and threw Cody high in the air. He was carried to a hospital and remained there two weeks. Pawnee Bill says that the first time he had seen Cody free from liquor that summer was when Cody rejoined the show in Chicago. The following season there was substituted a simulated "Buffalo Chase, by Buffalo Bill and Pawnee Indians."[21]

While the show played the Chicago Driving Park, October 17 to 20, Cody was sobered in more ways than one. Nate Salsbury was

[19] Walsh, The Making of Buffalo Bill, 228–30; Salsbury, "The Origin of the Wild West Show," Colorado Magazine, Vol. XXXII, No. 3 (July, 1955), 207.

[20] Programs, the Wild West, 1883: Brighton Beach, Coney Island; Gentleman's Driving Park, West Fairmont, September 4–8; Chicago Driving Park, October 17–20—in Denver Public Library; Leonard and Goodman, Buffalo Bill, King of the Old West, plate 28, p. 224.

[21] Shirley, Pawnee Bill, 102–103.

playing in a theater there, and, Nate says, "Cody came to see me and said that if I did not take hold of the show he was going to quit the whole thing. He said he was through with Carver and that he would not go through such another summer for a hundred thousand dollars." He had not made that much, but neither had the season been a failure. He wrote Julia late in the season that he had not made much money, but that he had spent freely for advertising and also in fitting up facilities at Coney Island, as a build-up for the following year.[22]

Cody was called home from Chicago by the illness of his eleven-year-old daughter Orra Maude, which resulted in her death on October 24. His family was then reduced to two daughters, Arta, born in 1866, and the baby, Irma Louise, born on February 9, 1883. Orra's death came at a time when Cody was talking of a petition for divorce. In a letter to Julia he said that Lulu had tried to ruin him financially that summer. His domestic difficulties no doubt added to his discouragement and may account for some of his heavy drinking.

Cody's final break with Dr. Carver came when the Evil Spirit proposed a winter tour. Instead, the Cody-Carver Wild West closed its season at Omaha, and the partners divided their physical assets by the toss of a coin. Cody kept the Deadwood stagecoach.

Carver made his winter tour in partnership with Captain Jack Crawford. Their Wild West played Nashville, Atlanta, Augusta, Charleston, Columbus, Montgomery, Mobile, and New Orleans. In 1884, Carver took his show to Canada and in 1885 to New England, where he tangled with Buffalo Bill's Wild West. A series of court actions followed. Carver's version is that he won his case but lost his show. In 1886, Dr. Carver's Wild West was combined with W. W. Cole's New Colossal Show, and for two following seasons with the circus of Adam Forepaugh, Jr.

Carver's revived Wild West toured Europe in 1889 and Australia in 1890 and 1891. In 1892 he gave an outdoor Wild West in the afternoon and used the same company in a melodrama, *The Scout,* in theaters at night. Despite his persistence, Dr. Carver's Wild West won neither lasting fame nor immediate fortune, and he

[22] Salsbury, "The Origin of the Wild West Show," *Colorado Magazine,* Vol. XXXII, No. 3 (July, 1955), 207; *Letters from Buffalo Bill,* 20-21.

remained embittered and intensely jealous of the greater success of Buffalo Bill. Carver nevertheless continued trouping until 1927. His final attraction was a troupe of diving horses, which he exhibited at fairs, with a girl rider plunging forty feet from a diving platform into a pool with her horse.[23]

When Carver and Cody parted in the fall of 1883, it was John Peter Altgeld, later governor of Illinois, who drew up the contract of partnership by which Cody, Salsbury, and Bogardus undertook to carry on the enterprise to be known as "Buffalo Bill's Wild West —America's National Entertainment." Nate, or Nathan, Salsbury was a person of quite different temperament from the Evil Spirit, although he also was a showman. Born in Freeport, Illinois, on February 28, 1846—Cody was just two days older—Nate ran away from home at fifteen and enlisted in the Union Army during the Civil War. In later years General Sherman recalled Nate's gay singing of "Oh! Susannah" during a period of hardship in the Georgia campaign. Nate was captured and imprisoned at Andersonville. After the war he began the study of law, but was attracted by amateur theatricals and served a stage apprenticeship in stock companies at Grand Rapids, Detroit, and Baltimore. After achieving some success at the Boston Museum, he was employed as leading heavy man at Hooley's Theater in Chicago. He then organized his own company for comedy entertainment, "The Troubadours," with which he toured successfully for twelve years, including a trip to Australia. For this company he wrote the farcical dramas *Patchwork*, which had a run of eighteen months, and *The Brook*, which he is said to have completed in eight hours, close to Ned Buntline's record. Nate Salsbury played *The Brook* continuously for five years.

The partnership of Cody and Salsbury has generally been regarded as ideal in outdoor show annals, with Cody providing the showmanship out front before the public and Salsbury the behind-the-scenes business management that led to success. Salsbury's name appeared as joint proprietor on all billing, and his picture

[23] W. F. Carver to William Garnett, June 29, Sept. 12, 1926, and press releases attached; "The Letters of Doc Carver," *Outdoor Life—Outdoor Recreation*, Vol. LXV, Nos. 4-6, Vol. LXVI, No. 1 (April to July, 1930).

was frequently used beside that of Cody, but he never appeared in the arena and was little known to the public that flocked to see Buffalo Bill. That Salsbury was not entirely happy in his self-effacing role is apparent in articles he wrote but did not allow to be published during his lifetime. His references to Cody's earlier career reflect more legend than fact and indicate a lack of intimacy as well as a lack of admiration. Considering their long successful partnership, Salsbury's resentment of Cody would seem surprising were it not characteristic of show business. Nate had been a star; he might have been willing to share the limelight, but to have it turned entirely on his partner aroused jealousy. There is no evidence that Cody was ever aware of it. If he was, he said nothing; that was characteristic, too.

Salsbury had wanted Buffalo Bill as a figurehead, as he said himself, but things did not quite work out that way. Cody insisted on a share in management, particularly in personnel. Nate's admiration for that greatest of press agents, Major Burke, was strictly limited. In Nate's words: "I should never have put this relation of the origin of the Wild West Show on paper if there had not been in all the years that have passed a most determined effort on the part of John Burke and other hero-worshippers who have hung on to Cody's coat tails for their sustenance to make Cody the originator of the show for in doing so they can edge in their own feeble claims to being an integral part of the success of the show. The men I speak of were all participants in the failure that followed the first venture by Cody and were retained in the management of the show by me at the request of Cody, who lives in the worship of those who bleed him. . . .

"In his peculiar position of almoner general to the newspaper men of the world Burke has more personal friends than any man I ever knew. I do not believe there is another man in the world who could have covered as much space in the newspapers of the day as John Burke has done and I do not believe there is another man in the world in his position that would have had the gall to exploit himself at the expense of the show as much as John Burke!

"Burke and Keen and the rest of the Codyites who have followed the show from the day I took hold of it have never forgiven me for taking the reins of management out of their hands where they had been placed by Cody and Carver. . . . Mr. Keen is honest and able in his department but that lets him out."[24]

Salsbury's low opinion of Burke was not shared by a later partner in the show, Pawnee Bill. When Lillie was first employed to manage the show, he was asked to get rid of Burke and Louis E. Cooke, the general agent, because of their extravagant spending. Said Lillie, "I would not have been more surprised had they asked for my resignation." He noted that Burke "was the highest salaried press agent in the country. He knew more managing editors and owners of big publications, and called them by their first names, than any man who ever lived." And Lillie told the owners, "As for Burke's excessive expense account, I do not believe we did half enough entertaining the press, for I never in my life saw such liberal treatment of any show, any place, as was accorded us by the press of New York City." The upshot was that Lillie bought out the group that held control of the show.[25]

Salsbury almost admits Burke's value, but very grudgingly, and it is apparent that his prejudices were all to the fore as he wrote these papers. As they were never published by him, it is possible that they did not represent the view he held at all times. Whatever his opinions, there can be no doubt of Salsbury's abilities nor of the necessity of them for the show's success, even though he may have exaggerated its previous failure. These abilities became apparent as he met his first problem—that of ending the celebrating that had marked the inaugural year.

When Nate visited his property, ready to open the season at St. Louis in the spring of 1884, he found Cody "surrounded by a lot of harpies called old timers who were getting as drunk as he at his expense. . . . He had taken a plug hat from someone in the crowd, and jammed it on his head, and as his hair was long and thick in those days, a more ridiculous figure could not be imagined than he cut with his arm around White Beaver while they rehearsed the exploits of the frontier to the gaping gang of bloodsuckers that surrounded them."

[24] Salsbury, "The Origin of the Wild West Show," *Colorado Magazine,* Vol. XXXII, No. 3 (July, 1955), 207–208.
[25] Shirley, *Pawnee Bill,* 186–87.

Salsbury protested in a letter which he hoped Bill would read in a sober moment. It drew this reply from Cody: "Your very sensible and truly rightful letter has just been read and it has been the means of showing me just where I stand. And I solemnly promise you that after this you will never see me under the influence of liquor. I may have to take two or three drinks today to brace up on; that will be all as long as we are partners. I appreciate all you have done. Your judgment and business is good and from this on I will do my work to the letter. This drinking surely ends today and your pard will be himself, and on deck all the time."[26]

From this episode stems one of the most famous of Buffalo Bill legends. The story has been told that Nate limited Bill to one drink a day, whereupon Bill poured his drink of whiskey in a schooner with capacity to last him through the day. By the time Gene Fowler got to the story in *Timberline*, it had grown to twelve drinks a day poured in twelve huge tumblers. Gene goes on to tell how Nate sued Bill under their contract, but the judge before whom the case was heard held that the contract specified glasses of whiskey without limitation on size. Of course, there never was such a contract and Nate never sued Bill—but it makes a good story. Bennett Cerf, in a recent retelling of the story, took out some exaggeration—he made it only ten glasses a day.[27]

While no version greatly exaggerates Cody's capacity, it will surprise many to learn that there is evidence that Cody stuck pretty well to his bargain to quit drinking on the job. This is not intended to imply that he quit drinking altogether, or that he did not take an occasional fall off the wagon on the job, as the Old Army expression of Bill's day put it.

Cody once wrote to Captain Jack Crawford, "I would have answered at once from Frisco, but I was on a hell of a toot and I seldom attend to anything but hoof her up when I am that way." His planned fall from the wagon came regularly when the show season closed and he returned to North Platte. Dexter Fellows, who traveled with the show as press agent and knew a two-fisted drinking man when he saw one, records an occasion, when the

[26] Walsh, *The Making of Buffalo Bill*, 233; Fellows and Freeman, *This Way to the Big Show*, 90–92.

[27] Gene Fowler, *Timberline*, 46–48; Bennett Cerf, "Cerfboard," *This Week*, New York *Herald-Tribune*, August 5, 1951.

show closed at North Platte, and the entire show, with the exception of Annie Oakley and Johnny Baker, went on a memorable binge. But Fellows should also be credited when he states: "No doubt during the winters there were big doings at his camp, but while he was with the show, except for that visit to his home State, I never saw him under the influence of liquor. . . . Because of the need to entertain, Cody kept a stock of liquor in his private car, but I never saw any in his tent on the show grounds. In fact, when General Fitzhugh Lee visited him in Richmond, Cody had to send a messenger to the car to provide the nephew of General Robert E. Lee with the drink of his choice." Lee had heard that Cody made "the best old-fashioned cocktail ever put together. . . . When the messenger brought back the makings, Cody mixed the drink, pouring only a small one for himself."[28]

Ed Goodman, son of Bill's sister Julia, gave Johnny Baker no such exceptional reputation for sobriety as did Fellows, but he did report to his mother from the show grounds in Philadelphia in 1886, "Uncle Will never touches a drop I dont think I never hear of his doing so." William McDonald, Cody's business representative in North Platte, states emphatically that Cody quit drinking altogether, under doctor's orders, during the last nine years of his life. Cody had the reputation of never having missed a performance on account of drinking in all his years of show business.[29]

The second year of the Wild West offered an all-star bill of authentic western celebrities that never again would be assembled. In addition to two of the proprietors, Buffalo Bill and Captain Bogardus—the third proprietor, Nate Salsbury, continued with his Troubadours to keep the 1884 pot boiling—all billing featured Major Frank North, the Pilot of the Prairie; "Oklahoma" Payne, the Progressive Pioneer; "Buck" Taylor, King of the Cow-Boys; and Con Groner, the Cow-Boy Sheriff of the Platte. North and Payne were dead before another season opened.

Captain David L. Payne, "Oklahoma" Payne, was the foremost organizer of the "Boomers" who attempted to force the opening of the Oklahoma District of Indian Territory to settlement. Cattle

[28] Cody to Crawford, April 22, 1879, MS Denver Public Library; Fellows and Freeman, *This Way to the Big Show*, 90–92.
[29] *Letters from Buffalo Bill*, 26; interview, William McDonald.

companies had been permitted to lease lands not actually occupied by Indians. Payne and his followers saw this as a flagrant favoring of rich cattle barons at the expense of poor settlers. They proposed to force the issue by moving in, regardless of federal law.

Cody bought forty shares in Payne's colony in 1882. Early in 1884, when Payne had exhausted his funds in the Boomer fight, Cody offered the Captain a place in the show. Said the show program: "While waiting for certain developments in his still continued contest, Capt. Payne will accompany, for recreation only, his old friend Buffalo Bill's 'Wild West,' to renew again the cherished project so dear to the progressive spirit of the Oklahoma Raiders." It is unlikely that Payne made many appearances in the show, for developments came rapidly during 1884. In June his colony assembled near the Indian Territory border. Troops were called and Payne was arrested and haled into court. Eventually indictments against him were dismissed, but his part in the contest was over, for while planning reorganization of his colony, he died suddenly on November 26.[30]

William Levi Taylor, "Buck" Taylor, was the first and original "King of the Cowboys." His name has almost faded into oblivion, but undeservedly so, for he was America's first cowboy hero, in fact as well as in fiction. "Cowboy," before Buffalo Bill's Wild West, was a word of evil connotation. President Chester A. Arthur in his annual message to Congress in 1881 denounced a band of "armed desperadoes known as 'Cowboys,'" as menaces to the peace of Arizona Territory. Even a Buffalo Bill biography speaks of "cowboys and rough characters" as apparently synonymous, although the same book reprints a spirited defense of the cowboy, written by Texas Jack Omohundro. Programs and heralds of Buffalo Bill's Wild West were careful to explain that the six-foot-five Buck Taylor was "amiable as a child," although he was advertised to throw a steer by the horns or tail and tie him singlehanded, pick up a handkerchief from the ground while riding a horse at full speed, and master the worst of bucking broncos.

The first publication with a cowboy hero was *Buck Taylor, King of the Cowboys*, which was written by Ingraham for Beadle's

[30] Carl Coke Rister, *Land Hunger*, 107, 154; Buffalo Bill's Wild West program, 1884.

Half-Dime Library in 1887. It was followed by *The Wild Star Riders, Buck Taylor, the Saddle King, The Lasso King's League, The Cowboy Clan, Buck Taylor, the Comanche Captive*, and *Buck Taylor's Boys; or, The Red Riders of the Rio Grande*. The titles indicate that the dime-novel Buck Taylor had little more to do with cows than did Owen Wister's popular classic cowboy hero in *The Virginian*.

The real Buck Taylor was born at Fredericksburg, Gillespie County, Texas, in November, 1857. His father, a Texas cavalryman, was killed in the Civil War; and his mother died when he was six; he once said, "I was dependent on myself at an age when ordinary children are still in the nursery. . . . There was only one thing to do; which was to be a cowpuncher. . . . By the time I was 14 I was able to ride and rope with some of the best of them and was known around our section as the best cowpuncher of my age that had ever been seen." He drifted east and landed on Buffalo Bill's Nebraska ranch. He was another of Cody's many youthful protégés; Buck says he learned to read and write there, and he was on hand when the Wild West was organized. He suffered a broken leg while performing in London in 1887. Cody gave him a gambling concession while he was recovering. He bought a ranch in the Sweetwater country of Wyoming in 1890. He superintended the Cowboy Tournament and Wild West in Denver in 1892. He died in Downingtown, Pennsylvania, in 1924.[31]

Con Groner, cowboy sheriff of the Platte, had broken up Doc Middleton's gang, capturing six members and balking their plot with followers of Jesse James to hold up a Union Pacific train at Garnett Station, six miles east of North Platte. Jesse James literature has little to say of Groner, but the show's publicity credited him with catching "over fifty murderers, more than that number of horse thieves, cattle cutters, burglars, and outlaws. Even the nomenclature of the West was in its infancy; by "cattle cutter" is meant rustler.

Colonel Homer W. Wheeler was present when Con Groner made his reputation as an Indian fighter. During the winter of

[31] James D. Richardson (ed.), *A Compilation of the Messages and Papers of the Presidents* (New York, 1897), X, 4640–41; Clarence E. Ray, *Buffalo Bill, the Scout*, 55, 84–90; Logan, *Buckskin and Satin*, 27–30; Henry Nash Smith, *Virgin Land*, 110 ff.; A. Johannsen, *The House of Beadle and Adams*.

1877–78, Wheeler was ordered from Fort McPherson with forty men of Company H, Fifth Cavalry, to pursue a band of Indian marauders. At North Platte he picked up a guide, Dave Perry, who told him the Indians had raided the Barton and Keith ranch, about forty miles distant. When the troop arrived there, some twenty cowmen under Sheriff Groner offered their aid. Wheeler asked Groner and his men to locate the Indian trail while the soldiers got their meal and fed their horses, but on no account to follow the trail. When Wheeler and his troop caught up, they learned that Groner's men had found the Indians setting up wickiups to go into camp and had fired on them, frightening them off. As a result, Wheeler never did catch the Indians.[32]

These were the celebrities, and it may be noted that North Platte was heavily represented by North, Taylor, and Groner, a further indication that the Wild West derived from the Old Glory Blow Out. A guest star was Cody's drinking companion, White Beaver, or Dr. Frank Powell, who was occasionally practicing medicine at La Crosse, Wisconsin. It was announced that Powell would put on his shooting act with the show at some of the larger cities. David Franklin Powell, the hero of the green room fight during Buffalo Bill's engagement in a Chicago theater, was born in Kentucky in 1847 and had his medical education at the University of Louisville. His path crossed that of Cody many times. Possibly the first time was when Powell, as deputy grand master of Nebraska, conferred Masonic degrees on Cody at the Platte Valley Lodge in Cottonwood Springs while Powell was serving at Fort McPherson and North Platte Barracks as army contract surgeon. He also served at Fort Laramie and at Camp Stambaugh.

Powell is said to have received his name "White Beaver" from Rocky Bear of the Sioux, whose daughter's life Powell saved by his medical skill. Rocky Bear recognized the appropriateness of the name because Powell claimed membership in the Beaver clan of the Senecas through his mother, who was of Iroquois descent. After Wee-Noo-Sheik, chief of the Winnebagoes, was pulled through a serious illness in 1876, Powell became chief medicine man of that tribe, an asset to him during his years as a physician in Wisconsin. Almost a charlatan—the stairway leading to his office in La Crosse

[32] Wheeler, *Buffalo Days*, 206–209; Walsh, *The Making of Buffalo Bill*, 234–35.

was lined with exhibits of his surgery preserved in alcohol—he alternated medical practice with show business, dealt in Indian remedies, and did exhibition shooting.[33]

More generally recognized than some of the headliners was John Y. Nelson, a colorful figure with long, flowing beard. He, with his Sioux wife and five children in Indian costume, dominates the front row in many pictures of the personnel of Buffalo Bill's Wild West. Nelson guided Brigham Young to Utah in 1847 and was a scout with Cody at Fort McPherson in 1869. He was the interpreter in some of the Buffalo Bill Combinations on the stage, and served in the same capacity in the Wild West show, also doubling as cowboy and stagecoach driver and throwing up glass balls for Cody to shoot. His daughter Rose, the littlest one in the pictures, became Mrs. Rose Ecoffey and professionally Princess Blue Waters, carrying on the family tradition by managing a troupe of Indians for rodeos and other appearances.[34]

Fred Mathews drove the Deadwood coach. Seth Hathaway was Pony Express rider. Among the cowboys were Bill Bullock, Jim Lawson, Bud Ayers, Dick Bean, Utah Frank, Bronco Bill, Montana Joe, and Blue Hall—a colorful set of appellations.

The second year of the show got off to a good start when Chicago turned out one crowd counted at 41,448, an unusually large attendance for that period. Colonel Ingraham entertained the press in advance of the New York opening on June 16 at the Polo Grounds. The critics commented on the excellence of the riding acts and the roping as adding variety to an exhibition that had been overloaded with shooting the year before. Actually the program, despite Nate Salsbury's low opinion of it in 1883, was very little changed. Races made up one-third of the numbered events. The buffalo chase had replaced the unfortunate attempt to ride buffalo. The new concluding spectacle was described as "Attack on Settler's Cabin by Indians and Rescue by Buffalo Bill with his Scouts, Cowboys, and Mexicans." This act remained on the bill for many years.

Bad luck began to dog the tour at Hartford. There Frank North was thrown from his horse when a saddlegirth broke and was

[33] Charles H. L. Johnston, *Famous Scouts*, 279–95.
[34] Bert L. Hall, *Roundup Years*, 224, 398, 450, 534.

trampled by one of the horses. He remained in a hospital for several months, rejoined the show briefly, but left it again in New Orleans early in 1885, and died in Columbus, Nebraska, on March 14.

One-a-day performances in the East did not bring in the money very fast, and the partners decided to keep the show on the road during the winter. The World's Industrial and Cotton Exposition was scheduled in New Orleans that winter—the Wild West in later years was to have some of its greatest successes in connection with expositions, but not this time. Pony Bob Haslam was made advance agent, a task to which he brought no experience and little capacity. At Cincinnati he hired a steamboat to convoy the show southward. The stops he arranged along the way proved bad guesses, and the steamboat tour ran in the red. Then came disaster.

Near Rodney Landing, Mississippi, the showboat collided with another river steamer and sank within an hour. Wagons, camp equipage, arms, ammunition, donkeys, buffalo, and one elk were lost. Captain Bogardus lost all his exhibition equipment. The Deadwood coach, the band wagon, and the horses were saved, and there was no loss of life among personnel.

Cody telegraphed Salsbury, who was appearing with the Troubadors at Denver: "Outfit at bottom of the river, what do you advise?" Nate was just ready to go on stage to sing when the message arrived. He asked the orchestra leader to repeat the overture to give him time to think. Then he wrote his reply: "Go to New Orleans, reorganize, and open on your date," and went on with his show. Both partners proved showmen on this occasion. Those who rate Cody as having little capacity for management must give him full credit here. Within eight days he rounded up herds of buffalo and elk, wagons, and other equipment. The show opened on time.[35]

In New Orleans it rained for forty-four days straight—never missing show time. On one of those days only nine persons bought tickets, and the ticketseller suggested that the show be canceled. "If nine people came out here in all this rain to see us, we'll show," Cody said, again proving himself a showman. At the end of winter

[35] Cody, *Story of the Wild West*, 698–99; *Letters from Buffalo Bill*, 19–21 (letter, on p. 19, should be dated 1885); Walsh, *The Making of Buffalo Bill*, 240–41.

the Wild West was $60,000 in the red. Cody summed up his assets—about the same number of horses as last summer, twenty-five Indians in the saddle, seven Mexicans, and eight cowboys. Some of the Indians had to return home to do their spring plowing, but he had sent Frank North to recruit more and raise some money—however it was on this trip that Frank North died. Then Bill made a promise in a letter to Nate: "As I told you that I am to do my best for another season yet next winter when the show is laid up for winter I am going to get on a drunk that is a drunk. Just to change my luck I will paint a few towns red hot—but till then I am staunch and true—With my shoulder to the wheel."

In a postscript to this letter, Cody said, "Johnie Baker is shooting to beat L. breaks balls in the air like an old timer. I want to star him this summer." All the luck was not bad at New Orleans. Also showing there during the rainy winter had been the Sells Brothers Circus, and some of its performers had been over to the Wild West lot for a visit. One of them was Annie Oakley.[36]

[36] Walsh, *The Making of Buffalo Bill,* 242–45.

Indians in the Buffalo Bill show

Courtesy Fred B. Hackett

The show Indians playing ping-pong behind the scenes

Courtesy Denver Public Library Western Collection
Photograph by John C. Hemment

"Little Sure Shot" herself

Annie Oakley at the height of her career.

Courtesy M-G-M Photos

LITTLE SURE SHOT

PHOEBE ANN MOSES WAS BORN on August 13, 1860, in a cabin in Darke County, Ohio, the fifth child of Susan and Jacob Moses. Her name was to change several times, the first time when four older sisters began calling her "Annie." After a son and another daughter were born, Annie's father died of exposure in a blizzard in March, 1866. The widow married again, but her second husband died after adding one more daughter to the family.

When she was seven, Annie often fed the family with quail caught in traps she made. She once told an interviewer: "I was eight years old when I made my first shot, and I still consider it one of the best shots I ever made. I saw a squirrel run down over the grass in front of the house, through the orchard and stop on the fence to get a hickory nut. I decided to shoot it and ran into the house to get a gun which was hanging on the wall and which I knew to be loaded. I was so little I had to jump up on a chair and slide it down to the mantel and then to the ground. I laid the gun on the railing of the porch, and then recalled that I had heard my brother say about shooting: 'It is a disgrace to shoot a squirrel anywhere but in the head because it spoils the meat to hit him elsewhere.' I took the remark literally and decided, in a flash, that I must hit that squirrel in the head, or be disgraced. It was a wonderful shot, going right through the head from side to side. My mother was so frightened when she learned that I had taken down the loaded gun and shot it that I was forbidden to touch it again for eight months."[1]

Annie was offered a chance to go to school in exchange for helping Mrs. Crawford Eddington, wife of the superintendent of the county poor farm. Annie learned to sew while working on clothing for the inmates. She became interested in needlework, and in later years her fine embroidery was almost as notable as her shooting. A farmer's family offered pay in addition to schooling for her help with a baby, but there she was beaten and half-starved and kept in virtual slavery for two years until she ran away. When she made it home, a forty-mile walk, she learned that her mother had been married a third time, to Joseph Shaw, a Civil War veteran with a pension, a small farm, and a large mortgage. Her older sisters had married.

Names had been changed frequently in that family, and ten-year-old Annie had become embittered about hers because of derision in a rhyme about "Moses Poses." As the eldest bearing that name, she decided to change it to "Mozee." She altered family records, had "Mozee" cut on tombstones, and carried on a lifetime feud with her brother John, who continued to call himself "Moses."[2]

When Annie got her gun back, the mortgage was the target. She supplied game to the general store of Charles Ketzenberger in Greenville. He talked a mailman into taking the surplus to a Cincinnati hotelkeeper, Jack Frost. When Annie at the age of fifteen visited her older sister Lyda, Mrs. Joseph Stein, in Cincinnati, Frost was curious about the girl who shot squirrels in the eye. He put up fifty dollars for a Thanksgiving Day match with his guest Frank Butler, who in partnership with Billy Graham did exhibition shooting between the acts of a stock company show. Butler thought a joke was being played on him when he found his opponent to be a little girl in a pink gingham dress and sunbonnet,

---

[1] Margaret C. Getchell, "An American Woman Who Could Have Shot Kaiser," *Philadelphia Public Ledger*, May 18, 1919. See also Courtney Ryley Cooper, *Annie Oakley, Woman at Arms;* Annie Fern Swartwout, *Missie;* Walter Havighurst, *Annie Oakley of the Wild West;* Fred Stone, *Rolling Stone* (New York, London, 1945); and Holbrook, *Little Annie Oakley.*

[2] Swartwout, *Missie,* 41–42.

dragging an ancient rifle bigger than she was, but he lost by one pigeon. The acquaintance thus started resulted in their marriage a year later, on June 22, 1876.

Frank had run away from home in Ireland and shipped to New York. There he made his way after the manner of a hero of Horatio Alger, Jr. Frank went from street Arab to show business, as dog trainer and in a shooting act. He had a broken marriage behind him, and this one, to a sixteen-year-old country girl, had everything against it, especially when she beat him at his own game and became world famous. Yet he abandoned his career to become her manager, and they were happy and inseparable until their deaths within twenty days of each other in 1926.

Billy Graham was ill one night, and disappeared from history. The act became Butler and Oakley—a stage name Annie pulled out of thin air for the occasion. They played in stock companies and variety shows, and eventually joined Sells Brothers Circus, an Ohio aggregation organized in 1872 by Lewis, Ephraim, Allen, and Peter Sells of Dublin. That show played New Orleans at the same time as Buffalo Bill's unhappy engagement there. For some reason the Wild West looked good to the Butlers and they opened negotiations to join it.

Cody and Salsbury were reluctant; they were long on shooting acts and short on salary for any kind of talent. However, Bogardus withdrew from the partnership, and when Butler proposed to put their act on trial for three days, they were invited to join at Louisville. Annie once wrote, "I went right in and did my best before 17,000 people, and was engaged in fifteen minutes." Of Cody she said, "I traveled with him for seventeen years—there were thousands of men in the outfit during that time, Comanches, cowboys, Cossacks, Arabs, and every kind of person. And the whole time we were one great family loyal to a man. His words were more than most contracts. Personally I never had a contract with the show after I started. It would have been superfluous."[3]

When Bill introduced her to the company, he said, "This little Missie here is Miss Annie Oakley. She's to be the only white woman with our show. And I want you boys to welcome and protect her."

[3] Annie Oakley, "Tribute to Col. Cody," *Cody Enterprise*, February 20, 1946; Swartwout, *Missie*, 78.

Ever afterward she was "Little Missie" to Cody. That she was one of the greatest single assets the Wild West ever had is without question. The show's advertising rarely named performers. After watching her first rehearsal, Nate Salsbury ordered seven thousand dollars' worth of printing featuring Annie on billboards and in heralds.

No woman in outdoor show business has been so long remembered—and this was true before the Rodgers and Hammerstein musical, *Annie, Get Your Gun,* the motion picture version of it, or Annie's appearance in comic books and on television. These developments would not have startled her; although she had never traveled west of Cincinnati except in show business, she appeared in such melodramas as *The Western Girl,* in which her shooting was represented as devoted to the "rescue of the U.S. soldier." Unaccountably she missed being a dime-novel heroine.

Explaining the impact that made her remembered, Dexter Fellows said, "She was a consummate actress, with a personality that made itself felt as soon as she entered the arena. Even before her name was on the lips of every man, woman, and child in America, the sight of this frail girl among the rough plainsmen seldom failed to inspire enthusiastic plaudits. Her entrance was always a very pretty one. She never walked. She tripped in, bowing, waving, and wafting kisses. Her first few shots brought forth a few screams of fright from the women, but they were soon lost in round after round of applause. It was she who set the audience at ease and prepared it for the continuous crack of firearms which followed." She always appeared early in the program, usually in second spot. Fellows is one of the few who does not go all out for her as America's sweetheart. He scores her mainly as a tightwad. She rarely joined other troupers in a holiday in town. Daily she filled her small pitcher with lemonade from a big one provided for Cody. She drank no liquor, but occasionally took a glass of beer—when someone else was buying.[4]

One of Butler's acts had been to shoot an apple from the head of a trained dog. Annie added to this trick by shooting a cigarette being smoked by her husband, by hitting a dime held in his fingers, and by slicing a playing card in two. After two clay pigeons had

[4] Fellows and Freeman, *This Way to the Big Show,* 73.

been released, she would leap over a table, pick up her gun, and bring down both targets. Her shooting of card targets gave rise to a slang term "Annie Oakley" for a pass or complimentary ticket, often punched so that they can be identified when counting receipts. One card target that she used was about five by two inches in size with a small picture of Annie at one end and a one-inch heart-shaped bull's-eye at the other. Such cards, after being hit, were thrown into the audience as souvenirs. The story that they were good for admission to the show is unlikely—a scramble for them while firearms were being used would have been dangerous.[5]

Annie proved her skill in many formal shooting contests. In April, 1884, at Tiffin, Ohio, she broke 943 out of 1,000 glass balls thrown in the air, using a Stevens .22-caliber rifle. At Cincinnati, in February, 1885, she broke 4,772 out of 5,000 glass balls at fifteen yards' rise with shotguns in nine hours, loading her own guns. At Gloucester, New Jersey, in 1888, a bet of $5,000 was made that she could not kill forty out of fifty pigeons, thirty yards' rise. She killed forty-nine. Challenged by Miles Johnson, champion of New Jersey, the following day, she defeated him with another forty-nine. She never lost her skill; at Pinehurst, North Carolina, in April, 1922, she broke one hundred targets straight at sixteen yards. Although she met all comers in America or abroad, she never was advertised as woman champion. The programs, with surprising restraint, introduced her as the "Celebrated Shot, who will illustrate her dexterity in the use of Fire-arms," and she was billed as "The Peerless Wing and Rifle Shot." A program biography did not claim her 943 out of 1,000 as a record, but noted that Dr. Ruth had made 944. A record book issued for publicity purposes included her occasional defeats.[6]

She gained another title of more lasting fame, "Little Sure Shot," conferred on her by Sitting Bull. The famous Sioux leader, who had gone to Canada after the defeat of Custer, returned to the United States and surrendered in 1881. After two years as technical prisoner of war, he was sent to Standing Rock Reservation.

---

[5] Elmo Scott Watson, in *Publishers' Auxiliary,* 1926, conducted a symposium on "Annie Oakleys"; Ban Johnson was credited with originating the phrase. The card target described was given to me by Mrs. Swartwout.

[6] Programs, Buffalo Bill's Wild West, 1893–98; Peter P. Carney, *Greatest of Modern Dianas* (Pinehurst, N. C., n.d.).

On September 2, 1884, he joined other Sioux at St. Paul for a tour of fifteen cities, arranged by Ehle and Alvaren Allen. Since Annie says that he saw her performance in a St. Paul theater, it was probably at this time. He became much excited over her shooting, shouting, *"Watanya cicilia,"* dubbing her "Little Sure Shot." After the show he exchanged photographs with her and adopted her into the Hunkpapa Sioux as his daughter.[7]

This photograph of Annie saved the day when Burke was trying to sign up Sitting Bull for appearance in the Wild West. Sitting Bull had been treated with little consideration on the Allen tour, and was reluctant. When Burke spotted the picture of Annie in his tipi and promised that Sitting Bull would see "Little Sure Shot" every day, he was persuaded. He signed a contract on June 6, 1885, agreeing to appear with the show for four months at $50 a week. He got an advance of two weeks' pay, a bonus of $125, and sole right to sell his photographs and autographs. Five Sioux warriors went with him for $25 a month each, three women for $15 each, and William Halsey, interpreter, for $60. Burke agreed to pay the expenses of the party to join the show at Buffalo, and back to Standing Rock at the end of the season.[8]

Sitting Bull was cast as a villain in the United States and was often hissed when he paraded the arena—there was much curiosity to see him, nevertheless—but as the Wild West toured Canada, playing Montreal, Ottawa, Kingston, Toronto, and Hamilton, he was honored by mayors and members of Parliament, and stole the show. The Canadian government had been less ready to recognize him when he was an unwelcome refugee a few years previously. It was in Montreal that William Notman took the photographs of Sitting Bull and Buffalo Bill that appeared in programs with the caption, "Foes in '76—Friends in '85."[9]

Opinions differ on whether Sitting Bull enjoyed being exhib-

[7] Stanley Vestal, *Sitting Bull* (1932 ed.), 256, (1957 ed., 250); Willoughby M. Babcock, Minnesota Historical Society, to Don Russell, August 1, 1956, on St. Paul newspapers, September 2–11, 1884; Swartout, *Missie,* 70–71; extract from Annie Oakley's MS autobiography copied for me by Mrs. Swartwout.

[8] *Middle Border Bulletin* (Friends of the Middle Border, Mitchell, S. D.), Vol. III, No. 2 (Autumn, 1943), text of contract.

[9] Elmo Scott Watson, "The Photographs of Sitting Bull," *The Westerners Brand Book* (Chicago), Vol. VI, No. 6 (August, 1949); Vestal, *Sitting Bull* (1932 ed.), 256, (1957 ed., 250).

ited, but he liked being introduced to strangers and was unhappy when not given attention. He had a natural bent for personal publicity and took full advantage of his contract rights in photographs and autographs, learning to trace his name crudely. He also learned the technique of selling such personal possessions as his pipe pouch by maintaining a reserve stock. Both Annie Oakley and Johnny Baker attest that what money Sitting Bull did not send home to his family, he squandered on newsboys, bootblacks, and other urchins who hung about his tent. He could not understand how there could be such obvious poverty in the midst of the white man's apparent wealth. On this tour he was granted his wish to tell his troubles to the President of the United States. He met General Carr and other old opponents and learned much. Sitting Bull observed: "The white people are so many that if every Indian in the West killed one every step they took, the dead would not be missed among you. I go back and tell my people what I have seen. They will never go on the war-path again."[10]

It was Sitting Bull's only season in show business, but there is no indication that he was dissatisfied. Cody sent him home as agreed, giving him a gray trick horse to which he had become attached and a white sombrero, size eight. One day one of his relatives wore the hat, angering Sitting Bull, who said, "My friend Long Hair gave me this hat. I value it very highly, for the hand that placed it upon my head had a friendly feeling for me." This incident indicates that Sitting Bull left the show with a high regard for Cody, and it is to be remembered in connection with the tragic killing of Sitting Bull after Cody was barred from negotiating with him.[11]

As Cody had promised, he featured Johnny Baker as "The Cow-boy Kid" in 1885. Con Groner and Buck Taylor were top stars; others named were Broncho Bill Irving, Coyote Bill Bullock, and Antonio Esquivel, champion *vaquero*, long one of the show's outstanding horsemen. The return from Canada was at Detroit, and stands were played at Saginaw and Columbus before closing

[10] DeCost Smith, *Indian Experiences* (Caldwell, 1943), 188; George Creelman, *On the Great Highway* (Boston, 1901), 201–302; C. R. Cooper, *Annie Oakley*, 124; Vestal, *Sitting Bull* (1932 ed.), 256–57, (1957 ed., 250–51); Walsh, *The Making of Buffalo Bill*, 255–56.
[11] Vestal, *Sitting Bull* (1932 ed.), 257, (1957 ed., 251).

the season at Columbus. Within five months Buffalo Bill's Wild West had been seen by a million persons for a profit of $100,000, the first successful outdoor show season for Buffalo Bill. Perhaps Annie Oakley had brought luck to the show; perhaps Sitting Bull was the big attraction. Not yet did Cody feel safely in the big money, however. He returned to the stage for the last time that winter, playing *The Prairie Waif* with Buck Taylor in a schedule that included Kansas City and Topeka in February, 1886. Thereafter the Wild West required the full attention of Cody and Salsbury, and its profits made their theater appearances unnecessary.[12]

A long-extended stay in one location was a successful experiment in 1886. Erastus Wiman operated a summer resort called "Erastina" on Staten Island. Buffalo Bill's Wild West showed there for six months. There Lillian Smith, fifteen-year-old rifle-shot, joined Annie Oakley in trick shooting. Lillian could hit a plate thirty times in fifteen seconds, break ten balls hung from strings and swinging around a pole, and fire four times after a glass ball had been thrown into the air, breaking it with the last shot. Born in Coleville, Mono County, California, she had started riding as soon as she could sit a saddle and had begun shooting when seven. She claimed forty mallards and redheads in a day. At her first attempt at glass balls she made 323 successive shots without a miss and broke 495 out of 500, using a Ballard .22.

Seth Clover was another marksman, using marbles as targets. Johnny Baker, under Annie's coaching, was developing into her rival. That rivalry became one of the show's features; many spectators hoped to be present when Johnny outshot Annie, but it never happened. When asked years later whether it had been planned that way, Johnny admitted frankly that he never could quite make it.

The shooting of Buffalo Bill was also one of the headlined features. The program was careful to point out that Cody was not a "fancy shot," but rather "a practical all-around shot." It stated that "Mr. Cody will give an exhibition of his ability by shooting objects thrown in the air while galloping at full speed, executing difficulties that would receive commendation if accomplished on

[12] *Kansas City Times*, February 1, 1886; *Topeka Daily Citizen*, February 8, 1886, files at KSHS.

foot, and which can only be fully appreciated by those who have attempted the feat while experiencing a rapid pace while occupying 'a seat in the saddle.' "

In the 1902 program, an advertisement quoted Cody as saying, "As you know, I always use Winchester rifles and Winchester ammunition. I have used both exclusively for over twenty years for hunting and in my entertainments." A number of detractors, beginning with Dr. Carver, made much of Bill's "trickery" in using small shot fired from a rifle instead of rifle bullets. It is said that both Dr. Carver and Cody used rifle bullets at their first performance—and got a big bill from a greenhouse owner eight blocks away! It is obvious that firing heavy bullets from horseback in directions determined by the cast of a glass ball would be highly dangerous. A gun expert says Cody used "the .44/40 W.C.F. shot cartridges with a thin paper bullet which dropped off from the shot charge after it left the muzzle, but did protect it from leading the rifling. The charge was about 20 grains of black powder, a half charge or 'midrange load' and ¼ ounce No. 7½ chilled shot. At 20 yards, the average range at which Cody shot the glass balls, the pattern was about two or three inches across." He quotes Johnny Baker as saying that it was quite as difficult to hit the target with shot as with a single rifle ball. Few skeet or trap shooters would expect perfect scores while firing their shotguns from horseback.[13]

What kind of scores did Cody make? While he had done some exhibition shooting from the stage, he was a bit diffident about matching himself against such experts as Carver and Bogardus during his first year in an outdoor show. In writing to his sister during the Wild West's first season, Cody said, "I am improving wonderfully in shooting, don't take a back seat from Carver or Roger [Bogardus]. Tell Al I broke 87 glass balls out of one hundred thrown from a trap 21 yards rise with a shotgun riding a horse at full speed. I have broken 76 out of a hundred with a rifle running full speed." That statement seems to settle the question of shotgun and rifle on horseback.[14]

A. B. (Pinnacle Jake) Snyder was breaking horses at the ranch

[13] Program, Buffalo Bill's Wild West, 1902, pp. 2, 13–14; William C. L. Thompson, "The Guns of Buffalo Bill," *Guns*, Vol. II, No. 3–15 (March, 1956).
[14] *Letters from Buffalo Bill*, 20, quoted by permission of Mrs. Foote.

at North Platte in March, 1892, when one of the boys reported swans on a lake north of the ranch buildings. Cody drove with a visitor in the buckboard, and found the swans swimming in the middle of the lake. Said Cody, "If I can get them lined up right I won't need but one bullet." Jake reports, "Sure enough, when the swans were swimming even with their heads in line, Cody drew a bead and got 'em both with the one shot, and that a long one and a sixty-mile wind blowing to boot." Jake's comment: "Cody's reputation as a dead shot with most any kind of gun was well known at that time but there are some in these times who'd like to make folks believe that his marksmanship was exaggerated and that he actually wasn't such a good shot after all. Well, the best they've told about old Bill's shooting was no exaggeration."[15]

Less is of record regarding his pistol-shooting ability, and no claims were made that he was a quick-draw artist, did any fanning, indulged in personal gunplay, or habitually wore a pistol. However, Bat Masterson said of Cody, "He was an expert horseman and could shoot a pistol with deadly accuracy, while riding his horse at full speed." Bat also said that Cody "would ride his horse full tilt into a herd of buffalo and with a pistol in either hand and the bridle reins between his teeth, was almost sure to bring down that day's supply of meat at the first run. With six shots in each pistol, he had often killed as many as eight buffalo on a run. This feat was never equalled, although many times attempted by men who fancied they could ride and shoot as well as Cody." Bat notes that Cody was never engaged in a deadly duel with a white man, "perhaps due to the fact that he was never called upon for such a purpose," implying that his marksmanship was too widely known.[16]

The 1886 program was not all shooting. American Horse, the younger of that name, headed the Indians. Doc Middleton, the Nebraska bandit whom Sheriff Con Groner had pursued, was there along with his pursuer. An English spectator described the riding of a black mare called "Dynamite" by Jim Mitchell: "It was necessary for four men to hold her and she had to be blindfolded before he could get on her, and then letting out a scream like a woman in

[15] A. B. Snyder (as told to Nellie Irene Yost), *Pinnacle Jake*, 50–51.

[16] W. B. ("Bat") Masterson, "Colonel Cody—Hunter, Scout, Indian Fighter," *Human Life* magazine (New York, 1907).

pain, she made a headlong dash and plunged with all her force into a fence, turning completely over head first and apparently falling upon the rider. . . . Poor Jim was dragged out, bleeding and maimed, and led away. What was the astonishment of the multitude, when the other refractory animals had had their sport, to see Dynamite again led out, and the cowboy, limping and pale, come forward to make another attempt to ride her. . . . For fifteen minutes the fight went on between man and beast. . . . The cowboy got upon her back by some superhuman skill, and then he was master."[17]

Another famous bucker was "White Emigrant," purchased for the show in March, 1886, at Woodland, California, by James Willoughby, known as "Jim Kid." In 1884, Jim had won the championship of Montana by riding White Emigrant, his prize being a $260 outfit, including saddle, bridle, spurs, chaps, and lariat. Here is demonstrated how rodeo kept pace with the Wild West. State championships were unknown before 1883.

The Wild West was attracting the attention of notables. General Sherman attended on the opening day at Erastina. Mark Twain, who later contributed to Cody's fame with a story—perhaps not among his best—called "A Horse's Tale," about Buffalo Bill's horse, commented that the Wild West "brought back to me the breezy, wild life of the Rocky Mountains, and stirred me like a war song. Down to its smallest details, the show is genuine—cowboys, vaqueros, Indians, stage coach, costumes and all; it is wholly free from sham and insincerity and the effects it produced upon me by its spectacles were identical with those wrought upon me a long time ago by the same spectacles on the frontier. . . . It is often said on the other side of the water that none of the exhibitions which we send to England are purely and distinctively American. If you will take the Wild West show over there you can remove that reproach."[18]

P. T. Barnum said, "They do not need spangles to make it a real show." Mrs. Custer called the Wild West "that most realistic

[17] Cody, *Story of the Wild West*, 716, quoting the *London Era*.

[18] Printed in *Harper's Monthly*, Vol. CXIII, Nos. 675, 676 (August, September, 1906); *New York Dispatch*, July 18, 1886.

and faithful representation of a western life that has ceased to be, with advancing civilization."[19]

Thomas A. Edison was a visitor, but his genius was not employed in attempting another innovation—the first night performances. Lamps, gas flares, and the use of much red fire for the Indian dances and the attack on the stagecoach comprised the first lighting effects. The shooting acts suffered in the poor light, and Cody demanded that something be done. An inventive genius of the back lot soaked wads of cotton in alcohol and glued them to the clay pigeons, lighting the flares just before the trap was sprung. Often the pigeon went one way and its light another. Then came a night when this was corrected. The clay targets were all well lighted—but Annie Oakley chalked up ten straight misses, and Bill followed with the same zero score. The inventor had fastened his lights to the pigeons with masses of court plaster—the predecessor of adhesive tape—and the shot went through without breaking them![20]

The Erastina engagement proved so great a success—one July week's attendance totaled 193,960—that Madison Square Garden was leased from Adam Forepaugh for a winter exhibition. Under the direction of Louis E. Cooke, the polysyllabic promoter, there was inaugurated "a gigantic new era and departure in colossally realistic scenic production"—his own words for it. Steele MacKaye wrote a scenario for this pageant-like exhibition, called *The Drama of Civilization*. Matt Morgan devised scenic effects, and Nelse Waldron, inventor of the first double or moving stage used in a theater, was in charge of mechanical effects. Their plans were so vast that it was necessary to raise the roof of the Garden twenty-five feet to take care of them.

In one scene, a mining camp, Deadwood City in the Black Hills, was reproduced with its tavern, post office, stage station, and other structures, all to be destroyed by a cyclone. Lew Parker, stage manager, says MacKaye wanted something more realistic than the traditional stage effects produced by silks and tin sheets, and suggested a winnowing machine. Parker pointed out that a winnowing machine sucked air in, but did not blow it. Then, says

[19] Elizabeth Custer, *Tenting on the Plains*, 46.
[20] C. R. Cooper, *Annie Oakley*, 146–51.

Parker, "I saw a machine in a window revolving, with a handkerchief in front of it, which was being blown out. I interviewed the
gentleman inside and asked him what its object was. He said it was
a ventilator. By placing one of those machines in one wall of a
building, it blew fresh air into the building; and another machine
on the opposite side of the building, revolving the same way, blew
out foul air, keeping up a current of fresh air all the time." It might
be supposed that Parker had discovered a device known as an
electric fan, but not so; this ventilator was driven by a steam
engine. Parker ordered three fans, five feet in diameter. His next
problem was steam power. The Stevenson Car Company, across
Twenty-seventh Street, allowed him to run a pipe under the street
and use steam from the factory at night. As there was no time to
get a permit to take up the paving, Parker had a trench dug across
the street, the pipe laid, and the street repaved, between midnight
and three-thirty one morning. The cyclone was a great success.
One hundred bags of dried leaves were opened in front of the fans,
and the leaves blew across the stage quite realistically.[21]

Queen Victoria's Golden Jubilee—celebrating the fiftieth year
of her reign—was scheduled for 1887, in connection with which
American promoters organized "An Exhibition of the Arts, Indus-
tries, Manufactures, Products and Resources of the United States,"
commonly known as the American Exhibition. Prime movers in
this project were Colonel Henry S. Russell, president; John Robinson Whitley, director-general; and Vincent Applin, secretary.
They offered their facilities and a percentage of the gate receipts
to Cody and Salsbury for Buffalo Bill's Wild West as a feature of
their program. The partners accepted.

[21] *New York Dispatch*, July 18, 1886; L. Parker, *Odd People I Have Met*, 37–
39, 83–84.

BEFORE THE CROWNED HEADS OF EUROPE

THE INVASION OF ENGLAND by Buffalo Bill's Wild West in 1887 was, beyond much question, the most successful ever made by an American aggregation. It made Buffalo Bill a world figure and contributed to a large degree to the traditional view in England of the American West as one of the romantic and adventurous areas of the world. The show attracted great interest in England, and that interest, reflected back to the United States, gave impetus to the rapidly growing Buffalo Bill legend.

John M. Burke could not forecast so overwhelming a reception, and anticipated Charles Lindbergh, who, it may be recalled, took with him letters of introduction on his famous first overseas flight to Paris. Burke, as public relations director, collected letters of introduction and endorsement for Cody from army officers with whom he had served. The response, in a series of brief notes dated between December 25, 1886, and February 14, 1887, was more enthusiastic than would ordinarily be evoked by a press agent's appeal. Sherman, then the only living four-star general, recalled that Cody had guided him in 1866 "up the Republican, then occupied by the Cheyennes and Arapahoes as their ancestral hunting grounds." Lieutenant General Sheridan, then commanding general of the army, commended Cody as a scout who "served in my command on the western frontier for many years. He was always ready for duty, and was a cool, brave man, with unimpeachable character." General Crook testified to the "very efficient service" rendered by Cody as a scout in 1876, and praised the Wild West Exhibition as "the most realistic performance of the kind I have ever seen." General Merritt called Buffalo Bill "the superior of any scout I ever knew. He was cool and capable when surrounded by dangers, and his reports were always free from exaggeration." Said General Miles, "Your services on the frontier were exceedingly valuable," and he regarded "your Exhibition as not only very interesting but practically instructive."

General Emory stated, "Mr. Cody was chief guide and hunter to my command when I commanded the District of North Platte, and he performed all his duties with marked excellence." Brigadier General H. C. Bankhead, who had once arrested Cody in an argument over a mule, made it, "I fully and with pleasure indorse you as the veritable 'Buffalo Bill,' U. S. Scout, serving with troops operating against hostile Indians in 1868 on the plains. I speak from personal knowledge, and from reports of officers and others, with whom you secured renown by your services as scout and successful hunter." Colonel W. B. Royall, to whom Bill had once delivered buffalo on the hoof, said, "He filled every position and met every emergency with so much bravery, competence, and intelligence as to command the general admiration and respect of the officers, and became Chief of Scouts of the Department." General James B. Fry wrote, "Recalling the many facts that came to me while I was Adjutant-General of the Division of the Missouri, under General Sheridan, bearing upon your efficiency, fidelity, and daring as a guide and scout over the country west of the Missouri River and east of the Rocky Mountains, I take pleasure in observing your success in depicting in the East the early life of the West." General John H. King recommended Cody "as a man who has a high reputation in the army as a Scout. No one has ever shown more bravery on the Western plains than yourself."

Colonel N. A. M. Dudley, who had been major in the Third Cavalry during Cody's services with that regiment said, "I often recall your valuable services to the Government, as well as to myself, in years long gone by, specially during the Sioux difficulties, when you were attached to my command as Chief of Scouts. Your indomitable perseverence, incomprehensible instinct in discovering the trails of the Indians, particularly at night, no matter how dark or stormy, your physical powers of endurance in following the enemy until overtaken, and your unflinching courage as exhibited on all occasions, won not only my own esteem and admiration, but that of the whole command." Colonel James W. Forsyth wound it up: "Your army career on the frontier, and your present enterprise of depicting scenes in the Far West, are so enthusiastically approved and commended by the American people and the most prominent men of the U. S. Army, that there is nothing left for me to say."[1]

This is an impressive representation of the highest-ranking army officers of the period, all of whom had personal knowledge of Cody's career as a scout, and all of whom praised his services. It formed solid backing for presenting to far-away London—almost as far away in distance in 1887 as Buffalo Bill now is from us in time—the showman as one who had actually been all that he was represented to be.

However, it is characteristic of the Buffalo Bill legend that of all the endorsements collected by Major Burke, the one that was most effective had in it a touch of the phony. This was a document from Governor John M. Thayer of Nebraska appointing and commissioning the Hon. William F. Cody as "aide-de-camp of my staff with the rank of Colonel" to date from March 8, 1887. It was a very ordinary sunburst title, little valued in the United States, but abroad a Governor's aide, commissioned in the National Guard, sounded important.

Army officers backed Colonel Cody by presenting him with a jeweled sword, and of this the press of England took notice. From that time forward it was "Colonel Cody," and even to his intimates he was "the Colonel." Major Burke devised a style for publicity use: "Col. W. F. Cody, Chief of Scouts, U. S. Army." This was deceptive, probably intentionally so. It seemed to imply that Cody was chief of scouts of the entire army, with the rank of colonel. No such appointment ever existed.

Buffalo Bill's Wild West was incorporated on February 26,

---

[1] The letters appear in most programs and heralds after 1887, for example, program, Buffalo Bill's Wild West, Chicago, 1893, pp. 15–18.

1887—Cody was forty-one that day—with each of the partners holding thirty-five shares of stock, the remaining thirty of a total of one hundred being divided among Frank C. Maeder, Milton E. Milner, and William D. Guthrie. Frank Maeder, theatrical agent and manager, was a brother of Fred Maeder, who wrote the first Buffalo Bill melodrama. Directors were elected two days later, Salsbury's forty-first birthday. An added touch of sentiment was the chartering of the *State of Nebraska* of the State Line, Captain Braes, for the voyage to the Old World. By this time the Cowboy Band, long led by William Sweeney, was organized, and it played "The Girl I Left Behind Me" as the ship sailed from New York on Thursday, March 31. Newspaper reporters counted 83 saloon passengers, 38 steerage passengers, and 97 Indians, backing up Cody's boast of "a company of more than two hundred"; 180 horses, 18 buffalo, 10 mules, 10 elk, 5 wild Texas steers, 4 donkeys, and 2 deer.[2] Cody also mentioned bears. The previous year a moose had been trained to draw a sleigh, but London newspapers fail to mention this act or an Indian riding an elk, another novelty.

The Indians had a superstition that any of their race attempting to cross the ocean would waste away and die. When seasickness struck the company, the death-song was heard frequently. Cody tried to reassure them, although, as he admits, "sick as a cow with a hollow horn myself." Annie Oakley, who was immune, says the worst came as the ship rolled in a stormy sea for forty-eight hours until a damaged rudder could be repaired. Smoother sailing followed, and all recovered. Cody and Red Shirt, chief of the Sioux, addressed a Sunday meeting, and Salsbury revived acts from the Troubadors for shipboard entertainment. No Indians succumbed; the only loss in an unusually rough passage was one horse.

At Gravesend on April 16, British officials waived regulations in honor of the American Exhibition. Despite threats of rinderpest and foot-and-mouth disease, the cattle and buffalo were released after a brief quarantine. The importation of ammunition was banned, but the supply was turned over to an army arsenal and issued as needed. A tug flying the American flag, with a band playing "The Star-Spangled Banner" brought a committee headed by

[2] London *Era*, April 23, 1887; London *Evening News,* undated clippings, 1887; Cody, *Story of the Wild West,* 702.

Lord Ronald Gower, directors of the exhibition, Major Burke, and newspapermen to welcome the Wild West. Three trains took the show from the port of London to the Midland station; and before the day was over, camp was set up, ready for the first performance, not scheduled until May 9. The speed of the movement, a development of the American railroad circus, attracted wide attention.

American publicity methods also attracted attention. One newspaper denounced the posters as "mural enormities . . . colossal daubs, splashes of red and yellow." The *Globe* commentator was moved to verse:

> I may walk it, or 'bus it, or hansom it: still
> I am faced by the features of Buffalo Bill.
> Every hoarding is plastered, from East-end to West,
> With his hat, coat, and countenance, lovelocks and vest.[3]

Distinguished visitors came to the camp. Henry Irving, England's leading actor, soon afterward recognized with a knighthood, had written in the *Era* praising the Wild West, which he had seen at Erastina. Ellen Terry, leading actress; Mary Anderson, once of Louisville, Kentucky, where a theater was named for her; Charles Wyndham; and John L. Toole were other show people who came, as did Justin McCarthy, member of Parliament and author of the melodrama, *If I Were King,* long played by E. H. Sothern and later made into the musical, *The Vagabond King*.

The Wild West had been recruited to larger size than ever before, with consequent lack of experience, and had moved from the indoor confines of Madison Square Garden to an arena bounded by a track more than one-third of a mile in circumference. Flattering invitations and distinguished visitors curtailed time for rehearsals and taxed the Colonel's talents as a showman. William Ewart Gladstone, former prime minister, showed up with a party on April 25, two weeks before the opening, and a partial show was given for him. It was worth it, for "the manly frankness of this splendid specimen of the American Backwoodsman highly interested Mr. Gladstone, and he remained in conversation with him for some time." He inspected Old Charlie, Cody's horse, he inter-

[3] April 26, 1887.

viewed Red Shirt, and he said that the Americans had surpassed Englishmen as horsemen and hoped the exhibition would stir up British emulation and lead to further development of what he might call a noble art.[4]

On May 5, Albert Edward, prince of Wales—afterward King Edward VII—accepted an invitation to attend a special perform-ance. In the party were the Princess of Wales, Alexandra; their children, the Princesses Victoria Louise, Maud, and Louise; Prin-cess Alexandra's brother, Crown Prince Frederick of Denmark; the Comtesse de Paris; the Marquis of Lorne; and their attendants. The ground was muddy and the show ill rehearsed, but when the Indians, "yelling like fiends, galloped out from their ambuscade and swept around the enclosure like a whirlwind, the effect was instantaneous and electric," says Cody, boasting justifiably. "The Prince rose from his seat and leaned eagerly over the front of the box, and the whole party seemed thrilled by the spectacle. 'Cody,' I said to myself, 'you have fetched 'em!' From that moment we were right—right from the word 'Go.' Everybody was in capital form—myself included—and the whole thing went off grandly."[5]

The Prince wanted to see everything. He insisted on tramping through mud to inspect the stables and quite won Bill's heart by inquiring about Old Charlie. Red Shirt received the contents of the Prince's cigaret case, and, says Cody, "The Royal party cottoned greatly to John Nelson's half-breed papoose." Formally introduced were Cody, Salsbury, Burke, Frank Richmond (the announcer), Lillian Smith, and Annie Oakley. Annie had original ideas about the etiquette due the occasion:

"I had heard a great deal about how women tried to flirt with the Prince while the gentle Princess held her peace and now it all ran before me. An English-born lady would not have dared to have done as I did—they must speak to royalty according to the station of the Royal personages. The Prince's hand came over the low front of the box as they all rose to their feet. I ignored it and quickly proffered my hand to his Princess. She did not offer the tips of her fingers, expecting me to kneel down and kiss them, but took my hand gently in her own, saying: 'What a wonderful little girl.' Nor

[4] *Pall Mall Gazette*, April 28, 1887.
[5] Cody, *Story of the Wild West*, 728.

was His Highness displeased at what I had dared to do, for he, too, shook my hand warmly when I turned from the Princess to him, and after I had bowed far enough to turn my back, he made this remark, loud enough for the whole assembly to hear: 'What a pity there are not more women in the world like that little one!' "[6]

The command performance for Queen Victoria was the high spot to date for Buffalo Bill's Wild West. In more than a quarter of a century since the death of her consort, Prince Albert, the Queen had not attended any kind of public entertainments, although she had commanded some companies to give plays privately at Windsor Castle. However, when it was explained that the Wild West could not feasibly be brought in its entirety to the castle grounds, she agreed to go to the Earl's Court arena. Having broken one precedent, she was ready for another. When the American flag was presented according to the usual Wild West custom, the Queen rose from her seat and bowed deeply and impressively toward the banner, and as her entire party joined in the salute, says Cody, "there arose such a genuine heart-stirring American yell from our company as seemed to shake the sky. It was a great event. For the first time in history, since the Declaration of Independence, a sovereign of Great Britain had saluted the star-spangled banner, and that banner was carried by a member of Buffalo Bill's Wild West!" British sovereigns have gladly saluted a great number of American flags since, but before that time there was little occasion for doing so.[7]

Queen Victoria came at five o'clock in the afternoon of May 11 with a strict requirement that she should see everything within one hour. She was so pleased that she stayed for the entire program, fifteen minutes overtime, and then commanded that Buffalo Bill and leading members of the company be presented to her. These included Nate Salsbury, Annie Oakley, Lillian Smith, two

---

[6] C. R. Cooper, *Annie Oakley*, 173; Agnes Wright Springs, *Buffalo Bill and His Horses*, 7–9; List of Distinguished Vivitors, from the *Special Daily Journal of the American Exhibition*, NSHS, Buffalo Bill Museum, Lookout Mountain, Colo.; L. Parker, *Odd People I Have Met*, 4, 90–94.

[7] Cody, *Story of the Wild West*, 735–37; Thomas W. Handford, *Queen Victoria: Her Glorious Life and Illustrious Reign* (n.p., Franklin Printing & Publishing Co., 1901), 277–78; M. Willson Disher, *Pleasures of London* (London, 1950), 277–78.

Indian women with their babies, and Red Shirt, whose kingly dignity was commended.

This visit resulted in another command performance on June 20 for the Jubilee guests. Probably no commercial entertainment was ever attended by more members of royalty than appeared on this occasion. The audience included the King of Denmark, the King of Greece, the King of the Belgians, the King of Saxony, the Crown Prince and Princess of Germany (he was soon to become Kaiser Wilhelm II), Crown Prince Rudolph of Austria (within two years of his tragic suicide at Mayerling), the Crown Prince of Sweden and Norway, Prince George of Greece, the hereditary Prince and Princess of Saxe-Meiningen, Prince Louis of Baden, Princesses Victoria, Sophie, and Margaret of Prussia, the Prince and Princess of Wales, Prince Albert Victor and George of Wales (Prince George became King George V), and the Princesses Victoria and Maude of Wales and Marie Victoria and Alexandria of Edinburgh.

It was on this occasion that the Deadwood coach carried four kings, those of Denmark, Greece, Belgium, and Saxony, along with the Prince of Wales, with Buffalo Bill as driver, during the simulated attack by Indians. In 1871, President Grant had appointed General Robert Cumming Schenck as minister to the Court of St. James's, and that envoy had conferred upon London society a great boon—a knowledge of the game of poker. The Prince of Wales was speaking as an apt pupil when he said to Cody, "Colonel, you never held four kings like these before."

"I've held four kings," said Cody, "but four kings and the Prince of Wales makes a royal flush, such as no man ever held before."[8]

This is the way Cody first told it, but later versions add a happy afterthought by quoting Cody as saying, "four kings and the Royal Joker." It is one of the Colonel's tall tales that may well have happened—the four kings and the Prince were there on June 20.

Not all of the royalty appeared that day. There were others—the King and Crown Prince of Sweden, the Queen of the Belgians, Queen Kapiolani of Hawaii (not yet the fiftieth state) and the Princess who became Queen Liliuokalani, the Grand Duke Michael of Russia, the Comte de Paris who claimed to be King of France,

[8] Cody, *Story of the Wild West,* 742–43; L. Parker, *Odd People I Have Met,* 92.

Prince Debanwanza of Siam, the Crown Prince of Portugal, the Crown Prince of Bavaria, and a number of dukes and duchesses. British political figures included Robert Peel, John Bright, and Campbell-Bannerman; General Viscount Wolseley, foremost soldier of Europe, saw the Wild West, as did Sarah Bernhardt, Adelina Patti, Christine Nilsson, Chauncey Depew, and James G. Blaine.

Besides all these, twenty to forty thousand persons paid to see each performance. What did they get for their shillings? An English critic was impressed by the size of the enclosure at Earl's Court, cleverly increased in illusion by picturesque scenery of the West enclosing half the circle. In the opening spectacle the entire company was drawn up against this background—Indians in war paint and feathers; Mexicans headed by Antonio Esquivel and Andrés Rozzalo; cowboys led by Buck Taylor; and "the renowned Sergeant Bates," described as "equally celebrated" with Buffalo Bill himself. Sergeant Bates has long since ceased to be equally celebrated with Buffalo Bill; he was a Civil War veteran who had achieved notoriety by tramping about the United States carrying an American flag and giving patriotic lectures.

The pony express was demonstrated. An emigrant train with teams of oxen and mules, was attacked by Indians and rescued by cowboys. On the roof of the Deadwood stagecoach a scout "fights bravely, discharging his revolver right and left, scouts and cowboys happen to be near, and after a few minutes' furious firing the Indians retire, unhurt but beaten." The reporter called the attack on the settler's cabin "a very vivid incident."

The fighting scenes were interspersed with feats of skill, and no one complained of being bored. "Mustang Jack performed the startling feat of clearing a horse sixteen hands high, having previously covered thirteen feet with a standing leap." The buffalo hunt was "immensely realistic." Novel to Londoners were the bucking horses. Some escaped while being saddled and had to be pursued and lassoed—no chutes were used in those days. Antonio Esquival was praised as top rider, but honorable mention went to Buck Taylor, Jim Kidd (who had recently married Lillian Smith), Dick Johnson, Jim Mitchell, and Tom Webb.

Said the *London Review*: "Buffalo Bill's specialty is shooting while riding at full gallop, and he does this to wonderful perfection." Lillian Smith cleared off twenty balls from a swinging target, smashed a glass ball revolving horizontally at high speed, and "struck eggs in rapid and slow motion." She and Annie Oakley competed in a horse race in addition to their shooting.

Seen for the first time was the square dance on horseback, performed in many a later-day rodeo. "The girls and the Colonel and the King of Cowboys rode a Virginia reel, and one of the girls induced her horse to jump to music and to stand on his hind legs to bow." The trick horsewoman was Emma Lake, sometimes billed as Emma Lake Hickok, daughter of Agnes Lake, circus owner who had been married to Wild Bill Hickok shortly before his unfortunate encounter with Jack McCall at Deadwood.[9]

Times had changed since Annie Oakley was the only woman in the Wild West. There were now at least a dozen, including the wife of the settler whose cabin was attacked, "Ma" Whitaker, in charge of the costume department; the pistol-packing Mrs. Georgie Duffy, rough rider of Wyoming; and Miss Dell Ferrel, a rider from Colorado.

English newspapers were even kind to another celebrity who rode with Colonel Cody in the grand entrance—Gabriel Dumont, exiled chieftain of Riel's Rebellion in Canada—although it might have occurred to someone that he could be charged with treason. He was mentioned as casually as Con Groner, the cowboy sheriff.

William Sweeney's Cowboy Band of thirty-six musicians "upsets all one's previous ideas about the correct costume of musicians, but they play with spirit," was one comment. They wore gray shirts, slouch hats, and moccasins, rode matched horses on parade, and played a half-hour concert of classical and popular music preceding the performance. Why the band should play "Garry Owen" during the exciting melee depicting Custer's last fight mystified the London reporter. In America, "Garry Owen" is remembered only as the marching song of Custer's Seventh Cavalry.

From May 9 to October 31 these scenes were recreated day after day, but the performances were only a part of Buffalo Bill's

[9] *Birmingham Gazette*, November 7, 1887; *London Illustrated News*, April 16, 1887; *The Metropolitan*, April 30, 1887; *Scraps*, May 7, 1887; *Letters from Buffalo Bill*, 27–33; Cody, *Story of the Wild West*, 731–33.

London success. He was lionized to an extent that brought some unfavorable comment. "The Buffalo Bill furore is becoming ridiculous," said one journal in criticizing Lord Beresford for inviting Cody to the Coaching Club meet. "There is a want of congruity in the companionship of an illustrious officer who fills an important position in the Government with a gentleman chiefly famed as an adroit scalper of Indians." You cannot please everyone—there are those in America who accuse Cody of not killing or scalping any Indians. Another London writer suggested "the advantage of the introduction of a little scalping," in the show, his idea being that the Indians be allowed to win one of the fights, making their victory realistic by seizing the wigs and daubing the victims with carmine. Cody thought nothing would satisfy this visitor short of a real massacre.[10]

A less enthusiastic critic saw the Wild West as an "overgrown circus . . . neither more nor less than a hippodrome on an enormous scale. All the best of it we have seen before, either at Covent Garden or at Olympia." The *Birmingham Gazette* writer that agreed that it was "a mixture of circus, menagerie, and melodrama," yet found "the show was so good that it can stand . . . all the mirth provoked by the splendid superlatives on the programme." *The Indicator*, however, indicated that, "It is not a company of professional circus riders which has accompanied Mr. Cody to England. The men have learned the arts they practice in the daily exercise of frontier life."[11]

A former United States minister to the Court of St. James's was less than pleased with the performances of the unofficial ambassador of good will. Wrote James Russell Lowell, "I think the true key to this eagerness for lions—even of the poodle sort—is the dullness of the average English mind." But back home *Life* magazine, then a humorous weekly sparked by John Kendrick Bangs, was thrilled, and amused, by Cody's success. Bangs took up the cudgel for Cody against the poet who had produced such basic Americana as *The Bigelow Papers*, but was in 1887, in the editor's opinion, both stuffed shirt and Anglophile. Lowell, dis-

[10] Unidentified clipping, Salsbury scrapbook; *Serio-Comic, Jr.*, April 13, 1887; Cody, *Story of the Wild West*, 732.
[11] C. R. Cooper, *Annie Oakley*, 166–67; *Birmingham Gazette*, November 7, 1887; *The Indicator*, April 15, 1887; unidentified clipping, Salsbury scrapbook.

missed as minister when the Democratic party returned to office, stayed on in England. In August, *Life* jibed that "Messrs. Blaine, Phelps, Lowell and Buffalo Bill, America's Big Four, are all in London"; and again, "With Dana, Pulitzer, Blaine, Buffalo Bill, Red-Shirt, Lowell, Flower, et al., in Europe, it seems funny they had to fall back on a Coburg for that Bulgarian throne." Few weeks went by without some joke about Buffalo Bill. *Life* was amused when John L. Sullivan, the heavyweight champion, became a favorite of the Prince of Wales, along with Buffalo Bill—and Lowell. "We are doing a vast deal in these days for our British cousins," *Life* editorialized. "We sent them our Buffalo Bill, and for months he has delighted all sizes and conditions of them, and might, apparently, continue to delight them for years to come at great profit. Just as Bill pulls up his stakes, along comes John Sullivan from Boston, and consoles the Britishers to that degree that the Wild West's departure is hardly noticed."[12]

Marshall P. Wilder, a dwarf who was comedian, entertainer, and author, enjoying a successful tour abroad, declared that "the greatest, most unapproachable, thoroughly howling success that America ever sent to London was Buffalo Bill." Wilder found it not strange that this was so, for "the great mass of the English people think of America as a place principally infested by Indians, bears, and hunters, and they took Bill and his show as a sample." Added to this were the many noble and wealthy hunters whom Cody had guided in the West. "First they learned to like him, and then they heartily respected him, and he never did anything to make them change their opinion of him—he could not, for in spite of the prairie style which was his at that time, he was born well and well-bred, and had always kept his heart and his manners in good working order. . . . Bill always seemed to know exactly what to do and say. . . . I must express my pride and delight, as an American, at the figure Bill cut in society. He fills a full-dress suit as gracefully as he does the hunter's buckskins, carries himself as elegantly as any

[12] Francis Hyde Bangs, *John Kendrick Bangs* (New York, 1941), 74–78; *Life*, Vol. X (August 11, 1887), 74; *ibid.* (July 14, 1887), 18; *ibid.* (August 25, 1887), 109; *ibid.* (November 3, 1887), 253; *ibid.* (November 17, 1887), 272; *ibid.* (November 24, 1887), 286. Edmund John Phelps was U. S. minister; Charles A. Dana, editor, *New York Sun;* Joseph Pulitzer, publisher, *New York World;* Benjamin Orange Flower, editor, *American Spectator.*

English gentleman of leisure, uses good grammar, speaks with a drawing-room tone of voice, and moves as leisurely as if he had nothing to do all his life but exist beautifully. He tells a good joke, but knows when not to carry the fun too far. Every friend he has made over there I am sure he has kept. I ought to know, for most of them have told me so themselves."[13]

Buffalo Bill's Wild West remained in London through October, quite overshadowing the American Exhibition of which it was a part. The exhibition got off to a bad start with the British public when, because of its private nature, President Grover Cleveland declined to allow his name to appear as sponsor—although seven dukes were on the list and it was officially opened by the Prince of Wales. Cleveland relented, or repented, and sent a felicitous cablegram for the opening ceremonies. British newspapermen found little to write about except Frederic Auguste Bartholdi's diorama of New York harbor, including his Statue of Liberty, dedicated less than seven months before the exhibition opened. One reporter recorded that we "did not come to the exhibit to see the false teeth and the Christmas cards"; and another added, "Nor are we likely to undertake a tour to West Brompton for the purpose of looking at such doubtless ingenious but decidedly ugly things as coffee-mills, stoves, Gatling guns, hand machines for executing embroidery presumed to be artistic, liquid fish-glue and an ironclad branduster." Many notables rushed off to see Buffalo Bill's Wild West before the president of the exhibition had finished welcoming them to the grounds.

There can be little doubt that Buffalo Bill was the main attraction. At the conclusion of the American Exhibition, its sponsors called a meeting to propose a court of arbitration to settle differences between the British Empire and the United States. A fisheries treaty had expired and was not renewed, ending reciprocity, and some ill feeling had developed. The London *Times* credited the good will built up by Buffalo Bill and his Wild West as contributing to the favor with which the proposal was received.

Colonel Cody "found himself the hero of the London season," said *The Times*. "Notwithstanding his daily engagements and his

[13] Marshall P. Wilder, *The People I've Smiled With* (Akron, New York, Chicago, 1899), 108–21.

punctual fulfillment of them, he found time to go everywhere, to see everything, and to be seen by all the world. All London contributed to his triumph, and now the close of his show is selected as the occasion for promoting a great international movement with Mr. Bright, Lord Granville, Lord Wolseley, and Lord Lorne for its sponsors. Colonel Cody can achieve no greater triumph than this, even if he some day realizes the design attributed to him of running the Wild West show within the classic precincts of the Colosseum at Rome."[14]

Sparked by this encouragement, the Colonel and has daughter Arta took a two weeks' trip to Italy to look over the Colosseum. He found it unsuitable for the purpose.

At the close of the London engagement, Annie Oakley quit the show. The reasons for the break are not entirely clear. At the written request of the Prince of Wales, Cody had arranged a match for her with the Grand Duke Michael of Russia. She won, 47 to 36, out of 50 clay pigeons apiece. The Grand Duke was courting one of the Prince's daughters, and some newspapers took occasion to lampoon him, with consequent publicity for Annie. She was invited to Wimbledon, to the London Gun Club, and to society events. It is suggested that all this attention aroused Cody's jealousy, but it seems quite as likely that it was felt that her extracurricular activities were interfering with her show appearances. The break came when she accepted an invitation to Berlin for an exhibition at Charlottenburg Race Course under the patronage of Crown Prince Wilhelm.[15]

Buffalo Bill's Wild West started its tour on November 5 at Aston Lower grounds, Birmingham—admission one shilling; reserved seats, one to three shillings extra. "In spite of London's lavish praise," said the *Gazette,* "Birmingham's thousands insisted on their right to criticize. . . . There was nothing remarkable about the 'genuine buffalo hunt.' Of course the buffaloes were genuine. There was nothing very remarkable about the roping and riding of 'wild' Texas steers by cowboys and Mexicans. Of course the steer was wild. It took half a dozen men to lasso it and hold it by the tail; and it did jump when a rope had been tied round its body and a

[14] November 1, 1887.
[15] C. R. Cooper, *Annie Oakley,* 190–92; Swartwout, *Missie,* 142–43, 150–51.

cowboy rode on its back. . . . The Indian war cry is a decided failure. It is apparently a shrill and feeble screech, and not at all the blood-curdling yell that Fenimore Cooper and other writers have led us to believe. . . . I fear, too, that the 'war dance' as performed at Aston has not made a great impression on the popular mind. It is a tame—one might say almost a childish—jig, without rhythm or measure, and thus another hallucination of our boyhood is disposed of."

That was the sum of objections. The *Birmingham Gazette* concluded: "The show is worth seeing—it is worth anybody's while to put himself to some trouble to go and see it. Nothing like it has ever been shown in Birmingham before. A better idea of the dangers pioneers confront, of the resource and skill that difficulties bring out, of the way in which the Wild West has been 'settled' and civilized, can be obtained from one visit to this exhibition than by reading a score of histories and a cartload of descriptions."[16]

On November 14 it was announced that the "entire electrical installation from the American Exhibition in London was being installed." This seems to have been ten carbon arc lights with a total of 150,000 candlepower. Those who remember arc lights will not be much impressed.

Two performers had been absent in the interests of publicity. Broncho Charley Miller and Marve Beardsley—and Marve was an undoubted original Pony Express rider—started a six-day race on their horses at Agricultural Hall, Islington, London, on November 7, against two cyclists, Richard Howell of Leicester and W. M. Woodside of Philadelphia. In that day a six-day bicycle race was a novelty, and the bicycles ridden were those with a high wheel in front and a small wheel in the rear. At the end of the first day the cyclists totaled 137 miles and seven laps, and Buffalo Bill's pony express riders had 136 miles and six laps. At the end of the second day the horsemen had 272 miles and the cyclists 271 miles and seven laps. The race was run eight hours a day, horses being changed every hour, using thirty horses. The average pace was about twenty miles an hour. The cowboys won the £300 prize by

16 *Birmingham Gazette*, November 4, 5, 7, 16, 1887, photostats, and summaries of other articles through December 7, and *Birmingham Post*, November 3–December 1, supplied by A. B. Gregory.

two miles and two laps. Miller and Beardsley had each ridden 407 miles, Woodside made 422 miles, and Howell, 389.[17]

At Manchester race course, Salford, "the largest theater ever seen in the world, heated by steam, and illuminated by the electric light" was being erected. The previous year's indoor exhibition at Madison Square Garden was the model for the winter engagement that opened there on December 17. For the "Depiction of American Pioneer History," $40,000 worth of "Grand Natural Scenic Effects" was supplied by Matt Morgan, of New York, an English artist who had gone to America as cartoonist for *Frank Leslie's Weekly*. There were seven panoramas, each two hundred feet long, worked on drums thirty feet high.

This "Page of Passing History" opened with the primeval forest, with Indians—Cody had plenty of Indians—demonstrating dances, sign language, customs, and a fight between tribes. A triumph of scenic and stage management represented a prairie fire periling an emigrant train with an accompanying stampede of wild animals. "This scene," said the *Sunday Chronicle*, "is one of the grandest ever placed before the public, and fairly baffles description." Lew Parker explained how it was done: "The grass rows used in the prairie fire were graded from twenty-six feet high in the rear to three feet in front, giving the appearance of immense distance. The fire scene was most realistic. At that time we had no electric devices to help us out. I devised a steam curtain some distance in front of the burning grass and we forced the elk, buffalo, and bears across the stage behind the steam effect, which gave the appearance of the animals going through a mountain of fire and smoke."

A cattle ranch scene gave opportunity for exhibitions by Miss Emma Hicock [*sic*], America's Queen of the Saddle, and Miss Lillian Smith, "the California Girl," with fancy rifle shooting. The sixth episode was Custer's Last Fight, long the crowning spectacle of the Wild West. In the final scene, Deadwood City was destroyed by an artificial cyclone supplied by the Blackman Air Propellor Company.[18]

[17] *Illustrated London News*, New York Edition, Vol. I, No. 29 (November 26, 1887); *Broncho Charlie, A Saga of the Saddle: The Autobiography of Broncho Charlie Miller* (as told to Gladys Shaw Erskine), 251–55.
[18] Program, Inaugural Invitation Exhibition of Buffalo Bill's Wild West, Manchester, December 17, 1887; summaries, *Manchester Evening News* and *Manchester*

During the first few weeks the Wild West repeated its London success. Dignitaries assembled from far and near to present the Colonel with a rifle, and he entertained them with an Indian-style rib-roast feast. His Worship, the Mayor of Salford proclaimed three new streets in the area to be Cody Street, Buffalo Street, and Bill Street. But there were signs that the triumph was over. It had been planned to stay abroad for two years, but on January 10, 1888, Salsbury left to arrange for a summer tour back home. In February the business in Manchester fell off sharply. There was some talk of returning to London, but fear of losing reputation if the Wild West failed to repeat its previous success caused the management to remain in Manchester and take the losses.[19]

The final performance there was given on April 30, with "Farewell Day" announced for Tuesday, May 1, when a program of sports was given—another forecast of rodeo. It included racing, and one race went wrong, departure of the troupe was delayed, and the race was run over. This was a ten-mile relay race in which Antonio Esquival rode successively thirteen broncos against English Thoroughbreds ridden by J. Latham for B. Goodall, horse-breeder of Altrincham. Esquival was more adept at changing horses because of his experience in the pony express act, and he won the £500 stake.[20]

The delayed departure from Manchester was made on May 4, and on May 5 the final performance in England was given at Hull. The triumph there was a fitting close to the first visit abroad of Buffalo Bill's Wild West. The *Hull News* recorded: "Numerous excursion trains were run to Hull not only from the immediate neighborhood, but from the West Riding and the Midland districts, and large numbers of persons were brought to the town. The Holderness road during the latter part of the morning and the afternoon presented a lively scene, for as early as eleven o'clock the spectators began to enter the ground, and the trams and waggonettes plying in that direction were heavily laden, the traffic being for a time congested, and was only carried on with difficulty, so

---

Guardian, December 2, 1887–May 4, 1888, supplied by Mr. Sidney Horrocks, librarian, the Manchester Public Libraries Reference Library.

[19] *Letters from Buffalo Bill*, 33–34.

[20] *Manchester Evening News*, April 30, May 1, 1888; *Manchester Guardian*, May 2, 1888.

great was the crowd of vehicles. Early in the afternoon very many thousands had gathered on the field and the grand stand, for entrance to which a charge of 5s. each was made, was quite filled." This was the grandstand of the Hull Football Field. Two playing fields were thrown together for the Wild West, and temporary stands were also erected.[21]

Buffalo Bill's Wild West sailed from the Alexandra Dock, Hull, on May 6, 1888, on the *Persian Monarch*. The voyage was uneventful except for the death of Old Charlie, Cody's veteran horse, ridden by him since the beginning of the Wild West. Old Charlie was buried at sea on May 17. The troupe was given a tumultuous welcome in New York harbor, and went immediately to Erastina to open another engagement there.

Life's two-page cartoon in its mid-December issue was titled "The Triumph of the West." The artist, Charles Dana Gibson, centered it on the familiar figure of Buffalo Bill, rifle in hand, on his white horse, receiving the homage of Queen Victoria and her court and preceded by three peers in their robes. The British Lion, garbed as an Indian with tomahawk in his belt, stalked alongside. Pages and dancing girls surrounded the hero. In the background a huge float drawn by representative citizens and driven by the Prince of Wales enthroned John L. Sullivan.[22]

While the objective, of course, was to make British enthusiasms look slightly ridiculous, *Life's* attitude was also that of pointing out with amusement British interest in the frontiersman to the dismay of Anglophiles and sophisticates who took their culture second-hand from Europe and could see no merit in a character so uncouth.

However it be interpreted, the cartoon in *Life* emphasized one fact—that in 1887 the man of the year was William F. Cody.

[21] *Hull News*, May 5, 7, 12, 1888; *Eastern Morning News*, May 7, 1888; *Hull Times*, May 12, 1888, copies from Mr. R. F. Drewery, D.P.A., F.L.A., chief librarian, City and County of Kingston upon Hull Public Libraries.
[22] *Life*, Vol. X (December 15, 1887), 348–49.

BUFFALO BILL AND THE BUFFALO

As BUFFALO BILL'S WILD WEST arrived in Birmingham, England, the *Birmingham Gazette* on November 4, 1887, noted, "Additional interest is attached to the buffaloes by the fact that they are almost the only survivors of what is nearly an extinct species. According to Colonel Cody there are not so many buffaloes on the whole American continent as there are in the exhibition." If he meant buffalo in a wild state within the United States, that was no exaggeration, but even the unqualified statement would have been difficult to disprove at that particular moment. That the exhibition was depicting scenes that were already historic was dramatically shown by the fact that the founding of Buffalo Bill's Wild West in 1883 almost exactly coincided with the extermination of the buffalo.

The destruction of the vast herds that once roamed the North American continent took place largely between 1870 and 1883. In three of those years 3,700,000 buffalo were killed in the southern herd alone; it ceased to exist after 1875. The hide hunters did not realize that the northern herd was gone at the end of the winter of 1882–83. That fall they outfitted as usual only to meet total failure, for they found no buffalo.

The end came so quickly that the Smithsonian Institution found itself without presentable specimens, and by 1886 it was feared that the bison would become entirely extinct before any could be obtained. An expedition organized that year was fortunate in finding enough wild buffalo in Montana Territory to make a comprehensive scientific display. The report by William T. Hornaday on "The Extermination of the American Bison" in the annual report of the Smithsonian Institution for 1887 is credited with being instrumental in saving the buffalo from extinction.

Cody's name looms large in this report. On its first page he is mentioned in a reference to "Cabeza de Vaca—or, in other words, 'Cattle Cabeza,' the prototoype of our own distinguished 'Buffalo Bill.'"

In taking account of the surviving buffalo, fourth on the census of those in captivity is the herd of Hon. W. F. Cody. Says the report: "The celebrated 'Wild West Show' has, ever since its organization, numbered among its leading attractions a herd of live buffaloes of all ages. At present this herd contains eighteen head, of which fourteen were originally purchased of Mr. H. T. Groome, of Wichita, Kansas, and have made a journey to London and back. As a proof of the indomitable persistence of the bison in breeding under most unfavorable circumstances, the fact that four of the members of this herd are calves which were born in 1888 [1887?] in London, at the American Exposition, is of considerable interest. The herd is now [December, 1888] being wintered on General Beale's farm near the city of Washington. In 1886–87, while the Wild West Show was at Madison Square Garden, New York City, its entire herd of twenty buffaloes was carried off by pleuro-pneumonia. It is to be greatly feared that sooner or later in the course of its travels the present herd will also disappear, either through disease or accident."[1]

This statement points up how important the scientist considered Cody's eighteen buffalo in connection with the preservation of the species. At the end of 1888, of 256 buffalo in captivity, only two herds were larger than Buffalo Bill's. S. L. Bedson, of Stony Mountain, Manitoba, was a pioneer in breeding buffalo, and from ten in 1877 he had produced seventy by 1888, when he sold his herd to Charles J. Jones, of Garden City, Kansas, known as "Buffalo Jones."

[1] *Annual Report of . . . the Smithsonian Institution . . . June 30, 1887*, Part II, 367–548; see particularly pp. 373, 460. See also Martin S. Garretson, *The American Bison;* E. Douglas Branch, *The Hunting of the Buffalo.*

Jones, like Bedson, had experimented with cross-breeding bison and cattle, and carried on a lively publicity campaign for his "cattalo." Prior to his purchase of the Bedson herd, Buffalo Jones owned fifty-seven buffalo, most of which he had captured personally in Texas. Some he rounded up and drove to his ranch with the aid of tamed buffalo, but as he had little luck in taming grown buffalo or even in keeping them alive after capture, he turned his attention to calves, which he lassoed, threw, tied, and hobbled. His total of 140 was by far the largest herd in private hands. Charles Allard of the Flathead Indian Reservation in Montana had thirty-five. Charles Goodnight, rancher, had thirteen from the last of the Texas herd in Paloduro Canyon near his home in Clarendon, Texas. At Bismarck Grove, Kansas, the Santa Fe Railroad maintained ten buffalo as a tourist attraction. Similarly, John H. Garin had four at a summer resort at Glen Island, near New York. The number in zoos was small: Philadelphia had ten; there were four in Cincinnati; four in Central Park, New York City; seven in Lincoln Park, Chicago; and a pair at the National Museum, Washington. Abroad were two at Manchester, England; one in London; one in Liverpool, purchased from Buffalo Bill; two in Dresden, Germany; and one in Calcutta, India. Frederick Dupree, of the Cheyenne agency, Dakota Territory, had nine; Dr. V. T. McGillicuddy had four at Rapid City; and fourteen more were held singly or in pairs. The total was 216 kept for breeding purposes and 40 for exhibition. The Yellowstone Park herd was estimated at 200. The estimate on the remaining wild buffalo in the United States was eighty-five—twenty-five in Texas, twenty in Colorado, twenty-six in Wyoming, ten in Montana, and four in Dakota. Adding an estimated 550 in Canada, the survivors of the millions of only a decade before totaled only 1,091.[2]

This destruction was brought about almost entirely by hide hunters who got fifty cents to a dollar and a quarter for each skin. Employing the still-hunt system, instead of the horseback chase of Buffalo Bill, the hide hunters could kill forty to sixty animals a day. Sometimes a large number could be killed from a single spot,

[2] Hornaday, "The Extermination of the American Bison," *Smithsonian Annual Report, 1887*, Part II, 460–64. See also Col. Henry Inman, *Buffalo Jones' Forty Years of Adventure;* Zane Grey, *The Last of the Plainsmen* (Chicago, 1911); J. Evetts Haley, *Charles Goodnight, Cowman and Plainsman* (Norman, 1949); Julia B. Mc-Gillycuddy, *McGillicuddy, Agent.*

for buffalo were little disturbed by the noise of shooting or by the death struggles of the victims.

Contrary to much opinion expressed since that time, Hornaday felt that the Indian was as much responsible for the destruction of the buffalo as the white hide hunter. Sitting Bull's Sioux on returning from Canada made huge inroads in the diminishing northern herd. He pointed out that the Indians used such methods as driving a herd over a cliff, or surrounding it, and slaughtering numbers far in excess of what they needed or could use, and took sadistic pleasure in the killing. True, they did not hunt for sport, but, says Hornaday, "I have yet to learn of an instance wherein an Indian refrained from excessive slaughter of game through motives of economy, or care for the future, or prejudice against wastefulness."

It has been suggested also that natural causes might have contributed to the decline. Years of drought are many in the plains area, and little is known about the effect of a scarcity of grass on the numbers of buffalo in the years when it was impossible to count them. Yet the blizzard of 1885–86 had no effect on the buffalo; Jones determined to attempt to domesticate them after seeing "thousands upon thousands of carcasses of domestic cattle." He records, "When I reached the habitat of the buffalo, not one of their carcasses was visible, except those which had been slain by the hunters. Every animal I came across was as lively and nimble as a fox."[3]

Because Cody acquired his pseudonym by killing buffalo, it is assumed that he was among those largely responsible for the extermination of the animals. The buffalo killed by Cody were used for food. Hornaday finds that all of the buffalo killed for food reduced the herds very little. During the three years of the heaviest slaughter of the southern herd, when 1,200,000 buffalo a year were killed, only 50,000 a year were used for food. Many were slaughtered for their tongues alone, at twenty-five cents a tongue. The killing was carelessly wasteful. In the first year of heavy slaughter in the south, 1872, it was estimated that only one hide was recovered for every three buffalo killed. As numbers decreased, hide hunters became more efficient. In the second year they took one

---

[3] Hornaday, "The Extermination of the American Bison," *Smithsonian Annual Report*, 1887, Part II, 506–507; Inman, *Buffalo Jones*, 47–48.

hide from every two buffalo killed; and in the third year, 100 hides for every 125 animals killed.

Buffalo Bill was a professional meat hunter only during the few months he was employed for the Kansas Pacific contractors. The 4,280 animals he killed then was, of course, a trifling number among the millions extant. That figure has been mentioned so frequently that it is sometimes assumed to be the total number he killed. He hunted buffalo to feed troops throughout his scouting career and guided many hunting parties, yet down to 1884, when he killed his last buffalo, it seems doubtful that his total approached 10,000. Hornaday estimates the total killed by all hunting parties at 10,000, and is sure that many individual hide hunters could claim as many as all the foreign sportsmen.

It would be dramatic to record that Hornaday's report resulted in immediate action to preserve the species. Actually, few persons cared. General Sheridan and other army officers had said that elimination of the buffalo would end the Indian problem. Few historians will deny that they were right. Both cowmen and nesters were agreed that the buffalo must go. The end of the buffalo east of the Mississippi River had gone almost unheralded except on the Great Seal of the state of Indiana. Congress was reluctant to act, although Canada in 1889 passed a law to protect the buffalo. There was no protection for buffalo anywhere in the United States except in Yellowstone Park, and little enough there.

Troops on duty in Yellowstone were ordered to protect the buffalo herd, but when they caught a poacher skinning a buffalo, he was released because there was no way to bring a citizen to trial in an area that had no civil government. The soldiers, however, took other measures. As the fellow was defiant and obnoxious, they beat the tar out of him before turning him loose. There were no civil authorities to whom he could complain.

During the winter of 1893–94 the Yellowstone herd drifted out of the park. By spring only twenty survivors were counted, and it was not certain that some had not been counted more than once. That year an act was passed providing a fine and imprisonment for killing a Yellowstone Park buffalo. Buffalo Jones was employed to build up the herd. He bought eighteen from the Allard heirs and three from Goodnight.

At this point Buffalo Bill's eighteen seem important. His part in the preservation of the species was not inconsiderable. The show provided a market for domesticated animals, encouraging that activity. When Cody lost his herd in 1886, he got two surplus buffalo from the Philadelphia zoo for $300. Before going to London, he offered Buffalo Jones $1,000 a head. Cody sold one buffalo to the zoo in Liverpool. It is probable that he was responsible for those reported in zoos at London and Manchester.[4]

Much more important than this occasional brokerage, however, was the propaganda value of Buffalo Bill's exhibition to the Smithsonian Institution's cause—at the start almost the only popular support. It was Buffalo Bill's show that was making the West appear romantic to a contemporary generation, and buffalo came to characterize the Wild West. Thousands of the show's spectators had never before seen a buffalo. Their interest contributed to the sentimental reaction that saved the species from extinction. Others probably were more active than Cody in the campaign that was not safely won until well along in the 1920's, but Buffalo Bill's Wild West was important in that long crusade. By the 1950's the number of buffalo in the United States was held at 9,000, with about 300 killed each year as surplus.

Experience taught Cody to abandon the idea of roping or riding buffalo as an entertainment feature, but few persons then or since realized the difficulties of the brief spectacle of the buffalo hunt that was a fixture in Buffalo Bill's Wild West programs. Almost three-quarters of a century later an outdoor showman was advertising "the world's only trained buffalo," and it was no exaggeration, for the buffalo is almost untamable. Buffalo Jones broke a team of seven-year-old bulls to draw a wagon, but had to use a windlass to control the lines. One of this pair had killed its former owner. Adult wild buffalo would not live in captivity; they would break their necks plunging over embankments or crush their skulls against any barrier strong enough to hold them.

When Michel Pablo sold the herd started by C. A. Allard to

[4] W. F. Cody to Rudolph J. Schaefer, May 15, 1915, in Buffalo Bill Museum, Lookout Mountain, for his last buffalo; Garretson, *The American Bison*, 190–91; Hornaday, "The Extermination of the American Bison," *Smithsonian Annual Report, 1887*, Part II, 461, 464; Kirke Mecham (ed.), "The Annals of Kansas, 1887," *Kansas Historical Quarterly*, Vol. XX, No. 4 (November, 1952), 286.

the Canadian government in 1907, it took him and a band of experienced cowboys three years to round up and deliver the buffalo. After six decades of attempted taming, a half-dozen ranches were raising buffalo for meat by the mid-twentieth century. With little of this experience to draw on, Cody transported buffalo around the country and to England and the Continent, and put on a mock buffalo hunt in which, an English commentator declared, he found "nothing remarkable."[5]

It is possible that the publicity given Buffalo Bill and Buffalo Bill's Wild West contributed to the common acceptance of the word "buffalo" as applied to this animal which scientific purists insist should be called a "bison." The question of nomenclature has given rise to a perennial gag, perhaps originated by "Believe It or Not" Robert Ripley, that Buffalo Bill never shot a buffalo. Martin Garretson, secretary of the American Bison Society, refutes this statement, for he saw Buffalo Bill shoot and kill an animal that all scientists would accept as a buffalo. In 1888, while the Wild West was at Erastina, one of the attractions was a pair of water buffalo from India. On the day Garretson visited the show, one of the water buffalo got loose and mixed with the herd of American bison, and an old bull ripped the India animal wide open. Cody saw that the water buffalo was done for and sent for Johnny Baker to kill it, but Johnny happened to have his rifle dismounted for cleaning. Cody then went to his tent, got his rifle, and with one shot killed the suffering buffalo.[6]

Pawnee Bill Lillie has received much credit for his contribution to the preservation of the buffalo, but his work came much later. It was not until 1902 that Lillie purchased the Casey herd of buffalo in Missouri and established his Buffalo Ranch near Pawnee, Oklahoma. Pawnee Bill's experience with the original Wild West in 1883 had aroused his interest in show business. In 1885 he took a troupe of Indians on tour with the Healy and Bigelow Medicine Show. He toured another season with Buffalo Bill's Wild West in 1886. Sells Bros. circus featured Pawnee Bill's Historical Wild

[5] *This Week, New York Herald Tribune,* October 14, 1956; *Chicago Sunday Tribune Magazine,* October 14, 1956; Grey, *Last of the Plainsmen,* 49, 51; Walter Noble Burns, "The Last Stand of the Buffalo," *Saturday Evening Post* (March 23, 1912), 16–18, 53–55.

[6] Garretson, *The American Bison,* 239–41.

West in 1887, and in 1888 Lillie went out alone, with 165 horses and mules, 84 Indians, 50 cowboys and *vaqueros*, and 30 trappers, hunters, and scouts. The band was led by Edward Jonathan Hoyt, Buckskin Joe, who had been scout against Ute Indians, and later was to head Buckskin Joe's Wild West. Other stars were Trapper Tom, Lillie's companion in early adventures; Oklahoma Al Lillie, Bill's brother, as pistol shot; and May Lillie, Bill's wife. He had married May Manning, a Philadelphia girl, in 1886 and taught her to shoot. She became an outstanding Wild West Show performer. Pawnee Bill's show played St. Joseph, Kansas City, Indianapolis, and Philadelphia with only moderate financial return.[7]

Meanwhile Annie Oakley and Frank Butler, returning from Europe that spring, signed up, sight unseen, with a show, probably that of Charles M. Southwell of Philadelphia. They found that its cowboys could not ride, and that, with the exception of a few unhappy Indians, it had been recruited from no further west than Pennsylvania. Learning that Pawnee Bill with a genuine cow country outfit was having box office troubles, Annie and Frank promoted a merger.

The combined shows drew big crowds at Gloucester Beach, New Jersey. In the fall they started south, playing fairs, but unfavorable contracts and bad weather melted away profits. Buckskin Joe withdrew, and the show was attached by the sheriff at Easton, Maryland. Pawnee Bill could not pay his hotel bill, and his trunks were seized. Fortuitously he was rescued when the Wichita Board of Trade employed him to head the Boomer movement as successor to Captain Payne. Before he could organize a new Boomer invasion of Indian Territory, however, he was called off. Prospects for legal opening of the territory looked too good to take a chance. Pawnee Bill is said to have led a colony of Boomers in the Oklahoma run of 1889. He was back in show business that summer with Adam Forepaugh's circus.

The failure of Pawnee Bill's Wild West in 1888 has been attributed in part to vicious warfare carried on by Buffalo Bill's Wild West. It could not have been a very extensive campaign, as the Buffalo Bill show made only a short tour that year. After leaving

[7] DeWolff, *Pawnee Bill*, 45–49; Shirley, *Pawnee Bill*, 118–32, 148–50; Gordon W. Lillie to Don Russell, August 30, 1938.

Erastina and the New York area, it made stops in Philadelphia, Baltimore, and Washington, closing at the Richmond Exposition and going into winter quarters—the first time the show had disbanded in two years and seven months.

Annie Oakley, after failure of the Pawnee Bill show, appeared in a variety bill at the opening of Tony Pastor's Opera House in New York, scheduled a few shooting matches, and took the part of "Sunbeam" in a melodrama, *Deadwood Dick*. Then she settled whatever disagreement she may have had with Cody and Salsbury and rejoined Buffalo Bill's Wild West for the season of 1889.

A European tour had been planned, and it was to prove a long one. The *Persian Monarch* was again engaged. The destination was Havre, with showing scheduled at the *Exposition Universale* in Paris. The opening performance was attended by President Sadi Carnot, members of his cabinet, and Ministers Whitelaw Reid and Louis MacLean. Royalty were not as conspicuous at Paris as at Queen Victoria's Jubilee, but Shah Naz-er-el-den of Persia attended and Queen Isabella of Spain rode in the Deadwood coach. Paris became as enthusiastic as had London for western books, cowboy and *vaquero* saddles and hats, and Indian baskets, bows, and moccasins.

Rosa Bonheur, the most famous animal painter of her day, spent most of her time in the back lot of the show during its seven months' run at the Paris Exposition, and at least seventeen paintings resulted. Next to her "Horse Fair," probably most widely reproduced of her paintings is that of Buffalo Bill on his white horse, which was copied on posters, heralds, couriers, programs, postcards, and in many books. Cody is said to have been critical of the great artist's depiction of himself and to have had the face repainted by Robert Lindneux.

Six Bonheur paintings represent buffalo: *Les bisons,* a group of four; *Étude de bison,* a study of a young buffalo; *Bisons fuyant l'incendies,* buffalo fleeing a prairie fire; *Peaux rogues attaquant des bisons,* redskins attacking bisons; *Le chasse aux bisons,* buffalo chase, and *Étude de Rosa Bonheur fait chez Buffalo Bill in 1889,* which study in Buffalo Bill's camp was a side view of his favorite Buffalo bull, Old Barney.

Indiens de Buffalo Bill also fascinated her; this title was given

350

Pawnee Bill and Buffalo Bill

Courtesy Denver Public Library Western Collection
Photograph by D. F. Barry

A Letter from Cody to his Cousin Lydia, 1894

"I love children," he wrote, inviting her to the show. "Bring them all."

to a picture of two mounted Indians. There were at least four more. A photograph shows Rosa Bonheur and Cody with Red Shirt and Rocky Bear. Others among the seventy-two Indians with the show who may have been her models were Cut Meat, American Bear, Flat Iron, Tall Horse, and Kills Plenty.[8]

While the Wild West was in Paris, it recovered one of its strayed performers. Black Elk had missed the boat two years previously at Hull, and was stranded there with five other Indians. They made their way to London, where they were employed in Mexican Joe's show. Joe took them to Paris, where Black Elk became seriously ill. He was cared for by a French family. After his recovery they heard that Buffalo Bill was in Paris and took Black Elk to him. Black Elk said, "He was glad to see me. He had all his people give me three cheers. Then he asked me if I wanted to be in the show or if I wanted to go home. I told him I was sick to go home. So he said he would fix that. He gave me a ticket and ninety dollars. Then he gave me a big dinner. Pahuska had a strong heart."[9]

Buffalo Bill's Indians were allowed to come and go like other employes of the show, and as Europeans had a great curiosity about the red men, they were treated with much consideration. A few remained in Europe. Others wandered off, and some found their way back to America. Among these was one White Horse, who told a tall tale of cruelty and starvation in the Wild West camp, which was printed in the *New York Herald*. When this story got to Berlin, Major Burke went into action. He invited the consul general and the secretary of legation there, as well as the consul in Hamburg, to inspect the Indians. All three agreed that "they are certainly the best looking, and apparently the best fed Indians we have ever seen." Their report was sent to the European edition of the *New York Herald* in Paris, and that newspaper editorially expressed satisfaction and even took pride in pointing out, "It shows the value of an international newspaper that stories wilder than the Wild West itself can be so promptly sat upon and refuted." However, since Cody felt it necessary to clarify the matter with the Commissioner of Indian Affairs, he decided to take all the In-

[8] Anna Klumpke, *Rosa Bonheur* (Paris, 1908); Leigh Jerrard, "Rosa Bonheur Revealed as a Painter of Westerns," *The Westerners Brand Book* (Chicago), Vol. X, No. 6 (August, 1953).

[9] *Black Elk Speaks* (as told to John G. Neihardt), 232.

dians home that fall instead of making an 1890–91 winter tour as had been planned.[10]

After the Paris Exposition the Wild West toured southern France, including Lyon and Marseille, then chartered a ship to Spain. A landing of American Indians at Barcelona 398 years after Columbus returned there from his discovery of America was an opportunity not overlooked by Major Burke. The Indians were photographed in front of the Columbus statue, where one of them observed, "It was a damned bad day for us when he discovered America." In all respects save publicity the Barcelona visit was a mistake. The city was in partial quarantine for typhoid fever and Spanish influenza. Frank Richmond, popular announcer of the show, died here, as did four Indians. Annie Oakley was seriously ill, and seven ailing Indians were sent home.

As soon as possible the show moved on by way of Sardinia and Corsica to Naples, where it opened on January 26, 1890. In Rome mounted Indians were photographed in front of St. Peter's—Pope Leo XIII received a Wild West delegation—and in temporary camp at the Colosseum, the nearest Buffalo Bill came to putting on a show in that ancient arena. The tour brightened when Don Onorio Herzog of Sermonetta, Prince of Teano, challenged the cowboys to ride his untamed stallions of the Cajetan breed, wildest and most unmanageable in Italy. Twenty thousand spectators saw the contest on March 4. "The brutes made springs into the air, darted hither and thither in all directions, and bent themselves into all sorts of shapes, but all in vain," wrote the Rome correspondent of the *New York Herald*. "In five minutes the cow-boys had caught the wild horses with the lasso, saddled, subdued, and bestrode them."

After this Roman triumph the show moved to Florence, Bologna, and Milan. At Verona, Buffalo Bill fulfilled his ambition of exhibiting the Wild West in an ancient Roman amphitheatre, that of Diocletian, built A.D. 260 and restored by Napoleon. On April 16 the inventors of the canoe tried out the gondola in the Grand Canal of Venice, for the benefit of photographers. The next move was by

[10] Carolyn Thomas Foreman, *Indians Abroad*, 203–204; program, Buffalo Bill's Wild West, 1893, pp. 34–35. See also Chauncey Yellow Robe, "The Menace of the Wild West Show," *Quarterly Journal of the Society of American Indians*, Vol. II, No. 3 (July–September, 1914), 224–28.

Innsbruck and the Tyrol to Munich. The days of Buffalo Bill are commemorated in Munich in a museum dedicated to Karl May, a German writer of Wild West juveniles, immensely popular in Europe. One of its prides is a painting of Custer's last fight by Elk Eber, who obtained his information from a Sioux woman, eyewitness of the fight, who left Buffalo Bill's Wild West to be married in Germany.[11]

The summer tour included Vienna, Berlin, Dresden, Leipzig, Bonn, Coblentz, and Frankfurt, the season ending at Stuttgart. Nate Salsbury set up winter quarters at Benfield, Alsace Lorraine. Burke and the Indians took ship at Antwerp for Philadelphia, and went on to Washington.

[11] National Park Service, *Custer Battlefield National Cemetery* (1943); *Life*, June 21, 1948, p. 58; Hermann Eber, in *The Westerners Brand Book* (Chicago), Vol. V, No. 5 (July, 1948), 32, denied the report that Elk Eber was the son of a Sioux woman with a certified birth certificate.

25

THE LAST WAR TRAIL

THE SIOUX WAR OF 1876–77, which at first appeared small, proved to be among the greatest of all Indian wars. The Sioux war of 1890–91 at one stage caused more alarm and appeared to be of far greater proportions than any previous Indian trouble, but in the outcome it was inconsequential. The Sioux, after their experiences following the defeat of Custer, had no desire to tangle with troops again. Despite much provocation from governmental policies applied with little understanding of their needs, they showed surprising patience. Indian agents and the do-good friends of the Indian agreed on a simple solution to the Indian problem, namely, to make over the Indian into an imitation white man as soon as possible. Friends of the Indian in the East were ready to force the Indian to become a farmer by applying the adage that those who did not work should not eat. Indian agents could readily see that no amount of farm work would make the Sioux self-supporting on the kind of land assigned them as reservations, but were sure the hard work would be good for them. The climax came when, after three years of drought that caused the abandonment of Dakota lands by experienced white farmers, the Indian Bureau cut Sioux rations upon discovering that the reservation rolls had been padded. With all the padding, the rations had been inadequate, and a total crop failure meant that the Sioux were actually starving.

In their despair there came to the Sioux a savior, an actual Messiah. A fanatical religious movement swept through the Plains tribes, gaining momentum as conditions became riper for it. The new religion was an odd mixture of Christian teaching and the traditional Indian happy hunting ground. It was said that the Messiah, who had been rejected and slain by the white men, had returned to earth on behalf of the Indians. He would bring with him all of the Indians who had died, and all of the departed horses and buffalo. As he started walking from west to east, a wave of new earth many feet deep would accompany him, covering the white man and all his works and returning to the living Indian and his departed ancestors a world as it had been before Columbus made his landfall. All that was necessary to bring this about was to dance the Ghost Dance and await the second coming of the Messiah. Never before had so many diverse peoples had anything in common. From the Rocky Mountains to the Missouri River, from North Dakota to Indian Territory, all tribes were dancing the Ghost Dance, to the alarm of the many settlers who were filling the West under the assumption that the Indian wars were over. When the name of Sitting Bull became associated with this movement, the alarm increased, for despite a campaign to deflate the reputation of Sitting Bull, in the minds of the general public he was still the one Indian held most largely responsible for the Custer disaster.

There actually was a Messiah. His name was Wo-vo-ka, or Jack Wilson, a Paiute Indian of Nevada, who had dreams and visions, and perhaps by some form of self-hypnosis had caused others to see the same dreams and visions. His ideas possibly were derived from Smowhala of the Wanapum tribe in Oregon, whose cult of the Dreamers figured in the Nez Percé outbreak in 1877. Spiritual leadership from such remote areas had become possible with advancing civilization, which in some directions was moving more rapidly than even the Indian agents suspected. Inter-tribal warfare had stopped, permitting Indians to range farther than they had ever dared in their primitive nomadism. They rode on trains, for many railroads had agreed to carry them free. Thus as news of the new Messiah spread across the plains, many Indians went to see for themselves.

Sitting Bull of the Arapahoes—not to be confused with Sitting

Bull of the Hunkpapa Sioux, as he may have been at the time—went to see Wo-vo-ka and came back converted, to teach the new cult on the Southern Plains. Ahpiaton of the Kiowas was more skeptical; he had worshiped the new Messiah from afar for three years, and was amazed to find that Wo-vo-ka was unable to recognize him or to converse in the Kiowa language. Lieutenant Hugh L. Scott, who became chief of staff of the army during World War I, persuaded General Merritt to forego trying to disarm eight tribes of the Southern Plains and not to interfere with the Ghost Dance. Said Scott, "The Indian was then most susceptible to Christianity; the name of Jesus was on every tongue, and had I been a missionary I could have led every Indian on the Plains into the church."[1]

On the Northern Plains the Sioux desperately felt the need of spiritual leadership. Three emissaries, Kicking Bear, Short Bull, and Porcupine, went to seek the Messiah. They traveled by horseback, afoot, and by rail, from South Dakota across Montana to the land of the Crows, and then to the Shoshones—both tribes traditional enemies—and then to the Nevada camp of Wo-vo-ka. They returned as enthusiastic missionaries. Kicking Bull took the Ghost Dance to the camp of Sitting Bull on Grand River.

It seems improbable that Sitting Bull, a medicine man in his own right, was personally an ardent believer in the Messiah or the Ghost Dance, but he did nothing to discourage Kicking Bear. Opinions differ as to whether he sought to take advantage of the excitement for more ambitious ends. The two opinions that counted most at the time were that he did. Major General Nelson A. Miles, commanding the Division of the Missouri with headquarters in Chicago, believed, "It was a threatened uprising of colossal proportions, extending over a far greater territory than did the confederation inaugurated by the Prophet and led by Tecumseh, or the conspiracy of Pontiac, and only the prompt action of the military prevented its execution."[2]

James McLaughlin, Indian agent at Standing Rock, was convinced "that the new religion was managed from the beginning, as far as the Standing Rock Sioux were concerned, by Sitting Bull,

[1] H. L. Scott, *Some Memories of a Soldier*, 155. See also James Mooney, "The Ghost Dance Religion," *Fourteenth Annual Report, Bureau of American Ethnology* (Washington, 1896); Paul Bailey, *Wovoka* (Los Angeles, 1957).

[2] Nelson A. Miles, *Serving the Republic*, 238.

who . . . having lost his former influence over the Sioux, planned to import and use it to re-establish himself in the leadership of the people, whom he might then lead in safety in any desperate enterprise which he might direct."[3]

If Sitting Bull had lost his former influence, McLaughlin had little to worry about. Actually this was wishful thinking. McLaughlin had done everything in his power to destroy Sitting Bull's influence and had not succeeded. It was Indian Bureau policy to destroy the influence of chiefs, on the theory that they had led their people to war. The hope for peace, in the official view, was in the younger generation. The policy did not work. It was the younger generation who took up the Ghost Dance and were spoiling for a fight, while elder chiefs, like Red Cloud, counseled prudence. McLaughlin was considered the ablest Indian agent of his time, his wife was a Sioux, and he had a great deal of sympathy for the Indians—but no understanding. He represented the prevailing Indian Bureau policy: he banned the sun dance; he discouraged Indian habits and customs; repeatedly he says Indians had no history and no traditions. He judged Indians in accordance with their willingness to adopt white ways, and Sitting Bull was not among those who were willing to do so. McLaughlin never has a kind word for him: "Crafty, avaricious, mendacious, and ambitious, Sitting Bull possessed all the faults of an Indian and none of the nobler attributes which have gone far to redeem some of his people from their deeds of guilt. . . . Even his people knew him as a physical coward, but the fact did not handicap the man in dealing with his following." McLaughlin, in his efforts to discredit Sitting Bull, was a principal advocate of the story that at the Custer fight Sitting Bull "took to the hills, there to make medicine, while the fight was in progress."[4]

McLaughlin, on October 14, 1890, sent Lieutenant Chatka of his Indian police to eject Kicking Bear from Sitting Bull's camp, which Chatka succeeded in doing. "That night," says McLaughlin, "Sitting Bull broke his peace-pipe, which he had kept sacredly since his surrender at Fort Buford in 1881." McLaughlin recommended the arrest of Sitting Bull and his removal to some remote

---

[3] James McLaughlin, *My Friend, the Indian*, 238.
[4] *Ibid.*, 25, 180, 182, 192, 263.

military prison. The Indian Bureau turned the recommendation over to the army, to McLaughlin's disappointment. On November 17, McLaughlin, accompanied only by an interpreter, went to Sitting Bull's camp, where he found a Ghost Dance in progress.

McLaughlin must be given credit for courage; he upbraided Sitting Bull for taking part in the Ghost Dance and for leading his people astray. Sitting Bull challenged McLaughlin to go with him to "seek for the men who saw the Messiah; and when we find them, I will demand that they show him to us, and if they cannot do so I will return and tell my people it is a lie." This certainly seems a straightforward offer, but McLaughlin, who apparently knew nothing of Wo-vo-ka or of the expedition of Kicking Bear, Short Bull, and Porcupine that had succeeded in finding him, replied that "such an attempt would be like catching up with the wind that blew last year," and tried to get Sitting Bull to come in to the agency. This Sitting Bull refused to do.[5]

It was at this point that Buffalo Bill enters the picture. Most of those who have written about the incident have considered it the height of absurdity; those on both sides of the argument regarding the attitude and intentions of Sitting Bull seem to agree that there was no merit in Colonel Cody's intrusion. Just why there was not seems obscure.

Cody's return from Europe had nothing to do with the troubles among the Sioux—his only concern as he set out was the charge that the Indians of the Wild West show were being mistreated. However, he dropped his plan to join Major Burke and the Indians in Washington to argue the matter, for on his arrival in New York he was handed a telegram from General Miles requesting him to come to Chicago as soon as possible. Cody reported within thirty-six hours. Miles, convinced that he was faced with a widespread Indian war, wanted information about the Bad Lands country, with which Cody was familiar. Whether the mission to Sitting Bull was the purpose of Miles' telegram to Cody or was an afterthought is not clear.

Cody says: "Miles said that Sitting Bull had his camp somewhere within forty or fifty miles of the Standing Rock Agency, and was haranguing the Indians thereabout, spreading the Messiah

[5] *Ibid.*, 192, 207.

talk and getting them to join him. He asked me if I could go immediately to Standing Rock and Fort Yates, and thence to Sitting Bull's camp. He knew that I was an old friend of the chief and he believed that if any one could induce the old fox to abandon his plans for a general war I could. . . . I was sure that if I could reach Sitting Bull he would at least listen to me."[6]

It seems clear that Cody had no other intention than to have a talk with Sitting Bull and to try to persuade him not to start a war —few now believe Sitting Bull ever had any idea of starting a war. There can be no doubt that Cody was also authorized to invite Sitting Bull to a conference with General Miles, which would serve the purpose also of getting the Indian leader out of the troubled area. Cody, of course, could not take Sitting Bull from the reservation without some authority. That authority was given thus:

Confidential
Headquarters, Division of the Missouri
Chicago, Ill., Nov. 24, 1890

Col. Cody,

You are hereby authorized to secure the person of Sitting Bull and and [sic] deliver him to the nearest com'g officer of U. S. Troops, taking a receipt and reporting your action.

NELSON A. MILES
Major General
Comd. Division

On the back of a visiting card the General wrote in pencil:

Com'd'g officers will please give Col. Cody transportation for himself and party and any protection he may need for a small party.

NELSON A. MILES[7]

It probably never occurred to either Cody or Miles that acting under these orders Cody was to arrest Sitting Bull forcibly in his camp in the midst of the Sioux nation. But to everyone who had

[6] Cody, *Autobiography*, 305–306; Cody, *True Tales of the Plains*, 234–35.
[7] Original in Buffalo Bill Museum, Lookout Mountain, Colo.

ever read a Buffalo Bill dime novel—and that would include almost all his contemporaries except Buffalo Bill himself—he would be expected to do just that: McLaughlin was horrified; his words: "The threat came on us like a bolt from the blue, and though bloodshed was averted for the moment, I knew that affairs might get beyond control at any time. The threat took form in Colonel William F. Cody (Buffalo Bill) who arrived at the agency on November 28, with an order signed by General Miles, then division commander, directing military officers to supply Colonel Cody with whatever assistance was necessary in arresting Sitting Bull." McLaughlin had planned to have Sitting Bull arrested by Indian police on ration day, alternate Saturdays, when all Indians except Sitting Bull came to the agency. "I knew that any attempt by outside parties to arrest Sitting Bull would undoubtedly result in loss of life, as the temper of the ghost-dancers was not to be doubted," he continued.[8] This sounds strange only eleven days after McLaughlin had visited the camp of Sitting Bull and had not been molested, although he was no friend of Sitting Bull, whereas Cody was. Sitting Bull had been willing to accompany McLaughlin to investigate the Messiah. There is no reason to suppose he would not be as willing to accompany Cody to see General Miles.

McLaughlin telegraphed the Commissioner of Indian Affairs: "William F. Cody (Buffalo Bill) has arrived here with commission from Gen. Miles to arrest Sitting Bull. Such a step at present is unnecessary and unwise, as it will precipitate a fight which cannot be averted. A few Indians still dancing, but it does not mean mischief at present. I have matters well in hand, and when proper time arrives can arrest Sitting Bull by Indian police without bloodshed. I ask attention to my letter of November 19. Request Gen. Miles order to Cody be rescinded and request immediate answer."[9]

Officers of the Eighth Cavalry and Twelfth Infantry at Fort Yates, commanded by Lieutenant Colonel William F. Drum, conspired with McLaughlin to delay Cody until an answer was received. Cody had never scouted with either of these regiments, and their officers may have regarded him only as showman and dime-novel hero. That they knew little about him is evidenced by

[8] McLaughlin, *My Friend, the Indian,* 209–10.
[9] *Ibid.*

the method they adopted. They invited Cody to the Officers' Club, assuming that by working in relays they could get him drunk and leave him under the table. A final report on this campaign by Assistant Surgeon Alonzo R. Chapin, apparently the only survivor, says, "Colonel Cody's capacity was such that it took practically all the officers in details of two or three at a time to keep him interested and busy through the day."[10]

Cody appreciated the hospitality, but did not allow it to interfere seriously with anything he planned to do. He slept late, but was on his way by eleven o'clock. With him were Pony Bob Haslam and White Beaver Powell, who had known Sitting Bull in the show. Also named are Steve Burke and Bully White. It has commonly been assumed that Cody was accompanied by newspapermen. The fact that no other episode in his later career is so poorly covered proves he was not. He had no idea that there was any need for haste. Cody and his party stopped for a visit with an old soldier, William Presley Zahn, married to a Sioux woman and living on the reservation. They met Louis Primeau, interpreter, who took it on himself to tell Cody that Sitting Bull was on his way to the agency by another road with John M. Carignan, agency teacher. Cody crossed over to the other road, but missed Carignan, who had taken Sam Clover, a Chicago newspaperman, to see the Ghost Dance—and Clover had photographed it, another indication that the situation was far from tense.[11]

Meanwhile, McLaughlin had his answer; his plea, involving two departments, had been referred to President Harrison, and the President ordered Cody recalled. With all the delays, Cody was headed off before he got to Sitting Bull's camp on Grand River. Sitting Bull called on Carignan to ask about his visitors, and was told Cody was at the agency and wanted to see him, but, of course, Sitting Bull would not go to the agency.

McLaughlin was now called upon to make good his boast that he had matters well in hand and could arrest Sitting Bull without bloodshed. He was ordered by the Commissioner to "co-operate

[10] Vestal, *Sitting Bull* (1932 ed.), 287 (1957 ed., 281).

[11] Frank Bennett Fiske, *Life and Death of Sitting Bull*, 37–40; Vestal, *New Sources of Indian History*, 2–3; Vestal, *Sitting Bull* (1932 ed.), 287–88, (1957 ed., 280–81); E. A. Brininstool, "Buffaloing Buffalo Bill," *Hunter-Trader-Trapper*, Vol. LXXVI, No. 4 (April, 1932), 18.

with and obey the orders of the military officers commanding," and when the War Department on December 12 ordered Colonel Drum to arrest Sitting Bull, the Fort Yates commander was cautioned to "call on Indian agent to co-operate and render such assistance as will best promote the purpose in view." McLaughlin protested that "a military demonstration would precipitate a collision and bloodshed," and again urged that "if I could make provision to make the arrest by Indian police, at an opportune time and in my own way, there would be no necessity for shedding blood."[12]

Sitting Bull provoked a decision by sending a letter that has been interpreted as a request for a pass to go to Pine Ridge Agency, where the Messiah was expected to visit, but which McLaughlin viewed as a defiance of his orders. The first interpretation seems more reasonable, as Indians, except in Buffalo Bill dime novels, did not ordinarily notify an official that they were going on the warpath. McLaughlin mobilized forty-three Indian police under Lieutenant Bullhead. Two troops of the Eighth Cavalry under Major E. G. Fechét were to stand by at Owl Creek, eighteen miles from Sitting Bull's camp, to receive the prisoner. Fortunately Major Fechét moved to within three miles of the scene of the proposed arrest.

McLaughlin's insistence that the arrest would be bloodless shows that he had little knowledge of the enmities he was unloosing. The Indian police, authorized in 1878, were an Indian Bureau device for civilizing the Indian by depriving him of tribal government, thus putting an end to the power and influence of chiefs. The fact that Indian police were answerable only to the agent was in direct conflict with Indian ideas of democracy, and sending Indian police to arrest a leader of the stature of Sitting Bull was a direct challenge. In addition, there was personal enmity between Lieutenant Bullhead and Catch-the-Bear, head of Sitting Bull's personal following. Just a few months before, Bullhead had claimed a sack in which Catch-the-Bear had put his rations and seized it, dumping Catch-the-Bear's rations on the ground. Catch-the-Bear had warned Bullhead, "Look out in the future. I am going to get you."[13]

12 McLaughlin, *My Friend, the Indian*, 211–12.

362

An hour before dawn on December 18, 1890, the Indian police seized Sitting Bull, asleep in his cabin. At first he made no resistance, but as they tried to dress him roughly, he became angry. He demanded that they saddle his horse—the horse Buffalo Bill had given him in friendship. Sitting Bull's supporters gathered. As the police dragged and pushed Sitting Bull out of his cabin, Catch-the-Bear, with a Winchester repeating rifle in his hand, came through the crowd, calling for Bullhead. As Bullhead answered, Sitting Bull called out, "I am not going. Take action." Catch-the-Bear immediately fired, hitting Bullhead in the leg. As he fell, Bullhead fired at Sitting Bull, who was also shot from behind by Red Tomahawk. Either wound would have been fatal. The police got the worst of the fighting and were besieged in the cabin. In half an hour eight of Sitting Bull's followers were killed, including Catch-the-Bear. Four Indian police were killed outright, and Lieutenant Bullhead and his second-in-command, Sergeant Shavehead, were fatally wounded.

As the shooting started, Sitting Bull's horse caught his cue for his act in Buffalo Bill's Wild West and began going through his tricks. While bullets flew around him, he sat down in the middle of the battleground and raised one hoof, to the terror of the Indian police, who supposed the spirit of Sitting Bull had entered his horse. The horse was unhurt, and was ridden to Fort Yates with the news. Cody recovered him, and he was ridden by the cavalry standard bearer in the Wild West at the Chicago Columbian Exposition in 1893.

Two messengers got through to the cavalry, which dashed to the rescue, backed by a Gatling rapid-fire gun and a breech-loading steel Hotchkiss gun. Major Fechét reported, "The Indians fell back from every point upon the approach of the troops, not showing any desire to engage in hostile action against the soldiers." The troops and Indian police withdrew to Fort Yates, taking their dead with them. There Sitting Bull was buried, to rest in peace until 1953, when relatives kidnaped his remains and reburied them at Mobridge.[14]

[13] Vestal, *Sitting Bull* (1932 ed.), 287–88 (1957 ed., 180–81); George E. Hyde, *A Sioux Chronicle*, 29 ff.
[14] *Report of the Secretary of War*, 1891 (52 Cong., 1 sess., *House Ex. Doc 1*,

Some newspapers at the time accused McLaughlin of deliberately getting Sitting Bull killed. This is exaggeration, but the incident reflects little credit to his judgment, his understanding of the Sioux, or his boast that he had the situation well in hand. And these shortcomings leave little weight for his condemnation of Buffalo Bill's attempt to arrest Sitting Bull.

Cody was apparently unaware of McLaughlin's part in his recall. In *True Tales of the Plains,* Cody says, in tortuous locutions undoubtedly supplied by Major Burke: "Left to himself, in conjunction with his coadjutor, the army officer, that most efficient and famous among the best Indian agents, Major James McLaughlin (now Inspector) would have probably brought about a peaceful solution. . . . Some well-meaning philanthropists, who divined a sinister motive in my action . . . impressed President Harrison that it would create a war, ending in the death of Sitting Bull. So the commander-in-chief, the President, was constrained to act (afterward, in Indianapolis, to express regret for it to me personally) and my mission was countermanded at the threshold almost of the hostile camp."[15]

Cody was defeated by his own legend. It has been popular to ridicule his mission as a publicity stunt, which ignores the point of view of General Miles, who at the moment was far from being interested in promoting Buffalo Bill's Wild West. According to his information at the time—which may seem exaggerated because it did not happen—General Miles was faced with a great uprising of the Sioux under the leader who was generally credited (except by McLaughlin) with master-minding the Custer disaster. General Miles had available the only white man for whom Sitting Bull had ever been known to express friendship. Miles had employed Cody as a scout and had found him, as other officers who had employed him had also reported, to be fearless, capable, and level-headed. From what is now known of Sitting Bull's attitude at that time, it seems highly improbable that he was planning an uprising and entirely reasonable to suppose that he would have been willing to talk to Cody and Miles.

Part 2), I, 196–97; Vestal, *New Sources of Indian History,* 29; *Sioux County Pioneer-Arrow,* Fort Yates, April 3, 17, 1953; *Mobridge Tribune,* April 16, 1953.
[15] Pages 254–56.

Just about that General Miles said in his annual report to the Secretary of War: "It was the design of the division commander *to anticipate the movements of the hostile Indians and arrest and overpower them in detail before they had time to concentrate in one large body,* and it was deemed advisable to secure, if possible, the principal leaders and organizers, namely Sitting Bull and others, and remove them for a time from that country. To this end authority was given on November 25, 1890, to William F. Cody, a reliable frontiersman who has had much experience as chief of scouts, and who knew Sitting Bull very well, and had perhaps as much influence over him as any living man, to proceed to the Standing Rock Agency to induce Sitting Bull to come in with him, making such terms as he (Cody) might deem necessary, and if unsuccessful in this, to arrest him quietly and to remove him quickly from his camp to the nearest military station. He was authorized to take a few trusty men with him for that purpose. He proceeded to Fort Yates on the Standing Rock Reservation, and received from Lieut. Col. Drum, commanding, the necessary assistance, but his mission was either suspected, or made known to the friends of Sitting Bull who deceived him as to his whereabouts. This had the effect of delaying the arrest for a time." In the last sentence General Miles obviously evaded pin-pointing blame for the failure. In his later memoir he merely credited "adverse influence that was used to defeat my purpose."[16]

The killing of Sitting Bull came very near provoking the general war his arrest was intended to prevent. Many of his followers fled to the Bad Lands, reaching one of the most recalcitrant bands, that led by Big Foot of the Minneconjous, just as he had agreed to bring his followers into the agency. The story of supposed treachery in the attempt to arrest Sitting Bull threw the Minneconjous into a panic, but by this time Miles had troops converging from all angles, and wherever Big Foot's band turned, it was faced by military force. At Wounded Knee Creek on December 29, 1890, the Seventh Cavalry (not unmindful of Custer's defeat) intercepted Big Foot's band and ordered its members to surrender all arms. While the troopers were moving in to enforce this order, a shot was fired,

[16] *Report of the Secretary of War,* 1891, I, 145 (italics his); Miles, *Serving the Republic,* 238.

by a Ghost Dance zealot, it is generally conceded. Both sides were jittery. General Miles thus described what followed: "A general mêlée and massacre occurred, in which a large number of men, women, and children were killed and wounded."[17]

"Massacre" it has commonly been called. Although Buffalo Bill re-enacted the Battle of Wounded Knee both in the Wild West and in motion pictures, he was not among those present. He was not put on any pay roll for the Sitting Bull mission, but a voucher dated February 28, 1891, shows that he was paid $505.60 as "reimbursement of expenses in complying with order by Gen. Miles." Cody went to his home in North Platte after Miles's order had been rescinded.[18]

Cody had been commissioned a brigadier general as aide-de-camp on the staff of Governor John M. Thayer of Nebraska on November 23, 1889, and this commission was activated on January 6, 1891, when Governor Thayer issued the following order:

> My dear General
> As you are a member of my Staff, I have detailed you for special service; the particular nature of which was made known during our conversation.
> You will proceed to the scene of the Indian troubles and Communicate with General Miles.
> You will in addition to the special service refered [sic] to, please visit the different towns, if time permit, along the line of the Elkhorn Rail-road, and use your influence to quiet excitement and remove apprehensions upon the part of the people.
> Please call upon General Colby, and give your views as to the probability of the Indians breaking through the cordon of regular troops; your superior knowledge of Indian character and mode of warfare, may enable you to make suggestions of importance.
> All Officers and members of the State Troops, and all others, will please extend to you every courtesy.[19]

While the nature of the "special service" is not disclosed, the

[17] Miles, *Serving the Republic,* 242.
[18] Original in Buffalo Bill Museum, Lookout Mountain, Colo.
[19] Facsimile in program, Buffalo Bill's Wild West, 1893, p. 53. Brigadier General L. W. Colby was the commanding general of the Nebraska National Guard.

tenor and substance of the order suggests what it may have been. The presence of the National Guard along the Nebraska border was a necessary precaution, yet a source of worry to General Miles, for the irresponsible action of some local officer might precipitate the general war Miles was trying desperately to avoid. General Cody's roving assignment would have been called after World War I a liaison mission. As an officer of the National Guard, as a citizen of Nebraska, and as a former scout for the Regular Army he had the confidence of all parties. Here the Buffalo Bill legend was an asset, for if he failed to report any dime-novel heroics, it might be considered a rather dull war.

General Cody found all quiet along the border and proceeded to Pine Ridge Agency, which was headquarters for the campaign. The place was overrun with war correspondents, some twenty-five newspapermen being present. Major Burke also was at Pine Ridge, having brought the Wild West show Indians there. About fifty of them were employed as Indian police and in a company of scouts sent to Fort Robinson for duty under Lieutenant Taylor. On December 8, Dr. D. F. Royer, the Indian agent at Pine Ridge, was ordered to investigate the pay, clothing, food, and general welfare of the Buffalo Bill show Indians. He and Special Agent Cooper reported that all of them spoke in highest praise of Mr. Cody and his treatment of them while abroad, and not one made a complaint. Commented the *Lincoln* (Nebraska) *Journal,* "This is a pretty effectual denial of the various charges lodged against Buffalo Bill and his managers."

With Burke at his elbow, General Cody entered the journalistic competition, contributing dispatches to the *New York Herald* and the *New York Sun*. In the *Herald,* Cody urged prompt attention to the Indian's rights, his complaints, and his necessities, and concluded, "I think it looks like peace, and if so, the greater the victory." This statement, undoubtedly inspired by General Miles, made top headlines, which is not surprising, for it seemed paradoxical from the swashbuckling and jingoistic Buffalo Bill of legend.

The campaign was over only a few days after General Cody received his orders from Governor Thayer. On January 11, General Miles announced its end in commendatory orders, including the

following addressed to Brigadier General W. F. Cody: "I am glad
to inform you that the entire body of Indians are now camped near
here (within a mile and a half). They show every disposition to
comply with the orders of the authorities. Nothing but an accident
can prevent peace being re-established, and it will be our ambition
to make it of a permanent character. I feel that the State troops can
now be withdrawn with safety, and desire through you to express
to them my thanks for the confidence they have given your people
in their isolated homes."[20]

On January 16 the Indians formally surrendered, giving up
some, at least, of their weapons and delivering nineteen leaders as
hostages. On that day Buffalo Bill rode with General Miles and his
two aides, both notable Indian fighters, Captain Frank Baldwin
and Captain Marion P. Maus. General Miles reviewed all the
troops present, probably the largest assembly of Regular Army organizations since the Civil War, adding to the review's primary
purpose in overawing the Indians. It was midwinter, with snow
on the ground, and General Miles found the scene "weird and in
some respects desolate," marking the end of the war power of the
Sioux, although even he did not fully realize that it also marked
the end of the Indian wars. It was fitting that Cody should see the
finish. It was his last service for the government.

Cody emerged from the brief winter campaign with one material honor—he had served actively in the rank of brigadier general. The title, however, sat a little heavy with him, although he
made some use of it. The preface to Alexander Majors' *Seventy
Years on the Frontier* was signed "General W. F. Cody." Major
Burke's book, published the same year, 1893, was compiled "with
the authority of General W. F. Cody." The following year a dime
novel, *Wild Bill, the Wild West Duellist,* was signed by "General"
Cody.

A possibly apochryphal story may account for his dropping the
title. The story goes that one day while at Pine Ridge Cody was
approached by one of his Indian friends—and it should be recalled
that the state militia was not always held in high esteem in Regular
Army circles in those days.

"You General Cody now, not Colonel Cody?" the Indian asked.

[20] *Ibid.*

"Yes, I am a brigadier general now," Bill responded.

"You big general same as General Brooke and General Miles?"

"Well, not exactly," Cody admitted. "My commission is in the Nebraska National Guard."

"M'lish, oh hell," snorted the Indian disgustedly.[21]

On March 30, 1895, Governor Silas A. Holcomb issued a new commission to Cody as aide-de-camp on the staff of the commander-in-chief of Nebraska forces, this time with the rank of colonel. No doubt the demotion was at Cody's request. Thereafter he returned comfortably to the familiar "Colonel" Cody.

The nineteen prisoners of war of the Ghost Dance disturbance were sent to Fort Sheridan, Illinois. Their punishment, one historian remarks, was a queer one. They were sent to Europe with Cody's Wild West show. In March the previous order of the Commissioner of Indian Affairs was overruled, and Cody was permitted to enroll one hundred Indians for his show in Europe. Among the prisoners allowed to join the show were Kicking Bear, Short Bull, Lone Bull, Mash the Kettle, Scatter, and Revenge, along with the peacemakers Long Wolf, No Neck, Yankton Charley, and Black Heart.[22]

The prisoners would learn much about the white man's world before they returned home and they would live better than they had on the reservation, but perhaps they would not be much reformed, for they were hired to return to the old Indian ways the Ghost Dance cult had advocated. The Indians left from Philadelphia on the Red Star steamer *Switzerland* and landed at Antwerp, joining the show at Strasbourg.

[21] Walsh, *The Making of Buffalo Bill*, 289.
[22] Hyde, *A Sioux Chronicle*, xiii, 318; *Martin's World Fair Album-Atlas and Family Souvenir* (Chicago, 1892); *Fort Sheridan Tower*, March 17, 1944.

"CONGRESS OF ROUGH RIDERS

OF THE WORLD"

NATE SALSBURY HAD NOT BEEN IDLE while his partner was on the warpath. From his vantage point in central Europe, the vice-president and general manager was putting into effect at last the idea that had been his in the first place—a show "that would embody the whole subject of horsemanship." Until March there was no assurance that the Indians would be allowed to return to Europe. It was necessary to be prepared to reorganize the show drastically, and as the show was in Europe, recruiting horsemen of various nationalities would be economical.

Whatever weight was given practical considerations, a display of various types of horsemanship was no small attraction in the horse-and-buggy age. It proved one of the most successful innovations in the history of the show, and by 1893 the title was changed on all show paper to read "Buffalo Bill's Wild West and Congress of Rough Riders of the World." Within five years Lieutenant Colonel Theodore Roosevelt was to give wider fame to the term "Rough Riders." Where Cody got the inspiration for using it is not recorded, but it is old cowboy talk—the bronc buster who was given the least-broken horses was said to be "riding the rough string." An Illinois cavalry regiment in the Civil War was called "rough riders."

As organized in 1891, Buffalo Bill's Wild West had 640 "eating members." There were 20 German soldiers, 20 English soldiers, 20

United States soldiers, 12 Cossacks, and 6 Argentine Gauchos, which with the old reliables, 20 Mexican *vaqueros*, 25 cowboys, 6 cowgirls, 100 Sioux Indians, and the Cowboy Band of 37 mounted musicians, made a colorful and imposing Congress of Rough Riders.

The 1891 tour resumed the swing through Europe. Karlsruhe, Mannheim, Mainz, Wiesbaden, Cologne, Dortmund, Duisburg, Krefeld, and Aachen were stops in Germany. Annie Oakley wrestled Prince Regent Luitpold of Bavaria to the ground to get him out of the way of the famous bucking bronco "Dynamite"—a more intimate contact with royalty than other performers had. The Prince had gone with her to a practice session.

Kaiser Wilhelm II, whose interest in the American West had been aroused by the journalist Poultney Bigelow when they were schoolmates at Potsdam, was a frequent patron. One time the Kaiser demanded that Annie shoot the ashes from a cigarette held in his mouth. During World War I, when it was popular to consider him solely responsible for that conflict, Annie publicly expressed regret that she did not miss that shot and hit the Kaiser.

Unwittingly Buffalo Bill's Wild West was giving the German army lessons in logistics for war. The American outdoor show had become a huge establishment compared to the traditional one-ring circus of Europe. It had adopted the special railway train, making possible long jumps to cities large enough to support a big show. Its pay roll, maintenance, and other costs were enormous; the season was short. The ideal was to give a morning street parade and afternoon and evening performances each day—occasionally three performances—which meant split-second timing in packing, moving, and setting up at the next show town. German officers watched these procedures with interest. American shows originated the method of unloading a train of flatcars in continuous procession by linking the cars with runways and using a single ramp at the end for bringing all vehicles to the ground, in order—virtually ready for the parade. This method was applicable to the unloading of artillery and other heavy military equipment.

The Buffalo Bill show served three meals a day to all employees, and the German army's rolling kitchens were developed after observation of the show's methods. Annie Oakley wrote: "We never moved without at least forty officers of the Prussian Guard standing all about with notebooks, taking down every detail of the performance. They made minute notes on how we pitched camp—the exact number of men needed, every man's position, how long it took, how we boarded the trains and packed the horses and broke camp; every rope and bundle and kit was inspected and mapped."[1]

The enthusiasm of the Kaiser and of his army for Buffalo Bill was matched by that of the civilian population, and the American West has continued popular in Germany as embodying some of the romance of far-away places. That this widespread interest got its main stimulus from Buffalo Bill's Wild West is indicated by a continued interest in Cody. Translations of Buffalo Bill dime novels were read in Germany long after they had disappeared in the United States, and a new series by new authors was going strong in 1950.

When the show reached Holland, Queen Wilhelmina attended, recalling her pleasure in it at the London Jubilee. From Brussels, Belgium, a detour was made to show the American flag on the battlefield of Waterloo. The Wild West then embarked at Antwerp to cross the North Sea to Grimsby, where a tour of provincial Great Britain began.

The *Liverpool Mercury* on July 7 welcomed "a piece of the Wild West bodily transported to our midst. . . . It is not a show in the ordinary acceptance of the term, because the actors are each and all real characters—men who have figured not on the stage, but in real life. . . . The exhibition, moreover, is not merely entertaining, but most instructive." John Y. Nelson, Jim Mitchell, and Antonio Esquival were among the stars noted, along with Annie Oakley, Johnny Baker, and C. L. Daly, pistol marksman.

At Manchester a benefit performance was given for nineteen survivors of the charge of the Light Brigade at Balaclava. Other stops were at Leeds, Sheffield, Stoke-on-Trent, Nottingham, Leicester, and Birmingham. At Cardiff, Wales, a six-day stand, September 21 to 27, brought in £10,000, nearly $50,000 in those days. Bristol, Brighton, and Portsmouth engagements followed. In August a company was organized under direction of Thern Camfield to play in theaters and to continue through the winter. The Wild

[1] C. R. Cooper, *Annie Oakley,* 236.

West went to Glasgow, where Steele MacKaye's indoor pageant was revived in the East End Exhibition Building. As Colonel Cody planned a trip home, added attractions were needed. Lew Parker went to Boulogne, France, where he employed Sam Lockart's performing elephants. Learning that Henry M. Stanley had just landed in Hamburg with a group of Zulus, Parker signed up thirty men and thirty women of the African tribe. When they arrived in Glasgow, they were lined up opposite the Indians for press photographers. Broncho Bill called on Rocky Bear to try the sign language of the plains. To everyone's surprise, the Zulu chief understood and responded in similar sign language.[2]

Cody had several reasons for returning to North Platte. He had complained through the season of "feeling poorly" and of being very nervous over the continued strain—although, he hastened to add, "I am shooting better than I ever did in my life." In December he had "hay fever or grippe or something." There were worries at home, too. He had directed Al Goodman to build a big barn with "shelter enough to keep all our stock at home this winter," a change from the open-range days in Nebraska. The Colonel's daughter Arta, who had accompanied him on his first trip abroad, had married Horton Boal. They wanted to run the North Platte ranch. Mrs. Cody sided with them, and Al Goodman resigned and returned to Kansas with Julia.[3]

The season of 1892 opened with a return to Earl's Court, London. Queen Victoria was eager to see the Cossacks, led by Prince Ivan Rostomov Macheradse, billed as a direct descendant of Mazeppa. As the Cossack act took only twelve minutes, enough of the show was added to make up an hour's performance on the grounds of Windsor castle, with Nate Salsbury explaining the acts to the Queen and her guests. Cody was again presented to the Queen, after which Colonel McNeill, the Queen's equerry, took the men to his apartments to offer them refreshments. As Nate Salsbury pulled no punches in discussing the shortcomings of his partner, Nate's exact words are quoted: "We compromised by another act of self-sacrifice on my part, for as Cody did not drink anything that summer, I did duty for both of us in a glass of wine." This incident

---

[2] L. Parker, *Odd People I Have Met*, 83–85.
[3] *Letters from Buffalo Bill*, 37–40.

was publicized to the great satisfaction of the Salvation Army in England, which made propaganda of Cody's abstinence.[4]

This command performance assured a successful season, which, of course, could not match the enthusiasm for novelty that marked 1887. There can be little question, however, that Buffalo Bill's Wild West and Congress of Rough Riders of the World hit its high point at the World's Columbian Exposition in Chicago in 1893. The Wild West was ruled off the exposition grounds, but Salsbury with forethought had leased a lot between Sixty-second and Sixty-third streets near the entrance. It is said that there were those who mistook the entrance to Buffalo Bill's Wild West for the entrance to the Columbian Exposition and, after seeing the show, came away well satisfied.[5]

It must not be supposed, however, that Buffalo Bill's Wild West ran away with the Columbian Exposition. Of all world's fairs it probably rates the highest in general interest and lasting influence. It was one of a very few that did not run in the red. Of 27,539,041 persons who saw the "White City" between May 1 and October 30, 1893, admiring its classic architecture or its Little Egypt on the Midway, 716,881 paid admission on one day, October 9, Chicago Day, and that likely still stands as a record for the number of persons buying tickets to a place of entertainment. The success of the exposition contributed to the success of Buffalo Bill, for no one considered that he had seen the fair unless he had also seen the Wild West. It was a show worth seeing. A veteran Chicago city editor, who from his vantage spot in newspaper work had seen just about everything worth seeing once, told me that he considered Buffalo Bill's Wild West in 1893 the greatest show he had ever seen in his life.

Major General Hugh L. Scott paid it almost the same tribute in saying, "That was the most realistic show I have ever seen." In attesting the genuineness of Cody's Indians, Scott told of visiting the show in 1884, when he recognized Red Shirt and Shunkamanito Ota, alias Yankton Charley, who had guided General Mackenzie

[4] Nate Salsbury, "Wild West at Windsor," *The Colorado Magazine*, Vol. XXXII, No. 3 (July, 1955), 208–11.

[5] Harry Hanson, *The Chicago* (Rivers of America Series) (New York, Toronto, 1942), 327; John Moses and Paul Selby, *The White City* (Chicago, 1893), 152.

into the Cheyenne village for his 1876 victory. In 1884, said Scott, "one seldom met Oglalas in Philadelphia."[6]

Crowds were turned away from the Wild West on the opening day, a 130,000-attendance day for the Fair. Adam Forepaugh's circus attempted to compete, but made not a dent in Buffalo Bill's business. It had been called the most successful year in outdoor-show history, with profits estimated at from $700,000 to $1,000,000. The Wild West cashed in on a long accumulation of public interest. Since its first invasion of the Old World six years previously, the show had played only one season in the United States, that of 1888. The show's appearances before the crowned heads of Europe, Cody's dramatic victory in the controversy over the treatment of Indian performers, and his part in the last of the Indian wars had been widely acclaimed.

The biggest publicity event of that summer was the Thousand-Mile Cowboy Race, long a legend among western cowmen. Early in the previous winter, stockmen at Chadron, Nebraska, and Sturgis, South Dakota, talked of organizing a riding party to visit the exposition. The idea developed into an endurance race to advertise the stamina of the western horse. Chadron put up $1,000, to which Cody added $500 on condition that the finish be at the Wild West arena. Chadron was approximately one thousand miles from Chicago, and to beat a French endurance record of fifty miles a day, the cowboy race was run in thirteen days, an average of seventy-seven miles a day. Each rider was allowed two horses, which he could ride alternately, leading the other. Humane societies protested the race, and Governor Altgeld of Illinois issued a proclamation against it. The objections were withdrawn, however when the humane societies were invited to supervise the race.

There were ten entrants, of whom five finished. John Berry, riding horses owned by Jack Hale and George Boland of Sturgis, came in first. Joe Gillespie, stock farmer of Chadron, was second. Others who finished were Charley Smith, a stockman; James H. Stephens, known as "Rattlesnake Pete," a cowboy; and George Jones, called "Stub," riding horses owned by G. E. Lemmon. Doc Middleton, one-time bandit who formerly had been in the Wild

[6] Scott, *Some Memories of a Soldier,* 171–73.

West, rode for the honor of Chadron, but gave up at Dixon, Illinois, after one of his horses was injured.[7]

The Cowboy Race, newspaper publicity, the growing flood of dime novels might arouse curiosity, but it was the show itself that drew the crowds. What was it like? The 1893 program proved so successful that it remained virtually unchanged for nearly a decade. Here it is:

> *Overture,* "Star Spangled Banner". . . . Cowboy band, Wm. Sweeny, Leader.
>
> 1—*Grand Review* introducing the Rough Riders of the World and Fully Equipped Regular Soldiers of the Armies of America, England, France, Germany, and Russia.
>
> 2—*Miss Annie Oakley,* Celebrated Shot, who will illustrate her dexterity in the use of Fire-arms.
>
> 3—*Horse Race* between a Cowboy, a Cossack, a Mexican, an Arab, and an Indian, on Spanish-Mexican, Broncho, Russian, Indian, and Arabian Horses.
>
> 4—*Pony Express.* The Former Pony Post Rider will show how the Letters and Telegrams of the Republic were distributed across the immense Continent previous to the Railways and the Telegraph.
>
> 5—*Illustrating a Prairie Emigrant Train Crossing the Plains.* Attack by marauding Indians repulsed by "Buffalo Bill" with Scouts and Cowboys. N. B.—The Wagons are the same as used 35 years ago.
>
> 6—*Group of Syrian and Arabian Horsemen* will illustrate their style of Horsemanship, with Native Sports and Pastimes.
>
> 7—*Cossacks,* of the Caucasus of Russia, in Feats of Horsemanship, Native Dances, etc.
>
> 8—*Johnny Baker,* Celebrated Young American Marksman.
>
> 9—*A Group of Mexicans* from Old Mexico, will illustrate the use of the Lasso, and perform various Feats of Horsemanship.
>
> 10—*Racing Between Prairie, Spanish and Indian Girls.*
>
> 11—*Cowboy Fun.* Picking Objects from the Ground, Lassoing Wild Horses, Riding the Buckers.
>
> 12—*Military Evolutions* by a Company of the Sixth Cavalry of the United States Army; a Company of the First Guard Uhlan

[7] G. E. Lemmon, *Developing the West,* reprinted from *Belle Fourche Bee,* 1943, Installment I, pp. 6–7; Harry Barnard. *Eagle Forgotten* (New York, 1938), 178–79; *Chicago Herald,* June 28, 1893.

Regiment of His Majesty King William II, German Emperor, popularly known as the "Potsdamer Reds"; a Company of French Chasseurs (Chasseurs a Cheval de la Garde République Français); and a Company of the 12th Lancers (Prince of Wales' Regiment) of the British Army.

13—*Capture of the Deadwood Mail Coach by the Indians,* which will be rescued by "Buffalo Bill" and his attendant Cowboys. N.B.—This is the identical old Deadwood Coach, called the Mail Coach, which is famous on account of having carried the great number of people who lost their lives on the road between Deadwood and Cheyenne 18 years ago. Now the most famed vehicle extant.

14—*Racing Between Indian Boys on Bareback Horses.*

15—*Life Customs of the Indians.* Indian Settlement on the Field and "Path."

16—*Col. W. F. Cody* ("Buffalo Bill"), in his Unique Feats of Sharpshooting.

17—*Buffalo Hunt,* as it is in the Far West of North America—"Buffalo Bill" and Indians. The last of the only known Native Herd.

18—*The Battle of the Little Big Horn,* Showing with Historical Accuracy the scene of Custer's Last Charge. [Early in the season the spectacle was: *Attack on a Settler's Cabin*—Capture by the Indians—Rescue by "Buffalo Bill" and the Cowboys.]

19—*Salute.* *Conclusion.*[8]

The staff included Cody, president; Salsbury, vice-president and manager; Burke, general manager; Albert E. Sheible, business representative; Carter Couturier, advertising agent; Jule Keen, treasurer; L. J. Loring, orator; Lew Parker, contracting agent; and William Langen, supply agent. The only credit was "Wild West scenery by A. Bender."

Vincenzo (often Vincent) Orapeza, was a top roper of all time and teacher of Will Rogers. Antonio Esquival headed the *vaqueros* and Jim Mitchell, the cowboys. John Y. Nelson was still on hand with his Sioux family. John Shangrau was in charge of the Military Hostages. Indians included Kicking Bear, Short Bull, Plenty Horses, No Neck, Rocky Bear, Young-Man-Afraid-of-His-Horses, and Jack Red Cloud, son of the famous Red Cloud. Two Indian

[8] Buffalo Bill's Wild West and Congress of Rough Riders of the World, Historical Sketches and Programme, 1893, and variant.

children attracted notice, John Burke No Neck, found beside his slain father at Wounded Knee and adopted by Major Burke, and Little Emma, pictured on the program.

It was a show of fast action from the moment Buffalo Bill swept off his sombrero and boomed, "Ladies and Gentlemen, permit me to introduce to you a Congress of Rough Riders of the World," until Custer fell dead at the Little Big Horn. The run of the Deadwood coach never failed to thrill. The Pony Express ride forever immortalized that heroic failure. The buffalo hunt was a spectacle rarely attempted elsewhere. In the numbers entitled "Cowboy Fun" and the Mexicans "illustrating the use of the Lasso" were the beginnings of rodeo.

A successful formula had been found, and there were few changes in the years immediately following. New in 1894 were "South American Gauchos (First appearance in the United States) Riding, throwing the bolas, etc.," and "Hurdle Race between Primitive Riders mounted on Western Broncho Ponies that never jumped a hurdle until three days before the opening of the present exhibition." That season was played in Greater New York. A covered grandstand seating 20,000 persons was erected at Ambrose Park, South Brooklyn, adjoining the Thirty-ninth Street ferry, for two performances a day, rain or shine, at fifty cents general admission. With expenses $4,000 a day, attendance was not large enough. By mid-July, only a year after his most profitable season, Cody was complaining that he was in the tightest squeeze of his life. In January, 1895, he asked Salsbury to go on his note for $5,000. Salsbury had become ill at the close of the 1894 season and never was able to resume active management of the show. A deal was made with James A. Bailey to provide transportation and local expenses for a share in profits.[9]

The junior partner of Barnum and Bailey is the forgotten man in popular acclaim, but his is the greater circus name of the two. It should be; he picked it out for that purpose. James Anthony McGinness, an orphan boy who ran away with a circus from Pontiac, Michigan, attached himself to an advance agent claiming descent from Hachaliah Bailey, circus pioneer who brought the first ele-

[9] *Ibid.*, 1894; *Letters from Buffalo Bill*, 41–42; Walsh, *The Making of Buffalo Bill*, 309.

phant to America. It sounded like a good circus name, so James became James A. Bailey. By the time he was thirty, he was half-owner of the Cooper and Bailey Circus. When an elephant was born on its lot, Barnum offered $100,000 for it. Bailey broadcast Barnum's telegram on billboards and heralds. Barnum knew when he was licked, and joined Bailey. When Adam Forepaugh died in 1890, Barnum and Bailey acquired the Forepaugh and Sells Brothers Circus. Barnum died in 1891, leaving Bailey in control of the two largest circuses. In controlling also the routing of Buffalo Bill's Wild West, Bailey could run strong opposition to his principal competition, the five Ringling brothers.

For twelve years the Wild West had generally played long runs at expositions or in large cities, but the poor returns in New York in 1894 indicated it was time to try something else. Bailey provided railway cars and equipment to send the show to 131 stands in 190 days in 1895 over a route of 9,000 miles. This required fifty-two railway cars, ten more than Barnum and Bailey used, and fourteen more than transported Ringling Brothers.

The ailing Salsbury, meanwhile, tried a new venture to recoup their fortunes in "Black America," an effort to apply the Wild West formula to the Deep South. The versatile Lew Parker, who was a veteran of minstrel shows, was named contracting agent to put the show together. It employed three hundred Negroes, transported in fifteen railway cars. Within three weeks Salsbury was ready to drop the plan, but Cody urged that it be given further trial. Unfortunately, the glamour of Wild West would not translate into this medium, and it failed.[10]

The barnstorming tours of Buffalo Bill's Wild West, however, proved highly profitable. In 1896 the show traveled 10,000 miles to 132 stops. In 1897 it played 104 cities. Colonel Cody was not happy over that kind of trouping; he was growing older, he had long been plagued by ill health, and he had an increasing burden of management. But the one-day stands made Buffalo Bill more widely known and seen than ever before. New fields opened for the publicity talents of Major Burke—such as the peace treaty between the Sioux and the Chippewas.

[10] L. Parker, *Odd People I Have Met*, 29; Walsh, *The Making of Buffalo Bill*, 310.

When Buffalo Bill's Wild West played Ashland, Wisconsin, on September 11, 1896, it was brought to Colonel Cody's attention that Wisconsin's Chippewas were still technically at war with the Sioux. Of course, all Indian tribes were theoretically at war with all other tribes at all times unless an alliance had been negotiated, but the hereditary enmity of the Sioux and Chippewas had been unusually bloody. While no overt act had occurred in threescore years, it seemed fitting that a pact of eternal friendship be signed. Lieutenant William Allen Mercer, agent for the Chippewas, fell for the idea and summoned a tribal grand council. Colonel Cody provided envoys extraordinary and plenipotentiary representing the Sioux Nation from personnel scheduled to attack the Deadwood stagecoach at the evening performance. A suggestion that the treaty ceremony be held in the big tent as part of the show was rejected; said the conference's secretary, "Col. Cody refused to commercialize it." After preliminaries on the lawn of the Chequamegon Hotel, the speeches and ceremony took place back of the big tent. Chief Flat Iron headed the Sioux delegates; Chiefs Cloud, Blackbird, and Buffalo signed for the Chippewas. It is one Indian treaty that was never violated.[11]

It was a time when the American male provided himself with a lodge sword instead of golf clubs or a bowling ball, when the popular sport was to drill with the Uniform Rank, Knights of Pythias, with the Modern Woodmen of America, carrying nickel-plated axes, or with the Knights Templar, and to parade in the fanciful costumes of these orders. Innovations for a long New York engagement of the Wild West in 1897 reflected this interest. One was "U. S. Artillery Drill, by Veterans from Capt. Thorpe's Battery D, Fifth Regiment, U. S. Artillery." Captain Frank Thorp (Cody's spelling had not improved) probably did not accompany his veterans who put on the colorful maneuvers of the horse-drawn artillery. Another was "Sixth U. S. Cavalry. Veterans from Col. Sumner's celebrated Regiment at Fort Myer, Va., in military exercises and an exhibition of athletic sports and horsemanship." Samuel S. Sumner was a Fifth Cavalry comrade of Cody's.

[11] *Ashland Daily Press,* September 11, 1896; Guy M. Burnham, *The Lake Superior Country in History and Story* (Ashland, Wis., 1930); information from Paul Vanderbilt, Wisconsin State Historical Society.

Even more spectacular was the "Zouave Infantry Drill by the celebrated Aurora Zouaves. Ten years interstate champions." The Zouave drill and uniform of baggy red trousers, gold-braided blue vest, and red fez derived from the Zouaoua tribe in French service in Algeria in the 1830's. Captain Elmer E. Ellsworth popularized the idea in the United States with his drill company of Chicago Zouaves that won national honors in 1860. (Ellsworth, as colonel of the New York Fire Zouaves, was the first Union officer killed in the Civil War.) The drill was executed in a double-time half-step with the men in close order, touching elbows, and consisted of intricate wheelings and patterns, usually performed in sequence without orders other than whistle signals. Its climax was wall-scaling, in which a human pyramid was formed and used as steps by the rest of the men, who were tumbled to the top, the last two or three being drawn up the wall by their rifles and rifle-slings. It has often been revived when a group can be found willing to undergo the strenuous training necessary.

Despite this heavy load of military events, obviously there was room in 1898, the summer of the Spanish-American War, for a "Color Guard of Cuban Veterans, on leave of absence to give their various wounds time to heal." Undoubtedly a more popular innovation in 1898 was "A Bevy of Beautiful Rancheras, genuine and famous frontier girls in feats of daring equestrianism." The press agents failed to put over their coinage of "ranchera," but the glamour of the cowgirl had been added to the Wild West.

The press agents, however, deserve a hand for the programs, heralds, and couriers extolling Buffalo Bill's Wild West, for no more colorful or elaborate show paper ever was issued, and certainly none more instructive. A herald is a handbill, a single sheet of paper. A courier is an advertising booklet. One copyrighted by the Courier Company of Buffalo in 1898 contained thirty-two pages and was cut out in the shape of a buffalo head. Another was a cut-out of a profile of an Indian's head. A cut-out in fanciful design featuring the profiles of Buffalo Bill and Pawnee Bill had half its pages in full color, reproducing the lithographed posters used on billboards, along with paintings by Frederic Remington and Joe Scheurle. *The Rough Rider* was a sixteen-page magazine, sixteen by ten inches in size, with many illustrations and a number of long articles. It was first used in 1899 and was continued after the merger with Pawnee Bill.

Elaborate programs profusely illustrated started with the show itself in 1883 and reached their top in quality and brilliance of color-lithographed covers in the 1890's. For the small sum of one dime a customer got sixty-four pages of text and pictures, mostly about and by Buffalo Bill. Not all the facts were accurate, but most of them were; indeed, these programs contained much more truth about the West than can be salvaged from infinite hours of movie and television watching. The back cover in 1893 showed in color a Prentiss Ingraham concept of a Sioux stronghold in a canyon steeper than even Albert Bierstadt painted, but the text included documentation on Cody's last war trail in 1890–91.

In 1895 it was noted that the exhibition was "under the auspices of that great triumvirate of entrepreneurs, Nate Salsbury, James A. Bailey, and Colonel W. F. Cody," and that "Bailey has been for years the most successful and widely known and popular caterer to the amusement of the public." Thereafter his name disappears from programs, but not his influence. No doubt he was responsible for adding advertising to the programs—as much as sixteen pages in a wraparound—extolling such products as Columbia bicycles, New Brunswick tires for same, Yucatan chewing gum, Le Roy cigarettes, Gibbs patented rubber-cushioned horseshoe, and Mrs. Winslow's Soothing Syrup. You could learn from the John B. Stetson Company that "Years ago we made specially for Colonel Cody the 'Buffalo Bill,' a soft hat of quite tremendous proportions. This style has been adopted and worn ever since by him and many of his Western companions"—the origin of the cowboy's ten-gallon hat. The reader was told that for over twenty years Colonel Cody had used Winchester rifles and Winchester ammunition, that Miss Annie Oakley had used Stevens rifles for seventeen years, and that "Johny" Baker used a double-barreled Parker in all his exhibition shooting.

Most of the sixty-four pages in the "Historical Sketches and Programme" concerned Buffalo Bill, and the impression made by all publicity matter is that the great attraction was Buffalo Bill himself. This makes it more surprising that he should have had so many imitators and that some of them became quite successful.

Some forty to fifty Wild West shows flourished, or failed to flourish, during Cody's lifetime.

The Great Indian Congress of thirty-one tribes at the 1898 Trans-Mississippi Exposition at Omaha was, of course, "not a Wild West show, but a serious ethnological exhibition." Its general manager was Colonel Frederic T. Cummins, born in 1859 at Council Bluffs, the son of Hiram Cummins, an Indian trader. Cummins had prospected in the Black Hills, at Helena, and at Coeur d'Alene, and had been a cowboy for the Wadsworth brothers' ranch along the Little Missouri. Omaha continued its fair in 1899 as the Greater American Exposition, and the Indian Congress stayed on. Colonel Cummins repeated his ethnological exhibition for the Pan-American Exposition at Buffalo in 1901, then took it on a tour of New England and to Madison Square Garden in 1903. After showing at the Louisiana Purchase Exposition at St. Louis in 1904, he resumed touring. Between 1907 and 1912, Colonel Cummins' Wild West and Indian Congress visited Great Britain, Belgium, Germany, Switzerland, France, and Italy.[12]

Colonel Cummins featured many western celebrities. Calamity Jane "was never connected with any other public exhibition," his publicity declared, although she had been before the public in 1896 at Kohl and Middleton's Palace Museum in Minneapolis. Martha Jane Canary signed herself "Mrs. Burke" in the not-too-authentic autobiography she sold at the Pan-American Exposition. She was a character in Buffalo Bill dime novels and is mentioned in a number of show programs, but she never appeared in Buffalo Bill's Wild West.

Red Cloud was in the Indian Congress at the Pan-American Exposition, and Chief Joseph of the Nez Percés was in Cummins' show at Madison Square Garden in 1903. Such Buffalo Bill show veterans as Red Shirt, American Horse, Flat Iron, and Jack Red Cloud, also appeared with Cummins. Rain-in-the-Face was on view at the Chicago Columbian Exposition, but he never signed up with either Cody or Cummins. Geronimo of the Chiricahua Apaches was less exclusive. He was with Cummins at the Omaha,

[12] Octave Thanet, "The Trans-Mississippi Exposition," *Cosmopolitan*, Vol. XXV, No. 6 (October, 1898), 612; Richmond C. Hill, *A Great White Indian Chief* (published by Young Buffalo Wild West and Col. Fred Cummins Far East Combined, 1912).

Buffalo, and St. Louis expositions, and put in two or three seasons with Pawnee Bill's Historic Wild West.

On June 11, 1905, Geronimo appeared at a roundup staged at the Miller brothers' 101 Ranch in Oklahoma Territory for the National Editorial Association. A buffalo hunt in which a buffalo was killed to feast the guests, roping and riding contests, and an attack on a wagon train by two hundred Indians, along with a cavalry band, proved that the Miller brothers could round up a Wild West without going far from their own property. Star of the show was Lucille Mulhall, outstanding among early-day cowgirl riders. The Miller brothers—Joe C., Zack T., and George L.—were sons of George W. Miller, who had founded the 101 Ranch in 1892. Fame of the 1905 roundup inspired an invitation to bring their show to the Jamestown Exposition in 1907. When they took it to Brighton Beach, New York, Edward Arlington persuaded them to go into show business permanently. The Miller Bros. 101 Ranch Wild West opened at Ponca City, Oklahoma, April 14, 1908. From then through 1916 it took a top place, developing such stars as Tom Mix, Buck Jones, and Mabel Normand of the silent motion pictures, Bill Pickett of bulldogging fame, and Tad Lucas, rodeo cowgirl rider.[13]

One of the oddest of Wild West shows was that of Cole Younger and Frank James. Cole had been pardoned from the Minnesota penitentiary where he was serving a life sentence for the Northfield bank robbery. Frank, brother of Jesse James, had surrendered his guns to the governor of Missouri personally, and cases against him were nol-prossed for lack of proof. The reformed robbers sought to turn an honest penny, but every grift and con man in the country thought it was old home week when the Cole Younger and Frank James Wild West opened in 1903. The survivors of the train-robbery gang could not make a go of it.

Colonel Zach Mulhall, father of Lucille, started a Wild West. The combination of Dr. W. F. Carver's Wild West with the circus of Adam Forepaugh, Jr., was emulated by his sister and her husband with the Luella Forepaugh–Fish Wild West, also billed as

---

[13] Ellsworth Collings and Alma Miller England, *The 101 Ranch* (Norman, 1938); Fred Gipson, *Fabulous Empire* (Boston, 1946); information from Harley Lichtenberger, Lombard, Ill.

the "Great Forepaugh Wild West." Jim and Kid Gabriel, who had been in the Buffalo Bill show, but not in the 1893 Cowboy Race, billed their show as the "Gabriel Brothers Champion Long Distance Riders Wild West" when they played Delmar Gardens, outside the world's fair grounds at St. Louis in 1904. Many imitators incorporated "buffalo" in their names, as Missoula Buffalo's Wild West, the Buffalo Ranch Wild West, and Buffalo Tom's Wild West. Most successful of these was Young Buffalo's Wild West and Frontier Days, organized by Vernon C. Seaver. In 1912 he merged with Colonel Cummins. Buffalo Bill's Wild West Combined with Pawnee Bill's Great Far East was paralleled by Young Buffalo Wild West and Col. Fred Cummins' Far East Combined.[14]

[14] Guy Weadick, "The Old and the New Wild West," *Billboard*, December 29, 1934; Charles H. Tompkins, "Gabriel Brothers Wild West," *The Westerners Brand Book* (Chicago), Vol. XIII, No. 8 (Chicago, 1956), 64.

THE DIME-NOVEL HERO

BUFFALO BILL'S WILD WEST was an international institution. Hundreds of thousands of spectators saw Cody in person, read of his exploits in show programs, and were exposed to the publicity devices of Major Burke and his cohorts. Millions more never had that opportunity. The show made only a few extended tours, and even then played only in the larger cities. Many a boy of that era never saw the lithographed posters advertising Buffalo Bill's Wild West, even though they were distributed for considerable distances around each city on the schedule, in the hope of attracting farmers who might drive in for the day or others who might take an excursion to see the show by steam railway line or, in the twentieth century, by electric interurban line.

Yet no community, however small, lacked lithographs of Buffalo Bill. At newsstands, drugstores, general stores, railway stations, and on trains dime novels were offered for sale; they were as widely distributed in their day as are the quarter books and comic books of a later generation, and resemble both those publications in many respects. The dime novels were similarly denounced as corrupters of youth and as inciting crime. Their lurid covers, however, did not exploit sex. Just as all the quarter books are not sold for a quarter and just as the comic books are not necessarily comic, so the dime novel was not necessarily a novel and did not necessarily sell for a dime. "Dime novel" is generally accepted as the designation of a type of publication containing one complete story of considerable length and issued periodically, usually weekly. Many, perhaps most, dime novels sold for five cents, upped to six during World War I. Others were fifteen and even twenty cents. The dime novel as made famous by the house of Beadle and Adams contained a story of about 70,000 words; the stories in their Half-Dime Library were about half as long. The subject matter ranged from reprints of the works of Scott and Dickens to crime and detective stories, and, perhaps most popular of all, stories of frontier adventure, not yet called "Westerns," a term that came into general use during the Zane Grey period. The first dime novel is generally conceded to be *Malaeska; the Indian Wife of the White Hunter*, by Mrs. Ann S. Stephens, issued by Irwin P. Beadle and Company, in June, 1860. The first highly successful one, No. 8 in the series, is *Seth Jones; or the Captives of the Frontier*, by Edward S. Ellis, which proved pioneer exploits to be the right line. During the Civil War, dime novels were scattered in a hundred circling camps and Beadle and Adams were on their way.

Ned Buntline has generally received far too much credit for his contribution toward making Buffalo Bill a dime-novel hero and for making the dime novel about the West popular. True, he wrote in 1869 the first Buffalo Bill story, *Buffalo Bill, the King of Border Men*, which ran serially in Street and Smith's *New York Weekly*. He produced three more. *Texas Jack; or Buffalo Bill's Brother*, by Lone Star, in DeWitt's Ten-Cent Romances might be counted as a fifth on no better evidence than that it appeared in 1873 while Ned was still trouping with Jack and Bill in *The Scouts of the Prairie*. Counting all reprints, fourteen publications constitute Ned Buntline's contribution to Buffalo Bill literature.

In contrast to Ned Buntline's fourteen, the total number of Buffalo Bill dime novels, including reprints and counting all dated publications issued in the United States, comes to 1,700, as nearly as it can be figured out. The reprints, sometimes under variant or totally different titles, were numerous, several series being made up entirely of reprints. The total number of different Buffalo Bill dime novels comes to 557, again as nearly as it can be figured out. No complete file of them exists. Neither the 1,700 total nor the 557 originals include series issued outside the United States, which would add several hundred reprints and translations and many originals printed in England, Germany, Italy, Spain, France, and elsewhere. Not counted are twenty-two dime novels signed by Buffalo Bill as author, reprinted to make a total of forty-seven issues. Also not counted are paperback biographies of Buffalo Bill not issued as dated publications.[1]

All Buffalo Bill stories, with the exception of those written by Ned Buntline, are commonly attributed to Colonel Prentiss Ingraham. He also has received too much credit. He wrote not more than 121 of the 557 original stories. Many a book and article will tell you that he wrote 211, but that is an erroneous deduction based upon the deceptive fact that his name appears as author of 211 issues of the Buffalo Bill Border Stories published by Street and Smith. Despite this convincing evidence, he had not written half of them, probably not more than 73 of the 211. And therein is as complicated a plot as any Colonel Ingraham ever devised for his hero.

Three authors unknown to fame and unmentioned in Buffalo Bill literature each wrote almost as much about Buffalo Bill as did Prentiss Ingraham and far more than Ned Buntline. They are W. Bert Foster, with 136 titles; William Wallace Cook, with 119; and the Reverend John Harvey Whitson, with 59. Ingraham, however, was the largest producer of Buffalo Bill fiction if measured either by inches or by wordage, for 67 of his 121 titles were each a book-length dime's worth, twice as long as the five-cent productions of Messrs. Foster, Cook, and Whitson.

Ingraham's first Buffalo Bill story may have been *The Crimson Trail; or, On Custer's Last Warpath*, "as witnessed by Hon. W. F. Cody," which ran in six issues of the Street and Smith *New York*

[1] These figures and much data in this chapter are derived from J. Edward Leithead, of Philadelphia, foremost expert on Buffalo Bill dime novels, both in personal letters and in his articles in *Dime Novel Round-Up*, as follows: "Buffalo Bill Novels in Paper-book Format" (June, 1949); "Buckskin Men of Forest and Plain" (March, May, June, July, October, November, 1953); "The Wild West Shows Pass in Grand Review" (September, October, 1954); "Four-footed Friends of Our Dime Novel Heroes" (June, 1957); and "By the Author of Buffalo Bill" (May, June, July, 1958). Data concerning Beadle and Adams dime novels are derived from Albert Johannsen personally and from his *The House of Beadle and Adams;* see also his "Alfred Bronaugh Taylor, a Beadle Author," in *Dime Novel Round-Up* (December, 1957).

Weekly beginning September 25, 1876. If Hon. W. F. Cody had anything to do with this, he worked fast, for he was still scouting in Montana Territory as late as September 6. Ingraham quarreled with Francis S. Smith, perhaps over this story, and did no more Buffalo Bill fiction for Street and Smith until 1901. Ingraham got into the Buffalo Bill business permanently by writing a play for Cody in 1879, following it immediately, presumably as publicity backing for the play, with the dime novel *Buffalo Bill, the Buckskin King,* published serially in the *Saturday Journal* and promptly reprinted in Beadle's Dime Library.

In 1880 came *Dashing Dandy, the Hotspur of the Hills; or, The Pony Prince's Strange Pard,* a Buffalo Bill serial also reprinted in the Dime Library. In 1881, Ingraham wrote three shorter Buffalo Bill stories for Beadle's Half-Dime Library and started off Beadle's Boy's Library with the semi-biographical *Adventures of Buffalo Bill from Boyhood to Manhood.* Ingraham was not yet making a career of Buffalo Bill. Credited to him also this year was a dime novel signed by Dr. Frank Powell, known as White Beaver, *The Doomed Dozen; or, Dolores, the Danite's Daughter.* This was later rehashed into a Buffalo Bill story, as were also three other stories about Wild Bill published in 1882. Ingraham also continued a steady output of sea and pirate stories, such as *The Magic Ship, Ocean Guerrillas, The Giant Buccaneer,* and *Monte Cristo Afloat; or The Wandering Jew of the Sea.* The last title suggests that Ingraham might have plagiarized Alexandre Dumas and Eugene Sue at one fell swoop. Undoubtedly he did.

Colonel Ingraham was among those present at the launching of Buffalo Bill's Wild West, and wrote publicity for that exhibition, but whether he wrote dime novels to advertise the show or took advantage of the show to publicize his dime novels is anyone's guess. It can be guessed plausibly, however, that Buffalo Bill paid out little for publicity in the show's early years. In 1883, the opening year of the show, Ingraham wrote two Buffalo Bill dime novels, but none at all for two years following. However, from 1886 through 1889, he averaged two Buffalo Bill serials a year in Beadle's *Banner Weekly.* In the Half-Dime Library on February 1, 1887, he introduced the first cowboy hero of fiction in *Buck Taylor, King of the Cowboys,* as Buck in his own person was billed in the Wild

West that year. Ingraham wrote one more tale about Buck Taylor in 1889 and five more in 1891.

From 1890 onward, during the years Buffalo Bill's Wild West hit its peak in popularity and prosperity, there was a notable increase in Buffalo Bill dime novels, suggesting a more direct tie-up with show publicity. The Street and Smith Log Cabin Library, issued from 1889 to 1897, had seven Buffalo Bill stories by various authors, including reprints of two by Ned Buntline that had previously appeared in their *New York Weekly* and their Sea and Shore Series. But Ingraham soon stepped into the lead and began to devote himself more extensively to the glorification of Buffalo Bill. In 1890 he had three new stories for the *Banner Weekly* and three for the Half-Dime Library, while three of his serials dating from 1886 and 1887 were printed for the first time in the Dime Library. In 1891 four new serial stories ran in *Banner Weekly*, and three old ones turned up in the Dime Library. In 1892, when the Wild West was planning for its triumph at the Chicago world's fair, Ingraham wrote nine original Buffalo Bill novels for the Dime Library, keeping up this average, with the aid of reprints, for two more years. Then he doubled it. In 1895, Ingraham wrote three serials for the *Banner Weekly*, eight original stories for the Dime Library, and five more for the Half-Dime Library, while three reprints appeared in the Dime Library, for a total of nineteen. He hit his peak in 1896 with twenty-three Buffalo Bill dime novels in all categories.

In 1897, Beadle and Adams began to hit the skids and suspended the *Banner Weekly*, leaving Buffalo Bill dangling with an Ingraham serial cut off after two installments. The hero was rescued by a printing of the complete story in the Half-Dime Library. Despite these adverse circumstances, Ingraham got eleven Buffalo Bills launched in 1897. But the house of Beadle and Adams came to an end on February 23, 1898, with Dime Library No. 1009, *Buffalo Bill's Dead-shot Dragoon,* a serial Ingraham had written for the *Banner Weekly* two years earlier. M. J. Ivers and Company took over the Dime Library and the Half-Dime Library, continuing them with reprints until 1905. Apparently their rights to the Buffalo Bills were restricted, for after Ingraham's last two serials in the Dime Library were reprinted, there were no others except a reissue of Ned Buntline's sole Buffalo Bill story in that library.

Although Ingraham was without a market, he at first refused to deal with Street and Smith, charging they had given him "a dirty deal." Gilbert Patten, author of the Frank Merriwell dime novels, egged on by Arthur Grissom, editor of *Smart Set*, persuaded Ingraham to see Ormond G. Smith, son of the editor with whom Ingraham had quarreled, and peace was made. It is reasonable to suppose that the publicity department of Buffalo Bill's Wild West had not viewed the idleness of Ingraham without concern, and may have taken a hand. No author was ever treated more handsomely by a publisher than was Colonel Ingraham by Street and Smith. Not only did they give him full credit for all the Buffalo Bill stories he had written for rival publishers, but also they put his name on most of those anyone else had written, including their own writers.

It came about thus: In 1901, Street and Smith started a five-cent weekly called Buffalo Bill Stories. It ran to 591 issues, each signed anonymously "by the author of *Buffalo Bill*," whatever that meant. Ingraham probably wrote No. 1 in this series and perhaps twenty-five to thirty more original stories. Also used in this weekly were his sixty-seven long stories about Buffalo Bill that had appeared between 1879 and 1897 in Beadle's Dime Library, the twenty-three about half as long from the Half-Dime Library, and the doctored Dr. Frank Powell and Wild Bill stories. The longer stories were good for two or even three issues under new titles. Street and Smith also poured into the hopper seven Buffalo Bill stories by Ned Buntline and other authors that had appeared in their *New York Weekly,* Sea and Shore Series, and Log Cabin Library. Ingraham died in 1904, but the weekly continued, and when the supply of reprints wore thin, half a dozen or more authors were employed from time to time to write new stories about Buffalo Bill.

Here is the chain of events that led to Street and Smith's eventually attributing all of the Buffalo Bill stories to Ingraham. In 1907, while Buffalo Bill Stories still continued, a new fifteen-cent book-size Far West Library was started, each issue combining two, three, and in some cases even four of the weekly stories into one. Its first 85 issues were signed "by the author of *Buffalo Bill*" as usual, but the rest of the 211 were attributed to Howard W. Erwin, a nom de plume invented for this occasion, apparently for no particular reason. This series came to an end when the available stories were exhausted, whereupon the entire 211 were reprinted in a new series—with some of the titles changed—called Buffalo Bill Border Stories, this time all of them signed "by Colonel Prentiss Ingraham, author of *Buffalo Bill*." Actually eight or ten authors were represented, and as some of them were Street and Smith editors, it seems unlikely they had forgotten that Ingraham did not write all of them. More likely, they had begun to consider his name an asset. Ingraham's name also appeared as author in a third series of reprints called the Great Western Library.

Who were the other authors? Even in the days of prosperity for Beadle and Adams, Ingraham did not have exclusive rights to Buffalo Bill. Ingraham's last appearance in the Dime Library was its No. 1029, *Buffalo Bill in Arizona; or, Buckskin Sam's Shadow Trail.* Buckskin Sam was Major Sam S. Hall, who had a notable career as a Texas Ranger. Besides getting away with fighting on both sides in the Civil War and becoming a dime-novel character, Major Hall was also a writer of that form of literature, and among his not inconsiderable output is *Buffalo Bill, The Prince of the Platte; or, Buffalo Bill's Long Trail*, which appeared in the American Library.

Leon Lewis, one of the most popular and prosperous of dime-novel writers, produced only two about Buffalo Bill, but one of them is of interest in that it is the earliest to show a direct tie-up between a dime novel and Wild West show publicity. This is *Daredeath Dick, The King of the Cowboys; or, In the Wild West with Buffalo Bill*, which ran serially in the *Banner Weekly* from November 6, 1886, to January 15, 1887, and was reprinted as Beadle's Dime Library No. 629 on November 12, 1890. In this story Bill's faithful companion is not Wild Bill, Texas Jack, White Beaver, or any other Scout of the Plains, but none other than Nate Salsbury! Nate's qualification for his unaccustomed role is his experience as an actor, which enables him to adopt in a trice a disguise no one can penetrate, a requirement in all dime novels involving crime. Daredeath Dick, the titular hero, actually has little to do with running down the outlaw band known as Jay Hawks (a name not yet appropriated by Kansans), who had wrecked the Wild West show's train in an attempt to steal its treasure chest. Yet this fictitious King of the Cowboys may qualify, by the narrowest of margins, as the first cowboy hero, an honor claimed for Buck Taylor. The Daredeath Dick serial was concluded in the *Banner Weekly* of January 15, 1887. The first Buck Taylor dime novel appeared in the Half-Dime Library on February 1. Daredeath Dick is a character so weakly drawn, playing so minor a part in the story named for him, that any such claim is a technicality. Leon Lewis, however, anticipated the erudite cowboys of Eugene Manlove Rhodes. One of Daredeath Dick's companions is a cowboy pianist and another is distinguished for his elegant language.

The other story by Leon Lewis is *Buffalo Bill's Ban; or, Cody to the Rescue,* published in the *Banner Weekly* in 1889 and in the Dime Library in 1893. Leon's real name was Julius Warren Lewis. His first story signed "Leon Lewis" is *Red Knife; or, Kit Carson's Last Trail,* so Buffalo Bill was not far afield for him, although his specialty was sea stories. His wife, Harriet, was his collaborator. Some books were signed by both of them; she wrote some signed by his name; each wrote independently; and both used various pen names—a most versatile team. He died in 1920.

One more story in Beadle's Dime Library barely qualifies as a Buffalo Bill yarn, but it was the first by a writer who became one of the four top producers of Buffalo Bill literature. It is another of the half-dozen or so featuring the Wild West show, and as its title indicates, it related to the engagement at the Columbian Exposition in 1893. It was *Chicago Charlie, the Columbian Detective; or, The Hawks of the Lakeside League.* It was signed Lt. A. K. Sims, one of the pseudonyms used by Rev. John Harvey Whitson. Whitson was born in a log cabin at Seymour, Indiana, on December 28, 1854, but was homesteading near Garden City, Kansas, when he began writing for Beadle. He wrote a number of early western novels in hard covers: *Barbara, A Woman of the West, The Rainbow Chasers,* and *Justin Wingate, Ranchman.* Many factual articles by Whitson appeared in *The Youth's Companion.* As a staff writer for Street and Smith he took over the Frank Merriwell stories while their originator, Patten (Burt L. Standish), was managing a baseball team. Similarly Whitson exchanged the Burt L. Standish by-line for "by the author of *Buffalo Bill*" for some fifty-nine issues of Buffalo Bill Stories. Whitson was ordained a Baptist minister in 1898, taught Bible history and literature at the Ward-

Belmont School for Girls in Nashville, Tennessee, and became head of the department of religious education at Hardin College, Mexico, Missouri. He died in 1936.

In Beadle's Half-Dime Library, besides twenty-three Buffalo Bill stories by Ingraham, there were two by Captain Alfred B. Taylor, both published in 1881. They were *Buffalo Billy, the Boy Bullwhacker; or, The Doomed Thirteen,* and *Buffalo Bill's Bet; or, The Gambler's Guide.* When they were reprinted in The Pocket Library, Ingraham was named as author. Taylor was captain in the Fifth Cavalry during Cody's service with that regiment; and, although his stories show little reflection of that association, it may be assumed that he was thereby inspired to write them. That he did write them is confirmed by Captain Price's regimental history, which reports Taylor "engaged in mercantile and literary pursuits at New York City until the fall of 1881." An obvious deduction is that Ingraham edited and sponsored the stories, and that the publishers later issued them under his name, assuming he had written them under one of his numerous pseudonyms.

Buffalo Bill's Wild West was the setting for one more number of the Half-Dime Library. This was *Cool Colorado in New York; or, The Cowboy's Fight for a Million,* published in 1897. The author was Albert W. Aiken; it was natural for him to write of show business, for he was a popular actor in melodrama as well as a prolific author of dime novels. This, however, was his sole story about Buffalo Bill.

Frank Tousey, a leading dime-novel publisher from about 1875 until well into the twentieth century, got into the Buffalo Bill business with at least six stories, five of which appeared in Tousey's Wide Awake Library and were reprinted in his Pluck and Luck series. Two are by W. Howard Van Orden, who used the pen-name Paul Bradden in writing *Buffalo Bill's Boy Bronco Breaker; or, The Youngest Hero on the Plains,* and *Little Quick Shot; or, Buffalo Bill's Wild West in Europe.* Little Quick Shot was not, as might be suspected, Annie Oakley ("Little Sure Shot"), who escaped the dime-novel writers only to fall into the hands of Rodgers and Hammerstein (*Annie Get Your Gun*), the movies, the comic books, and television. Van Orden's hero was a boy and was fictitious.

All of the authors who wrote Buffalo Bill stories for Tousey used pen-names, few of which have been identified. *Buffalo Bill's Chum* was signed by Captain Ralph Fenton when it appeared in the Wide Awake Library; "by an Old Scout" in Pluck and Luck as *Buffalo Bill's Boy Chum; or, In the Wild West with the King of Scouts;* and by Frank Forrest when the longer form of the title began serially in *Happy Days* on May 9, 1896.

Robert Maynard was the name signed in Wide Awake Library to *In the Wild West; or, On the Plains with Buffalo Bill,* but when the title was turned around to *On the Plains with Buffalo Bill; or, Two Years in the Wild West* for two appearances in Pluck and Luck, "an Old Scout" took the by-line. *Out with Buffalo Bill* in Wide Awake Library also became Old Scout's in Pluck and Luck.

S. A. D. Cox wrote all of Tousey's Three Chums Weekly as "Harry Moore." One of its numbers was *Three Chums with Buffalo Bill's Wild West.* There were two imitation Buffalo Bill stories in the Wide Awake Library, *Buffalo Bill Jr. and His Band of Dead Shots,* by Allyn Draper, who got around to Junior before television did, and *Little Buffalo Bill, or, The Boy Scout of the Rio del Norte,* by Lt. E. H. Kellogg, a Civil War veteran who died in 1898.

Another stray, author unknown, is *Buffalo Bill's Boyhood Days: The Adventures of the Famous Scout,* No. 26 in Young Sports Library.

But the publisher who brought out the first Buffalo Bill story and the last, as well as most of them in between, was Street and Smith. After the first Buffalo Bill by Ned Buntline in 1869 and the two that accompanied Ned's stage venture with Cody in 1872, Street and Smith showed little interest until the publicity splurge over Buffalo Bill's Wild West in the 1890's. Then the two 1872 Ned Buntline serials were dredged out in 1890 for the Sea and Shore Series and were reprinted again in 1891 in the Log Cabin Library.

The Log Cabin Library also contributed five more stories to the Buffalo Bill list. Probably they had previously appeared in *New York Weekly.* Three were by St. George Henry Rathborne, a Street and Smith editor, born in Covington, Kentucky, in 1854 and surviving until 1938. Between 1868 and 1935 he wrote a wide variety of fiction, from *Sure Shot, the Hunter Chief* to a series on Boy Scouts in the world war and including sixty about his character "Doctor Jack." Rathborne used the pseudonym E. W. Wheeler (not to be confused with Edward Lytton Wheeler, author of the Deadwood Dick stories) for *Buffalo Bill's Best Bower; or, The Soldier Scout's Last Trail; Buffalo Bill's Border Bravos; or, The Trail Through the Land of Death;* and *Buffalo Bill's Long Trail; or, The King of the Plains.*

Rathborne did not have exclusive use of the name E. W. Wheeler, for Robert Russell used it for *Buffalo Bill the Border King; or, The White Queen of the Sioux and the Girl Rifle Shot.* Russell, however, used the name W. B. Lawson—a pseudonym also occasionally used by Rathborne—for *Buffalo Bill at Wounded Knee; or, The Battle Secret of the Bad Lands.*

Robert Russell's two dime novels help to enlighten the strange doings of Street and Smith, whereby Colonel Ingraham became exclusively the author of Buffalo Bill.

Robert Russell's *Buffalo Bill at Wounded Knee,* "by W. B. Lawson," became in Buffalo Bill Stories, "by the author of *Buffalo Bill,*" two stories with two new titles, No. 45, *Buffalo Bill in the Bad Lands,* and No. 46, *Buffalo Bill's Trail of the Ghost Dancers.* The two issues were reassembled as a single story in the Far West Library No. 8, again with a new title, *Buffalo Bill's Bravery,* but still "by the author of *Buffalo Bill.*" The same title was used in Buffalo Bill Border Stories No. 3, but this time the title page said the story was by Colonel Prentiss Ingraham. Ingraham stayed on as author of the same title in Great Western Library No. 42.

Similarly, Robert Russell's *Buffalo Bill, the Border King,* first published as "by E. W. Wheeler," became *Buffalo Bill's Comrades,* "by the author of *Buffalo Bill,*" as Far West Library No. 5. When the same title appeared as Buffalo Bill Border Stories No. 10, it was signed "by Colonel Prentiss Ingraham," and so continued in Great Western Library No. 49.

Buffalo Bill, the Border King was the title of Buffalo Bill Stories No. 1 in 1901, but this was not at all *Buffalo Bill, the Border King* that Robert Russell wrote under the name of W. B. Lawson and that later was wrongly attributed to Colonel Ingraham. On the contrary, Colonel Ingraham probably was the author of the first issue of Buffalo Bill Stories. This is the same *Buffalo Bill, the Border King* that was No. 1 in the Far West Library, "by the author of

Buffalo Bill" but credited to Ingraham as No. 1, Buffalo Bill Border Stories, and as No. 40, Great Western Library.

Of course, no one would confuse either Russell's or Ingraham's *Buffalo Bill, the Border King* with Ned Buntline's *Buffalo Bill the King of the Border* and certainly not with Ingraham's *Buffalo Bill, the Buckskin King*.

Buffalo Bill Stories ran for 591 weeks, then was succeeded in 1912 by the similar New Buffalo Bill Weekly, entirely made up of reprints from the previous series, running 364 issues to September 1, 1919, when it was discontinued. No author was ever named in either series; all 955 issues were "by the author of *Buffalo Bill*."

Buffalo Bill Stories, the first of the two series, was the last publication to produce original dime novels about Buffalo Bill. Ingraham probably wrote twenty-five or thirty new stories before his death in 1904, but most of the first 135 numbers, running for two and one-half years, were reprints from Beadle's Dime Library and Half-Dime Library and from Street and Smith's Log Cabin Library. Their authors included Ingraham, Ned Buntline, Rathborne, Russell, Taylor, and possibly other Beadle authors. Original stories were used from No. 139 to No. 551, and the number of new stories is, as nearly as has been determined, 446 of the 591 total. The new stories were written by Ingraham, Foster, Cook, Whitson, and Laurana Sheldon, the only woman to write Buffalo Bill dime novels. She wrote a dozen or so.

W. Bert Foster, anonymous in his contributions and unmentioned in any previous book about Buffalo Bill, actually wrote more titles than anyone else, although, as has been explained, Ingraham was far in the lead in number of words. When it was decided to make Pawnee Bill the partner of Buffalo Bill in dime novels as well as in the Wild West show—another indication of the close affiliation of show publicity and paperback literature—Bert Foster was chosen to launch the new series. Considerable fanfare and advance advertising preceded the appearance of Buffalo Bill Stories No. 481, *Buffalo Bill's Ultimatum; or, Facing Terrors with Pawnee Bill.* The masthead of the colored cover was changed to include a medallion with the heads of Cody and Lillie, such as was used in show advertising. This was continued with slight variation to the end of the publication. Its successor, the New Buffalo Bill Weekly, also featured the two faces, continuing to use them long after the partners' Wild West show folded.

The series with Pawnee Bill in each subtitle started in 1910, when Cody was trying desperately to retire and pass his mantle on to his partner. Seventy-four original stories had Pawnee Bill as the companion of Buffalo Bill, twenty-six of them by Foster, besides others in which old stories were reprinted with the name of Wild Bill, Texas Jack, White Beaver, or some other companion of Buffalo Bill changed to Pawnee Bill. In Chapter VII of *Buffalo Bill's Leap in the Dark; or, The Outcasts of Santibell,* Alkali Pete addresses Pawnee Bill as "Hickok," indicating a slip in the substitution of names. Despite this sharp practice, however, Wild Bill retained his leadership as the faithful companion in the long run, besides being the hero of more dime novels on his own account than any other of Cody's associates.

Bert Foster began selling fiction at the age of seventeen—that would be in the late 1880's—and was editing a newspaper at twenty-one, while growing a beard to add to the appearance of maturity. At some such early age he had a book, *The Heron's Nest,* to his credit. He came to New York to write exclusively for *Argosy* magazine, and was so prolific that he used seven pen names in that publication. Frank Munsey is said to have had a superstition that he needed a Foster story for the first issue of any new magazine he launched. Foster began writing for Street and Smith about 1906. Besides Buffalo Bill Stories, he contributed to the New Nick Carter Weekly, the New Magnet Weekly (Harrison Keith tales), Diamond Dick Jr. Weekly, Rough Rider Weekly, and Bowery Boy Library. His mystery serials *Six to Six* and *Findings Is Keepings* saw book publication.

Foster wrote railroad stories under the name of Jared L. Fuller, hard-luck stories as John Boyd Clark, and girls' books as Amy Bell Marlowe. He wrote the first ten books of the Cornerhouse Girls series, the first dozen or so of the Ruth Fielding stories, and launched the Oriole Series. *Caroline of the Corners* and *Caroline of the Sunny Heart* became silent motion pictures starring Bessie Love. He signed James A. Couper to a number of Cape Cod stories, such as *Sheila of Big Wreck Cove, Cap'n Jonah's Fortune, Tobias of the Light,* and *Cap'n Abe, Storekeeper.* Two of them became movies. His historical novels included *With Ethan Allen at Ticonderoga, With Washington at Valley Forge, The Eve of War,* and *The Last Galleon.*

His cowboy characters "Two-gun" Homer Stillson and "Poke" Fellows ran through several years of stories in *Ace-High* magazine. The poker-playing partner derived from "Poke" Carew, who appeared in a 1908 Buffalo Bill dime novel. His poet and minstrel companion was more the Roy Rogers type of cowboy.

Foster did most of his writing in longhand on a drawing board while wearing a green eyeshade. His wife, Myrtle Juliette Corey, who wrote many western stories under that name, typed his manuscripts, which he usually corrected so heavily that a second copy was needed—a painstaking method for so prolific an author. Few dime-novel writers took so much care, and their work shows it. Foster died at Fort Lee, New Jersey, in the 1930's.[2]

William Wallace Cook was another versatile and prolific writer. He actually wore himself out at his many tasks on occasion, and had to retire to a sickbed, arising as frequently to take on a new and often entirely different load. He was born in Marshall, Michigan, on April 11, 1867, the son of Charles Ruggles Cook and Jane Elizabeth Bull Cook. When he was fifteen, living at Ottawa, Kansas, he won a certificate of honorable mention for a contribution to Frank Leslie's *Boys and Girls Weekly.* A few weeks later he left high school there and went with his parents to Chicago, where he enrolled in the Bryant and Stratton Business College. On completing his course, he became a stenographer for a subscription book-publishing house. He had a great advantage among writers of his time in his training on the typewriter. He was a reporter for the *Chicago Morning News* and had his first fiction success with the sale of a short story, and then a serial, to the *Detroit Free Press.* Soon he was contributing regularly to Elverson's *Saturday Night* and the *Chicago Ledger,* and occasionally to the *Banner Weekly, Puck,* and the *Ladies World.* He was married on February 28, 1891, to Anna Gertrude Slater of Madison, Wisconsin. She approved his resigning a job as paymaster for a firm of contractors to devote all

---

[2] Information about Foster from Mr. Leithead, who knew Foster personally and also obtained much data from Mrs. Foster.

his time to writing. He commended himself to Street and Smith in 1894 by taking over a type of serial developed by them for their *New York Weekly* and signed by the company-owned pseudonym Julia Edwards. He followed this with stories in imitation of Archibald Clavering Gunther.

Overwork and a threat of tuberculosis retired Cook to a ranch near Phoenix, Arizona, in 1895. When he returned to New York, he had only a few hundred dollars left, and he did not get back into full production until 1898. His ready facility in imitating the style and subject matter of other writers gave him employment for ten years turning out nickel weekly stories and serials for Klondike Kit Library, Do and Dare Weekly, Boys of America, Red Raven Library, Paul Jones Weekly, Might and Main, Rough Rider Weekly, and Bowery Boy Library. After 1911 he turned his talents to pulp magazines, such as Street and Smith's *Top Notch,* that had begun to replace dime novels. In the 1920's he wrote scenarios for silent motion pictures. He was the author of at least two clothbound books, *His Friend the Enemy,* 1903, and *Wilby's Dan,* 1904. Late in life he returned to his birthplace, Monroe, Michigan, where he died on July 20, 1933. He is said to have earned $300,000 during his lifetime of writing.

With his versatility and imitative talent, it was inevitable that he would be called upon to write Buffalo Bill stories in emergency. Street and Smith records show he wrote twenty-three numbers in 1907, forty-nine in 1908, seven in 1909, and forty in 1910. Thus for two of these years he wrote almost all issues of the weekly. The fantastic character of his tales is indicated by such titles as *Buffalo Bill's Balloon Escape, Buffalo Bill in the Aztec City, Buffalo Bill's Aztec Runners; or, The Hate of the Gilded Mexican, Buffalo Bill in Old Mexico; or, The Red Priests of Zataclin, Buffalo Bill, the White Whirlwind,* and *Buffalo Bill in the Land of Spirits.*[3]

Some twenty authors—sixteen of them identifiable—created the 557 or so original Buffalo Bill dime novels printed and reprinted for a total of 1,700 dated publications in the United States. Around the world there were many more, some of them original stories, but

[3] Stanley A. Pachon, "William Wallace Cook," in *Dime Novel Rround-Up,* Vol. XXV, No. 300 (September, 1957).

Buffalo Bill, the Border King, 1896

Buffalo Bill in *Pluck and Luck,* 1901

most of them reprinted, adapted, or pirated from American models. In England, The ORIGINAL Buffalo Bill Library of the Aldine Publishing Company, Ltd., reached No. 700 with *Buffalo Bill's Red Rescuer*. The same publisher's Buffalo Bill 1d Library, heralded as a "Splendid New Series," included such titles as *Buffalo Bill and the Mormons, Buffalo Bill's Boy Pards, Buffalo Bill Afloat, Buffalo Bill's Life Story,* and biographies of Texas Jack and Wild Bill. Aldine's Buffalo Bill Novels: New Series at four pence, were long stories such as *Buffalo Bill's Triple Trail,* but not all of them were Buffalo Bill stories. This publisher also advertised two books by Wingrove Willson, *Buffalo Bill—Chief of Scouts,* and *More Adventures with Buffalo Bill.* Newnes' New Redskin Library included *Buffalo Bill and Buckskin Sam,* a rehash of Ned Buntline's story about Dove Eye, and *Buffalo Bill and the Utes.* None of these were dated publications. Most of them were issued after World War I.

Buffalo Bill Die Sioux-Schlacht am Grabstein was No. 122 of a series in German published in Dresden using colored lithographs from Street and Smith weekly issues in which the original English titles were included in the cut. This one was *Buffalo Bill and the Lost Miners; or, Hemmed in by Redskins.* Similarly *Buffalo Bill's 'Frisco Feud* became *Der Kampf im Sakramento-Fluss.* Even a limited knowledge of German indicates these translations are not very close. The price was 20 pfennigs, 25 heller, or 20 centimes, showing that these publications got around. A similar format was used for translations into French, Italian, and Spanish. As late as 1936, Buffalo Bill dime novels were displayed on newsstands in Barcelona. Germany went on an American West binge after World War II. A new Buffalo Bill series copyrighted in 1949 and 1950 was written by authors with such American-sounding pseudonyms as Tex Richards, Johnny Briggs, and Ted Clark. This series got into Cody's Kansas boyhood, a subject generally avoided in the United States except by Ned Buntline. Uncle Elijah, the slaveholder, becomes a deep-dyed villain. *Der erste Indianer* is a German version of Cody's killing his first Indian. Other easily translated titles are *Der Pony Express Reiter* and *Spion für General Sherman.* These are small magazines of thirty-two pages with colored covers reminiscent of the dime novel, although the art work is somewhat modernized. This is small-town stuff; the text is printed by a newspaper in Goslar. In Germany, Buffalo Bill has also appeared in comic books and in albums for bubble-gum cards.[4]

In the United States the gaudy colored-cover nickel magazine such as the New Buffalo Bill Weekly meant "dime novel" to the latest generation able to hide that form of literature behind atlas-sized geographies. The last issue of that series appeared in 1919, some two years after the death of Buffalo Bill. Street and Smith continued the book-size paperbacks for several years longer, starting their Great Western Library in January, 1927. For its first twenty-five issues it alternated Diamond Dick stories by W. B. Lawson with Buffalo Bill stories ostensibly by Colonel Ingraham. Buffalo Bill proved the more durable, and from No. 26 to the end only Buffalo Bill stories were used. The last of the series, No. 156, was published in December, 1932—sixty-three years after Ned Buntline launched Buffalo Bill as a dime-novel hero.

What kind of person was the Buffalo Bill depicted by a score of authors in 1,700 weekly publications? His alikeness under so many hands would be surprising were it not for the fact that no one of them seems to have had any particular talent for describing or developing a character. The dime-novel Buffalo Bill was the perfect hero and therefore generally colorless. One suspects that he sometimes became uninteresting to his authors, who occasionally relegated him to a background role as *deus ex machina*, while giving some one of his companions the lead.

Generally—except in Buntline—he speaks grammatical and somewhat stately English, while the actually courtly Wild Bill indulges in what passes for frontiersman dialect. Buntline makes Cody's language a little more human in spots, but gives him noble thoughts. Ingraham occasionally makes the hero less than infallible; the Ingraham plots demand frequent capture by Indians, and it is not unknown for a desperado to get the drop on our hero. However, in these cases it is only necessary for Bill to give a few

[4] Ruth Q. McBride, "Turbulent Spain," *National Geographic Magazine*, Vol. LXX, No. 4 (October, 1936), 399, 405; English titles are listed in *Old Timers Mart* (July–August, 1954, December, 1958), published by Ralph F. Cummings, Fisherville, Mass., who supplied samples; information on German dime novels from Dr. Gertrude Hafner, Graz, Austria, Joseph Balmer, Zurich, Switzerland, and Manfred S. Bordasch, Hannover, West Germany.

minutes thought to the most desperate situation to come up with an ingenious plan that foils the villain. Rather too often Bill offers the unspeakable dastard a duel after the Code of the West—the same code that is familiar in movies and television and little found in anything factual about the West. But even in cases where the heroine's life or honor is at stake, Bill is taking less risk than appears because of his uncanny accuracy and speed with all sorts of weapons. Happily, in these ante-movie days it was not always necessary for him to defeat the villain in hand-to-hand fisticuffs.

There were juvenile delinquents in those days, and dime novels had little competition in getting the full blame for them. It must be admitted that dime-novel morality is not always above reproach. Buntline, the great rascal of his day who wrote much of his output from jail cells, offended little. He gives Buffalo Bill frequent temperance lectures to direct at Wild Bill (who slips occasionally). Buntline's Buffalo Bill says on one occasion, "I never should have trusted that man. I knew he was a gambler, and out here they're always close kin to a robber."[5] Ingraham, however, makes Cody an expert gambler. In *Buffalo Bill's Blind Trail* the hero captures a stagecoach robber. Instead of turning over his captive to legal authorities, as morality would require, Bill learns that the robber has been driven to a life of crime by heavy gambling losses, jeopardizing the mortgage on his dear old mother's home. Bill then connives at covering up the crime, hunts out the gambler, and in a fair game with a new deck of cards, wins back the holdup man's losses. Of course that brings about the robber's reform, which, after all, is the object of penology.

Most dime novels about real persons were pseudo-biographical, basing the stories on some factual background, but rarely did a Buffalo Bill dime novel bear any relation to anything ever done by the real Cody. Despite a popular opinion to the contrary expressed in much writing about Ned Buntline, the works by that author were no exception. Buntline spent several weeks on the plains with Cody before writing his first story, and one wonders why, as there is not a word in it about Bill as a scout at Summit

[5] Ned Buntline, *Buffalo Bill and His Adventures in the West* (New York, J. S. Ogilvie & Co., 1886), a reprint of his first Buffalo Bill story, confirmed by comparison with facsimile of *New York Weekly* (December 23, 1869).

Springs, the killing of Tall Bull, or any of the events of the postwar period in the West.

The story opens with Buffalo Bill's father shot down and killed on his own doorstep by one Jake M'Kandlas. The elder Cody, it may be recalled, was stabbed not shot, was not killed, was not at home at the time, and was not attacked by anyone named M'Kandlas. This is the closest Buntline gets to any real event in Buffalo Bill's life. The name M'Kandlas bears a striking resemblance to Mc-Canles, and while Buffalo Bill vows vengeance in this first chapter, the reader is not surprised when the revenge is taken care of by Wild Bill Hitchcock—a spelling of Hickok that has official standing—in a later chapter, wherein Wild Bill takes on singlehanded the eleven—count them—members of the M'Kandlas gang, by far the largest number of McKandlases or McCanleses executed by Wild Bill in any version of the story—indeed, historians allow him only three.

As we "leap over a lapse of years" to Chapter II, it is 1861, and Buffalo Bill is returning from a trip on the plains with Wild Bill and Dave Tutt, a name that will be recognized as that of another of Wild Bill's victims. Sure enough, in a later chapter, Wild Bill kills Dave Tutt in a traditional western gun duel. Something of the sort the real Wild Bill actually did. With the two principal villains taken care of by Wild Bill, there may seem little for the titular hero to do, but he keeps reasonably busy. Cody is provided with fictitious twin sisters named Lillie and Lottie, who make a career of being rescued. They get themselves kidnaped by that "fiend incarnate," Jake M'Kandlas, by Dave Tutt, by a tribe of Indians, or by a band of Border Ruffians, in almost every chapter. Every two or three pages one or the other of them faces "a fate worse than death" from some "fiend in human shape"—these traditional dime-novel clichés actually appear in the story.[6]

Of course, Buffalo Bill has a fight with Indians, and, "Oh, it was a grand as well as a fearful sight, to see him, bare-headed and bespattered with blood and brains, dash here and there, Powder Face kicking, plunging and snorting as he dashed his red hoofs into the dead and dying, while the Indians, utterly terror mad,

[6] *Ibid.*, 120, 147, 151, 154, 235.

sought only to escape." Casualties in this fight are not recorded by the author of this story "founded entirely on fact," but he tells of another occasion when Bill with only 43 men pursued a band of guerrillas, including M'Kandlas and Dave Tutt, totaling 200, killed 150 of them, and lost only four scouts killed, although it is admitted that half of the 43 were wounded. The wound incurred by the half-man unhappily is not described.

This history continues by recording that Buffalo Bill with his victorious company of scouts led the advance of the army to the Battle of Pea Ridge—a fight the real Cody never claimed to have taken part in. In this battle Wild Bill was killed by a couple of amazons named Ruby Blazes and Sallie Perkins in revenge for Tutt and M'Kandlas, a highly unfortunate event for Wild Bill since it occurred before he had done any of the things for which he gets a modest place in history, except, of course, to dispose of sundry McCanleses. He was indeed still very much alive when Buntline wrote this story.

Only one episode described by Buntline in these pages seems to have entered in any way the Buffalo Bill tradition. That was his rescue from a drunken sergeant of a girl called here Louise or Louisa La Valliere, obviously intended for Louisa Frederici. This story appears in some books about Buffalo Bill as fact, although nothing of the kind is hinted at in any autobiographical work.

This may be the only Buffalo Bill story among the 557 in which our hero is provided with a sweetheart. Occasionally in later stories he is allowed to rescue a fair damsel, but her heart is always bestowed elsewhere.

Prentiss Ingraham handled romance after a manner that no doubt delighted the small boys who were the best customers for his stories. He even used the word in the title of *Buffalo Bill's Blind Trail; or, Mustang Madge, the Daughter of the Regiment, A Story of Wild West Romance*. This 1892 story runs to thirty pages, three columns to the page in type almost under the range of human vision. In its 70,000 words are enough characters, plots, sub-plots, and mysteries to last for two or three volumes. One of the many characters is a young lieutenant who takes part in some of the Indian fights. Occasionally his name is on the same page as that of the heroine, but there is no indication of any closer contact between them until you reach the last two paragraphs. Colonel Ingraham concludes his romance thus:

"And what of Mustang Madge?

"I need now only remark that she at last married one of the gallant Fifth, and that one was the lucky Otey Onderdonk, who was the envy of every young officer of the post, for in the unknown Daughter of the Regiment, the Prairie Waif, he secured a pearl beyond price."

You never would have guessed it—and this story far antedates O. Henry, who is supposed to have invented the surprise ending.

Ingraham is not far behind Buntline in using the type of phrasing that is commonly associated with the dime novel. The Colonel's particular forte was alliteration, as many of his titles indicate and as is indicated by the names of some of the characters in this story. Bessie Bond, the Border Beauty, is one of his many mystery figures. Associated with the less reputable Emerald Ed is Keno Kate, the Faro Fairy.

Like Buntline, Ingraham used real names. One in this story is Captain Alfred Taylor, who wrote a couple of Buffalo Bill dime novels on his own account. The faithful companion is Surgeon Frank Powell, known as White Beaver and also as Fancy Frank, the Surgeon Scout—more alliteration. Texas Jack also enters the story; he was a favorite character and appeared in many dime novels long after his death.

This is not the story with the famous opening, "Another redskin bit the dust," but Ingraham did nearly as well. It starts:

"It is a ride for life, and the Indians catch the hindmost; but once there we can stand them off until we can get aid from the fort, so let us be off."

As you may guess, the troops were being guided to a pass where "we can stand off a tribe of redskins," which, next to a cave, was the most common feature of the landscape in the dime-novel West. In *Buffalo Bill's Buckskin Pards,* Colonel Ingraham finds a cañon that "can be defended by your outfit against a couple of hundred Indians" on page 30; "a natural breastwork where they [the Indians] could have kept back a much larger force than their own" on page 67; and a place where "six men could, in that waste, stand off a large attacking force" on page 95. Buntline also had no difficulty in finding at need a spot that could be "defended by a few against the approach of thousands." In military history Thermopylae seems to have been the only such place that was at hand when it was needed, but when the Greek Army tried it again in World War II, the pass had mysteriously widened out until a couple of German army corps slipped through somewhere around the edges.

The number of Indians killed by Buffalo Bill and his pards in such places was truly enormous, but however great the number, let it be said to Bill's credit that he always tarried to bury his dead. Unlike the twentieth-century paperback mysteries, the dime novels never left a lot of corpses lying around. While there is never any mention of Bill's carrying pick and shovel while on his perilous dashes for life, those implements were never lacking after he had, with "deadly aim, desperate daring, and great strength," disposed of a desperado who had temporarily "got him in his power." Decent burial of the dead became so prevalent a custom of the dime-novel West that even Sitting Bull was constrained to adhere to it, contrary to the custom of the Sioux, who generally put their dead on high, exposed platforms.[7]

Occasionally—but not often—Ingraham used plots bearing a slight resemblance either to actual events in Cody's life or to those that became legendary. It was widely believed, probably from the frequent representation of the fight as a Wild West spectacle, that Buffalo Bill got to the Little Big Horn just a little too late to save Custer. In *Buffalo Bill's Grip; or, Oath-bound to Custer*, we find Cody on the field when "hardly yet had the thirsty ground drunk up the crimson tide that had flowed from death-wounds given to man and beast alike." The dead Custer's right hand "held his sword-hilt, and the blade was buried in the body of a painted chief, and was probably the last act of the dying leader of the three hundred slaughtered troopers." Ingraham got this detail from Cassilly Adams' picture made famous by Anheuser Busch, for Custer carried no sword on the campaign. Just as Buffalo Bill was holding himself "oath-bound to Custer," he was captured by Bill Bevins, outlaw and renegade who had led the Indians in the fight—the

[7] Prentiss Ingraham, *Buffalo Bill's Return* (Great Western Library No. 69), 91–92; *Buffalo Bill's Buckskin Pards* (Buffalo Bill Border Stories No. 14), 153.

story of a white renegade in Sitting Bull's camp is one of the persistent legends of the Custer fight. Bill's life is saved for the time being by a beautiful Indian girl named Feather Feet, and he escapes in time to take "the first scalp for Custer" by killing Yellow Hand in a fantastic knife fight on a cliff, far above the troopers of the Fifth Cavalry.

Anyone trying to reconcile this story with anything that happened will be as confused as dime-novel readers must have been when they came to read Ingraham's *Buffalo Bill with General Custer*, for in that story Cody is presented as a survivor of the fight itself. He opens his eyes on the gory field of battle to find that "a red man lay across him, and he was entangled with his dead horse." Again he is captured by the Indians, but this time no beauteous maiden rescues him. His experiences in the Sioux camp are not particularly enlightening, for Ingraham had little knowledge of Indian ways. In *Buffalo Bill the Border King*, Ingraham describes Indians walking posts as sentinels and chiefs making "grand rounds." Had the Indians used any such services of security, Tall Bull might have lived to fight another day.

Ingraham makes some use of western folklore. His Mad Hunter bears some resemblance to Bigfoot, the terror of the Oregon Trail.[8] A note of realism is added by naming such actual associates of Cody as General Miles, Colonel Royall, Major Frank Baldwin, and Lieutenant Edward L. Keyes. But Ingraham's greatest quality was an awareness of time and place. His "Fort Beauvoir" in *Buffalo Bill's Blind Trail* somehow comes to life with its array of frontier characters, its contests in horsemanship and shooting, and its entertainments for visitors. It relays a vivid impression of life at a frontier army post during the period of the Indian wars.

Subject matter began to grow thin after a few hundred Buffalo Bill stories had been published, but, surprisingly, by far the best work on them was done by the late-comer, W. Bert Foster. His stories have closely knit plots, they use modern short-story techniques, and their characters occasionally come to life. By this time Buffalo Bill was following a pattern later extensively used by radio's Lone Ranger, riding about redressing wrongs and aiding in law

8 Porter Morgan Ward, "Bigfoot: Man of Myth," *Montana*, Vol. VII, No. 2 (April, 1957), 19–23.

enforcement. Just as the Lone Ranger is accompanied by the faithful Tonto, so Buffalo Bill is provided with an Indian friend, "Little Cayuse of the Piutes." Here again western folklore was drawn upon, for there was a Little Cayuse, or at least a lively legend about him, only he was a Pawnee, not a Paiute.

According to Cy Warman and William Lightfoot Visscher, Little Cayuse was only two years old when a trapper known only as Whipsaw bought him for a knife from a Sioux who had captured him in a raid. When Little Cayuse was four years old, Whipsaw took charge of a Pony Express station along the Platte. It was then that the boy earned his name, for he could hear the Pony Express rider approaching long before anyone else, and would shout, "Cayuse, cayuse" until the relief rider was aroused. His keen ears also detected Indian raiders. On one occasion his alertness enabled three men at the station to ambush six Sioux who had killed the express rider and attempted to steal the station's horses. Little Cayuse was found kicking and firing shots into the body of one of the Sioux, who was identified by the scar on his face as the one who had captured and sold the boy. Little Cayuse's abilities, as described, made him useful in Buffalo Bill's entourage.[9]

For the scout, in these stories, had accumulated quite a following of frontier characters who seemed to have little to do except to have one weekly adventure after another. This is the period when Pawnee Bill was Cody's right-hand man and hero of the subtitle in every issue. Wild Bill was not entirely forgotten, for unlike Ned Buntline, who killed off Wild Bill before he had a chance to walk the streets of Abilene or Hays City, these latter-day writers gave Hickok a prolonged post mortem career. The actual date of the stories is somewhat vague, but Wild Bill's frequent use of an electric flashlight proves he must have survived Jack McCall's bullet by a couple of decades, for Thomas A. Edison only got around to the invention of the electric light about the time Wild Bill was being buried at Deadwood's Mount Moriah.

Wild Bill, however, does not appear in all these stories, and when he does, his part is often a minor one. More prominent is a fictional scout, Nick Nomad, whose frontier dialect is possibly in-

---

[9] William Lightfoot Visscher, *A Thrilling and Tuthful History of the Pony Express,* 63–68.

tended for comic relief. The real comedy role, however, is reserved for the Baron Willum von Schnitzenhouser, for those were the days when a German dialect was the stock in trade of the comedian in vaudeville, burlesque, and melodrama, the days of Weber and Fields and of Charles Follon Adams' "Leedle Yawcob Strauss." Despite the handicap of being a typed dialect character, the Baron is such a good-natured blunderer that it is easy to see why the dashing Buffalo Bill tolerates him. In one story the Baron takes the lead, and his blundering pays off.

This story, *Buffalo Bill's O.K.*, starts with the Baron losing all his funds gambling. Returning to the hotel, he finds that Buffalo Bill, Nomad, and Little Cayuse have gone, leaving him a note to follow by train. Having no funds, the Baron plays hobo. After the freight car he is riding on top of is cut off at a mine siding, he learns that four villains have kidnaped and are holding a Denver capitalist there. The Baron follows them into the mine, which serves as the customary dime-novel robbers' cave in this story, and rescues the victim. Meanwhile, one of the bandit gang has posed as the capitalist in a mine deal involving Pawnee Bill. This sets the stage for "Pawnee Bill's Warning" (the subtitle), which gets "Buffalo Bill's O.K." The chase after the bandits follows. However, not all the bandits are rounded up. Some of them had to be saved for next week. This story has one other unusual feature—there are no female characters whatever. The dime-novel West had become a man's world—for boy readers.

Foster occasionally got far off the beaten track of Buffalo Bill legend. *Buffalo Bill Overboard* is a story of Mississippi steamboat gamblers. *Buffalo Bill and the Eight Vaqueros* is about Mexican bandits. *Vaqueros* were more familiar to Cody in show business than in his western career. In *Buffalo Bill's Royal Flush,* the villains are, believe it or not, Russians. Sounding even more up to date is the title, *Buffalo Bill and the Russian Plot.*

At selecting titles that made much more exciting reading than his stories, however, William Wallace Cook excelled. His *Buffalo Bill Among the Blackfeet* uses a plot he employs frequently. A girl comes west in search of her missing father [brother, sweetheart], reported slain by Indians [kidnaped by bandits]. With the aid of Buffalo Bill she always finds her man, but under circumstances of great mystery. The Wizard, for example, is a misplaced Edison who uses marvelous electrical inventions to overawe the Blackfeet. In *Buffalo Bill's Diamond Mine; or, The Bedouins of the Plains,* the mad father has discovered the secret of popping into and out of a mysterious spring connected with a cave. This confuses the Pawnee Bedouins no end, and they never do find his hidden diamonds. In *Buffalo Bill on the Deadwood Trail; or, Cat Eye, the Sioux Renegade,* the girl joins the bandit gang seeking her father, while her father joins the same band seeking revenge on Cat Eye for the presumed murder of the daughter. In *Buffalo Bill and the Mad Millionaire; or, The Redskin Rovers,* it is the father who employs Buffalo Bill. The daughter, for some not too clearly defined reason, is living in a secret room of a house full of trap doors and mysterious passageways. The fathers in all these stories are mad, but Cook made a discovery of which psychiatrists might take note. When restored to their long-lost daughters, these madmen invariably recover their reason.

Most of his colorless heroines could stay lost without too much harrowing of the reader's emotions. An exception is Sally Dorman, who, with rifle, pistol, and knife, slaughters quite as many Night Hawks as did Buffalo Bill in *Buffalo Bill's Dance of Death; or, The Night Hawks of Snake River.* Sally was too busy to be hunting for any missing madman. Sometimes it is the villain who is mad, as in *Buffalo Bill in the Land of Wonders; or, The Mad Chief of* the Modocs. It makes little difference. Cook succeeded in writing stories without characters. His villains are not very villainous, his heroines are not very heroic, and his heroes spend most of their time untying knots in the ropes that hold them captive. Cook also got along without plot or setting. His stories did have action—so much of it that sometimes he ran short of space and had to wind it up in a synopsis paragraph. It is a tribute to the vitality of the Buffalo Bill legend that the weekly issues could survive stories no better than some of his.

John H. Whitson apparently wrote in intentional imitation of Foster, using the same cast of characters, the Baron and all the others, and some of the same tricks of phrasing. His stories are slower paced than those of Foster and perhaps less well plotted, but full of suspense and action. *Buffalo Bill at the Copper Barriers;*

or, Pawnee Bill's Cave of Aladdin opens with the escape of the Apache Kid—a real Chiricahua Apache who carried on his own private war with United States forces—from jail in Yuma, Arizona. The partners pursue him to Mexico and become involved in one of the familiar dime-novel caves, full of secret passages and, in this case, of Aztec gods as well. Much farther off the trail usually followed by the scouts is *Buffalo Bill and the Lost Indian,* a tale of an educated Indian who seeks to lead a revolt of his people. He is a somewhat involved character for a dime novel, and it keeps Buffalo Bill busy protecting a Miss Hunt from the Indian leader's attentions. Sex almost sneaked into this one, but not very far.

Stories by other authors got even farther away from the real Buffalo Bill—one laid in the "then Territory of Washington" is about as far as you can get from his usual haunts. This is *Buffalo Bill and the Amazon; or, Pawnee Bill and the Timber Thieves.* Before Pawnee Bill was written into it, it was *Buffalo Bill and the Timber Thieves; or, The Camp of the Secret Clan.* The author probably is Laurana Sheldon. One of its characters is Nick Wharton, who seems to have been the original of the later Nick Nomad. This story of fist fighting among rival lumbermen is closer to the Hollywood Western than it is to the tradition of Buffalo Bill.

As much might be said of *Buffalo Bill and the War Hawk; or Pawnee Bill and the Five Nations,* except that the scene is Nebraska in the Indian-fighting days. St. George Rathborne is probably responsible for this amalgamation of Western and detective story. The "War Hawk" is Wally Burt, a mysterious New York tenderfoot, who displays considerable nonchalant courage as he faces villains red and white. He turns out to be a detective who gets his man and musters up courage to speak of love to Grace Winslow, a pioneer heroine. With both sex and crime, this particular story is far out of line.

These few examples are perhaps sufficient to indicate that the 1,700 dime novels about Buffalo Bill contributed little to what has been accepted and believed about him as a person. It is only necessary to read the titles to know that the majority of them deal with wholly imaginery and fantastic situations—*Buffalo Bill and the Klan of Kan, Buffalo Bill and the Headless Horseman, Buffalo Bill and the Rope Wizard, Buffalo Bill's Lassoed Spectre, Buffalo Bill and the Sorceress,* and *Buffalo Bill and the Nihilists,* for example.

Yet Ned Buntline was not alone in claiming veracity for such wild tales. For years the Street and Smith publications bore this announcement with the list of back numbers on the back cover:

"Buffalo Bill is more popular today than he ever was, and, consequently, everybody ought to know all there is to know about him. In no manner can you become so thoroughly acquainted with the actual habits and life of this great man, as by reading the New Buffalo Bill Weekly." But no one was expected to believe it, for the preceding sentence in the same announcement said, "These stories have been read exclusively in this weekly for many years, and are voted to be masterpieces of Western adventure fiction."

Which were they, fact or fiction? It seems improbable that even juvenile readers accepted them as actual fact. It was sufficient to know that this fictional hero existed in actual fact. Gene Autry, Roy Rogers, Hopalong Cassidy, and the Lone Ranger were exploited in circus and rodeo and aroused a similar curiosity, but small fry do not necessarily assume that these personages have actually performed the derring-do of screen, television, or radio drama. With Buffalo Bill, however, they had a hero whose fictional exploits had been paralleled by real adventures in a historical period.

Buffalo Bill was no inconsiderable figure in this dime-novel world. In fact, no other actual person was hero of so many of these stories; and even of the many fictional characters who gave their names to long series, only one figured in more dime novels than Buffalo Bill. That was Nick Carter, the detective, who, of course, goes on and on. Jesse James probably ranks third.

The dime novels had little impress on the saga of the Buffalo Bill legend because there were so many of them. Dime novels about other historical characters usually bore some relation to actualities, but the numerous writers of the numerous Buffalo Bill stories were forced far afield for their plots. It is a safe assumption that no one person ever read all of them. Indeed, no one has ever seen a complete collection of Buffalo Bill dime novels.[10] Their publishers

[10] The Library of Congress has a large collection of Beadle and Adams and other early dime novels, but none of later issues.

recognized that they had a changing readership and found it safe to repeat stories and titles after some nine to eleven years.

Yet while no one remembered very long anything that Buffalo Bill did in any one dime novel, the cumulative effect of this constant stream of Buffalo Bill weeklies was enormous. Few youngsters of the time could have failed to read at least one Buffalo Bill story, and no one at all could have failed to be conscious of the kaleidoscopic color covers that were ever changing but always present to view.

Nothing that William F. Cody did in life, not all the traveling of Buffalo Bill's Wild West nor all the efforts of Major Burke and his corps of press agents, did as much to impress the name of Buffalo Bill upon several generations not only of young Americans but also of boys and men throughout the world as the dime novels. Of twenty-five million words, only two have survived—Buffalo Bill—but that survival in itself has contributed enormously to the legend. The glamour attached to Buffalo Bill and the West he personified has been reflected in billions more of words than have been strung together in the never ending stream of Westerns—books, melodrama, musical comedy, motion pictures, radio, television, even ballet and grand opera.

The dime-novel Buffalo Bill never crumbled into the dust of the pulp paper he was printed on. He still exists, a very real part of the American tradition.

BUFFALO BILL DIME NOVELS—A COMPILATION

	Originals	Reprints
Street & Smith's New York Weekly*	1	7(?)
Beadle's Dime Library	67	
Beadle's Half-Dime Library	26	1
Beadle's Boy's Library	1	
Saturday Journal*		2
Banner Weekly*		31
Pocket Library		6
Beadle's Dime Biographical Library		2
Saturday Library	1	
Young Sports Library (No. 26)	1	
De Witt's Ten-Cent Romances (No. 102)	1	

Tousey's Pluck and Luck		5
Tousey's Wide Awake Library	5	1
Tousey's Three Chums Weekly	1	
*Happy Days**		6(?)
Street & Smith's Sea and Shore Library		2
Street & Smith's Log Cabin Library	7	7
Buffalo Bill Stories	446	145
New Buffalo Bill Weekly		364
Far West Library		211
Buffalo Bill Border Stories		211
Great Western Library		143
Totals	557	1,143
Aggregate		1,700

* Stories published serially are counted as reprints even when they preceded dime-novel publication.

THE HERO LESS HEROIC

AT THE VERY TIME Buffalo Bill was reaching the height of his fame
as a dime-novel hero, he let his public down. Any other man fifty-
two years old and responsible for an enterprise employing 467
persons might have been excused for missing the Spanish-American War, but not Buffalo Bill, who was currently being represented by Colonel Ingraham as seeking each month ever new and
perilous adventures. And Cody did miss the war, after talking a
great deal about it.

The Spanish-American War was the last war in which volunteers rushed to the colors in disorderly or, rather, unorganized
fashion. It had been suggested that cowboys would make ideal
cavalry. That this idea stemmed from the glorification of the cowboy in Buffalo Bill's Wild West was indicated when a unit recruited
in the West, officially the First Regiment of United States Volunteer Cavalry, was universally known as the "Rough Riders." Its
lieutenant colonel, Theodore Roosevelt, was almost as good a publicity man as Major Burke. There were also Second and Third regiments, but they saw no fighting and got little publicity.

It was to be expected that Buffalo Bill would be among the
first to offer his services, and he did so on April 18, 1898, proposing
to raise a company of cavalry scouts. He also offered 400 horses—
the show carried 453 that year—and George Burch, the show's chief

of cowboys, stood ready to recruit 2,000 cowboys for the Rough Riders. Nothing more is heard of the company of scouts or the 400 horses, but Cody's services were promptly accepted by the commanding General of the Army, Nelson A. Miles, with an appointment to his staff. Cody sent two horses, "Knickerbocker" and "Lancer," to Washington to be sent with headquarters property whenever a move should be made.[1]

Buffalo Bill's Wild West, with added patriotic features including Cuban insurgent veterans, opened in Greater New York before war was declared. When war was declared on April 25, it was announced that Colonel Cody would continue with the show until his services were needed. On April 29, Cody wrote a friend, "I will have a hard time to get away from the show—but if I don't go—I will be forever damned by all—I must go—or lose my reputation. And General Miles offers me the position I want. George, America is in for it, and although my heart is not in this war—I must stand by America."[2]

The show moved on to Philadelphia and then to Washington, finding Miles still there, for the commanding general himself was having difficulty in getting to the front. General Miles was believed to have political ambitions, and there were those in the capital who did not desire to see him add further military laurels. Colonel Cody and his show went on to Hartford, and General Miles went to Tampa, Florida, early in June to see how Major General William R. Shafter was getting along with the Fifth Corps, scheduled to go to Cuba as soon as the navy had cleared the way. Miles, finding that Shafter, a corpulent man, was seriously affected by the intense heat, telegraphed for permission to accompany the expedition, but received no reply. On the day after the expedition sailed, Miles was recalled to the capital on important business, which proved to be connected with the famous "message from García" brought by Lieutenant A. S. Brown, who had penetrated Cuban jungles to find the rebel leader.

On July 1, Shafter's corps won the battles of El Caney and San Juan Hill. Roosevelt and the Rough Riders had their day of glory when they charged the hill, but they never got to prove that cow-

[1] Clifford P. Westermeier, *Who Rush to Glory*, 34, 44–46, 119.
[2] Cody to George Everhart, April 29, 1898, copy from Ralph G. Newman.

boys made good cavalrymen, for they fought on foot. Their horses were left in Florida, along with four troops to take care of them. On July 3, Admiral William T. Sampson's fleet destroyed the Spanish fleet off Santiago.

On July 7, General Miles left Washington hurriedly to accompany reinforcements to Cuba. There is no indication that he sent for Buffalo Bill at this time. When Miles arrived, he found negotiations for Spanish surrender in progress. He stayed until the formal surrender on July 17.

On July 21, General Miles sailed for Puerto Rico with 3,300 men, and this time he did send for Cody. The show had moved on to Detroit and westward. Miles fought six small and forgotten battles in Puerto Rico, but it was already apparent that the war was nearly over, and hostilities ceased on August 13, following the signing of the peace protocol and the declaring of an armistice on August 12. When Cody reported that it would cost $100,000 to close the Wild West, he was advised by Miles to stay at home. The General rode Buffalo Bill's horses in Puerto Rico and then brought them back to Washington.

Cody's decision to remain with his show was not unheroic. He headed no small organization to be abandoned in mid course. There can be no doubt that Cody would rather have gone than stayed—his April 29 letter shows how he felt about it. But when he and his press agents had talked loud of his volunteering, they had reckoned without those responsible for financial investment in his exhibition and those whose livelihood depended on it. Not in 1898 or in any other year did Cody make enough to quit, while at the same time he was also making too much to quit.

He had been caught talking big and performing little.

Yet in this same year, 1898, Cody enjoyed what Dexter Fellows calls "the happiest day in his life during the years I was with him." It was Cody Day at the Trans-Mississippi Exposition in Omaha, and old friends and neighbors gathered to do him honor. Among them was Alexander Majors of the Pony Express firm, who recalled how he had employed the boy Billy and had given him "a man's pay because he can ride a pony just as well as a man can." Majors told that Billy had been paid twenty-five dollars in half-dollars for his first month's work, and that he had taken his pay home to his mother and spread the money out over the table.

"I have been spreading it ever since," Cody interjected. The homefolk of Nebraska knew how true that was, but they did not know that Majors himself, his freighting empire long since vanished, was one of the beneficiaries.

Others who honored Cody included Edward Creighton, who had built the first telegraph line across the plains and thus had ended the riding of the Pony Express; Governor Silas A. Holcomb, who had commissioned Cody colonel in 1895; Senator John M. Thurston; and A. D. Jones, the first postmaster of Omaha.[3]

In 1899 the Rough Riders of the World included sixteen of Roosevelt's Rough Riders, among them Tom Isbell and William McGinty. The spectacle was the Battle of San Juan Hill. Featured were the war horses Knickerbocker and Lancer, which Cody had intended to ride, but Miles actually rode at the front. Adding to the Spanish-American War atmosphere were eight Cubans, three Filipinos, and seven Hawaiians. This was getting away from Wild West. The season of 1900 was largely a repetition of 1899. These were years of long tours with many one-day stands.

The show was brought up to date in 1901 with a spectacle, "The Allied Powers at the Battle of Tien-Tsin and the Capture of Pekin," an event of the preceding year when an international force had rescued diplomats besieged by the Boxer rebels in China. Uniforms of the Ninth Regiment of United States Infantry, United States Marines, British Marines, Welsh Fusiliers, East Indian Sikhs, and German, Russian, French, and Japanese forces were represented in the pageant. "The Management of the Wild West have taken a little dramatic license in massing troops where there was only desultory fighting," the program apologized while trying to give the impression that the sham battle was somewhat larger than the real thing.

A Gatling gun drill was another added feature. This gun, directed by that sturdy Indian fighter, Captain James Parker, had won considerable acclaim at Santiago. It was a machine gun of several barrels fired in succession, mounted on a light artillery car-

[3] Fellows and Freeman, *This Way to the Big Show*, 158.

riage. An interchange of wheels between gun and caisson was a spectacular feature of the drill, and the gun fired blanks with exciting noise and speed.

A demonstration by the United States Life-Saving Service included "the firing of the shot carrying a line over the mast of the doomed vessel; the planting of the sand-anchor and connecting a hawser from it to the mast by means of the shot-carried line; the rigging of a breeches-buoy on the hawser and working it to and fro, over the surf, with the rescued mariners."

As the show train left Charlotte, North Carolina, on October 28, 1901, for its last engagement of the season at Danville, Virginia, its second section had a head-on collision with a freight train. One hundred and ten horses were killed, including the Colonel's mount, "Old Pap"; only two survived. No person was killed, but Annie Oakley suffered serious internal injuries. She had fired her last shot for Buffalo Bill. After several operations she recovered slowly. It was more than a year before she was back in show business; on November 12, 1902, she opened in *The Western Girl,* a melodrama written by Langdon McCormick. White-haired after the wreck, she never regained her old-time vigor, but her shooting skill returned. She toured in 1912 with the Young Buffalo Wild West and Col. Cummins Far East Combined show.

After a long tour from coast to coast in 1902 with more stops than ever before, the Colonel returned to Cody, Wyoming, in November for the opening of the Irma Hotel, named for his daughter. He did not tarry long, for Bailey sent the show to Europe that winter, this time for a tour of more than four years. On Christmas Eve, 1902, Nate Salsbury died. The show opened in London as scheduled two days later, with flags at half-staff. It was the end of an era for Colonel Cody and for Buffalo Bill's Wild West.

Cody's visits to the West in these years were not as heroic as the contemporary dime novels would lead one to believe, despite their advertised objective of revealing "all there is to know about him." Many were concerned with investments and speculation. Perhaps he met a few deep-dyed villains on these expeditions, but he seems to have failed to foil all their plots. His most inglorious appearance came in 1905, when his stage was a Wyoming courtroom, and the melodrama (or perhaps farce) was a divorce suit he brought against Lulu.

Their trouble was of long standing and involves details of his private life—he did have one, of sorts, despite all the efforts of press agents and dime-novel writers. Lulu never forgot nor forgave him for kissing the girls good-bye at the close of his theatrical season of 1877. Five years later Bill made a startling discovery. During all the time the show was on the road he had been sending Lulu money to buy property and then, in 1882, he learned that she had bought everything in her name alone, and she refused to let him have any part of it. He did not even have a home to go to; there was no welcome for him at "Welcome Wigwam," the house on which he had lavished money at North Platte.[4]

It may be argued that Lulu distrusted Bill's business sense. She had good occasion to distrust it in the matter that brought on this crisis. Bill's grandfather had once owned a tract of land that became a part of downtown Cleveland, Ohio. One of Bill's uncles sold it. Other members of the family brought suit to recover $15,-000,000 they claimed by right of inheritance. The case dragged on for years, and Bill, being the most affluent plaintiff, poured money into it with high hopes for his sisters as well as for himself. These hopes were not shared by Lulu, who refused to sign a paper in connection with the suit or allow Bill to use any of the property she had bought to raise funds for the endless legal processes. Of course, she was right; the suit came to nothing.

Bill, needing a partner he could trust on his home grounds, turned to Al Goodman, husband of his sister Julia. Al and Julia had been managing the farm of Uncle Joseph Cody at Valley Falls, Kansas, the former Grasshopper Falls. Al drove one hundred mares to North Platte and spent some time on Cody's ranch in 1882. In a letter to Julia, who remained at Valley Falls, Bill said that all the news he had from home came from Al, as Lulu had quit writing to him.[5]

The next year, 1883, Cody started the Wild West, another project in which Lulu had no faith. She not only refused to let him use any of the money he had sent her, but she also tried to tie up everything in sight against the crash she was sure would follow. This time she was wrong, as Bill squeaked through and went on to big

[4] *Letters from Buffalo Bill,* 18.
[5] *Ibid.,* 19, 21; Mrs. Goodman MS.

success. He was so incensed at what he called flatly her attempts to ruin him financially that he entered a petition for divorce. Nothing came of it this time.[6]

In November, 1885, Al Goodman became manager of the North Platte properties. Bill and Lulu were still estranged, and as Lulu was occupying Welcome Wigwam, the Goodmans had to put up with a small house on the ranch that winter with their family of nine, in addition to ten hired hands and such assorted casualties from the Wild West show as Bill sent home to recuperate. Bill planned a house of fifteen rooms with porches ten feet wide—not the skimpy six feet Al suggested. Appropriately it was called "Scout's Rest," and that name was painted on the barn in letters large enough to be read from the Union Pacific a mile away.

During 1886, while the house was being built, Cody had many suggestions. A contractor offered to supply all material, move off the old house, and complete the new one for $3,500. Cody wondered whether that was too much. Mr. Welch, the contractor, included the painting in his price, but the Goodmans could pick the color. Cody left most details to them, but he made one reservation for himself: there should be a sideboard, with decanters and glasses, in his room upstairs, and a large bed, so that if any of his guests got drunk, he could put them to bed.[7] It may be noted that a period of serious domestic difficulty coincided with his heavy drinking during his first Wild West season, and it will be recalled that after his promise to Nate Salsbury to quit drinking on the job, he also warned that after the season closed, he would "get on a drunk that is a drunk." These were the years when his sprees at North Platte between tours became proverbial.

Truly this new home was Scout's Rest. Julia Goodman says that while she lived there, she entertained everyone from royalty to cowboys. Bill usually brought a group of house guests with him at season's end, and some of them were as perennial visitors as the scouts who were there all the time. Bill's hospitality was widely known. Frank C. Huss recalled, "On our way to North Platte, while passing the home of William F. Cody, some of the older boys said they thought Bill was at home. Some 15 of us rode over to the ranch,

---

[6] *Letters from Buffalo Bill*, 21.
[7] *Ibid.*, 23–25; Mrs. Goodman MS.

about a mile south of the road. Cody was at home and sitting on the veranda. After hand shaking and introductions, we were asked what we would have to drink. Each called for his favorite and each was supplied. There must have been a big supply on hand!"[8]

All this extravagant hospitality was expensive, but Scout's Rest Ranch was not the complete liability it has sometimes been supposed. As much because of interest in agricultural development as because it belonged to Buffalo Bill, Omaha newspapers kept an eye on it, and reported Al Goodman a progressive and competent manager. A correspondent for the *Omaha Herald* in 1885 was impressed by the herd of 125 blooded cattle—Herefords, Polled Angus, and Shorthorns, including an imported pedigreed Hereford bull named "Earl Horace"—at a period when western ranchmen were just beginning to improve their stock from the original Texas longhorns.

Ten years later, in 1895, a reporter for the *Omaha Bee* described Scout's Rest Ranch as one of the finest improved farms in western Nebraska. "Until the past year this has been more properly a stock ranch, and as such was originally planned by its owner. But the decline in the profits of horse raising changed the order of things." In partnership with Isaac Dillon, owner of an adjoining farm, Colonel Cody had built a twelve-mile irrigation ditch, capable of watering 6,000 acres, of which 1,000 acres had been broken and planted. Of 4,000 acres in the ranch—the same figure as was given in 1885—1,200 acres were in corn; one hundred acres of alfalfa in bloom "presents, perhaps, the most striking appearance to be seen"; fifty acres were in broomcorn; and an ordinary farm had been converted into an oatfield. There was also a meadow. The ranch worked eighty horses and employed thirty men, the number rising to fifty or sixty at certain seasons. The reporter was convinced that all this was profitable.[9]

Not all of Cody's investments were as rewarding. Dr. Frank Powell, White Beaver, was prolific in get-rich-quick ideas, and always got Cody's backing. As early as 1884 they were in partnership, producing Yosemite Yarrow Cough Cream and Wonder

[8] B. L. Hall, *Roundup Years*, 133.
[9] *Omaha Herald*, December 6, 1885, cited by Foote, in *Letters from Buffalo Bill*, 22; *Omaha Bee*, July 14, 1895, NSHS.

Worker at La Crosse, Wisconsin, where Dr. Powell practiced medicine after a fashion. Later they offered White Beaver's Cough Cream, the Great Lung Healer, at fifty cents a bottle. They joined with Lieutenant Frederick Schwatka in a project to colonize 2,500,-000 acres of land in Mexico. Schwatka, an officer of the Third United States Cavalry during Cody's scouting with that regiment, became an experienced Arctic explorer. In 1878 he had started a three-year search for Sir John Franklin, missing since 1845. In 1883 and 1884, Schwatka had explored the sources of the Yukon; in 1886, he had headed an expedition to Alaska. Perhaps he should have confined his interests to Alaska, for the Mexican venture failed, although Cody and Powell had agreed to supply five hundred colonists a year and Powell accompanied Buffalo Bill's Wild West to Europe in 1889 in furtherance of the project.[10]

No more appropriate promoters could have been found than Cody and Powell for "Panamalt," designed in 1893 as a substitute for both alcoholic beverages and coffee. The partners hoped for big business among the Mormons, who banned coffee, but in the hard times of 1894 the Panamalt factory was forced to close. Cody's hotel and livery service at Sheridan, Wyoming, also failed during that same year.

Meanwhile the domestic scene brightened. There was some sort of reconciliation in 1887. Lulu weakened in her resolution to stay away from show business and went to New York. Ed Goodman, son of Al and Julia, who was with the show selling programs, was busy denying he had said anything about the family troubles of his Uncle Will and Aunt Lue. Before the show sailed for England, Lulu had gone in a huff; while enjoying his triumph abroad, Bill wrote to Julia inquiring if Lulu were home and what she had to say, and instructing Al to give her what money she needed. On his few and brief visits home in these years, Bill stayed at Scout's Rest with Lulu still at Welcome Wigwam, although their relations seem to have reached a status where they tolerated each other.

Writing from England in 1891, Bill told Al that if Mrs. Cody had any grain or grass to be cut on her place, to have it done, and if she was not home, to have it done regardless. "I often feel sorry

[10] Hebbard, "Notes on Dr. Powell," *Wisconsin Magazine of History*, Vol. XVI, No. 6 (Summer, 1958), 308–309; label from H. S. Cody.

for her," Bill wrote. "She is a strange woman, but don't mind her—remember she is my wife—and let it go at that. If she gets cranky just laugh at it, she can't help it. I am glad that Julia does not worry much about her, you know how she will talk, but people know Julia now and Mrs. C's talk don't hurt her."[11]

Arta usually sided with her mother—Cody complained that Arta would not answer his letters—but she accompanied her father to London in 1887. After her marriage to Horton Boal in 1890, Mrs. Cody urged that Boal take over the ranch, as Al Goodman was not well and was unable to oversee it efficiently. Cody could not approve; he urged Al to stay on even if he had to ride around in a buggy to direct the ranch work. Al resigned in 1891 and moved back to Kansas, and Boal took over. Even then Lulu did not move to Scout's Rest, and when Welcome Wigwam burned, Cody bought a new house for her in North Platte. Yet she and Irma came to Chicago while Buffalo Bill's Wild West showed there in 1893. Again there was a quarrel, and they did not visit the show lot again until 1898.

When Boal had no success in running the ranch, Al Goodman was persuaded to return. Julia took more persuading, even when assured that no one was in the house but Al. Eventually Al and Bill went to Denver to talk her into it. This time the Goodmans stayed until 1899, when they moved into North Platte because of Al's serious illness. He died in 1901.

Lulu was intensely jealous of members of Bill's family and of everything he did for them. Bill was loyal to his sisters and eager to share his wealth with them—and neither they nor members of their families were reluctant to accept it. In 1893, Helen was married for a second time, to Hugh A. Wetmore, editor of the *Duluth Press*. Cody built them a printing plant and got some return from that investment, as Helen's *Last of the Great Scouts* was first printed there. Wetmore contributed to the Cody legend with a narrative poem, *Buffalo Bill and Yellow Hand*. Whether this should be considered an asset may be determined from some extracts:

> *"I know ye, Long Hair," yells Yellow Hand*
> *A-ridin' out from his pesky band*
> *(A reg'lar bluff o' the Indian brand).*

[11] *Letters from Buffalo Bill*, 27–48.

"You kill heap Injun, I kill heap white;
My people fear you by day or night;
Come, single-handed, an' you me fight."

"I'll go ye!" quick as a thunder-clap
Says Bill, who jest didn't care a rap;
"Stan' by, an' watch me an' the varmint scrap."

With relatives and friends, Cody was generous, and he backed them in a number of unprofitable ventures. Many of his own investments were in failures verging on the ridiculous. However, it would be hard to prove that he was not farsighted in his development of the Big Horn Basin country of Wyoming, including the founding of the city of Cody. The development did not proceed rapidly enough for him to gain much profit—and there were other complications in his finances—but much of what he planned came to substantial and lasting success. The Cody Chamber of Commerce stands ready to prove it.

Cody once said that he first became interested in the Big Horn area as a result of Professor O. C. Marsh's expedition in search of fossils in that region. Cody long remembered what the professor said about the richness of the soil and possibilities of oil and mineral wealth. In 1895, Cody joined George T. Beck, Bronson C. Rumsey, Sr., and others in the construction of the Cody Canal, a project of the Shoshone Land and Irrigation Company. It had been proposed to name a town at DeMaris Springs for Cody. The company also laid out a townsite, calling it Shoshone, but that name was rejected for a post office because of possible confusion with the Shoshoni Indian agency. Charles Emery Hayden, engineer, said Beck, Nate Salsbury, Ed Goodman, Charles Gilette, and Hobo Jones then conspired to annex the name of Cody before the DeMaris Springs townsite got around to it. The Cody post office was established in August, 1896, with Ed Goodman, son of Julia, as first postmaster. The water project eventuated in the construction of Shoshone Dam, called the highest in the world, at 328 feet, when completed in 1910. It was renamed the Buffalo Bill Dam in 1946.[12]

In 1895, Cody also began moving cattle to Wyoming. Constant

---

[12] Arlan W. Coons, in *Cody Enterprise*, February 20, 1946; Harold E. Briggs, *Frontiers of the Northwest* (New York, London, 1940), 440–41.

bickering with Lulu over management of the North Platte property as a factor in this shift. Another of the Goodman boys, Henry, drove a herd from Scout's Rest Ranch to Hyannis, where it was shipped to Sheridan. Henry then went to Deadwood to pick up another herd from the Colonel's old friend and hunting companion, Mike K. Russell. Mike's Black Hills herd wore the TE brand, which he made over to Cody, and that was the origin of Buffalo Bill's famed TE Ranch. The TE was once rated at 4,600 acres, but Cody also owned the Carter ranch near by, of similar size, and eventually added Irma Lake Ranch, Sweeney Ranch, and Rock Creek Ranch to his Big Horn Basin holdings.

Cody was instrumental in persuading Charles E. Perkins, president of the Burlington Railroad, to extend a branch of that line to Cody in 1901. A corollary was the establishment of the Cody Road to Yellowstone Park, built by the government at an original cost of $50,000. That was big spending in those days, and there was objection that the route was impracticable, but President Theodore Roosevelt said, "My old friend Buffalo Bill has hit the trail up there, and if he was good enough to guide such men as Sheridan, Sherman, Carr, Custer, and Miles with their armies through uncivilized regions, I would take chances on building a road into the middle of eternity on his statement, and Bill says it is all right, as he has been over it on horseback."[13]

Bill planned a line of stagecoaches for Cody Road. He established his hunting lodge, Pahaska Tepee, which became a permanent tourist attraction (and still is) at the park entrance, and he proposed something very like a dude ranch for the TE. The Buffalo Bill Barn at Cody was another link in the tourist route. In 1901 the Colonel founded the Cody Military College and International Academy of Rough Riders.

But the big event for his namesake town was the opening of the Irma Hotel on November 18, 1902. The Irma Hotel still operates in faded glory, boasting Charles Schreyvogel's painting of the *Battle of Summit Springs* and other paintings by Henry R. Lewis and Charles S. Stobie in its imposing lobby. The hotel was too big for the town in 1902, and Bill is said to have lost five hun-

[13] "P. I. W." [Wellman], in the *Kansas City Times*, July 14, 1937; "W. H. G.," in the *Kansas City Star*, March 21, 1946.

dred dollars a month operating it; by the time the town was big enough to support the hotel, its streets were cluttered with motor courts. There was no thought of such a development as the champagne corks popped in 1902.

When Buffalo Bill's Wild West played Washington in 1899, Colonel J. H. Peake had been invited to Bill's tent and found before he left that he had agreed to publish a newspaper in a town that as yet existed largely in Bill's imagination. Yet he went to press with the first issue of the *Cody Enterprise* on August 31, 1899, and it was firmly established in 1902 to report the grand opening. For eastern coverage, at the suggestion of Dexter Fellows, press agent with the show, Charles Wayland Towne of the *Boston Herald* was invited to the opening. The presence of H. C. Morrill, president of the Lincoln Land Company, which had developed townsites along the Burlington right-of-way since 1880, proved that Buffalo Bill had learned a lesson since his unfortunate attempt to found Rome along the Kansas Pacific in his earlier years.

There was a gathering of the Cody clan, and the engagement of Irma to Lieutenant Clarence Stott was announced at the opening. They were married the following February, but Stott died shortly of pneumonia. Irma was married again, to Frederick H. Garlow. Arta was there with her children, Clara and William Cody Boal. Bill's sister Eliza died early in 1902; the three other sisters were widows. Julia Goodman was managing the hotel. Helen Wetmore was helping to run the *Cody Enterprise*. May Bradford was not in Cody in 1902, but came a year later. She afterward married Louis Decker. Of Julia's children, Ed was postmaster, Henry had driven cattle to the TE Ranch, and Finley, Walter, and Josephine were with their mother. The Boston reporter escorted Josephine to the grand ball.

Buffalo Bill, in white tie and tails and wearing rimless glasses, read a prepared dedicatory speech from manuscript. "Isn't Uncle awful!" exclaimed Josephine. But he was not drinking, under doctor's orders. In deference to him, the old scouts also abstained.

The old scouts were there in full force. Dr. Frank Powell stood ready to give up patent medicines and Indian remedies to devote his undoubted promotional talents to the Colonel's ever widening interests. Others were Charlie Christy, called "Roman Nose," Mike

Russell, original owner of the TE brand, and Charles Stewart Stobie, known as "Mountain Charlie." After the festivities Cody and the scouts went hunting, taking along the Boston reporter, Towne.[14]

This hunting party was outstanding in its personnel as well as in its recording. Towne became an authority on the West and co-author with his cousin, Colonel Edward Norris Wentworth, of those livestock classics, *Shepherd's Empire*, *Pigs: From Cave to Corn Belt*, and *Cattle and Men*. When Colonel Cody read Towne's account of the opening of the Irma Hotel in the *Boston Herald*, with its description of cowboys in chaps and spurs, he was ready to run the young reporter off the reservation, for he was proud of the frontier town's dress suits—he had worn one himself. But Fellows persuaded the Colonel that the *Herald* account was good publicity in Boston, and Towne stayed on, spending a year as guest and publicity man at the Irma.

Stobie, born in Baltimore on March 18, 1845, went west in 1865, by wagon train to Denver, teaming up with California Joe Milner. They were in three Indian fights between Fort Kearny and Fort Sedgwick. Stobie was the only white man with a Ute war party that fought Arapahoes and Cheyennes; he scouted for Major Jack Downing against the same tribes, and was scout with Jim Baker at the White River Ute Agency under Major D. C. Oakes. Returning to Chicago, Stobie studied art under G. P. A. Healy. Stobie painted Sitting Bull, Standing Bear, Little Wolf, Frank North, and Kit Carson, and was also notable as a photographer.[15]

Cody did not wear a dress suit on the hunting trip, but he did wear a black flower-embroidered shirt. Towne records more poker playing than shooting—but no drinking—and that the Colonel dedicated the poker jackpots to his sister May's charity in Denver, described as a home for "deflowered frails," although Cody admitted that he had no idea how much good would be done with

[14] Charles Wayland Towne, "Preacher's Son on the Loose" (MS), and interview, May, 1957; Charles Stewart Stobie, Diary, 1902 (MS, SHSC); Fellows and Freeman, *This Way to the Big Show*, 153; James W. Hook, "Seven Months in Cody, Wyoming, 1905-1906," *Annals of Wyoming*, Vol. XXVI, No. 1 (January, 1954).

[15] Charles Stewart Stobie, "With the Indians in Colorado," *Colorado Magazine*, Vol. VII, No. 2 (March, 1930), 75-76; "Crossing the Plains to Colorado in 1865," *ibid.*, Vol. X, No. 6 (November, 1933), 201-12; see also pp. 234-36, in *ibid.*, "The Charles S. Stobie Collection."

the money, as he dared not visit the place. Cody demonstrated that he retained his old skill with the Winchester by hitting a tin can thrown into the air twice before it hit the ground, and he got two out of five mountain sheep at an estimated 1,500 yards, with one shot apiece.

Stobie's diary records that on November 23, 1902, at Ish-a-woo-at Creek, Powell Mountain, Wyoming, he made an "oil color study of mountain back of camp with teepees and Cody." The original painting hangs in the Irma Hotel, and it has often been reproduced. The hunting party returned on December 6, and the Colonel sailed for England on December 15.

During this year the Colonel got around to the subject of divorce again. On March 21 he wrote Julia, "I have tried & tried to think that it was right for me to go on through all my life, living a false lie—Just because I was too much of a Morral coward to do otherwise, But I have decided that if the Law of man can legally join together the same law can legally unjoin. And that it's more honorable to be honest than to live a life of deceit. There is no use of my telling you of my Married life—more than that it grows more unbearable each year—Divorces are not looked down upon now as they used to be—people are getting more enlightened. Some of the very best people in the world are getting divorced every day. They say it's better than going on living a life of misery for both. God did not intend joining two persons together for both to go through life miserable. When such a mistake was made—A law was created to undo the mistake. As it is I have no future to look forward to—no happiness or even contentment. Lulu will be better contented. She will be her absolute master—I will give her every bit of the North Platte property. And an annual income. If she will give me a quiet legal separation—if she won't do this then it's war and publicity. I hope for all concerned it may be done quietly."[16]

Apparently he did sign over the North Platte property to Lulu with the expectation that she would agree to a divorce, but she did not, and while Cody was in England in 1903, Lulu's meddling with affairs in Wyoming caused trouble with his sisters. Lulu refused to sign a deed for a place called "Cody View," which Bill had given to Helen. Helen quarreled with Bill, and Bill told Julia to

[16] *Letters from Buffalo Bill,* 49.

get Helen out of Cody before he returned. Later he relented and gave Helen his interest in the *Cody Enterprise*. Julia, under pressure from Lulu, threatened to leave the Irma Hotel, but Bill persuaded her to stay. However, all seemed quiet when Bill returned for a brief visit late in 1903. He promised May to build her a house, but business was so bad in the summer of 1904 that he professed inability to spare that much cash.

Cody returned home on November 3, 1904, bringing friends from England for another big hunt. Also on the hunt were Lieutenant General Miles, Dr. Powell, Major Burke, and Iron Tail. Walter Goodman, Julia's youngest son, only twelve years old, got his first elk, which was mounted under his Uncle Will's direction.

On New Year's Day, Arta, whose first husband, Horton Boal, had died in 1902, was married again, to Dr. Charles W. Thorp. On January 30, 1904, she died in Spokane, Washington. She was to be buried beside Kit and Orra in Rochester, New York. Cody telegraphed his wife urging that they forget all past differences. Lulu replied by accusing him of breaking Arta's heart and causing her death. They traveled on the same train, but she refused to speak to him. At the Auditorium Hotel in Chicago she made a scene, denouncing Cody and his sisters. When the journey was resumed, she threatened to express her full opinion of Bill at the grave of their daughter.

Depositions in the Colonel's plea for divorce were taken before Judge Charles Scott in Cheyenne, Wyoming, in February and March, 1905. Mrs. Cody's defense made much of Bill's drinking, but testimony was also offered that she did some drinking herself on occasion; that when she did, she became quarrelsome and abusive; that her language was often vulgar; and that she sometimes refused to feed Bill's guests and otherwise insulted them.

Of value here are the impressions of Dan Muller, who as a boy lived at Scout's Rest. Dan was fond of both of the Codys, and he found Lulu a kind, motherly woman, who gave him even-tempered affection, although Bill was responsible for his being there, as the orphan son of an old friend. Dan tells of Bill's coming home at the close of show season with his cronies, giving Lulu a bare word of greeting, but showing interest in everyone else on the ranch before getting on with the refreshment and entertainment of his guests.

While Bill held forth with them in the dining room, Lulu ate her meal at the kitchen table with Dan. This is what Bill meant when he charged that she refused to entertain his friends.[17]

It cannot be said that the reputation of either was enhanced by charges brought at the divorce hearing. It seemed to be a contest to see which could bring the most absurd specifications.

The Colonel charged that his wife had tried to poison him. The incident on which this charge was based took place on the day after Christmas in 1900. Mrs. John Boyer, wife of the superintendent at Scout's Rest Ranch, testified: "She gave him Dragon's Blood. It was a drug she had. She gave it to him in his coffee." When Cody drank it, he collapsed and found himself unable to speak. The defense intimated that this was no uncommon condition for the Colonel after drinking certain liquids at North Platte. However, more details were brought out about Dragon's Blood. It was a love potion Lulu had obtained from a gypsy; it was supposed to cause the return of the Colonel's affection, perhaps even to cure him of drinking. Mrs. Boyer told of switching the cups on one occasion, with the result that the concoction made Mrs. Cody sick. The witness admitted she did not believe that Mrs. Cody was attempting to poison her husband.

Another witness, Mrs. H. S. Parker, testified that Mrs. Cody was jealous of the attentions paid the Colonel by Queen Victoria and Queen Alexandra. Judge Scott immediately expunged from the record the testimony concerning the queens as "manifestly unjust, preposterous, false, and brutal." This jealousy was in fact so preposterous that it weakened considerably the credibility of everything Lulu had to say about other women in Bill's life.

When Lulu went to Chicago in 1893, she heard rumors of his association with Olive Clemons. Lulu went to the house where he lived during the show season, found no Olive Clemons there, but wrecked the place on general principles. At the conclusion of the trial Judge Scott asked Mrs. Cody's attorneys to strike out all charges relating to Cody's conduct in Chicago.

In 1898, Mrs. Cody went to New York and stopped at the Astoria. When she called Bill's room at the Hoffman House, the

[17] Muller, *My Life with Buffalo Bill*, 46–60, 75–80; interview with Charles S. Sweetland, who prepared Muller's book for publication.

phone was answered by a voice she identified as that of Bessie Bell. On this occasion Lulu wrecked her own room, breaking mirrors and vases, the cost of which Bill paid, but not cheerfully.

Bessie Isbell of Washington, D. C., began to travel with Buffalo Bill's Wild West in 1900 as a press agent—and a good one, Bill said. He had given her a silver-mounted saddle, but denied that it was a token of affection, as well he might. On a visit to the Big Horn country she was "sick all over the ranch," according to testimony, which mentioned that Bill had kissed her good-bye. Bill could not remember that he had. Judge Scott also asked Mrs. Cody's attorneys to strike out all charges relating to Bessie Isbell.

In the trial there was only passing mention of Katherine Clemmons, an actress Cody had met during his first London engagement, when he called her "the finest looking woman in the world." Impressed by her appearance, or by what he mistook for acting ability, Cody financed for her a tour of England during which she played in *Theodore*. He then brought her to the United States and bought the play *A Lady of Venice* for her, in which she flopped at a cost to him of $50,000. She was indignant because Bill went off bear hunting and declined to add to his losses. Cody is quoted as saying, "I would rather manage a million Indians than one soubrette." She afterward married Howard Gould, who sued her for divorce in 1907, naming Cody. Dan Muller tells a story of Gould's attorneys coming to Cody at a time when his financial situation was desperate to offer him $50,000 to testify against Katherine. Cody told them to get the hell out of his tent, and meant it.

After asking the attorneys for Mrs. Cody to amend their answer by striking out all charges naming other women, Cody's conduct in Chicago, and early excesses at Fort McPherson, Judge Scott handed down the decision that "all the allegations in the amended answers of the said defendant, Louisa Cody, are true, and that the allegations in the plaintiff's petition and amended petition and supplemental petition are hereby disproved." Cody lost the suit and had to pay Mrs. Cody's court costs, amounting to $318. The case was dismissed on March 23, 1905.[18]

[18] *The Westerners Brand Book* (Chicago), Vol. II (1945–46), 27–31; *Letters from Buffalo Bill*, 60–61; Arthur Sears Henning, "More Memoirs," *Chicago Tribune*, January 8, 1954; *Denver Post*, March 11, 12, 1904; *Nebraska State Journal*, November 29, 1896.

There was one woman in Bill's life about whom Lulu apparently knew nothing. This was Nadeau Piatt, between whom and Cody a series of letters is extant, each starting with the salutation "Dear B.B." and each signed, "B. B." On his end of the correspondence, "B. B.," of course, means Buffalo Bill, and on hers, "Beautiful Baby," which she was, according to a photograph preserved with the letters. What comes between "Dear B. B." and the signature "B. B." is disappointing to anyone seeking scandal in Cody's life, for the letters relate mostly to the comings and goings of Cody's sisters, nieces, and nephews and other minor gossip. A record that in 1912 Cody and Maud G. Thomas of Pima County, Arizona, sold the Aurora mine in that county to Aurora Piatt indicates that the Piatt family had some connection with Cody's Arizona mining ventures, which cost him more money than all the women in his life, possibly even including Lulu.[19]

As early as 1902, Colonel D. B. Dyer, a former Indian agent, interested Cody in a mine prospect containing tungsten, gold, and lead. The Cody-Dyer Mining and Milling Company was formed, and Cody wrote to Julia on March 13, 1903, that the long-sought vein of ore had been struck after seven months of night-and-day drilling, and predicted that the mine would begin to pay off within four months. As soon as the roads were passable, wagons would haul ore to the Grand Encampment smelter, and their own mill would be built during the summer. In June the roads were not yet passable because of late heavy snows, and two months' work had been lost.

Despite setbacks, Cody never lost faith in Dyer, although it is probable that Cody never saw the mine until he went there at the close of the show season in 1910 with Mr. and Mrs. Johnny Baker. The Campo Bonito mine is about seven miles northeast of Oracle in Pima County. It is in the Catalina Mountains in the region of the fabled Mine with the Iron Door, which inspired a novel by Harold Bell Wright. The legend tells of a vein so heavy with gold that Spanish adventurers put up an iron door to guard their treasure. Then all were killed by Apaches and the secret was lost. Cody backed an old scout, William Neal, in a quest for the lost mine. Neal eventually decided that it had been buried by an earthquake

[19] Cody file, Western History Department, Denver Public Library.

in 1878. Cody did not stay long on this first visit, as he went to North Platte for Christmas, then to Wyoming for a brief stay, and started back to the Arizona mine in January. However, he was called to Pasadena by the serious illness of his sister Helen, who died there on February 8, 1911.[20]

The stop in North Platte signified a reconciliation with Lulu, which had been effected on July 28, 1910. Even in the midst of her denunciation of him while being interviewed about the divorce suit, Lulu had interjected, "Will is one of the kindest and most generous of men." While the Wild West was touring in the area, Bill's grandson William Cody Boal urged Bill to come to North Platte. When he arrived, he found Lulu there; the family contrived to leave them in a room together, and when they came out, all was forgiven—or at least they agreed to go on as they had before.

When the Wild West played Kansas City in September, 1911, Cody was interviewed while visiting Dyer at his home in Beaumont, on the site of the Battle of the Little Blue. Reporters described Dyer's country place as having forty-seven rooms and notable for its collection of antiques. The partners were optimistic; they controlled forty-five claims and had driven a dozen tunnels into them. A steel manufacturer in Pittsburgh was buying their sheelite, a high-grade tungsten ore—tungsten had replaced carbon filament in electric lighting, and the metal had a big future. The partners put a new quartz mill into operation on October 16. After the show closed at Richmond, Cody hastened to Oracle. He was joined there by Lulu, and they stopped, or at least Mrs. Cody stopped, at the Mountain View Hotel, which had been built by Neal, the scout who had hunted the Mine with the Iron Door. Cody dashed about, to the mine, to Tucson, where he was a member of the Pueblo Club, and elsewhere promoting mine business, sometimes leaving Lulu knitting on the verandah of the Mountain View for months at a time.[21]

They came back in 1912. That Christmas, Buffalo Bill played Santa Claus for two hundred children he had gathered in from fifty to one hundred miles around in the recesses of the Catalina

[20] *Letters from Buffalo Bill*, 52–56; Cody scrapbook, Arizona Pioneers Historical Society, Tucson (hereafter referred to as APHS).

[21] *Kansas City Star*, September 3, 1911; *Arizona Daily Star*, February 23, 1946; *Arizona Republic*, April 3, 1956.

Mountains, most of them miners' children of Spanish-Mexican descent who had had little previous contact with Santa Claus. There was a program of entertainment—Bill's sixth cousin, John Franklin Cody of London, Ontario, beat Professor William Sweeney, leader of the Cowboy Band, in the fat men's race—but the big show was the children themselves, whose one day of happiness was the most substantial production of the Campo Bonito mine.[22] Within a year Bill was trying to sell it at any price. He hoped for help from his Canadian cousins, from an invention Thomas A. Edison was reported to have patented that would reduce low-grade ores, from Johnny Baker, who went to London on a stock-selling venture. A half-century later the machinery at Camp Bonito was rusting away unused. The Mountain View Hotel's verandah still stood, but it had been many a year since it had heard the creak of Lulu's rocking chair.

Through 1912, Cody had dropped half a million dollars into those Arizona mine shafts. One-sixth of that amount would have saved him from disaster in 1913. Nothing that he touched outside of show business ever made him any money, yet those ventures that cost him the most, Scout's Rest Ranch, the development of Cody, and even the Arizona mines, seem plausible investments. The investments that appear ridiculous, such as that in White Beaver's Cough Cream, cost him comparatively little.

Also, as Lulu had said, he was the kindest and most generous of men. He filled his pockets with silver dollars to hand out to anyone who asked. He made thousands of loans to old scouts and out-of-luck showmen that he never expected to see repaid. This sort of lavishness he could afford, as he could the Christmas party for the children of the Catalina Mountains.

He was least the hero in his relations with women. His long estrangement from Lulu makes it easy to suppose that he sought other female companions, but the stories rest only on rumor and speculation. Lulu blocked his divorce suit, but all her charges concerning women were stricken from the record. As Howard Gould failed in his divorce suit against Katherine Clemmons and she was

[22] Unidentified clipping, Cody scrapbook, APHS, dated December 30, 1912; Winget, *Pipe Dreams, Seventh Smoke: Buffalo Bill as Santa Claus* (1925).

awarded separate maintenance against him in 1909, two more court hearings failed to prove anything against Cody.

Buffalo Bill was never less than a hero to children. Dozens of photographs show him surrounded by children in his tent on the show's back lot. They were not publicity pictures; many were snapped by parents who had wangled an interview for their off-spring. It was not an act. Cody really liked children, and he was one of those rare adults who keep their promises to children. From Europe he sent back stamps for Walter Goodman's collection and took much trouble seeking out post cards for Josie. In Paris he bought the finest of Jumeau dolls for Irma. When Walter at twelve shot his first elk under his Uncle Will's tutelage, it was a long-planned treat. As early as August 13, Uncle Will had written Josie that he intended to take her brother on his November hunt and followed it up two weeks later to Mrs. Goodman with full instructions: "Tell him to have his horse ready. If he wants a gun to practice with tell Mr. Schwoob to fit him out and I will pay him, for he must have a gun a 30 30 that he can Kill big game with, he must kill and Elk."[23]

On one occasion he had promised his grandson, William Cody Boal, a ride in the Deadwood coach in the show "if he would hold on dog-gone tight." He did not forget his promise, even though he did forget the boy's name, for when the time came, Cody ordered, "Put little Mr. — er — What's-his-name in the coach," then in an aside, "Blame my Skeets if I hadn't forgot the boy's name and he is named after me." It is an idiosyncrasy many will recognize when even the most familiar of names flits away when wanted suddenly. The expletives used on this annoying occasion, however, were such as made Buffalo Bill a hero to parents as well as to their offspring, for he rarely used profanity, generally confining himself to "Dog-gone it," or "Dog my cats."

Children of show troupers—and in later years there were many of them—had their daily story hour with the Colonel. And, of course, there were the thousands and hundreds of thousands of children who came to the Wild West. The show was primarily for

[23] *Letters from Buffalo Bill,* 58–59; Eleanor St. George, *The Dolls of Yesterday* (New York, 1948), 140–41.

them and was directed to them. A few came as guests, for the out-door show world was beginning to see the publicity value of free seats for orphans and other unfortunates in charitable institutions.

Lydia Sarah Cody was Bill's first cousin once removed; that is, her grandfather, Philip, was the brother of Bill's father, Isaac. Lydia, who had taught social science in Columbia University, was engaged in social welfare work in New York City when Buffalo Bill's Wild West was playing at Ambrose Park, Brooklyn. She wrote to the Colonel on behalf of a group of boys in which she was interested, and received the following reply:

Aug 1st 1894

Dear Cousin Lydia

Your letter was a happy surprise. I will be delighted to see you. I enclose you a Card that will Admit you—And as many as you wish to bring. Any day except Saturday. Come direct to my headquarters—I love children, bring them all—

Lovingly

Cousin

WILL CODY[24]

William Frederick Cody at times fell short of the heroic role in which he was cast in the dime novels. On occasion he could do foolish things; on occasion he could appear ridiculous. But the idol of many generations of children can be forgiven many faults when he can say sincerely, "I love children—bring them all."

[24] Quoted by permission of Miss Lydia S. Cody, Cleveland.

Cover of *The Buffalo Bill Stories*, 1907

Buffalo Bill and children

Courtesy Fred B. Hackett

29

"A SERIES OF FAREWELL EXHIBITIONS"

THE LAST EUROPEAN TOUR of Buffalo Bill's Wild West started inauspiciously with the death of Nate Salsbury just before the opening performance. Before the show returned to America, the sponsor of its tour, James A. Bailey, was also dead.

It has been said that Bailey kept the Wild West in Europe for four successive seasons to keep it out of competition with his circuses in the United States. While that may have been a factor in his management, it is not the whole story. The success of the Wild West was also his personal interest, and he may have felt that it was then a better show for Europe than for the United States. This barnstorming tour of Europe was a continuation of the tours Bailey had directed since 1895 in the United States, during which he had tried to route the show to every city large enough to support it.

He also traded territory with his Barnum and Bailey Circus, which had made a successful tour of Europe from 1897 to 1902. This had the practical aspect of permitting an exchange of transportation and other equipment. Unhappily, Barnum and Bailey returned home to find its leadership seriously threatened by the rapidly growing Ringling Brothers, which had become firmly entrenched in most of the desirable locations. Bailey at length gave up fighting and made a deal with the Ringlings, letting them in on the management of the third large circus, Adam Forepaugh and

Sells Brothers, and dividing territory with them. Keeping Buffalo Bill abroad fitted in with this program.[1]

Early crowds at Earl's Court were large and enthusiastic, but business soon dropped to a moderate level. King Edward VII, who as Prince of Wales had done much to make the 1887 season a happy memory, delayed his visit until March 14, 1903, three weeks before the show was scheduled to leave London. With the King were Queen Alexandra, the Duke of Connaught, the Duke of York, Princess Mary, and King Edward's grandson who became Edward VIII and Duke of Windsor. Before leaving, the sovereign remarked that "George and May must see it," so the future King George V and Queen Mary made it four successive rulers who were patrons of Buffalo Bill's Wild West.

The royal party stayed to the end of the show and then visited the back lot. King Edward unbent when an Indian child seized his umbrella, asking, "Would you like that umbrella, young man?" The boy was too shy to answer. This incident was the center of interest in a painting by Arthur Jule Goodman, which was reproduced in lithographed posters and in heralds, couriers, and programs.[2]

Sir Robert Baden-Powell, hero of Mafeking and founder of boy-scouting, who was a great admirer of Buffalo Bill, was another visitor. There was no shortage of nobility and notables—only of commoners. Cody still hoped for a big summer, "then quit the show business for ever," an idea he had expressed most seasons. But bad luck and bad weather dogged his steps. Snow fell the day before the show opened at Manchester on April 13—and at that opening performance Cody was thrown when his horse stumbled and fell. Bill's ankle was badly sprained and he was taken to a hotel, but he appeared in the arena in a carriage that night. However, he had to continue appearances in a carriage for seven weeks. After Liverpool, Birmingham, Dudley, Swindon, Bristol, and Leicester, Cody complained of the nervous strain and told Julia, "I do not go to

[1] Earl Chapin May, *The Circus from Rome to Ringling* (New York, 1932), 170–72; Marian Murray, *Circus: From Rome to Ringling* (New York, 1956), 152, 210, 248, 290, 299; John and Alice Durant, *Pictorial History of the American Circus* (New York, 1957), 312, 317; Esse Forrester O'Brien, *Circus* (San Antonio, 1959), 62, 77–78; Chindahl, *A History of the Circus in America*, 143–46.

[2] Original in Buffalo Bill Museum, Cody, Wyo.; lithograph poster, Stafford & Co., Netherfield near Nottm., England, 1903.

hotels any more for I haven't the strength to be even talked to."
Yet in September, when less optimistic of getting rich from his
Arizona mines, he wrote, "I will make more money after this with
the show for I will be sole owner. I am buying the Salsbury interest." He did not make it. At Bradford on October 6, he wrote of a
narrow escape from disaster: "We have had fifty hours steady of
the worst cold rain And wind storms I ever experienced in All my
life. We stood it off for 43 hours but had to give up. And to night
have lost our first show this season. We commenced pulling at 8 15.
At 8 37 a house adjoining our big top was blown down and fell on
our seats. had we had an audience in there would have been many
killed so we were lucky to not attempt a show." The season closed
at Burton-on-Trent on October 23, and the show went into winter
quarters at Stoke-on-Trent. The Colonel returned to Wyoming and
the TE Ranch. The season summed up 333 performances, with one
canceled. Street parades had numbered only seven.[3]

The 1904 season opened at Stoke-on-Trent on April 25. Most of
May was spent in Wales and Cornwall, then the show turned back
toward London and its suburbs, playing Windsor, York, and New-
castle-on-Tyne. On July 20 it entered Scotland. Its engagement in
Glasgow August 1 to 6 was rated its biggest week as a traveling
show, being exceeded only at the Chicago Columbian Exposition
in 1893. Business at Edinburgh was also big. The Wild West returned to England at Carlyle on September 15. The final performance was at Hanley, closing one of its best seasons. Winter quarters
were again at Stoke-on-Trent. The Colonel returned to Wyoming,
for an enjoyable hunt in the Rockies and a less enjoyable divorce
hearing in February and March.

The season of 1905 in France was one of ups and downs. As it
had cost $150,000 to winter the show, it was fortunate that the ups
came first. The Paris engagement from April 2 to June 4 was called
the most prosperous in tent history. The program was the most
elaborate ever issued for the show, devoting eighty pages to *Le
Dernier des Grands Éclaireurs,* a biography of Cody by René
d'Hubert with a title that clearly infringed that of Helen Cody
Wetmore's volume.

[3] Charles Eldridge Griffin, *Four Years in Europe with Buffalo Bill;* Jake Posey,
"With Buffalo Bill in Europe," *Bandwagon* (October, 1953); *Letters from Buffalo
Bill,* 51–58.

The twenty-four events included maneuvers of artillery and exercises of cavalry, of Arabs, Japanese, Cossacks, Zouaves, and French and English soldiery, as well as of veterans of the Sixth United States Cavalry and the Tenth United States Cavalry. The spectacle was again *"Le Dernier Combat du General Custer."* There were also the Pony Express, *"Un convoi d'émigrants travers-ant les plaines," "Attaque du Dead Wood Mail Coach,"* and cow-boy *"divertissements."* Johnny Baker was shooting headliner and equestrian director. Joe Esquival was chief of cowboys, while Vincent Orapeza, champion of the lasso, was chief of the *vaqueros.*

The war chief and head of all Indians in the show was now, and for subsequent years, Iron Tail, called the Indian on the buffalo nickel—James Earle Fraser once explained that he used both Iron Tail and Two Moon as models for the coin. In French translation Iron Tail was *Queue de Fer.* Others named in the program were Hard Whip, chief of the Cheyennes, as *Tape Dure;* Comes First of the Oglalas as *Premier Arrivé;* Black Heart of the Arapahoes as *Cœur Noir;* Blue Shield of the Brulés as *Bouclier Bleu;* and Lone Bear of the Indian Police as *Ours Solitaire.* Luther Standing Bear reveals that all was not on the up-and-up in these tribal designations. As interpreter in England in 1902, he had charge of seventy-five Sioux who were divided into four tribes so that each tribe would have horses of one color. Thus some Sioux played the parts of Arapahoes and Cheyennes.[4]

A ticket costing 50 centimes (really a thin dime, or 9.65 cents) admitted the bearer to the "Annexe," or side show, where he could see Mlle Octavia, snake charmer; Princess Nouma Hawa, twenty-one years old and only fifty centimeters tall, less than one foot, eight inches; Aaron Moore, an enormous giant Negro who topped two meters, fifty centimeters, or eight feet, two and one-half inches; Fred Walters, the blue man; and Professor Griffin, sword swallower. G. A. Giovannis offered trained birds and monkeys, and there were also a monkey theater, Professor Sackatto's trained hares, a troupe of Chinese acrobats and contortionists, and the Zeldas, magicians.

One-day stands followed at Chartres, Alençon, Fleury, St. Lô,

[4] Luther Standing Bear, *My People the Sioux* (ed. by E. A. Brininstool), 245–72; Program, Paris, 1905.

and Cherbourg; with two days at Rouen and Havre, then Arras, Douai, Calais, Boulogne, Armentières, and the first four days of July at Lille. Bailey made his last visit to the show at Lille on July 4. After three days at Reims there were stops at Charleville, Sedan, Verdun, Luneville, and Belfort, while Lyons held the show for ten days. On August 20 the Shah of Persia was a visitor at Vichy. Marseille was played November 1 to 12, the season closing there. Cody did not escape competition. J. T. McCaddon's International Shows, featuring a Wild West, billed towns ahead of the Buffalo Bill show, but Cody beat them so soundly that the rival show collapsed and its owner fled to England to escape his creditors. It reminded Bill of his victory over Doc Carver's show "when he jumped in ahead of me in 1885. And tryed to take my route away from me. Well I followed right behind him. And billed and advertised the same towns he did. And kept it up until I broke him. And he was sold out at sheriff sale. Well I have done the very same thing with this Maccaddore Circus & Wild West, they were sold out two days ago."[5] But the fight was costly.

Even more expensive was an outbreak of glanders among the broncos, first noticed on July 10. In one day forty-two horses were shot by order of the government, and by the end of the season two hundred of the three hundred horses in the show had been destroyed. For many days Jake Posey, boss hostler, drove twelve horses each day to an incinerator near Marseille. Cody and the show were heavily in debt at the end of the season, but the serious blow was the death of Bailey on March 22, 1906. Among his effects was found a note for $12,000, signed by Cody in the show's more prosperous days in London. Cody said he had paid it, and if he said so, he had. This note, his other debts, and the knowledge that Mrs. Bailey and the other heirs were mainly interested in getting out of show business hung over Cody's head for three years. He no longer talked of retirement after one more good season—he planned for five years more, pointing out that sixty-four was the age of retirement of his army friends.

At Marseille on March 4, 1906, before Bailey's death, the show experienced the biggest opening week of the European tour. It moved on to Nice, then into Italy at Genoa, La Spezia, Livorno,

[5] *Letters from Buffalo Bill,* 65; Cody's spelling or handwriting.

and Rome. In April, Cody felt sufficiently prosperous to give $5,000 to the victims of the eruption of Mount Vesuvius and $1,000 to the sufferers of the San Francisco earthquake and fire. The Austro-Hungarian Empire was entered on May 12 at Trieste. Agram (Zagreb) and Graz were good for two days each, and Vienna for three weeks. From Vienna, Cody sent an agent to New York to arrange for railway transportation for his farewell tours of America—and he put "tours" in the plural. In Europe he used fifty cars, each fifty-four feet long and eight feet wide, moved in three sections. There were twenty-two flats, eighteen orange stock cars, nine red sleepers, including one box sleeper, and an advance car.

A stop at Budapest was followed by a month of one-day stands in Hungary. A brief excursion across the Russian border was discouraging, but business picked up again in August in Germany. Bill was boasting the best-behaved company he had ever had—"No swearing or drinking in my Company since I got good." The tour included Zittau, Weimar, Eisenach, Fulda, Hanau, Saarbrücken, Metz, Luxemburg, and München-Gladbach. On September 10 the show crossed into Belgium at Verviers, playing Namur, Charleroi, Mons, four days in Brussels, two days in Antwerp, and two in Ghent. The season closed in Arles, France, on October 30.[6]

By November 23, Cody was back in New York, writing Julia from his office in the Bailey Building, "I am very busy as I have no partner I must put the show together alone. So I will be here some time. I am at My desk every morning at 8 30 and work all day. And office work is not my fort."[7] That the Colonel was fully capable of managing his own affairs when necessity arose is demonstrated in his 1907 program, which was a return to first principles. Gone were the battle of San Juan Hill, the siege of Peking, the side show, and other concessions to the circus and to the contemporary.

The spectacle was the Battle of Summit Springs, going back to 1869 for an Indian fight in which Bill had participated and which historically had dramatic possibilities. General Carr and other former officers of the Fifth Cavalry were asked for their recollections of the fight, for use in heralds, couriers, and programs.

Nothing could be more in the character of the Wild West of

[6] *Ibid.*, 67; Griffin, *Four Years in Europe with Buffalo Bill.*
[7] *Letters from Buffalo Bill*, 68.

dime novel and melodrama than the scene thus described in the program: "The Great Train Hold-up and Bandit Hunters of the Union Pacific will be a scene representing a train hold-up in the Western wilds. The bandits stop the train, uncouple the engine from the coaches, rob the express car and blow open the safe. Meanwhile the passengers are lined up and despoiled of their valuables. The scene ends with the arrival of the Bandit Hunters of the Union Pacific, who capture or kill the robbers." It was billed as "a real passenger train pulled by a practical locomotive," but an honest press agent explained: "To transport and operate a real railroad engine would, of course, be out of the question, but an adequate substitute had been found in the application of a motor car to the purpose. What conforms to the driving wheels of the car are in reality the driving wheels of the locomotive, increased to a size which conforms, together with the tender and cars, to a faithful reproduction of the locomotive and cars in vogue during the earlier days. The engine and cars are in every way practical and form a unit capable of carrying a train-load of passengers over the rough country roads and fields which our exhibition must of necessity travel upon and through." Mechanical effects, including puffings of the engine, black smoke, and an electric headlight, were devised by Miller Reese Hutchison, president of the Universal Motor Car Company of New York, and made by the Funk Engineering Company of Hoboken.[8]

With this show Buffalo Bill opened the 1907 season in Madison Square Garden and toured for two years of numerous one-day stands—the only two years of his life he operated without a partner. He owned only one-third of the show, and that third was heavily mortgaged. The Salsbury share had been taken over by the Bailey heirs. They were the widow, Mrs. Ruth L. Bailey; her brother, Joseph T. McCaddon; W. W. Cole, famed circus man long associated with Barnum & Bailey; and Albert A. Stewart, of the Strobridge Lithographing Company. They formed the Bailey Estate Trust, which sold the Bailey interest in Adam Forepaugh and Sells Brothers to its co-owners, Ringling Brothers, in 1906. The next year the Ringlings bought the badly run-down Barnum and Bailey

[8] *The Rough Rider*, Vol. IV (1907); program, 1907; courier, 1907.

show. Negotiation with Cody was hampered by the dispute over the note he said he had paid. The Bailey Estate sounded out Major Gordon W. Lillie on a merger with his Pawnee Bill show.[9]

Those who have written of Cody's partnerships, including the partners themselves, have depicted astute businessmen who kept the show going despite Cody's wild investments and irresponsible extravagances. Yet the same show program that advertised "Homes in the Big Horn Basin, Shoshone Irrigation Company, W. F. Cody, President" not only revealed that Salsbury was a director in this project, but also gave equal space to "The Reservation at Salsbury Beach, Long Branch—apply for terms and particulars to Nate Salsbury, 30 West 96th Street, New York." If it cost Cody $50,000 to mistake other attractions of Katherine Clemmons for acting ability, it was Salsbury who made a similarly bad investment in *Black America*.

Major Lillie was no slouch at throwing money around, nor had he a continuously successful record in show business. His first venture in 1888 failed dismally, despite the aid of Annie Oakley. He tried again in 1890, and by 1893, Pawnee Bill's Historical Wild West, Mexican Hippodrome, Indian Museum, and Grand Fireworks Exhibition boasted three hundred men and women and two hundred horses, specifying "beautious, dashing, daring and laughing Western girls who ride better than any other women in the world." In 1894 he took his show to the International Industrial and Fine Arts Exhibition at Antwerp. According to Lillie himself, his mistake was in touring Belgium afterward. In that small country everyone with money enough to see a show had been to the fair. His animals and equipment were seized; he was rescued by a speculator who took a chance that the show would do better in Holland. It did. Queen Wilhelmina patronized it, and Lillie made enough to get home. He was threatened with foreclosure before the 1895 season opened on account of debts contracted to get the show going. Another backer came to the rescue, and that season Lillie paid off his debts. In 1905 he enlarged his show as Pawnee Bill's Historic Far West and Great Far East. This was the origin of the "Far East"; he never had a show called "Pawnee Bill's Far

[9] Richard E. Conover, "Notes on the Barnum & Bailey Show," *Bandwagon* (March–April, 1959).

East," which became his end of the combination title. After the 1907 season, Lillie sold his trains and wagons and billed his show for the entire season of 1908 at Wonderland Park, Boston.

Parallel with Cody's investment in Cody, Wyoming, was Pawnee Bill's in Pawnee, Oklahoma. There he was president of the Arkansas Valley National Bank, chairman of the Board of Trade, donor of a $55,000 schoolhouse, head of the school board, and director in many enterprises. His Buffalo Ranch was so named because he kept on it a herd of buffalo and thus gained some credit as a preserver of that animal. More profitable were his herds of two hundred to three hundred Angora goats and three hundred to four hundred mules. There, at a time when Cody was burying his money in the mine at Oracle, his partner Lillie invested in a $75,000 Bungalow—that type of house was new then, and the word was capitalized. At its grand opening in 1910, publicity experts Burke, Cooke, and Winch estimated the furnishings and ornaments at $100,000 to $200,000, including especially commissioned paintings by Charles Schreyvogel, E. W. Deming, Charles H. Stephens, E. W. Lenders, and H. H. Cross.[10]

In June, 1908, Lillie broached the subject of merger to Cody at Keene, New Hampshire, but gave up after Cody flatly refused to consider changing the name of the show to include Pawnee Bill. In friendly shop talk on the show's routing, Lillie said he had always found business bad in New England after June 20 and forecast an upturn in New York, despite haying season, and advised Cody to set up all his extra seats when he got to Michigan. All of these suggestions proved accurate, and when the first Michigan city filled all the seats on a rainy day, Cody was ready to team up with Lillie. A further incentive was that Cody had been having trouble with Cooke, general manager representing the Bailey estate, and in a fit of temper, had knocked Cooke down. The Bailey heirs threatened to close the show unless Cody apologized. He did, and probably was ready to admit he was wrong, as he usually regretted his occasional flare-ups.

The show title agreed upon was "Buffalo Bill's Wild West com-

[10] Shirley, *Pawnee Bill*, 133–47; De Wolff, *Pawnee Bill*, 45–49; Souvenir, Pawnee Bill's Historic Wild West, 1893?; souvenir of Buffalo Ranch and Its Owners, 1911.

bined with Pawnee Bill's Great Far East," affectionately shortened by those who took part in it to the "Two Bills Show." Lillie toiled on plans at winter headquarters in Bridgeport, the former Barnum headquarters, and at offices in the Bailey Building, Twenty-eighth Street and Broadway, New York. One night he saw *Via Wireless*, an elaborately staged melodrama produced by the Shuberts. He hunted out the artist responsible for the settings and ordered scenery and stage effects. Besides costing $7,700, three times what he expected, his scenic piece left no room in Madison Square Garden for the entrance of the Deadwood stagecoach, covered wagons, and artillery. For three days they struggled with the problem; Cooke reported Cody in tears, and Johnny Baker, arena director, hostile. Lillie made his peace with Baker, and between them they worked out a fast-moving show. General Miles and the governors of New York and New Jersey attended the opening. The new show was a big success, with the huge Garden sold out for the last two weeks of the run.

Then the Bailey heirs lowered the boom on Lillie. They demanded that he discharge Cooke, the very man over whom they had threatened to close out Cody, and Burke, objecting that too much had been spent on advertising and publicity. Unlike Salsbury, Lillie had a high opinion of Burke's abilities as press agent; moreover, he had promised Cody that Burke and Baker would not be disturbed. The Bailey heirs contended that Lillie should pay no attention to Cody, since they controlled his one-third interest through notes and bill of sale. Lillie was trapped. He had paid $50,000 for a one-third interest, assuming he had only to get along with Cody. Instead, he was outvoted two to one. After threatening legal action, the Bailey estate offered to sell out for $66,666.66, which put a valuation of $100,000 on the show and indicated they had cheated Lillie in the original deal. However, Lillie accepted the offer after demanding that they cancel Cody's disputed note for $12,000. Despite all their sharp practice, Lillie got a bargain, for the show grossed $60,000 at its next stand in Philadelphia.[11]

Lillie was now sole owner, but he treated Cody with great generosity. He gave Cody the canceled note, declined interest on other notes he had taken over, and proposed that they be equal partners,

[11] Shirley, *Pawnee Bill*, 177–91.

with Cody's share to be paid out of earnings. Lillie recognized, as the Bailey heirs never did, that the show's great asset was Buffalo Bill himself; without him, its physical property was of little more value than what Lillie had had before the merger.

In the program the Great Far East had a far less important place than in the title and billing; it was merely the seventh episode in a total of eighteen. It was a show within a show, "a dream of the Orient," with a camel caravan, Rossi's Musical Elephants, acrobatics by Bedouin Arabs and Imperial Japanese, Australian boomerang throwers, Singhalese and Russian dancers, a Hindu fakir who "caused a beautiful young lady of the Orient to gracefully float in the air without any visible means of support," and Whirling Dervishes, Dahomeans, South Sea natives, Soudanese, Moors, Persians, Musselmen, and Syrians, making up "An Ethnological Congress of Strange Tribes, Clans, Races, and Nations of Peculiar People." Still it was very like a circus.

Of seventeen other episodes, only one offered anything new to patrons of Buffalo Bill's Wild West. This was "Football on Horseback . . . seen with this exhibition for the first time in any arena." It was played with a round ball, some five feet in diameter. Indians and cowboys were opponents; when a signal was given, horses rushed forward and "with a sharp, quick turn," struck the ball "with their chest to the right and left," while the goal defenders tried to halt progress by surrounding the ball. There were few rules, but it was spectacular and long a popular feature.

The Battle of Summit Springs, the Great Train Hold-up, Devlin's Zouaves, and other acts were an almost exact repetition of the Buffalo Bill program of the previous year, and much of it could have been seen any year since 1883. From the Pawnee Bill show came one star, Mexican Joe, lasso expert. He was José Barrera of San Antonio, who had been with Pawnee Bill since 1898.

More Far East acts were added in 1910. Rhoda Royal, who at some times had circuses under his own name, showed twenty high-school horses. Ray Thompson had Texas range horses manège-trained in circus-type performance. Maximilian Gruber and Miss Adeline—she had won a Paris beauty contest—used an elephant, a horse, and a Shetland pony. Mr. and Mrs. Bert Davis were the clowns "Uncle Joe" and "Aunt Malinda." Herr Schmergel's musical elephants, with beautiful Dalmatian lady accompanists, replaced the $1,000-a-week Rossi troupe.

If Lillie considered Cody's desire for retirement a motive in his acceptance of the merger, he dismissed the idea when he found that Cody was in no financial condition to retire. He probably knew that Cody had planned to retire "after just one more good season" every year since 1872. However, in 1910, the year set by Cody long in advance, all publicity was directed toward that end. Posters and Programs were blazoned, "Buffalo Bill Bids You Good Bye." Pawnee Bill was groomed as successor, and dime novels poured from the presses featuring Pawnee Bill as the faithful companion of Buffalo Bill. In overlooking the seriousness with which Cody took all this, Lillie made an error that led to eventual disaster.

A "Valedictory, Personal Announcement" said, "This farewell visit will positively be my last appearance in person, in the towns and cities of the present tour," concluding, "on the honor of Buffalo Bill . . . my present visit will positively be my last 'Hail and farewell' in the saddle, to you all." A slightly later version hedged a bit: "I have determined to retire from active service at the expiration of a final and complete tour of the American continent. Therefore, following a series of 'Farewell Exhibitions' which I hope to give in 1910 and 1911, I shall personally abandon the arena." A still later version substituted the years "1911 and 1912." Eventually loopholes were sought in the "series" of farewell exhibitions and even in the phrase "in the saddle." But Cody himself meant it when he made his farewell speech at the end of the Madison Square Garden engagement in May, 1910.

He said: "I am about to go home for a well-earned rest. Out in the West I have my horses, my buffaloes, my sturdy, staunch old Indian friends—my home and my green fields, but I never see them green. When my season is over the hillsides and the meadows have been blighted by a wintry frost and the sere and yellow leaves cover the ground. I want to see nature in its prime, to enjoy a rest from active life. My message to you to-night is one of farewell. Thirty years ago you gave me my first welcome here. I am grateful for your continued loyal devotion to me. During that time many of my friends among you and many of those with me have been long since gathered to the great unknown arena of another life—there

450

are only a few of us left. When I went away from here each year before I merely said good night—this time it will mean good-bye. To my little friends in the gallery and the grown-ups who used to sit there, I thank you once again. God bless you all—good-bye."

Frank Winch reports, "There was not a dry eye in the Garden," but it is strange that this tearful record appears in his book written as publicity matter for an extension of the series of "farewell exhibitions" through 1912, including more last appearances in Madison Square Garden.[12]

The show's take in 1910 was one million dollars, of which $400,-000 was profit. Lillie put a good share of his in the new Bungalow at Buffalo Ranch, then sold a friend of his, Thomas Smith, of Beaver Falls, Pennsylvania, a share in the show for $40,000, with which they bought the show's winter quarters and equipment from the Ringling Brothers. Cody spent most of the winter at the Oracle mine and left most of his share of the profits there.

On May 24, 1911, a rail wreck near Lowell, Massachusetts, scattered Wild West and Far East over the landscape. The congress of strange people lassoed and rounded up elephants, camels, and buffalo, paraded into Lowell, and set up tents without missing a performance. Business was poor in New England mill towns. As the show swung into the South in September and October, it struck four weeks of bad weather and heavy losses. Cody suffered from *la grippe* and was miserable. With profits low, he offered to sell Scout's Rest Ranch to Lillie for $100,000. Of this, $80,000 went to Mrs. Cody and $20,000 toward Cody's debt of $30,000 to Lillie. The rest was covered by a transfer to Lillie of a $10,000 mortgage on the Irma Hotel. Through this deal Cody was actually half-owner of the show at the end of 1911—and the Arizona mine was producing and selling tungsten ore.

In 1912 the show's profits came to $125,000. That was not enough for Cody. At Oracle, production costs had proved too heavy for profitable operation. The Colonel actually did retire at the close of the 1912 season, but he could not make it stick.[13]

[12] Winch, *Thrilling Lives of Buffalo Bill and Pawnee Bill*, 217–24.
[13] *Letters from Buffalo Bill*, 70–73; Shirley, *Pawnee Bill*, 199–206; Walsh, *The Making of Buffalo Bill*.

ADDED TO AND GIVEN WITH A CIRCUS

HARRY H. TAMMEN AND FREDERICK G. BONFILS were probably the most amoral and unscrupulous partners ever to publish a newspaper. Tammen, born in Baltimore, started work at the age of seven as porter's helper in a beer garden and at twenty-one was head bartender in the Palmer House, Chicago. He went to the Windsor in Denver in the same capacity, and Cody probably first knew him there. Tammen quit bartending to open a free museum and curio shop. On a visit to Chicago he met Bonfils, who had a sizable stake made in an illicit lottery. They bought the *Denver Post* in 1894, furbished it with red and black headlines, and made it noisy, vulgar, and highly successful. Within ten years it had the most circulation and profits of any newspaper in Denver.[1]

Tammen, an instinctive showman, bought a dog and pony show. The name of the Post's sports editor, Otto C. Floto, had a circus sound to Tammen, so it became the Floto Dog and Pony Show. It prospered, and Tammen sought for it an imposing and traditional circus name. He found a William Sells, bought his name, and the dog and pony show became the Sells-Floto Circus. Its posters and bills bore portraits of sports editor Floto and the four Sells brothers, recently of the Adam Forepaugh and Sells Brothers, purchased from the Bailey estate by Ringling Brothers and discon-

[1] Fowler, *Timberline*, 38, 46–48.

tinued when they found Barnum and Bailey equipment too run down to put both big circuses on the road. However, the Ringlings had no desire to see a name for which they had paid heavily used in competition against them. In 1909 they filed a suit in equity against the Sells-Floto Circus and Tammen and Bonfils personally, seeking to restrain them from using the name Sells. The court held that no law could prevent William Sells from attaching his name to a circus, but it enjoined Tammen and Bonfils from using the portraits of Lewis, Ephraim, Peter, and Allen Sells. This partial victory is said to have cost Tammen and Bonfils $260,000.

Having picked a fight with the most powerful circus combination, Tammen and Bonfils had no intention of stopping. Their slogan, "Not in the circus trust," met with some sympathy, for the Ringlings also could be high-handed. Tammen persuaded some cities to adopt a circus license based on number of railroad cars. This worked out that Sells-Floto paid $300 to Ringling's $5,000. When Ringling Brothers sought to play Denver, Tammen said blandly, "We own a circus and we don't want any other circus coming to town. The mayor does what we tell him to do."[2] In the course of this battle, Tammen cast his eye on Buffalo Bill's Wild West and Pawnee Bill's Far East as a large show independently owned that would add strength to his side of the argument. It was a baleful eye for Cody.

At the end of the 1912 season, Cody discovered that the gold and tungsten of Oracle was insufficient to finance his retirement. His debts had been reduced, but he still owed too much to quit show business. Lillie had been advancing the cost of keeping the show in winter quarters, $40,000, collecting Cody's share from later earnings. This winter he asked Cody to try to raise $20,000. While visiting his sister Mrs. Decker in Denver, the Colonel met Tammen, always genial and friendly. It took no time at all for Tammen to learn that Cody was shopping for a loan and less for Tammen to lend Cody $20,000 for six months at 6 per cent.

An announcement in the *Denver Post* on February 5, 1913, stated: "Colonel W. F. Cody (Buffalo Bill) put his name to a contract with the proprietors of the Sells-Floto Circus, the gist of

2 Bob Taber, "Ringling and Sells-Floto Battles," *Bandwagon* (March–April, 1959).

which is that these two big shows consolidate for the season of 1914 and thereafter. The Pawnee Bill interests now associated with Colonel Cody's Wild West Show are not included in this agreement—the idea being that the Sells-Floto Circus shall continue in its entirety and the 'Buffalo Bill Exposition of Frontier Days and the Passing of the West' with the historic incidents associated with them, shall also be preserved, added to, and given with the circus performance."[3]

That announcement is devious on its face. Tammen first says the two shows are consolidated, then in the next breath says they are not. His long-winded designation indicates that he is not claiming the title, "Buffalo Bill's Wild West"—perhaps he had learned something in the Sells litigation—but implies that he has acquired Cody's personal services. It appeared that Cody had disposed of his share of the partnership in return for the loan. The legality of such an arrangement is doubtful, as Lillie, after a threat of foreclosure because of a forgotten debt of Cody's, had incorporated the show in New Jersey.

When Lillie asked what it was all about, Cody telegraphed, "Pay no attention to press reports; I have done nothing that will interfere with our show." Eager as he was to retire, it is unlikely he would have knowingly signed such an agreement. It might have been a condition he assumed would be canceled when the loan was paid—or perhaps Cody did not read the agreement he signed and did not know what the conditions were. A good guess is that no such agreement had been signed or mentioned anywhere except in the *Denver Post*.

Tammen's ways were devious. Such an agreement was of no immediate importance to him. The important thing was that Lillie believed Cody had signed it, and Lillie reacted just as Tammen expected. Convinced that Cody had double-crossed him and would leave at the end of the season, he refused to worry further about Cody's debts. In a simple partnership he could have been held responsible for them, but since the show had been incorporated, he felt safe in leaving Cody to get out of his scrape the best way he could.

Tammen, however, could not have foreseen the difficulties the

[3] *Letters from Buffalo Bill*, 73–76; Fowler, *Timberline*, 376.

show faced that year. Its last tour started with bad routing, and 1913 was a flood year. In early spring the show ran into cold and freezing rains in a South poverty stricken by cheap cotton. Twice canvas was blown down by high winds. Cody was seriously ill in Knoxville. For a hundred successive stands the show lost money—one matinee in good weather netted only $7.15. The Indians saw the handwriting on the wall—or the leanness of fare in the dining tent—and deserted in such numbers that for the first time Colonel McCune was sent to Pine Ridge to recruit in mid-season. By the time he had signed up replacements, there was nowhere for them to go.[4]

The biggest blunder, next to Cody's borrowing from Tammen, was Lillie's scheduling Denver. To appear in Tammen's bailiwick on July 21, within a few days of the due date on Cody's note, was asking for trouble for Cody, and apparently Lillie was so angry at Cody that he did not care—which was what Tammen had counted on. Lillie admits he was warned what would happen; a friend in the United States Printing and Lithographing Company said Tammen controlled, and would foreclose, the show's note for $60,000, owed for the customary posters, programs, and other show paper printed at the beginning of each season. Lillie would not believe that Tammen would wreck the show, not realizing that all Tammen wanted from it was Buffalo Bill himself.

Legal advisers of the *Denver Post* were among attorneys for the lithographers that took court action. When Cody saw sheriff's men on the lot, he sent Thomas A. Smith to the ticket window to get the day's receipts, in the hope of paying off the show people, but the sheriff's men got there first. Some Indians had to sell their show costumes to get back to the reservation. A well-wisher sent Cody $500; Cody applied all of it to helping stranded workers.

Lillie rushed off to New Jersey to file a petition in bankruptcy, but was forestalled when Denver attorneys filed a petition in involuntary bankruptcy for two creditors claiming $340 for merchandise and $36 for stock feed. The *Denver Post* assailed Lillie for refusing to apply his interests in Cody's North Platte property and the Hotel Irma to the show's debt. Cody was induced to sue Lillie

[4] Maurice Frink, "Buffalo Bill's Last Raid on the Sioux," *Denver Post* (*Empire Magazine*), August 26, 1957; *Letters from Buffalo Bill*, 73-74.

for an accounting and to ask that their partnership be dissolved. Tammen attached the show for Cody's $20,000 note. The trap was complete; Lillie was blocked at every turn. While he managed to save much of his personal fortune, he never succeeded in making a comeback in show business.

At a deferred auction on September 15, two friends of Cody's bid against each other for his horse "Isham," knocked down at $150 to Colonel C. J. Bills, of Lincoln, who sent it to TE Ranch for Cody. The Pawnee Bill band wagon, with gilded wood carving depicting the landing of Columbus on one side and Pocahontas rescuing Captain John Smith on the other, brought $250, harness included. Colonel Cody's spider phaeton went for $30.00; a prairie schooner, $20.00; baggage wagons, $150.00 apiece. Cody's silver-mounted saddle sold for $25.00; Lillie's for $50.00; McClellan cowboy saddles, $2.50 and $1.00; Indian pads and bridles, 25 cents apiece. Eight oxen brought $780. Also sold were 144 horses, 6 camels, 4 sacred cows, and 11 burros. Among the buyers were the Miller Brothers 101 Ranch, the Bison motion picture company, and F. W. Biddle, circus man. Tammen bought only a pair of black mules.[5]

Cody once referred to Tammen as "the man who had my show sold at sheriff sale, which broke my heart."[6] The colonel was old, ill—only four years from his death—and tired. In the last season he dropped his shooting act from horseback, appearing in the show seated in his spider phaeton. Last-minute efforts to save the show must have taken much out of him. As he went to TE Ranch—to see it in summer for the first time—he might seem broken, washed up, through, finished.

He was nothing of the sort; instead, he made an immediate and startling comeback. He turned down an offer to appear in variety in London at $2,500 a week, demanding $5,000. Tammen, still as affable as when he persuaded Cody to sign the note that ruined him, forwarded "with love and good cheer" an offer to appear in motion pictures. Cody refused, but it gave him an idea—a series of historical films depicting events in his life and the Old West with the original cast, so far as available. He took the idea to Tammen

---

[5] *Denver Republican*, August 22, September 16, 1913; *Bandwagon* (September–October, 1958), 9–10; Fowler, *Timberline*, 377–81.
[6] *Letters from Buffalo Bill*, 76.

and Bonfils, and they fell in with it. The Secretary of War was visiting Denver, and he approved the use of army troops for the project. General Miles, now retired, enthusiastically offered to take part. The Secretary of the Interior permitted use of Pine Ridge Reservation and agency Indians. The Essanay Film Company of Chicago helped in organizing "The Col. W. F. Cody (Buffalo Bill) Historical Pictures Company."

Essanay meant "S" and "A." The "S" was George K. Spoor, who started making movies in 1895 when they were first projected on a screen. In 1903 a woman in Denver inquired whether he could supply a film a day. He asked Tammen, an old acquaintance, to investigate. Tammen reported the request came from the owner of a storeroom theater who planned to show motion pictures exclusively for five cents' admission. Previous demand for film had been for fillers in vaudeville or for advertising promotion. Tammen's report encouraged Spoor to step up production.

The "A" was Gilbert M. Anderson. In 1903 he directed and had a small part in *The Great Train Robbery*, the first movie that told a story and the first Western film. It was shown in tents, in storerooms, and along with vaudeville bills. Nickelodeons, like the one in Denver, sprang up everywhere. In 1907, Anderson became Spoor's partner. At their Argyle Street studio in Chicago he took male leads, directing and producing as he went along. He took a company on location in Wyoming and became Broncho Billy Anderson, first of Western film stars. In making six hundred Broncho Billy films in Wyoming and later at Niles, California, he had a large share in the creation of the cowboy legend. It was logical that Essanay should line up the old master who had invented the glamour of the West.[7]

By early fall of 1913 all was ready for picture-making at Pine Ridge. The Twelfth Cavalry, six hundred strong, was there, as were General Miles and other Indian Wars veterans—Generals Frank Baldwin and Jesse M. Lee and Colonel Marion P. Maus. Leading the Indians were Short Bull, No Neck, Woman's Dress, Flat Iron, and others who had been in Buffalo Bill's Wild West. Again the

[7] Carl Guldager, "Movie Pioneer in Flashback to When Industry Was Born," *Chicago Daily News*, October 9, 1943; Jack McPhaul, "Movies First Cowboy Star Recalls His Work in Chicago," *Chicago Sun-Times*, April 29, 1951; Museum of Modern Art Film Library, Series I, Program I, *The Great Train Robbery*.

signal for the dash that led to Cody's killing Yellow Hand was given by Lieutenant King—now General King, for he had commanded a brigade in the Philippine Insurrection. The Battle of Wounded Knee, last of the spectacles in the Two Bills Show, was staged again, but more authentically, for General Miles insisted on exact fidelity. It is said that he demanded that the six hundred cavalrymen march past the cameras until the eleven thousand of his 1891 command had been recorded—but that some of the marching was past cameras in which no film was turning.

Eight one-reel subjects were made, sometimes billed for eight successive Saturday afternoons. The "Historical Pictures" created no great sensation, but neither had Sarah Bernhardt's *Queen Elizabeth* the previous year. It was a time when nickelodeons filled their seats by showing anything that moved, and the Buffalo Bill pictures moved as much as the rest of them.

Cody went out for the 1914 season with Sells-Floto Circus and Buffalo Bill's Wild West—Two Big Institutions Joined Together at One Price of Admission—twenty-five cents. The Colonel got $100 a day, plus 40 per cent of receipts above $3,000. He introduced the show from the saddle, but did no shooting or other acts. He spent much time in promotion, meeting newspapermen and prominent citizens. He drew much of his pay in advance, hoping to keep ahead of debts, although still optimistic for his Arizona mine and Wyoming investments. Johnny Baker went to London to shoot in the Anglo-American Exhibition, and while there sought to interest English capital in the mine at Oracle and to get bookings for Historical Pictures.

In April and May, Cody boasted of good health; but when the season closed in October, he was so ill that he went directly to his sister's home in Denver. There he recovered quickly and went to the TE Ranch, where he killed a deer by moonlight. He spent the winter scheming new ways to make money to pay his debts. One idea was a dude ranch at De Maris Springs. On February 26, 1915, old friends gathered to pay their tribute and express their faith in him on his sixty-ninth birthday.

While still sick in Denver, Cody had been persuaded by Tammen to sign up for another season. By this time Cody should have learned to take a close look at anything offered for his signature by

Tammen, but the Colonel afterward said that he had failed to notice that this time the 40 per cent was for receipts above $3,100 instead of $3,000. Since he signed up again, under not quite so much compulsion, it is probable he had not had too bad a time. That is the opinion of Karl L. King, then bandmaster with the show. He says, "Colonel Cody was with Sells-Floto for the two *full* seasons of 1914 and 1915. I was mailman on the show in addition to being bandmaster, so saw him every day. He kept pretty much to himself in his private dressing tent. Had a certain amount of dignity about him that I admired. Was a handsome man for his age and still looked wonderful on a horse. He made a definite impression on me, and it is one of my favorite memories of my years in show business. In other words I liked the old boy."

King composed and dedicated to Cody an intermezzo, *Passing of the Red Man*. King also composed *On the Warpath* for the Indian number and *Wyoming Days* for the cowboy riding act. Merle Evans, bandmaster in the 1916 show, recalls that Cody liked *Passing of the Red Man*, and "used to come to the band stand during the concert with the Wild West show and ask me to play it for him."[8] Another loyal friend was the Sells-Floto press agent, Courtney Ryley Cooper, outstanding writer on the circus—he grew up in show business.

The season of 1915 proved a nightmare. The show opened on April 13; by May 27, Cody could report only four days of sunshine. That meant no percentage profits, but he was getting his one hundred dollars a day, he was in good health, and he was treated with consideration, having a private car with a porter, a cook, and a carriage driver. Lulu was with him, and no additional charges were made for her.

When the admission price was upped from 25 to 50 cents, he was hopeful that the increase would bring in some of his 40 per cent. However, he discovered that old advertising was being used and that patrons expecting to see a twenty-five cent show were held up for double the price. Cody called this graft and robbery and warned press agents and advance men not to use his name or

---

[8] Karl L. King to Don Russell, June 10, 1954, December 29, 1958; K. L. King, *Passing of the Red Man* (Oskaloosa, Ia., 1916); K. L. King, *On the Warpath* (Oskaloosa, Ia., 1915); Merle Evans to Gene Russell, October, 1958.

picture in connection with any such misleading advertising.

At Fort Madison, Iowa, the show lot was near a swamp, and was flooded by a sudden storm that endangered a thousand women and children. The Colonel and only five of the show crew stayed to carry out the children and help the women, while the rest of the four hundred circus men fled in a panic that threatened to stampede the audience.

The main tent was old and its ropes were rotten. Cody feared it would fall down on an audience and that he would be blamed as an experienced showman who should have known it to be unsafe. When he threatened to leave the show unless conditions were corrected, Tammen sprang another legal bombshell.

As Cody told it: "After everything was sold of the Buffalo Bill-Pawnee Bill show at the sheriff's sale in Denver I asked him if he was satisfied. He said yes and that I should be satisfied as my debts were paid. I said are you paid in full he said yes. Now as I am going to leave him, I got a letter from him yesterday August 21 Saying that Lawyers and thieves had gotten away with all the money and I still owed him $20,000. And wanted to commence takeing it out of my wages. Such things won't let me get well. I haven't been well all summer. Of course I have got to see Tammen and I have got evidence enough to land him in the Penitentiary. . . . I may not stay with this show two weeks probly not a day. I am going to Denver to see Tammen. I expect to pull off a big hunt this fall but I am in such bad luck that might fall down—I am very tired nervous and discouraged."[9]

While the Colonel was writing wildly to old friends seeking help—and even Pawnee Bill tried to aid him, although a suit against Lillie in Cody's name was still pending in the courts—Tammen saw that he had stirred up more than he had bargained for. Cody did not have to go to Denver; Tammen came to Lawrence, Kansas, to see Cody—and when he got there, he was afraid to go in the Colonel's tent. And well he might have been, for there was fire in the old scout's eye, and he had written to a friend, "This man is driving me crazy. I can easily kill him but as I avoided killing in the bad days I don't want to kill him. But if there is no justice left I will."[10]

[9] *Letters from Buffalo Bill,* 76; Walsh, *The Making of Buffalo Bill,* 351–52.

Cody sat tight in his tent and made Tammen come to him, as he did after assurances that it would be safe to do so. The result was a compromise. Tammen got what was probably his only objective: the Colonel agreed to stay with the show to the end of the season. Tammen in return dropped all claims against Cody's $100 a day. He refused to make any commitment on the claim for the $20,000 debt and threatened to sue for $100,000 if Cody left before the end of the tour.

When the Sells-Floto-Buffalo Bill shows folded up the worn-out tent after the annual farewell dinner in Fort Worth, Texas, on October 14, 1915, Buffalo Bill boasted that he had never missed a performance, although the circus had given 366 shows in 183 days over a route that totaled 16,878 miles. He figured that the show owed him $18,000 on his percentage of profits, for business had been good toward the close of the tour, but he did not expect to collect it, and was glad to be through with Tammen even at that price. Actually he was not, quite.

Cody went on a lecture tour with his motion pictures, starting at New Rochelle, New York, on February 11, 1916, and ending in New York City on March 5. Tammen claimed an interest in the pictures, but was talked out of it by Spoor.

When Cody proposed to revive Buffalo Bill's Wild West, Tammen warned that he owned that name and planned to continue using it. He demanded $5,000 if the name "Buffalo Bill" appeared in any other show. Here is another of the strange contradictions in Tammen's nature. If he had any valid claim, the name was worth much more than $5,000. He had spent much more in money, time, and legal machinations in seeking to acquire it. He probably knew that he could not prove any such claim. He also knew that he and Cody could drag each other through courts indefinitely. The chances are that he wanted to be generous and let Cody off the hook—so he merely squeezed out one last petty sum from a highly profitable bargain.

During that winter Cody, as usual, cast about for other ways of making money—rather desperate ones at times, including his perennial optimism over the value of the mine at Oracle. He dabbled a little in oil. There was a proposal to sell prints of Rosa Bonheur's

[10] *Ibid.*, 352.

painting of him. And during that winter he wrote the series of articles for *Hearst's International* magazine that were published, not without editing and expansion, under the title, "The Great West That Was," beginning in August, 1916, and reprinted after his death as the last of his many autobiographies.

Wild West poster

depicting visit of King Edward VII and Queen Alexandra of England to the show on March 14, 1903. From a lithograph by Stafford & Co., Netherfield near Nottm., Eng., from a painting by Arthur Jule Goodman.

Cover of *New Buffalo Bill Weekly*, 1916

THE LAST STANDS

PREPAREDNESS WAS THE WATCHWORD in 1916. With the first world war in its second year, Americans were finding it ever more difficult to be "neutral in fact as well as in name," as President Wilson had urged at the outset, but almost all could agree on the necessity for "preparedness." Colonel Cody had talked it on his tour with the motion pictures and was unquestionably sincere in seeking to contribute in his own way to the patriotic cause. A "Pageant of Preparedness" was an obvious spectacle for a Wild West show. He proposed the idea to the Chief of Staff of the U.S. Army, Major General Hugh L. Scott, and got immediate approval and aid in recruiting soldiers on reserve furlough and in obtaining artillery pieces.

In casting about for a show, Cody sought backing to buy the Miller Brothers and Arlington 101 Ranch Wild West, which had a good reputation but never seemed quite sure of itself financially. The Millers had chosen 1914 to tour Europe, but at the outbreak of war horses and vehicles were impressed by the British government. They got back with a few trained animals. For the season of 1915 they signed up Jess Willard, Kansas cowboy who became world heavyweight champion by knocking out Jack Johnson on April 5 of that year. In 1916, Willard went to Sells-Floto, which suggests that Tammen might have swapped him for Buffalo Bill.

Cody failed to get a share in the ownership, but made a deal by which he was paid $100 a day and one-third of all profits over $2,750 daily—in one week he made $4,161.35. The show was billed "Miller & Arlington Wild West Show Co., present The Military Pageant Preparedness, 'Buffalo Bill' (himself) Combined with the 101 Ranch Shows." The Pageant of Preparedness featured batteries of field guns and charging cavalry. Madam Marantette and her high-jumping horses and Arabian and Japanese acrobats were on the program, but it was mainly "Real Wild West," as advertised, with Tommy Kirnan and Hank Durnell demonstrating the Pony Express and other familiar events. Cody found it a happy show; he wrote W. H. Curtis from Baltimore on May 31: "Say Billy its so different with this show—no friction. Johny Baker has full charge of the rear and Mr. Geo. Arlington and Mr. Bixby in front. I have full access all over. Parades out on time baring late arrieving, which no one can help. Our business fine. We had a capacity matinee and turned them away tonight."[1]

There was one city in the United States where the word "preparedness" held no magic that summer. That was Chicago, governed by the powerful Republican political machine of Mayor William Hale Thompson. "Big Bill" had discovered that Chicago was the "sixth German city in the world"; he already knew that all those German-American citizens had votes and that few French-Americans or Anglo-Americans lived in Chicago. He denounced the hue and cry for preparedness. The military pageant preparedness did not seem a good idea for that city, but some publicity genius found a solution. From August 19 to 27, Buffalo Bill (himself) Combined with the 101 Ranch Shows became the Chicago Shan-Kive and Round-up.

Shan-Kive was inadequately explained in the program as Indian for "a good time." Round-up meant rodeo, a term so little known in 1916 that the program interpreted its single mention: "Pendleton, Ore., and Cheyenne, Wyo., look forward to their annual fall round-up with the same eagerness as an Illinois farmer in the corn belt anticipates the county fair. At Los Angeles, Cal., the season would not be complete without the Rodeo, which is

[1] Cody to W. H. Curtis, Baltimore, May 31, 1916, photostat from Mr. Curtis.

another name for round-up. At Calgary and Winnipeg the big fall cowboy meet is called a stampede."

Turning the show into a rodeo followed a line of development that had been parallel since Buffalo Bill's Wild West originated in North Platte's 1882 Old Glory Blow Out, which was essentially a rodeo. Rodeo became a national institution with the world championships staged by Tex Austin in Chicago beginning in 1925 and those at Madison Square Garden in 1926. By that time the promotors sought to dissociate themselves from Wild West shows, but it is strange to find that note in the Shan-Kive program, which stated, "The Chicago Round-Up is not a Wild West Show, although amusement features are not neglected"—quite overlooking the fact that it had been a Wild West Show the week before, and would be again the week after the Chicago engagement. Here is, however, the direct transition from the Wild West show that barely survived Buffalo Bill to the rodeo that was its heir and successor, with more program events in common than is generally realized.[2]

Mayor Thompson was pleased rather than deceived by the transition from preparedness pageant to Shan-Kive, for "a good time" was right down his alley, and so was Round-up, for he fancied himself a cowboy and was identified with the ten-gallon hat, even on his campaign buttons. He consented to be "Honorary Director General" of the Shan-Kive. Buffalo Bill was "Judge Supreme" of contests and was also named with J. C. Miller of the 101 Ranch to the panel of "Honorary Judges."

The Pageant of Preparedness was banished. The program listed "Artillery Drill by Veteran Members of the U. S. Artillery" and "Roman Riding by Regulars of the U. S. Cavalry," as well as boasting 88,000 square feet of scenery and 15,000,000 candle-power illumination, which features no doubt constituted the Pageant of Preparedness whenever the aggregation desisted from not being a Wild West show.

Cowboys' steer bulldogging attracted the greatest attention among events judged for world-championship honors. Ed Lindsey, one of the all-time great steer wrestlers, and Bill Pickett, Texas

---

[2] Official program, World's Championship Rodeo Contest, Tex Austin, manager, Chicago, 1925, 1926, 1927, 1928; Foghorn Clancy, *My Fifty Years in Rodeo* (San Antonio, 1952), 54–56, 70.

Negro cowboy, were tied at eleven seconds in the first day's contest. Pickett is the reputed originator of this event. In 1903 he became so incensed at a longhorn he was trying to corral that he took after it at full speed, leaned from his horse and grabbed the steer by the horns and twisted its neck, throwing it off its feet. Clay McGonigal, headlined roper and bronc rider, bet Bill he could not do it again. Bill did, and soon was getting twelve dollars a week for demonstrating his new-found skill. The Millers hired him, and he appeared at their 1905 roundup, at the Jamestown Exposition, and in their Wild West. In 1908, Bill tried his art on the fighting bulls of Mexico City. *El toro's* neck is too thick to twist, but Bill hung on long enough to win his bet. According to Zack Miller, Bill sunk his teeth in the steer's nostrils to bring him down, and it was the bite that gave the event its name "bulldogging." Chicago rules stated, "Positively no biting allowed." Bill Pickett died on the 101 Ranch on April 2, 1932, when he followed a rope too close to a rearing bronco that came down and trampled him.[3]

Other world championship events were bucking-horse riding, trick and fancy roping, wild-horse racing, and steer roping. Contests were also held in bucking-bull riding with saddle and bucking-mule riding. The program claimed 1,200 contestants with 800 horses, and such prizes were offered as $1,000 for the best all-around cowboy or cowgirl and several first places at $500. However, the idea that this was a sports contest did not quite get over; the *Chicago Tribune* ungenerously referred to it as "the Roundup, the Wild West show at Lincoln and Polk streets."[4]

Lucille Mulhall was billed as "World's Lady Champion" in roping and tying wild steers. She was the first girl to rope and tie a steer, according to Will Rogers. When she appeared at the age of fourteen at a Roosevelt Rough Riders' Reunion at Oklahoma City on July 6, 1900, the *New York World* said, "Little Miss Mulhall, who weighs only 90 pounds, can break a bronco, lasso and brand a steer, and shoot a coyote at 500 yards. She can also play Chopin, quote Browning, construe Virgil, and make mayonnaise

---

[3] *Chicago Tribune*, August 19, 1916; Vincent Lockhart, "Canadian Site of First Rodeo," *Amarillo Sunday News and Globe*, August 14, 1938, p. F-21; Collings and England, *The 101 Ranch*, 171–72; Gipson, *Fabulous Empire*, 225–26, 259–60; Clancy, *My Fifty Years in Rodeo*, 21–22.

[4] August 20, 23, 24, 1916.

dressing. She is a little ashamed of these latter accomplishments, which are a concession to the civilized prejudices of her mother." Her father, Colonel Zach Mulhall, staged a show in Madison Square Garden in 1905 that brought Will Rogers to fame when he roped a steer that escaped into the grandstand. The steer got away from Lucille, and Tom Mix missed a cast at it, but the story that Bill Pickett was hazing the steer probably exaggerates the all-star cast present. Will describes Lucille's cowgirl attire as a divided skirt of gray whipcord or gray broadcloth that came down long over patent-leather boot-tops, a white silk shirtwaist, and a small, stiff-brimmed hat. She retired in 1917 and died in an auto accident in 1941.[5]

The *Tribune,* which undoubtedly resented the connection of Mayor Thompson with the cowboy spectacle, was altogether favorable in its review, noting the ovation given Buffalo Bill when he presented the Rough Riders. Chicago was always kind to Cody, and in no great city was he more at home. There, in 1913, the Showman's League of America was organized, with Cody as its first president, and his memory is kept alive there by the homeless troupers of the outdoor-show world who turn to that organization in time of trouble.

The Shan-Kive moved on and again became a Wild West show; Edith Zantlinger dropped No. 57 from her back to resume trap and fancy shooting with no prize money offered, and Iron Tail again led the attack on the Deadwood stagecoach. The spectacle was the attack on Columbus, New Mexico, by the Mexican band of Pancho Villa, which was close to the news, for it had occurred early that year.

As the season wore on, the show's profits dropped. Cody heard that holders of the Medal of Honor were eligible for pay, and in June he wrote a pathetic letter to the adjutant general applying for it, saying, "I need that ten dollars a month in my business as it rains all the time." He signed William F. Cody on show stationery with his name and picture blazoned across the top third of it, but thought it necessary to add in a corner the explanation, "Bill Cody

[5] "Lucille Mulhall Carried Feminist Banner into the Cattle Country," in *Kansas City Star,* January 11, 1941; Homer Croy, *Our Will Rogers* (New York, Boston, 1953), 96–100; Gipson, *Fabulous Empire,* 235–37.

of the Old Army."[6] His information was incorrect, as *Army Regulations, 1913,* then in effect, authorized no payments to medal holders. Additional pay of two dollars a month was allowed enlisted men to whom a certificate of merit was granted. The regulations also stated that the medal could be awarded to a person "provided he was at the time of the gallant act or acts an officer, noncommissioned officer, or private in the Army of the United States." When Cody was awarded the medal, this provision was ignored, for he was a civilian employee. For this reason his name was stricken from the list of Medal of Honor holders by a board of review about this time. It is unlikely that Cody ever heard of this action.

The rain he had complained of, and the cold, continued into July. Then it became hot and humid. An epidemic among children cut business further. Yet late in the year Cody was optimistic. He boasted that he had not missed a parade or a performance; his health was so much improved that he was planning for his own show next season. He admitted in a letter to Julia that he had been so unwell earlier in the year that he had been afraid to propose new ventures. There had been times when Johnny Baker had thought that the Colonel could not make a performance. Often he was helped on his horse behind the scenes, but the old scout toughed it out and no audience suspected anything was wrong.

The season closed on November 4. Cody planned to be with his sister May in Denver for a four-day visit by the seventeenth before going to Wyoming. He had planned to return to May's during the winter to write the articles requested by Hearst in continuation of the autobiographical series. When he arrived at May's, he was exhausted; the final weeks of the show had been more of a strain than he had realized. He got to the TE Ranch for a few weeks' rest, returning to Denver in early December. Then he contracted a cold, with complications so alarming that his wife and Irma were summoned. By the time they arrived, he was up and around again. Dr. J. H. East ordered him to cut down on smoking, after which a heart condition showed improvement. On January 3, Cody went to Glenwood Springs, hoping to benefit from its waters.

[6] Cody to the Adjutant General, Boston, June 14, 1916, facsimile in Walsh, *The Making of Buffalo Bill,* 258.

Two days later he suffered a nervous collapse, and was brought back to Denver. On January 8 it was publicly announced that he was dying. He lingered on for two days more.

On the afternoon of January 9 he was baptized and received into the Roman Catholic church by Father Christopher V. Walsh, assistant at the Cathedral of the Immaculate Conception. Mrs. Cody no doubt urged this decision upon him, but Colonel Cody was deeply religious, although not previously a member of any church. His mother was a Methodist, and he had attended that church as a boy. Expressions of religious sentiment are frequent in his family letters. The Very Reverend George A. Beecher, Episcopal missionary bishop of western Nebraska, who knew Cody in North Platte and traveled for a time with the Wild West in Europe, said of him, "I learned to respect this man for his virtues, and to be patient with his faults. . . . I am not trying to present any brief for Colonel Cody as a representative Churchman or professing Christian. . . . I know Cody was never guilty of betraying a friend, and that he never placed a false advertisement in any department of his famous show." Cody contributed generously to the building of every church erected during his lifetime in Cody, Wyoming.[7]

At 12:05 o'clock on January 10, 1917, William Frederick Cody crossed the Great Divide. President Woodrow Wilson and General Scott were among the first to offer sympathy. Said General Miles, "Colonel Cody was a high-minded gentleman, and a great scout. He performed a great work in the West for the pioneers and for the generations coming after them and his exploits will live forever in history." Former President Theodore Roosevelt, in accepting an honorary vice-presidency in the Buffalo Bill Memorial Association, called Cody "an American of Americans. . . . He embodied those traits of courage, strength, and self-reliant hardihood which are vital to the well-being of the nation."

The legislature of Colorado by special resolution ordered that Cody's body lie in state in the rotunda of the capitol on Sunday, the day of the funeral. A crowd estimated at 25,000 passed in single file between lines of soldiers from Fort Logan.

[7] Rev. Felician A. Foy (ed.), *The 1954 National Catholic Almanac*, 50th Anniversary Edition, 208–209; *Denver Post*, January 10, 11, 12, 15, 1917; *Denver Times*, January 11, 12, 1917; *Rocky Mountain News*, January 11, 12, 1917; Bishop George A. Beecher, *A Bishop of the Great Plains* (Philadelphia, 1950), 112, 154–55.

"Step lively, please; big crowd behind; step along; hurry up, folks," cried a master of ceremonies with high silk hat and cane, reminiscent of the Colonel's recent circus engagement.

Governor Julius G. Gunter of Colorado, Governor John B. Kendrick of Wyoming, Lieutenant Governor Edgar Howard of Nebraska, and official delegations from the legislatures of those three states led the funeral procession to the hall of Denver Lodge No. 17, B. P. O. E., where services were held. Infantry and the regimental band from Fort Logan preceded the hearse. Behind it was led Buffalo Bill's last white horse, "McKinley," saddled and bridled, with reversed stirrups. Civil War veterans with fife and drum corps; the National Order of Cowboy Rangers, seventy strong; two hundred Elks, fifty Boy Scouts, fourteen women of the Women's Relief Corps, and Spanish-American War veterans marched to the dirges. Represented were the Showmen's League of America, the Royal Arch Masons of North Platte, Palestine Commandery No. 13, Knights Templars of North Platte, and Mecca Temple of the Ancient Arabic Order of the Mystic Shrine of New York.

At the lodge hall, a quartet sang Cody's favorite song, "Tenting Tonight on the Old Camp Ground." John W. Springer, banker, delivered the Elks' eulogy, following one by Albert U. Mayfield of the Cowboy Rangers. The Elks' chaplain, the Reverend Charles H. Marshall, pastor of St. Barnabas Episcopal Church, then read the burial service, but there was no burial. The coffin was taken to Olinger's mortuary to be placed in a crypt until spring.

Buffalo Bill was to be buried on top of Lookout Mountain near Denver. The *Denver Post* of Tammen and Bonfils started a drive for pennies from school children—"no child permitted to contribute more than 5 cents"—to build a monument. It was reported that Cody himself had chosen the site, although it was also reported, elsewhere, that Cody had picked a mountain near Cody, Wyoming. Mrs. Cody fell in with the Denver idea, as did Johnny Baker, who arrived just after the Colonel's death in a race across the country from New York.

The memorial association was permanently organized before the month was out, with Mayfield of the Cowboy Rangers as president, W. H. Wheadon of the Elks as treasurer, and John C. Shaffer, publisher of the *Rocky Mountain News,* heading the advisory council, with the names of Tammen and Bonfils modestly bringing up the rear.

The city of Cody, which had gone into public mourning for its patron, was disgruntled. Mrs. Cody was forced to issue a signed statement denying published reports that she had discouraged the erecting of monuments to Cody's memory other than at his grave. In the long run, the Wyoming city got the monument, carved by Gertrude Vanderbilt Whitney, and a museum as well, while the *Denver Post's* grandiose plan fell short. No monument other than a sizable gravestone was ever erected on Lookout Mountain.

It was almost five months after Buffalo Bill's death that they got him in a grave, carved from the heart of granite and lined with cement, with a steel vault, so that the body could not be stolen for Cody, Wyoming, North Platte or Omaha, Nebraska, Arlington National cemetery, or any other place that contended for Homer dead, through which the living Homer begged his bread with circuses. Buffalo Bill rests safely, surrounded by restaurants, souvenir stands, and side shows.

"A day has passed," wrote Gene Fowler on June 3, 1917. "With it we have turned a page that cannot be rewritten." All morning three thousand motorcars toiled up the seven and one-half miles of Lookout Mountain—and the motorcars of 1917 toiled on the mountain roads of that era, although the Lariat Trail had been an achievement in 1913. "The roads are excellent in their wealth of view," said Mr. Fowler, but he neglected other detail except to say that "at first the pitch of the road is gradual. It becomes more abrupt on the ascent. Its trend is ever upward." You see why they waited until June. Mrs. Cody had to stop and rest a half-mile from the grave.

Although it had been announced that the coffin would not be opened, it was, at Mrs. Cody's order, because Colonel J. P. Boggs, an old friend, had come from Mattoon, Illinois, to pay his last respects. For two hours a throng filed by, two abreast, parents holding children shoulder high. Then they got on with the ceremonies, in charge of Golden City Lodge No. 1, Ancient Free and Accepted Masons, acting for the North Platte lodge of which the Colonel had been a member. The Masonic burial ritual was read, as was an original poem dedicated to the scout by A. F. Beeler. The lamb-skin apron of Masonry was dropped into the grave. Quince Record, chief musician of the Fifth Ohio Infantry in the Spanish-American War, sounded "Taps." The national flag was raised. A salute of eleven guns, that for a brigadier general, was fired by Colorado's Battery B.[8]

Denver's gaudiest funeral was over. From its start under the dome of the capitol to its end months later on Lookout Mountain, it was a strange mixture of deserved tribute and flamboyant show-manship that was typical of the life of Buffalo Bill and has so con-fused those who have tried to understand him.

Major John Burke would have understood, and would have reveled in it, but he was not there to hear the salute of a brigadier general fired over the grave of Buffalo Bill. The great press agent died on April 12, 1917, just thirteen weeks after his idol.

"At rest here by his request"—so says the bronze plate on the stone marker at the head of his grave. There lies a man six feet, three-fourths inch in height, weighing in his prime 218 pounds, recognized by his goatee, his mustache, his long hair—was that Buffalo Bill? In later years, as his long hair turned white, it also thinned, and he wore a toupee. Once it came off with his hat as with sweeping gesture he introduced the Rough Riders of the World. He swore he would never wear it again—but he did. That false hair was buried in concrete—but not the Buffalo Bill of the Wild West.

[8] *Denver Post,* June 3, 4, 1917.

Buffalo Bill and "Isham" at the TE Ranch, Wyoming

Courtesy Denver Public Library Western Collection

Buffalo Bill in 1915

glad to leave the saddle for the less strenuous buggy seat.

32

"LET MY SHOW GO ON"

"LET MY SHOW GO ON," was the slogan adopted by those who owned the name "Buffalo Bill's Wild West." The slogan was supposed to represent Cody's dying words, but since at the time he had no show to go on, it seems unlikely he said any such thing. In his last season, the billing read, "Miller & Arlington Wild West Show Co., Inc. present 'Buffalo Bill' (himself) Combined with the 101 Ranch Shows," and "himself" was about all Buffalo Bill contributed to the combination. Yet, oddly enough, after Buffalo Bill was dead, it was the Buffalo Bill part of this combination that went on, while Miller and Arlington and the 101 Ranch Shows retired, not to revive their show until 1925.

Johnny Baker put the show together, and Jess Willard bought into it. The billing of the 1917 show was "Buffalo Bill Wild West Show Co., Inc., Ray O. Archer Presents JESS WILLARD (Himself in the Flesh) and the BUFFALO BILL Wild West Show and Circus, Johnny Baker, Arena Director; Harry Clarence, Arena Announcer." So the Buffalo Bill show did go on, for that year at least. It featured Tex McLoud, champion roper of Idaho; Chester Byers, champion roper of the world; and Hank Darnell, champion roper of South America. Merle Evans was bandmaster, as he had been the previous season. Two Lance was head chief, Iron Cloud led the Sioux, and Flying Hawk, the Arapahoes. The familiar acts were on the program—Pony Express, emigrant train, stagecoach holdup, quadrille on horseback, cowboy fun, Devlin's Zouaves, artillery drill, Cossacks, Arabs, and Japanese. In the circus, formerly Far East, part were Rhoda Royal's high-school horses, Madam Marantette's liberty horses, Emily Stickney and Fred Collier in riding acts, and Baby May and Baby Emma, each described as the most wonderfully trained elephant in the world. Jess Willard and Johnny Baker kept it on the road until November, but wartime restrictions, added to the usual hazards of outdoor-show business, got the best of them, and they could not bring the show out another season.

Tammen and Bonfils had had enough of show business by 1920, and sold to Edward M. Ballard and Jerry Mugivan, who formed the American Circus Corporation, controlling Sells-Floto, Hagenbeck Wallace, John Robinson's, Yankee Robinson, Gollmar Brothers, Al G. Barnes, and Sparks. On the letterhead of their stationery appeared "Buffalo Bill's Wild West—Let My Show Go On," but it never did, for they failed to activate it. In 1929 they sold out to Ringling Brothers. There lies the name "Buffalo Bill's Wild West," suppressed with many another historic show name in the same locker where Sells-Floto finally came to rest alongside Adam Forepaugh and Sells Brothers.

Miller Brothers successfully revived the 101 Ranch Wild West in 1925. Joe Miller died in 1927 and George in 1929. When Zack could not pay his performers in 1931, they wrecked his show. He tried to revive it for Chicago's Century of Progress in 1933, but could not repeat Buffalo Bill's 1893 triumph; the show lasted only a few days. Zack kept on trying until his death in 1952. Colonel Tim McCoy, who had an after-show with Ringling Brothers–Barnum and Bailey for several seasons, tried Wild West in the grand manner in 1938, but failed in a few weeks. The day of the Wild West show was over—but its legitimate successor, rodeo, grew and flourished.

Commercial reprinting of Buffalo Bill dime novels ended in 1932. Their decline, however, indicated no lack of popularity of fiction about the West. About the time of Cody's death, Zane Grey and his competitors became so prolific that "Western" became recognized as a distinctive type of printing-press product. Melodramas such as were played by the Buffalo Bill Combination were not seen in theaters after World War I, but they lived on in Saturday afternoon movies and eventually became "adult Westerns" of television.

In the decade after Cody's death, many an obituary of an old-timer made it a point of distinction that "He fought with Buffalo Bill," or "He was in the Buffalo Bill show." But as Cody's companions died, there were fewer left to contradict the last-scout-to-leave-Custer and the scout who shot at Yellow Hand just before Cody did, whose garrulous reminiscences coincided with the fad of the 1920's for debunking celebrities. A theory was advanced that Buffalo Bill was largely, if not entirely, the creation of press-agentry. Reconsideration of the evidence inclines toward agreement that the Colonel's entourage had as little regard for facts as many present-day practitioners in their field, but, to make a fine distinction, that there was more extravagance than there was exaggeration in their work. They were rarely intentionally mendacious, although not above juggling a quotation to point it in a desired direction. Major Burke kept Buffalo Bill's name before the public, but by a rehash of the same old recipe from year to year; his "historical sketches and programme" was reprinted annually unchanged for a decade. The thesis that press agents desperately sought new material to prop up a waning reputation is disproved by their failure ever to hunt out official records of Cody's scouting.

For a decade and more after Cody's death, sketches of him were found frequently in school texts, quoted from or based on his autobiographies and such books as that of his sister Mrs. Wetmore.[1] Since then there has never been any dearth of juvenile biographies, a class of literature approved by educational authorities for "supplementary reading" if its vocabulary meets the proper level, despite any blithe disregard of historical fact. Regardless of the valiant efforts of Prentiss Ingraham, Bert Foster, and their contemporaries in hundreds of dime novels, writers of these "educational" works find new and fantastic adventures for Buffalo Bill, with a scanty framework of fact supporting masses of misinforma-

[1] Wilbur Fisk Gordy, *Leaders in Making America* (New York, 1923), 368–72; W. W. Thiesen and Stirling A. Leonard, *Real Life Stories, A Seventh Reader* (New York, 1929); James Witt Sewell, *Citizenship Readers: Makers of America* (Philadelphia, 1930), 204–11.

tion. When in one of them the Cody family is described as entering Kansas after the manner of the Oklahoma run of 1889, that may be due to ignorance, but the boy Cody's encounters with bandits immediately thereafter is sensationalism of a type that gave dime novels a bad name with school authorities of another generation. Much more shoddy work is done in the name of legendry and folklore, which have scholastic respectability, although too often legend is regarded as any lie the scholar is too lazy to investigate.

Serious historians have been inclined to shy away from mention of Cody; they are disconcerted by the Ned Buntline legend, invented by dabblers in popular history who readily believe in a super-colossal Paul Bunyan of writers. It is difficult to find anything ever said about Buffalo Bill that was more extravagantly untrue than some statements made by recent rediscoverers of Ned Buntline.

All that has been said and done by the debunkers and the writers of historical pap, however, has had surprisingly little effect on the heroic legend of Buffalo Bill in public opinion. That legend, not at all concerned with facts, approaches truth more nearly than the others. It is to be found in casual reading of newspapers, magazines, and books, where the name of Buffalo Bill turns up in discussion of subjects having no remote connection with William F. Cody, his life, or his works. The writer may use it to evoke recognition of an epoch of westward expansion or as a symbol for one of its aspects—scout, Indian fighter, cowboy, hunter, horseman, covered wagon, stagecoach, dime novel, or showman. The names of Custer, Wild Bill Hickok, Sitting Bull, Geronimo, Jesse James, Billy the Kid, Wyatt Earp, and Bat Masterson are readily recognized, particularly with the aid of movies and television, but each was a champion in only a single event in that great rodeo of the plains and the mountains in the last half of the nineteenth century. The man of many lives and legends, the all-around champion in popular opinion—publicity opinion, if you will—was Buffalo Bill. You need name no other.

The legend, even when it most nearly approaches the life, is still far from the person who was Billy to childhood acquaintances, Will and Uncle Will to members of his family, Mr. Cody to army men of his scouting days, the Colonel to associates of his show career, and Buffalo Bill to the world at large. Can we get some idea of the real William Frederick Cody behind the legend—or does anyone care?

To those in search of a hero, he may fall somewhat short, not because his deeds did not deserve acclaim, for they did, but because he contributed so largely to the acclaim they received. That he allowed himself to be exploited as a hero, and made a living at it, was resented by many contemporaries. Some assumed the deeds attributed to him to be fictitious when they found him reticent in discussing them. His intimates agree that he was not boastful and that he often deprecated extravagances printed about him. Army officers who employed him found him quiet and lacking in braggadocio. It is quite possible that he considered his exploits of little importance, and it is abundantly evident that he had no sense of himself as a historical figure. Yet most of his life was given to stressing the westward movement of which he was a part. It is notable that the word "show" was not used; it was an exhibition, historical and educational; and it is notable also that it was honest in its re-enactment and free from fakery.

He was hail-fellow-well-met with anyone and an easy mark for a touch on any flimsy excuse. In his own time there were few who disliked Bill Cody. For every one whose violent jealousy sought to disparage Cody's fame, there was another who took it all back after one meeting with Buffalo Bill.

He was a boy who never grew up; yet in spite of the many lives he lived, he was no drifter. Astonishing as it may seem, from the age of twenty-two years, he was a remarkably steady young man. From 1868 to 1913, Cody was continuously employed, at first as scout, then as actor, finally as showman. For more than forty years he followed this most precarious of occupations, showmanship, without a failure or even a serious setback. It must be added that when he did fail, he did it completely. His drinking bouts were notorious, yet he never missed a scouting assignment or a show performance for this reason.

To those who saw him introducing a Congress of Rough Riders of the World, he looked every inch the hero. Dr. J. N. Hall, who examined Cody during his last illness, wrote, "I have never examined a man past his seventy-first year who assumed on rising, so nearly the ideal position of the soldier. His height was about 5 ft., 10 in. [elsewhere 6 feet, ¾ inches]; weight, 170 pounds, of wiry build, and, of course with no superfluous fat. There is certainly a very close relationship between such an ideal build and ideal posture and the ability to stand up under long and unusual stress. I could readily believe that such a man, in his youth, could have ridden four of the daily routes of a pony express rider, aggregating something like three hundred and eighty miles, without stopping for sleep."[2]

Physical endurance was one of the assets that made Cody outstanding as a scout. Others were total recall of any terrain he had ever seen, knowledge of Indian ways and unusual ability as a trailer, expert marksmanship, and informed courage. These made possible his several long rides through country reported teeming with hostile Indians, where other scouts feared to venture. His courage was not recklessness. He was confident that he knew the terrain and that he knew how to avoid the Indians. He did his job so well that he had few adventures on such rides. The same qualities made him an invaluable guide. When his scouting was successful, he was dependable in a fight. So say the reports of officers who employed him. His marksmanship was further valued when as a buffalo hunter he fed the troops in emergencies. His horsemanship was another asset. When he enlisted for the Civil War, he gave his occupation as teamster. He showed that he was an expert driver when he saved the expedition of 1868–69 a week of winter marching by taking the supply train over a route that seemed impassable for wagons. He was employed only briefly as a stagecoach driver, but he took the reins himself on important occasions in his show.

In Buffalo Bill's Wild West, it was the staging of the show itself that was in Cody's charge. He had the ability to dramatize a way of life that must have been prosaic enough and often boring to those who lived it. Every event programmed in Buffalo Bill's Wild West has retained its glamour, and it is difficult now to realize that the glamour was not already there. J. Frank Dobie has noted that "heroizing Andrew Jackson as a fighter against unhorsed Indians east of the Mississippi became obsolete even before boys ceased to

[2] Dr. J. N. Hall, *Tales of Pioneer Practice*, 121.

read the romances of James Fenimore Cooper. The whole tradition of Indians fighting afoot has faded from the popular mind. On the other hand the tradition of fighting the wild-riding Indians of the West remains on screen and in pulp fiction almost as alive as it was when Buffalo Bill's arena presented it in pageant form."[3] If there is any doubt that this is Cody's influence, it may be recalled that the Wild West never programmed the wars of his time against the Modocs and Apaches, who wore no feathered headdresses and fought on foot. But when Hollywood glamorized Geronimo and Cochise, the Apaches wore feathers and rode ponies—and sometimes spoke Sioux! And when a television adult Western gets around to Captain Jack, Bogus Charley, Shacknasty Jim, and the other Modocs who fought in the Lava Beds, you may count on it that they will trail feathers from the backs of their mustangs. The public expects Indians in movies and on television to wear headdresses and ride ponies because Cody employed Sioux and other tribes of the plains in Buffalo Bill's Wild West. Similarly, cowboys wear ten-gallon Stetsons, not because such a hat was worn in early range days, but because it was part of the costume adopted by Buffalo Bill for his show.

The least-noticed asset that Buffalo Bill brought to his legend was his sense of humor. He at least never took himself seriously, and was always ready to tell a joke or a tall tale at his own expense. He felt ridiculous in perpetually playing the hero; he so expressed himself from the melodrama stage. Often, in telling of outstanding achievements, he brings in a touch of the incongruous. Most commentators take these tall tales solemnly, the literal-minded regarding them as bare-faced lies. A wider uncritical opinion, almost subconsciously, finds here a chance to laugh with Cody and to go along with him in not taking himself too seriously. That makes it easy to regard him, almost facetiously, as the symbol of all that is heroic and glamorous in the West without bothering too much to know whether he actually had been all that the image invokes. He is one hero we can treat with little respect and no awe.

In an age that is skeptical of heroism, anyone who does bother to find out what William F. Cody really amounted to may turn up a record that is impressive in its universal acclaim from a wide

[3] J. Frank Dobie, *The Mustangs* (Boston, 1952), 43.

variety of sources as well as in its lack of any hint that he ever faltered or blundered. What more could possibly be asked of a hero? If he was not one, who was?

Even so, it is difficult to assess his importance, which has little to do with his days of heroism. It is to be remembered that the West was still unconquered when he began to exploit it. His effect upon the westward movement must have been significant. Reporters commented that it was boys and young men who filled the theaters for his stage shows. While he was still commuting between jobs as actor and scout, between shooting glass balls and shooting buffalo, between grease paint and war paint, how many, from generations growing up between 1872 and 1917, followed him into the West, no one can say. The West would not have been the same without them.

It cannot be said that they found the West less glamorous or less romantic than he had painted it, for if they had, the West of Buffalo Bill would not have become a legend. He could scarcely have put this over had he not been a part of it, had he not been genuine. It was Finley Peter Dunne's sage Mr. Dooley who once observed that the farther one gets from a period the better he can write about it, because "you are not subject to interruptions by people who were there." Most of those who had anything derogatory to say waited until Cody was no longer around to interrupt.

But in the long run it is the legend that wins. Expunge the name of Buffalo Bill from the pages of histories. Deny the entire story of his life as fabrication. Tie the red tape again around the bundles of army reports that tell his real story, as I did after brief exposure in these pages, and bury them again in the steel files of the National Archives. Forget him.

Indians in Sioux war bonnets still ride through a thousand movies. The cavalry still rides to the rescue. The Deadwood stagecoach and the covered wagon still cut deep ruts in the trails of America's traditions. Natives' beards grow long and tourists' pocketbooks grow light every summer at a hundred rodeos and frontier celebrations. The cowboy hero nightly lights up hundreds of thousands of television screens, and keeps hundreds of printing presses rolling. A cow bolts a loading platform to wander through city streets, and some newspaper reporter is sure to write,

"The days of Buffalo Bill returned here today when police were called. . . ."

In the words attributed to the dying William Frederick Cody, which he probably never said, and never needed to say, "Let my show go on."

BIBLIOGRAPHY

I. Manuscripts, Documents, and Newspaper Files

Arizona Pioneers Historical Society, Tucson. Scrapbook and file. (Cited in footnotes as APHS.)

Buffalo Bill Memorial Museum, Lookout Mountain, Colo. Documents.

Buffalo Bill Museum, Cody, Wyo. Manuscripts, documents.

Colorado, State Historical Society of, Denver. Letters, manuscripts, documents, newspaper clippings. (Cited in footnotes as SHSC.)

Custer Battlefield Museum, Montana. Clippings and photographs, with notes by Mrs. George A. Custer on Grand Duke Alexis hunt.

Denver Public Library, Western History Department. Nate Salsbury papers, scrapbooks, photographs, programs, Cody correspondence.

Goodman, Julia Cody. "Memoirs of Buffalo Bill," 163 handwritten (pencil) pages, dated April, 1926, given by her to H. S. Cody, who lent it to me. (Cited in footnotes as Mrs. Goodman MS.)

Kansas State Historical Society, Topeka. Manuscripts, documents, newspaper files. (Cited in footnotes as KSHS.)

National Archives, Washington, D. C. Post Returns and Medical History, Fort McPherson; letters received, District of the Republican, Department of the Platte, Division of the Missouri; muster rolls, Fifth U. S. Cavalry; files of Generals Merritt and Carr, Office of the Adjutant General; reports of persons hired; compilation of Cody record, Office of the Quartermaster General.

Nebraska State Historical Society, Lincoln. Mrs. Julia Cody Goodman scrapbook, clippings, letters, manuscripts, file on Yellow Hand controversy. (Cited in footnotes as NSHS.)

Newberry Library, Chicago. Program, pamphlets, newspaper files.

Office of the Quartermaster General, QM 201 AP-C (A & C Div.), Cody, William F., May 19, 1939, transcript prepared at the request of Rep. Thomas F. Ford. (Cited in footnotes as O.Q.M. 1939.)

Wyoming State Historical Society, Cheyenne. Newspaper clippings, file.

II. Books, Articles, and Miscellaneous Printed Materials

(From the voluminous Buffalo Bill literature, this selected list includes books of a general biographical character and items most frequently cited. Items cited only once or only in one chapter are generally not repeated in this list.)

Armes, Col. George A. *Ups and Downs of an Army Officer.* Washington, 1900.

Beals, Frank Lee. *Buffalo Bill.* Chicago, 1943.

Black Elk Speaks, as told to John G. Neihardt. New York, 1932.

Blake, Herbert Cody. *Blake's Western Stories.* Brooklyn, 1929.

Blaut, Jacob. "Who Killed Yellow Hand?," *Winners of the West,* Vol. II, No. 9 (August, 1925), 7.

Bourke, John G. *On the Border with Crook.* New York, 1891.

Branch, E. Douglas. *The Hunting of the Buffalo.* New York, London, 1929.

Brininstool, E. A. "Buffaloing Buffalo Bill," *Hunter-Trader-Trapper,* Vol. LXXVI, No. 4 (April, 1932), 18.

———. *Fighting Indian Warriors.* Harrisburg, 1953.

———. "Two Tales about Buffalo Bill," *Adventure* (July, 1921).

———, ed. Who Killed Yellow Hand," *Outdoor Life—Outdoor Recreation,* Vol. LXV, No. 2 (February, 1930). The stories of Beaver Heart and Josie Tangleyellowhair, as taken down February 13 and May 27, 1929, by C. B. Lohmiller, superintendent, Lame Deer Agency; Willis Rowland, interpreter.

Bruce, Robert. *The Fighting Norths and Pawnee Scouts.* New York, 1932.

Buel, J. W. *Heroes of the Plains.* New York, St. Louis, 1882.

Buffalo Bill: His Life & Stirring Adventures in the Wild West. London, n. d.

Buffalo Bill and His Wild West Companions. Chicago, n. d.

Buffalo Bill's store vovestikke, En Fortaelling fra det vestlige Amerika, Oversat fra engelsk. (In Norwegian.) St. Paul, n. d.

Buffalo Bill's Wild West programs, 1883–1908.

Buffalo Bill's Wild West, combined with Pawnee Bill's Great Far East, programs, 1909-13.

Burke, John M. *"Buffalo Bill" from Prairie to Palace.* Chicago, New York, 1893.

Burnham, Maj. Frederick Russell. *Taking Chances.* Los Angeles, 1944.

Bushell, William. *The Life of Captain Adam Bogardus.* Lincoln, Ill., n. d. [1956].

Cahill, Luke. "An Indian Campaign and Buffalo Hunting with 'Buffalo Bill,'" *The Colorado Magazine,* Vol. IV, No. 4 (August, 1927).

Carver, Dr. "The Letters of Doc Carver," ed. by Raymond W. Thorp, *Outdoor Life—Outdoor Recreation,* Vol. LXV, Nos. 4, 5, 6; Vol. LXVI, Nos. 1, 2 (April–July, 1930).

Cattermole, E. G. *Famous Frontiersmen, Pioneers, and Scouts.* Chicago, New York, n. d.

Chambers, Julius. *News Hunting on Three Continents.* New York, 1921.

Chapman, Arthur. *The Pony Express.* New York, London, 1932.

Cleaveland, Agnes Morley. *Satan's Paradise.* Boston, 1952.

Cody, Louisa Frederici, in collaboration with Courtney Ryley Cooper. *Memories of Buffalo Bill.* New York, London, 1920.

Cody, Lydia S. *The Cody Family in America.* Kissimmee, Fla., 1954. See also under Cody Family Association.

Cody, William Frederick. *The Adventures of Buffalo Bill.* New York, 1904. New York, Boblin Sales Company, n. d. (wrappers). (Cited as Cody, *Adventures.*)

———. *An Autobiography of Buffalo Bill (Colonel W. F. Cody).* Illustrated by N. C. Wyeth. New York, 1920. (Cited in footnotes as Cody, *Autobiography.*) Binder's title: *Buffalo Bill's Life Story: An Autobiography.* Serialized as "The Great West That Was, 'Buffalo Bill's' Life Story," *q.v.*

———. *Buffalo Bill's Own Story of His Life and Deeds* . . . including a full account of his death and funeral by . . . William Lightfoot Visscher. Chicago, 1917. Also published as *Life and Adventures of "Buffalo Bill."* New York, 1927; Golden, Colo., 1939.

———. "Famous Hunting Parties of the Plains," *Cosmopolitan,* Vol. XVII, No. 2 (June, 1894).

———. Fighting and Trapping Out West," *Murray's Magazine* (June, 1887).

———. "The Great West That Was, 'Buffalo Bill's' Life Story," *Hearst's Magazine* (August, 1916, to July, 1917).

———. *Letters from Buffalo Bill.* Ed. by Stella Adelyne Foote. Billings, Mont., 1954.

———. *The Life of Hon. William F. Cody, Known as Buffalo Bill, the Famous Hunter, Scout and Guide: An Autobiography.* Hartford, 1879. Also *Prospectus of.* (Cited in footnotes as Cody, *Life.*)

———. "Riders of the World," *Metropolitan,* Vol. II, No. 15 (August, 1900).

———. "Rounding Up Indians," *Harper's Round Table,* Vol. XII, No. 15 (January, 1899).

———. *Story of the Wild West and Camp-fire Chats.* N. p., 1888; Philadelphia, 1888; Chicago, 1888; Boston, 1889. Also published as *The History of the Wild West.* Chicago, 1901.

———. *True Tales of the Plains.* New York, 1908.

———. "The Wild West in Europe," *Sunday Magazine,* May 12, 1907.

———. Introduction to *Hoofs, Claws and Antlers of the Rocky Mountains by the Camera.* Denver, 1902.

———. Prefaces. See Inman and Majors.

Cody Family Association publications:

Our Cody Family Directory 1925. Descendants of Philip and Martha Cody of Beverly, Mass., presented by Sherwin Cody, Hiram S. Cody, Luther M. Cody. Printed in West Somerville, Mass.

The Cody Family Directory 1927. Descendants of . . . . Prepared by Luther M. Cody, secretary, N. p.

The Cody Family Directory 1936. Descendants of . . . . Prepared by Luther Morrill Cody, first secretary, and Ernest William Cody, secretary-treasurer since 1931. Inc. N. p., Hotels Statler.

The Cody Family Handbook-Directory 1941. Descendants of Philip and Martha at Beverly, Massachusetts, 1698. Introductory Notes by Ernest William Cody, secretary-treasurer. Printed at London, Ont.

The Cody Family Association Directory 1952. Descendants of . . . . The joint effort of Ernest William Cody, secretary-treasurer, and his wife: Ella Jean Cody, assistant secretary. London, Ontario.

The Cody Family in America 1698. Descendants of Philip and Martha, Massachusetts, Biographical and Genealogical. Published by Lydia S. Cody, chairman, Historical Board. Kissimmee, Fla., printed by Cody Publications, Inc., 1954. (Bound book of 257 pp.)

The Piercing of the Veil. By Ernest William Cody. The Cody Family Association, London, Ontario, 1957. (Four-p. printed pamphlet and two inserted pp. of illustrations and documents).

Coe, Jeffrey. *The Picture Story of Buffalo Bill.* Illustrated by Percy Lasson. New York, 1954.

Collections of the Kansas State Historical Society. Vol. X (1907–1908),

Vol. XII (1911–12), Vol. XIII (1913–14), Vol. XV (1919–22), Vol. XVI (1923–25), Vol. XVII (1926–28).

Collier, Edmund. *The Story of Buffalo Bill*. New York, 1952.

Connelley, William E. *Wild Bill and His Era*. New York, 1933.

——, ed. "The Topeka Movement," *Collections of the Kansas State Historical Society*, XIII (1913–14). Topeka, 1915.

Cook, James H. *Fifty Years on the Old Frontier*. New Haven, 1923. Reprinted, Norman, 1957.

Cooper, Courtney Ryley. *Annie Oakley, Woman at Arms*. New York, 1927.

—— "The Life and Times of Buffalo Bill," Bell Syndicate, *Kansas City Star*, April 4, 11, 18, 25, May 2, 9, 16, 23, 30, June 6, 1926.

Cooper, Frank C. *The Stirring Lives of Buffalo Bill and Pawnee Bill*. New York, 1912.

Cooper, Tex. "I Knew Buffalo Bill," *Frontier Times*, Vol. XXXIII, No. 2 (Spring, 1959).

Courtney, W. B. "The Prairie Prince," *Collier's*, April 14, 21, 28, May 12, 19, 1928.

Crawford, Capt. Jack. *The Poet Scout: Being a Selection of Incidental and Illustrative Verses and Songs*. San Francisco, 1879.

——. *The Poet Scout: A Book of Song and Story*. New York, London, 1886.

Croft-Cooke, Rupert, and W. S. Meadmore. *Buffalo Bill: The Legend, the Man of Action, the Showman*. London, 1952.

Croy, Homer. *Trigger Marshal: The Story of Chris Madsen*. New York, 1958.

——. "How Buffalo Bill Killed Chief Yellow Hand," *American Weekly* (June 8, 1958).

Custer, Elizabeth Bacon. *Tenting on the Plains*. New York, 1887.

Custer, Gen. George A. *My Life on the Plains*. New York, 1874.

D'Aulaire, Ingri and Edgar. *Buffalo Bill*. Garden City, N. Y., 1952.

Davies, Gen. H. E. *Ten Days on the Plains*. New York, 1871.

DeBarthe, Joe. *Life and Adventures of Frank Grouard*. Ed. by Edgar I. Stewart. Norman, 1958. First published, St. Joseph, Mo., 1894.

DeWolff, J. H. *Pawnee Bill*, N. p., 1902.

Dodge, Col. Richard Irving. *Our Wild Indians*. Hartford, 1882.

Dodge, Theodore Ayrault. *Riders of Many Lands*. New York, 1894.

Downer, Harry E. *History of Davenport and Scott County, Iowa*. Volume I. Chicago, 1910.

Drury, John. *Historic Midwest Houses*. Minneapolis, 1947.

Dunn, Roy Sylvan. "Buffalo Bill's Bronc Fighter," *Montana*, Vol. VII, No. 2 (Spring, 1957).

Dunraven, the Earl of. *Canadian Nights*. New York, 1914.

———. *The Great Divide*. London, 1876.

Fellows, Dexter W., and Andrew A. Freeman. *This Way to the Big Show*. New York, 1936.

Finerty, John F. *Warpath and Bivouac*. Chicago, 1890.

Fishwick, Marshall W. *American Heroes: Myth and Reality*. Washington, 1954.

Fiske, Frank Bennett. *Life and Death of Sitting Bull*. Fort Yates, N. D., 1933.

Foreman, Carolyn Thomas. *Indians Abroad*. Norman, 1943.

Forsyth, Bvt. Brig. Gen. George A. *The Story of the Soldier*. New York, 1900.

Fowler, Gene. *A Solo in Tom-Toms*. New York, 1946.

———. *Timberline: A Story of Bonfils and Tammen*. New York, 1933.

Fox, S. M. *The Seventh Kansas Cavalry*. Topeka, 1908.

Frackelton, Dr. Will. *Sagebrush Dentist*, as told to Herman Gastrell Seely. Chicago, 1941; Pasadena, 1947.

Frederick, J. V. *Ben Holladay, the Stagecoach King*. Glendale, 1940.

Frink, Maurice. "Buffalo Bill's Last Raid on the Sioux," *Denver Post Empire Magazine*, August 26, 1957.

Fryxell, F. M. "The Codys in LeClair," *Annals of Iowa* (July, 1929).

Garland, W. W. "Ten Days with Col. Cody," *The Pony Express*, Vol. XXII, No. 2 (July, 1955).

Garretson, Martin S. *The American Bison*. New York, 1938.

Garst, Shannon. *Buffalo Bill*. New York, 1948.

———. *The Story of Buffalo Bill*. Indianapolis, New York, 1938.

Godfrey, Lt. Edward Settle. *The Field Diary of . . . .* Ed. by Edgar I. and Jane R. Stewart. Portland, Ore., 1957.

Gowdy, George. *Young Buffalo Bill*. Boston, 1955.

Green, Jules. "Death of Yellow Hand, Cheyenne Chief," as told to Ellis T. Pierce, *Winners of the West*, Vol. VI, No. 10 (September, 1929).

Griffin, Charles Eldridge. *Four Years in Europe with Buffalo Bill*. Albia, Ia., 1908.

Grinnell, George Bird. *The Fighting Cheyennes*. New York, 1915; Norman, 1956.

———. *Pawnee Hero Stories and Folk Tales*. New York, 1889.

———. *Two Great Scouts and Their Pawnee Battalion*. Cleveland, 1928.

Hall, Bert L. *Roundup Years*. Kennebec, S. D., 1954.

Hall, Dr. J. N. *Tales of Pioneer Practice*. Denver, 1937.

Hall, Jesse A., and LeRoy T. Hand. *History of Leavenworth County, Kansas*. Topeka, 1921.

Hanson, Joseph Mills. *The Conquest of the Missouri.* New York, 1946.

Havighurst, Walter. *Annie Oakley of the Wild West.* New York, 1954.

———. *Buffalo Bill's Great Wild West Show.* New York, 1957.

Hawkeye, Harry (Paul Emilius Lowe). *Buffalo Bill, King of Scouts.* Baltimore, 1908.

Hebberd, Mary Hardgrove. "Notes on Dr. David Franklin Powell, Known as 'White Beaver,'" *Wisconsin Magazine of History,* Vol. XVI, No. 6 (Summer, 1952).

Heitman, Francis B. *Historical Register and Dictionary of the United States Army.* 2 vols. Washington, 1903.

History of Scott County, Iowa. Chicago, 1882.

Hochschild, Harold K. *Township 34.* New York, 1952.

Holbrook, Stewart H. *Little Annie Oakley and Other Rugged People.* New York, 1948.

Holmes, Louis A. "William F. Cody and the Nebraska Legislature," *The Westerners Brand Book* (Chicago), Vol. XIV, No. 12 (February, 1958).

Hook, James W. "Seven Months in Cody, Wyoming, 1905–1906," *Annals of Wyoming,* Vol. XXVI, No. 1 (January, 1954).

Hornaday, William T. "The Extermination of the American Bison," *Annual Report of the Board of Regents of the Smithsonian Institution for the Year ending June 30, 1887,* Part II, Washington, 1889.

Hunton, John. *John Hunton's Diary.* Ed. by L. G. (Pat) Fleming, 2 vols. Lingle, Wyo., 1956, 1959.

Hyde, George E. *The Pawnee Indians.* Denver, 1951.

———. *A Sioux Chronicle.* Norman, 1956.

Inman, Col. Henry. *Buffalo Jones' Forty Years of Adventure.* Topeka, 1899.

———. *The Old Santa Fe Trail.* Preface by W. F. Cody. New York, 1897.

———, and Col. William F. Cody. *The Great Salt Lake Trail.* New York, 1898.

Jelinek, George. *Ellsworth, Kansas, 1867–1947.* Salina, Kan., 1947.

———. *Ninety Years of Ellsworth and Ellsworth County History.* Ellsworth, Kan., 1957. Title on wrappers: "The Ellsworth Story."

Jerrard, Leigh. "Rosa Bonheur Revealed as a Painter of Westerns," *The Westerners Brand Book* (Chicago), Vol. X, No. 6 (August, 1953).

Johannsen, Albert. *The House of Beadle and Adams and Its Dime and Nickel Novels: The Story of a Vanished Literature.* Norman, 1950.

Johnston, Charles H. L. *Famous Scouts.* Boston, 1910.

Keim, DeB. Randolph. *Sheridan's Troopers on the Borders.* Philadelphia, 1885.

Bibliography

Kelsey, D. M. *History of Our Old West.* Chicago, 1903.

King, Capt. Charles. *Campaigning with Crook: The Fifth Cavalry in the Sioux War of 1876.* Milwaukee, 1880.

———. *Campaigning with Crook and Stories of Army Life.* New York, 1890.

———. "Friend Defends Buffalo Bill; Tells of Fight with Indian," *New York World*, March 31, 1929.

———. "Long Distance Riding," *Cosmopolitan*, Vol. XVI, No. 1 (January, 1894).

———. *Memories of a Busy Life.* Reprinted from *Wisconsin Magazine of History*, Vol. V, Nos. 3, 4; Vol. VI, Nos. 1, 2 (March–December, 1922).

———. "My Friend, Buffalo Bill," as told to Don Russell, *Cavalry Journal*, Vol. XLI, No. 173 (September–October, 1932).

———, and Brig. Gen. W. C. Brown. *Map, Big Horn and Yellowstone Expedition of 1876.* Denver, 1930. King's diary in margin.

Leonard, L. O. "Buffalo Bill's First Wild West Rehearsal," *Union Pacific Magazine* (August, 1922).

Lemmon, G. E. *Developing the West.* Reprinted from *Belle Fourche Bee*, n. d.

Leonard Elizabeth Jane, and Julia Cody Goodman. *Buffalo Bill, King of the Old West.* Ed. by James Williams Hoffman. New York, 1955.

Life and Adventures of Buffalo Bill, The. London, 1887.

Logan, Herschel C. *Buckskin and Satin.* Harrisburg, 1954.

———. "Royal Buffalo Hunt," *American Rifleman*, Vol. C, No. 10 (October, 1952).

Madsen, Chris. "Chris Madsen Finds the Spot," *Winners of the West*, Vol. IX, No. 12, Vol. XII, No. 1 (November, December, 1934).

Majors, Alexander. *Seventy Years on the Frontier.* With a preface by "Buffalo Bill." Ed. by Col. Prentiss Ingraham. Chicago, 1893.

Masterson, W. B. (Bat). "Colonel Cody—Hunter, Scout, Indian Fighter," *Human Life* magazine (1907).

McCoy, Robert B. "Guns of the Wild West Show," *Guns*, Vol. V, No. 2–50 (February, 1959).

McCreight, M. I. "Buffalo Bill as I Knew Him," *True West*, Vol. IV, No. 6 (July–August, 1957).

McGillicuddy, Julia B. *McGillicuddy, Agent.* Stanford, Calif., 1941.

McLaughlin, James. *My Friend, the Indian.* Boston, New York, 1926.

Miles, Nelson A. *Personal Recollections.* Chicago, New York, 1896.

———. *Serving the Republic.* New York, London, 1911.

Miller, Broncho Charlie. *Broncho Charlie, a Saga of the Saddle: The*

Autobiography of Broncho Charlie Miller, as told to Gladys Shaw Erskine. London, 1935.

Mills, Anson. *Big Horn Expedition, August 15 to September 30, 1874, Companies B and D, Second Cavalry, Companies F, H, and M, Third Cavalry, Company H, Fourth Cavalry, Company D, Thirteenth Infantry, Commanded by Capt. Anson Mills, Third Cavalry.* 16-p. pamphlet. N. p., n. d.

————. *My Story.* Ed. by C. H. Claudy. Washington, 1916.

Monaghan, Jay. *The Great Rascal.* Boston, 1952.

————. "The Stage Career of Buffalo Bill," *Journal of the Illinois State Historical Society*, Vol. XXXI, No. 4 (December, 1938).

Mueller, Harold L., and Chris Madsen. "Four Score Years a Fighter," *The Farmer-Stockman*, Vol. LIV, Nos. 9–24; Vol. LV, Nos. 1–4 (May 1, 1941–February 15, 1942).

Muller, Dan. *My Life with Buffalo Bill.* Chicago, 1948.

Nebraska Ned. *Buffalo Bill and His Daring Adventures in the Romantic Wild West.* Baltimore, 1915.

North, Maj. Frank. *Journal of an Indian Fighter: The 1869 Diary of Major Frank North.* Ed. by Donald F. Danker. Reprinted from *Nebraska History*, Vol. XXXIX, No. 2 (June, 1958).

North, Capt. L. H. "My Military Experiences in Colorado," *The Colorado Magazine*, Vol. XI, No. 2 (March, 1934).

————. "Pioneering with Capt. Luther H. North," *Winners of the West*, Vol. XI, No. 10 (September, 1934).

O'Connor, Richard. *Bat Masterson.* Garden City, N. Y., 1957.

————. *Wild Bill Hickok.* Garden City, N. Y., 1959.

Pachon, Stanley A. "William Wallace Cook," *Dime Novel Round-Up*, Vol. XXV, No. 300 (September, 1957).

Parker, Gilbert. *Tarboe, the Story of a Life.* New York, London, 1927.

Parker, Lew. *Odd People I Have Met.* N. p., n. d.

Peck, Robert Morris. Reminiscences, *National Tribune*, May 9, 1901.

Pocock, Roger. *Captains of Adventure.* Indianapolis, 1913.

Posey, Jake. "With Buffalo Bill in Europe," *Bandwagon* (October, 1953).

Price, George F., compiler. *Across the Continent with the Fifth Cavalry.* New York, 1883.

Ralph, Julian, and Frederic Remington. "Behind the 'Wild West' Scenes," *Harper's Weekly*, Vol. XXXVIII, No. 1965 (August 18, 1894).

Ray, Clarence E. *Buffalo Bill, the Scout.* Chicago, n. d. [1891].

————. Buffalo Bill and the Heroes of the Plains. Chicago, n. d.

Reckmeyer, Clarence. "The Battle of Summit Springs," *The Colorado Magazine*, Vol. VI, No. 6 (November, 1929).

Report of the Adjutant General of the State of Kansas, 1861–1865, Vol. I, Leavenworth, 1867; Vol. II, also published as *Official Military History of Kansas Regiments During the War for the Suppression of the Great Rebellion*. Leavenworth, 1870.

Rister, Carl Coke. *Border Command*. Norman, 1944.

———. *Land Hunger*. Norman, 1942.

Root, Frank A., and W. E. Connelley. *The Overland Stage to California*. Columbus, 1950.

Rough Rider, The. Vol. IV, 8th ed., Buffalo Bill's Wild West, 1907; Vol. V, 11th ed., Buffalo Bill's Wild West Combined with Pawnee Bill's Great Far East, 1910.

Roth, Charles B. "The Biggest Blow Since Galveston," *The Denver Westerners Monthly Roundup*, Vol. XII, No. 1 (January, 1956).

Russell, Don. "The Duel on the War Bonnet," *Journal of the American Military History Foundation*, Vol. 1, No. 2 (Summer, 1937).

———. "The Wild West and Buffalo Bill," *Facts*, Vol. III, No. 2 (August, 1943).

Sabin, Edwin L. *Buffalo Bill and the Overland Trail*. Philadelhpia, 1914.

Salsbury, Nate. "The Origin of the Wild West Show," "Wild West at Windsor," "At the Vatican (1890)," *The Colorado Magazine*, Vol. XXXII, No. 3 (July, 1955).

Schuchert, Charles, and Clara Mae LeVene. *O. C. Marsh, Pioneer in Paleontology*. New Haven, 1940.

Scott, Maj. Gen. Hugh Lenox. *Some Memories of a Soldier*. New York, London, 1928.

Sell, Henry Blackman, and Victor Weybright. *Buffalo Bill and the Wild West*. New York, 1955.

Settle, Raymond W. and Mary Lund. *Empire on Wheels*. Stanford, Calif., 1949.

———. *Saddles and Spurs*. Harrisburg, 1955.

Shackleford, William Yancey. *Buffalo Bill Cody, Scout and Showman*. Girard, Kan., 1944.

Sheridan, P. H. *Personal Memoirs*. 2 vols. New York, 1888.

Shirley, Glenn. *Pawnee Bill*. Albuquerque, 1958.

Smith, Henry Nash. *Virgin Land*. Cambridge, 1950.

Snyder, A. B. *Pinnacle Jake*, as told to Nellie Irene Yost. Caldwell, Ida., 1951.

Spring, Agnes Wright. *Buffalo Bill and His Horses*. Fort Collins, Colo., 1948.

————. *Cheyenne and Black Hills Stage and Express Routes.* Glendale, 1949.

Standing Bear, Luther. *My People the Sioux.* Ed. by E. A. Brininstool. Boston, New York, 1928.

Stevenson, Augusta. *Buffalo Bill, Boy of the Plains.* Indianapolis, New York, 1948.

Stevenson, E. L. "Those Carver Yarns," *Outdoor Life—Outdoor Recreation,* Vol. LXV, No. 8 (August, 1930).

Stone, Eloise Duvel. *Buffalo Bill, the Life of Wm. F. Cody.* N. p., 1948.

Swartwout, Annie Fern. *Missie.* Blanchester, Ohio., 1947.

Tarbeaux, Frank. *The Autobiography of . . . ,* as told to Donald Clarke Henderson. N. Y., 1930.

Thomas, Chauncey. "Buffalo Bill's Last Interview," *Outdoor Life,* Vol. XXXIX, No. 5 (May, 1917).

Thompson, William C. "The Guns of Buffalo Bill," *Guns,* Vol. II, No. 3–15 (March, 1956).

Thorp, Raymond W. *Spirit Gun of the West.* Glendale, 1957.

Twain, Mark (Samuel L. Clemens). *A Horse's Tale.* N. Y., 1907.

Vestal, Stanley. "The Duel with Yellow Hand," *Southwest Review,* Vol. XXVI, No. 1 (Autumn, 1940); reprinted in Elizabeth Matchett Stover, ed., *Son-of-a-Gun-Stew.* Dallas, 1945.

————. *New Sources of Indian History.* Norman, 1934.

————. *Sitting Bull, Champion of the Sioux: A Biography.* Norman, 1957. First printed, Boston, New York, 1932.

————. *Warpath and Council Fire.* New York, 1948.

Visscher, William Lightfoot. *A Thrilling and Truthful History of the Pony Express.* Chicago, 1908.

————. " 'Buffalo Bill,' Some Reminiscences of William F. Cody," *The Scoop* (April, 1917).

Walsh, Richard J., with Milton S. Salsbury. *The Making of Buffalo Bill.* Indianapolis, 1928.

Webb, William Edward. *Buffalo Land.* Cincinnati, Chicago, 1872.

Wector, Dixon. *The Hero in America.* New York, 1941.

Wells, Capt. James M. *"With Touch of Elbow."* Philadelphia, 1909.

Westermeier, Clifford P. *Trailing the Cowboy.* Caldwell, Ida., 1959.

————. *Who Rush to Glory.* Caldwell, Ida., 1958.

Wetmore, Helen Cody. *Last of the Great Scouts.* Chicago, Duluth, 1899.

————, and Zane Grey. *Last of the Great Scouts (Buffalo Bill).* New York, Grosset and Dunlap, 1899, 1918. A reprint of the above item with foreword and afterpiece by Grey added.

Wheeler, Col. Homer W. *Buffalo Days.* Indianapolis, 1923.

Bibliography

Wilder, Marshall P. *The People I've Smiled With*. Akron, Ohio, 1899.
———. *The Sunny Side of the Street*. New York, London, 1905.
Williams, Henry Llewellyn. *Buffalo Bill in the Wild West*. London, n. d.
Willson, Wingrove. *Buffalo Bill—Chief of Scouts*. London, n. d.
———. *More Adventures with Buffalo Bill*. London, n. d.
Wilstach, Frank J. *Wild Bill Hickok, the Prince of Pistoleers*. Garden City, N. Y., 1926.
Wilstach, John. "Buffalo Bill's Last Stands," *Esquire*, Vol. XXI, No. 6 (June, 1944).
Winch, Frank. "Buffalo Bill—Frontiersman," *Ace-High*, Vol. XLVII, No. 3 (January–September, 1929).
———. *Thrilling Lives of Buffalo Bill and Pawnee Bill*. New York, 1911.
Winget, Dan. *Anecdotes of "Buffalo Bill."* Chicago, 1927.
———. *Pipe Dreams, Smoker*. 8 issues. Clinton, Iowa, 1925–27.

THE DIME NOVELS (A LIST)

I. FICTION SIGNED BY BUFFALO BILL (in order of publication)

The Haunted Valley; or, A Leaf from a Hunter's Life, Vickery's Fireside Visitor, April, 1875.

The Pearl of the Prairies; or, The Scout and the Renegade, New York Weekly, August 9, 1875.

Deadly Eye, the Unknown Scout
Saturday Journal (hereafter SJ), September 11–October 23, 1875; No. 55, Beadle's Half-Dime Library (½DL), August 13, 1878; No. 39, The Pocket Library (PL), October 8, 1884; combined with *The Prairie Rover* as No. 27, Beadle and Adams Twenty Cent Novels, July 5, 1877.

Prairie Prince, the Boy Outlaw; or, Trailed to His Doom, Saturday Evening Post, October 16, 1875.

The Prairie Rover; or, The Robin Hood of the Border, SJ, October 23–November 20, 1875; No. 68, ½ DL, November 12, 1878, as *The Border Robin Hood; or, The Prairie Rover;* No. 52, PL, January 7, 1885; combined with *Deadly Eye, the Unknown Scout,* as No. 27, Twenty Cent Novels, *Deadly Eye; or, The Prairie Rover,* July 5, 1877.

Kansas King; or, The Red Right Hand, SJ, March 25–May 27, 1876; No. 3, ½DL, October 22, 1877; No. 2, PL, January 23, 1884; No. 1038, ½DL, June 15, 1897.

The Phantom Spy; or, The Pilot of the Prairie, SJ, September 23–November 18, 1876; No. 19, ½DL, December 17, 1877; No. 1029, ½DL,

494

April 13, 1897; No. 6, PL, as *The Prairie Pilot; or, The Phantom Spy*, February 20, 1884.

The Crimson Trail; or, On Custer's Last Warpath, "as witnessed by W. F. Cody," *New York Weekly,* September 25–October 30, 1876; No. 180, Diamond Dick Library, 1896, by Buffalo Bill; No. 7, Nugget Library, 1889, by Prentiss Ingraham.

Lost Lulu; or, The Prairie Cavalier, SJ, May 11–August 3, 1878; No. 52, Beadle's Dime Library (DL), October 9, 1878, as *Death Trailer, the Chief of Scouts; or, Life and Love in a Frontier Fort.*

Gold Bullet Sport; or, The Knights of Chivalry, SJ, March 29–May 31, 1879; No. 83, DL, December 17, 1879 (subtitle, *The Knights of the Overland*).

Fancy Frank of Colorado; or, The Trapper's Trust, SJ, February 14–April 17, 1880; No. 158, ½DL, August 3, 1880; No. 117, PL, April 7, 1886.

Wild Bill, the Whirlwind of the West, Beadle's Weekly, BW, May 26–August 18, 1883; No. 319, DL, December 3, 1884.

The Pilgrim Sharp; or, The Soldier's Sweetheart, No. 243, DL, June 30, 1883.

Texas Jack, the Prairie Rattler; or, The Queen of the Wild Horses, BW, August 18–October 27, 1883; No. 304, DL, August 20, 1884.

White Beaver, the Exile of the Platte; or, A Wronged Man's Red Trail, BW, February 23–May 3, 1884; No. 394, DL, May 12, 1886.

The Wizard Brothers; or, White Beaver's Red Trail, BW, May 3–June 26, 1884; No. 397, DL, June 2, 1886.

White Beaver's One-arm Pard; or, Red Retribution in Borderland, BW, July 26–October 18, 1884; No. 401, DL, June 30, 1886, *The One-arm Pard.*

Red Renard, the Indian Detective; or, The Gold Buzzards of Colorado, BW, October 18, 1884–January 10, 1885; No. 414, DL, September 29, 1886.

The Dead Shot Nine; or, My Pards of the Plains, The Banner Weekly, succeeded *Beadle's Weekly* (BW), November 14, 1885–February 6, 1886; No. 599, DL, April 16, 1890.

Montebello, the Magnificent; or, The Gold King of Colorado, BW, February 6–May 1, 1886; No. 639, DL, January 28, 1891, *The Gold King.*

Wild Bill, the Dead Center Shot; or, Rio Grande Ralph, the Cowboy Chief, No. 800, DL, February 21, 1894.

Wild Bill, the Wild West Duelist; or, The Girl Mascot of Moonlight Mine, No. 807, DL, April 11, 1894 (by General W. F. Cody).

THE LIVES AND LEGENDS OF BUFFALO BILL

White Beaver's Still Hunt; or, The Miner Marauder's Death-track, No. 820, DL, July 11, 1894.

Texas Jack, the Lasso King; or, The Robber Rangers of the Rio Grande, BW, August 25–November 17, 1894; No. 969, DL, May 29, 1897.

The Ranch King Dead-Shot; or, Texas Jack's Proxy, No. 839, DL, November 21, 1894.

The Dread Shot Four; or, My Pards of the Plains, BW, April 10–May 22, 1897; unfinished in last issue of *The Banner Weekly*; No. 973, DL, June 16, 1897.

The White Captive, 10 Story Book, September, 1903.

II. Buffalo Bill Dime Novels (alphabetically by author, and in order of publication, including first serial appearance)

Aiken, Albert W. *Cool Colorado in New York; or, The Cowboy's Fight for a Million*, No. 518, ½DL, June 28, 1897.

Cook, William Wallace. 119 titles, Street & Smith's Buffalo Bill Stories (BBS), 1907–10, including Nos. 255–81, 284–91, 296–99, 302–34, 373–75, 388–90, 423–25, 441–46, 507–509.

Cox, S. A. D. (Harry Moore). *Three Chums with Buffalo Bill's Wild West*, No. 52, Tousey's Three Chums Weekly.

Erwin, Howard W. Pen name signed to No. 86–211, Far West Library.

Fenton, Captain Ralph (Frank Forrest; An Old Scout, real name unknown). *Buffalo Bill's Chum*, Nos. 463, 1305, Tousey's Wide Awake Library, No. 632, Pluck and Luck Library, *Buffalo Bill's Boy Chum; or, In the Wild West with the King of Scouts*, by An Old Scout; same in *Happy Days*, by Frank Forrest, beginning May 9, 1896.

Foster, W. Bert. 136 titles, BBS, 1906–11, including Nos. 282–83, 292–95, 300–301, 335–72, 376–87, 391–411, 450–506.

Hall, Major Samuel Stone (Buckskin Sam). *The Prince of the Platte; or, Buffalo Bill's Long Trail*, No. 35, Saturday Library.

Ingraham, Col. Prentiss (Maj. Dangerfield Burr). *Buffalo Bill, the Buckskin King; or, Wild Nell, the Amazon of the West*, SJ, November 29, 1879–February 14, 1880; No. 92, DL, April 21, 1880.

———. *Dashing Dandy, the Hotspur of the Hills; or, The Pony Prince's Strange Pard*, SJ, August 7–October 30, 1880; No. 117, DL, January 19, 1881.

———. *Gold Plume, the Boy Bandit; or, The Kid-glove Sport*, No. 204, ½DL, June 21, 1881; No. 1046, ½DL, No. 155, PL.

———. *Bison Bill, the Prince of the Reins; or, The Red Riders of the Overland*, No. 216, ½DL, September 13, 1881; No. 185, PL.

——. *Grit, the Bravo Sport; or, The Woman Trailer,* No. 222, ½DL, October 25, 1881; No. 197, PL.

——. *Adventures of Buffalo Bill from Boyhood to Manhood,* Beadle's Boy's Library No. 1, December 14, 1881; No. 2, *ibid.,* New Series; No. 388, PL, June 17, 1891, *The Pony Express Rider; or, Buffalo Bill's Frontier Feats.*

——. *The League of Three; or, Buffalo Bill's Pledge,* BW, November 18, 1882–February 10, 1883; No. 329, DL, February 11, 1885.

——. *Buffalo Bill's Grip; or, Oath-bound to Custer,* BW, January 13–March 10, 1883; No. 362, DL, Sept. 30, 1885.

——. *Buffalo Bill's Bonanza; or, The Knights of the Silver Circle,* BW, May 22–August 21, 1886; No. 644, DL, February 25, 1891.

——. *Buffalo Bill's Swoop; or, The King of the Mines,* BW, August 14–November 6, 1886; No. 667 DL, August 5, 1891.

——. *Buffalo Bill's Secret Service Trail; or, The Mysterious Foe,* BW, January 29–April 23, 1887; No. 682, DL, November 18, 1891.

——. *Buffalo Bill's Big Four; or, Custer's Shadow,* BW, August 6–October 29, 1887; No. 750, DL, March 8, 1893.

——. *Buffalo Bill's Double; or, The Desperado Detectives,* BW, June 9–September 1, 1888; No. 757, DL, April 26, 1893.

——. *Silk-ribbon Sam, the Mad Driver of the Overland; or, Buffalo Bill's Twelve,* BW, November 3, 1888–January 26, 1889; No. 765, DL, June 21, 1893, as *Buffalo Bill's Dozen.*

——. *The Hercules Highwayman; or, The Mounted Miners of the Overland,* No. 644, ½DL, November 26, 1889.

——. *Buffalo Bill's Brand; or, The Brimstone Brotherhood,* BW, September 28–December 21, 1889; No. 781, DL, October 11, 1893.

——. *Buffalo Bill's Boys in Blue; or, The Brimstone Band's Blot-out,* BW, December 21, 1889–March 15, 1890; No. 830, DL, September 19, 1894.

——. *Butterfly Billy, the Pony Rider Detective; or, Buffalo Bill's Boy Pard,* No. 650, ½DL, January 7, 1890.

——. *Butterfly Billy's Man Hunt; or, One More Trail,* No. 656, ½DL, February 18, 1890.

——. *Buffalo Bill's Buckskin Braves; or, The Card Queen's Last Game,* BW, March 15–June 7, 1890; No. 874, DL, July 24, 1895.

——. *Butterfly Billy's Bonanza; or, The Spectre Soldier of the Overland,* No. 662, ½DL, April 1, 1890.

——. *The Three Bills—Buffalo Bill, Wild Bill and Band-box Bill; or, The Bravo in Broadcloth,* BW, June 7–August 30, 1890; No. 882, DL, September 18, 1895.

——. *The Texan's Double; or, Buffalo Bill's Secret Ally*, BW, August 30–November 22, 1890; No. 895, DL, December 18, 1895.

——. *Gentleman Jack, the Man of Many Masks; or, Buffalo Bill's Peerless Pard*, BW, November 22, 1890–February 21, 1891; No. 904, DL, February 19, 1896, as *Buffalo Bill's Tangled Trail*.

——. *Red Butterfly; or, Buffalo Bill's League*, BW, February 14–May 9, 1891; No. 909, DL, March 25, 1896.

——. *Go-Wan-Go, the Redskin Rider; or, Buffalo Bill and the Surgeon-Scout*, BW, May 9–August 4, 1891; No. 915, DL, May 6, 1896.

——. *Velvet Bill's Vow; or, Buffalo Bill's Quandary*, BW, August 1–October 24, 1891; No. 921, DL, June 17, 1896.

——. *Buffalo Bill's Blind Trail; or, Mustang Madge, the Daughter of the Regiment*, No. 691, DL, January 20, 1892.

——. *Buffalo Bill's Buckskin Brotherhood; or, Opening Up a Lost Trail*, No. 697, DL, March 2, 1892.

——. *Buffalo Bill Baffled; or, The Deserter Desperado's Defiance*, No. 710, DL, June 1, 1892.

——. *Buffalo Bill's Scout Shadowers; or, Emerald Ed of Devil's Acre*, No. 716, DL, July 30, 1892.

——. *Buffalo Bill on the War Path; or, Silk Lasso Sam, the Will-o'-the-Wisp of the Trails*, No. 722, DL, August 24, 1892.

——. *Buffalo Bill's Body-guard; or, The Still Hunt of the Hills*, No. 727, DL, September 28, 1892.

——. *Buffalo Bill's Beagles; or, Silk Lasso Sam, the Outlaw of the Overland*, No. 731, DL, October 26, 1892.

——. *Buffalo Bill and His Merry Men; or, The Robin Hood Rivals*, No. 735, DL, November 23, 1892.

——. *Buffalo Bill's Blind; or, The Masked Driver of Death Canyon*, No. 739, DL, December 21, 1892.

——. *Buffalo Bill's Flush Hand; or, Texas Jack's Bravos*, No. 743, DL, January 18, 1893.

——. *Buffalo Bill's Mascot; or, The Death Valley Victim No. 13*, No. 761, DL, May 24, 1893.

——. *Buffalo Bill's Sweepstake; or, The Wipe-out at Last Chance*, No. 769, DL, July 19, 1893.

——. *Buffalo Bill's Spy-shadower; or, The Masked Man of Grand Canyon*, No. 777, DL, September 13, 1893.

——. *Buffalo Bill's Dead Shot; or, The Skeleton Scout of the Colorado*, No. 787, DL, November 22, 1893.

——. *Buffalo Bill's Winning Hand; or, The Masked Woman of the Colorado Canyon*, No. 794, DL, January 10, 1894.

———. *Buffalo Bill's Death-knell; or, The Red Hand Riders of the Rockies,* No. 812, DL, May 16, 1894.

———. *Buffalo Bill's Red Trail; or, The Road Rider Renegade Rundown,* No. 816, DL, June 13, 1894.

———. *Buffalo Bill's Volunteer Vigilantes; or, The Mysterious Men in Blue,* BW, July 14–October 6, 1894; No. 956, DL, February 17, 1897.

———. *Montebello, the Gold King; or, Buffalo Bill's Best Bower,* No. 822, DL, July 25, 1894.

———. *Buffalo Bill's Sharp-shooters; or, The Surgeon Scout to the Rescue,* No. 826, DL, August 22, 1894.

———. *Buffalo Bill's Life Raffle; or, The Doomed Three,* BW, November 17, 1894–February 16, 1895; No. 984, DL, September 1, 1897.

———. *Buffalo Bill's Red-skin Ruse; or, Texas Jack's Death Shot,* No. 845, DL, January 2, 1895.

———. *Buffalo Bill's Double Dilemma; or, The Great Scout's Big Three,* No. 851, DL, February 13, 1895.

———. *Buffalo Bill's Royal Flush; or, The Pony Rider's Death Run,* No. 857, DL, March 27, 1895.

———. *Buffalo Bill's Death-charm; or, The Man with the Scar,* No. 863, DL, May 8, 1895.

———. *Buffalo Bill's Marked Bullet; or, The Spectre Slayer of the Colorado,* BW, May 11–August 3, 1895; No. 989, DL, October 6, 1897.

———. *Buffalo Bill's Crack-shot Pard; or, The Tenderfoot in the Wild West,* No. 929, ½DL, May 14, 1895.

———. *Buffalo Bill's Road-agent Round-up; or, The Mysterious Masked Men in Black,* No. 869, DL, June 19, 1895.

———. *Buffalo Bill's Boy Mascot; or, Jack Jarvis' Hold-up,* No. 936, ½DL, July 2, 1895.

———. *Buffalo Bill's Lone Hand; or, The Unknown Dead-shot,* BW, August 3–November 2, 1895; No. 994, DL, November 10, 1897.

———. *Buffalo Bill's Tough Tussle; or, The Buckskin Boss Boy,* No. 942, ½DL, August 13, 1895.

———. *Buffalo Bill's Snap-shot; or, Wild Kid's Texas Tally,* No. 948, ½DL, September 24, 1895.

———. *Buffalo Bill's Grim Guard; or, The Chinaman in Buckskin,* BW, November 7, 1895–February 6, 1896; No. 1000, DL, December 22, 1897.

. *Buffalo Bill's Life-stake; or, The Pledged Three,* No. 890 DL, November 13, 1895.

———. *Buffalo Bill's Mazeppa-chase; or, Dick Dearborn's Death Ride,* No. 958, ½DL, December 3, 1895.

———. *Buffalo Bill's Decoy; or, The Arizona Crack-shot*, No. 964, ½DL, January 14, 1896.

———. *Buffalo Bill's Rough Riders; or, Texas Jack's Sharp-shooters*, No. 900, DL, January 22, 1896.

———. *Buffalo Bill's Death-deal; or, The Wandering Jew of the Wild West*, BW, February 1–April 25, 1896; No. 1004, DL, January 19, 1898.

———. *Buffalo Bill's Rush-ride; or, Sure-shot, the High Flyer*, No. 968, ½DL, February 11, 1896.

———. *Buffalo Bill's Rifle-shots; or, The Buckskin Bravo's Lone Trail*, No. 975, ½DL, March 31, 1896.

———. *Buffalo Bill's Dead-shot Dragoon; or, The Hidden Home of Shadow Valley*, BW, May 2–August 1, 1896; No. 1009, DL, February 23, 1898.

———. *Buffalo Bill's Fighting Five; or, The Black Lariat's Blot-out*, No. 981, ½DL, May 12, 1896.

———. *Buffalo Bill's Lasso-throwers; or, Shadow Sam's Short-stop*, No. 988, ½DL, June 30, 1896.

———. *Buffalo Bill's Bluff; or, Dusky Dick, the Sport*, No. 927, DL, July 29, 1896.

———. *Buffalo Bill's Secret Six; or, Velvet Val, the Spotter Sport*, BW, August 8–October 31, 1896; M. J. Ivers & Co., No. 1013, DL, June, 1898.

———. *Buffalo Bill's Drop; or, Dead-shot Ned, the Kansas Kid*, No. 995, ½DL, August 18, 1896.

———. *Buffalo Bill's Decoy Boys; or, The Death Rivals of the Big Horn*, No. 1000, ½DL, September 22, 1896.

———. *Buffalo Bill's Black Pard; or, The Gold Boomers of the Big Horn*, No. 936, DL, September 30, 1896.

———. *Buffalo Bill's Sure-shots; or, Buck Dawson's Big Draw*, No. 1007, ½DL, November 10, 1896.

———. *Buffalo Bill's Block Game; or, Rounding Up the Mounted Riders of the Overland*, No. 943, DL, November 18, 1896.

———. *Buffalo Bill's Texan; or, The Dog Detective*, No. 1013, ½DL, December 22, 1896.

———. *Buffalo Bill in Arizona; or, Buckskin Sam's Travel Trail*, BW, January 2–March 27, 1897; M. J. Ivers & Co., No. 1029, DL, October, 1899.

———. *Buffalo Bill at Bay; or, The Gold-seeker's Doom*, 950 DL, January 6, 1897.

————. *Buffalo Bill's Blue Belt Brigade; or, Sunflower Sam of Shasta,* No. 960, DL, March 17, 1897.

————. *Buffalo Bill's Invincibles; or, The Sable Shadower's Sublime Sacrifice,* No. 964, DL, April 14, 1897.

————. *Buffalo Bill in Disguise; or, The Boy Boomer at Danger Divide,* BW, May 1–15, 1897; No. 1052, ½DL, September 21, 1897.

————. *Buffalo Bill's Pony Patrol; or, The Mysterious Boy of the Overland,* BW, May 15–22, 1897 (unfinished); 1040, ½DL, June 29, 1897.

————. *Buffalo Bill's Relentless Trail; or, The Unknown Slayer of the Black Cavalry,* No. 979, DL, July 28, 1897.

————. *Buffalo Bill's Daring Deed; or, The Scourge of the Gold Trail,* No. 1007, DL, February 9, 1898.

————. 25 to 30 titles, Buffalo Bill Stories, 1901–1904.

————. Reprints in New Buffalo Bill Weekly, Far West Library, Buffalo Bill Border Stories, Great Western Library.

Judson, Edward Zane Carroll (Ned Buntline). *Buffalo Bill, the King of Border Men,* Street & Smith's *New York Weekly,* beginning December 23, 1869; No. 40, People's Library, July 1, 1881; *Buffalo Bill and His Adventures in the West* (bound), 1886; *Buffalo Bill* (bound), n. d.

————. *Buffalo Bill's Best Shot; or, The Heart of Spotted Tail, New York Weekly,* May 25, 1872; No. 23, Sea and Shore Series, September, 1890; No. 127, 384, Log Cabin Library, 1891; No. 3, Log Cabin Library, Pocket Edition, 1900; No. 147, Buffalo Bill Series, 1897.

————. *Buffalo Bill's Last Victory; or, Dove Eye, the Lodge Queen, New York Weekly,* July 8, 1872; reprinted December 5, 1886; No. 5 Sea and Shore Series, October, 1890; No. 128, Log Cabin Library, August 27, 1891; No. 386, Log Cabin Library, Pocket Edition, 1898.

————. *Will Cody, the Pony Express Rider; or, Buffalo Bill's First Trail,* BW, April 18–July 25, 1885; No. 517, DL, September 19, 1888, *Buffalo Bill's First Trail;* No. 517, M. J. Ivers & Co., DL, 1899.

Lewis, Julius Warren (Leon Lewis). *Daredeath Dick, King of the Cowboys; or, In the Wild West with Buffalo Bill,* BW, November 6, 1886–January 15, 1887; No. 629, DL, November 12, 1890.

————. *Buffalo Bill's Ban; or, Cody to the Rescue,* BW, March 16–June 8, 1889; No. 773, DL, August 16, 1893.

Lone Star (probably E. Z. C. Judson). *Texas Jack; or, Buffalo Bill's Brother,* No. 102, DeWitt's Ten Cent Romances, 1872.

Maynard, Robert (pen name, real name unknown). *In the Wild West; or, On the Plains with Buffalo Bill,* No. 735, Frank Tousey's Wide

Awake Library; Nos. 163, 725, Pluck and Luck Library, *On the Plains with Buffalo Bill; or, Two Years in the Wild West*, by An Old Scout.

Old Scout, An (see also Ralph Fenton and Robert Maynard). *Out with Buffalo Bill; or, Six New York Boys in the Wild West*, No. 39, Frank Tousey's Pluck and Luck Library; originally in Wide Awake Library, author not traced.

Powell, Frank (attributed to Prentiss Ingraham). *The Doomed Dozen; or, Dolores, the Danite's Daughter*, No. 158, DL, November 2, 1881.

Rathborne, St. George Henry (E. W. Wheeler; see also Robert Russell). *Buffalo Bill's Best Bower; or, The Soldier Scout's Last Trail*, No. 134, Log Cabin Library, 1890; also No. 394.

——. *Buffalo Bill's Border Bravos; or, The Trail Through the Land of Death*, No. 145, Log Cabin Library, 1890; also No. 390.

——. *Buffalo Bill's Long Trail; or, The King of the Plains to the Rescue of the Deadwood Coach*, No. 160, Log Cabin Library, 1890; also No. 395.

——. Some original stories; also reprints, Buffalo Bill Stories.

Russell, Robert (W. B. Lawson, E. W. Wheeler). *Buffalo Bill at Wounded Knee; or, the Battle-secret of the Bad Lands*, by W. B. Lawson, No. 103, Log Cabin Library, 1890?; also No. 288.

——. *Buffalo Bill, the Border King; or, The White Queen of the Sioux and the Girl Rifle Shot*, by E. W. Wheeler, No. 152 Log Cabin Library, 1890?; also No. 392; No. 59, Log Cabin Library, Pocket Edition, 1898.

Sawyer, Eugene T. Possible author of 3 titles, Buffalo Bill Stories.

Sheldon, Laurana. 12 titles, Buffalo Bill Stories, including Nos. 159–61, 163–71.

Taylor, Captain Alfred B. *Buffalo Billy, the Boy Bullwhacker; or, The Doomed Thirteen*, No. 191, ½DL, March 22, 1881; No. 160, PL, as "by Col. Prentiss Ingraham."

——. *Buffalo Bill's Bet; or, The Gambler Guide*, No. 194, ½DL, April 12, 1881; No. 165, PL, as "by Col. Prentiss Ingraham."

Van Orden, W. Howard (Paul Braddon). *Buffalo Bill's Boy Bronco Breaker; or, The Youngest Hero on the Plains*, No. 917, Frank Tousey's Wide Awake Library; probably also in *Happy Days*.

——. *Little Quick Shot; or, Buffalo Bill's Wild West in Europe*, No. 1003, Frank Tousey's Wide Awake Library; probably also in *Happy Days*.

Whitson, Rev. John Harvey (Lt. A. K. Sims). *Chicago Charlie, the Co-*

lumbian Detective; or, The Hawks of the Lakeside League, No. 776, DL, September 6, 1893.

———. 59 or more titles, Buffalo Bill Stories, 1909–12, including Nos. 412–22, 447–49, 507–51, 580–82.

Unknown author. *Buffalo Bill's Boyhood Days: The Adventures of the Famous Scout,* No. 26, Young Sport's Library.

INDEX

The text of *The Lives and Legends of Buffalo Bill* has been set in eleven-point Caledonia type, with two points of space between lines. Caledonia is an original type design by W. A. Dwiggins, cut in 1940 for the Linotype as a refinement of Scotch faces of the early nineteenth century. Both the twelve-point Linotype Gothic of the chapter titles and the limited use of handset Beton Open for display have been selected to complement the Caledonia and to recall the flavor of William F. Cody's times.

UNIVERSITY OF OKLAHOMA PRESS
NORMAN